Resources for Teaching

MIDDLE SCHOOL

Science

NATIONAL SCIENCE RESOURCES CENTER

The National Science Resources Center (NSRC) is operated by the National Academy of Sciences/National Academy of Engineering/Institute of Medicine and the Smithsonian Institution to improve the teaching of science in the nation's schools. The NSRC collects and disseminates information about exemplary teaching resources, develops and disseminates curriculum materials, and sponsors outreach activities, specifically in the areas of leadership development and technical assistance, to help school districts develop and sustain hands-on science programs.

SMITHSONIAN INSTITUTION

The Smithsonian Institution was created by act of Congress in 1846 in accordance with the will of Englishman James Smithson, who in 1826 bequeathed his property to the United States of America, "to found at Washington, under the name of the Smithsonian Institution, an establishment for the increase and diffusion of knowledge among men." The Smithsonian has since evolved into an institution devoted to public education, research, and national service in the arts, sciences, and history. This independent federal establishment is the world's largest museum complex and is responsible for public and scholarly activities, exhibitions, and research projects nationwide and overseas. Among the objectives of the Smithsonian is to apply its unique resources to enhance preschool through grade 12 education and adult education. I. Michael Heyman is secretary of the Smithsonian Institution.

NATIONAL ACADEMY OF SCIENCES

The National Academy of Sciences is a private, nonprofit, self-perpetuating society of distinguished scholars engaged in scientific and engineering research, dedicated to the furtherance of science and technology and to their use for the general welfare. Upon the authority of the charter granted to it by the Congress in 1863, the Academy has a mandate that requires it to advise the federal government on scientific and technical matters. Dr. Bruce M. Alberts is president of the National Academy of Sciences.

NATIONAL ACADEMY OF ENGINEERING

The National Academy of Engineering was established in 1964, under the charter of the National Academy of Sciences, as a parallel organization of outstanding engineers. It is autonomous in its administration and in the selection of its members, sharing with the National Academy of Sciences the responsibility for advising the federal government. The National Academy of Engineering also sponsors engineering programs aimed at meeting national needs, encourages education and research, and recognizes the superior achievements of engineers. Dr. William A. Wulf is president of the National Academy of Engineering.

INSTITUTE OF MEDICINE

The Institute of Medicine was established in 1970 by the National Academy of Sciences to secure the services of eminent members of appropriate professions in the examination of policy matters pertaining to the health of the public. The Institute acts under the responsibility given to the National Academy of Sciences by its congressional charter to be an adviser to the federal government and, upon its own initiative, to identify issues of medical care, research, and education. Dr. Kenneth I. Shine is president of the Institute of Medicine.

NATIONAL RESEARCH COUNCIL

The National Research Council was organized by the National Academy of Sciences in 1916 to associate the broad community of science and technology with the Academy's purposes of furthering knowledge and advising the federal government. Functioning in accordance with general policies determined by the Academy, the Council has become the principal operating agency of both the National Academy of Sciences and the National Academy of Engineering in providing services to the government, the public, and the scientific and engineering communities. The Council is administered jointly by both Academies and the Institute of Medicine. Dr. Bruce M. Alberts and Dr. William A. Wulf are chairman and vice chairman, respectively, of the National Research Council.

Resources for Teaching

MIDDLE SCHOOL

Science

**National
Science
Resources
Center**

Smithsonian Institution

**National Academy of Sciences
National Academy of Engineering
Institute of Medicine**

NATIONAL ACADEMY PRESS

Washington, D.C.   1998

NATIONAL ACADEMY PRESS • 2101 Constitution Avenue, N.W. • Washington, D.C. 20418

NOTICE: *Resources for Teaching Middle School Science* was developed by the National Science Resources Center. The views expressed in this book are solely those of its contributors and do not necessarily reflect the views of the National Academy of Sciences, the National Academy of Engineering, the Institute of Medicine, the Smithsonian Institution, or The Merck Institute for Science Education.

Library of Congress Cataloging-in-Publication Data

National Science Resources Center (U.S.).
    Resources for teaching middle school science / National Science
Resources Center.
       p. cm.
    Includes indexes.
    ISBN 0-309-05781-7 (pbk.)
    1. Science—Study and teaching (Secondary) 2. Curriculum
planning. I. Title.
Q181.N3862   1998
07.1′273—dc21   98-12987

Printed in the United States of America

National Science Resources Center
Arts and Industries Building, Room 1201
Smithsonian Institution
Washington, D.C. 20560

Douglas Lapp, Executive Director
Sally Goetz Shuler, Deputy Director for Development,
    External Relations, and Outreach
Evelyn M. Ernst, Information Dissemination Director
Dean Trackman, Publications Director

Project Development Team

Evelyn M. Ernst, Director
Barbara K. Johnson, Research Associate
Dorothy Sawicki, Project Managing Editor
Rita C. Warpeha, Resource/Database Specialist
Max-Karl Winkler, Cover Illustrations
Abigail Porter, Writer Consultant

Cover and photo credits appear on p. 479.

National Academy Press

Sally Stanfield, Editorial Coordination
Francesca Moghari, Cover Design
Liz Clark, Isely &/or Clark Design,
    Book Design
Linda C. Humphrey, Page Layout

Major support for
Resources for Teaching Middle School Science
was provided by a grant from
The Merck Institute for Science Education

CONTENTS

PART 4. ANCILLARY RESOURCES

APPENDIXES

THE INDEXES 449

FOREWORD

Educators, school administrators, and state and local officials are developing science programs consistent with the National Science Education Standards (NSES) to achieve the national goal of "scientific literacy for all students." Selecting effective standards-based curriculum materials from the wide array of available resources is a key step in this process.

Resources for Teaching Middle School Science, produced by the National Science Resources Center (NSRC), provides authoritative, up-to-date information that greatly simplifies this task. This new volume is the second in a series of resource guides that the NSRC is developing to assist with the teaching of science in kindergarten through twelfth grade. *Resources for Teaching Elementary School Science* was published in 1996. In the future, the NSRC plans to develop additional resource guides for high school science teachers.

This NSRC guide provides extensive, annotated bibliographies of middle school curriculum materials in the major scientific disciplines. These materials were evaluated by panels of teachers and scientists who used carefully developed criteria based on the National Science Education Standards. (For quick reference, the NSES content standards for grades 5-8 are included in an appendix.)

One of the clear messages of the standards is that the challenge of science education reform extends to all those who have an influence on science education, such as research scientists, engineers, museum curators, and government officials. In this spirit, this resource guide is designed to help science teachers find additional sources of assistance outside the classroom. The guide includes lists of local, state, and national organizations that can give assistance, such as museums, science-technology centers, and professional scientific and governmental organizations. Many of these organizations have programs and materials that can be used to enrich the teaching of science.

The development of resource guides is just one of the ways that the NSRC is helping to bring about the national goal of scientific literacy for all students. Since its inception in 1985, the NSRC has had a significant impact on science education reform in school districts throughout the country through its information dissemination, materials development, and outreach programs. The NSRC's sponsoring organizations, the Smithsonian Institution and the National Academy of Sciences—along with the National Academy of Engineering and the Institute of Medicine—take pride in the publication of this new resource guide and in the continuing contributions of the NSRC to the improvement of science education.

BRUCE M. ALBERTS
President
National Academy of Sciences

I. MICHAEL HEYMAN
Secretary
Smithsonian Institution

PREFACE

The National Science Resources Center (NSRC) is pleased to announce the publication of *Resources for Teaching Middle School Science*—a guide to curriculum materials and other resources for teaching science in grades six through eight. The guide is the culmination of several years of intense work. The NSRC would like to thank The Merck Institute for Science Education, which provided the major support for the development of this publication.

Resources for Teaching Middle School Science is the second in the NSRC's series of resource guides for kindergarten through twelfth grade; the first was *Resources for Teaching Elementary School Science,* published in 1996. Although the style and structure of the two guides are the same, this volume has several new features that we believe will make it particularly valuable for middle school teachers. Some of the changes reflect the greater complexity of middle school science curriculum materials; others provide additional kinds of information about resources that are available to teachers of science in grades six through eight. Let me briefly mention some of the specific changes. Readers will find additional background information in the "Introduction to the Guide."

In the section on curriculum materials, a new chapter has been added. It focuses on an important subject area for middle school—environmental science—and complements the chapters on physical, life, earth and space, and multidisciplinary and applied science. The categories in which the curriculum titles are organized—core materials, supplementary units, and science activity books—remain the same as in the elementary guide.

Readers will notice that a reading level is included for the core curriculum titles. Together with the recommended grade level, which the guide also provides, the reading level can help educators gauge the appropriateness of core curriculum materials for particular groups of middle school students.

As was the case with the elementary school guide, all curriculum materials annotated in this volume are "standards-based." This means that the materials were found by panels of scientists and teachers to meet the NSRC's "Evaluation Criteria for Middle School Science Curriculum Materials." These criteria are based on the goals and principles identified in the *National Science Education Standards* (NSES), and they address important characteristics that are stressed in the NSES—for example, inquiry, science content, pedagogy, age-appropriateness, and assessment. (The NSRC middle school evaluation criteria are reproduced in appendix B.)

Two features of this middle school guide relate directly to the National Science Education Standards. First, a "Key to Content Standards" is provided in each annotation of core and supplementary material. This key identifies the specific NSES content standards that the curriculum material addresses. Second, for readers who want to refer to the full text of the relevant NSES content standards, the National Science Education Standards for grades five through eight are reprinted in appendix C.

In developing this guide, the NSRC focused mainly on the evaluation of print curriculum materials. We have, however, developed a chapter entitled "Sources of Information on Educational Software and Multimedia Programs." This chapter can help teachers access reviews of computer software and other multimedia instructional resources.

The sections of the guide focusing on teacher reference materials and on ancillary resources (such as museums, science and technology centers, and professional scientific associations) are in the same format as in the NSRC's elementary school guide. Each of the hundreds of entries in these sections, however, includes information about programs, services, publications, and other forms of assistance specifically relevant to middle school science.

The NSRC is grateful to Evelyn M. Ernst, NSRC Program Director for Information Dissemination and general editor of *Resources for Teaching Middle School Science,* for shepherding this guide through all stages of its development—from formulation of the evaluation criteria through panel review to publication. We would also like to thank the NSRC's parent institutions, the National Academy of Sciences, the National Academy of Engineering, the Institute of Medicine, and the Smithsonian Institution, for their support in helping the NSRC carry out this project.

Our search for materials for this guide was comprehensive, and the evaluation process was extensive and thorough. We believe that this compilation will prove to be a valuable resource for middle school science teachers. We look forward to hearing from readers about the effectiveness of the guide in meeting their needs, together with any suggestions they may have for its improvement.

DOUGLAS LAPP
Executive Director
National Science Resources Center
January 1998

ACKNOWLEDGMENTS

Resources for Teaching Middle School Science is the first volume of its kind to focus exclusively on curriculum materials and other resources for teaching middle school science. The challenging task of producing this extensive compilation required coordinated efforts on a number of fronts. It could not have been accomplished without the hard work and dedication of a core group of staff, combined with the efforts of a large number of teachers, scientists, and other professionals.

This guide was brought to fruition with generous support from The Merck Institute for Science Education, with continuing encouragement from its director, Carlo Parravano. Special thanks go to Evelyn M. Ernst, project director and general editor, for her tireless efforts in fashioning this useful and versatile guide from the vast array of diverse material submitted for consideration. Thanks also go to her staff and to the consultants who participated in the work on the volume. Research associate Barbara K. Johnson helped organize and manage the complex, structured review of hundreds of curriculum materials, and she also helped research information for all major sections of the guide. Resource/database specialist Rita C. Warpeha cataloged the materials received for review and verified the extensive array of information provided in the publishers and suppliers list in appendix A. Consultant Abigail Porter made a significant contribution to the guide by preparing the first drafts of more than 400 curriculum annotations on the basis of the reviewers' evaluations. Retha Rutkowski, reading specialist with Fairfax County Public Schools in Virginia, analyzed curriculum materials for reading level. As developmental and managing editor for the project, Dorothy Sawicki participated in all aspects of the editing, scheduling, and production of the guide and drafted overview and introductory material.

Providing logistical support and helping with manuscript preparation tasks during various phases of the project were Sarah Lanning, Lynn Portmann, James Munton, and Scott Stefanski. The administrative and photographic skills of Matt Smith, NSRC editorial assistant, are gratefully acknowledged. The NSRC also appreciates the cooperation of Inez Cohen, principal of Rocky Run Middle School in Chantilly, Virginia, and her school for participating in a photo shoot for the guide.

The NSRC wishes to recognize the assistance of the many hundreds of organizations and individuals who contributed time and effort to the information-gathering and review stages of the manuscript. Special thanks go to the reviewers of the various parts of the manuscript: Marilyn Decker, Associate Director for Programs and Science at the Center for the Enhancement of Science and Math Education in Boston, Mass.; Charles N. Hardy, former NSRC Deputy Director for Information Dissemination, Materials Development, and Publications (1995-96); Becky Smith, former Elementary Science/Social Sciences Curriculum Materials Editor with the Mesa Public Schools in Mesa, Ariz.; and Dean Trackman, NSRC Publications Director. The NSRC also acknowledges with gratitude the technical review of the section on "Museums and Other Places to Visit" carried out by the Association of Science-Technology Centers under the direction of Ellen Griffee and Franklin Boyd.

And, finally, this guide would not have been possible without the support of the many teachers and scientists who reviewed curriculum materials. Following is a list of their names and affiliations.

CURRICULUM REVIEW PANEL

GEORGIANA F. ABOKO-COLE
Director, Center for Preprofessional Education, College of Arts and Sciences, Howard University, Washington, D.C.

LORA ADAMS
Teacher, Prince George's County Public Schools, Charles Carroll Middle School, New Carrollton, Md.

JANE ALBERT
Teacher, Howard County Public Schools, Mount View Middle School, Marriottsville, Md.

MARJAY D. ANDERSON
Professor and Chair, Comprehensive Sciences Department, Howard University, Washington, D.C.

HAROLD BAER
Retired. Center for Biologics Evaluation and Research, Food and Drug Administration, Washington, D.C.

MARY BAILEY
Teacher, Fairfax County Public Schools, Langston Hughes Middle School, Reston, Va.

GINO C. BATTISTONE
Biochemist (retired), U.S. Army Institute of Dental Research, Walter Reed Army Medical Center, Washington, D.C.

PAULA BATZER
Teacher, Charles County Public Schools, Piccowaxen Middle School, Newburg, Md.

RICHARD BERENDZEN
Professor, Department of Physics, American University, Washington, D.C.

OTTO BERGMANN
Professor, Department of Physics, George Washington University, Washington, D.C.

WILLIAM C. BURTON
Geologist, U.S. Geological Survey, Reston, Va.

LYNN CARRUBBA
Teacher, Frederick County Public Schools, Monocacy Middle School, Frederick, Md.

IDA CHOW
Executive Officer, Society for Developmental Biology, Bethesda, Md.

BARBARA CHRISTIAN
Teacher, Fairfax County Public Schools, Franklin Middle School, Chantilly, Va.

ANNA COBLE
Associate Professor, Department of Physics and Astrophysics, Howard University, Washington, D.C.

KATHRYN DAVIS
Teacher, Fairfax County Public Schools, Rocky Run Middle School, Chantilly, Va.

LARRY DAVIS
Computer Scientist, User Technology Associates, Department of Defense High Performance Computing Modernization Office, Arlington, Va.

ROBERT EHRLICH
Professor, Department of Physics and Astronomy, George Mason University, Fairfax, Va.

RICHARD FENICHEL
Pharmacologist (retired), Wyeth-Ayrest, Princeton, N.J.

ANNA FORTIER
Microbiologist, Entremed, Rockville, Md.

SUSAN GDOVIN
Microbiologist, University of Maryland, College Park, Md.

MARIA GIOVANNI
Molecular Biologist, National Eye Institute/National Institutes of Health, Bethesda, Md.

BROOK GREEN
Teacher, Frederick County Public Schools, Thurmont Middle School, Thurmont, Md.

TERESA HEIN
Instructor, Department of Physics, American University, Washington, D.C.

RACHELLE S. HELLER
Professor, Department of Electrical Engineering and Computer Science, George Washington University, Washington, D.C.

TERRY HUFFORD
Professor, Department of Biological Sciences, George Washington University, Washington, D.C.

MARILYN IRVING
Professor, Department of Curriculum and Instruction, Howard University, Washington, D.C.

PATRICIA JACOBBERGER-JELLISON
Geologist, Smithsonian Institution, Washington, D.C.

PHILIP B. JOHNSON
Physicist, Lockheed Martin Corporation, Manassas, Va.

THERESE JOHNSTON
Teacher, Alexandria City Schools, George Washington Middle School, Alexandria, Va.

ELLA JORDAN
Teacher, Howard County Public Schools, Ellicott Mills Middle School, Ellicott City, Md.

HOWARD KAPLAN
Retired. Department of Biology and Environmental Science, University of the District of Columbia, Washington, D.C.

DONALD KELSO
Associate Professor, Department of Biology, George Mason University, Fairfax, Va.

ROBERT KNOWLTON
Associate Professor, Department of Biological Sciences, George Washington University, Washington, D.C.

DONALD W. KUPKE
Professor, Department of Chemistry, University of Virginia, Charlottesville, Va.

JACQUELINE LEE
Teacher, Fairfax County Public Schools, Rocky Run Middle School, Chantilly, Va.

PETER LEVIN
Assistant to Counselor to the President, The White House, Washington, D.C.; and Associate Professor of Electrical and Computer Engineering and Supervisor of Computation, Fields Laboratory, Worcester Polytechnic Institute, Worcester, Mass.

RAMON LOPEZ
Associate Research Scientist, Department of Astronomy, University of Maryland, College Park, Md.; Director of Education and Outreach, American Physical Society, College Park, Md.

PETER LYTTLE
Geologist, U.S. Geological Survey,
Reston, Va.

LEONARD C. MAXIMON
Professor, Department of Physics, George
Washington University, Washington, D.C.

TED A. MAXWELL
Associate Director, Collections and
Research, National Air and Space
Museum, Smithsonian Institution,
Washington, D.C.

NATALIE MEYERS
Teacher, Howard County Public Schools,
Clarksville Middle School, Clarksville, Md.

CYNTHIA B. MILLER
Teacher, Frederick County Public
Schools, Governor Thomas Johnson
Middle School, Frederick, Md.

HENRY MILNE
Teacher, Montgomery County Public
Schools, Cabin John Middle School,
Rockville, Md.

GWENDOLYN MINOR
Teacher, Fairfax County Public Schools,
Kilmer Middle School, Vienna, Va.

VERNON MORRIS
Assistant Professor, Chemistry and
Atmospheric Sciences, Howard University and Center for Atmospheres,
Washington, D.C.

LINDA NEWSOME
Teacher, Prince George's County Public
Schools, Benjamin Tasker Middle School,
Bowie, Md.

MARY ANN PETERSON
Teacher, Arlington Public Schools,
Williamsburg Middle School, Arlington, Va.

MARY QUEEN
Teacher-Facilitator of Middle School
Science, Frederick County Public
Schools, Ballenger Creek Middle School,
Frederick, Md.

NINA ROSCHER
Professor and Chair, Department of
Chemistry, American University,
Washington, D.C.

JAN RUEHLE
Teacher, Loudoun County Public
Schools, Farmwell Station Middle
School, Ashburn, Va.

CHRISTINA M. SAX
Molecular Biologist, National Institutes of
Health, Bethesda, Md.

CONSTANCE SKELTON
Teacher, Arlington Public Schools,
Williamsburg Middle School, Arlington, Va.

MAENETTE B. (DONNA) SMITH
Teacher, Prince George's County Public
Schools, Walker Mill Middle School,
Capital Heights, Md.

DOUGLAS R. SPICHER
Teacher, Prince George's County Public
Schools, Hyattsville Middle School,
Hyattsville, Md.

GEORGE C. STEPHENS
Professor and Chair, Department of
Geology, George Washington University,
Washington, D.C.

SUSAN STEWARD
Teacher, Arlington Public Schools,
Gunston Middle School, Arlington, Va.

JOSEPHINE R. STONE
Teacher, Prince George's County Public
Schools, Martin Luther King, Jr.,
Academic Center, Beltsville, Md.

MILLICENT T. TATE
Teacher, Prince William County Public
Schools, Fred Lynn Middle School,
Woodbridge, Va.

JOSEPH TEACH
Teacher, District of Columbia Public
Schools, Jefferson Junior High School,
Washington, D.C.

BERNHARD TRAMS
Teacher, Montgomery County Public
Schools, Eastern Middle School, Silver
Spring, Md.

CLARENCE WADE
Professor, Department of Chemistry,
University of the District of Columbia,
Washington, D.C.

MARTHA WEISS
Assistant Professor, Department of
Biology, Georgetown University,
Washington, D.C.

DAVID WILLIAMS
Adjunct Faculty Member, Department of
Chemistry, George Mason University,
Fairfax, Va.

RENEKKI WILSON
Teacher, District of Columbia Public
Schools, Roper Middle School,
Washington, D.C.

NATHANIEL W. WOODRICK
Director, Institute for Science, Space and
Technology, Howard University,
Washington, D.C.

NANCY ZELLER
Adjunct Professor, Department of Biology,
American University, Washington, D.C.

Building a compass

PART 1

INTRODUCTION
TO THE GUIDE

PART 1

Classroom teachers and school administrators often ask the National Science Resources Center (NSRC), which is sponsored jointly by the Smithsonian Institution and the National Academy of Sciences, for guidance in identifying effective science curriculum materials at the middle school level. *Resources for Teaching Middle School Science,* the second in the NSRC's series of resource guides, is a compendium of useful information that can provide such guidance. The volume reviews curriculum materials—hands-on, inquiry-centered materials that align with the National Science Education Standards—and sources of assistance for teaching middle school science.

The central focus of *Resources for Teaching Middle School Science* is to provide guidance in identifying and evaluating middle school science curriculum materials and resources. The volume addresses this objective in the following ways:

- It identifies a broad spectrum of middle school science curriculum materials, published from about 1987 to 1998, that are pedagogically and scientifically sound and that are in alignment with the National Science Education Standards.

- It provides descriptive annotations for these materials, totaling about 400 individual books and units. These annotations include the recommended grade level, a description of major concepts and activities presented in the material, and bibliographic and ordering information. For some categories of materials, a series or program overview is also included, as is a reading level and a key to the National Science Education Standards that are addressed in the materials.

- The appendixes include the comprehensive set of criteria that were used by scientists and teachers in evaluating middle school materials for this volume. These evaluation criteria emphasize a hands-on, inquiry-centered approach to science education, addressing the goals and principles defined in the *National Science Education Standards*. The criteria can be used by science curriculum adoption committees at the local, state, or regional levels.
- The appendixes also include excerpts from the *National Science Education Standards*—specifically, the content standards for grades five through eight.
- The guide describes a variety of reference works of particular relevance for middle school science teachers. It also identifies sources of authoritative reviews of computer software and multimedia programs that can help teachers keep abreast of this fast-moving field.

- The guide includes information about 700 facilities and organizations throughout the United States that offer programs and resources to enhance and support hands-on middle school science. Several facilities in Canada are also included.

While the materials and resources listed here can be used to improve an existing program or to design a complete curriculum, it should be emphasized that the guide is not a recipe for a middle school science program. Neither the National Science Education Standards nor this guide was designed to prescribe a curriculum. Ultimately, it is up to teachers, schools, and local entities to select the particular materials that best fit their needs.

The curriculum materials annotated in the guide have not been ranked or assigned ratings. They have all achieved the general objectives set by the evaluation criteria. Their inclusion indicates that scientists and teachers have judged them to be effective materials.

Beyond that, each item is unique and accomplishes its learning objectives in its own individual fashion. Thus, ranking could be misleading. What might be considered very useful in one classroom might be less appropriate elsewhere because of different needs and circumstances. The full array of materials presented here provides sufficient diversity to enable teachers and schools to select what best suits their own needs.

Contents of the Guide

Resources for Teaching Middle School Science is organized in three major parts—

- Part 2, "Middle School Science Curriculum Materials,"
- Part 3, "Reference Materials,"
- Part 4, "Ancillary Resources."

An overview sets the stage for each part, describing and discussing the types, sources, and organization of the information presented. Following each overview are individual chapters containing annotations.

A boxed "nuts-and-bolts" section in each chapter gives detailed information about the annotations.

Part 2, "Middle School Science Curriculum Materials," includes six chapters. The first five contain annotations to curriculum materials, arranged by scientific discipline or field. These six chapters are—

- Chapter 1, "Physical Science,"
- Chapter 2, "Life Science,"
- Chapter 3, "Environmental Science,"
- Chapter 4, "Earth and Space Science,"
- Chapter 5, "Multidisciplinary and Applied Science,"
- Chapter 6, "Sources of Information on Educational Software and Multimedia Programs."

In the first five chapters, the annotations are subdivided in the following categories: Core Materials, Supplementary Units, and Science Activity Books. These categories are described in the Part 2 "Overview."

Part 3, "Reference Materials," includes three chapters—

- Chapter 7, "Books on Teaching Science,"
- Chapter 8, "Science Book Lists and Resource Guides,"
- Chapter 9, "Periodicals."

Chapter 7 focuses on reference materials that offer guidance in learning theory and pedagogical techniques specifically for the middle school teacher. Chapter 8 annotates directories and other sourcebooks, including guides to materials and to science trade books for students. Chapter 9 offers a carefully chosen collection of periodical titles for teachers and students. It includes a recommended grade level for each student publication.

Part 4, "Ancillary Resources," includes two chapters—

- Chapter 10, "Museums and Other Places to Visit,"
- Chapter 11, "Professional Associations and U.S. Government Organizations."

Chapter 10 presents a wealth of information for the enrichment of middle school science education. The two large subsections in the chapter identify some 600 facilities throughout the United States and several in Canada to which middle school teachers can take their students for hands-on, inquiry-centered science experiences.

Chapter 11 then highlights more than 100 institutions, such as federal government organizations and professional societies, that are engaged in active efforts to provide information, services, or materials for the enhancement of middle school science teaching and learning.

Resources for Teaching Middle School Science also contains four appendixes. Appendix A, "Publishers and Suppliers," provides addresses and contact information for obtaining the curriculum and reference materials annotated in the chapters.

Appendix B, "NSRC Evaluation Criteria for Curriculum Materials," briefly discusses how the middle school criteria were developed, and indicates that they may be used by school district science curriculum adoption committees. The criteria are reproduced in the appendix in a format appropriate for school district use.

Appendix C, "National Science Education Standards: Content Standards for Levels 5-8," contains material reprinted from the *National Science Education Standards* for the convenience of readers. A brief introduction discusses the standards and explains how they relate to the other information contained in the guide.

Appendix D, "Overviews of Core and Supplementary Programs with Titles Annotated in This Guide," lists, by program, the individual titles annotated in the sections "Core Materials" and "Supplementary Units" in the five curriculum chapters. A brief description of each science program is also provided.

An extensive set of indexes provides access to the resources annotated in the guide. Title, name, and subject indexes are included, as well as special indexes that focus on particular aspects of the curriculum materials—for example, on the core and supplementary materials according to the content standards they address. Two indexes help readers locate materials at a specific grade level in a specific area of science. Another index covers the major topics addressed in the curriculum materials.

What Is Not Included in the Guide

Several kinds of teaching resources are not reviewed in *Resources for Teaching Middle School Science*—for example, computer software and audiovisual materials (such as films, videotapes, and videodiscs). Instead, the guide concentrates on print curriculum materials, although it does indicate when software and audiovisuals are components of a program. For information on science computer software and audiovisual materials—which can play an important role in the science classroom and can be integrated with print materials and kits to enrich science teaching—readers are referred to Chapter 6, "Sources of Information on Educational Software and Multimedia Programs."

This guide also does not attempt to review the vast number of science trade books that can be used to enrich students' knowledge and understanding. Many teachers use such books as an integral part of their science curriculum, and the NSRC urges teachers to supplement hands-on activities in the classroom with extensive reading of science trade books. For sources of current information on science trade books, readers are referred to Chapter 8, "Science Book Lists and Resource Guides," and Chapter 9, "Periodicals."

PART 2

MIDDLE SCHOOL SCIENCE CURRICULUM MATERIALS

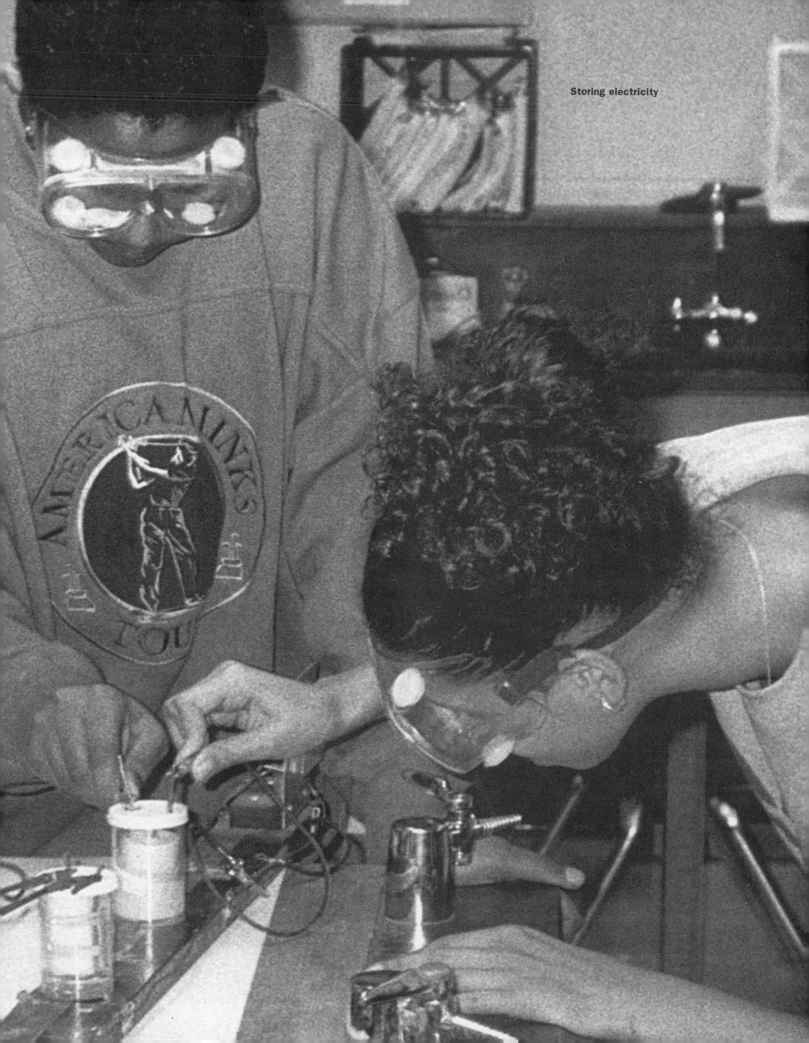

Storing electricity

The first five chapters in part 2 of *Resources for Teaching Middle School Science* include annotations for an extensive selection of currently available print curriculum materials, produced between 1987 and 1998, for teaching hands-on, inquiry-centered science in grades six through eight. These materials were selected for inclusion in the guide on the basis of a set of evaluation criteria, developed by the National Science Resources Center, that incorporate the goals and principles defined in the *National Science Education Standards.*

The five chapters and examples of the topics they include are—

- Chapter 1, "Physical Science," which includes materials on such topics as the chemistry of matter, heat energy, electricity and magnetism, and sound and light.
- Chapter 2, "Life Science," which includes materials on topics such as cells, plants and animals, heredity, human biology and health, and biodiversity.
- Chapter 3, "Environmental Science," which includes materials on topics such as acid rain, global warming, and pollution. (These materials may approach their subject from the perspective of the life, physical, and/or earth sciences, but the overall topic is of an "environmental" nature.)
- Chapter 4, "Earth and Space Science," which includes materials on topics such as the earth and other planets, earthquakes, rocks and minerals, weather, and oceanography.

- Chapter 5, "Multidisciplinary and Applied Science," which includes materials on widely varying topics, such as matter and energy in the biosphere, the technology of paper, and transportation systems. Materials in this chapter relate to several scientific disciplines, integrate scientific disciplines, or focus on the application of scientific processes.

The last chapter in part 2— Chapter 6, "Sources of Information on Educational Software and Multimedia Programs"— directs readers to some of the periodicals, directories, and organizations that specialize in reviewing computer software and other multimedia instructional materials appropriate for middle school science classrooms.

The extensive indexes at the end of the guide, including the index of topics addressed in curriculum materials, can help readers locate annotations on particular subjects.

The Organization of Materials in Chapters 1–5

Because instructional materials are designed to be used in different ways, the NSRC has identified three categories for classifying different types of science curriculum materials. The annotations in the curriculum chapters are placed in these three categories:

- **Core materials** are substantial enough to form the foundation of a comprehensive middle school science curriculum.
- **Supplementary units** often consist of a series of activity-centered lessons. These units can provide enrichment for inquiry-based science teaching but may not have the depth or focus of core curriculum units.
- **Science activity books** offer a selection of ideas and activities to facilitate science learning. These materials are generally too broad in scope or specific in focus to serve as the foundation of a comprehensive science program.

The placement of materials in these three categories implies no judgment as to the quality or merit of the materials reviewed. All of the materials annotated in this guide are considered to be effective teaching materials.

The Annotations

This section provides an explanation of how the information in the annotations is organized.

- **Alphabetical arrangement of annotations by title, with entry numbers.** The annotations in chapters 1 through 5 are arranged alphabetically by title in each category. In addition, each annotation has a two-part entry number. (The chapter number is given before the period; the number after the period locates the entry within that chapter. For example, the first entry number in chapter 1 is 1.1; the second entry in chapter 2 is 2.2, and so on.) The entry numbers within each curriculum chapter run consecutively through Core Materials, Supplementary Units, and Science Activity Books.

(The indexes locate each title by its entry number.)

- **Bibliographic information.** The bibliographic information is based on the actual volumes reviewed. (Some titles may have been revised or updated since materials were submitted for review.)

- **Program overviews for core and supplementary units.** Most core and supplementary units are developed in the context of a curriculum series or program. A brief description of the series or program is presented with each title in these categories in order to provide readers with a more complete picture of the material. (*See also* appendix D.)

- **Recommended grade level.** The narrative description of each item is preceded by the grade level recommended by teacher reviewers during the NSRC review of curriculum materials. The recommendations reflect the reviewers' judgment of the levels for which the learning activities would be most appropriate. In some instances, the recommended grade level may differ slightly from the publisher's advertised level.

- **Reading level.** A reading level is indicated for core materials. This designation, which appears immediately after the recommended grade level, was provided by a reading specialist using the Edward Fry Readability Scale. Together with the recommended grade level, it can help teachers gauge whether material is appropriate for their students not only conceptually but in terms of students' reading ability. (On occasion, a unit did not have student reading selections of sufficient length to use this reading scale, so the reading level could not be included.)

- **Description of the curriculum material.** The curriculum annotations were written specifically to provide information and assistance to those involved in teaching classes and designing programs in middle school science. These descriptions focus on what students will learn and do. Each annotation describes the organization of the piece of curriculum material and the support it provides for teachers. The descriptions of some core materials and supplementary units are subdivided into parts that describe the different components—for example, Student Edition, Teacher's Guide, Supplementary Laboratory Manual, and so forth—to give as complete a view of the material as possible within the space limitations of this volume.

- **Unit structure and time required for completion.** Information is given about the internal structure of a unit and, where available, about the length of time needed to complete it—for example, the number of lessons or class periods, the suggested length of lessons, or the overall time required.

Such information is taken directly from the unit, textbook, or activity book itself, although not all books or units state this information consistently.

- **Key to content standards: 5-8.** After the narrative description of each core and supplementary unit is a list of the content standards for grades 5-8 that are characterized by that unit or textbook. The content standards are from the *National Science Education Standards* (NSES) (*see* appendix C, which contains the reprinted text of the NSES content standards for grades 5-8).

- **Ordering information.** Each entry in the curriculum chapters ends with information on the cost of the materials and where they can be ordered. The cost information should be checked with publishers or distributors

before ordering, since prices are subject to change. (Appendix A, "Publishers and Suppliers," provides addresses and contact information.)

NSRC's Review of Curriculum Materials

To gather curriculum materials for review, the NSRC issued general invitations to publishers to submit materials and attempted to obtain any that were not forthcoming. Many hundreds of titles were reviewed in the course of the NSRC review process. Among these were any titles that had been annotated in NSRC's first guide in the series—*Resources for Teaching Elementary School Science*—that were appropriate for sixth-grade science courses. Such materials were reviewed according to the NSRC's "Evaluation Criteria for Middle School Science Curriculum Materials" and are included here if they met the criteria.

The review process developed by the NSRC for the selec-

tion of curriculum materials involved panels of teachers and scientists. The teachers were experienced and knowledgeable in the teaching of middle school science, with most being lead science teachers or master teachers who had taught in school districts with effective science programs. Their backgrounds included participation in numerous science curriculum development activities; they had training and experience teaching students with different learning styles and abilities and had taught student populations representing diverse cultural and ethnic backgrounds. The panels also included individuals with experience and training in cooperative learning, assessment strategies, the integration of curriculum, and the use of modern technology. Reviewers had experience with a variety of instructional materials for middle school science programs and were able to use the NSRC evaluation criteria effectively to identify differences and to recognize strengths and weaknesses in curriculum materials.

The scientists on the panel had expertise in one of four areas—life science, earth science, physical science, and applied science or technology. Every effort was made to match each scientist reviewer with curriculum materials relevant to his or her area of expertise. The scientists on the panel included teaching professors, working scientists, and others with an understanding of pre-college science education.

NSRC's Curriculum Evaluation Criteria

Consistent with the NSRC's philosophy of science teaching and with the National Science Education Standards, the materials included in this guide are hands-on and inquiry-centered. Briefly described, such materials provide opportunities for students to learn through direct observation and experimentation; they engage students in experiences not to confirm the "right" answer but to investigate the nature of things and to arrive at explanations that are scientifically correct and satisfying to young adolescents. These experiences offer students opportunities to experiment productively, to ask questions and find their own answers, and to develop patience, persistence, and confidence in their ability to tackle and solve real problems.

The evaluation criteria developed by the NSRC are based on the goals and principles defined in the *National Science Education Standards*. The NSRC evaluation criteria are also informed by the experience gained by the NSRC in its ongoing review of science curriculum materials under the auspices of the National Academy of Sciences and the Smithsonian Institution; and in its outreach work with teachers, superintendents, principals, and science curriculum coordinators across the United States.

The evaluation criteria that the NSRC developed are organized in the following sections:

- **Pedagogical appropriateness.** These criteria elaborate on the following key questions: Do the materials promote effective middle school science teaching and learning? Are inquiry and activity the basis of the learning experiences? Are the topics addressed in the unit and the modes of instruction developmentally appropriate?

- **Science content and presentation.** These criteria address whether the science content is accurate, up to date, and effectively presented. Specific issues addressed include the following: Do the suggested investigations lead to an understanding of basic science concepts and principles? Is the writing style interesting and engaging, while respecting scientific language? Which of the subject matter standards from the *National Science Education Standards* does the material focus on?

- **Organization and format; materials, equipment, and supplies; and equity issues.** The criteria on organization and format include questions about the presentation of information—for example, whether the suggestions for instructional delivery are adequate and whether the print materials for students are well written, age appropriate, and compelling in content. The criteria concerning hands-on science materials focus on questions such as the clarity and adequacy of instructions on manipulating laboratory equipment and the inclusion of appropriate safety precautions. Criteria addressing equity issues include the question of whether the material is free of cultural, racial, gender, and age bias.

The NSRC evaluation criteria are reprinted in appendix B, "NSRC Evaluation Criteria for Curriculum Materials." Teachers, curriculum specialists, curriculum developers, principals, superintendents, and those involved in various aspects of science education reform may find the criteria not only instructive, but useful as an instrument for reviewing instructional materials for local adoption.

CHAPTER 1

PHYSICAL SCIENCE

1.1 **Chemistry of Matter.** 3rd ed. Anthea Maton, Jean Hopkins, Susan Johnson, and others. Prentice Hall Science Integrated Learning System series. Upper Saddle River, N.J.: Prentice Hall, 1997.

Program Overview The Prentice Hall Science Integrated Learning System series is a program for middle school or junior high school students. Designed to cover all relevant areas of science, this program consists of 19 books, each in a particular topic area, such as sound and light, the planet earth, and chemistry of matter. Seven science themes are incorporated into the program; the themes are energy, evolution, patterns of change, scale and structure, systems and interactions, unity and diversity, and stability. For each unit, teaching materials, ancillary student materials, and some optional components are available.

Student Edition **Recommended grade level: 8+. Reading level: 12.** The textbook *Chemistry of Matter,* which introduces students to the chemical properties of matter, is organized in 5 chapters: (1) "Atoms and Bonding," (2) "Chemical Reactions," (3) "Families of Chemical Compounds," (4) "Petrochemical Technology," and (5) "Radioactive Elements." Students learn about ionic, covalent, and metallic bonds and about how to predict bond type. They also learn about chemical reactions, chemical equations, and the energy associated with chemical reactions. They study the nature of solutions and the factors that affect the rate of solution and solubility. Students also investigate acids, bases, and salts, as well as carbon compounds, petrochemical technology, and polymerization. They are introduced to the properties of radioactive elements, find out how nuclear reactions (including transmutation, fission, and fusion)

occur, and learn about the uses and dangers of radioactivity.

Each chapter includes a lab investigation. Students explore the melting points and conductivity of ionic and covalent compounds, and they see how the concentration of a substance affects reaction rate. They also experiment with acids and bases to discover their properties, and discover how natural and synthetic polymers compare in strength, absorbency, and resistance to chemical damage.

Each chapter contains comprehensive reading sections that introduce major science concepts. Suggestions are provided for activities in which students "find out by doing," "find out by reading," and "find out by writing." Other skills-oriented activities are also suggested—for example, growing salt crystals and testing the pH of common household substances.

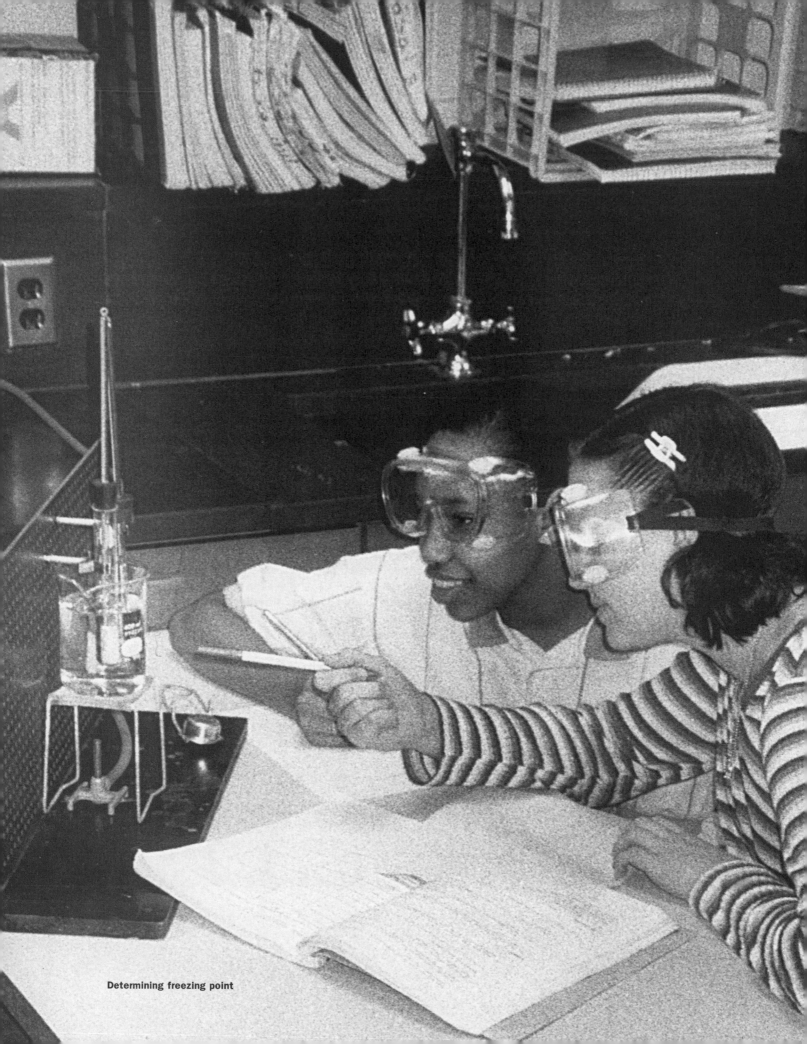

Determining freezing point

Other features include problem-solving challenges, science career descriptions, and science connections to real-world events or issues. The student edition closes with readings on 3 topics: the "bucky ball" carbon molecule, the use of plant material for fuel, and silicon-based plastics and other new materials.

Teacher's Edition In the teacher's wraparound edition, each chapter begins with a 2-page planning guide and a 2-page preview that summarizes each section within the chapter. The teacher's edition also provides suggestions for teaching, guiding, integrating, and closing lessons, as well as enrichments, extensions, and answers to questions in the student text.

Supplementary Laboratory Manual The supplementary lab manual provides 15 additional investigations directly correlated with the information presented in the student textbook. Examples of investigations include the synthesis of copper oxide by heating copper metal in air, the decomposition of water by electrolysis, performing a double replacement reaction, determining the effect of temperature on the solution process, and determining the amount of vitamin C in a sample of fruit juice.

Program Resources and Support Materials A variety of materials, including some optional components, is available. A teacher's resource package contains the student edition

ABOUT THE ANNOTATIONS IN "PHYSICAL SCIENCE— CORE MATERIALS"

Entry Numbers
Curriculum materials are arranged alphabetically by title in each category (Core Materials, Supplementary Units, and Science Activity Books) in chapters 1 through 5 of this guide.

Each curriculum annotation has a two-part entry number: the chapter number is given before the period; the number after the period locates the entry within that chapter. For example, the first entry number in chapter 1 is 1.1; the second entry in chapter 2 is 2.2; and so on.

The entry numbers within each curriculum chapter run consecutively through Core Materials, Supplementary Units, and Science Activity Books.

Order of Bibliographic Information
Following is the arrangement of the facts of publication in the annotations in this section:

- **Title of publication**
- **Number of edition,** if applicable
- **Authors** (an individual author or authors, an institutional author, or a project or program name under which the material was developed)
- **Series title**
- **Series developer,** if applicable
- **Place of publication, publisher, and date of publication**

Recommended Grade Level and Reading Level
The grade level for each piece of material was recommended by teacher evaluators during the development of this guide. In some instances, the recommended grade level may differ slightly from the publisher's advertised level. The Fry Readability Scale was used to determine the approximate reading level of core materials.

Key to Content Standards: 5-8
The key lists the content standards for grades 5-8 from the *National Science Education Standards* (NSES) that are addressed in depth by the item. A key is provided for core materials and supplementary units. (*See* appendix C.)

Price and Acquisition Information

Ordering information appears at the end of each entry. Included are—

- **Prices** (of teacher's guides, student books, lab manuals, and kits or units)
- **Publisher/supplier** (The name of a principal publisher/supplier, although not necessarily the sole source, for the items listed in the price category. Appendix A, "Publishers and Suppliers," provides the address, phone and fax numbers, and electronic ordering information, where available, for each publisher and supplier.)
- **Materials** (various sources from which one might obtain the required materials)

Readers must contact publishers/suppliers for complete and up-to-date listings of the program resources and support materials available for a particular unit. Depending on the developer, these items may be required, optional, or both; they may be offered individually and/or in kits, packages, or boxes. Materials may change with revised editions. The prices given in this chapter for selected resources or materials are based on information from the publishers and suppliers but are not meant to represent the full range of ordering options.

Indexes of Curriculum Materials

The multiple indexes on pp. 449-78 allow easy access to the information in this guide. Various aspects of the curriculum materials—including titles, topics addressed in each unit, grade levels, and standards addressed—are the focus of seven separate indexes. For example, titles and entry numbers are listed in the "Title Index" on pp. 450-54. The "Index of Authors, Series, and Curriculum Projects," on pp. 455-57, provides entry numbers of any annotated titles in a particular series.

Overviews of Core and Supplementary Programs

Appendix D, "Overviews of Core and Supplementary Programs with Titles Annotated in This Guide," on pp. 441-48, lists, by program or series, the individual titles annotated in the sections "Core Materials" and "Supplementary Units" in the five curriculum chapters.

and annotated teacher's editions of both the textbook and the lab manual, as well as a test book, an activity book, a review-and-reinforcement guide, and English and Spanish audiotapes for auditory and language learners. Other available materials include interactive videodiscs, transparencies, assessment materials, English and Spanish guides for language learners, a study guide, a teacher's desk reference, and a booklet of product-testing activities.

Key to Content Standards: 5-8 (see app. C)

UNIFYING CONCEPTS AND PROCESSES: Systems, order, and organization; change, constancy, and measurement.
SCIENCE AS INQUIRY: Abilities necessary to do scientific inquiry; understandings about scientific inquiry.
PHYSICAL SCIENCE: Properties and changes of properties in matter; transfer of energy.
SCIENCE AND TECHNOLOGY: Understandings about science and technology.
SCIENCE IN PERSONAL AND SOCIAL PERSPECTIVES: Natural hazards; risks and benefits; science and technology in society.
HISTORY AND NATURE OF SCIENCE: Science as a human endeavor; history of science.

Prices: Student edition (ISBN 0-13-423351-4), $9.97. Teacher's edition (ISBN 0-13-423120-1), $22.97. Teacher's resource package, $112.97. (Contact publisher/supplier for complete price and ordering information.)
Publisher/supplier: Prentice Hall.
Materials: Available locally, or from commercial suppliers.

1.2 **Electricity and Magnetism.** 3rd ed. Anthea Maton, Jean Hopkins, Susan Johnson, and others. Prentice Hall Science Integrated Learning System series. Upper Saddle River, N.J.: Prentice Hall, 1997.

Program Overview The Prentice Hall Science Integrated Learning System series is a program for middle school or junior high school students. Designed to cover all relevant areas of science, this program consists of 19 books, each in a particular topic area, such as sound and light, the planet earth, and electricity and magnetism. Seven science themes are incorporated into the program; the themes are energy, evolution, patterns of change, scale and structure, systems and interactions, unity and diversity, and stability. For each unit, teaching materials, ancillary student materials, and some optional components are available.

Student Edition **Recommended grade level: 8+. Reading level: middle 10.** Concepts that students explore in *Electricity and Magnetism* include the atomic basis of electric charge, static electricity, voltage, current, and resistance. They also learn about magnetism and magnetic poles, fields, lines of force, domains, the earth's magnetic force, and compasses. Then they are introduced to electromagnetism and electromagnetic induction. Students gain an understanding of the real-world application of these concepts as they learn how electronic devices such as vacuum tubes, transistors, integrated circuits, radios and televisions, and computers work. The safe use of electricity is discussed.

In laboratory investigations, students produce electricity from a lemon, they plot a magnetic field using a bar magnet, and they investigate what factors affect the strength of an electromagnet and what materials are attracted to it.

Electricity and Magnetism has 4 chapters: (1) "Electric Charges and Currents," (2) "Magnetism," (3) "Electromagnetism," and (4) "Electronics and Computers." Each chapter contains comprehensive reading sections that introduce major science concepts. Suggestions are provided for activities in which students "find out by doing," "find out by reading," and "find out by writing." Other skills-oriented activities are also suggested—for example, using common materials to observe static electricity and writing a report about the discovery and history of lodestones. Each chapter includes a formal lab investigation.

Other features include problem-solving challenges, science career descriptions, and science connections to real-world events or issues. The student edition closes with readings on 3 topics: the search for superconductors, the possible danger of electromagnetic radiation to humans, and the potential for the development of a "living" computer some day.

Teacher's Edition In the teacher's wraparound edition, each chapter begins with a 2-page planning guide and a 2-page preview that summarizes each section within the chapter. The teacher's edition also provides suggestions for teaching, guiding, integrating, and closing lessons, as well as enrichments, extensions, and answers to questions in the student text.

Supplementary Laboratory Manual The supplementary lab manual provides 7 additional investigations directly correlated with the information presented in the student textbook. Examples of activities include constructing series and parallel circuits and measuring their current and voltage, using bar magnets and iron filings to explore magnetism and magnetic fields, investigating electromagnetic induction, and constructing a simple computer circuit that converts decimal numbers into binary numbers.

Program Resources and Support Materials A variety of materials, including some optional components, is available. A teacher's resource package contains the student edition and annotated teacher's edition of both the textbook and the lab manual, as well as a test book, an activity book, a review-and-reinforcement guide, and English and Spanish audiotapes for auditory and language learners. Other available materials include videotapes, interactive videodiscs, transparencies, assessment materials, English and Spanish guides for language learners, a study guide, a teacher's desk reference, and a booklet of product-testing activities.

Key to Content Standards: 5-8 (see app. C)

UNIFYING CONCEPTS AND PROCESSES: Systems, order, and organization; change, constancy, and measurement.

SCIENCE AS INQUIRY: Abilities necessary to do scientific inquiry; understandings about scientific inquiry.

PHYSICAL SCIENCE: Transfer of energy.

SCIENCE AND TECHNOLOGY: Understandings about science and technology.

SCIENCE IN PERSONAL AND SOCIAL PERSPECTIVES: Risks and benefits; science and technology in society.

HISTORY AND NATURE OF SCIENCE: Nature of science; history of science.

Prices: Student edition (ISBN 0-13-423344-1), $9.97. Teacher's edition (ISBN 0-13-423112-0), $22.97. Teacher's resource package, $112.97. (Contact publisher/supplier for complete price and ordering information.) *Publisher/supplier:* Prentice Hall. *Materials:* Available locally, or from commercial suppliers.

1.3 **Exploring Physical Science.** 2nd ed. Anthea Maton, Jean Hopkins, Susan Johnson, and others. Prentice Hall Exploring Life, Earth, and Physical Science series. Upper Saddle River, N.J.: Prentice Hall, 1997.

Program Overview The Prentice Hall Exploring Life, Earth, and Physical Science series is a program for middle school students. Designed to cover all relevant areas of science, this integrated program consists of 3 textbooks (1 for each major discipline) and incorporates 7 science themes—energy, evolution, patterns of change, scale and structure, systems and interactions, unity and diversity, and stability. Each of the 3 year-long courses contains about 6 units. The units are also available, possibly with some modifications, as individual textbooks in the Prentice Hall Science Integrated Learning System series (*see*, e.g., 1.1). For each course, teaching materials, ancillary student materials, and some optional components are available.

Student Edition **Recommended grade level: 7-8. Reading level: middle 7.** *Exploring Physical Science* offers a complete course on matter and energy. The units in this textbook are entitled (1) "Matter: Building Block of the Universe"; (2) "Chemistry of Matter"; (3) "Motion, Forces, and Energy"; (4) "Heat Energy"; (5) "Electricity and Magnetism"; and (6) "Sound and Light." Throughout the course, students learn about physical and chemical changes, the classification of matter, atoms and bonding, radioactivity, energy and its role in motion, forces and machinery, electricity and magnetism, electronics and computers, the nature and characteristics of waves, and optical instruments.

Examples of the lab investigations that students conduct during the 6 units are these: determining how concentration affects reaction rate, producing electricity from a lemon, building a shoe-box-sized model of a solar collector, exploring the connection between mass and inertia, observing the physical and chemical properties of a lighted and an unlighted candle, exploring how a change in mass affects the velocity of an object if its kinetic energy is kept constant, and recording the temperatures of different regions of an electromagnetic spectrum.

Each of the 6 units in *Exploring Physical Science* typically has 4 to 6 chapters. Each chapter contains comprehensive reading sections that introduce major science concepts. Other skills-oriented activities are also suggested for discovering, doing, calculating, thinking, and writing about science. The activities range from observing and explaining how many paper clips can stick to the surface of a bar magnet to writing a report about quarks. Each chapter includes a laboratory investigation as well as a review and study guide.

Other features of this textbook include problem-solving challenges, science connections to real-world events or issues, and careers in science. An "Activity Bank" at the back of the book provides at least 1 additional laboratory investigation for each chapter. Examples include calculating the density of objects with an irregular shape, growing and observing crystals, testing foods for fats and starches, measuring the effects of phosphates on plant growth, building and flying paper airplanes to calculate speed and distance, and building a simple model of a passive solar heating system.

Teacher's Edition In the teacher's wraparound edition, each chapter begins with a 2-page planning guide and a 2-page preview that summarizes each section within the chapter. The teacher's edition also provides suggestions for teaching, guiding, integrating, and closing lessons, as well as enrichments, extensions, and answers to questions in the student text.

Supplementary Laboratory Manual The supplementary lab manual provides 61 additional investigations directly correlated with the information presented in the student textbook. Examples include investigating phase changes; examining the properties of ionic and covalent compounds; testing the tensile strengths of cotton, polyester, and cotton-covered polyester threads; determining the center of gravity of an irregularly shaped object; using balls to investigate energy and falling motion; constructing series and parallel circuits and measuring their current and voltage; and constructing a pinnacle viewer and a periscope.

Program Resources and Support Materials A variety of support materials is available, including a box of teaching resources (with activities, worksheets, and assessment materials for each chapter), a teacher's desk reference, an integrated science activity book, a computer test bank, videos, videodiscs, transparencies, a classroom manager guide, and a book of product-testing activities.

Key to Content Standards: 5-8 (see app. C)

UNIFYING CONCEPTS AND PROCESSES: Systems, order, and organization; change, constancy, and measurement.
SCIENCE AS INQUIRY: Abilities necessary to do scientific inquiry; understandings about scientific inquiry.
PHYSICAL SCIENCE: Properties and changes of properties in matter; motions and forces; transfer of energy.
SCIENCE AND TECHNOLOGY: Abilities of technological design; understandings about science and technology.

SCIENCE IN PERSONAL AND SOCIAL PER-SPECTIVES: Science and technology in society.
HISTORY AND NATURE OF SCIENCE: Science as a human endeavor; nature of science; history of science.

Prices: Student edition (ISBN 0-13-418716-4), $41.47. Teacher's edition (ISBN 0-13-422-8332), $70.47. Lab manual, teacher's edition (1995), $24.47. Teaching resources, $306.47. (Contact publisher/supplier for complete price and ordering information.) *Publisher/supplier:* Prentice Hall. *Materials:* Available locally, or from commercial suppliers.

1.4 **Floating and Sinking.** Science and Technology for Children (STC) series. Developed by National Science Resources Center (Washington, D.C.). Burlington, N.C.: Carolina Biological Supply, 1995.

Program Overview The Science and Technology for Children (STC) series consists of 24 inquiry-centered curriculum units for grades 1-6, with 4 units at each grade level. Students learn about topics in the life, earth, and physical sciences. The technological applications of science and the interactions among science, technology, and society are addressed throughout the program. The STC units, each of which takes about 16 class sessions to complete, encourage participatory learning and the integration of science with mathematics, language arts, social studies, and art. The components of an STC unit are a teacher's guide, a student activity book with simple instructions and illustrations, and a kit of materials.

Teacher's Guide **Recommended grade level: 5-6. Reading level: 7.** *Floating and Sinking* introduces students to the phenomenon of buoyancy through a series of investigations

with freshwater and saltwater. Students first make and test predictions about which objects will float or sink. Then they consider the variables involved. After calibrating a spring scale for weighing objects, they use the scale to investigate weight and buoyant force. Students design and construct clay boats and explore how weight can be distributed to make a sinker into a floater. They load the boats with marbles to test the efficiency of the designs. To investigate the effect of size on buoyancy, students build and test aluminum-foil boats of different sizes but with the same design. They measure buoyant force by pulling objects under water, compare the apparent weights of objects in and out of water, and construct a hydrometer to compare the buoyancy of objects in freshwater and saltwater. In the final activity, students apply what they have learned to predict whether a mystery cylinder will float or sink. Throughout the unit, students make and test predictions, record observations and test results, and construct charts and graphs to facilitate data analysis.

Floating and Sinking is a 16-lesson unit. The teacher's guide includes a unit overview, the 16 lesson plans, an annotated bibliography, reproducible masters, and instructions on repairing the spring scale. The module includes science background information, detailed instructions on planning for and conducting each activity, an extensive assessment component, and extensions for integration and enrichment. The student activity book that accompanies this unit provides helpful illustrations and directions for completing activities.

Key to Content Standards: 5-8 (see app. C)

UNIFYING CONCEPTS AND PROCESSES: Systems, order, and organization; evidence, models, and explanation; change, constancy, and measurement; form and function.

SCIENCE AS INQUIRY: Abilities necessary to do scientific inquiry; understandings about scientific inquiry.
PHYSICAL SCIENCE: Properties and changes of properties in matter; motions and forces.
SCIENCE AND TECHNOLOGY: Abilities of technological design; understandings about science and technology.
SCIENCE IN PERSONAL AND SOCIAL PER-SPECTIVES: Science and technology in society.
HISTORY AND NATURE OF SCIENCE: Science as a human endeavor; nature of science; history of science.

Prices: Teacher's guide (ISBN 0-89278-726-0), $24.95. Student activity book (ISBN 0-89278-727-9), $3.75. Unit, $429.95. *Publisher/supplier:* Carolina Biological Supply. *Materials:* Available locally, from commercial suppliers, or in kit.

1.5 **Food Chemistry.** Science and Technology for Children (STC) series. Developed by National Science Resources Center (Washington, D.C.). Burlington, N.C.: Carolina Biological Supply, 1994.

Program Overview The Science and Technology for Children (STC) series consists of 24 inquiry-centered curriculum units for grades 1-6, with 4 units at each grade level. Students learn about topics in the life, earth, and physical sciences. The technological applications of science and the interactions among science, technology, and society are addressed throughout the program. The STC units, each of which takes about 16 class sessions to complete, encourage participatory learning and the integration of science with mathematics, language arts, social studies, and art. The components of an STC unit are a teacher's guide, a student activity book with simple instructions and illustrations, and a kit of materials.

Teacher's Guide **Recommended grade level: 5-6. Reading level: 6.** In *Food Chemistry,* students investigate the basic nutrients in foods they eat. They conduct a series of physical and chemical tests to discover which nutrients—starches, glucose, fats, and proteins—are in common foods. They learn about the role nutrients play in human growth and development, read about the importance of vitamins and other nutrients, and examine food labels for nutritional information. In a final activity, students apply testing techniques they learn in the unit to analyze the nutritional components of a marshmallow. Throughout the unit, students gather, organize, and interpret data. By comparing results from tests, they learn the important concept that chemical tests are not always clearly positive or negative.

Food Chemistry is a 16-lesson unit. The teacher's guide includes a unit overview, the 16 lesson plans, an annotated bibliography, reproducible masters, and instructions for making test solutions and papers. The module includes science background information, detailed instructions on planning for and conducting each activity, an extensive assessment component, and extensions for integration and enrichment. The student activity book that accompanies this unit provides helpful illustrations and directions for completing activities.

Key to Content Standards: 5-8 (see app. C)

UNIFYING CONCEPTS AND PROCESSES: Systems, order, and organization; evidence, models, and explanation; change, constancy, and measurement; form and function.
SCIENCE AS INQUIRY: Abilities necessary to do scientific inquiry; understandings about scientific inquiry.
PHYSICAL SCIENCE: Properties and changes of properties in matter.
SCIENCE AND TECHNOLOGY: Understandings about science and technology.

SCIENCE IN PERSONAL AND SOCIAL PERSPECTIVES: Personal health; science and technology in society.
HISTORY AND NATURE OF SCIENCE: Science as a human endeavor; nature of science; history of science.

Prices: Teacher's guide, $24.95. Student activity book, $3.75. Unit, $349.95. *Publisher/supplier:* Carolina Biological Supply. *Materials:* Available locally, from commercial suppliers, or in kit.

1.6 Glencoe Physical Science.
Charles W. McLaughlin and Marilyn Thompson. Glencoe Life, Earth, and Physical Science series. New York, N.Y.: Glencoe/McGraw-Hill, 1997.

Program Overview The Glencoe Life, Earth, and Physical Science series includes 3 full-year courses—one in life, one in earth, and one in physical science—for students in grades 8 and above. Four major themes are developed: (1) energy, (2) systems and interactions, (3) scale and structure, and (4) stability and change. An extensive set of materials and resources, including many optional components, is available for students and teachers.

Student Edition **Recommended grade level: 8. Reading level: middle 9.** *Glencoe Physical Science* is divided into 7 units: (1) "Physical Science Basics"; (2) "Energy and Motion"; (3) "The Nature of Matter"; (4) "Kinds of Substances"; (5) "Interactions of Matter"; (6) "Waves, Light, and Sound"; and (7) "Electricity and Energy Resources."

During this course, students learn about motion and forces; acceleration and momentum; energy; simple machines; solids, liquids, and gases; atomic structure; chemical bonds; organic and biological compounds; solutions; chemical reactions; acids, bases, and salts; waves and sound; light; mirrors and lenses; electricity; magnetism and its uses; electronics and computers; nuclear reactions; and energy sources.

Sample lab activities in this textbook include making a model of a simple accelerometer, constructing a pendulum to compare the exchange of potential and kinetic energy, and constructing and analyzing a model of a 4-stroke engine. Students also design an experiment to show the relationship between the temperature and volume of a gas, they compare the solubility of a solute at different temperatures, and they distinguish between weak and strong acids by comparing ease of ionization.

Glencoe Physical Science has 25 chapters in its 7 units. Each chapter begins with a self-guided activity in which students make observations and generate questions about chapter concepts and topics. Reading sections on science concepts are then interwoven with various types of activities, including open-ended activities, minilabs (activities that can be done in class or at home), and skill-building or problem-solving activities. In activities for designing their own experiments, students brainstorm hypotheses, make a decision to investigate a hypothesis that can be tested, plan procedures, and think about why their hypothesis was supported or not. At the end of each unit is a cooperative "project" investigation, designed for students to work on throughout the unit.

Special features of the textbook include "connect to" marginal notes that relate basic questions in physics, chemistry, earth science, and life science to one another. The book also provides "science and society" features that invite students to confront real-life problems; profiles of people in science; and reading selections about connections between science, history, literature, and the arts.

Teacher's Edition The wraparound teacher's edition provides information on curriculum integration, assessment, planning, and meeting the diverse needs of students. Each chapter contains a 4-page planning guide; strategies for preparing, teaching, and closing lessons; answers to in-text questions; tips on connecting physical science to other sciences, disciplines, or community resources; and different assessment options.

Supplementary Laboratory Manual The supplementary lab manual offers 1 or more additional labs for each chapter. It has set-up diagrams, data tables, and space for student responses. Examples of investigations include observing how the concentration of a liquid affects its viscosity, using a calorimeter to determine the specific heat of a metal, distinguishing between physical and chemical changes, and using indicators to test unknown solutions for starch and sugar. In other investigations, students determine the relationship between reaction rate and temperature for the decomposition of sodium hypochlorite, measure the effects of distance and direction on light intensity, and record the growth patterns of plants grown from seeds that have been exposed to different amounts of radiation.

Program Resources and Support Materials *Glencoe Physical Science* offers an extensive list of support materials and program resources, including the following: activity and reinforcement worksheets, science integration activities that relate earth and life science to specific physical science chapters, a critical-thinking/problem-solving book, a concept-mapping book, chapter review masters, a study guide, enrichment worksheets, a book on multicultural connections, technology-integration masters, assessments, computer test banks, color transparencies, a Spanish resources book, and interactive CD-ROM and videodisc programs.

Key to Content Standards: 5-8 (see app. C)

UNIFYING CONCEPTS AND PROCESSES: Systems, order, and organization; change, constancy, and measurement. **SCIENCE AS INQUIRY:** Abilities necessary to do scientific inquiry; understandings about scientific inquiry. **PHYSICAL SCIENCE:** Properties and changes of properties in matter; motions and forces; transfer of energy. **SCIENCE AND TECHNOLOGY:** Abilities of technological design; understandings about science and technology. **SCIENCE IN PERSONAL AND SOCIAL PERSPECTIVES:** Science and technology in society. **HISTORY AND NATURE OF SCIENCE:** Science as a human endeavor; nature of science.

Prices: Student edition (ISBN 0-02-827879-8), $41.79. Teacher's edition (ISBN 0-02-827880-1), $57.86. Student lab manual, $8.25. Teacher's lab manual, $14.00. Teacher's classroom resources, $321.87. (Contact publisher/supplier for complete price and ordering information.) ***Publisher/supplier:*** Glencoe/McGraw-Hill. ***Materials:*** Available locally, or from commercial suppliers.

1.7 Hard As Ice. Michigan Science Education Resources Project. New Directions Teaching Units. Lansing, Mich.: Michigan Department of Education, 1993.

Program Overview The New Directions Teaching Units focus on developing scientific literacy and conceptual understanding. They were designed to reflect the ideas about teaching, learning, and curriculum in the Michigan Essential Goals and Objectives for K-12 Science Education, which were developed by the Michigan Science Education Resources Project. Several New Directions Teaching Units can be used with middle school students.

Teacher's Guide **Recommended grade level: 5-6.** *Hard As Ice* introduces students to the concept of molecules and the molecular structure of matter. It helps them develop an understanding of the many different forms of water on earth and of the changes that occur when solids melt into liquids and liquids freeze into solids. During the unit, students write detailed descriptions of the different forms of water found on earth; they observe and measure the weight and temperature of different forms of water (such as slush, crushed ice, and snow); and they discuss ways in which people use water in everyday life. They construct an explanation in molecular terms for why ice is hard and water is flowing, and they make ice and develop an explanation of what happens when water freezes. Students experiment with chocolate or crayons to observe the process of melting in substances other than water. They also freeze substances other than water and explain the change in terms of molecules. They figure out whether snow is a solid, a liquid, or something else.

Although some lessons in *Hard As Ice* refer to examples from the history and geography of Michigan, these lessons could easily be adapted for other regions of the country.

This unit has 11 lessons and requires approximately 17 class sessions to complete. The teacher's guide contains background information; lab preparation notes; answers to questions posed in the unit's separate, reproducible student pages; and information about student misconceptions and how to address them.

Key to Content Standards: 5-8 (see app. C)

UNIFYING CONCEPTS AND PROCESSES: Systems, order, and organization; evidence, models, and explanation; change, constancy, and measurement. **SCIENCE AS INQUIRY:** Abilities necessary to do scientific inquiry; understandings about scientific inquiry.

PHYSICAL SCIENCE: Properties and changes of properties in matter; transfer of energy.
SCIENCE AND TECHNOLOGY: Abilities of technological design.

Price: $18 (including an audiotape). *Publisher/supplier:* Battle Creek Area Math/Science Center. *Materials:* Available locally, or from commercial suppliers.

1.8 Heat Energy. 3rd ed. Anthea Maton, Jean Hopkins, Susan Johnson, and others. Prentice Hall Science Integrated Learning System series. Upper Saddle River, N.J.: Prentice Hall, 1997.

Program Overview The Prentice Hall Science Integrated Learning System series is a program for middle school or junior high school students. Designed to cover all relevant areas of science, this program consists of 19 books, each in a particular topic area, such as sound and light, the planet earth, and heat energy. Seven science themes are incorporated into the program; the themes are energy, evolution, patterns of change, scale and structure, systems and interactions, unity and diversity, and stability. For each unit, teaching materials, ancillary student materials, and some optional components are available.

Student Edition **Recommended grade level: 8+. Reading level: early 8.** *Heat Energy* introduces students to heat as a form of energy as they learn about conduction, convection, and radiation. Students study about the nature of temperature as a measure of the kinetic energy of molecules, and they learn to measure heat transfer indirectly by measuring changes in temperature. They also relate heat transfer to phase changes and identify heat of fusion and heat of vaporization. Then they explore thermal expansion and its practical applications. Students also study

practical applications of heat, such as the use of the principles of heat energy in direct and indirect heating systems, insulation, cooling systems, and heat engines.

In lab investigations, students measure the temperature of a mixture of hot and cold water, comparing it with the temperatures of the original hot and cold samples. In a second investigation they build a shoe-box-sized solar collector.

Heat Energy has 2 chapters: (1) "What is Heat?" and (2) "Uses of Heat." Each chapter contains comprehensive reading sections that introduce major science concepts. Suggestions are provided for activities in which students "find out by doing," "find out by reading," and "find out by writing." Other skills-oriented activities are also suggested— for example, calculating the number of calories in a food product and finding out what the R-value of insulating materials is based on. Each chapter includes a lab investigation.

Other features of this book include problem-solving challenges, science career descriptions, and science connections to real-world events or issues. The student edition closes with readings on 3 topics: (1) a female scientist who is doing research on a sulfur-eating microbe, (2) the "greenhouse effect," and (3) solar energy houses.

Teacher's Edition In the teacher's wraparound edition, each chapter begins with a 2-page planning guide and a 2-page preview that summarizes each section within the chapter. The teacher's edition also provides suggestions for teaching, guiding, integrating, and closing lessons, as well as enrichments, extensions, and answers to questions in the student text.

Supplementary Laboratory Manual The supplementary lab manual provides 5 additional investigations directly correlated with the informa-

tion presented in the student textbook. Examples include determining the heat of combustion of a candle and constructing a solar furnace with the capacity to boil water.

Program Resources and Support Materials A variety of materials, including some optional components, is available. A teacher's resource package contains the student edition and annotated teacher's editions of both the textbook and the lab manual, as well as a test book, an activity book, a review-and-reinforcement guide, and English and Spanish audiotapes for auditory and language learners. Other available materials include interactive videodiscs, transparencies, assessment materials, English and Spanish guides for language learners, a study guide, teacher's desk reference, and a booklet of product-testing activities.

Key to Content Standards: 5-8 (see app. C)

UNIFYING CONCEPTS AND PROCESSES: Systems, order, and organization; change, constancy, and measurement.
SCIENCE AS INQUIRY: Abilities necessary to do scientific inquiry; understandings about scientific inquiry.
PHYSICAL SCIENCE: Properties and changes of properties in matter; transfer of energy.
SCIENCE AND TECHNOLOGY: Abilities of technological design; understandings about science and technology.
SCIENCE IN PERSONAL AND SOCIAL PERSPECTIVES: Science and technology in society.
HISTORY AND NATURE OF SCIENCE: Nature of science; history of science.

Prices: Student edition (ISBN 0-13-423294-1), $9.97. Teacher's edition (ISBN 0-13-423104-X), $22.97. Teacher's resource package, $112.97. (Contact publisher/supplier for complete price and ordering information.) *Publisher/supplier:* Prentice Hall. *Materials:* Available locally, or from commercial suppliers.

1.9 **Introductory Physical Science.** 6th ed. Uri Haber-Schaim, Reed Cutting, H. Graden Kirksey, and Harold A. Pratt. Belmont, Mass.: Science Curriculum, 1994.

Program Overview *Introductory Physical Science* is a full-year course focused on the study of matter leading to the development of the atomic model. The course addresses 3 broad areas: the empirical framework for developing an atomic model, an introduction to the atomic model, and the electric dimension of the atomic model. This division provides natural breaking points for spreading the course over more than a year, if preferred.

Student Edition **Recommended grade level: 8+. Reading level: middle 7.** The central theme of *Introductory Physical Science,* a lab-centered textbook, is the study of matter leading to the development of the atomic model. The topics that students study include the following: volume and mass, mass changes in closed systems, properties of substances and objects, solubility, the separation of mixtures, compounds and elements, radioactivity, the atomic model of matter, sizes and masses of molecules and atoms, electric charge, atoms and electric charge, and cells and charge carriers.

Students perform 47 experiments. Sample lab activities include using the water displacement method to measure the volume of a solid, finding the density of a liquid, and comparing the concentrations of saturated solutions. In other lab activities, students distill a mixture of liquids and examine the properties of the fractions. They also examine the mass ratio of reactants and products in a single replacement reaction, conduct flame tests, and determine the quantity of charge needed to release one atom of zinc from a solution containing zinc.

In its 12 chapters, *Introductory Physical Science* offers reading sections that lay the groundwork for new concepts and for labs. Also provided are directions for experiments and a large selection of problems designed to reinforce ideas immediately after the ideas are encountered in the text or laboratory. The introduction of new ideas is based on students' experiences in the laboratory; new terms are consistently introduced after the need for them has been established.

The laboratory instructions in this textbook provide a minimum of directions and raise questions to call students' attention to the important parts of an experiment. Most labs take between 45 and 50 minutes and can be completed by students individually or in pairs. Some experiments are designed to familiarize students with an instrument or technique; others require them to record data carefully, draw graphs, and calculate results. Each chapter ends with a set of problems for review, as well as applications and extensions.

Teacher's Guide and Resource Book The teacher's guide and resource book includes the following: information on the structure of the course; science background information for each chapter or experiment; suggestions for guiding students' experiments; tips on conducting prelab and postlab discussions; and answers to the problems at the end of each chapter.

Assessment Guide The Assessment Guide contains 2 sets of tests—multiple choice questions and essay questions—for each of the 12 chapters. The sets differ in degree of difficulty. In addition, a series of lab tests is available, as is diagnostic software for Macintosh computers for the chapter tests. The software allows teachers to provide individual test scores, overall class results, and

a diagnostic interpretation, or analysis, of many of the wrong choices.

Key to Content Standards: 5-8 (see app. C)

UNIFYING CONCEPTS AND PROCESSES: Systems, order, and organization; evidence, models, and explanation; change, constancy, and measurement. **SCIENCE AS INQUIRY:** Abilities necessary to do scientific inquiry; understandings about scientific inquiry. **PHYSICAL SCIENCE:** Properties and changes of properties in matter. **HISTORY AND NATURE OF SCIENCE:** Nature of science.

Prices: Student edition (ISBN 1-882057-04-X), $31. Teacher's edition (ISBN 1-882057-05-8), $60. Assessment package, $35. *Publisher/supplier:* Science Curriculum (textbooks and guides). Delta Education (materials kit). *Materials:* Available locally, from commercial suppliers, or in kit.

1.10 **Levers and Pulleys.** Full Option Science System (FOSS) series. Developed by Lawrence Hall of Science (Berkeley, Calif.). Hudson, N.H.: Delta Education, 1993.

Program Overview The Full Option Science System (FOSS) program is a K-6 science curriculum consisting of 27 stand-alone modules. The 8 modules for grades 5-6 are organized under topics in the life, physical, and earth sciences and in scientific reasoning and technology. They can be used in any order. The FOSS program is designed to engage students in scientific concepts through multisensory, hands-on laboratory activities. All modules of the program incorporate 5 unifying themes—(1) pattern, (2) structure, (3) interaction, (4) change, and (5) system. The components of a FOSS module are a teacher's guide and a kit of materials.

Teacher's Guide **Recommended grade level: 5-6.** In *Levers and Pulleys*, students discover that these 2 types of simple machines are important in their daily lives. They are first introduced to the parts of a lever. Then they construct their own Class 1 levers and experiment to determine the relationship between load and effort for maximum advantage. Subsequently, they explore Class 2 and Class 3 levers, determine the advantage gained by using each, and look at common tools that are applications of each class. Students apply their knowledge of load, effort, and advantage to assemble and investigate 4 different 1- and 2-pulley systems. They discover the mechanical advantages and disadvantages of each system. Throughout the unit, students work in pairs or in small groups to construct their own simple machines; conduct their own experiments; and gather, record, and interpret their own data.

Levers and Pulleys consists of 4 activities, requiring a total of 16 class sessions of about 45 minutes each. The teacher's guide includes a module overview, the 4 individual activity folios, duplication masters (in both English and Spanish) for student sheets, and an annotated bibliography.

. The module includes science background information, detailed instructions on planning for and conducting each activity, an extensive assessment component, and extensions for integration and enrichment.

Key to Content Standards: 5-8 (see app. C)

UNIFYING CONCEPTS AND PROCESSES: Systems, order, and organization; evidence, models, and explanation; change, constancy, and measurement; form and function.
SCIENCE AS INQUIRY: Abilities necessary to do scientific inquiry; understandings about scientific inquiry.
PHYSICAL SCIENCE: Motions and forces; transfer of energy.

SCIENCE AND TECHNOLOGY: Abilities of technological design.
HISTORY AND NATURE OF SCIENCE: Nature of science.

Prices: Teacher's guide (ISBN 0-7826-0059-X), $101. Complete module, $539. *Publisher/supplier:* Delta Education. *Materials:* Available locally, from commercial suppliers, or in kit.

1.11 **Magnets and Motors.** Science and Technology for Children (STC) series. Developed by National Science Resources Center (Washington, D.C.). Burlington, N.C.: Carolina Biological Supply, 1991.

Program Overview The Science and Technology for Children (STC) series consists of 24 inquiry-centered curriculum units for grades 1-6, with 4 units at each grade level. Students learn about topics in the life, earth, and physical sciences. The technological applications of science and the interactions among science, technology, and society are addressed throughout the program. The STC units, each of which takes about 16 class sessions to complete, encourage participatory learning and the integration of science with mathematics, language arts, social studies, and art. The components of an STC unit are a teacher's guide, a student activity book with simple instructions and illustrations, and a kit of materials.

Teacher's Guide **Recommended grade level: 6. Reading level: 7.** In *Magnets and Motors,* students are introduced to electromagnetism and electromagnetic motors. They experiment with magnets, make a compass, observe and investigate magnetism's connection with electricity. They develop an understanding of how a motor works, and they experiment with 3 different electric motors, including 2 that they make. During the unit, students apply previous learning to make and

test hypotheses and learn how to design and conduct controlled experiments. Students use activity sheets and a science journal to record their questions, ideas, observations, and results of experiments.

Magnets and Motors is a 16-lesson unit. The teacher's guide includes a unit overview, the 16 lesson plans, an annotated bibliography, and reproducible masters. A well-organized student activity book provides instructions for carrying out the activities. Appendixes include background information and instructions for setting up a classroom learning center.

The module includes science background information, detailed instructions on planning for and conducting each activity, an extensive assessment component, and extensions for integration and enrichment.

Key to Content Standards: 5-8 (see app. C)

UNIFYING CONCEPTS AND PROCESSES: Systems, order, and organization; evidence, models, and explanation; change, constancy, and measurement.
SCIENCE AS INQUIRY: Abilities necessary to do scientific inquiry; understandings about scientific inquiry.
PHYSICAL SCIENCE: Properties and changes of properties in matter; motions and forces; transfer of energy.
SCIENCE AND TECHNOLOGY: Abilities of technological design.
SCIENCE IN PERSONAL AND SOCIAL PERSPECTIVES: Science and technology in society.
HISTORY AND NATURE OF SCIENCE: Science as a human endeavor; nature of science; history of science.

Prices: Teacher's guide (ISBN 0-89278-726-0), $24.95. Student activity book (ISBN 0-89278-727-9), $3.75. Unit, $479.95. *Publisher/supplier:* Carolina Biological Supply. *Materials:* Available locally, from commercial suppliers, or in kit.

1.12 **Matter: Building Block of the Universe.** 3rd ed. Anthea Maton, Jean Hopkins, Susan Johnson, and others. Prentice Hall Science Integrated Learning System series. Upper Saddle River, N.J.: Prentice Hall, 1997.

Program Overview The Prentice Hall Science Integrated Learning System series is a program for middle school or junior high school students. Designed to cover all relevant areas of science, this program consists of 19 books, each in a particular topic area, such as sound and light, the planet earth, and matter—building block of the universe. Seven science themes are incorporated into the program; the themes are energy, evolution, patterns of change, scale and structure, systems and interactions, unity and diversity, and stability. For each unit, teaching materials, ancillary student materials, and some optional components are available.

Student Edition **Recommended grade level: 8+. Reading level: middle 7.** *Matter: Building Block of the Universe* introduces students to the nature of matter. They study the general properties of matter (mass, weight, volume, and density); inertia; phases of matter and phase changes; chemical properties and chemical changes; the classification of matter (as mixtures, solutions, elements, and compounds); the use of chemical symbols, formulas, and equations; the development of the atomic model; and the forces that govern the behavior of subatomic particles. Students also read about the development of the periodic table and gain an understanding of metals, nonmetals, and metalloids.

In lab investigations, students explore the connection between mass and inertia, and they also observe the physical and chemical properties of a lighted and an unlighted candle and use marshmallows to make models of chemical reactions. Students then perform exercises with mystery objects in a shoe box to see how indirect evidence is used to build a model, and they identify elements using flame tests.

Matter: Building Block of the Universe has 5 chapters: (1) "General Properties of Matter"; (2) "Physical and Chemical Changes"; (3) "Mixtures, Elements, and Compounds"; (4) "Atoms: Building Blocks of Matter"; and (5) "Classification of Elements: The Periodic Table." Each chapter contains comprehensive reading sections that introduce major science concepts. Suggestions are provided for activities in which students "find out by doing," "find out by reading," and "find out by writing." Other activities are also suggested—for example, making models of the Thomson atom and the Rutherford atom and reading a poem by Carl Sandburg about fog (a colloid). Each chapter includes a formal lab investigation.

Other features include problem-solving challenges, science career descriptions, and science connections to real-world events or issues. The student edition closes with 3 readings: about physicist Shirley Ann Jackson, acid rain, and the possibility of factories in space.

Teacher's Edition In the teacher's wraparound edition, each chapter begins with a 2-page planning guide and a 2-page preview that summarizes each section within the chapter. The teacher's edition also provides suggestions for teaching, guiding, integrating, and closing lessons, as well as enrichments, extensions, and answers to questions in the student text.

Supplementary Laboratory Manual The supplementary lab manual provides 12 additional investigations directly correlated with the information presented in the student textbook. Examples include determining the density of several liquids; observing physical and chemical changes; determining the solubility of potassium nitrate; relating electrons and probability; and investigating the relative activities of zinc, copper, and lead.

Program Resources and Support Materials A variety of materials, including some optional components, is available. A teacher's resource package contains the student edition and annotated teacher's editions of both the textbook and the lab manual, as well as a test book, an activity book, a review-and-reinforcement guide, and English and Spanish audiotapes for auditory and language learners. Other available materials include interactive videodiscs, transparencies, assessment materials, English and Spanish guides for language learners, a study guide, a teacher's desk reference, and a booklet of product-testing activities.

Key to Content Standards: 5-8 (see app. C)

UNIFYING CONCEPTS AND PROCESSES: Systems, order, and organization; evidence, models, and explanation; change, constancy, and measurement. **SCIENCE AS INQUIRY:** Abilities necessary to do scientific inquiry; understandings about scientific inquiry. **PHYSICAL SCIENCE:** Properties and changes of properties in matter; transfer of energy. **SCIENCE IN PERSONAL AND SOCIAL PERSPECTIVES:** Science and technology in society. **HISTORY AND NATURE OF SCIENCE:** Science as a human endeavor; history of science.

Prices: Student edition (ISBN 0-13-423369-7), $9.97. Teacher's edition (ISBN 0-13-423138-4), $22.97. Teacher's resource package, $112.97. (Contact publisher/supplier for complete price and ordering information.) *Publisher/supplier:* Prentice Hall. *Materials:* Available locally, or from commercial suppliers.

1.13 **Mixtures and Solutions.** Full Option Science System (FOSS) series. Developed by Lawrence Hall of Science (Berkeley, Calif.). Hudson, N.H.: Delta Education, 1993.

Program Overview The Full Option Science System (FOSS) program is a K-6 science curriculum consisting of 27 stand-alone modules. The 8 modules for grades 5-6 are organized under topics in the life, physical, and earth sciences and in scientific reasoning and technology. They can be used in any order. The FOSS program is designed to engage students in scientific concepts through multisensory, hands-on laboratory activities. All modules of the program incorporate 5 unifying themes—(1) pattern, (2) structure, (3) interaction, (4) change, and (5) system. The components of a FOSS module are a teacher's guide and a kit of materials.

Teacher's Guide **Recommended grade level: 5-6.** *Mixtures and Solutions* introduces students to some concepts of basic chemistry—mixture, solution, concentration, saturation, and chemical reaction. Activities include separating mixtures using the techniques of sifting, dissolving, filtering, and evaporating. Other activities involve making saturated solutions of salt and citric acid and then comparing the solubility of these 2 substances in water; determining the relative concentration of salt solutions; and observing chemical reactions that result in the formation of a gas and a precipitate and then applying the techniques of filtering and evaporation to separate some of the reaction products.

Mixtures and Solutions consists of 4 activities, requiring a total of 13 class sessions to complete. The teacher's guide includes a module overview, the 4 individual activity folios, duplication masters (in both English and Spanish) for student sheets, and an annotated bibliography.

The module includes science background information, detailed instructions on planning for and conducting each activity, an extensive assessment component, and extensions for integration and enrichment.

Key to Content Standards: 5-8 (see app. C)

UNIFYING CONCEPTS AND PROCESSES: Systems, order, and organization; change, constancy, and measurement. **SCIENCE AS INQUIRY:** Abilities necessary to do scientific inquiry; understandings about scientific inquiry. **PHYSICAL SCIENCE:** Properties and changes of properties in matter. **SCIENCE AND TECHNOLOGY:** Abilities of technological design. **HISTORY AND NATURE OF SCIENCE:** Nature of science.

Prices: Teacher's guide (ISBN 0-7826-0081-6), $101. Complete module, $469. *Publisher/supplier:* Delta Education. *Materials:* Available locally, from commercial suppliers, or in kit.

1.14 **Motion, Forces, and Energy.** 3rd ed. Anthea Maton, Jean Hopkins, Susan Johnson, and others. Prentice Hall Science Integrated Learning System series. Upper Saddle River, N.J.: Prentice Hall, 1997.

Program Overview The Prentice Hall Science Integrated Learning System series is a program for middle school or junior high school students. Designed to cover all relevant areas of science, this program consists of 19 books, each in a particular topic area, such as motion, forces and energy; the planet earth; and cells—building blocks of life. Seven science themes are incorporated into the program; the themes are energy, evolution, patterns of change, scale and structure, systems and interactions, unity and diversity, and stability. For each unit, teaching materials, ancillary student materials, and some optional components are available.

Student Edition **Recommended grade level: 8+. Reading level: late 6.** *Motion, Forces, and Energy* introduces students to the interactions of forces that make all physical activity possible. Students explore motion, frame of reference, and the difference between speed and velocity. They learn about the concepts of acceleration and motion, about force and its relationship to motion, and about Newton's 3 laws of motion and the concept of gravitation. Students study forces in fluids and learn about Archimedes' principle and Bernoulli's principle. They explore the subjects of work, power, mechanical advantage, and simple machines; kinetic energy and potential energy; energy conservation; and the law of conservation of energy.

In lab investigations, students make a distance-time graph of constant speed and compare the falling rates of objects with different masses. They also explore the relationship between the density of an object and its buoyancy in a fluid. They observe and measure how pulleys can make work easier, and they explore how a change in mass affects the velocity of an object if its kinetic energy is kept constant.

Motion, Forces, and Energy has 5 chapters: (1) "What Is Motion?"; (2) "The Nature of Forces"; (3) "Forces in Fluids"; (4) "Work, Power, and Simple Machines"; and (5) "Energy: Forms and Changes." Each chapter contains comprehensive reading sections that introduce major science concepts. Suggestions are provided for activities in which students "find out by doing," "find out by reading," and "find out by writing." Other skills-oriented activities are also suggested—for example, calculating the velocity and acceleration of a falling drop of water and writing a report about people who developed an accurate understanding of the solar system. Each chapter includes a formal lab investigation.

Other features include problem-solving challenges, science career descriptions, and science connections to real-world events or issues. The student edition closes with 3 readings: about the African-American astronaut Guion Bluford, the use of robots in manufacturing, and hypersonic planes.

Teacher's Edition In the teacher's wraparound edition, each chapter begins with a 2-page planning guide and a 2-page preview that summarizes each section within the chapter. The teacher's edition also provides suggestions for teaching, guiding, integrating, and closing lessons, as well as enrichments, extensions, and answers to questions in the student text.

Supplementary Laboratory Manual The supplementary lab manual provides 14 additional investigations directly correlated with the information presented in the student textbook. Examples of investigations include: constructing an accelerometer and using it to determine the direction of acceleration; exploring how surface area, texture, and weight influence friction; determining how buoyancy relates to the apparent loss of mass of an object; investigating how different positions of the effort, resistance, and fulcrum affect the mechanical advantage of the lever; and experimenting to determine how various factors affect the behavior of a pendulum.

Program Resources and Support Materials A variety of materials, including some optional components, is available. A teacher's resource package contains the student edition and annotated teacher's editions of both the textbook and the lab manual, as well as a test book, an activity book, a review-and-reinforcement guide, and English and Spanish audiotapes for auditory and language learners. Other available materials include interactive videodiscs, trans-parencies, assessment materials, English and Spanish guides for language learners, a study guide, a teacher's desk reference, and a booklet of product-testing activities.

Key to Content Standards: 5-8 (see app. C)

UNIFYING CONCEPTS AND PROCESSES: Systems, order, and organization; change, constancy, and measurement. **SCIENCE AS INQUIRY:** Abilities necessary to do scientific inquiry; understandings about scientific inquiry. **PHYSICAL SCIENCE:** Motions and forces; transfer of energy. **SCIENCE AND TECHNOLOGY:** Abilities of technological design; understandings about science and technology. **SCIENCE IN PERSONAL AND SOCIAL PERSPECTIVES:** Science and technology in society.

Prices: Student edition (ISBN 0-13-423278-X), $9.97. Teacher's edition (ISBN 0-13-423088-4), $22.97. Teacher's resource package, $112.97. (Contact publisher/supplier for complete price and ordering information.) *Publisher/supplier:* Prentice Hall. *Materials:* Available locally, or from commercial suppliers.

1.15 Sound and Light. 3rd ed. Anthea Maton, Jean Hopkins, Susan Johnson, and others. Prentice Hall Science Integrated Learning System series. Upper Saddle River, N.J.: Prentice Hall, 1997.

Program Overview The Prentice Hall Science Integrated Learning System series is a program for middle school or junior high school students. Designed to cover all relevant areas of science, this program consists of 19 books, each in a particular topic area, such as sound and light, the planet earth, and cells—building blocks of life. Seven science themes are incorporated into the program; the themes are energy, evolution, patterns of change, scale and structure, systems and interactions, unity and diversity, and stability. For each unit, teaching materials, ancillary student materials, and some optional components are available.

Student Edition **Recommended grade level: 7-8. Reading level: middle 7.** *Sound and Light* introduces students to the nature, characteristics, types, and interactions of waves. Students learn about the properties of sound, the wave nature of sound, and the mechanism of hearing. They also explore the wave nature of light, the electromagnetic spectrum, light reflection and refraction, light and color, the mechanism of vision, mirrors, lenses, optical instruments, and light technology (such as lasers, fiber optics, and holography).

In lab investigations, students use a Slinky to observe the characteristics of a wave; they experiment with tuning forks to explore sympathetic vibration, resonance, interference, beats, and the Doppler effect; they record the temperatures produced by different colors of light; and they observe the images formed by a convex lens.

Sound and Light has 4 chapters: (1) "Characteristics of Waves," (2) "Sound and Its Uses," (3) "Light and the Electromagnetic Spectrum," and (4) "Light and Its Uses." Each chapter contains comprehensive reading sections that introduce major science concepts. Suggestions are provided for activities in which students "find out by doing," "find out by reading," and "find out by writing." Other skills-oriented activities are also suggested—for example, using a barometer to forecast the weather and examining 2 microclimates in a neighborhood. Each chapter includes a formal lab investigation.

Other features include problem-solving challenges, science career descriptions, and science connections to real-world events or issues. The student edition closes with 3 readings: about a sculptor who uses light and colors to create his art, the dangers of noise pollution, and "solar sailing" rockets.

Teacher's Edition In the teacher's wraparound edition, each chapter begins with a 2-page planning guide and a 2-page preview that summarizes each section within the chapter. The teacher's edition also provides suggestions for teaching, guiding, integrating, and closing lessons, as well as enrichments, extensions, and answers to questions in the student text.

Supplementary Laboratory Manual The supplementary lab manual provides 7 additional investigations directly correlated with the information presented in the student textbook. Examples of investigations include observing the behavior of water waves in a ripple tank, determining the speed of sound in air, measuring the heating effects of the sun and observing how different materials change these effects, and comparing the images formed by convex and concave lenses.

Program Resources and Support Materials A variety of materials, including some optional components, is available. A teacher's resource package contains the student edition and annotated teacher's editions of both the textbook and the lab manual, as well as a test book, an activity book, a review-and-reinforcement guide, and English and Spanish audiotapes for auditory and language learners. Other available materials include interactive videodiscs, transparencies, assessment materials, English and Spanish guides for language learners, a study guide, a teacher's desk reference, and a booklet of product-testing activities.

Key to Content Standards: 5-8 (see app. C)

UNIFYING CONCEPTS AND PROCESSES: Systems, order, and organization; change, constancy, and measurement; form and function.
SCIENCE AS INQUIRY: Abilities necessary to do scientific inquiry; understandings about scientific inquiry.
PHYSICAL SCIENCE: Transfer of energy.
SCIENCE AND TECHNOLOGY: Abilities of

technological design; understandings about science and technology.
SCIENCE IN PERSONAL AND SOCIAL PERSPECTIVES: Science and technology in society.

Prices: Student edition (ISBN 0-13-423286-0), $9.97. Teacher's edition (ISBN 0-13-423096-5), $22.97. Teacher's resource package, $112.97. (Contact publisher/supplier for complete price and ordering information.) ***Publisher/supplier:*** Prentice Hall. ***Materials:*** Available locally, or from commercial suppliers.

1.16 **Structures.** Insights series. Developed by Education Development Center (EDC). Dubuque, Iowa: Kendall/Hunt, 1997.

Program Overview The Insights program, for grades K-6, consists of 17 modules, several of which are appropriate for middle school. Topics in the program reflect a balance of life, physical, and earth sciences. Insights modules integrate science with the rest of the curriculum, particularly with language arts and mathematics. The activities support cultural, racial, and linguistic diversity. Each module requires about 25 class sessions to complete. The components of an Insights module are a teacher's guide and a kit of materials.

Teacher's Guide **Recommended grade level: 6.** Students develop an understanding of some of the basic principles of structures in this unit. The concepts covered include live load (the weight of a structure's own materials) and dead load (added weight), tension and compression, and the relationship of materials and shape to structure and strength. Students first look at structures in their school neighborhood and record the variety of sizes, shapes, materials, and functions they find. Then they explore how these characteristics affect a structure's ability to remain standing. Students learn to build standing structures using straws

and paper clips, index cards, and other materials. Next they explore how dead load and live load affect the stability of their straw structures. They are challenged to increase the ability of their structures to support live loads while increasing the dead load as little as possible. Then students eliminate any extra straws until they reduce the structure to only the "necessary" straws. In the process they learn that the arrangement of beams, columns, and diagonal supports in a framework is important in helping make the structure strong enough to support loads. Students work primarily in groups of 4. They have many opportunities for drawing and recording information.

Structures consists of 13 Learning Experiences, requiring at least 24 class sessions to complete. The teacher's guide includes a unit overview, the 13 Learning Experiences, reproducible masters for student sheets, and annotated lists of additional resources to use with the module.

The module includes science background information, detailed instructions on planning for and conducting each activity, an extensive assessment component, and extensions for integration and enrichment.

Key to Content Standards: 5-8 (see app. C)

UNIFYING CONCEPTS AND PROCESSES: Systems, order, and organization; evidence, models, and explanation; form and function.
SCIENCE AS INQUIRY: Abilities necessary to do scientific inquiry; understandings about scientific inquiry.
PHYSICAL SCIENCE: Motions and forces.
SCIENCE AND TECHNOLOGY: Abilities of technological design; understandings about science and technology.
HISTORY AND NATURE OF SCIENCE: Nature of science.

Prices: Teacher's guide (ISBN 0-7872-3345-5), $68.90. Materials kit, $209.90. ***Publisher/supplier:*** Kendall/Hunt. ***Materials:*** Available locally, from commercial suppliers, or in kit.

Physical Science—Supplementary Units

1.17 **Bubble Festival.** Jacqueline Barber and Carolyn Willard. Great Explorations in Math and Science (GEMS) series. Berkeley, Calif.: Lawrence Hall of Science, 1992.

Program Overview The Great Explorations in Math and Science (GEMS) series includes more than 50 teacher's guides and handbooks for preschool through grade 10. About 35 of these are appropriate for middle school. The series also includes several assembly presenter's guides and exhibit guides. New guides and handbooks continue to be developed, and current titles are revised frequently. The series is designed to teach key science and mathematics concepts through activity-based learning. The time needed to complete GEMS units varies from about 2 to 10 class sessions.

Teacher's Guide **Recommended grade level: 5-7.** In *Bubble Festival*, students participate in a variety of bubble activities in a learning-station format. The unit's 12 classroom tabletop activities provide open-ended explorations in an informal, student-centered setting. Students experiment with bubble formation, bubble behavior, and bubble geometry. They make bubble measurements, investigate surface tension, and discover different colors and patterns. "Activity Task Cards for Volunteers" explain the learning goals of each activity, suggest additional questions to ask students, and explain how to maintain stations so they are safe and ready for successive groups. Blackline masters of

ABOUT THE ANNOTATIONS IN "PHYSICAL SCIENCE—SUPPLEMENTARY UNITS"

Entry Numbers
Curriculum materials are arranged alphabetically by title in each category (Core Materials, Supplementary Units, and Science Activity Books) in chapters 1 through 5 of this guide.

Each curriculum annotation has a two-part entry number: the chapter number is given before the period; the number after the period locates the entry within that chapter. For example, the first entry number in chapter 1 is 1.1; the second entry in chapter 2 is 2.2; and so on.

The entry numbers within each curriculum chapter run consecutively through Core Materials, Supplementary Units, and Science Activity Books.

Order of Bibliographic Information
Following is the arrangement of the facts of publication in the annotations in this section:

- **Title of publication**
- **Number of edition,** if applicable
- **Authors** (an individual author or authors, an institutional author, or a project or program name under which the material was developed)
- **Series title**
- **Series developer,** if applicable
- **Place of publication, publisher, and date of publication**

Recommended Grade Level
The grade level for each piece of material was recommended by teacher evaluators during the development of this guide. In some instances, the recommended grade level may differ slightly from the publisher's advertised level.

Key to Content Standards: 5-8
The key lists the content standards for grades 5-8 from the *National Science Education Standards* (NSES) that are addressed in depth by the item. A key is provided for core materials and supplementary units. (*See* appendix C.)

Price and Acquisition Information

Ordering information appears at the end of each entry. Included are—

- **Prices** (of teacher's guides, student books, lab manuals, and kits or units)
- **Publisher/supplier** (The name of a principal publisher/supplier, although not necessarily the sole source, for the items listed in the price category. Appendix A, "Publishers and Suppliers," provides the address, phone and fax numbers, and electronic ordering information, where available, for each publisher and supplier.)
- **Materials** (various sources from which one might obtain the required materials)

Readers must contact publishers/suppliers for complete and up-to-date listings of the program resources and support materials available for a particular unit. Depending on the developer, these items may be required, optional, or both; they may be offered individually and/or in kits, packages, or boxes. Materials may change with revised editions. The prices given in this chapter for selected resources or materials are based on information from the publishers and suppliers but are not meant to represent the full range of ordering options.

Indexes of Curriculum Materials

The multiple indexes on pp. 449-78 allow easy access to the information in this guide. Various aspects of the curriculum materials—including titles, topics addressed in each unit, grade levels, and standards addressed—are the focus of seven separate indexes. For example, titles and entry numbers are listed in the "Title Index" on pp. 450-54. The "Index of Authors, Series, and Curriculum Projects," on pp. 455-57, provides entry numbers of any annotated titles in a particular series.

Overviews of Core and Supplementary Programs

Appendix D, "Overviews of Core and Supplementary Programs with Titles Annotated in This Guide," on pp. 441-48, lists, by program or series, the individual titles annotated in the sections "Core Materials" and "Supplementary Units" in the five curriculum chapters.

signs for the learning stations are provided for each activity. Literature and writing extensions are included.

Key to Content Standards: 5-8 (see app. C)

UNIFYING CONCEPTS AND PROCESSES: Systems, order, and organization; evidence, models, and explanation; change, constancy, and measurement. **SCIENCE AS INQUIRY:** Abilities necessary to do scientific inquiry; understandings about scientific inquiry. **PHYSICAL SCIENCE:** Properties and changes of properties in matter. **SCIENCE AND TECHNOLOGY:** Abilities of technological design.

Price: $16 (ISBN 0-912511-80-X). *Publisher/supplier:* LHS GEMS. *Materials:* Available locally, or from commercial suppliers.

1.18 **Bubble-ology.** Reprinted with revisions. Jacqueline Barber. Great Explorations in Math and Science (GEMS) series. Berkeley, Calif.: Lawrence Hall of Science, 1992.

Program Overview The Great Explorations in Math and Science (GEMS) series includes more than 50 teacher's guides and handbooks for preschool through grade 10. About 35 of these are appropriate for middle school. The series also includes several assembly presenter's guides and exhibit guides. New guides and handbooks continue to be developed, and current titles are revised frequently. The series is designed to teach key science and mathematics concepts through activity-based learning. The time needed to complete GEMS units varies from about 2 to 10 class sessions.

Teacher's Guide **Recommended grade level: 5-8+.** In *Bubble-ology,* students use bubbles to investigate light and color, aerodynamics, chemical composition, surface tension, and technology. During this unit, they create an ideal bubble-blowing instrument, determine which brand of dishwashing liquid will make the biggest bubble, test the effect of different amounts of glycerin on the size of bubbles, apply Bernoulli's principle to keep a bubble aloft, and use color to predict bubble survival.

Bubble-ology consists of 6 activities requiring 8 to 10 class sessions of 45 to 60 minutes each. The module includes a brief introduction, a materials list, detailed instructions for preparing and conducting the lessons, and extension ideas. Useful summary outlines and reproducible student worksheets are included.

Key to Content Standards: 5-8 (see app. C)

UNIFYING CONCEPTS AND PROCESSES: Systems, order, and organization; evidence, models, and explanation; change, constancy, and measurement.
SCIENCE AS INQUIRY: Abilities necessary to do scientific inquiry; understandings about scientific inquiry.
PHYSICAL SCIENCE: Properties and changes of properties in matter; transfer of energy.
SCIENCE AND TECHNOLOGY: Abilities of technological design.

Price: $9 (ISBN 0-912511-11-7).
Publisher/supplier: LHS GEMS.
Materials: Available locally, or from commercial suppliers.

1.19 **Changes in Matter.** Mary Atwater, Prentice Baptiste, Lucy Daniel, and others. Unit 32. Macmillan/McGraw-Hill Science series. New York, N.Y.: Macmillan/McGraw-Hill School Publishing, 1995.

Program Overview The Macmillan/McGraw-Hill Science series is a comprehensive, activity-based, K-8 science curriculum made up of 42 stand-alone units, 18 of which are designed for grades 6-8. The series is constructed around 7 major themes: (1) systems and interactions, (2) scale and structure, (3) stability, (4) energy, (5) evolution, (6) patterns of change, and (7) models. The subject of each unit—for example, changes in matter—is presented from the perspective of one or more of these themes. One theme is designated as the "major theme" for a unit, and any others are treated as "related themes." For each unit, a wide range of materials, including some optional components, is available for students and teachers.

Student Edition **Recommended grade level: 7-8.** *Changes in Matter* contains 7 lessons that discuss the physical and chemical properties of matter and examine how the chemical properties of matter determine its interaction with other substances. The organizing themes for this unit are systems and interactions (major theme) and scale and structure (related theme).

Each of the 7 lessons in this unit typically requires 5 days for completion. During the unit, students observe and identify the physical properties of different materials, describe the effect of temperature changes on the 3 phases of matter, and distinguish between chemical and physical properties of matter. They also learn about the structure of atoms, discover how different elements are categorized in the periodic table, and explore the interac-

tion of elements in chemical systems to form compounds. Students then study acids and bases, and learn to describe and distinguish different mixtures (such as solutions, colloids, and suspensions).

Sample activities include comparing the densities of corn oil, baby oil, corn syrup, and water; identifying an unknown substance using chemical properties of matter; and classifying substances as metals or nonmetals. Other activities include observing copper plating, identifying acids and bases using red cabbage juice as an indicator, and observing the separation of a mixture using paper chromatography.

Each lesson contains narrative information and a series of sequential, hands-on activities—such as an introductory "minds-on" activity, short "try this" activities, and a longer "explore" activity. The latter, which is a lab activity, takes a class period to complete. Students use activity logs to record ideas, observations, and results.

Special unit features include curriculum links to language arts, literature, mathematics, music, and art; information about science careers; and narrative sections highlighting science, technology, and society connections.

Teacher's Planning Guide The teacher's planning guide, a spiral-bound, wraparound edition, provides information and strategies for teaching the 7 lessons in the student edition. Each lesson is introduced by a 4-page section that offers background information, a lesson planning guide, and assessment options. Marginal notes on the lesson pages provide discussion ideas, tips on meeting individual needs, suggestions for addressing misconceptions, assessment ideas, and curriculum connections.

Program Resources and Support Materials A wide range of materials, including some optional components, is available. Examples include consumable and nonconsumable activity materials; audio- and videotapes; interactive videodiscs; color transparencies; assessment materials; a teacher anthology of short stories, poems, fingerplays, and songs; trade books; teacher resource masters; activity cards; activity logs; a staff development package; concept summaries and glossaries for students acquiring English; and software with problem-solving simulations for students.

Key to Content Standards: 5-8 (see app. C)

UNIFYING CONCEPTS AND PROCESSES: Systems order, and organization; change, constancy, and measurement. SCIENCE AS INQUIRY: Abilities necessary to do scientific inquiry; understandings about scientific inquiry. PHYSICAL SCIENCE: Properties and changes of properties in matter. SCIENCE AND TECHNOLOGY: Understandings about science and technology. SCIENCE IN PERSONAL AND SOCIAL PERSPECTIVES: Science and technology in society. HISTORY AND NATURE OF SCIENCE: History of science.

Prices: Student edition (ISBN 0-02-276132-2), $7.06. Teacher's planning guide (ISBN 0-02-276080-6), $55.98. Unit package, $116.88. Activity materials kit, $94.00. (Contact publisher/supplier for complete price and ordering information.) *Publisher/supplier:* McGraw-Hill. *Materials:* Available locally, from commercial suppliers, or in kit.

1.20 Chemical Interactions. Judith Mabel. Delta Science Module (DSM) series. Hudson, N.H.: Delta Education, 1994.

Program Overview The Delta Science Module (DSM) series has 51 life, physical, and earth science units for grades K-8 that emphasize science concepts, science content, and process skills. The series includes 12 modules for grades 5-6 and 8 modules for grades 6-8. Each requires about 3 to 4 weeks to complete and includes a teacher's guide and materials for a class of 32 students.

Teacher's Guide Recommended grade level: 7-8. *Chemical Interactions* introduces students to the world of chemical reactions. In this module, students compare the densities of 3 different liquids, explore the inverse relationship between the pressure and volume of a gas, and differentiate between solutions and suspensions. Students then learn about the structure of an atom and the properties of protons, neutrons, and electrons, and are introduced to the concept of an isotope. They build models to demonstrate the 3-dimensional structure of molecules and test various covalent and ionic compounds to see how the type of bond between atoms in the compounds affects the characteristics of those compounds. Then students simulate chemical reactions with models, draw and construct models of isomers of organic compounds, distinguish between saturated and unsaturated fats, and explore the effect of double bonds on their melting points. They use indicators to measure pH and identify common household acids and bases, they discover that bases neutralize acids, they conduct a controlled experiment to determine the factors necessary for oxidation to occur, and they carry out a double replacement reaction and observe the formation of a precipitate.

The 13 activities in *Chemical Interactions* generally take between 30 and 60 minutes each and can be done by students working individually or in groups. In addition to directions for activities, the teacher's guide provides a module overview, a schedule of activities, objectives for each activity, background information, materials management and preparation tips, sample answers to discussion questions, teaching suggestions, and reinforcement activities. Also included are reproducible activity sheets for student work and a performance-based assessment. A "connections" feature at the end of each activity provides suggestions for extending or applying the concepts addressed.

Key to Content Standards: 5-8 (see app. C)

UNIFYING CONCEPTS AND PROCESSES: Systems, order, and organization; evidence, models, and explanation; change, constancy, and measurement. SCIENCE AS INQUIRY: Abilities necessary to do scientific inquiry; understandings about scientific inquiry. PHYSICAL SCIENCE: Properties and changes of properties in matter. SCIENCE AND TECHNOLOGY: Understandings about science and technology. SCIENCE IN PERSONAL AND SOCIAL PERSPECTIVES: Science and technology in society. HISTORY AND NATURE OF SCIENCE: Science as a human endeavor; history of science.

Prices: Teacher's guide (ISBN 0-87504-160-4), $27.95. Kit, $379.00. Refill package, $52.00. *Publisher/supplier:* Delta Education. *Materials:* Available locally, from commercial suppliers, or in kit.

1.21 **Chemical Reactions.** Reprinted with revisions. Jacqueline Barber. Great Explorations in Math and Science (GEMS) series. Berkeley, Calif.: Lawrence Hall of Science, 1993.

Program Overview The Great Explorations in Math and Science (GEMS) series includes more than 50 teacher's guides and handbooks for preschool through grade 10. About 35 of these are appropriate for middle school. The series also includes several assembly presenter's guides and exhibit guides. New guides and handbooks continue to be developed, and current titles are revised frequently. The series is designed to teach key science and mathematics concepts through activity-based learning. The time needed to complete GEMS units varies from about 2 to 10 class sessions.

Teacher's Guide **Recommended grade level: 7-8+.** *Chemical Reactions* contains directions for a 2-part activity that is, in essence, an observation and investigation of a dramatic chemical reaction. In part 1 of the activity, students carefully observe 3 chemicals—calcium chloride, baking soda, and phenol red. They then combine these chemicals in a Ziplock bag and observe the reaction.

In part 2 of the activity, students experiment to find out which of the reactants caused the reaction to release heat. Combining the chemicals in different ways, they encounter different reactions with respect to temperature, color, and the production of gas. Through their own experiments and deductions, students discover which reactants cause the reaction to get hot.

Each part of the activity takes 45 to 60 minutes, plus follow-up sessions. The guide includes directions, extensions, brief background information, and student record sheets.

Key to Content Standards: 5-8 (see app. C)

UNIFYING CONCEPTS AND PROCESSES: Systems, order, and organization; evidence, models, and explanation; change, constancy, and measurement. **SCIENCE AS INQUIRY:** Abilities necessary to do scientific inquiry; understandings about scientific inquiry. **PHYSICAL SCIENCE:** Properties and changes of properties in matter; transfer of energy.

Price: $9 (ISBN 0-912511-13-3). *Publisher/supplier:* LHS GEMS. *Materials:* Available locally, or from commercial suppliers.

1.22 **Color Analyzers.** Reprinted with revisions. Cary I. Sneider, Alan Gould, and Cheryl Hawthorne. Great Explorations in Math and Science (GEMS) series. Berkeley, Calif.: Lawrence Hall of Science, 1993.

Program Overview The Great Explorations in Math and Science (GEMS) series includes more than 50 teacher's guides and handbooks for preschool through grade 10. About 35 of these are appropriate for middle school. The series also includes several assembly presenter's guides and exhibit guides. New guides and handbooks continue to be developed, and current titles are revised frequently. The series is designed to teach key science and mathematics concepts through activity-based learning. The time needed to complete GEMS units varies from about 2 to 10 class sessions.

Teacher's Guide **Recommended grade level: 5-8+.** In *Color Analyzers*, students investigate light and color while experimenting with diffraction gratings and color filters. The unit's activities include using diffraction gratings to look at light sources and using colored light filters to decipher and invent secret messages. These activities draw students into investigations of light and color and help them discover why different objects appear to be different colors. Activities to provide additional experiences with light perception are suggested.

Color Analyzers includes 4 sessions of 30 to 60 minutes each. The lesson plan for each session includes an overview, a list of materials, blackline masters of student worksheets, and complete instructions for planning and conducting the activity. Background information for the teacher, summary outlines, and reproducible student worksheets are included. A class set of diffraction gratings and color filters accompanies the teacher's guide.

Key to Content Standards: 5-8 (see app. C)

UNIFYING CONCEPTS AND PROCESSES: Systems, order, and organization; change, constancy, and measurement. **SCIENCE AS INQUIRY:** Abilities necessary to do scientific inquiry; understandings about scientific inquiry. **PHYSICAL SCIENCE:** Transfer of energy.

Prices: $31.50 (ISBN 0-912511-14-1). Consumable kit, $5.50. *Publisher/supplier:* LHS GEMS. *Materials:* Available locally, or from commercial suppliers.

1.23 **Color and Light.** National Learning Center. Delta Science Module (DSM) series. Hudson, N.H.: Delta Education, 1994.

Program Overview The Delta Science Module (DSM) series has 51 life, physical, and earth science units for grades K-8 that emphasize science concepts, science content, and process skills. The series includes 12 modules for grades 5-6 and 8 modules for grades 6-8. Each requires about 3 to 4 weeks to complete and includes a teacher's guide and materials for a class of 32 students.

Teacher's Guide **Recommended grade level: 5-6.** In *Color and Light* students investigate the relationships between pigments, color filters, and the light that strikes them. In this module, students observe the properties of light by experimenting with prisms; they mix different colors of pigments, observing the new colors that form; and they use paper chromatography to separate a mixture of pigments. Students also use color filters and light sources to investigate and compare the processes of subtractive and additive color mixing. They see how colored light can affect the way colored objects look, observe how primary colors can be used to produce full-color images, and learn to create colors by combining primary colors. Students then observe the effect that color filters have on what we see, apply their knowledge of how color filters affect sight to create the illusion of a 3-dimensional object from a 2-dimensional drawing, explore afterimages, and make and use multicolored wheels to observe the "persistence of vision" phenomenon.

The 13 activities in *Color and Light* generally take 30 to 60 minutes each and can be done by students working individually or in groups. In addition to directions for activities, the teacher's guide provides a module overview, a schedule of activities, objectives for each activity, background information, materials management and preparation tips, sample answers to discussion questions, teaching suggestions, and reinforcement activities. Also included are reproducible activity sheets for student work and a performance-based assessment. A "connections" feature at the end of each activity provides suggestions for extending or applying the concepts addressed.

Key to Content Standards: 5-8 (see app. C)

UNIFYING CONCEPTS AND PROCESSES: Evidence, models, and explanation; change, constancy, and measurement. **SCIENCE AS INQUIRY:** Abilities necessary to do scientific inquiry; understandings about scientific inquiry. **PHYSICAL SCIENCE:** Transfer of energy. **SCIENCE AND TECHNOLOGY:** Understandings about science and technology.

Prices: Teacher's guide (ISBN 0-87504-113-2), $27.95. Kit, $309.00. Refill package, $42.00. *Publisher/supplier:* Delta Education. *Materials:* Available locally, from commercial suppliers, or in kit.

1.24 Discovering Density. Reprinted with revisions. Jacqueline Barber, Marion E. Buegler, Laura Lowell, and Carolyn Willard. Great Explorations in Math and Science (GEMS) series. Berkeley, Calif.: Lawrence Hall of Science, 1993.

Program Overview The Great Explorations in Math and Science (GEMS) series includes more than 50 teacher's guides and handbooks for preschool through grade 10. About 35 of these are appropriate for middle school. The series also includes several assembly presenter's guides and exhibit guides. New guides and handbooks continue to be developed, and current titles are revised frequently. The series is designed to teach key science and mathematics concepts through activity-based learning. The time needed to complete GEMS units varies from about 2 to 10 class sessions.

Teacher's Guide **Recommended grade level: 6-8+.** In *Discovering Density*, students learn about the concept of density through 5 hands-on activities using liquids. In the first activity, students layer colored "mystery liquids" of different densities in a drinking straw and discover that some liquids float on top of others. They experiment with colored salt solutions and discover that water containing different amounts of salt also forms layers. Drawing on these 2 experiments, students learn to define density and to distinguish weight from density. In the third and fourth activities, they create their own mixtures of liquids of different densities using "secret formulas." They predict how the liquids will layer and then test their predictions. In the final activity, students observe how temperature affects the density of a liquid, then apply their understanding of density to explain some real-life situations. Directions for the activities are clear and concise.

Discovering Density contains 5 sessions of 25 to 50 minutes each. The lessons include helpful suggestions for group work, discussion, and classroom management. Background information, literature connections, and reproducible student record sheets are also contained in the guide.

Key to Content Standards: 5-8 (see app. C)

UNIFYING CONCEPTS AND PROCESSES: Systems, order, and organization; evidence, models, and explanation; change, constancy, and measurement. **SCIENCE AS INQUIRY:** Abilities necessary to do scientific inquiry; understandings about scientific inquiry. **PHYSICAL SCIENCE:** Properties and changes of properties in matter.

Price: $10.50 (ISBN 0-912511-17-6). *Publisher/supplier:* LHS GEMS. *Materials:* Available locally, or from commercial suppliers.

1.25 **Electrical Connections.** Bob Roth. Delta Science Module (DSM) series. Hudson, N.H.: Delta Education, 1994.

Program Overview The Delta Science Module (DSM) series has 51 life, physical, and earth science units for grades K-8 that emphasize science concepts, science content, and process skills. The series includes 12 modules for grades 5-6 and 8 modules for grades 6-8. Each requires about 3 to 4 weeks to complete and includes a teacher's guide and materials for a class of 32 students.

Teacher's Guide **Recommended grade level: 6-8.** *Electrical Connections* offers 13 activities to increase students' understanding of static and current electricity, electrical circuits, and simple electrical energy converters. The activities are designed to give students concrete experiences building, operating, and analyzing electrical circuits and their applications.

Students first construct an electroscope to detect and investigate the behavior of static charges. Then they are introduced to the concepts of electrical energy source, energy receiver, and energy converter as they construct simple, then more complex, electrical circuits using batteries, bulbs, wires, and switches. Students build a galvanometer and use it to compare currents in different circuits, they test various arrangements of lightbulbs and a galvanometer and determine that current is conserved in both series and parallel circuits, and they investigate various factors (such as resistors or batteries) that affect current in electric circuits. Students then construct a simple motor and infer that a motor is an energy converter. Finally, they use simple circuits to model and analyze the operation of a 3-way switch and a dimmer switch.

The 13 activities in *Electrical Connections* take 30 to 60 minutes each and can be done by students working individually or in groups. In addition to directions for activities, the teacher's guide provides a module overview, a schedule of activities, objectives for each activity, background information, materials management and preparation tips, sample answers to discussion questions, teaching suggestions, and reinforcement activities. Also included are reproducible activity sheets for student work and a performance-based assessment. A "connections" feature at the end of each activity provides suggestions for extending or applying the concepts addressed.

Key to Content Standards: 5-8 (see app. C)

UNIFYING CONCEPTS AND PROCESSES: Systems, order, and organization; evidence, models, and explanation; change, constancy, and measurement. **SCIENCE AS INQUIRY:** Abilities necessary to do scientific inquiry; understandings about scientific inquiry. **PHYSICAL SCIENCE:** Transfer of energy. **SCIENCE AND TECHNOLOGY:** Understandings about science and technology. **HISTORY AND NATURE OF SCIENCE:** History of science.

Prices: Teacher's guide (ISBN 0-87504-158-2), $27.95. Kit, $379.00. Refill package, $59.50. *Publisher/supplier:* Delta Education. *Materials:* Available locally, from commercial suppliers, or in kit.

1.26 **Electromagnetism.** Delta Science Module (DSM) series. Hudson, N.H.: Delta Education, 1994.

Program Overview The Delta Science Module (DSM) series has 51 life, physical, and earth science units for grades K-8 that emphasize science concepts, science content, and process skills. The series includes 12 modules for grades 5-6 and 8 modules for grades 6-8. Each requires about 3 to 4 weeks to complete and includes a teacher's guide and materials for a class of 32 students.

Teacher's Guide **Recommended grade level: 5-7.** In *Electromagnetism,* students explore the unique relationship between electricity and magnetism and how this relationship can be manipulated to produce an electric current or a magnetic field. Students first review the properties of magnetism as they observe the interaction of magnets with ferrous and nonferrous objects; then they use iron filings and a magnet to explore magnetic-field patterns. They explore compasses and how they interact with magnets, and they discover that a ferrous object placed within the magnetic fields of 2 stacks of magnets becomes magnetized. Students then construct a circuit and observe that electric current flowing through a wire deflects a compass needle. They make and use an electromagnet and then a telegraph and a buzzer. Then they construct a simple motor, followed by a more elaborate motor with a 2-coil armature and brushes. They experiment to determine the effect of 2 electromagnetic fields on 1 ferrous object. Finally, they observe that a magnetic field can produce an electric current (that is, induction).

The 12 activities in *Electromagnetism* take 30 to 60 minutes each and can be done by students working individually or in groups. In addition to directions for activities, the teacher's guide provides a module overview, a schedule of activities, objectives for each activity, background information, materials management and preparation tips, sample answers to discussion questions, teaching suggestions, and reinforcement activities. Also included are reproducible activity sheets for student work and a performance-based assessment. A "connections" feature at the end of each activity provides suggestions for extending or applying the concepts addressed.

Key to Content Standards: 5-8 (see app. C)

UNIFYING CONCEPTS AND PROCESSES: Evidence, models, and explanation; change, constancy, and measurement. SCIENCE AS INQUIRY: Abilities necessary to do scientific inquiry; understandings about scientific inquiry. PHYSICAL SCIENCE: Transfer of energy. SCIENCE AND TECHNOLOGY: Abilities of technological design; understandings about science and technology.

Prices: Teacher's guide (ISBN 0-87504-130-5), $27.95. Kit, $349.00. Refill package, $37.00. *Publisher/supplier:* Delta Education. *Materials:* Available locally, from commercial suppliers, or in kit.

1.27 Energy and Communications: How Can We Send and Receive Information? New York Science, Technology and Society Education Project (NYSTEP). Problem-Solving Activities for Middle-Level Science series. Albany, N.Y.: NYSTEP, 1993.

Program Overview The Problem-Solving Activities for Middle-Level Science series consists of 8 stand-alone modules. Each module contains 2 to 6 units focused on technological and/or ethical aspects of issues involving science, technology, and society. The series was designed so that teachers might select modules and units that address local needs and draw on local community resources. A module requires 3 to 8 weeks to complete, depending on the units selected. Supplies and equipment may be required that are not typically part of a school's science inventory.

Teacher's Guide Recommended grade level: 7-8. *Energy and Communications* introduces students to different types of electronic communication and technology. During the module, students explore some of the trade-offs in communication technologies of different time periods. They build a series circuit and a parallel circuit to light a bulb, and then design, construct, and use a lightbulb telegraph communications system. In a unit on electromagnetism and sound, students make an electromagnet and use it to build a working speaker. Students then use lenses and other devices to investigate the various ways that light can be amplified, reduced, or manipulated. They also build a photophone and use it to send and receive messages. In a final unit they design, construct, and refine a telecommunications system that uses Lucite rods as an analogue for systems employing fiber optics.

Energy and Communications is designed to be completed over a 4- to 6-week period. The module is divided into 4 units, each of which has directions for its activities, a bibliography, interdisciplinary connections (to technology, social studies, language arts, mathematics, health, home and career skills, arts, and foreign languages/culture), and suggestions for extensions.

Key to Content Standards: 5-8 (see app. C)

UNIFYING CONCEPTS AND PROCESSES: Systems, order, and organization; evidence, models, and explanation; change, constancy, and measurement. SCIENCE AS INQUIRY: Abilities necessary to do scientific inquiry; understandings about scientific inquiry. PHYSICAL SCIENCE: Transfer of energy. SCIENCE AND TECHNOLOGY: Abilities of technological design; understandings about science and technology. SCIENCE IN PERSONAL AND SOCIAL PERSPECTIVES: Science and technology in society.

Prices: Teacher's guide: In New York State, free with attendance at work-shop; outside New York, $7. *Publisher/supplier:* New York Science, Technology and Society Education Project. *Materials:* Available locally, or from commercial suppliers.

1.28 Experimenting with Model Rockets. Reprinted with revisions. Cary I. Sneider. Great Explorations in Math and Science (GEMS) series. Berkeley, Calif.: Lawrence Hall of Science, 1991.

Program Overview The Great Explorations in Math and Science (GEMS) series includes more than 50 teacher's guides and handbooks for preschool through grade 10. About 35 of these are appropriate for middle school. The series also includes several assembly presenter's guides and exhibit guides. New guides and handbooks continue to be developed, and current titles are revised frequently. The series is designed to teach key science and mathematics concepts through activity-based learning. The time needed to complete GEMS units varies from about 2 to 10 class sessions.

Teacher's Guide Recommended grade level: 6-8+. *Experimenting with Model Rockets* is a "nuts-and-bolts" guide that introduces students to the concept of controlled experimentation. During the activities, students work in teams as they design, build, and launch different model rockets (and a control rocket) to find out why some rockets fly higher than others do. Students measure the altitude of each rocket as it is launched, compute the altitude of each rocket in meters, and display the results on graphs. They also discuss other rocket experiments they would like to perform.

A prerequisite for this unit is *Height-O-Meters*, another module in the GEMS series, in which students build simple cardboard instruments to measure the altitude of objects that are too high or far away to measure directly. In this rocketry unit, students use Height-O-Meters to track the altitudes of their model rockets.

The teacher's guide includes background information, step-by-step directions for the activities (which require 7 sessions of 50 minutes each), a Model Rocketry Safety Code, and a reproducible "Experimenter's Guide" for student work. Information on obtaining model rocketry materials and supplies is provided.

Key to Content Standards: 5-8 (see app. C)

UNIFYING CONCEPTS AND PROCESSES: Evidence, models, and explanation; form and function.
SCIENCE AS INQUIRY: Abilities necessary to do scientific inquiry; understandings about scientific inquiry.
PHYSICAL SCIENCE: Motions and forces.
SCIENCE AND TECHNOLOGY: Abilities of technological design; understandings about science and technology.

Price: $16 (ISBN 0-912511-20-6).
Publisher/supplier: LHS GEMS.
Materials: Available locally, or from commercial suppliers.

1.29 **Flight Lab.** Science Technology and Reading (STAR) series. Developed by Reading Is Fundamental (Washington, D.C.). Dubuque, Iowa: Kendall/Hunt, 1996.

Program Overview Designed for the upper elementary grades, the Science Technology and Reading (STAR) series consists of 8 thematic "labs" in the natural and physical sciences. Each lab focuses both on science activities and on a genre of children's literature, developing correlations between the science process and the process of reading. In addition to a teacher's guide for

each of the 8 labs, the STAR program includes a mentor's guide for scientists, engineers, and others assisting in the classroom.

Teacher's Guide **Recommended grade level: 5-7.** *Flight Lab* introduces activities on the science of flight with a collection of historical anecdotes tracing the development of flight science and technology. Students experiment with kites, parachutes, airfoils, gliders, and balloon rockets to learn about 4 forces acting on an aircraft in flight—lift, drag, thrust, and gravity. They measure altitude, wind speed, rate of descent, and flight distance. Information, procedures, and test data are recorded in student flight logs. Examples of cross-curricular activities include analyzing the elements of science fiction stories, constructing a flight history timeline, calculating and comparing flight times for airplanes throughout history, and drawing a scene as viewed from a hot air balloon.

Flight Lab provides a list of resources, including books, computer software, and audiovisual materials.

Key to Content Standards: 5-8 (see app. C)

UNIFYING CONCEPTS AND PROCESSES: Systems, order, and organization; evidence, models, and explanation.
SCIENCE AS INQUIRY: Abilities necessary to do scientific inquiry; understandings about scientific inquiry.
PHYSICAL SCIENCE: Motions and forces.
SCIENCE AND TECHNOLOGY: Abilities of technological design.
HISTORY AND NATURE OF SCIENCE: History of science.

Prices: Teacher's guide (ISBN 0-7872-1457-4), $21.90. Mentor's guide, $3.90. ***Publisher/supplier:*** Kendall/Hunt. ***Materials:*** Available locally, or from commercial suppliers.

1.30 **Forces and Machines.** Mary Atwater, Prentice Baptiste, Lucy Daniel, and others. Unit 39. Macmillan/McGraw-Hill Science series. New York, N.Y.: Macmillan/McGraw-Hill School Publishing, 1995.

Program Overview The Macmillan/McGraw-Hill Science series is a comprehensive, activity-based, K-8 science curriculum made up of 42 stand-alone units, 18 of which are designed for grades 6-8. The series is constructed around 7 major themes: (1) systems and interactions, (2) scale and structure, (3) stability, (4) energy, (5) evolution, (6) patterns of change, and (7) models. The subject of each unit—for example, forces and machines—is presented from the perspective of one or more of these themes. One theme is designated as the "major theme" for a unit, and any others are treated as "related themes." For each unit, a wide range of materials, including some optional components, is available for students and teachers.

Student Edition **Recommended grade level: 7-8.** *Forces and Machines* contains 5 lessons in which students explore the forces of friction and gravity and their interaction with objects in different systems. The organizing themes for this unit are systems and interactions (major theme) and energy (related theme).

Each of the 5 lessons in this unit typically requires 5 days for completion. During the unit students develop an understanding of friction and gravity; find out how one form of energy can be transformed into another; discriminate between potential and kinetic energy; calculate and measure energy using joules; define work, power, and momentum; and explore levers, pulleys, the wheel and axle, and the inclined plane as simple machines.

Sample activities include investigating the variables involved in frictional forces; observing if mass and height affect the motion of a skate rolling down a ramp; calculating the amount of work done in walking up stairs and the rate at which it was done; exploring how a lever changes the amount of force needed to do work; and investigating how an inclined plane affects the effort force.

Each lesson contains narrative information and a series of sequential, hands-on activities—such as an introductory "minds-on" activity, short "try this" activities, and a longer "explore" activity. The latter, which is a lab activity, takes a class period to complete. Students use activity logs to record ideas, observations, and results.

Special unit features include curriculum links to language arts, literature, mathematics, music, and art; information about science careers; and narrative sections highlighting science, technology, and society connections.

Teacher's Planning Guide The teacher's planning guide, a spiral-bound, wraparound edition, provides information and strategies for teaching the 5 lessons in the student edition. Each lesson is introduced by a 4-page section that offers background information, a lesson planning guide, and assessment options. Marginal notes on the lesson pages provide discussion ideas, tips on meeting individual needs, suggestions for addressing misconceptions, assessment ideas, and curriculum connections.

Program Resources and Support Materials A wide range of materials, including some optional components, is available. Examples include consumable and nonconsumable activity materials; audio- and videotapes; interactive videodiscs; color transparencies; assessment materials; a teacher anthology of short

stories, poems, fingerplays, and songs; trade books; teacher resource masters; activity cards; activity logs; a staff development package; concept summaries and glossaries for students acquiring English; and software with problem-solving simulations for students.

Key to Content Standards: 5-8 (see app. C)

UNIFYING CONCEPTS AND PROCESSES: Systems, order, and organization; change, constancy, and measurement. **SCIENCE AS INQUIRY:** Abilities necessary to do scientific inquiry; understandings about scientific inquiry. **PHYSICAL SCIENCE:** Motions and forces; transfer of energy. **SCIENCE AND TECHNOLOGY:** Understandings about science and technology.

Prices: Teacher's guide (ISBN 0-02-276087-3), $55.98. Student book (ISBN 0-02-276139-X), $7.06. Teacher's resource package, $91.92. Activity materials kit, $99.00. ***Publisher/supplier:*** McGraw-Hill. ***Materials:*** Available locally, from commercial suppliers, or in kit.

1.31 **Inventor's Lab.** Science Technology and Reading (STAR) series. Developed by Reading Is Fundamental (Washington, D.C.). Dubuque, Iowa: Kendall/Hunt, 1996.

Program Overview Designed for the upper elementary grades, the Science Technology and Reading (STAR) series consists of 8 thematic "labs" in the natural and physical sciences. Each lab focuses both on science activities and on a genre of children's literature, developing correlations between the science process and the process of reading. In addition to a teacher's guide for each of the 8 labs, the STAR program includes a mentor's guide for scientists, engineers, and others assisting in the classroom.

Teacher's Guide **Recommended grade level: 3-6.** The story of Lewis Latimer, an African-American inventor who was a colleague of Thomas Edison, provides the context for a series of investigations using electrical circuitry in *Inventor's Lab*. As apprentices, students construct simple electric circuits and an electromagnet. As journeymen they apply their skills and knowledge to build a model cottage with electrical sources, an electromagnetic crane, or an electronic quiz game. As inventors they are challenged to create an invention or a prototype of an invention. The unit includes additional activities to tie the inventor's lab to reading, social studies, art, and mathematics, including learning more about inventors by reading about their lives and careers, wiring a dollhouse, and building a better book bag.

Inventor's Lab provides a list of resources, including books, computer software, and audiovisual materials.

Key to Content Standards: 5-8 (see app. C)

UNIFYING CONCEPTS AND PROCESSES: Systems, order, and organization. **SCIENCE AS INQUIRY:** Abilities necessary to do scientific inquiry; understandings about scientific inquiry. **PHYSICAL SCIENCE:** Transfer of energy. **SCIENCE AND TECHNOLOGY:** Abilities of technological design; understandings about science and technology. **HISTORY AND NATURE OF SCIENCE:** Science as a human endeavor.

Prices: Teacher's guide (ISBN 0-7872-1455-8), $21.90. Mentor's guide, $3.90. ***Publisher/supplier:*** Kendall/Hunt. ***Materials:*** Available locally, or from commercial suppliers.

1.32 **Lenses and Mirrors.** National Learning Center. Delta Science Module (DSM) series. Hudson, N.H.: Delta Education, 1994.

Program Overview The Delta Science Module (DSM) series has 51 life, physical, and earth science units for grades K-8 that emphasize science concepts, science content, and process skills. The series includes 12 modules for grades 5-6 and 8 modules for grades 6-8. Each requires about 3 to 4 weeks to complete and includes a teacher's guide and materials for a class of 32 students.

Teacher's Guide **Recommended grade level: 5-7.** In *Lenses and Mirrors,* students investigate the refraction and reflection of light by lenses and mirrors as they come to understand how light can be manipulated to help us see things. In this module students investigate how light rays behave when they strike a reflective surface. They discover the connection between the location of an object and the apparent location of its reflection. Then they construct a pinhole viewer and learn why rays passing through a very small hole produce an inverted image. Students discover what happens when light is reflected off more than 1 mirror, investigate the reflection patterns produced by 2 mirrors joined at 1 edge, examine the reflections produced by 2 vertical mirrors and 1 horizontal mirror positioned to form a 3-way corner mirror, and observe the results when light rays strike concave and convex mirrors. In other activities they investigate lenses and discover that lenses change the appearance of things by causing light rays to converge or diverge. They also learn the difference between real and virtual images and the types of lenses and mirrors that produce them. They learn the different parts of the eye and how they work with the brain to produce images, and then learn how eyesight is tested and discuss how

lenses are used to correct eyesight. Finally, students design and conduct their own experiments with lenses and mirrors.

The 12 activities in *Lenses and Mirrors* take 30 to 60 minutes each and can be done by students working individually or in groups. In addition to direction for activities, the teacher's guide provides a module overview, a schedule of activities, objectives for each activity, background information, materials management and preparation tips, sample answers to discussion questions, teaching suggestions, and reinforcement activities. Also included are reproducible activity sheets for student work and a performance-based assessment. A "connections" feature at the end of each activity provides suggestions for extending or applying the concepts addressed.

Key to Content Standards: 5-8 (see app. C)

UNIFYING CONCEPTS AND PROCESSES: Evidence, models, and explanation; change, constancy, and measurement. **SCIENCE AS INQUIRY:** Abilities necessary to do scientific inquiry; understandings about scientific inquiry. **PHYSICAL SCIENCE:** Transfer of energy. **SCIENCE AND TECHNOLOGY:** Abilities of technological design; understandings about science and technology.

Prices: Teacher's guide (ISBN 0-87504-115-9), $27.95. Kit, $379.00. Refill package, $33.00. *Publisher/ Supplier:* Delta Education. *Materials:* Available locally, from commercial suppliers, or in kit.

1.33 **More Than Magnifiers.** Reprinted with revisions. Cary I. Sneider and Alan Gould. Great Explorations in Math and Science (GEMS) series. Berkeley, Calif.: Lawrence Hall of Science, 1991.

Program Overview The Great Explorations in Math and Science (GEMS) series includes more than

50 teacher's guides and handbooks for preschool through grade 10. About 35 of these are appropriate for middle school. The series also includes several assembly presenter's guides and exhibit guides. New guides and handbooks continue to be developed, and current titles are revised frequently. The series is designed to teach key science and mathematics concepts through activity-based learning. The time needed to complete GEMS units varies from about 2 to 10 class sessions.

Teacher's Guide **Recommended grade level: 6-8+.** In *More Than Magnifiers,* students investigate the properties and practical applications of lenses. Using readily available and inexpensive materials, students experiment and find out how lenses are used in magnifiers, simple cameras, telescopes, and projectors. They learn that lenses have properties that can be measured and that some lenses are better than others for certain purposes.

The 4 activities in *More Than Magnifiers* take 30 to 45 minutes each. The teacher's guide provides step-by-step directions for the activities and background information on the properties and functions of the lenses in the 4 devices constructed during the unit. "Going further" ideas at the end of each activity can help teachers design a unit for more advanced students. Summary outlines and reproducible student data sheets are provided.

Key to Content Standards: 5-8 (see app. C)

UNIFYING CONCEPTS AND PROCESSES: Systems, order, and organization; evidence, models, and explanation; change, constancy, and measurement. **SCIENCE AS INQUIRY:** Abilities necessary to do scientific inquiry; understandings about scientific inquiry.

PHYSICAL SCIENCE: Transfer of energy. **SCIENCE AND TECHNOLOGY:** Abilities of technological design.

Prices: $9 (ISBN 0-912511-62-1). Box of lenses, $21. *Publisher/supplier:* LHS GEMS. *Materials:* Available locally, or from commercial suppliers.

1.34 **Newton's Toy Box.** Carolyn Sumners. Delta Science Module (DSM) series. Hudson, N.H.: Delta Education, 1994.

Program Overview The Delta Science Module (DSM) series has 51 life, physical, and earth science units for grades K-8 that emphasize science concepts, science content, and process skills. The series includes 12 modules for grades 5-6 and 8 modules for grades 6-8. Each requires about 3 to 4 weeks to complete and includes a teacher's guide and materials for a class of 32 students.

Teacher's Guide **Recommended grade level: 6-8.** *Newton's Toy Box* introduces students to Newton's laws of motion as they experiment with familiar toys and objects. For example, they use wooden balls to review gravity, motion, and the relationship between mass and force; investigate the variables that affect air resistance when they construct a parachute and use it to slow the speed of falling objects; examine the parabolic path of a tossed ball; and experiment with a traditional "ball and cup" toy and explain how gravity and Newton's second law affect the toy. Students then calculate the speed of a toy car in 3 different situations and identify the degree of friction as the variable accounting for differences in speed. They use gravity (via ramps) to accelerate toy cars and determine which factors, such as starting height on the ramp, affect the cars' speed. They explore Newton's third law of motion—action and reaction—as they construct a come-back-can, and

describe its behavior in terms of potential and kinetic energy. Action and reaction is examined further with spring jumpers and student-assembled paper models of grasshoppers. Students experiment with clacking balls and describe the behavior in terms of momentum and transfer of energy, and create collisions with balls of different masses to test the law of conservation of momentum.

In conjunction with the unit's activities, students watch a video, *Toys in Space*, in which real astronauts experiment with some of the toys students are using. Students compare the behavior of the toys on earth with that of toys in a microgravity environment and see that many of the techniques they use to operate their toys depend on the earth's gravitational force.

The 15 activities in *Newton's Toy Box* each require 30 to 60 minutes and can be done by students working individually or in groups. In addition to directions for activities, the teacher's guide provides a module overview, a schedule of activities, objectives for each activity, background information, materials management and preparation tips, sample answers to discussion questions, teaching suggestions, and reinforcement activities. Also included are reproducible activity sheets for student work and a performance-based assessment. A "connections" feature at the end of each activity provides suggestions for extending or applying the concepts addressed.

Key to Content Standards: 5-8 (see app. C)

UNIFYING CONCEPTS AND PROCESSES: Systems, order, and organization; evidence, models, and explanation; change, constancy, and measurement. **SCIENCE AS INQUIRY:** Abilities necessary to do scientific inquiry; understandings about scientific inquiry.

PHYSICAL SCIENCE: Motions and forces. **SCIENCE AND TECHNOLOGY:** Abilities of technological design; understandings about science and technology.

Prices: Teacher's guide (ISBN 0-87504-156-6), $27.95. Kit, $349.00. Refill package, $5.50. *Publisher/supplier:* Delta Education. *Materials:* Available locally, from commercial suppliers, or in kit.

1.35 **Of Cabbages and Chemistry.** Reprinted with revisions. Jacqueline Barber. Great Explorations in Math and Science (GEMS) series. Berkeley, Calif.: Lawrence Hall of Science, 1993.

Program Overview The Great Explorations in Math and Science (GEMS) series includes more than 50 teacher's guides and handbooks for preschool through grade 10. About 35 of these are appropriate for middle school. The series also includes several assembly presenter's guides and exhibit guides. New guides and handbooks continue to be developed, and current titles are revised frequently. The series is designed to teach key science and mathematics concepts through activity-based learning. The time needed to complete GEMS units varies from about 2 to 10 class sessions.

Teacher's Guide **Recommended grade level: 4-8.** In the module *Of Cabbages and Chemistry*, students discover acids and bases and some of their properties by conducting experiments with red cabbage juice (a natural indicator) and common household liquids. In the first of 4 activities, students mix cabbage juice with various household liquids, then classify the liquids into groups according to the colors of the resulting mixtures. Next they share and compare their results in a classroom "scientific convention," relate their classifications to the terms "acid," "base," and "neutral," and then discover through hands-on experimentation that acids and bases are not discrete categories but points along a continuum. In the third and fourth activities, students investigate the concepts of concentration and neutralization and apply what they have learned by testing a variety of new liquids and household products. A short game, "Acids and Aliens from Outer Space," included at the end of the unit can be used as an assessment.

Of Cabbages and Chemistry includes 4 activities, requiring 4 to 8 sessions of 30 to 60 minutes each. The guide contains appropriate science background information, detailed lesson plans, reproducible masters of student data sheets, and ideas for extensions.

Key to Content Standards: 5-8 (see app. C)

UNIFYING CONCEPTS AND PROCESSES: Systems, order, and organization; change, constancy, and measurement.
SCIENCE AS INQUIRY: Abilities necessary to do scientific inquiry; understandings about scientific inquiry.
PHYSICAL SCIENCE: Properties and changes of properties in matter.

Price: $10.50 (ISBN 0-912511-63-X).
Publisher/supplier: LHS GEMS.
Materials: Available locally, or from commercial suppliers.

1.36 Oobleck: What Do Scientists Do? Reprinted with revisions. Cary I. Sneider. Great Explorations in Math and Science (GEMS) series. Berkeley, Calif.: Lawrence Hall of Science, 1994.

Program Overview The Great Explorations in Math and Science (GEMS) series includes more than 50 teacher's guides and handbooks for preschool through grade 10. About 35 of these are appropriate for

middle school. The series also includes several assembly presenter's guides and exhibit guides. New guides and handbooks continue to be developed, and current titles are revised frequently. The series is designed to teach key science and mathematics concepts through activity-based learning. The time needed to complete GEMS units varies from about 2 to 10 class sessions.

Teacher's Guide **Recommended grade level: 4-8.** In this unit, students investigate an unknown substance (said to come from another planet) called Oobleck, describe its physical properties, experiment to identify its unique characteristics, and hold a scientific convention to discuss the similarities and differences among their findings. Students then design a spacecraft that would be able to land and take off again on an ocean of Oobleck. They compare the scientific methods they employed with those of real scientists.

The format for the 4 activities (requiring 5 or 6 class sessions of 20 to 45 minutes each) includes a list of materials, suggestions for preparation, and directions for the activity. Background information and summary outlines are also provided.

Key to Content Standards: 5-8 (see app. C)

UNIFYING CONCEPTS AND PROCESSES: Systems, order, and organization; evidence, models, and explanation; change, constancy, and measurement.
SCIENCE AS INQUIRY: Abilities necessary to do scientific inquiry; understandings about scientific inquiry.
PHYSICAL SCIENCE: Properties and changes of properties in matter.
SCIENCE AND TECHNOLOGY: Abilities of technological design; understandings about science and technology.

Price: $9 (ISBN 0-912511-64-8).
Publisher/supplier: LHS GEMS.
Materials: Available locally, or from commercial suppliers.

1.37 Simple Machines. Delta Science Module (DSM) series. Hudson, N.H.: Delta Education, 1994.

Program Overview The Delta Science Module (DSM) series has 51 life, physical, and earth science units for grades K-8 that emphasize science concepts, science content, and process skills. The series includes 12 modules for grades 5-6 and 8 modules for grades 6-8. Each requires about 3 to 4 weeks to complete and includes a teacher's guide and materials for a class of 32 students.

Teacher's Guide **Recommended grade level: 5-7.** *Simple Machines* introduces students to simple machines and the concepts of force, work, friction, energy transfer, and mechanical advantage. During the module, students determine the amount of force necessary to move objects and calculate the amount of work done when an object is moved over a measured distance. They construct a lever and investigate mechanical advantage by experimenting with the position of the fulcrum, load, and effort. Students experiment with friction, and discover how wheels reduce the amount of friction between an object and the surface over which it moves. Students then assemble a toy tractor and discover the mechanical advantage of a wheel-and-axle simple machine, and they experiment with traction and how it improves the performance of their tractors. They also examine the structure of a gear and observe how gears interact to transfer force, and construct and use a pulley. They perform experiments with an inclined plane, finding that it allows them to do the same amount of work while exerting less force; discuss the properties of a wedge that permit it to be classified as a simple machine; discover that a screw consists of an inclined plane wrapped around a cylinder; and compare lists of simple machines found at home.

The 12 activities in *Simple Machines* generally take from 30 to 60 minutes each to complete, and can be done by students working individually or in groups. In addition to directions for activities, the teacher's guide provides a module overview, a schedule of activities, objectives for each activity, background information, materials management and preparation tips, sample answers to discussion questions, teaching suggestions, and reinforcement activities. Also included are reproducible activity sheets for student work and a performance-based assessment. A "connections" feature at the end of each activity provides suggestions for extending or applying the concepts addressed.

Key to Content Standards: 5-8 (see app. C)

UNIFYING CONCEPTS AND PROCESSES: Systems, order, and organization; evidence, models, and explanation; change, constancy, and measurement. **SCIENCE AS INQUIRY:** Abilities necessary to do scientific inquiry; understandings about scientific inquiry. **PHYSICAL SCIENCE:** Motions and forces. **SCIENCE AND TECHNOLOGY:** Understandings about science and technology.

Prices: Teacher's guide (ISBN 0-87504-119-1), $27.95. Kit, $279.00. Refill package, $15.00. *Publisher/supplier:* Delta Education. *Materials:* Available locally, from commercial suppliers, or in kit.

1.38 **Using Energy.** Mary Atwater, Prentice Baptiste, Lucy Daniel, and others. Unit 42. Macmillan/McGraw-Hill Science series. New York, N.Y.: Macmillan/McGraw-Hill School Publishing, 1995.

Program Overview
The Macmillan/McGraw-Hill Science series is a comprehensive, activity-based, K-8 sci-

ence curriculum made up of 42 stand-alone units, 18 of which are designed for grades 6-8. The series is constructed around 7 major themes: (1) systems and interactions, (2) scale and structure, (3) stability, (4) energy, (5) evolution, (6) patterns of change, and (7) models. The subject of each unit— for example, using energy—is presented from the perspective of one or more of these themes. One theme is designated as the "major theme" for a unit, and any others are treated as "related themes." For each unit, a wide range of materials, including some optional components, is available for students and teachers.

Student Edition Recommended grade level: 7-8.
Using Energy contains 5 lessons in which students discover how thermal energy is produced and investigate the effect of thermal energy on matter, examine the relationship between thermal energy and other forms of energy, and discuss different types of energy resources. The organizing theme for this unit is energy (major theme).

Each of the 5 lessons in the unit typically requires 5 to 8 days for completion. During the unit students define thermal energy and develop an understanding of the relationship between thermal energy and temperature. They also learn the difference between temperature and heat; compare and contrast conduction, convection, and radiation; and learn about the main sources of thermal energy, their relationships, and how they occur. Students discuss the difference between renewable and nonrenewable resources, and learn about the importance of energy conservation.

Sample activities include observing that objects become warmer with increasing motion, and experimenting with hot and cold water in plastic bags to discover that thermal energy moves from warmer objects to cooler objects. Other activities include

designing and testing an insulated box made to slow the melting of an ice cube, observing that different materials conduct heat at different rates, constructing a solar collector and comparing how long the solar collector and a traditional heat source such as a hot plate take to heat water, and calculating daily energy consumption and its cost.

Each lesson contains narrative information and a series of sequential, hands-on activities—such as an introductory "minds-on" activity, short "try this" activities, and a longer "explore" activity. The latter, which is a lab activity, takes a class period to complete. Students use activity logs to record ideas, observations, and results.

Special unit features include curriculum links to language arts, literature, mathematics, music, and art; information about science careers; and narrative sections highlighting science, technology, and society connections.

Teacher's Planning Guide
This teacher's planning guide, a spiral-bound, wraparound edition, provides information and strategies for teaching the 5 lessons in the student edition. Each lesson is introduced by a 4-page section that offers background information, a lesson planning guide, and assessment options. Marginal notes on the lesson pages provide discussion ideas, tips on meeting individual needs, suggestions for addressing misconceptions, assessments ideas, and curriculum connections.

Program Resources and Support Materials
A wide range of materials, including some optional components, is available. Examples include consumable and nonconsumable activity materials; audio- and videotapes; interactive videodiscs; color transparencies; assessment materials; a teacher anthology of short stories, poems, fingerplays, and songs; trade books; teacher

resource masters; activity cards; activity logs; concept summaries and glossaries for students acquiring English; and software with problem-solving simulations for students.

Key to Content Standards: 5-8 (see app. C)

UNIFYING CONCEPTS AND PROCESSES: Change, constancy, and measurement.
SCIENCE AS INQUIRY: Abilities necessary to do scientific inquiry; understandings about scientific inquiry.
PHYSICAL SCIENCE: Properties and changes of properties in matter; transfer of energy.
SCIENCE AND TECHNOLOGY: Understandings about science and technology.
SCIENCE IN PERSONAL AND SOCIAL PERSPECTIVES: Science and technology in society.

Prices: Student edition (ISBN 0-02-276142-X), $7.06. Teacher's planning guide (ISBN 0-02-276090-3), $55.98. Unit package, $115.68. Activity materials kit, $86.00. (Contact publisher/supplier for complete price and ordering information.)
Publisher/supplier: McGraw-Hill.
Materials: Available locally, from commercial suppliers, or in kit.

1.39 **Vitamin C Testing.** Reprinted with revisions. Jacqueline Barber. Great Explorations in Math and Science (GEMS) series. Berkeley, Calif.: Lawrence Hall of Science, 1990.

Program Overview The Great Explorations in Math and Science (GEMS) series includes more than 50 teacher's guides and handbooks for preschool through grade 10. About 35 of these are appropriate for middle school. The series also includes several assembly presenter's guides and exhibit guides. New guides and handbooks continue to be developed, and current titles are revised frequently. The series is designed to teach key science and mathematics concepts through activity-based learning. The time needed to complete GEMS units varies from about 2 to 10 class sessions.

Teacher's Guide **Recommended grade level: 4-8.** *Vitamin C Testing* offers an introduction to chemistry and nutrition by providing students with the materials and techniques needed to test the vitamin C content in common juices. Students learn to use the chemical technique titration. They compare the vitamin C content of different juices and graph the results. For more advanced study, students examine the effects of heat and freezing (or other treatment) on vitamin C content.

The skills developed in this unit include performing chemistry lab techniques, experimenting, analyzing data, and graphing and drawing conclusions. Summary outlines help the teacher guide students through the activities. All materials are available in local stores except for the indicator chemical (indophenol) and plastic vials, which can be ordered from a scientific supply company.

The lesson plans for the 4 sessions of 45 minutes each include an overview, a materials list, and detailed instructions for preparing for and conducting the activity. The guide includes reproducible masters of student data sheets.

Key to Content Standards: 5-8 (see app. C)

UNIFYING CONCEPTS AND PROCESSES: Evidence, models, and explanation; change, constancy, and measurement.
SCIENCE AS INQUIRY: Abilities necessary to do scientific inquiry; understandings about scientific inquiry.
SCIENCE AND TECHNOLOGY: Abilities of technological design.
HISTORY AND NATURE OF SCIENCE: Nature of science.

Price: $9 (ISBN 0-912511-70-2).
Publisher/supplier: LHS GEMS.
Materials: Available locally, or from commercial suppliers.

1.40 **What's in Our Food?** Module 2.4. Foundations and Challenges to Encourage Technology-based Science (FACETS) series. Developed by American Chemical Society (Washington, D.C.). Dubuque, Iowa: Kendall/Hunt, 1996.

Program Overview The Foundations and Challenges to Encourage Technology-based Science (FACETS) program consists of 3 series of 8 modules each for grades 6-8. Each module focuses on a topic in the life, earth, or physical sciences. The time needed to complete FACETS modules varies from 2 to 4 weeks. Each module consists of a student book and a teacher's guide.

Student Edition **Recommended grade level: 6-7.** The module *What's in Our Food?* introduces students to the subject of food additives. The major focus is on thickening agents used in commercial brands of vanilla ice cream. Working in teams, students investigate the effects of several variables—type and amount of thickener, temperature of the mixture, and mixing technique—on the thickness of the final product.

Among the activities in the unit, students examine food labels and identify and categorize additives. They conduct a controlled experiment to determine the effects of 3 thickening agents on a basic ice cream mixture, and they explore the effect of different mixture temperatures and mixing techniques on the thickening property of an additive. They also design and carry out a consumer-preference survey on the desirable thickness of ice cream. In the unit's final activity, students use their knowledge of thickeners to develop their own brand of vanilla ice cream.

What's in Our Food? is a 4-week module divided into 5 activities, which each take between 1 and 5 class periods to complete. A narrative section at the end of the module provides background information for students on mixtures, food additives, and consumer opinion surveys.

Teacher's Guide The wraparound teacher's guide includes a unit overview, a time line for completing the module, a materials list, background information, and teaching suggestions.

Key to Content Standards: 5-8 (see app. C)

UNIFYING CONCEPTS AND PROCESSES: Form and function.
SCIENCE AS INQUIRY: Abilities necessary to do scientific inquiry; understandings about scientific inquiry.
PHYSICAL SCIENCE: Properties and changes of properties in matter.

SCIENCE AND TECHNOLOGY: Abilities of technological design; understandings about science and technology.

Prices: Student edition (ISBN 0-7872-1449-3), $7.90. Teacher's guide (ISBN 0-7872-1463-9), $14.90. *Publisher/ supplier:* Kendall/Hunt. *Materials:* Available locally, or from commercial suppliers.

Physical Science—Science Activity Books

1.41 **Analysis.** Ron Marson. Task Card Series 10. Canby, Oreg.: TOPS Learning Systems, 1991.

Recommended grade level: 7-8+. In the 16 easy-to-follow activities in *Analysis*—which is one of the many units in the Task Card Series—students practice and become familiar with the analytical and problem-solving skills that scientists use in identifying substances. For example, students separate a mixture of salt and sand quantitatively, following directions on a flowchart; they develop a reaction table to use as a reference for identifying unknown powders; and they qualitatively analyze the composition of various mixtures of white powders, using testing agents that react in characteristic ways. They also investigate the properties of cabbage water as an acid–base indicator, and they study how beet juice interacts with acids and bases.

The activities in *Analysis* require commonly available materials (such as baking soda, sand, beets, and red cabbage leaves). Certain activities can be omitted or sequences changed to meet specific class needs. The unit contains reproducible "task cards" with directions for each activity, a reproducible pH scale for use in some activities, teaching notes with answers, and review questions.

Price: $8 (ISBN 0-941008-80-0). *Publisher/supplier:* TOPS Learning Systems. *Materials:* Available locally, or from commercial suppliers.

ABOUT THE ANNOTATIONS IN "PHYSICAL SCIENCE— SCIENCE ACTIVITY BOOKS"

Entry Numbers

Curriculum materials are arranged alphabetically by title in each category (Core Materials, Supplementary Units, and Science Activity Books) in chapters 1 through 5 of this guide.

Each curriculum annotation has a two-part entry number: the chapter number is given before the period; the number after the period locates the entry within that chapter. For example, the first entry number in chapter 1 is 1.1; the second entry in chapter 2 is 2.2; and so on.

The entry numbers within each curriculum chapter run consecutively through Core Materials, Supplementary Units, and Science Activity Books.

Order of Bibliographic Information

Following is the arrangement of the facts of publication in the annotations in this section:

- **Title of publication**
- **Number of edition,** if applicable
- **Authors** (an individual author or authors, an institutional author, or a project or program name under which the material was developed)
- **Series title**
- **Series developer,** if applicable
- **Place of publication, publisher, and date of publication**

Recommended Grade Level

The grade level for each piece of material was recommended by teacher evaluators during the development of this guide. In some instances, the recommended grade level may differ slightly from the publisher's advertised level.

Price and Acquisition Information

Ordering information appears at the end of each entry. Included are—

- **Prices** (of teacher's guides, activity books, and kits or units)
- **Publisher/supplier** (The name of a principal publisher/supplier, although not necessarily the sole source, for the items listed in the price category. Appendix A, "Publishers and Suppliers," provides the address, phone and fax numbers, and electronic ordering information, where available, for each publisher and supplier.)
- **Materials** (various sources from which one might obtain the required materials)

Readers must contact publishers/suppliers for complete and up-to-date ordering information, since prices are subject to change and materials may also change with revised editions. The prices given in this chapter are based on information from publishers and suppliers but are not meant to represent the full range of ordering options.

Indexes of Curriculum Materials

The multiple indexes on pp. 449-78 allow easy access to the information in this guide. Various aspects of the curriculum materials—including titles, topics addressed in each unit, and grade levels—are the focus of seven separate indexes. For example, titles and entry numbers are listed in the "Title Index" on pp. 450-54. The "Index of Authors, Series, and Curriculum Projects," on pp. 455-57, provides entry numbers of any annotated titles in a particular series.

1.42 **"The Best of Edison" Science Teaching Kits.** East Orange, N.J.: Charles Edison Fund, 1994.

Recommended grade level: 6-8. *"The Best of Edison"* is a compilation of more than 65 hands-on activities relating to electricity, energy sources and conservation, the environment, nuclear energy, and some of Thomas Edison's inventions. Among the activities, for example, students make a solar-powered hot dog cooker, build and test a model solar hot water heater, and investigate the water-holding capacity of soils. They also conduct a home energy audit, build a DC motor, and use a simple electroscope to detect the presence of static electricity on the surface of a phonograph record. The teacher's guide also includes a biography of Lewis Latimer, an African-American inventor and associate of Edison, and provides activities based on some of Latimer's experiments, such as building an air cooler.

"The Best of Edison" is presented in 3-ring-notebook format. It provides directions and limited background information. No student record sheets are supplied.

Price: $1. Publisher/supplier: Charles Edison Fund. **Materials:** Available locally, or from commercial suppliers.

1.43 **Brick Layers: Creative Engineering with LEGO Constructions.** Sheldon Erickson, Tom Seymour, and Martin Suey. Activities Integrating Mathematics and Science (AIMS) series. Fresno, Calif.: AIMS Education Foundation, 1994.

Recommended grade level: 5-8. *Brick Layers* contains 26 activities for students to explore mechanical and structural engineering concepts by experimenting with LEGO Dacta kits. In the first 18 activities, which focus on mechanical engineering principles, students learn about force, work, friction, and mechanical advantage by constructing and working with inclined planes, levers, wheels and axles, and gears. They discover, for example, how the effort position on a lever affects the amount of effort required, how the size of a slot car's drive wheel affects its performance, and how changing the size of the gears on a fishing reel affects the rate at which the line is reeled in.

In the last 8 activities, which focus on structural engineering, students learn that certain geometric shapes—such as the cycloid and the triangle—have special properties that make them useful in construction. They also learn that tension and compression are forces that are present and need to be considered in building structures. They build polygons and test them to see which ones are stable, use a LEGO gear and racks to draw a cycloid so that they can conceptualize what the ride of a bug would be like if it were on the rim of a moving bicycle, and construct the longest boom possible that has the least possible deflection.

Each activity includes background information, procedures, discussion questions, extensions, and reproducible student pages. Each activity also has a "guiding documents" section, which lists the activity's relevance to specific NCTM (National Council of Teachers of Mathematics) standards and Project 2061 Benchmarks (developed by the American Association for the Advancement of Science).

Price: Teacher's guide (ISBN 1-881431-62-2), $16.95. *Publisher/supplier:* AIMS Education Foundation. *Materials:* Available in LEGO Dacta kits.

1.44 **Crime Lab Chemistry.** Reprinted with revisions. Jacqueline Barber. Great Explorations in Math and Science (GEMS) series. Berkeley, Calif.: Lawrence Hall of Science, 1989.

Recommended grade level: 4-8. In *Crime Lab Chemistry*, students play the part of crime lab chemists to solve a mystery. They discover which of several black pens was used to write a ransom note. This guide capitalizes on students' enthusiasm for solving mysteries to develop such skills as analyzing data and making inferences. They use the process of paper chromatography to separate the pigments contained in the ink on the ransom note. This same technique is then used to analyze the ink in several pens. Students compare the chromatograms to determine which pen was used to write the note.

Crime Lab Chemistry requires 2 class sessions of 35 to 45 minutes each. The teacher's guide includes an introduction, detailed information on time and materials needed and on steps in advance preparation, as well as suggestions for other mysteries to be solved and summary outlines for both sessions.

Price: $9 (ISBN 0-912511-16-8). *Publisher/supplier:* LHS GEMS. *Materials:* Available locally, or from commercial suppliers.

1.45 **Electricity and Magnetism.** Robert Gardner. Yesterday's Science, Today's Technology Science Activities series. New York, N.Y.: Twenty-First Century Books, 1994.

Recommended grade level: 6-8. *Electricity and Magnetism* contains 17 simple activities in which students investigate some of the science and technology associated with electricity and explore how electricity is related to magnetism. The activities involve topics such as magnets and magnetic fields, electric charge, the connection between electricity and magnetism, battery technology, electromagnets, and the future of electricity generation. Students magnetize a needle and use it to make a simple compass, experiment with static charges, plate copper on old spoons using a battery, and build a simple electric generator, among other activities. This book was written for students, and they can do most of the activities without supervision, although several may require adult assistance because of the materials involved.

Each activity includes a brief historical or science background section on the scientific discoveries of people such as Michael Faraday and Thomas Edison. The narrative then guides students through the activity. A list of 15 follow-up activities and ideas is included.

Price: $16.98 (ISBN 0-8050-2850-1). *Publisher/supplier:* Von Holtzbrinck (VHPS). *Materials:* Available locally, or from commercial suppliers.

1.46 **Energy Bridges to Science, Technology and Society.** 3rd ed. Florida Middle School Energy Education Project. Tallahassee, Fla.: Florida State University and Florida Energy Office, 1994.

Recommended grade level: 7-8. *Energy Bridges to Science, Technology and Society* contains 26 activities related to different types of energy technologies, conservation, solar electricity, and the social implications of energy production and consumption. Among these activities, students make a model wind energy machine and also identify some of the problems in cleaning up ocean oil spills. They build and use a simple calorimeter, and they measure the ability of some common materials to hold heat. In other activities, students make recycled paper, compare the transmission of solar radiation through different materials, and build and use a solar box cooker.

Energy Bridges was designed to supplement existing middle or junior high school texts and laboratory investigations. The activities are independent of one another and are designed to be used in class, as laboratory experiments, or as out-of-class assignments.

Presented in a 3-ring-binder format, *Energy Bridges* includes reproducible student data sheets and instructions, as well as a brief teacher's guide with an answer key. Some of the information and examples in the unit are specific to Florida, where the volume was developed, but the unit can be used in other areas of the country as well.

Price: Free. *Publisher/supplier:* Energy and Environmental Alliance. *Materials:* Available locally, or from commercial suppliers.

1.47 **Experiments with Balloons.** Robert Gardner and David Webster. Getting Started in Science series. Springfield, N.J.: Enslow, 1995.

Recommended grade level: 6-8. In *Experiments with Balloons,* 1 of 4 books in the series Getting Started in Science, about 50 simple activities with balloons help students learn about topics such as the properties of gases, air pressure, electricity, density, and sound. Among other activi-

ties, students measure the "floating strength" of liquid-filled balloons. They also compare the densities of air, "lung air," and carbon dioxide. Students build a pressure gauge to compare the pressure of a small balloon with that of a big one, make a model lung, and use balloons to investigate static and electric charge.

Experiments with Balloons was written for students. They can do most of the activities without supervision, although several may require adult assistance because of the materials involved. The activities are largely narrative in form. Each contains questions to help guide students' inquiry. Some experiments are preceded by an explanation of a scientific principle.

Price: $18.95 (ISBN 0-89490-669-0). *Publisher/supplier:* Enslow. *Materials:* Available locally, or from commercial suppliers.

1.48 **Experiments with Bubbles.** Robert Gardner. Getting Started in Science series. Springfield, N.J.: Enslow, 1995.

Recommended grade level: 5-8. In *Experiments with Bubbles,* 1 of 4 books in the series Getting Started in Science, about 50 simple activities with bubbles help students investigate topics such as light, color, Bernoulli's principle, and surface tension. Among other activities, students measure the surface tension of a liquid using a balance beam, they explore how humidity and temperature affect the life span and size of bubbles, and they compare the images one sees in a bubble with those seen in concave and convex mirrors. They also see whether bubbles made from a colored liquid are the same color as the liquid.

Experiments with Bubbles was written for students. They can do most of the activities without supervision, although several may require adult supervision because of the

materials involved. The activities are largely narrative in form. Each contains questions to help guide students' inquiry. Some experiments are preceded by an explanation of a scientific principle.

Price: $18.95 (ISBN 0-89490-666-6). *Publisher/supplier:* Enslow. *Materials:* Available locally, or from commercial suppliers.

1.49 **Experiments with Motion.** Robert Gardner. Getting Started in Science series. Springfield, N.J.: Enslow, 1995.

Recommended grade level: 6-8. In *Experiments with Motion,* 1 of 4 books in the series Getting Started in Science, about 50 simple experiments help students investigate Newton's laws of motion, speed, gravity, acceleration, and friction. Among the activities, students see what effect mass has on a toy truck's acceleration, they make and experiment with a model parachute, and they compare the acceleration of falling objects of different masses. They also investigate inelastic and elastic collisions by experimenting with a homemade "rolling-sphere" toy. The activities involve materials such as bicycles, toy cars and trucks, wagons, marbles, modeling clay, and balloons.

Experiments with Motion was written for students. They can do most of the activities without supervision, although several may require adult supervision because of the materials. The activities are largely narrative in form. Each contains questions to help guide students' inquiry. Some experiments are preceded by an explanation of a scientific principle.

Price: $18.95 (ISBN 0-89490-667-4). *Publisher/supplier:* Enslow. *Materials:* Available locally, or from commercial suppliers.

1.50 **The Exploratorium Guide to Scale and Structure: Activities for the Elementary Classroom.** Barry Kluger-Bell and the School in The Exploratorium. Portsmouth, N.H.: Heinemann, 1995.

Recommended grade level: 4-8. In the 36 open-ended activities of *The Exploratorium Guide to Scale and Structure* (The Exploratorium is San Francisco's museum of science, art, and human perception.), students explore many of the physical principles of structure and experience how changing the scale of a structure affects its strength, stability, and design. The principal concepts addressed in this guide include balancing the forces of weight with the strength of materials; stability, tension, and compression; and the distribution of weight (torques) and balancing points (centers-of-mass).

Activities in the guide are organized in three parts: (1) "The Physics and Engineering of Structure," (2) "The Mathematics of Scale," and (3) "The Effect of Scale on Structure." Among the activities, students build structures such as towers or bridges using various materials (blocks, straws, toothpicks and clay, newspaper, and bamboo garden stakes). They use a variety of balance boards to explore the concept of balance. They also work with cubes and cones to understand the relative changes in length, area, and volume as an object scales up or down. Finally, students investigate the effect of scale on structure through a variety of simple activities involving the surface tension of water.

Each activity includes background information for the teacher, procedures, discussion suggestions, and extensions. Sample student record sheets and a resource guide with short descriptions of books for teachers and students and audiovisual materials are provided. Many of the activities require special work areas to accommodate the large scale of the building projects.

Price: $29.50 (ISBN 0-435-08372-4). *Publisher/supplier:* Heinemann. *Materials:* Available locally, or from commercial suppliers.

1.51 **Flights of Imagination: An Introduction to Aerodynamics.** Rev. ed. Wayne Hosking. Washington, D.C.: National Science Teachers Association, 1990.

Recommended grade level: 5-8+. *Flights of Imagination* provides instructions for its 18 activities, which use student-constructed kites, gliders, and airfoils to investigate fundamental principles of aerodynamics. Students explore questions such as how the wind makes a kite rise; why some kites require a tail; how a dihedral adds stability; and what effect different materials have on a kite's durability, construction time, and flight performance. The more quantitative investigations on topics such as aspect ratio, weight-to-area factor, wind speed and lift, and angle of elevation are more appropriate for secondary school students.

Flights of Imagination includes appendixes on when, where, and how to fly a kite. It also provides a safety code, glossary, and resource list.

Price: $10.50 (ISBN 0-87355-067-6). *Publisher/supplier:* National Science Teachers Association. *Materials:* Available locally, or from commercial suppliers.

1.52 **Floaters and Sinkers: Mass, Volume, and Density.** Rev. ed. Betty Cordel, David Lile, Mike McKibban, and others. Activities Integrating Mathematics and Science (AIMS) series. Fresno, Calif.: AIMS Education Foundation, 1995.

Recommended grade level: 6-8. During the 34 activities in *Floaters and Sinkers*, students investigate the basic concepts and principles of mass, volume, and density by working with familiar things. For example, they find out if the peel of an orange affects whether and why the orange will float or sink. Students also figure out how to make a fresh egg float in water, design an aluminum-foil boat to hold the maximum amount of cargo, and determine how much cargo a ship made from a tin can will carry so that the ship's waterline is at a predetermined level.

Each activity in *Floaters and Sinkers* includes background information for the teacher; procedures, discussion questions, and extensions; and reproducible student pages containing instructions, data sheets, and graphs. Each activity also has a "guiding documents" section, which lists the activity's relevance to specific standards of the National Council of Teachers of Mathematics and to Project 2061 Benchmarks.

Price: Teacher's guide (ISBN 1-881431-58-4), $16.95. *Publisher/supplier:* AIMS Education Foundation. *Materials:* Available locally, or from commercial suppliers.

1.53 **Flying Tinsel: An Unusual Approach to Teaching Electricity.** Grant Mellor. White Plains, N.Y.: Cuisenaire, 1993.

Recommended grade level: 6-8. Many of the 29 sequential activities on electricity in *Flying Tinsel* are adapted from or based on historic experiments by well-known scientists of the seventeenth through the nineteenth century. *Flying Tinsel* is organized in 3 units: (1) "Static Electricity," (2) "Current Electricity," and (3) "Electromagnetism." Students explore topics such as positive and negative charges; voltage, current, resistance, and their relationship to

Ohm's law; applications of the electromagnet; and electromagnetic induction. Among other activities, students work with acrylic rods to investigate electric charges, build a pie-tin electrophorous or "charge carrier," and make a Leyden jar out of a plastic milk jug. They also re-create the world's first battery by building a 2-layer voltaic pile and feeling its moderately shocking force. Then they observe that electric current can produce a magnetic force, and use their electromagnets to construct simple buzzer circuits and a telegraph. They also build a working speaker out of a metal wastepaper basket, a permanent magnet, and an electromagnet.

The activities in *Flying Tinsel* range from being strongly teacher-directed to being free-form investigations. The required materials are generally easy to find and relatively inexpensive. Each activity includes background information for teachers, historical notes when relevant, procedures, discussion suggestions, and extensions. Three short assessments are provided.

Price: Teacher's guide (ISBN 0-938587-33-1), $12.95. *Publisher/ supplier:* Cuisenaire/Dale Seymour. *Materials:* Available locally, or from commercial suppliers.

1.54 **Fundamentals of Physical Science.** 2nd ed. Janet Z. Tarino, with Iona R. Shawver. Science Is Fun series. Mansfield, Ohio: The Ohio State University Research Foundation, 1994.

Recommended grade level: 5-7. The 40 simple experiments in *Fundamentals of Physical Science* introduce students to the nature of scientific investigation; the classification and identification of matter; and the properties of solids, liquids, and

gases. During the first few experiments, which introduce science as a process, students calculate the number of beans in a jar as an introduction to sampling and variability in measurement; they develop an understanding of a grid or coordinate system; they collect data and prepare a graph, and interpret the data and the graph in order to determine the relationships between variables; and they design an experiment to find out how many drops of water can fit on a penny. These introductory experiments are freestanding and could be used by all science teachers regardless of program content.

In the book's 35 physical science experiments, which are designed to be performed in sequence, students do a series of simple activities to discover that air is a substance which takes up space, and they use air pressure to implode a metal can. They also investigate surface tension and capillary action in liquids, and they compare the crystalline patterns of solids. Other experiments teach students how scientists separate and identify substances in mixtures with techniques such as paper chromatography or through knowledge of the physical and chemical properties of substances.

Each activity includes numbered teaching steps, teaching hints, questions for the students, and extensions.

Price: $20. *Publisher/supplier:* The Ohio State University at Mansfield. *Materials:* Available locally.

1.55 **Fun with Chemistry: A Guidebook of K-12 Activities. Vol. 1.** Compiled and edited by Mickey Sarquis and Jerry Sarquis. Madison, Wis.: Institute for Chemical Education, University of Wisconsin, 1991.

Recommended grade level: 5-8+. This first volume of *Fun with Chemistry*

includes 53 chemistry activities and demonstrations. The activities in the first part of the book are arranged in sections on carbon dioxide, chemistry with foodstuffs, color changes, density, and "from the five and dime." Among these activities, students observe that carbon dioxide extinguishes the flame from a candle, compare the dissolving rate of sugar cubes with that of powdered sugar, experiment with density columns, and boil water in a paper pot.

The activities in the second part of the book, most of which are demonstrations, are intended for use by teachers familiar with handling special chemicals, supplies, and equipment, such as concentrated acids, reactive chemicals, or gas cylinders. Students "race" 3 balloons filled with 3 different gases (helium, air, and carbon dioxide). They also observe the effect of extremely low temperature on objects cooled with liquid nitrogen (such as a banana or a racquet ball).

Most of the activities in *Fun with Chemistry* take fewer than 15 minutes to set up. Activities have a grade-level recommendation, instructions for doing the activity, safety and disposal guidelines, extensions or variations, curriculum integration ideas, and an explanation of the chemical concepts involved. The volume also provides a list of suppliers; a list of readily available, inexpensive chemicals (such as common household chemicals); and an activity index sorted by key concepts.

Prices: $23 ($45 for volumes 1 and 2). *Publisher/supplier:* Institute for Chemical Education. *Materials:* Available locally, or from commercial suppliers.

1.56 Fun with Chemistry: A Guidebook of K-12 Activities. Vol. 2. Compiled and edited by Mickey Sarquis and Jerry Sarquis. Madison, Wis.: Institute for Chemical Education, University of Wisconsin, 1993.

Recommended grade level: K-8+. The second volume of *Fun with Chemistry* is a collection of 54 classroom-tested activities that can enhance teaching, are enjoyable and easy to do, and help make science relevant for students. Many of the activities take 15 minutes to set up and not much longer to conduct. The activities are arranged in 8 sections on the following themes: colorful separations, dyeing eggs, polymers, Cartesian divers, physical properties and changes, observing chemical changes, crystals, and our everyday world. Examples of these activities include analyzing the component colors of candy coatings (such as M&Ms) using chromatography, making and studying the properties of a polymer gel similar to Slime, putting an egg into a bottle with a neck smaller than the diameter of the egg, and simulating a tornado in a bottle.

Each activity has a recommended grade level, step-by-step procedures, an explanation of the chemical concepts involved, alternative methods for doing the activity, extensions, references, and a list of sources for finding materials. Safety and chemical disposal guidelines are included. An appendix provides a detailed list of where inexpensive materials can be acquired. The activities are indexed by key concept.

Prices: $27 ($45 for volumes 1 and 2). *Publisher/supplier:* Institute for Chemical Education. *Materials:* Available locally, or from commercial suppliers.

1.57 The Fusion Series: Personal Science Laboratory (PSL) Explorer Investigations for Grades 6-9. Personal Science Laboratory (PSL) series. Boulder, Colo.: Team Labs, 1996.

Recommended grade level: 6-8+. This curriculum guide contains 12 computer-based investigations—each on a different topic—that integrate science, mathematics, and technology. The investigations use special probes, interfaced with a personal computer, that allow students to conduct measurements and enter data directly into the software program—PSL Explorer—that guides students through the experiments. Topics covered include the electromagnetic spectrum, phase changes, rotational velocity, electrovoltaic cells, photosynthesis, seismic waves, and exothermic and endothermic reactions.

Among the activities, students devise a method to map out a landing zone for a prototype flying saucer using a distance probe as a surveying tool. They also identify sources of electromagnetic radiation outside of the visible range and measure the intensity of this radiation using a light probe. In other activities, they construct a battery from a banana, graph the phase change of a special type of chocolate from a liquid to a solid, construct a pendulum seismograph, use probes to explore the temperature at which water has the greatest density, and replicate the reactions that occur in hot packs and cold packs.

Students complete experiments by logging onto the computer, selecting an experiment, following a series of prompts or directions, entering data from activities or by having the probes directly transmit the information, and completing follow-up activities. The computer program also organizes student-generated experimental data into charts, graphs, and tables. Each activity includes step-by-step procedures, student pages, assessments, and extensions.

The entire series of investigations comes in a hard-copy version, on a CD-ROM, and on diskettes. In order to use the program, a school must acquire both the Personal Science Laboratory software and equipment (such as probeware).

Prices: Curriculum guide, $288. Middle School Comprehensive Pak, $3,390. (Contact the publisher/supplier for complete price and ordering information.) *Publisher/supplier:* Team Labs. *Materials:* Available locally, from commercial suppliers, or from Team Labs.

1.58 Gears. Enfield, Conn.: LEGO Dacta, 1993.

Recommended grade level: 4-6. This booklet contains information about gears, simple hands-on gear activities, and appropriate diagrams and illustrations. It is designed to be used with the LEGO Dacta Gear Set, which uses the popular LEGO construction blocks to teach about gears. Students first learn the definition of a gear. Then they build models that will gear up (increase speed) and gear down (increase force). They arrange gears so they turn in the same direction, in opposite directions, or at 90-degree angles to each other. They discover that how fast or how slowly one gear makes another turn depends on the number of teeth on the gear. Students are challenged to design and build a spinning sign and a moving target.

Each activity in *Gears* states the main idea involved and provides illustrated instructions, additional information, and extension ideas. The guide lists the process and critical-thinking skills involved in the activities.

Prices: Teacher's guide (ISBN 0-914831-82-8), $5.25. Classroom pack, $183.75. Individual set, $15.75. *Publisher/supplier:* LEGO Dacta. *Materials:* Available from LEGO Dacta.

1.59 How Everyday Things Work: 60 Descriptions and Activities. Peter Goodwin. Walch Reproducible Books. Portland, Maine: Walch, 1992.

Recommended grade level: 6-8. *How Everyday Things Work* describes the scientific principles behind 60 everyday objects, systems, and events. The simple exercises and activities in the book help increase students' understanding of these principles. Some of the topics and their everyday applications are mechanics (how trees stand up in the wind); electricity and magnets (2-way switches, television pictures); sound and light (how a stereo speaker works, printing color pictures); thermodynamics (ice skates, avalanches); and environmental science (how cars are made more fuel-efficient, how smog forms).

Each of the 60 topics consists of a reproducible student section and a teacher section. The section for teachers gives a further explanation of scientific ideas, background information, and answers to questions.

Price: $22.95 (ISBN 0-8251-1974-X). *Publisher/supplier:* Walch. *Materials:* Available locally.

1.60 Ice Cream Making and Cake Baking. Bernie Zubrowski. Models in Physical Science (MIPS) series. White Plains, N.Y.: Cuisenaire, 1994.

Recommended grade level: 6-8. *Ice Cream Making and Cake Baking* is 1 of 4 volumes in the Models in Physical Science (MIPS) series. Through the 7 activities in this unit, students investigate the 3 basic types of heat transfer—conduction, convection, and radiation. During these activities, students try to determine the best conditions for removing heat from a container, and they investigate how to prevent heat transfer. Students test containers of different materials, shapes, sizes, and thicknesses to see

how these factors affect the melting rate of ice cubes. Then, in an investigation led by the teacher, they test ways of obtaining a temperature high enough to bake a cake in a cardboard-box oven.

Next, students move to an investigation of the best way to cool cream to make ice cream. They observe the cooling rate of hot water when ice is added to the coolant water, and they observe the cooling rate of hot water when an ice-salt-water solution is used as the coolant. At the end of the unit, students use what they have learned to make ice cream and bake a cake. For several of the activities, students represent data graphically and mathematically.

The activities in *Ice Cream Making and Cake Baking* include reproducible student pages and a section for teachers providing background information, discussion guidelines, assessment suggestions, and extensions.

Prices: Teacher's guide (ISBN 0-938587-36-6), $12.50. Kit, $115.00. *Publisher/supplier:* Cuisenaire/Dale Seymour. *Materials:* Available locally, from commercial suppliers, or in kit.

1.61 Identification of Chemical Reactions Kit. Ronkonkoma, N.Y.: Lab-Aids, 1996.

Recommended grade level: 7-8. This simple kit—the *Identification of Chemical Reactions Kit*—contains instructions and lab materials for a single, hands-on activity: students mix or combine a variety of solutions, observe what happens, and determine if a chemical reaction has taken place. When deciding if a chemical reaction has taken place, students are asked to provide evidence (such as a color change or the formation of a gas or precipitate) in support of their answer. If students

are advanced in the study of chemistry, they should also be able to write an equation for the chemical reactions that take place. The kit comes with 7 solutions, which can be combined in 21 different ways to test for reactions. Some of the mixtures do not react. In most cases, however, a chemical reaction does occur with clear evidence for the student to observe and interpret.

The kit includes a short booklet for the teacher, 50 student worksheets/guides, 12 plastic trays with wells for mixing chemicals, and the 7 solutions (hydrochloric acid, sodium carbonate, sodium hydroxide, potassium chromate, calcium chloride, sodium hydrogen sulfite, and copper sulfate). Little background information or discussion of general principles is provided.

Price: $49.95. *Publisher/supplier:* Sargent-Welch. *Materials:* Available in kit.

1.62 Integrating Aerospace Science into the Curriculum: K-12. Robert D. Ray and Joan Klingel Ray. Gifted Treasury Series. Englewood, Colo.: Teacher Ideas Press, 1992.

Recommended grade level: 6-8+. *Integrating Aerospace Science into the Curriculum* is a resource guide designed to help incorporate in the K-12 science curriculum ideas, activities, and interdisciplinary projects related to the science and story of aerospace advances. The format consists of reading sections interwoven with ideas for activities and projects. Topics addressed in the book's 7 chapters include the history of flight; principles learned from experimenting with objects, such as balloons and kites, often thought to be simple toys; the development of aircraft during periods of war; and the development of today's space programs, including the Space Shuttle and the

National Aerospace Plane. Many of the project and activity ideas are suggestions rather than fully developed teaching outlines, although some do provide simple directions— for example, for students to design a space station, to make and fly a "heli-pencil," and to construct a wind vane. Each chapter has a bibliography. An appendix lists addresses for obtaining aerospace resource materials.

Price: $21.50 (ISBN 0-87287-924-0). *Publisher/supplier:* Teacher Ideas Press. *Materials:* Available locally.

1.63 **Introduction to pH Measurement Kit.** Ronkonkoma, N.Y.: Lab-Aids, 1971.

Recommended grade level: 7-8. *Introduction to pH Measurement Kit* is a lab kit for a 1-period activity that introduces students to different types of acid–base indicators. Students experiment by adding various combinations of solutions to wells in plastic lab trays, repeating the procedures with cabbage juice and a fresh red or blue flower (which contain anthocyanin, a "natural" indicator).

The kit contains materials, solutions, and instructions for the activity. It includes multiple copies of the student instruction sheet, pH paper, litmus paper, solutions (phenol red, phenolphthalein, bromthymol blue, hydrochloric acid, and sodium hydroxide), and 12 plastic lab trays. The chemicals are clearly marked and accompanied by safety data sheets.

Price: $40.10. *Publisher/supplier:* Sargent-Welch. *Materials:* Available in kit.

1.64 **LEGO Technic I Activity Center.** Enfield, Conn.: LEGO Dacta, 1990.

Recommended grade level: 4-6. *LEGO Technic I Activity Center* helps students learn fundamental concepts, skills, and processes related to physical science and technology. The Activity Center consists of 110 activity cards, designed to be used with the LEGO building materials that come in the Technic I kit. A teacher's guide and a supplement accompany the activity cards.

The activity cards are color-coded in 4 categories by activity type: (1) exploration cards introduce students to building materials and mechanical principles through informal activities; (2) during guided investigations students use step-by-step instructions to build models that demonstrate important mechanical principles, and then they conduct formal investigations and formulate concepts; (3) simulation activities require students to apply what they have learned in a problem-solving setting by building a working model or simulation of a machine from the real world; (4) invention activities require students to apply what they have learned in a more difficult problem-solving setting by inventing a machine or device that performs to given specifications.

In addition to activity type, cards can be grouped by curriculum areas or contextual themes. Curriculum topics include forces and structures, levers, pulleys, gears, wheels and axles, and energy and enrichment. Contextual themes include the following: Medieval Castle, The Farm, The Harbor, The Amusement Park, Getting Around, The Big Race, and Enrichment. The teacher's supplement contains additional information about each of the curriculum areas.

Activities are suggested for teachers to explore in preparing for class.

Price: Activity center, $110. (Contact the publisher/supplier for complete price and ordering information.) *Publisher/supplier:* LEGO Dacta. *Materials:* Available in LEGO Dacta kits.

1.65 **Levers.** Enfield, Conn.: LEGO Dacta, 1993.

Recommended grade level: 5-6. This booklet contains information about levers, simple hands-on lever activities, and appropriate diagrams and illustrations. It is designed to be used with the LEGO Dacta Pulleys Set, which uses the popular LEGO construction blocks to explore the 3 classes of levers. Students first learn the definition of a lever. Then they construct working models of first-, second-, and third-class levers and build models of devices that incorporate them. Students are challenged to design and build 2 devices: one that can pick up a weighted brick while being operated with one hand, and another that can be raised and lowered and locked into a raised and lowered position.

Each activity in *Levers* states the main idea involved and provides illustrated instructions, additional information, and extension ideas. The guide lists the process and critical thinking skills involved in the activities.

Prices: Teacher's guide (ISBN 0-914831-83-6), $5.25. Classroom pack, $183.75. Individual set, $15.75. *Publisher/supplier:* LEGO Dacta. *Materials:* Available from LEGO Dacta.

1.66 **Light.** Robert Gardner. Investigate and Discover series. New York, N.Y.: Julian Messner/Simon & Schuster, 1991.

Recommended grade level: 5-8. Many of the investigations and features in *Light* are related to exhibits at the Science Museum at the Franklin Institute in Philadelphia. Through the experiments and activities in this guide, students explore the shadows cast by objects in bright light and try to explain the shadows' shapes and sizes. They investigate how light is reflected, how images are formed, and where those images are. They produce pinhole images, experiment with refraction of light, and examine and attempt to explain the behavior of colored light and colored objects. In a final activity, students are introduced to the wave and particle models as explanations of the properties of light.

Each chapter features extensive science background information and up to 7 investigations, including experiments with step-by-step instructions and less-structured activities that encourage students to explore on their own, at home, or at school.

Price: $9.95 (ISBN 0-671-69042-6). *Publisher/supplier:* Silver Burdett Ginn. *Materials:* Available locally.

1.67 **Light.** Ron Marson. Task Card Series 17. Canby, Oreg.: TOPS Learning Systems, 1991.

Recommended grade level: 7-8+. During the 36 activities in *Light*—which is one of many units in the Task Card Series—students learn about the properties of light as they investigate the visible spectrum, lenses, reflection, refraction, waves, and how light is transmitted. For example, students discover that the angles of incidence and reflection are equal for light reflected by a plane mirror. They

examine how water waves in a pan model the behavior of light waves; and they create concave, planar, and convex water surfaces in a test tube and find out why these shapes produce images of different sizes. Students distinguish between color addition and subtraction as they mix colors by subtracting them from white light and adding them to a white background. In other activities, they construct and use working models of telescopes and microscopes.

The activities in *Light* require commonly available materials (such as rubber bands, dinner forks, and plastic soda bottles). Certain activities can be omitted or sequences changed to meet specific class needs. The unit contains reproducible "task cards" with directions for each activity, a reproducible protractor, teaching notes with answers, and review questions.

Price: $16 (ISBN 0-941008-87-8). *Publisher/supplier:* TOPS Learning Systems. *Materials:* Available locally, or from commercial suppliers.

1.68 **Machines.** Ron Marson. Task Card Series 22. Canby, Oreg.: TOPS Learning Systems, 1989.

Recommended grade level: 7-8. During the 16 activities in *Machines*—which is one of many units in the Task Card Series—students explore simple machines and find that machines save effort but never reduce work. For example, they build a simple lever (a meterstick that pivots on a rubber stopper) to discover how this lever either reduces effort or reduces the distance through which the effort is applied. They evaluate the efficiency of a movable wheel pulley, and they graph how the effort required to pull a cart up an inclined plane changes with its angle of inclination. Students also classify com-

mon machines (stairs, scissors, door knob, hatchet) as levers or inclined planes, and build a working model of a wheel and axle.

The activities in *Machines* require commonly available materials (such as paper clips, thread, cans, and baby food jars). Certain activities can be omitted or sequences changed to meet specific class needs. The unit contains reproducible "task cards" with directions for each activity, a reproducible protractor, teaching notes with answers, and review questions.

Price: $8 (ISBN 0-941008-99-1). *Publisher/supplier:* TOPS Learning Systems. *Materials:* Available locally, or from commercial suppliers.

1.69 **Machine Shop.** Donna Battcher, Sheldon Erickson, Karen Martini, and others. Activities Integrating Mathematics and Science (AIMS) series. Fresno, Calif.: AIMS Education Foundation, 1993.

Recommended grade level: 5-8. Journal entries about the uses of various simple machines and the forces that affect them provide a story line for the activities in *Machine Shop,* an activity book on the mechanics of physics, in which mathematics and science skills are tested and other disciplines are integrated. Students investigate the following topic areas: simple machines; friction; inclined planes; levers and leverage; force, energy, and energy conservation; wheels and belts; gears and tooth ratios; wheel and axle systems; and pulleys, wedges, and mechanical advantage. Among the activities, for example, students use a seesaw to explore the properties of effort, resistance, and torque; they construct and test a high-performance catapult; and they determine the mechanical advantage for different nuts and bolts.

Machine Shop provides reproducible student worksheets, including data charts, tables, and graphs. A complete lesson plan is included for each of the 23 activities.

Price: Teacher's guide (ISBN 1-881431-39-8), $16.95. *Publisher/supplier:* AIMS Education Foundation. *Materials:* Available locally, or from commercial suppliers.

1.70 The Magic Wand and Other Bright Experiments on Light and Color. Paul Doherty, Don Rathjen, and The Exploratorium Teacher Institute. The Exploratorium Science Snackbook Series. New York, N.Y.: John Wiley, 1995.

Recommended grade level: 6-8. *The Magic Wand and Other Bright Experiments on Light and Color* contains 25 activities for experimenting with and making observations about light and how it behaves. These activities are miniature versions of some of the most popular exhibits at The Exploratorium, San Francisco's museum of science, art, and human perception. For example, students investigate what happens when light waves meet and mix—in the thin film of a soap bubble or in the gap between two plates of glass. They make a pinhole in an index card and use it like a magnifying glass. They also use a colored filter to decode secret messages written with colored pens, and experiment with a cylindrical mirror to understand how light bounces off different surfaces.

Each activity begins with a drawing of the original full-sized exhibit at The Exploratorium and a photograph of the scaled-down version that students can make. Most of the activities require basic materials such as mirrors, magnifying glasses, fish tanks, and water. Each 15- to 30-minute activity includes a materials list, assembly directions, descriptions of how to use the completed exhibits, and explanations of the science involved in the exhibits. A section called "etc." offers additional scientific and historic facts. Most of the activities can be completed by one student, although some indicate the need for a partner or adult assistance.

Price: $10.95 (ISBN 0-471-11515-0). *Publisher/supplier:* Wiley. *Materials:* Available locally, or from commercial suppliers.

1.71 Magnetism. Ron Marson. Task Card Series 20. Canby, Oreg.: TOPS Learning Systems, 1991.

Recommended grade level: 7-8. During the 28 activities in *Magnetism*—which is one of many units in the Task Card Series—students learn about magnets, magnetic forces, and the connection between electricity and magnetism. For example, they construct a pin compass and observe how it can be magnetized and remagnetized to assume different orientations in earth's magnetic field. They also define and measure the angle of declination for various geographic locations to understand that earth's magnetic poles are paired with unlike geographic poles, and use index cards to construct a 3-dimensional model of a magnetic field. In other activities, students investigate the lines of force associated with electricity flowing through a coil, build and operate an electromagnet with a removable solenoid, and construct a reverse-poles motor. They also graph how the force of repulsion between 2 magnetic poles increases as the distance between them decreases.

Each activity in *Magnetism* has between 2 and 5 steps and requires commonly available materials (such as straight pins, aluminum wire, and washers). Certain activities can be omitted or sequences changed to meet specific class needs.

The unit contains reproducible "task cards" with directions for each activity, teaching notes with answers, and review questions.

Price: $13 (ISBN 0-941008-90-8). *Publisher/supplier:* TOPS Learning Systems. *Materials:* Available locally, or from commercial suppliers.

1.72 Metals. Robert C. Mebane and Thomas R. Rybolt. Everyday Material Science Experiments series. New York, N.Y.: Twenty-First Century Books, 1995.

Recommended grade level: 7-8. *Metals,* 1 of 5 activity books in a series on everyday materials, contains 16 simple experiments that help students learn about metals as materials— what they are made of, how they behave, and why they are important. For example, students explore how increasing temperature can change the size of a copper wire. They also make and test a fuse made from steel wool, copperplate a dime, and turn a nail into an electromagnet.

Designed to be student-directed, many of these stand-alone activities could be done at home or as teacher demonstrations. Experiments requiring adult supervision are clearly identified. Activities are narrative in form, containing questions to help guide inquiry. Science concepts or brief explanations for the results observed in the experiments are provided in the text. The text for each activity also includes a description of real-world applications related to the experiments—for example, how a magnetic resonance imaging (MRI) machine uses superconducting magnets to allow a doctor to "see" inside a person's body.

Price: $15.98 (ISBN 0-8050-2842-0). *Publisher/supplier:* Von Holtzbrinck (VHPS). *Materials:* Available locally, or from commercial suppliers.

1.73 Methods of Motion: An Introduction to Mechanics, Book One. Rev. ed. Jack E. Gartrell, Jr. Washington, D.C.: National Science Teachers Association, 1992.

Recommended grade level: 7-8. *Methods of Motion* contains 27 hands-on activities and demonstrations and 14 readings that introduce students to the concepts of mechanics. Organized in 6 modules, the activities address such topics as mass and force; constant speed versus acceleration; interactions of force, mass, and acceleration; applying the laws of motion; and "hidden" forces (such as friction and gravity) affecting motion. Sample activities include the following: building a simple inertial balance to demonstrate the concept of inertia, using a drip timer to calculate the speed and acceleration of a toy car, conducting marble races to discover if an object's mass affects the rate at which it rolls down an incline, and experimenting with a hair dryer blowing straight up to oppose the downward force of gravity acting on a ping pong ball.

The readings give detailed explanations of the concepts presented in the activities, and may be used as background information for the teacher or reproduced as student handouts.

Each of the 6 modules in *Methods of Motion* begins with an overview. Each activity includes a reproducible student worksheet and an activity guide for teachers. Activities typically require 40 to 60 minutes to complete. Each activity guide includes background information, teaching procedures and tips, technical notes, suggestions for extensions, and answers to activity questions. The equipment required for the activities consists mainly of inexpensive toys and other low-cost materials.

Price: $18.50 (ISBN 0-87355-085-4). *Publisher/supplier:* National Science Teachers Association. *Materials:* Available locally, or from commercial suppliers.

1.74 Metric Measure. Ron Marson. Task Card Series 6. Canby, Oreg.: TOPS Learning Systems, 1992.

Recommended grade level: 7-8. The 20 short activities in *Metric Measure*—which is one of many units in the Task Card Series—help students learn about using the metric system. For example, students define and write metric prefixes in terms of the decimal ladder, and practice translating these prefixes to their numerical equivalents. They model cubic meters, centimeters, and millimeters using cubes and string; and they discover that dry measure in cubic centimeters is equal to liquid measure in milliliters. In other activities, students construct a light-duty equal-arm balance sensitive to 5 milligrams, and they estimate the number of rice grains in a baby food jar by counting the grains in a small mass and multiplying by the whole.

The activities use readily available materials (such as newspaper, a meter stick, and string). Certain activities can be omitted or sequences changed to meet specific class needs. The unit contains reproducible "task cards" with directions for each activity, several reproducible centimeter grids, teaching notes with answers, and review questions.

Price: $9.50 (ISBN 0-941008-76-2). *Publisher/supplier:* TOPS Learning Systems. *Materials:* Available locally, or from commercial suppliers.

1.75 Motion. Ron Marson. Task Card Series 21. Canby, Oreg.: TOPS Learning Systems, 1990.

Recommended grade level: 7-8. The 36 short activities in *Motion*—which is one of the many units in the Task Card Series—help students explore and learn about Newton's 3 laws of motion. For example, students track

elastic collisions between spheres of equal and unequal mass, and compare static friction with moving friction. They also study vectors, speed, and acceleration. In other activities, students build a rotating jet balloon and describe its motion in terms of Newton's third law, they construct a rubber band catapult for use in a study of force and mass, and they show on a graph how acceleration is directly proportional to force and inversely proportional to mass.

The activities, which each have 2 to 5 steps, require commonly available materials (such as marbles, pennies, and index cards). Certain activities can be omitted or sequences changed to meet specific class needs. The unit contains reproducible "task cards" with directions and data charts for each activity, teaching notes with answers, and review questions.

Price: $16 (ISBN 0-941008-98-3). *Publisher/supplier:* TOPS Learning Systems. *Materials:* Available locally, or from commercial suppliers.

1.76 Mystery Festival. Kevin Beals and Carolyn Willard. Great Explorations in Math and Science (GEMS) series. Berkeley, Calif.: Lawrence Hall of Science, 1994.

Recommended grade level: 2-8. *Mystery Festival* contains instructions for organizing 2 make-believe crime scenes, or "mysteries," in a classroom. Student-detectives subsequently observe, investigate, and attempt to solve the mysteries. The mystery "Who Borrowed Mr. Bear?" is for younger students (grades 2-3), and "The Mystery of Felix" is for older students (grades 4-8). Working in teams, students gather evidence at the crime scene and then conduct hands-on forensic tests, such as a thread test, fingerprint comparisons, chromatography, pH tests, and powder tests at activity stations. Students learn to distinguish between evidence and inference. They develop their critical-thinking and problem-solving skills. Preparation for the 2 mysteries is substantial when using the unit for the first time.

Mystery Festival provides detailed information and planning instructions, and includes suggestions for pre-teaching games and for the use of parent volunteers.

Price: $25.50 (ISBN 0-912511-89-3). *Publisher/supplier:* LHS GEMS. *Materials:* Available locally, or from commercial suppliers.

1.77 Nuclear Energy: Student Activities. Rev. ed. New York Energy Education Project (NYEEP). Albany, N.Y.: NYEEP, 1988.

Recommended grade level: 7-8+. *Nuclear Energy* introduces students to facts and issues related to nuclear energy. For example, students learn the parts and structure of the atom, as well as basic terms related to radioactivity. They model the process of radioactive decay, and develop an awareness of the various sources of radiation. They also investigate nuclear fission and model the production of energy in a nuclear reactor through a game. They learn about the types and sources of radioactive waste and role-play the problems associated with waste disposal and storage. In other activities, students analyze the costs involved in the construction of a nuclear power plant, and learn about breeder reactors and nuclear fusion.

In addition to presenting science concepts, *Nuclear Energy* explains both the risks and benefits of nuclear energy. This activity book is interdisciplinary; many activities can also help teach reading for comprehension, group decision making, or use

of shop tools (students construct models in class).

Each of the 7 activities in *Nuclear Energy* includes reproducible data sheets for students, as well as background information for the teacher and discussion points, answers, and evaluation suggestions. A list of sources of energy information is provided.

Prices: In New York State, free with attendance at workshop; outside of New York, $4. *Publisher/supplier:* New York Science, Technology and Society Education Project. *Materials:* Available locally.

1.78 Off the Wall Science: A Poster Series Revisited. Harold Silvani. Activities Integrating Mathematics and Science (AIMS) series. Fresno, Calif.: AIMS Education Foundation, 1995.

Recommended grade level: 5-8. *Off the Wall Science* consists of 30 physical science activities from *AIMS Science Posters*, compiled in book form for ease of use. The open-ended activities cover topics such as buoyancy, surface tension, change of state, inertia, and center of gravity. For example, students compare the weights of objects when weighed in and out of water, investigate whether an orange floats or sinks in water, and observe the mixing of hot and cold water. They also make a homemade fire extinguisher; they measure whether a burning walnut shell or burning walnut meat produces more heat energy; and they make an electrical circuit using a battery, a bulb, foil wire, and a clothespin.

Most materials needed for the short investigations in *Off the Wall Science* are commonly available and inexpensive. Each activity includes background information, procedures, discussion questions, extensions, reproducible pages for students, and a "guiding documents" section that

lists the activity's relevance to Project 2061 Benchmarks.

Price: Teacher's guide (ISBN 1-881431-50-9), $16.95. *Publisher/supplier:* AIMS Education Foundation. *Materials:* Available locally, or from commercial suppliers.

1.79 Optics. Robert Gardner. Yesterday's Science, Today's Technology Science Activities series. New York, N.Y.: Twenty-First Century Books, 1994.

Recommended grade level: 6-8. *Optics,* an activity book in a series written for students, contains 15 activities for investigating scientific principles and technology involved in optics. Students learn about topics such as light and color, how light travels, reflections, refraction, sight, cameras, and color combinations. Among the activities, for example, they build a small *camera obscura,* design and construct a periscope, and make a microscope from 2 convex lenses. They also construct an apparatus to show that water can be used as a light guide, and they learn about the mathematics of color by experimenting with colored water in plastic tumblers.

For each activity in *Optics,* students read a brief historical or science background section. Colorful illustrations, together with directions and questions in the narrative, then guide them through the activities. Although students can do most of the activities without supervision, the materials involved in several may require the assistance of adults. The book includes a list of 9 follow-up activities and ideas; some of them might be appropriate for science fair projects.

Price: $16.98 (ISBN 0-8050-2852-8). *Publisher/supplier:* Von Holtzbrinck (VHPS). *Materials:* Available locally, or from commercial suppliers.

1.80 **Pendulums.** Ron Marson. Task Card Series 1. Canby, Oreg.: TOPS Learning Systems, 1992.

Recommended grade level: 7-8. The 20 easy-to-follow activities in *Pendulums*—one of many units in the Task Card Series—relate to the science of pendulums. In the first activity, students construct a support for a pendulum from a cereal box; the support has a length and amplitude background grid. Then they use this support for many activities in the module. For example, students explore and graph how the frequency of a pendulum varies with length. They evaluate the relative effects of length, amplitude, and bob weight on the period of a pendulum. They also examine a pendulum system with 2 distinct pivot points and develop an equation for calculating its period.

The activities in *Pendulums* require a stopwatch and readily available materials (such as paper clips, masking tape, and washers). Certain activities can be omitted or sequences changed to meet specific class needs. The unit contains reproducible "task cards" with directions for students, teaching notes with answers, and review questions.

Prices: $9.50 (ISBN 0-941008-71-1). *Publisher/supplier:* TOPS Learning Systems. *Materials:* Available locally, or from commercial suppliers.

1.81 **Personal Science Laboratory Light Experiments.** 2nd ed. Personal Science Laboratory (PSL) series. Boulder, Colo.: Team Labs, 1995.

Recommended grade level: 7-8+. This annotated teacher's guide on *Light Experiments,* part of the Personal Science Laboratory series, is designed to help teachers run and teach 8 microcomputer-based investigations that explore light. The investigations use special photomet-

ric and radiometric light probes, interfaced with a personal computer, that allow students to enter measurements or data directly into the software—PSL Excelerator—linked to the experiment. Topics covered include specular and diffuse reflection, angle of incidence, the relationship between light intensity and distance, polarization, the relationship between scattering and polarization, and light absorption by colored materials.

Among the investigations, students measure and compare light reflected from a planar mirror, a white surface, and a black surface. They also compare the reflective properties of planar, concave, and convex mirrors, and use a light probe and polarizing film to test the light passing through a box filled with soapy liquid to determine whether the light is polarized. In other experiments they use polarized light to distinguish between "left-handed" and "right-handed" chemicals, and measure how the intensity of transmitted light varies as the concentration of dye in a liquid increases.

Students complete the experiments by logging onto a computer, selecting an experiment, following a series of prompts or directions, entering data from the activities or having the probes directly transmit the information, and completing follow-up activities. The computer program also organizes student-generated experimental data into charts, graphs, and tables. The guide contains teaching notes and an introduction to Personal Science Laboratory hardware and software.

Prices: Teacher's guide, $44. Student-version master, $226. PSL hardware, $520. (Contact publisher/supplier for complete price and ordering information.) *Publisher/supplier:* Team Labs. *Materials:* Available locally, from commercial suppliers, or from Team Labs.

1.82 **Personal Science Laboratory Motion Experiments.** 2nd ed. Personal Science Laboratory (PSL) series. Boulder, Colo.: Team Labs, 1995.

Recommended grade level: 7-8+. This annotated teacher's guide on *Motion Experiments,* part of the Personal Science Laboratory series, is designed to help teachers run and teach 10 microcomputer-based investigations that explore motion. The investigations use special distance probes (they emit ultrasound pulses), interfaced with a personal computer, that allow students to enter measurements or data directly into the software—PSL Excelerator—linked to the experiment. Topics covered include velocity; acceleration; vectors; harmonic motion; the relationship among acceleration, force, and mass; and kinetic and potential energy.

Among the investigations, students study distance-versus-time and velocity-versus-time graphs and write descriptions of movements that would produce those graphs. They experiment with rolling cylinders on ramps and measure their acceleration. They also explore (and graph) the up-and-down movements made by a mass on a spring, and calculate the acceleration of free fall of a rolling cart with a mass on it.

Students complete the experiments by logging onto a computer, selecting an experiment, following a series of prompts or directions, entering data from activities or having the probes directly transmit the information, and completing follow-up activities. The computer program also organizes student-generated experimental data into charts, graphs, and tables. The guide contains teaching notes, limited background information on Newton's first law of motion, and an introduction to Personal Science Laboratory hardware and software.

Prices: Teacher's guide, $44. Student-version master, $226. PSL hardware, $455. (Contact publisher/supplier for complete price and ordering information.) *Publisher/supplier:* Team Labs. *Materials:* Available locally, from commercial suppliers, or from Team Labs.

1.83 Personal Science Laboratory pH Experiments. 2nd ed. Personal Science Laboratory (PSL) series. Boulder, Colo.: Team Labs, 1996.

Recommended grade level: 7-8+. This annotated teacher's guide on *pH Experiments,* part of the Personal Science Laboratory series, is designed to help teachers run and teach 10 microcomputer-based investigations that explore acids, bases, and pH. The investigations use special probes for pH and temperature, interfaced with a personal computer, that allow students to enter measurements or data directly into the software—PSL Excelerator—linked to the experiment. Topics covered include properties of acids and bases, titration as a method of analysis, acid-base indicators, antacids and neutralization, acid rain and the aquatic environment, volumetric analysis, and the molar heat of acid-base reactions.

Among the investigations, students determine the pH range of several indicators and compare the neutralization rates of several commercial antacids. They also determine the relative buffering capacity of a simulated lake system to observe the effects of acid rain, and they determine the concentration of phosphoric acid in colas.

Students complete the experiments by logging onto a computer, selecting an experiment, following a series of prompts or directions,

entering data from activities or having the probes directly transmit the information, and completing follow-up activities. The computer program also organizes student-generated experimental data into charts, graphs, and tables. The guide contains teaching notes, limited background information on the meaning and measurement of pH, and an introduction to Personal Science Laboratory hardware and software.

Prices: Teacher's guide, $44. Student-version master, $226. (Contact publisher/supplier for complete price and ordering information.) *Publisher/supplier:* Team Labs. *Materials:* Available locally, from commercial suppliers, or from Team Labs.

1.84 Personal Science Laboratory Temperature Experiments. 2nd ed. Personal Science Laboratory (PSL) series. Boulder, Colo.: Team Labs, 1995.

Recommended grade level: 7-8+. This annotated teacher's guide on *Temperature Experiments,* part of the Personal Science Laboratory series, is designed to help teachers run and teach 8 microcomputer-based investigations that explore heat and temperature concepts. The investigations use special temperature probes, interfaced with a personal computer, that allow students to enter measurements or data directly into the software—PSL Excelerator—linked to the experiment. Topics covered include temperature versus heat content, insulation, how heating and cooling affects liquids and solids, heat of crystallization, the relationship between heat and motion, regulating body temperature, and temperature changes in soil and water.

Among the investigations, students compare the cooling curves of water and paraffin. They mix various chemicals with water and discover

which reactions are endothermic and which are exothermic. They measure the insulating effect of a glove on the skin, and they also measure the temperature change of air as it is compressed in a flask.

Students complete the experiments by logging onto a computer, selecting an experiment, following a series of prompts or directions, entering data from activities or having the probes directly transmit the information, and completing follow-up activities. The computer program also organizes student-generated experimental data into charts, graphs, and tables. The guide contains teaching notes, background information on heat and temperature, and an introduction to Personal Science Laboratory hardware and software.

Prices: Teacher's guide, $44. Student-version master, $226. (Contact publisher/supplier for complete price and ordering information.) *Publisher/supplier:* Team Labs. *Materials:* Available locally, from commercial suppliers, or from Team Labs.

1.85 Physical Science Activities for Elementary and Middle School. 2nd ed. Mark R. Malone. CESI Sourcebook V. Washington, D.C.: Council for Elementary Science International (CESI), 1994.

Recommended grade level: 1-7. *Physical Science Activities for Elementary and Middle School,* a sourcebook of physical science activities, contains materials developed for teachers by teachers who have tested them with their own students. Topics include sound, light and color, electricity, forces and motion, simple machines, heat, matter, chemistry, and space. Activities include making a kazoo from a cardboard tube to investigate sound, making paper dolls dance from static electricity, predicting the velocity of a rolling ball by observing its motion along a rail, using shadows to tell time, and learning about bonding by making slime.

The lesson plan for each of the 119 activities in this guide includes the following components: a short description of the concepts and/or skills developed by the activity; a list of materials and equipment needed; suggestions for planning, organizing, and implementing the activities; ideas for extending the lesson; and a list of references.

Price: $19. *Publisher/supplier:* CESI. *Materials:* Available locally, or from commercial suppliers.

1.86 Plastics and Polymers. Robert C. Mebane and Thomas R. Rybolt. Everyday Material Science Experiments series. New York, N.Y.: Twenty-First Century Books, 1995.

Recommended grade level: 7-8. *Plastics and Polymers,* 1 of 5 activity books in a series on everyday materials, contains 16 simple experiments that help students learn about the physical properties of polymers and plastics. Examples of these experiments include examining some of the differences between high-density and low-density polyethylene, and using a polymer present in flour (that is, starch) to thicken a liquid. Students also compare the flow of heat through 2 different forms of polystyrene, and determine how the bouncing height of a tennis ball is affected by temperature.

Designed to be student-directed, many of these stand-alone activities could be done at home or as teacher demonstrations. The activities are narrative in form, and contain questions to help guide inquiry. No background material is supplied, but science concepts or brief explanations for the results observed in the

experiments are provided in the text.

Price: $15.98 (ISBN 0-8050-2843-9). *Publisher/supplier:* Von Holtzbrinck (VHPS). *Materials:* Available locally, or from commercial suppliers.

1.87 Pressure. Ron Marson. Task Card Series 16. Canby, Oreg.: TOPS Learning Systems, 1992.

Recommended grade level: 7-8. In the 32 easy-to-follow activities in *Pressure*—one of many units in the Task Card Series—students become familiar with some of the concepts and principles associated with pressure. For example, they estimate the average pressure, in newtons per square centimeter, that one exerts while standing on the floor. They use sandwich bags and rubber tubing to demonstrate how force increases as pressure is applied over larger areas, and they construct a model to understand how the diaphragm regulates air pressure in the chest cavity. Students also construct a U-tube manometer to investigate the relationship between pressure and fluid depth, and they design and build a vacuum pump. In other activities, they observe how changes in temperature and volume affect pressure, and they build an instrument that measures atmospheric pressure.

The activities in *Pressure* require readily available materials (such as Ping-Pong balls, candles, and cereal boxes). Each activity has between 2 and 5 steps. Certain activities can be omitted or sequences changed to meet specific class needs. The unit contains reproducible "task cards" with directions for activities, a reproducible pressure scale, teaching notes with answers, and review questions.

Price: $14.50 (ISBN 0-941008-86-X). *Publisher/supplier:* TOPS Learning Systems. *Materials:* Available locally, or from commercial suppliers.

1.88 Project SEED: Sourcebook of Demonstrations, Activities, and Experiments. 2nd ed. Alan Cromer and Christos Zahopoulos. Boston, Mass.: Northeastern University Center for Electromagnetics Research, 1993.

Recommended grade level: 6-8+. *Project SEED* (which stands for Science Education through Experiments and Demonstrations) describes dozens of inexpensive physical science demonstrations, activities, and experiments. This sourcebook was originally written for workshop leaders and teachers participating in a Project SEED teacher-training program but will be of value to other teachers as well. Although it does not include complete lesson plans and might need some adaptations for the classroom, it is useful for teachers who wish to increase their use of concrete demonstrations and experiments in teaching science.

Topics covered in *Project SEED* include measurement, density and buoyancy, pressure, work and simple machines, motion, earth as a planet, elements and compounds, sound, optics, temperature and heat, electricity, and magnetism. Teachers can learn, for example, how to use plastic soda bottles with holes to demonstrate Pascal's law, or how to set up an experiment that shows the decomposition of water, measure the sun's diameter by using a pinhole in a piece of paper, or make a battery with a copper wire, iron nail, and a lemon. Throughout, the emphasis is on ways of clarifying fundamental science concepts and principles rather than on pedagogy. The book makes regular use of the mathematics of ratios and proportions.

Price: $16.48 (ISBN 1-56870-117-9). *Publisher/supplier:* RonJon. *Materials:* Available locally, or from commercial suppliers.

1.89 **Projects That Explore Energy.** Martin J. Gutnik and Natalie Browne-Gutnik. An Investigate! Book. Brookfield, Conn.: Millbrook Press, 1994.

Recommended grade level: 7-8+. *Projects That Explore Energy* is a small activity book, written for students, containing directions for 11 simple science projects or experiments about what energy is and how it works. The book begins by introducing students to components of the scientific method: observation, classification, making an inference, prediction, formulating a hypothesis, testing the hypothesis, and drawing a conclusion. Simple directions that follow the scientific method then allow each student to complete the projects. (The projects could also be useful for individual student research or for hands-on activities for a whole class.)

The topics addressed in *Projects That Explore Energy* include the first law of thermodynamics, photosynthesis, food chains, fossil fuels, and alternative forms of energy. Among the projects, for example, students make and use a calorimeter, create and observe an aquatic food chain, observe the effect of motor oil on Elodea plants, build and use a solar cooker, and build and use a wind vane. Limited background information is provided.

Price: $15.40 (ISBN 1-56294-334-0). *Publisher/supplier:* Millbrook Press. *Materials:* Available locally.

1.90 **Pulleys.** Enfield, Conn.: LEGO Dacta, 1993.

Recommended grade level: 5-6. This booklet contains information about pulleys, simple pulley activities, and appropriate diagrams and illustrations. It is designed to go with the LEGO Dacta Pulley Set, which uses the popular LEGO construction blocks. Students first learn the definition of a pulley. Then they arrange pulleys to investigate the direction of rotation of the driver and the follower. They also find out how the turning ratio of one pulley to another is determined by the size of the pulleys. Students are challenged to design and build 2 devices: a conveyor-belt system that uses a belt drive to carry packages, and a boat mover that winches a boat onto the shore.

Each activity in *Pulleys* states the main idea involved and provides illustrated instructions, additional information, and extension ideas. The guide lists the process and critical-thinking skills involved in the activities.

Prices: Teacher's guide (ISBN 0-914831-84-4), $5.25. Classroom pack, $183.75. Individual set, $15.25. *Publisher/supplier:* LEGO Dacta. *Materials:* Available from LEGO Dacta.

1.91 **Quick Energy and Beyond: Ideas for the 90's.** Rev. ed. Compiled by Colorado Energy and Resource Educators. Estes Park, Colo.: Colorado Energy and Resource Educators, 1991.

Recommended grade level: 5-8. *Quick Energy and Beyond* contains 41 interdisciplinary activities related to energy. Among other activities, students observe the formation of oxygen as an aquatic plant carries out photosynthesis in a Ziplock bag. They also study the way a rubber band absorbs and releases heat, construct simple electric circuits, and observe the cooling effect of an ice-salt mixture. In other activities, students look for energy words hidden in a puzzle, and use multiplying skills to solve problems based on electric rates schedules. The "starter" activities in the book are designed to stimulate students' thinking about energy, its sources, and its future. Other activities focus on issues of energy consumption and on various aspects of energy production.

Many of the activities in *Quick Energy and Beyond* take fewer than 15 minutes to complete, require readily available materials, and require little teacher preparation (although there are some exceptions). Each activity includes brief information for the teacher, a reproducible page for students (with blank charts and directions), and extension ideas.

Price: $10. *Publisher/supplier:* National Energy Foundation. *Materials:* Available locally.

1.92 **Renewables Are Ready: A Guide to Teaching Renewable Energy in Junior and Senior High School Classrooms.** Rev. ed. Union of Concerned Scientists. Cambridge, Mass.: Union of Concerned Scientists, 1994.

Recommended grade level: 6-8+. *Renewables Are Ready* is a "pick-and-choose" guide of 12 multidisciplinary activities that emphasize group work and help teachers introduce students to various renewable energy technologies as well as to some of the political and economic conditions necessary for their implementation. Among the activities, for example, students discover where and how they get the energy they use. They also build a solar box cooker from simple materials, construct a wind machine for generating electricity, play a game that simulates some of the economic changes necessary to make renewables succeed as large-scale electricity sources, and participate in a mock public meeting to determine a site for a new energy facility in a community.

The guide provides directions for the activities. It also offers a list of lesson ideas on topics such as researching photovoltaic efficiency and designing a model waterwheel. It contains suggestions for student-led education and action projects, such as organizing a renewable energy fair and writing articles, and presents a short resource bibliography. Most of the activities in the guide take between 1 and 5 periods of 45 minutes each. They include instructions for teachers and reproducible handouts for students. The ideas suggested for the additional lessons and projects are often in note form rather than filled out.

Price: $5. *Publisher/supplier:* Union of Concerned Scientists. *Materials:* Available locally, or from commercial suppliers.

1.93 **Science Experiments: Chemistry and Physics.** Tammy K. Williams. Science Experiments Book 1. Lewistown, Mo.: Mark Twain Media, 1995.

Recommended grade level: 6-8. *Science Experiments: Chemistry and Physics* is an activity book containing 36 simple experiments that introduce students to concepts in chemistry and physics. The activities also help students become familiar with models, carefully controlled experiments, and simulations. A section on laboratory skills is also included.

In the section on chemistry, students create hydrogen gas from a chemical reaction, collect it in a balloon, and explode it; make an acid-base indicator from red cabbage; and separate salt from saltwater. In the physics section, students simulate the decay of radioactive particles, make convex and concave lenses from water drops, and investigate the properties of magnets. In the section on reviewing and strengthening laboratory skills, students classify objects by different appearances, conduct experiments to measure a water droplet's splatter

size, and construct balloon rockets to investigate Newton's third law.

The experiments in this volume involve both individual and group work. Reproducible directions, data charts, and graphs are supplied on tear sheets. No background material is provided.

Price: $10.95. *Publisher/supplier:* Carson-Dellosa. *Materials:* Available locally, or from commercial suppliers.

1.94 **Science Investigations for Intermediate Students.** Rev. ed. Carl Pfeiffer. SciQuest series. Fort Atkinson, Wis.: Nasco, 1994.

Recommended grade level: 6-8. *Science Investigations for Intermediate Students,* presented in 3-ring-binder format, provides directions for more than 100 physical science activities. Each activity is categorized by grade level. A wide range of concepts is covered: the properties of air and water, motion, simple machines, heat, light, sound, magnetism, electromagnetism, electricity, acids and bases, and earth and space science. Seven activities on food and nutrition are included. Among the activities, students investigate the periodic motion of a pendulum, explore the relationship between heat and temperature, experiment with magnets and iron filings to determine a magnetic line of force, build and use a sundial, and conduct simple chemical tests to identify the presence of carbohydrates in food.

Each activity in the volume includes reproducible directions, data sheets, and evaluation forms. No background material for teachers is supplied.

Prices: Teacher's guide, $25.00. Complete kit, $420.05. Set of 14 teacher videos (optional), $280.00. *Publisher/supplier:* Nasco. *Materials:* Available locally, from commercial suppliers, or in kit.

1.95 **Science Projects about Chemistry.** Robert Gardner. Science Projects series. Springfield, N.J.: Enslow, 1994.

Recommended grade level: 6-8. *Science Projects about Chemistry,* 1 of 6 in a series written for students, contains 34 simple experiments or activities related to chemical concepts, including matter, solutions, chemical composition, chemical reactions, and acids and bases. Among the activities, students compare the densities of air and carbon dioxide; they test a number of solids (such as starch, flour, and baking soda) to see if they are soluble in water; and they investigate the effect of temperature on the speed at which a seltzer tablet reacts with water. In other activities, they explore 4 acid-base indicators (cabbage juice, unsweetened grape juice, tumeric, and phenolphthalein); and they determine what fraction of air is oxygen.

Designed to be student-directed, many of the stand-alone activities in *Science Projects about Chemistry* could be done at home or as teacher demonstrations, or used as the basis for science fair projects. The activities are narrative in form; the text contains questions to help guide inquiry. No background material is supplied, but brief explanations for the results observed in the experiments are provided in the text. Most activities include suggestions of further investigations for students to conduct on their own.

Price: $18.95 (ISBN 0-89490-531-7). *Publisher/supplier:* Enslow. *Materials:* Available locally, or from commercial suppliers.

1.96 **Science Projects about Electricity and Magnets.** Robert Gardner. Science Projects series. Springfield, N.J.: Enslow, 1994.

Recommended grade level: 6-8. *Science Projects about Electricity and Magnets*, 1 of 6 in a series, contains 23 simple experiments or activities that allow students to investigate electricity and magnetism. For example, students test a number of materials to see how they behave with respect to magnets. They also build series and parallel circuits, investigate the conductivity of different materials, make a lightbulb, and build a tiny electric motor.

Designed to be student-directed, many of these stand-alone activities could be done at home or as teacher demonstrations, or used as the basis for science fair projects. The activities are narrative in form; the text contains questions to help guide inquiry. No background material is supplied, but brief explanations for the results observed in the experiments are provided in the text. Most activities include suggestions of further investigations for students to conduct on their own.

Price: $18.95 (ISBN 0-89490-530-9). *Publisher/supplier:* Enslow. *Materials:* Available locally, or from commercial suppliers.

1.97 **Science Projects about Light.** Robert Gardner. Science Projects series. Springfield, N.J.: Enslow, 1994.

Recommended grade level: 7-8. *Science Projects about Light*, 1 of 6 in a series written for students, contains 37 short experiments or activities related to light. The topics addressed in these activities, which emphasize the processes of science, include mirrors and lenses, light and color, absorbed heat and light, and the human eye and how it works. For example, students conduct experiments with curved mirrors, pinholes, and convex lenses. They also use a diffraction grating to find out which colors of light are absorbed and which are transmitted by a colored liquid. In other activities, they build a model solar collector and experiment with afterimages.

Designed to be student-directed, many of these stand-alone activities could be done at home or as teacher demonstrations, or used as the basis for science fair projects. The activities are narrative in form; the text contains questions to help guide inquiry. No background material is supplied, but brief explanations for the results observed in the experiments are provided in the text. Most activities include suggestions of further investigations for students to conduct on their own.

Price: $18.95 (ISBN 0-89490-529-5). *Publisher/supplier:* Enslow. *Materials:* Available locally, or from commercial suppliers.

1.98 **Science Projects about Temperature and Heat.** Robert Gardner and Eric Kemer. Science Projects series. Springfield, N.J.: Enslow, 1994.

Recommended grade level: 7-8. *Science Projects about Temperature and Heat*, 1 of 6 in a series written for students, contains 24 simple experiments or activities related to temperature and heat. Among these activities, which emphasize the processes of science, students explore how changes in temperature affect the volume of solids and liquids. They also build and use an air expansion thermometer, compare the specific heats of different metals, determine the latent heat of vaporization of water, and investigate how heating by radiation depends on color.

Designed to be student-directed, many of these stand-alone activities could be done at home or as teacher demonstrations, or used as the basis for science fair projects. The activities are narrative in form; the text contains questions to help guide inquiry. No background material is supplied, but brief explanations for the results observed in the experiments are provided in the text. Most activities include suggestions of further investigations for students to conduct on their own.

Price: $18.95 (ISBN 0-89490-534-1). *Publisher/supplier:* Enslow. *Materials:* Available locally, or from commercial suppliers.

1.99 **Simple and Motorized Machines Activity Pack.** Enfield, Conn.: LEGO Dacta, 1997.

Recommended grade level: 4-8. This literature pack is designed to teach students the principles of simple and motorized machines. The pack includes a teacher's guide with 31 sequential activities and student worksheet copymasters for each activity. The pack is designed to support LEGO Dacta simple and motorized machines sets. The activities are organized in 6 units:
(1) "Structures and Forces,"
(2) "Levers," (3) "Wheels and Axles,"
(4) "Gears," (5) "Pulleys," and
(6) "More Mechanisms." Students, for instance, can build models of a deck chair and a drawbridge and use them to investigate rigidity, flexibility, and linkages; construct a model of a wheeled vehicle and use it to explore friction, flywheels, and energy; design and build a mixing mechanism; and assemble a motorized model of a conveyor belt and use it to investigate how a motor can drive a system of pulleys.

Each activity requires students to identify a problem related to a simple machine and its principles, and then design, implement, and evaluate a solution. The activities are intended to be used by students working in pairs, and take approximately 45 minutes each. Some activities require the use of a 9-volt LEGO motor. The teacher's guide provides background information, notes on the student worksheets, sample answers to worksheet questions, and extension ideas.

Prices: Activity pack, $37.50. Motorized simple machines resource pack, $462.50. (Contact the publisher/supplier for complete price and ordering information.) *Publisher/supplier:* LEGO Dacta. *Materials:* Available in resource pack.

1.100 **The Sky's the Limit! with Math and Science.** Rev. ed. Stan Adair, Bill Barker, Dennis Ivans, and others. Activities Integrating Mathematics and Science (AIMS) series. Fresno, Calif.: AIMS Education Foundation, 1994.

Recommended grade level: 6-8. *The Sky's the Limit! with Math and Science* offers 23 classroom activities on the science of aerodynamics. Among the activities, students make and use a clinometer to find the heights of various objects. They also construct various symmetric shapes and explore their flight properties, investigate the behavior of a paper rotor, construct various parachutes and calculate their rates of descent, use toy water rockets to explore the effects of variables on thrust, and discover how the design of a paper airplane affects how long it will stay in the air. In other activities, students manipulate design features of paper airplanes so the airplanes can perform certain stunts, and they explore the flight characteristics of 3 simple paper kites.

Each activity includes procedures, discussion questions, extensions, and reproducible student record sheets or handouts. Connections to standards of the National Council of Teachers of Mathematics (NCTM)

and to Project 2061 Benchmarks are also listed.

Price: Teacher's guide (ISBN 1-881431-44-4), $16.95. *Publisher/supplier:* AIMS Education Foundation. *Materials:* Available locally, or from commercial suppliers.

1.101 **Soap Films and Bubbles.** Ann Wiebe. Activities Integrating Mathematics and Science (AIMS) series. Fresno, Calif.: AIMS Education Foundation, 1990.

Recommended grade level: 4-8. Students learn about molecules, surface tension, light waves, air pressure, and patterns by experimenting with soap film in *Soap Films and Bubbles.* In a series of introductory activities, students first explore the effects of wet and dry surfaces on bubbles. They discover that all free-floating bubbles are spherical in shape, and they explore various combinations of bubbles and the structures and patterns they form. Students construct models of water and soap molecules as they investigate surface tension and the chemistry of soap film. In advanced activities, students take a quantitative look at geometric shapes; they discover the mathematical relationship between the size of 2 equal rings and the distance soap film will stretch between them (catenary curves). They experiment to determine the minimum distances between given numbers of points (Steiner's problem). They find a formula relating the parts of polyhedrons.

Soap Films and Bubbles provides reproducible student worksheets, including data charts, tables, and graphs. A complete lesson plan is included for each of the 21 activities.

Price: Teacher's guide (ISBN 1-881431-25-8), $16.95. *Publisher/supplier:* AIMS Education Foundation. *Materials:* Available locally, or from commercial suppliers.

1.102 **Solutions.** Ron Marson. Task Card Series 12. Canby, Oreg.: TOPS Learning Systems, 1990.

Recommended grade level: 7-8+. The 28 easy-to-follow activities in *Solutions*—which is one of many units in the Task Card Series—constitute a mini-overview of the chemistry of solutions, including the subjects of solvents, solutes, dissolving, filtering, and purifying processes. For example, students compare and contrast a coarse suspension, colloidal dispersion, and a true solution. They clear a mixture of soil and water by settling and filtration so that they can observe how soil particles tend to sort by size. They build a simple solar distillation apparatus that will purify a true solution. They also discover how temperature influences the rate of dissolving, analyze various sources of drinking water for the presence of dissolved minerals, read and interpret a solubility graph, and find out that the solubility of some solutes in water decreases with increasing temperature.

The activities in *Solutions* require readily available materials (such as rice, sugar cubes, and plastic straws). Certain activities can be omitted or sequences changed to meet specific class needs. The unit contains reproducible "task cards" that include directions for each activity, teaching notes, and review questions.

Price: $13 (ISBN 0-941008-82-7). *Publisher/supplier:* TOPS Learning Systems. *Materials:* Available locally, or from commercial suppliers.

1.103 **Sound.** Ron Marson. Task Card Series 18. Canby, Oreg.: TOPS Learning Systems, 1990.

Recommended grade level: 7-8. The 20 short, easy-to-follow activities in *Sound* help students learn about the properties of sound, including frequency, pitch, and intensity. For example, students discover that sound is produced by vibrating objects; they measure frequency by counting cycles over measured units of time; and they discover that sound intensity increases with the amplitude of the vibrating source. In other activities, they observe how objects with the same natural frequency resonate as one is sounded in the presence of another; they investigate the mathematical relationship between vibrating wires that sound octaves apart; and they build a working model of a phonograph with cans, a piece of rolled paper, and a straight pin.

The activities, which have between 2 and 5 steps each, require readily available materials (such as dinner forks, plastic soda bottles, and rubber bands). Some basic mathematical skills are needed to conduct the activities. Certain activities can be omitted or sequences changed to meet specific class needs. The unit contains reproducible "task cards" with directions for each activity, teaching notes with answers, and review questions.

Price: $9.50 (ISBN 0-941008-6). *Publisher/supplier:* TOPS Learning Systems. *Materials:* Available locally, or from commercial suppliers.

1.104 **Sparks and Shocks: Experiments from the Golden Age of Static Electricity.** Developed by The Bakken Library and Museum (Minneapolis, Minn.). Dubuque, Iowa: Kendall/Hunt, 1996.

Recommended grade level: 6-8+. *Sparks and Shocks,* a well-organized, sequential activity book, contains 6 investigative experiments and 12 demonstrations on static electricity, adapted by the Bakken Library and Museum from the original studies of

scientists who lived during the eighteenth century. Concepts covered include positive and negative charge, conductors, electrization by induction, potential, and capacitance. During the experiments, students discover what materials attract what things when rubbed; they learn that some substances transmit electricity whereas others do not; and they make and use a Leyden jar.

In addition to clear and detailed instructions on how to conduct the demonstrations and experiments, the book offers historical background and anecdotes about famous scientists and their experiments. It also includes tricks on getting static-electricity experiments to work in unfavorable weather and provides student handouts, a chronology of the study of static electricity, and a resource guide. An equipment kit and video can be purchased but are not required, since the book contains a separate chapter of instructions for inexpensively building the equipment needed—for example, a thread electroscope, an electrostatic generator, Leyden jars, an electrophorous, and an electrometer.

Sparks and Shocks is an expanded, revised version of *The Bakken 18th Century Electricity Kit and Curriculum* published in 1991.

Prices: $14.95 (ISBN 0-7872-1644-5). Kit, $200.00. *Publisher/supplier:* Kendall/Hunt (book). Bakken Library and Museum (materials kit). *Materials:* Available locally, from commercial suppliers, or in kit.

1.105 **Structures.** Bernie Zubrowski. Models in Physical Science (MIPS) series. White Plains, N.Y.: Cuisenaire, 1993.

Recommended grade level: 5-8. *Structures* contains 5 model-building activities. These activities introduce students to the basic concepts of force, tension, compression, and equilibrium of forces underlying structures they

see in their everyday environment—for example, houses, apartment buildings, bridges, and television towers. Using simple, inexpensive materials such as plastic drinking straws, students build a model house and test its strength. In another activity, they investigate how a single column of straws responds to the force of a cup of nails. They also build and test a model bridge, build and test a model tower, and assemble and use a testing apparatus to compare the strength of several different kinds of truss designs. Students must solve a variety of problems in order to keep their drinking-straw models rigid and strong. The overall concept that connects all the investigations is that of the truss as a basic structural system. In the course of these activities, students also have opportunities to practice proportional reasoning and graphical representation.

The guide includes directions for the assembly and use of equipment and materials, suggestions for ways of introducing and leading the activities, ideas for follow-up discussions, and embedded assessments.

Prices: Teacher's guide (ISBN 0-938587-35-8), $11.50. Complete kit, $225.00. *Publisher/supplier:* Cuisenaire/Dale Seymour Publications. *Materials:* Available locally, or in kit.

1.106 **Students and Research: Practical Strategies for Science Classrooms and Competitions.** 2nd ed. Julia H. Cothron, Ronald N. Giese, and Richard J. Rezba. Dubuque, Iowa: Kendall/Hunt, 1993.

Recommended grade level: 8+. *Students and Research* contains background information, activities, experiments, and strategies designed to help educators teach students the skills they need to successfully conduct, analyze, and report an experiment. (*See also* 5.74—the student version of this teacher's guide.) The book is a guide to teaching the major concepts of experimental design. It helps students acquire better understanding of the ideas of variables, control, hypothesis, and methods of gathering and analyzing data.

Topics covered in *Students and Research* include techniques for helping students design experiments, generate ideas, construct tables and graphs, write simple and formal reports, use library resources, and apply descriptive and inferential statistics. Other topics include management strategies for classroom teaching and independent research, assessments, how to encourage parental and community support, methods for maximizing student success and attitudes about science competitions, and ideas for making effective oral presentations and displays. The volume includes blackline masters for the activities.

Price: $25.14 (ISBN 0-7872-0170-7). *Publisher/supplier:* Kendall/Hunt. *Materials:* Available locally.

1.107 **Sweet Success.** Terry Hilton. Making Use of Science and Technology series. Heslington, York, England: Chemical Industry Education Centre, University of York, 1993.

Recommended grade level: 8+. In *Sweet Success,* a unit with 3 activities, students investigate why large sugar crystals sometimes form in the fondant of Cadbury creme eggs. During the activities, students use a microscope to investigate the structure of fondants in products bought from local stores. They design an experiment to test the hypothesis that large crystals grow at the expense of small crystals in confectionery products. They also investigate the effects of temperature and agitation on crystal growth. In the role of chemical engineers, students devise speci-

fications for an industrial sugar crystallizer that would produce sugar crystals all the same size.

The equivalent of 2 or 3 lessons of 40 to 60 minutes each is needed if all 3 activities are used. The unit includes teacher directions, a list of required materials, instructions for preparing solutions, and student record sheets.

Price: $10 (ISBN 1-85342-536-2). *Publisher/supplier:* Chemical Industry Education Centre. *Materials:* Available locally, or from commercial suppliers.

1.108 **Targeting Students' Science Misconceptions: Physical Science Concepts Using the Conceptual Change Model.** Joseph Stepans. Riverview, Fla.: Idea Factory, 1996.

Recommended grade level: 6-8+. *Targeting Students' Science Misconceptions,* a teacher's guide containing directions for approximately 100 activities, is designed to help students identify and change their common, naive preconceptions and misconceptions about science topics. In doing these activities, students first state their ideas about a wide range of physical science concepts, and then they rethink or reconsider them after experimentation in the classroom.

Topics addressed in this guide include matter, density and buoyancy, air pressure, liquids, forces, levers, motion, pendulums, electricity, magnetism, heat, waves, sound, light and color, transformation of energy, and geometry. In an activity about force, work, and machines, for example, students are asked to decide which is the easiest way to move a heavy box from the floor to the top of a table (lifting straight up, using a pulley, or using an inclined plane). They try out the various options and come up with an answer based on their observations.

In addition to directions for activities, *Targeting Students' Science Misconceptions* includes background information for the teacher, a listing of representative student misconceptions related to each concept, a listing of sources of students' confusion and misconceptions, and teaching notes.

Price: $24.95 (ISBN 1-885041-12-8). *Publisher/supplier:* Idea Factory. *Materials:* Available locally, or from commercial suppliers.

1.109 **Thrill Ride!** Russell G. Wright. Event-Based Science series. Menlo Park, Calif.: Innovative Learning Publications, 1997.

Recommended grade level: 7-8+. In *Thrill Ride,* an event-based unit on force and motion, students design an exciting but safe amusement park ride that demonstrates Newton's laws of motion. First they watch a videotape and read actual newspaper stories about thrill rides and amusement parks. Then they are told that the major task of the module will be to design and build, in teams, a model of a thrill ride that demonstrates some of the basic laws of physics. *Thrill Ride* contains 5 science activities to provide students with the background information and skills they need for this task.

Among the activities, for example, students use Newton's laws of motion to design a ramp that can transport fragile materials safely. They analyze the energy transformations experienced on a slide, and they investigate the forces exerted on a person riding on a revolving ride. They also study the forces that influence the motion of a pendulum, and apply Newton's second law of motion to falling objects.

The module contains short reading sections called "discovery files," explanatory graphics, and profiles of professionals—a roller coaster engineer, an amusement park manager, and a physicist, for example—involved in developing and running amusement parks. Other information that students need to complete the task must be obtained from encyclopedias, textbooks, films, and other sources that they locate. Students can also engage in several interdisciplinary activities, such as determining the geographic factors that affect the success of theme parks, or writing a description of a trip to an amusement park.

The wraparound teacher's guide provides brief overview information on the module's structure and activities. It includes suggestions for guiding specific student activities, a scoring rubric for a performance assessment at the end of the unit, and a list of resources.

Prices: Teacher's guide with video, $18.00. Student book, $7.95. Classroom package, $115.00. *Publisher/ supplier:* Addison Wesley/Longman. *Materials:* Available locally.

1.110 **Tops and Yo-Yos.** Bernie Zubrowski. Models in Physical Science (MIPS) series. White Plains, N.Y.: Cuisenaire, 1994.

Recommended grade level: 6-8. *Tops and Yo-Yos* contains 8 activities that help students learn about rotational motion while collaboratively building and launching tops and yo-yos. The required materials are inexpensive, familiar objects such as plastic plates and drawer knobs, so students can easily experiment with them and alter their characteristics. Among the activities, students launch and time different tops to determine the characteristics that produce different spin times. They also design their own tops to see which kinds spin longest. They investigate the relationship between weight and spin time, and they assemble different

kinds of yo-yos and compare their spin times. Several of the investigations in *Tops and Yo-Yos* require data collection and representation.

The guide includes reproducible pages for students, directions for teachers on the assembly and use of equipment and materials, suggestions for introducing and leading the activities and for follow-up discussions, and embedded assessments. Many of the activities also include ideas for further investigations.

Prices: Teacher's guide (ISBN 0-938587-37-4), $12.50. Kit, $225.00. *Publisher/supplier:* Cuisenaire/Dale Seymour Publications. *Materials:* Available locally, from commercial suppliers, or in kit.

1.111 **Transportation.** Robert Gardner. Yesterday's Science, Today's Technology Science Activities series. New York, N.Y.: Twenty-First Century Books, 1994.

Recommended grade level: 6-8. In *Transportation,* 17 activities written for students help them investigate some of the science and technology associated with different types of transportation, such as cars, trains, boats, and airplanes. Topics addressed in the unit include friction, wheels, gears, ball bearings, air pressure, levitating magnets, Archimedes' principle, and aerodynamics. Among the activities, for example, students compare the forces needed to move a wagon on wheels or on rollers. They use a bicycle and a pair of spring scales to see how changing gears changes both speed and the force one has to exert on the pedals. They also compare the forces involved in floating a block of wood and a ball of clay in water, design paper airplanes, and use a water hose to demonstrate the action of a jet engine.

Each activity includes a brief historical or science background section on the scientific discoveries of

people such as James Watt, Henry Ford, and the Wright Brothers. Colorful illustrations, directions, and questions in the narrative then guide students through the activity. Although students can do most of the activities without supervision, several of them may require the assistance of adults. Some of the activities require materials such as a bike, wagon, or playground seesaw that may not be readily available. Many activities also need to be done outside.

Price: $16.98 (ISBN 0-8050-2853-6). *Publisher/supplier:* Von Holtzbrinck (VHPS). *Materials:* Available locally.

1.112 **Using the Learning Cycle to Teach Physical Science: A Hands-on Approach for the Middle Grades.** Paul C. Beisenherz and Marylou Dantonio. Portsmouth, N.H.: Heinemann, 1996.

Recommended grade level: 6-8. *Using the Learning Cycle to Teach Physical Science* discusses and gives examples of a science teaching strategy— the learning cycle—that emphasizes science as a process of inquiry rather than as a body of knowledge, and uses questions, activities, and experiences to guide students in constructing science concepts on their own. The first part of the book discusses the rationale for this approach and its use in teaching science. The second part then gives examples of how the cycle can be used to teach 6 basic physical science concepts: (1) Bernoulli's principle, (2) acids and bases, (3) properties of gases, (4) expansion and contraction of gases, (5) circuits, and (6) density.

A series of between 9 and 17 short activities is given for each of the 6 basic concepts. For example, for the learning cycle sequence on circuits, students are asked to see how many ways they can make a bulb light using a battery and copper wire (exploration phase). Following a discussion of student observations, the concept of circuit is introduced (concept introduction). Then they engage in a number of activities that lead to an understanding of the term "series circuit" or "parallel circuit" (application phase). Examples of questioning techniques to encourage thinking and understanding are also given.

The last part of the book offers an opportunity for teachers to develop their own learning cycle sequence. Randomly sequenced activities related to the concept of surface tension are presented. Using these activities and others they create, teachers can construct their own learning cycle sequence.

Price: $26.50 (ISBN 0-435-08376-7). *Publisher/supplier:* Heinemann. *Materials:* Available locally, or from commercial suppliers.

1.113 **The Wizard's Lab: Exhibit Guide.** Reprinted with revisions. Cary Sneider and Alan Gould. Great Explorations in Math and Science (GEMS)/Exhibit Guides. Berkeley, Calif.: Lawrence Hall of Science, 1992.

Recommended grade level: K-8. *The Wizard's Lab* provides 10 interactive exhibits that can be used in a variety of settings—for example, at a science center, at a classroom learning station, in a discovery room, or on family science night. The wide spectrum of stimulating activities in physical science offered in this guide includes the spinning platform, solar cells and light polarizers, resonant pendulums, magnets, lenses, the "human battery," the oscilloscope and sound, and the harmonograph. Most of the exhibits utilize common materials and equipment available from most hardware, electronics, or variety stores and lumberyards. The skills developed include observing, analyzing, and finding patterns.

The Wizard's Lab provides background information recorded on cards with cartoon wizard figures that briefly explains the principles behind each exhibit. Detailed and illustrated instructions for constructing each exhibit are included in the teacher's guide.

Price: $21 (ISBN 0-912511-71-0). *Publisher/supplier:* LHS GEMS. *Materials:* Available locally, or from commercial suppliers.

1.114 **World of Science and Electronics Integrated Learning System.** 2nd ed. Educational Technology Systems, Peter Michael Kellen, and Leslie Ivor Kacev. Teach Yourself Electronics Series. San Diego, Calif.: PLANETS Educational Technology Systems, 1993.

Recommended grade level: 8+. This wirebound instruction manual—*World of Science and Electronics Integrated Learning System*—comes with a small box of 50 electronic components and contains directions for 26 electronic building projects. Starting with very basic circuits, students can build electronic sirens, flashing LEDs (light-emitting diodes), an electronic time-delay circuit, a sound synthesizer, and other projects. Students also learn how transistors, capacitors, diodes, resistors, integrated circuits, and silicon-controlled rectifiers work.

The projects, designed to be followed in sequence, each include step-by-step assembly directions, a pictorial guide, assembly diagrams, and electronic schematic diagrams. A teacher's guide, student workbook, and add-on modules are available.

Prices: Teacher's guide with student workbook, $30.00. Software version of book, $99.95. Power kit (AC power), $99.95. Dura-kit (Battery-powered), $89.95. *Publisher/supplier:* PLANETS. *Materials:* Available in kit.

1.115 **Young America Hands-on Activities.** PACT 95. Glenview, Ill.: Scott Foresman, 1996.

Recommended grade level: 5-8+. *Young America Hands-on Activities* is a teacher's resource guide that offers an 11-week series of interdisciplinary activities related to boats and sailing. (The activities were originally part of an educational program based on the America's Cup Race in 1995. Students were to complete the activities as the America's Cup trials unfolded.) The activities, which are categorized by grade level, help students learn the science involved in how a boat floats and stays upright, what makes a sailboat move, how a fast boat can be designed and built, and what navigational skills a sailor needs. The importance of teamwork in building and sailing a boat is also emphasized. Among the activities, for example, students make an anemometer and use it to measure wind speeds, locate the center of mass and the center of buoyancy of a wooden hull, determine the best rudder design for a model boat, learn how to build a miniature plug (the male mold of a boat's hull) from a lines plan (a drawing of the shape of a boat's hull), find out how to use a navigation chart, and learn how to organize effective cooperative teams.

One activity per week is provided for each of 3 grade levels (grades K-4, 5-8, and 9-12). For each activity, directions, extensions, cross-curricular connections, and information on careers and people related to the world of boats and sailing are provided.

Prices: $15.95 (ISBN 0-673-40240-1). *Publisher/supplier:* Scott Foresman/Addison-Wesley.

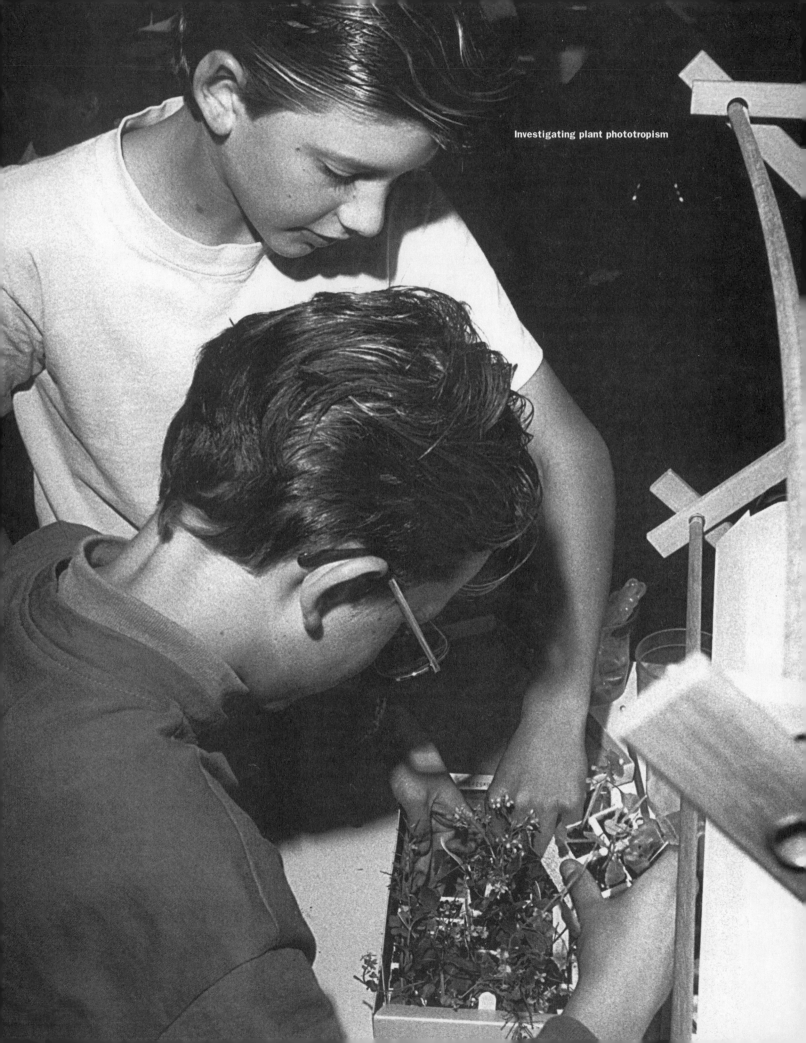

Investigating plant phototropism

CHAPTER 2

LIFE SCIENCE

2.1 **Cells: Building Blocks of Life.** 3rd ed. Anthea Maton, Jean Hopkins, Susan Johnson, and others. Prentice Hall Science Integrated Learning System series. Upper Saddle River, N.J.: Prentice Hall, 1997.

Program Overview The Prentice Hall Science Integrated Learning System series is a program for middle school or junior high school students. Designed to cover all relevant areas of science, this program consists of 19 books, each in a particular topic area, such as sound and light, the planet earth, and cells—building blocks of life. Seven science themes are incorporated into the program; the themes are energy, evolution, patterns of change, scale and structure, systems and interactions, unity and diversity, and stability. For each unit, teaching materials, ancillary student materials, and some optional components are available.

Student Edition **Recommended grade level: 7-8. Reading level: middle 7.** *Cells: Building Blocks of Life,* which introduces students to the cellular basis of life, is organized in 4 chapters: (1) "The Nature of Life," (2) "Cell Structure and Function," (3) "Cell Processes," and (4) "Cell Energy." During the course, students learn about several theories of the origin of life on earth. They also identify the basic characteristics of living things, learn about the organic compounds that are the building blocks of life, and examine the important structures of cells and their functions. Students compare a typical plant cell and a typical animal cell, and they study how materials pass into and out of cells through osmosis, diffusion, and active transport. They also examine the processes of growth and reproduction of cells, find out how cells obtain and use energy, and learn about and compare respiration and photosynthesis.

Each chapter includes a lab investigation. Students analyze their school lunch menu for the presence of 3 major food nutrients (carbohydrates, fats, and proteins). They also learn how to use a microscope to observe objects, and they look at prepared slides of mitosis in animal and plant cells. Students investigate the relationship between photosynthesis and respiration using Elodea and bromthymol blue solution (an indicator) in flasks.

Each chapter contains comprehensive reading sections that introduce major science concepts. Suggestions are provided for activities in which students "find out by doing," "find out by reading," and "find out by writing." Other skills-oriented activities are also suggested—for example, observing a piece of onion tissue under a microscope and writing a brief report on Melvin Calvin's discovery of the Calvin cycle.

Other features of the textbook include problem-solving challenges, descriptions of science careers, and science connections to real-world events or issues. The student edition closes with readings on 3 topics: (1) zoologist Fernando Nottebohm and his study of neurogenesis in bird brains, (2) the uses and abuses of human-growth hormone (HGH), and (3) a fictional account of people's being given attributes of plants to allow them to survive in a space colony.

Teacher's Edition In the teacher's wraparound edition, each chapter begins with a 2-page planning guide and a 2-page preview that summarizes each section within the chapter. The teacher's edition also provides suggestions for teaching, guiding, integrating, and closing lessons, as well as enrichments, extensions, and answers to questions in the student text.

Supplementary Laboratory Manual The supplementary lab manual provides 9 investigations directly correlated with the information presented in the student textbook. Examples of the investigations include studying the space requirements of seed plants; examining the structure and function of various cells, tissues, and organs in the chicken; observing the movement of molecules through a cell membrane; and using bromthymol blue and bromthymol yellow solutions to determine how carbon dioxide is exchanged between organisms and their environments.

ABOUT THE ANNOTATIONS IN "LIFE SCIENCE—CORE MATERIALS"

Entry Numbers

Curriculum materials are arranged alphabetically by title in each category (Core Materials, Supplementary Units, and Science Activity Books) in chapters 1 through 5 of this guide.

Each curriculum annotation has a two-part entry number: the chapter number is given before the period; the number after the period locates the entry within that chapter. For example, the first entry number in chapter 1 is 1.1; the second entry in chapter 2 is 2.2; and so on.

The entry numbers within each curriculum chapter run consecutively through Core Materials, Supplementary Units, and Science Activity Books.

Order of Bibliographic Information

Following is the arrangement of the facts of publication in the annotations in this section:

- **Title of publication**
- **Number of edition,** if applicable
- **Authors** (an individual author or authors, an institutional author, or a project or program name under which the material was developed)
- **Series title**
- **Series developer,** if applicable
- **Place of publication, publisher, and date of publication**

Recommended Grade Level and Reading Level

The grade level for each piece of material was recommended by teacher evaluators during the development of this guide. In some instances, the recommended grade level may differ slightly from the publisher's advertised level. The Fry Readability Scale was used to determine the approximate reading level of core materials.

Key to Content Standards: 5-8

The key lists the content standards for grades 5-8 from the *National Science Education Standards* (NSES) that are addressed in depth by the item. A key is provided for core materials and supplementary units. (*See* appendix C.)

Price and Acquisition Information

Ordering information appears at the end of each entry. Included are—

- **Prices** (of teacher's guides, student books, lab manuals, and kits or units)
- **Publisher/supplier** (The name of a principal publisher/supplier, although not necessarily the sole source, for the items listed in the price category. Appendix A, "Publishers and Suppliers," provides the address, phone and fax numbers, and electronic ordering information, where available, for each publisher and supplier.)
- **Materials** (various sources from which one might obtain the required materials)

Readers must contact publishers/suppliers for complete and up-to-date listings of the program resources and support materials available for a particular unit. Depending on the developer, these items may be required, optional, or both; they may be offered individually and/or in kits, packages, or boxes. Materials may change with revised editions. The prices given in this chapter for selected resources or materials are based on information from the publishers and suppliers but are not meant to represent the full range of ordering options.

Indexes of Curriculum Materials

The multiple indexes on pp. 449-78 allow easy access to the information in this guide. Various aspects of the curriculum materials—including titles, topics addressed in each unit, grade levels, and standards addressed—are the focus of seven separate indexes. For example, titles and entry numbers are listed in the "Title Index" on pp. 450-54. The "Index of Authors, Series, and Curriculum Projects," on pp. 455-57, provides entry numbers of any annotated titles in a particular series.

Overviews of Core and Supplementary Programs

Appendix D, "Overviews of Core and Supplementary Programs with Titles Annotated in This Guide," on pp. 441-48, lists, by program or series, the individual titles annotated in the sections "Core Materials" and "Supplementary Units" in the five curriculum chapters.

Program Resources and Support Materials A variety of materials, including some optional components, is available. A teacher's resource package contains the student edition and annotated teacher's editions of both the textbook and the lab manual, as well as a test book, an activity book, a review-and-reinforcement guide, and English and Spanish audiotapes for auditory and language learners. Other available materials include interactive videodiscs, transparencies, assessment materials, English and Spanish guides for language learners, a study guide, a teacher's desk reference, and a booklet of product-testing activities.

Key to Content Standards: 5-8 (see app. C)

UNIFYING CONCEPTS AND PROCESSES: Systems, order, and organization; evolution and equilibrium; form and function.

SCIENCE AS INQUIRY: Abilities necessary to do scientific inquiry; understandings about scientific inquiry.

LIFE SCIENCE: Structure and function in living systems; regulation and behavior; diversity and adaptations of organisms.

SCIENCE IN PERSONAL AND SOCIAL PERSPECTIVES: Science and technology in society.

HISTORY AND NATURE OF SCIENCE: Science as a human endeavor; nature of science; history of science.

Prices: Student edition (ISBN 0-13-423476-6), $9.97. Teacher's edition (ISBN 0-13-423237-2), $22.97. Teacher's resource package, $112.97. (Contact publisher/supplier for complete price and ordering information.) *Publisher/supplier:* Prentice Hall. *Materials:* Available locally, or from commercial suppliers.

2.2 Ecology: Earth's Living Resources. 3rd ed. Anthea Maton, Jean Hopkins, Susan Johnson, and others. Prentice Hall Science Integrated Learning System series. Upper Saddle River, N.J.: Prentice Hall, 1997.

Program Overview The Prentice Hall Science Integrated Learning System series is a program for middle school or junior high school students. Designed to cover all relevant areas of science, this program consists of 19 books, each in a particular topic area, such as sound and light, cells—building blocks of life, and ecology—earth's living resources. Seven science themes are incorporated into the program; the themes are energy, evolution, patterns of change, scale and structure, systems and interactions, unity and diversity, and stability. For each unit, teaching materials, ancillary student materials, and some optional components are available.

Student Edition **Recommended grade level: 7-8+. Reading level: early 9.** *Ecology: Earth's Living Resources* is organized in 4 chapters: (1) "Interactions among Living Things," (2) "Cycles in Nature," (3) "Exploring Earth's Biomes," and (4) "Wildlife Conservation." Students are introduced to interactions and connections among living things as they study topics including ecosystems, populations, competition, and symbiosis. They discover the effects of daily, lunar, and annual rhythms on living things. They learn about chemical cycles. They study about ecological succession and biomes. They also learn about extinct and endangered species, the causes of wildlife endangerment, and methods of wildlife conservation.

Each chapter includes a lab investigation. Students explore the effect of lawn fertilizer on an aquatic ecosystem. They observe the life cycle of a housefly, and they discover how different plants grow in different biomes. Students also construct a miniature ecosystem with aquatic plants, guppies, and pond snails.

Each chapter contains comprehensive reading sections that introduce major science concepts. Suggestions are provided for activities in which students "find out by doing," "find out by reading," and "find out by writing." Other skills-oriented activities are also suggested—for example, organizing a debate about the destruction of the rain forests. In another activity, students compare the organisms in mowed and unmowed areas of a backyard, field, or park lawn over a period of 6 weeks.

Other features of the textbook include problem-solving challenges, descriptions of science careers, and science connections to real-world events or issues. The student edition closes with readings on 3 topics: (1) the Biosphere II project in Arizona, (2) controversies generated by current wildlife conservation efforts, and (3) a fictional account of what Africa's animal population may be like 50 years from now.

Teacher's Edition In the teacher's wraparound edition, each chapter begins with a 2-page planning guide and a 2-page preview that summarizes each section within the chapter. The teacher's edition also provides suggestions for teaching, guiding, integrating, and closing lessons, as well as enrichments, extensions, and answers to questions in the student text.

Supplementary Laboratory Manual The supplementary lab manual provides 8 additional investigations directly correlated with the information presented in the student textbook. Examples include examining an outdoor ecosystem, observing schooling behavior in fish, and conducting an investigation to determine whether mental alertness in human beings changes predictably during a 24-hour period.

Program Resources and Support Materials A variety of materials, including some optional components, is available. A teacher's resource package contains the student edition and annotated teacher's editions of both the textbook and the lab manual, as well as a test book, an activity book, a review-and-reinforcement guide, and English and Spanish audiotapes for auditory and language learners. Other available materials include interactive videodiscs, transparencies, assessment materials, English and Spanish guides for language learners, a study guide, a teacher's desk reference, and a booklet of product-testing activities.

Key to Content Standards: 5-8 (see app. C)

UNIFYING CONCEPTS AND PROCESSES: Systems, order, and organization; change, constancy, and measurement; evolution and equilibrium. **SCIENCE AS INQUIRY:** Abilities necessary to do scientific inquiry; understandings about scientific inquiry. **LIFE SCIENCE:** Regulation and behavior; populations and ecosystems; diversity and adaptations of organisms. **SCIENCE IN PERSONAL AND SOCIAL PERSPECTIVES:** Populations, resources, and environments.

Prices: Student edition (ISBN 0-13-423443-X), $9.97. Teacher's edition (ISBN 0-13-423203-8), $22.97. Teacher's resource package, $112.97. (Contact publisher/supplier for complete price and ordering information.) *Publisher/supplier:* Prentice Hall. *Materials:* Available locally, or from commercial suppliers.

2.3 Ecosystems. Robert C. Knott and Herbert D. Thier. Science Curriculum Improvement Study 3 (SCIS 3) series. Hudson, N.H.: Delta Education, 1993.

Program Overview The Science Curriculum Improvement Study (SCIS) series focuses on the concepts and processes of science for grades K-6. The most current version of the series—SCIS 3—consists of 13 units: a kindergarten unit and 2 sequences of 6 units each in physical-earth science and life-environmental science for grades 1 through 6. Two units are designed for grade 6. The components of a SCIS 3 unit are a teacher's guide and a kit of materials.

Teacher's Guide **Recommended grade level: 6.** *Ecosystems* introduces students to physical and biological aspects of ecosystems in the world around them. The unit consists of 22 chapters organized in 5 sections: (1) "Reviewing Concepts and Creating Classroom Ecosystems," (2) "The Water Cycle," (3) "The Oxygen-Carbon Dioxide Cycle," (4) "Cycles in an Ecosystem," and (5) "Pollution."

The unit begins with students constructing aquarium-terrarium systems. They discover evidence of the water cycle as they observe evaporation and condensation in this system and in other experimental setups. Activities include the use of snails, ladybugs, aphids, daphnia, guppies, hornwort, and algae. Students use bromthymol blue (an indicator) to explore the role of plants and animals in the oxygen-carbon dioxide cycle, and they learn about the food-mineral cycle and investigate various aspects of the water cycle and water pollution. Diagrams of the 3 cycles illustrate the exchange and cycling of materials in an ecosystem. Students also study photographs of natural ecosystems, data

cards listing features of ecosystems, and maps showing the locations of 7 different ecosystems in the United States and Canada.

The teacher's guide includes an introduction to the unit, lesson plans for each of the 5 sections, a glossary, and blackline masters for a student journal. Science background information, detailed instructions on planning for and conducting each activity, an extensive assessment component, and extensions for integration and enrichment are provided.

Key to Content Standards: 5-8 (see app. C)

UNIFYING CONCEPTS AND PROCESSES: Systems, order, and organization; evidence, models, and explanation; change, constancy, and measurement.
SCIENCE AS INQUIRY: Abilities necessary to do scientific inquiry; understandings about scientific inquiry.
LIFE SCIENCE: Populations and ecosystems.
EARTH AND SPACE SCIENCE: Structure of the earth system.
SCIENCE IN PERSONAL AND SOCIAL PERSPECTIVES: Populations, resources, and environments; natural hazards; risks and benefits.

Prices: Teacher's guide (ISBN 0-87504-942-7), $39.50. Kit, $680.00.
Publisher/supplier: Delta Education. *Materials:* Available locally, from commercial suppliers, or in kit.

2.4 Ecosystems. Science and Technology for Children (STC) series. Developed by National Science Resources Center (Washington, D.C.). Burlington, N.C.: Carolina Biological Supply, 1996.

Program Overview The Science and Technology for Children (STC) series consists of 24 inquiry-centered curriculum units for grades 1-6, with 4 units at each grade level. Students

learn about topics in the life, earth, and physical sciences. The technological applications of science and the interactions among science, technology, and society are addressed throughout the program. The STC units, each of which takes about 16 class sessions to complete, encourage participatory learning and the integration of science with mathematics, language arts, social studies, and art. The components of an STC unit are a teacher's guide, a student activity book with simple instructions and illustrations, and a kit of materials.

Teacher's Guide **Recommended grade level: 5-6. Reading level: 6.** In *Ecosystems,* students learn about the interdependence of organisms and the natural environment by using 2-liter soda bottles to set up, observe, and experiment with 2 miniature ecosystems—an aquarium and a terrarium. After studying the 2 separate ecosystems, students connect them and observe the ecocolumn, noting any changes that may indicate an imbalance in the system. They read about aquatic and terrestrial organisms and pollution. They study habitat changes and conduct experiments simulating the effects of acid rain, road salt, and fertilizer. As a final activity, students in small groups investigate a real ecosystem in danger—the Chesapeake Bay. They read about the problems of the bay, analyze the situation from several points of view, propose possible solutions, and begin to grapple with the trade-offs involved in various solutions.

Ecosystems is a 16-lesson unit. The teacher's guide includes a unit overview, the 16 lesson plans, an annotated bibliography of additional resources, and information on maintaining live materials. Science background information, detailed instructions on planning for and conducting each activity, an extensive assessment component, and extensions for integration and enrichment are provided.

Key to Content Standards: 5-8 (see app. C)

UNIFYING CONCEPTS AND PROCESSES: Systems, order, and organization; evidence, models, and explanation; change, constancy, and measurement; evolution and equilibrium; form and function.
SCIENCE AS INQUIRY: Abilities necessary to do scientific inquiry; understandings about scientific inquiry.
LIFE SCIENCE: Structure and function in living systems; reproduction and heredity; regulation and behavior; populations and ecosystems.
EARTH AND SPACE SCIENCES: Structure of the earth system.
SCIENCE AND TECHNOLOGY: Abilities of technological design; understandings about science and technology.
SCIENCE IN PERSONAL AND SOCIAL PERSPECTIVES: Personal health; populations, resources, and environments; natural hazards; risks and benefits.
HISTORY AND NATURE OF SCIENCE: Science as a human endeavor; nature of science.

Prices: Teacher's guide (ISBN 0-89278-733-3), $24.95. Student activity book (ISBN 0-89278-734-1), $3.75. Unit, $389.95. ***Publisher/supplier:*** Carolina Biological Supply. *Materials:* Available locally, from commercial suppliers, or in kit.

2.5 **Experiments with Plants.** Science and Technology for Children (STC) series. Developed by National Science Resources Center (Washington, D.C.). Burlington, N.C.: Carolina Biological Supply, 1992.

Program Overview The Science and Technology for Children (STC) series consists of 24 inquiry-centered curriculum units for grades 1-6, with 4 units at each grade level. Students learn about topics in the life, earth, and physical sciences. The technological applications of science and the interactions among science, technology, and society are addressed throughout the program. The STC units, each of which takes about 16 class sessions to complete, encourage participatory learning and the integration of science with mathematics, language arts, social studies, and art. The components of an STC unit are a teacher's guide, a student activity book with simple instructions and illustrations, and a kit of materials.

Teacher's Guide **Recommended grade level: 6. Reading level: middle 7.** In *Experiments with Plants,* students learn how to design and conduct controlled experiments by using the 40-day life cycle of a *Brassica* plant as a vehicle for experimentation. They learn about the variables that affect plant growth and reproduction as they design and set up an experiment to manipulate an isolated variable. Students then plant seeds according to their experiment plans; they determine the effects of their experiments on the plants' life cycle through data collection, measurement, observation, and recording. After observing the entire life cycle, they communicate the results of their experiments. The unit concludes with 2 sets of experiments involving germination, geotropism, and phototropism. Some prior study of plants and plant life cycles is helpful, but not essential, for students in *Experiments with Plants.*

This is a 15-lesson unit. The teacher's guide includes a unit overview, the 15 lesson plans, an annotated bibliography of additional resources, and information on maintaining live materials. Science background information, detailed instructions on planning for and conducting

each activity, an extensive assessment component, and extensions for integration and enrichment are provided.

Key to Content Standards: 5-8 (see app. C)

UNIFYING CONCEPTS AND PROCESSES: Evidence, models, and explanation; change, constancy, and measurement.
SCIENCE AS INQUIRY: Abilities necessary to do scientific inquiry; understandings about scientific inquiry.
LIFE SCIENCE: Structure and function in living systems; reproduction and heredity; regulation and behavior.
HISTORY AND NATURE OF SCIENCE: Science as a human endeavor; nature of science; history of science.

Prices: Teacher's guide (ISBN 0-89278-680-9), $24.95. Student activity book (ISBN 0-89278-634-5), $3.75. Unit, $299.95. ***Publisher/supplier:*** Carolina Biological Supply. *Materials:* Available locally, from commercial suppliers, or in kit.

2.6 **Exploring Life Science.** 2nd ed. Anthea Maton, Jean Hopkins, Susan Johnson, and others. Prentice Hall Exploring Life, Earth, and Physical Science series. Upper Saddle River, N.J.: Prentice Hall, 1997.

Program Overview The Prentice Hall Exploring Life, Earth, and Physical Science series is a program for middle school students. Designed to cover all relevant areas of science, this integrated program consists of 3 textbooks (1 for each major discipline) and incorporates 7 science themes—energy, evolution, patterns of change, scale and structure, systems and interactions, unity and diversity, and stability. Each of the 3 year-long courses contains about 6 units. The units are also available, possibly with some modifications, as individual textbooks in the Prentice Hall Science Integrated Learning System series (*see*, e.g., 2.1). For each course, teaching materials, ancillary student materials, and some optional components are available.

Student Edition **Recommended grade level: 7-8+. Reading level: middle 11.** *Exploring Life Science* offers a complete course in life science. The units in this textbook are entitled (1) "Characteristics of Living Things," (2) "Monerans, Protists, Fungi, and Plants," (3) "Animals," (4) "Human Biology," (5) "Heredity and Adaptation," and (6) "Ecology." During the course, students learn about cells and cell processes and about how living things are classified by scientists. They study the characteristics of viruses, monerans, protists, fungi, plants with and without seeds, and the various groups of invertebrate and vertebrate animals. They investigate plant and animal structures, adaptations, reproductive processes, and growth patterns. They study human body systems, human reproduction and development, genetics and applied genetics, evolution, cycles in nature, and the earth's biomes.

Examples of the lab investigations that students conduct during the 6 units are these: observing a slime mold over 3 days, dissecting an owl pellet, observing what effect alcohol has on the growth of microorganisms, and making a model to represent recombinant DNA.

Each of the 6 units in *Exploring Life Science* typically has 3 to 6 chapters. Each chapter contains comprehensive reading sections that introduce major science concepts. Also included are suggested skills-oriented activities for discovering, doing, calculating, thinking, and writing about science. The activities range from comparing down and contour feathers, to making spore prints, to writing a report on human

fungal diseases. Each chapter includes a laboratory investigation as well as a review and study guide.

Other features of this textbook include problem-solving challenges, science connections to real-world events or issues, and careers in science. A "Science Gazette" feature at the end of each unit profiles prominent scientists—for example, paleontologist Jack Horner, physicist Stephen Hawking, and epidemiologist Veronica Broome. An "Activity Bank" at the back of the book provides at least one additional laboratory investigation for each chapter. Examples include using a microscope to observe the behavior of hydra, investigating the response of *Euglena* to light, growing a plant from a cutting, and exploring the process of making compost.

Teacher's Edition In the teacher's wraparound edition, each chapter begins with a 2-page planning guide and a 2-page preview that summarizes each section within the chapter. The teacher's edition also provides suggestions for teaching, guiding, integrating, and closing lessons, as well as enrichments, extensions, and answers to questions in the student text.

Supplementary Laboratory Manual The supplementary lab manual contains 70 investigations directly correlated with information presented in the student textbook. Examples include observing the movement of molecules through a cell membrane, culturing yeast cells, investigating germination inhibitors, examining bird adaptations, observing some human reflexes, and constructing a microhabitat.

Program Resources and Support Materials A variety of support materials is available, including a box of teaching resources with activ-

ities, worksheets, and assessment materials for each chapter. Other available materials are a teacher's desk reference, an integrated science activity book, a computer test bank, videos, videodiscs, transparencies, a classroom manager guide, and a book of product-testing activities.

Key to Content Standards: 5-8 (see app. C)

UNIFYING CONCEPTS AND PROCESSES: Systems, order, and organization; evidence, models, and explanation; change, constancy, and measurement; evolution and equilibrium; form and function.

SCIENCE AS INQUIRY: Abilities necessary to do scientific inquiry; understandings about scientific inquiry.

LIFE SCIENCE: Structure and function in living systems; regulation and behavior; populations and ecosystems; diversity and adaptations of organisms.

SCIENCE AND TECHNOLOGY: Understandings about science and technology.

SCIENCE IN PERSONAL AND SOCIAL PERSPECTIVES: Personal health; populations, resources, and environments; risks and benefits; science and technology in society.

HISTORY AND NATURE OF SCIENCE: Science as a human endeavor; nature of science; history of science.

Prices: Student edition (ISBN 0-13-418732-6), $41.47. Teacher's edition (ISBN 0-13-422841-3), $70.47. Lab manual, teacher's edition (1995), $24.47. Teaching resources, $306.47. (Contact publisher/supplier for complete price and ordering information.) ***Publisher/supplier:*** Prentice Hall. ***Materials:*** Available locally, or from commercial suppliers.

2.7 Food and Nutrition. Full Option Science System (FOSS) series. Developed by Lawrence Hall of Science (Berkeley, Calif.). Hudson, N.H.: Delta Education, 1993.

Program Overview The Full Option Science System (FOSS) program is a K-6 science curriculum consisting of 27 stand-alone modules. The 8 modules for grades 5-6 are organized under topics in the life, physical, and earth sciences and in scientific reasoning and technology. They can be used in any order. The FOSS program is designed to engage students in scientific concepts through multisensory, hands-on laboratory activities. All modules of the program incorporate 5 unifying themes—(1) pattern, (2) structure, (3) interaction, (4) change, and (5) system. The components of a FOSS module are a teacher's guide and a kit of materials.

Teacher's Guide **Recommended grade level: 5-6.** The unit *Food and Nutrition* helps students understand what food is, what its chemical components are, and how several nutrient groups contribute to making food healthful. Students test foods for their acid content, as well as for their vitamin C, fat, and sugar content. Next they learn how to read nutritional information on package labels, how to calculate the caloric content of foods, and how to use their own knowledge and the nutritional information from the packaging lists of product ingredients to plan and evaluate lunch menus. Activities involve students in measuring and comparing, observing, and analyzing.

Food and Nutrition consists of 4 activities, requiring about 10 sessions of 45 to 60 minutes each. The teacher's guide includes a module overview, the 4 individual activity folios, duplication masters (in English and Spanish) for student sheets, and an annotated bibliography. Sci-

ence background information, detailed instructions on planning for and conducting each activity, an extensive assessment component, and extensions for integration and enrichment are provided.

Key to Content Standards: 5-8 (see app. C)
UNIFYING CONCEPTS AND PROCESSES: Systems, order, and organization; evidence, models, and explanation; change, constancy, and measurement. **SCIENCE AS INQUIRY:** Abilities necessary to do scientific inquiry; understandings about scientific inquiry. **PHYSICAL SCIENCE:** Properties and changes of properties in matter. **LIFE SCIENCE:** Structure and function in living systems. **SCIENCE IN PERSONAL AND SOCIAL PERSPECTIVES:** Personal health.

Prices: Teacher's guide (ISBN 0-7826-0093-X), $101. Complete module, $429. *Publisher/supplier:* Delta Education. *Materials:* Available locally, from commercial suppliers, or in kit.

2.8 Glencoe Life Science. Lucy Daniel, Ed Ortleb, and Alton Biggs. Glencoe Life, Earth, and Physical Science series. New York, N.Y.: Glencoe/McGraw-Hill, 1997.

Program Overview The Glencoe Life, Earth, and Physical Science series includes 3 full-year courses—one in life, one in earth, and one in physical science—for students in grades 8 and above. Four major themes are developed: (1) energy, (2) systems and interactions, (3) scale and structure, and (4) stability and change. An extensive set of materials and resources, including many optional components, is available for students and teachers.

Student Edition **Recommended grade level: 8+. Reading level: early 7.** *Glencoe*

Life Science is divided into 7 units: (1) "Life," (2) "Heredity and Evolution," (3) "Diversity of Life," (4) "Plants," (5) "Animals," (6) "Ecology," and (7) "The Human Body." During this course, students learn about cells and cell processes and about patterns of heredity and how inherited changes can influence evolutionary trends. They learn how organisms are classified, and they examine the characteristics and life processes of monerans, protists, fungi, plants, and animals. Students are introduced to the fundamentals of ecology, including interaction of abiotic and biotic factors, characteristics of populations, the flow of energy, and the cycling of matter. They also study the systems of the human body and how they function, and they examine some basic health concepts.

Sample lab activities in this textbook include observing and comparing mitosis in plant cells and animal cells, using a dichotomous key to identify native cats of North America, designing and carrying out an experiment to determine what happens to proteins in the digestive system, and experimenting with models to observe the greenhouse effect.

Glencoe Life Science has 27 chapters in its 7 units. Each chapter begins with a self-guided activity in which students make observations and generate questions about chapter concepts and topics. Reading sections on science concepts are then interwoven with various types of activities, including open-ended activities, minilabs (activities that can be done in class or at home), and skill-building or problem-solving activities. In activities for designing their own experiments, students brainstorm hypotheses, make a decision to investigate a hypothesis that can be tested, plan procedures, and think about why their hypothesis was supported or not.

Special features of the textbook include "connect to" marginal notes that relate basic questions in physics, chemistry, earth science, and life science to one another. The book also provides "science and society" features that invite students to confront real-life problems; profiles of people in science; and reading selections about connections between science, history, literature, and the arts.

Teacher's Edition The wraparound teacher's edition provides information on curriculum integration, assessment, planning, and meeting the diverse needs of students. Each chapter contains a 4-page planning guide; strategies for preparing, teaching, and closing lessons; answers to in-text questions; tips on connecting earth science to other sciences, disciplines, or community resources; and different assessment options.

Supplementary Laboratory Manual The supplementary lab manual offers one or more additional labs for each chapter. It has setup diagrams, data tables, and space for student responses. Examples of investigations include exploring bacterial growth, comparing seeds, observing the responses of plants to light and gravity, investigating the effects of acid rain on the germination of bean seedlings, testing for carbohydrates in foods, and comparing the effects of different caffeine products on *Euglena*.

Program Resources and Support Materials *Glencoe Life Science* offers an extensive list of support materials and program resources, including the following: activity and reinforcement worksheets, science integration activities that relate earth and life science to specific physical science chapters, a critical-thinking/problem-solving book, a concept-mapping book, chapter review masters, a study guide, enrichment worksheets, a book on

multicultural connections, technology-integration masters, assessments, computer test banks, color transparencies, a Spanish resources book, and interactive CD-ROM and videodisc programs.

Key to Content Standards: 5-8 (see app. C)

UNIFYING CONCEPTS AND PROCESSES: Systems, order, and organization; evidence, models, and explanation; change, constancy, and measurement; evolution and equilibrium; form and function.

SCIENCE AS INQUIRY: Abilities necessary to do scientific inquiry; understandings about scientific inquiry.

LIFE SCIENCE: Structure and function in living systems; reproduction and heredity; regulation and behavior; populations and ecosystems; diversity and adaptations of organisms.

SCIENCE AND TECHNOLOGY: Abilities of technological design; understandings about science and technology.

SCIENCE IN PERSONAL AND SOCIAL PERSPECTIVES: Personal health; populations, resources, and environments; science and technology in society.

Prices: Student edition (ISBN 0-02-827737-6), $41.79. Teacher's edition (ISBN 0-02-827738-4), $57.86. Student lab manual, $8.25. Teacher's lab manual, $14.00. Teacher's classroom resources, $321.87. (Contact publisher/supplier for complete price and ordering information.) *Publisher/supplier:* Glencoe/McGraw-Hill. *Materials:* Available locally, or from commercial suppliers.

2.9 Heredity: The Code of Life. 3rd ed. Anthea Maton, Jean Hopkins, Susan Johnson, and others. Prentice Hall Science Integrated Learning System series. Upper Saddle River, N.J.: Prentice Hall, 1997.

Program Overview The Prentice Hall Science Integrated Learning System series is a program for mid-

dle school or junior high school students. Designed to cover all relevant areas of science, this program consists of 19 books, each in a particular topic area, such as sound and light, the planet earth, and heredity—the code of life. Seven science themes are incorporated into the program; the themes are energy, evolution, patterns of change, scale and structure, systems and interactions, unity and diversity, and stability. For each unit, teaching materials, ancillary student materials, and some optional components are available.

Student Edition Recommended grade level: 7-8+. Reading level: early 10. *Heredity: The Code of Life* introduces students to the science of genetics—from its beginnings in Mendel's experiments to current research in and applications of molecular genetics. The unit is organized in 4 chapters: (1) "What Is Genetics?" (2) "How Chromosomes Work," (3) "Human Genetics," and (4) "Applied Genetics." During the course, students learn about basic patterns of inheritance and principles of heredity and discover how these patterns and principles relate to probability. They learn about the chromosome theory of heredity and discover how chromosomes control the production of proteins. Students also apply the principles of genetics to understanding specific examples of heredity in humans, including the ABO blood groups, sickle-cell anemia, and Huntington disease. Finally, they are introduced to artificial methods of manipulating inheritance—such as selective breeding techniques and genetic engineering—and the application of these methods in agriculture and medicine.

Each chapter includes a lab investigation. Students complete a class survey of dominant and recessive human traits, such as hair color, hairline, and type of earlobe. They observe the growth of mutant (albino) corn sprouts as compared with that of normal corn sprouts. Students also study a human pedigree to trace the inheritance of sickle-cell anemia through 3 generations of a family, and they make models from construction paper to represent recombinant DNA.

Each chapter contains comprehensive reading sections that introduce major science concepts. Suggestions are provided for activities in which students "find out by doing," "find out by reading," and "find out by writing." Other skills-oriented activities are also suggested—for example, calculating the incidence of Down's syndrome in the United States and discussing the pros and cons of genetically engineered food plants.

Other features of this textbook include problem-solving challenges, descriptions of science careers, and science connections to real-world events or issues. The student edition closes with readings on 3 topics: (1) biologist Barbara McClintock's discovery of "jumping" genes, (2) the effect of humans on the rate of extinction of wild animals and plants, and (3) the Human Genome Project.

Teacher's Edition In the teacher's wraparound edition, each chapter begins with a 2-page planning guide and a 2-page preview that summarizes each section within the chapter. The teacher's edition also provides suggestions for teaching, guiding, integrating, and closing lessons, as well as enrichments, extensions, and answers to questions in the student text.

Supplementary Laboratory Manual The supplementary lab manual provides 5 additional investigations directly correlated with the information presented in the student textbook. Examples of the investigations include solving heredity problems, building a model of DNA, observing how the results of different gene combinations produce certain traits, and cloning a duckweed plant.

Program Resources and Support Materials A variety of materials, including some optional components, is available. A teacher's resource package contains the student edition and annotated teacher's editions of both the textbook and the lab manual, as well as a test book, an activity book, a review-and-reinforcement guide, and English and Spanish audiotapes for auditory and language learners. Other available materials include interactive videodiscs, transparencies, assessment materials, English and Spanish guides for language learners, a study guide, a teacher's desk reference, and a booklet of product-testing activities.

Key to Content Standards: 5-8 (see app. C)

UNIFYING CONCEPTS AND PROCESSES: Systems, order, and organization; evidence, models, and explanation; change, constancy, and measurement; evolution and equilibrium.
SCIENCE AS INQUIRY: Abilities necessary to do scientific inquiry; understandings about scientific inquiry.
LIFE SCIENCE: Reproduction and heredity; diversity and adaptations of organisms.
SCIENCE AND TECHNOLOGY: Understandings about science and technology.
SCIENCE IN PERSONAL AND SOCIAL PERSPECTIVES: Science and technology in society.
HISTORY AND NATURE OF SCIENCE: Nature of science; history of science.

Prices: Student edition (ISBN 0-13-423468-5), $9.97. Teacher's edition (ISBN 0-13-423229-1), $22.97. Teacher's resource package, $112.97. (Contact publisher/supplier for complete price and ordering information.) *Publisher/supplier:* Prentice Hall. *Materials:* Available locally, or from commercial suppliers.

2.10 Human Biology and Health. 3rd ed. Anthea Maton, Jean Hopkins, Susan Johnson, and others. Prentice Hall Science Integrated Learning System series. Upper Saddle River, N.J.: Prentice Hall, 1997.

Program Overview The Prentice Hall Science Integrated Learning System series is a program for middle school or junior high school students. Designed to cover all relevant areas of science, this program consists of 19 books, each in a particular topic area, such as sound and light, the planet earth, and human biology and health. Seven science themes are incorporated into the program; the themes are energy, evolution, patterns of change, scale and structure, systems and interactions, unity and diversity, and stability. For each unit, teaching materials, ancillary student materials, and some optional components are available.

Student Edition Recommended grade level: 7-8. Reading level: early 8. *Human Biology and Health* introduces students to human body systems, their interactions with one another, and how disorders and other factors affect the health of body systems. Over 9 chapters, students learn about the multicellular organization of the human body. They study the various systems of the human body, including the skeletal and muscular systems, the digestive system, the circulatory system, the respiratory and excretory systems, and the nervous and endocrine systems. In addition, students learn about the male and female reproductive systems and about human reproduction and development. They also read about the immune system and diseases and learn about effects of drugs, alcohol, and tobacco on the body.

Each chapter includes a lab investigation. Students examine the shape and arrangement of cells under a microscope, measure the number of calories used in 24 hours, measure pulse rate at different levels of activity, and determine where touch receptors are located on the body.

Each chapter contains comprehensive reading sections that introduce major science concepts. Suggestions are provided for activities in which students "find out by doing," "find out by reading," and "find out by writing." Other skills-oriented activities are also suggested—for example, calculating basal metabolic rate and constructing a chart to describe the changes that occur in the embryo and fetus during the first 3 months of pregnancy.

Other features of this textbook include problem-solving challenges, descriptions of science careers, and science connections to real-world events or issues. The student edition closes with readings on 3 topics: (1) how epidemiologist Claire Veronica Broome studies outbreaks of disease, (2) the issue of overexercising, and (3) bioengineering.

Teacher's Edition In the teacher's wraparound edition, each chapter begins with a 2-page planning guide and a 2-page preview that summarizes each section within the chapter. The teacher's edition also provides suggestions for teaching, guiding, integrating, and closing lessons, as well as enrichments, extensions, and answers to questions in the student text.

Supplementary Laboratory Manual The supplementary lab manual provides 17 additional investigations directly correlated with the information presented in the student textbook. Examples of the investigations include examining the structures of a long bone from a chicken leg and finding out how joints provide for movement of bones, determining the amount of vitamin C in fruit juice, and examining the circulation of blood in the capillaries of a goldfish's tail. Other investigations include measuring the effect of exercise on

the amount of carbon dioxide released from the lungs, observing a developing frog egg, and testing the effects of alcohol and tobacco smoke on seeds.

Program Resources and Support Materials A variety of materials, including some optional components, is available. A teacher's resource package contains the student edition and annotated teacher's editions of both the textbook and the lab manual, as well as a test book, an activity book, a review-and-reinforcement guide, and English and Spanish audiotapes for auditory and language learners. Other available materials include interactive videodiscs, transparencies, assessment materials, English and Spanish guides for language learners, a study guide, a teacher's desk reference, and a booklet of product-testing activities.

Key to Content Standards: 5-8 (see app. C)

UNIFYING CONCEPTS AND PROCESSES: Systems, order, and organization; change, constancy, and measurement; form and function.
SCIENCE AS INQUIRY: Abilities necessary to do scientific inquiry; understandings about scientific inquiry.
LIFE SCIENCE: Structure and function in living systems; reproduction and heredity; regulation and behavior.
SCIENCE IN PERSONAL AND SOCIAL PERSPECTIVES: Personal health; risks and benefits.

Prices: Student edition (ISBN 0-13-423435-9), $10.47. Teacher's edition (ISBN 0-13-423195-3), $22.97. Teacher's resource package, $112.97. (Contact publisher/supplier for complete price and ordering information.) *Publisher/supplier:* Prentice Hall. *Materials:* Available locally, or from commercial suppliers.

2.11 **Human Body Systems.** Insights series. Developed by Education Development Center (EDC). Dubuque, Iowa: Kendall/Hunt, 1997.

Program Overview The Insights program, for grades K-6, consists of 17 modules, several of which are appropriate for middle school. Topics in the program reflect a balance of life, physical, and earth sciences. Insights modules integrate science with the rest of the curriculum, particularly with language arts and mathematics. The activities support cultural, racial, and linguistic diversity. Each module requires about 25 class sessions to complete. The components of an Insights module are a teacher's guide and a kit of materials.

Teacher's Guide **Recommended grade level: 6.** *Human Body Systems* is designed to convey to students basic concepts about how 3 systems—the human circulatory, digestive, and respiratory systems—work together. As students explore these systems, beginning with the cell and the vital role it plays as a basic component of the body, they develop a sense of the size, location, and function of some of their internal organs. Students are introduced to the ideas that the individual parts of the body are all part of one larger system and that these parts work together to take in food, process it for energy, and get rid of waste. Students engage in a variety of activities that demonstrate how the 3 systems work interdependently to provide the cells in the body with the nutrients and energy they need.

Human Body Systems consists of 13 Learning Experiences, requiring a minimum of 24 class sessions. The teacher's guide includes an overview, the 13 Learning Experiences, reproducible masters for student sheets, and annotated lists of suggested readings and audiovisual materials. Science background information, detailed instructions on planning for and conducting each activity, an extensive assessment component, and extensions for integration and enrichment are also included.

Key to Content Standards: 5-8 (see app. C)

UNIFYING CONCEPTS AND PROCESSES: Systems, order, and organization; form and function.
SCIENCE AS INQUIRY: Abilities necessary to do scientific inquiry; understandings about scientific inquiry.
LIFE SCIENCE: Structure and function in living systems; regulation and behavior.
SCIENCE IN PERSONAL AND SOCIAL PERSPECTIVES: Personal health.

Prices: Teacher's guide (ISBN 0-7872-3343-9), $68.90. Materials kit, $398.90. ***Publisher/supplier:*** Kendall/Hunt. ***Materials:*** Available locally, from commercial suppliers, or in kit.

2.12 **Microworlds.** Science and Technology for Children (STC) series. Developed by National Science Resources Center (Washington, D.C.). Burlington, N.C.: Carolina Biological Supply, 1991.

Program Overview The Science and Technology for Children (STC) series consists of 24 inquiry-centered curriculum units for grades 1-6, with 4 units at each grade level. Students learn about topics in the life, earth, and physical sciences. The technological applications of science and the interactions among science, technology, and society are addressed throughout the program. The STC units, each of which takes about 16 class sessions to complete, encourage participatory learning and the integration of science with mathematics, language arts, social studies, and art. The components of an STC

unit are a teacher's guide, a student activity book with simple instructions and illustrations, and a kit of materials.

Teacher's Guide **Recommended grade level: 5-6. Reading level: 7.** *Microworlds* develops students' observational skills and allows them to become adept at using hand lenses, microscopes, slides, and related apparatuses to view living and nonliving specimens. Students make close observations of common objects with hand lenses and learn about different lenses and how they work. They use a microscope to observe inanimate objects such as hair and magazine photographs. Students explore the concept of field of view, prepare different types of slides, and examine the cells of an onion. Then they use their new expertise to view microscopic living organisms under magnification. Throughout the unit they record their observations by writing and drawing.

Microworlds is a 16-lesson unit. The teacher's guide includes a unit overview, the 16 lesson plans, and an annotated bibliography of additional resources. Science background information, detailed instructions on planning for and conducting each activity, an extensive assessment component, and extensions for integration and enrichment are provided. The appendixes include a supplementary drawing lesson and tips on caring for live cultures.

Key to Content Standards: 5-8 (see app. C)

UNIFYING CONCEPTS AND PROCESSES: Systems, order, and organization; evidence, models, and explanation; form and function.
SCIENCE AS INQUIRY: Abilities necessary to do scientific inquiry; understandings about scientific inquiry.
LIFE SCIENCE: Structure and function in living systems; diversity and adaptations of organisms.

SCIENCE AND TECHNOLOGY: Understandings about science and technology.
SCIENCE IN PERSONAL AND SOCIAL PERSPECTIVES: Science and technology in society.
HISTORY AND NATURE OF SCIENCE: Science as a human endeavor; nature of science; history of science.

Prices: Teacher's guide, $24.95. Student activity book, $3.75. Unit, $359.95. ***Publisher/supplier:*** Carolina Biological Supply. ***Materials:*** Available locally, from commercial suppliers, or in kit.

2.13 **Middle School Life Science.** Judy Capra (principal author) and Jefferson County Public Schools (Golden, Colo.). Dubuque, Iowa: Kendall/Hunt, 1991.

Program Overview *Middle School Life Science* is a full-year course organized around a series of learning cycles during which students work independently, with partners, and in small groups. They engage in hands-on laboratory activities to explore an idea or concept, develop the concept during class discussion and/or through readings or additional experiments, apply the concepts learned to other situations, and form connections between their new knowledge and other areas of inquiry.

Student Edition **Recommended grade level: 7. Reading level: early 8.** *Middle School Life Science* is a study of human biology, of people and the environment, and of choices people must make to stay healthy. The textbook is organized in 7 units: (1) "Ecosystems and Ecology," (2) "Body Structure," (3) "Foods and Digestion," (4) "Body Basics," (5) "Body Controls," (6) "Body Changes," and (7) "Cells and Genetics." When possible, the situations discussed relate to students' lives and involve general health topics such as fitness, nutrition, drug use, relationships with peers, and ecological topics such as recycling and environmental responsibilities.

The textbook's 7 units consist of 23 chapters, which provide activities and readings. Each chapter includes several activities—for example, constructing and observing a terrarium with decomposers and scavengers in it; examining microscope slides of muscle cells; observing the effect of saliva on protein, fat, and carbohydrate; and designing a poster on cancer awareness. The activities are used first to introduce concepts and then to reinforce these concepts by providing opportunities for students to apply what they have learned. The readings interspersed with the activities build on students' experiences and reinforce the activities. Each activity and reading is designated as core, recommended, or optional. The extensions provided are often interdisciplinary, with opportunities for exploring careers.

Teacher's Edition The teacher's guide, in 3-ring-binder format, contains information on the *Middle School Life Science* program, assessment options, strategies to use with reading assignments, unit overviews and materials lists, and directions and guidelines for teaching all activities. Answer keys and transparency keys are also provided.

A separate teacher's resource book contains additional material, arranged by chapter. Included are worksheets, blackline masters for transparencies, optional lessons, additional print materials, and a test item bank.

Key to Content Standards: 5-8 (see app. C)

UNIFYING CONCEPTS AND PROCESSES: Systems, order, and organization; change, constancy, and measurement; form and function.

SCIENCE AS INQUIRY: Abilities necessary to do scientific inquiry; understandings about scientific inquiry.

LIFE SCIENCE: Structure and function in living systems; reproduction and heredity; regulation and behavior; populations and ecosystems.

SCIENCE IN PERSONAL AND SOCIAL PERSPECTIVES: Personal health; natural hazards; risks and benefits; science and technology in society.

HISTORY AND NATURE OF SCIENCE: Science as a human endeavor; nature of science.

Prices: Student edition (ISBN 0-8403-5098-8), $43.90. Teacher's edition (ISBN 0-8403-5099-6), $69.90. Teacher's resource book, $109.90. *Publisher/supplier:* Kendall/Hunt. *Materials:* Available locally, or from commercial suppliers.

2.14 Parade of Life: Animals. 3rd ed. Anthea Maton, Jean Hopkins, Susan Johnson, and others. Prentice Hall Science Integrated Learning System series. Upper Saddle River, N.J.: Prentice Hall, 1997.

Program Overview The Prentice Hall Science Integrated Learning System series is a program for middle school or junior high school students. Designed to cover all relevant areas of science, this program consists of 19 books, each in a particular topic area, such as sound and light, the planet earth, and organisms that make up the animal kingdom. Seven science themes are incorporated into the program; the themes are energy, evolution, patterns of change, scale and structure, systems and interactions, unity and diversity, and stability. For each unit, teaching materials, ancillary student materials, and some optional components are available.

Student Edition Recommended grade level: 7-8+. Reading level: middle 9. *Parade of Life: Animals,* which introduces students to the organisms that make up the animal kingdom, is

organized in 5 chapters: (1) "Sponges, Cnidarians, Worms, and Mollusks"; (2) "Arthropods and Echinoderms"; (3) "Fishes and Amphibians"; (4) "Reptiles and Birds"; and (5) "Mammals." During the course, students briefly review the 5 kingdoms and their general characteristics, and they discuss the division of the animal kingdom into vertebrates and invertebrates. Then they study the general characteristics of the major groups of invertebrates. Students learn about the first groups of vertebrates to evolve—fishes and amphibians—and are introduced to reptiles and birds; they study the main characteristics of mammals; and they discuss the evolution of mammals into 3 distinct groups—monotremes, marsupials, and placental mammals.

Each chapter includes a lab investigation. Students observe how earthworms react to changes in moisture and light. They determine whether isopods prefer a wet or a dry environment. They observe the behavior of guppies in an aquatic environment over 2 weeks to determine the type of environment that is best suited to guppies. Also, they dissect an owl pellet and try to determine what an owl eats, and they describe the characteristics of hair seen under a microscope.

Each chapter contains comprehensive reading sections that introduce major science concepts. Suggestions are provided for activities in which students "find out by doing," "find out by reading," and "find out by writing." Other skills-oriented activities are also suggested—for example, observing the life of a mealworm over 4 weeks, and researching the effects of the accidental introduction of lampreys into the Great Lakes after the completion of the St. Lawrence Seaway.

Other features of the textbook include problem-solving challenges, descriptions of science careers, and science connections to real-world events or issues. The student edition closes with readings on 3 topics: (1) the efforts of Kenyan wildlife advocate Michael Werikhe to preserve the rhinoceros, (2) the impact of tuna net fishing on dolphins, and (3) a fictional account of future medical or societal use of a chemical that causes hibernation.

Teacher's Edition In the teacher's wraparound edition, each chapter begins with a 2-page planning guide and a 2-page preview that summarizes each section within the chapter. The teacher's edition also provides suggestions for teaching, guiding, integrating, and closing lessons, as well as enrichments, extensions, and answers to questions in the student text.

Supplementary Laboratory Manual The supplementary lab manual provides 18 additional investigations directly correlated with the information presented in the student textbook. Examples of the investigations include examining the external and internal structure of an earthworm, observing organisms that live in the soil, identifying the external parts of a perch and an anole, and using a simple classification key to identify some vertebrates.

Program Resources and Support Materials A variety of materials, including some optional components, is available. A teacher's resource package contains the student edition and annotated teacher's editions of both the textbook and the lab manual, as well as a test book, an activity book, a review-and-reinforcement guide, and English and Spanish audiotapes for auditory and language learners. Other available materials include interactive videodiscs, transparencies, assessment materials, English and Spanish guides for language learners, a study

guide, a teacher's desk reference, and a booklet of product-testing activities.

Key to Content Standards: 5-8 (see app. C)

UNIFYING CONCEPTS AND PROCESSES: Systems, order, and organization; evolution and equilibrium; form and function.
SCIENCE AS INQUIRY: Abilities necessary to do scientific inquiry; understandings about scientific inquiry.
LIFE SCIENCE: Structure and function in living systems; regulation and behavior; diversity and adaptations of organisms.

Prices: Student edition (ISBN 0-13-423484-7), $9.97. Teacher's edition (ISBN 0-13-423245-3), $22.97. Teacher's resource package, $112.97. (Contact publisher/supplier for complete price and ordering information.) ***Publisher/supplier:*** Prentice Hall. ***Materials:*** Available locally, or from commercial suppliers.

2.15 **Parade of Life: Monerans, Protists, Fungi, and Plants.** 2nd ed. Anthea Maton, Jean Hopkins, Susan Johnson, and others. Prentice Hall Science Integrated Learning System series. Englewood Cliffs, N.J.: Prentice Hall, 1994.

Program Overview The Prentice Hall Science Integrated Learning System series is a program for middle school or junior high school students. Designed to cover all relevant areas of science, this program consists of 19 books, each in a particular topic area, such as sound and light, the planet earth, and the classification of living things—monerans, protists, fungi, plants, and animals. Seven science themes are incorporated into the program; the themes are energy, evolution, patterns of change, scale and structure, systems and interactions, unity and diversity, and stability. For each unit, teaching

materials, ancillary student materials, and some optional components are available.

Student Edition Recommended grade level: 7-8+. Reading level: middle 7.
Parade of Life: Monerans, Protists, Fungi, and Plants introduces students to the ways that scientists classify living things. The unit is organized in 6 chapters: (1) "Classification of Living Things," (2) "Viruses and Monerans," (3) "Protists," (4) "Fungi," (5) "Plants without Seeds," and (6) "Plants with Seeds."

During the course, students learn about classification systems and the 7 major levels of taxonomic grouping. They study the parts of a virus and viral reproduction; they study the structures of monerans and how monerans obtain energy and reproduce; and they learn about 3 major groups of protists and the characteristics of several types of fungi. Students also analyze the adaptations necessary for plants to live on land, compare ferns to mosses and algae, learn about the process of photosynthesis, and study the patterns of growth in seed plants and the factors that affect growth.

Each chapter includes a laboratory investigation. Students develop a classification system for their shoes. They observe the growth of bacteria (monerans) in petri dishes with agar. They also observe some of the characteristics of a living slime mold over 3 days; compare the growth of mold on 3 substances (cheese, bread, and an apple slice); compare algae, mosses, and ferns using a hand lens and a microscope; and investigate how gravity affects the growth of a seed.

Each chapter contains comprehensive reading sections that introduce major science concepts. Suggestions are provided for activities in which students "find out by doing," "find out by reading," and "find out by writing." Other skills-oriented activities are also suggested—for example, calculating the reproductive capacity of bacteria and identifying the parts of plants from which various foods originate.

Other features of the textbook include problem-solving challenges, descriptions of science careers, and science connections to real-world events or issues. The student edition closes with readings on 3 topics: (1) the research of marine biologist Colleen Cavanaugh, who studies giant tube worms; (2) the pluses and minuses of pesticide use; and (3) the possibility of farming in outer space.

Teacher's Edition In the teacher's wraparound edition, each chapter begins with a 2-page planning guide and a 2-page preview that summarizes each section within the chapter. The teacher's edition also provides suggestions for teaching, guiding, integrating, and closing lessons, as well as enrichments, extensions, and answers to questions in the student text.

Supplementary Laboratory Manual The supplementary lab manual provides 13 additional investigations directly correlated with the information presented in the student textbook. Examples include trying to grow bacteria on common vegetables; culturing some yeast cells, determining their needs for growth, and observing their reproduction; and investigating the structures and functions of a leaf.

Program Resources and Support Materials A variety of materials, including some optional components, is available. A teacher's resource package contains the student edition and annotated teacher's editions of both the textbook and the lab manual, as well as a test book, an activity book, a review-and-reinforcement guide, and English and Spanish audiotapes for auditory and language learners. Other available materials include interactive videodiscs, transparencies, assessment materials, English and Spanish guides for language learners, a study guide, a teacher's desk reference,

and a booklet of product-testing activities.

Key to Content Standards: 5-8 (see app. C)

UNIFYING CONCEPTS AND PROCESSES: Systems, order, and organization; evolution and equilibrium; form and function.

SCIENCE AS INQUIRY: Abilities necessary to do scientific inquiry; understandings about scientific inquiry.

LIFE SCIENCE: Structure and function in living systems; reproduction and heredity; populations and ecosystems; diversity and adaptations of organisms.

SCIENCE IN PERSONAL AND SOCIAL PERSPECTIVES: Science and technology in society.

HISTORY AND NATURE OF SCIENCE: History of science.

Prices: Student edition (ISBN 0-13-225590-1), $9.97. Teacher's edition (ISBN 0-13-225608-8), $22.97. Teacher's resource package, $112.97. (Contact publisher/supplier for complete price and ordering information.) *Publisher/supplier:* Prentice Hall. *Materials:* Available locally, or from commercial suppliers.

Life Science—Supplementary Units

2.16 **Animals in Action.** Reprinted with revisions. Katharine Barrett. Great Explorations in Math and Science (GEMS) series. Berkeley, Calif.: Lawrence Hall of Science, 1991.

Program Overview The Great Explorations in Math and Science (GEMS) series includes more than 50 teacher's guides and handbooks for preschool through grade 10. About 35 of these are appropriate for middle school. The series also includes several assembly presenter's guides and exhibit guides. New guides and handbooks continue to be developed, and current titles are revised frequently. The series is designed to teach key science and mathematics concepts through activity-based learning. The time needed to complete GEMS units varies from about 2 to 10 class sessions.

Teacher's Guide **Recommended grade level: 6-8.** In *Animals in Action*, students investigate animal behavior by observing live animals. They first observe and describe the behavior of young animals—for example, gerbils, hamsters, guinea pigs, or chicks—enclosed in a large classroom corral. Then they introduce stimulus objects, such as food or shelter, and observe how each animal responds. On the basis of information in *Animals in Action,* students discuss the humane treatment of animals. Teams of students then design, conduct, and evaluate their own animal-behavior experiments, using small organisms such as crayfish, isopods, crickets, or garden snails. Findings are discussed at a simulated scientific convention.

ABOUT THE ANNOTATIONS IN "LIFE SCIENCE— SUPPLEMENTARY UNITS"

Entry Numbers
Curriculum materials are arranged alphabetically by title in each category (Core Materials, Supplementary Units, and Science Activity Books) in chapters 1 through 5 of this guide.

Each curriculum annotation has a two-part entry number: the chapter number is given before the period; the number after the period locates the entry within that chapter. For example, the first entry number in chapter 1 is 1.1; the second entry in chapter 2 is 2.2; and so on.

The entry numbers within each curriculum chapter run consecutively through Core Materials, Supplementary Units, and Science Activity Books.

Order of Bibliographic Information
Following is the arrangement of the facts of publication in the annotations in this section:

- **Title of publication**
- **Number of edition,** if applicable
- **Authors** (an individual author or authors, an institutional author, or a project or program name under which the material was developed)
- **Series title**
- **Series developer,** if applicable
- **Place of publication, publisher, and date of publication**

Recommended Grade Level
The grade level for each piece of material was recommended by teacher evaluators during the development of this guide. In some instances, the recommended grade level may differ slightly from the publisher's advertised level.

Key to Content Standards: 5-8
The key lists the content standards for grades 5-8 from the *National Science Education Standards* (NSES) that are addressed in depth by the item. A key is provided for core materials and supplementary units. (*See* appendix C.)

Price and Acquisition Information

Ordering information appears at the end of each entry. Included are—

- **Prices** (of teacher's guides, student books, lab manuals, and kits or units)
- **Publisher/supplier** (The name of a principal publisher/supplier, although not necessarily the sole source, for the items listed in the price category. Appendix A, "Publishers and Suppliers," provides the address, phone and fax numbers, and electronic ordering information, where available, for each publisher and supplier.)
- **Materials** (various sources from which one might obtain the required materials)

Readers must contact publishers/suppliers for complete and up-to-date listings of the program resources and support materials available for a particular unit. Depending on the developer, these items may be required, optional, or both; they may be offered individually and/or in kits, packages, or boxes. Materials may change with revised editions. The prices given in this chapter for selected resources or materials are based on information from the publishers and suppliers but are not meant to represent the full range of ordering options.

Indexes of Curriculum Materials

The multiple indexes on pp. 449-78 allow easy access to the information in this guide. Various aspects of the curriculum materials—including titles, topics addressed in each unit, grade levels, and standards addressed—are the focus of seven separate indexes. For example, titles and entry numbers are listed in the "Title Index" on pp. 450-54. The "Index of Authors, Series, and Curriculum Projects," on pp. 455-57, provides entry numbers of any annotated titles in a particular series.

Overviews of Core and Supplementary Programs

Appendix D, "Overviews of Core and Supplementary Programs with Titles Annotated in This Guide," on pp. 441-48, lists, by program or series, the individual titles annotated in the sections "Core Materials" and "Supplementary Units" in the five curriculum chapters.

Background information, easy-to-follow lesson plans for each of the 5 sessions, requiring 45 minutes each, and a small-animal resource guide are included in this unit.

Key to Content Standards: 5-8 (see app. C)

UNIFYING CONCEPTS AND PROCESSES: Systems, order, and organization; evidence, models, and explanation. **SCIENCE AS INQUIRY:** Abilities necessary to do scientific inquiry; understandings about scientific inquiry. **LIFE SCIENCE:** Regulation and behavior. **HISTORY AND NATURE OF SCIENCE:** Nature of science.

Price: $10.50 (ISBN 0-912511-10-9).
Publisher/supplier: LHS GEMS.
Materials: Available locally, or from commercial suppliers.

2.17 Biodiversity: Understanding the Variety of Life. Scholastic Science Place series. Developed in cooperation with Liberty Science Center (Jersey City, N.J.). New York, N.Y.: Scholastic, 1997.

Program Overview The Scholastic Science Place series is a K-6 program with 42 units, 6 for each grade level. The 6 units for grade 6 are organized under topics in the life, earth, and physical sciences. Three key themes—(1) scale and structure, (2) systems and interactions, and (3) patterns of change—are incorporated into the program. For each unit, teaching materials, student materials, and some optional components are available.

Student Edition Recommended grade level: 6-8. Through the activities in *Biodiversity: Understanding the Variety of Life*, students learn that people make choices that affect the survival of their own and other species. The lessons are grouped under 3 subconcepts of biodiversity: (1) Scientists use various methods to measure earth's biodiversity. (2) The variety of species and habitats changes with time. (3) Knowledge of biodiversity helps people make decisions about the environment.

In this unit, students use a transect to take a sample of species in the schoolyard and discover the variety of species present. They observe soil-dwelling organisms as they explore how conditions in habitats affect diversity. Students classify unknown organisms to discover some difficulties involved in measuring biodiversity. They examine fossils to learn about extinct species. In other activities, students make a model of competition and explore how competition affects biodiversity. They investigate the effects of catastrophes, overpopulation, and pollution on a habitat.

Biodiversity is a 17-lesson unit consisting of approximately 20 class sessions, typically 60 to 95 minutes in duration.

Teacher's Edition The conceptual goals of the unit are presented in the lesson-by-lesson story line in the teacher's guide. Each lesson also includes background information; a complete lesson plan, including suggestions for assessing performance and integrating the curriculum; and a list of the materials required. For each lesson there is also a list of the relevant National Science Education

Standards (developed by the National Research Council) and Project 2061 Benchmarks (developed by the American Association for the Advancement of Science).

Key to Content Standards: 5-8 (see app. C)

UNIFYING CONCEPTS AND PROCESSES: Systems, order, and organization; change, constancy, and measurement.
SCIENCE AS INQUIRY: Abilities necessary to do scientific inquiry; understandings about scientific inquiry.
LIFE SCIENCE: Regulation and behavior; populations and ecosystems; diversity and adaptations of organisms.
SCIENCE AND TECHNOLOGY: Abilities of technological design.
SCIENCE IN PERSONAL AND SOCIAL PERSPECTIVES: Populations, resources, and environments; natural hazards; risks and benefits.
HISTORY AND NATURE OF SCIENCE: History of science.

Prices: Student edition (ISBN 0-590-95536-5), $7.95. Teacher's edition (ISBN 0-590-95463-6), $27.00. Unit, $275.00. Consumable kit, $48.00.
Publisher/supplier: Scholastic.
Materials: Available locally, from commercial suppliers, or in kit.

2.18 Communicable Diseases. Module 2.1. Foundations and Challenges to Encourage Technology-based Science (FACETS) series. Developed by American Chemical Society (Washington, D.C.). Dubuque, Iowa: Kendall/Hunt, 1996.

Program Overview The Foundations and Challenges to Encourage Technology-based Science (FACETS) program consists of 3 series of 8 modules each for grades 6-8. Each module focuses on a topic in the life, earth, or physical sciences. The time

needed to complete FACETS modules varies from 2 to 4 weeks. Each module consists of a student book and a teacher's guide.

Student Edition Recommended grade level: 7. In the module *Communicable Diseases,* students design an educational package on communicable diseases for young children. In preparation for this project, they explore some of the ways in which communicable diseases are spread and controlled. Among the activities, students use various levels of magnification to view and draw small organisms, such as bacteria. They engage in a simulation to explore how communicable diseases can spread and how contact tracing sometimes works in identifying the path of communicable diseases in a population.

In other activities, students explore the conditions under which certain types of bacteria grow best. They also design an experiment to determine which of the materials used to kill bacteria in people's houses actually do so. In the final activity, students use their research findings and other information they have collected to develop the educational package for younger readers.

Communicable Diseases is a 3- to 4-week module divided into 5 activities, which each take between 1 and 5 class periods to complete. A narrative section at the end of the module provides background information for students on cells and infection, bacteria, viruses, and staying healthy.

Teacher's Guide The wraparound teacher's guide includes a unit overview, a time line for completing the module, a materials list, background information, and teaching suggestions.

Key to Content Standards: 5-8 (see app. C)

UNIFYING CONCEPTS AND PROCESSES: Evidence, models, and explanation. **SCIENCE AS INQUIRY:** Abilities necessary to do scientific inquiry; understandings about scientific inquiry. **LIFE SCIENCE:** Structure and function in living systems. **SCIENCE AND TECHNOLOGY:** Abilities of technological design. **SCIENCE IN PERSONAL AND SOCIAL PERSPECTIVES:** Personal health; risks and benefits.

Prices: Student edition (ISBN 0-7872-1468-X), $7.90. Teacher's guide (ISBN 0-7872-1469-8), $14.90. *Publisher/supplier:* Kendall/Hunt. *Materials:* Available locally, or from commercial suppliers.

2.19 **DNA—From Genes to Proteins.** Betty B. Hoskins. Delta Science Module (DSM) series. Hudson, N.H.: Delta Education, 1994.

Program Overview The Delta Science Module (DSM) series has 51 life, physical, and earth science units for grades K-8 that emphasize science concepts, science content, and process skills. The series includes 12 modules for grades 5-6 and 8 modules for grades 6-8. Each requires about 3 to 4 weeks to complete and includes a teacher's guide and materials for a class of 32 students.

Teacher's Guide **Recommended grade level: 7-8.** *DNA—From Genes to Proteins* introduces students to the structure and function of DNA. During the unit, students observe variations in the characteristics of classmates' features—for example, eye

color, tongue roll, or earlobe attachment; they learn that the appearance of visible body features such as skin color depends on the types and amount of proteins in cells; and they observe a microslide image of a cheek cell. Students also construct a model to help them visualize the 3-dimensional structure of a eukaryotic (nucleus-bearing) cell.

In other activities, students use strands of yarn to model DNA; use a 2-dimensional paper model to observe that DNA is made up of paired building blocks with a backbone of sugar and phosphate; model the process of DNA replication; model transcription and translation; and learn the related concepts of genes, chromosomes, and genome. Students also use models to demonstrate DNA mutations at the base-pair level, and they examine the similarities and differences between bacteria, virus particles, and animal cells to see why bacteria and virus particles can be more easily manipulated for genetic engineering. Students learn about recombinant DNA, find out about the technique and applications of DNA fingerprinting, and learn about the Human Genome Project and discuss its implications.

The 13 activities in *DNA—From Genes to Proteins* take 30 to 60 minutes each and can be done by students working individually or in groups. In addition to directions for activities, the teacher's guide provides a module overview, a schedule of activities, objectives for each activity, background information, materials management and preparation tips, sample answers to discussion questions, teaching suggestions,

and reinforcement activities. Also included are reproducible activity sheets for student work and a performance-based assessment. A "connections" feature at the end of each activity provides suggestions for extending or applying the concepts addressed.

Key to Content Standards: 5-8 (see app. C)

UNIFYING CONCEPTS AND PROCESSES: Systems, order, and organization; evidence, models, and explanation. **SCIENCE AS INQUIRY:** Abilities necessary to do scientific inquiry; understandings about scientific inquiry. **LIFE SCIENCE:** Structure and function in living systems; reproduction and heredity. **SCIENCE IN PERSONAL AND SOCIAL PERSPECTIVES:** Science and technology in society. **HISTORY AND NATURE OF SCIENCE:** History of science.

Prices: Teacher's guide (ISBN 0-87504-162-0), $27.95. Kit, $349.00. Refill package, $8.50. *Publisher/supplier:* Delta Education. *Materials:* Available locally, from commercial suppliers, or in kit.

2.20 **Earthworms.** Reprinted with revisions. Robert C. Knott, Kimi Hosoume, and Lincoln Bergman. Great Explorations in Math and Science (GEMS) series. Berkeley, Calif.: Lawrence Hall of Science, 1991.

Program Overview The Great Explorations in Math and Science (GEMS) series includes more than 50 teacher's guides and handbooks for preschool through grade 10. About 35 of these are appropriate for middle school. The series also includes several assembly presenter's guides and exhibit guides. New guides and handbooks continue to be developed, and current titles are revised frequently. The series is designed to teach key science and mathematics concepts through activity-based learning. The time needed to complete GEMS units varies from about 2 to 10 class sessions.

Teacher's Guide **Recommended grade level: 5-7.** The 3 lessons in *Earthworms* provide students an opportunity to develop science process skills while learning about the responses of earthworms to temperature, wetness, and soil compaction. In the first lesson, students observe how the worms move and turn themselves over and how the organism's skin looks and feels. Then students practice locating and counting the pulse rates of earthworms. In the second and third lessons, they measure the pulse rate of earthworms at different temperatures and graph the results. In discussing why earthworms respond as they do, students learn about cold-blooded animals.

Each lesson in *Earthworms* includes a materials list, preparation steps, and directions for activities and discussion. The guide also includes background information, summary outlines for each lesson, reproducible data sheets, and suggestions for related reading.

Key to Content Standards: 5-8 (see app. C)

UNIFYING CONCEPTS AND PROCESSES: Systems, order, and organization; evidence, models, and explanation; change, constancy, and measurement. **SCIENCE AS INQUIRY:** Abilities necessary to do scientific inquiry; understandings about scientific inquiry.

LIFE SCIENCE: Structure and function in living systems; regulation and behavior. **HISTORY AND NATURE OF SCIENCE:** Nature of science.

Price: $9 (ISBN 0-912511-19-2). *Publisher/supplier:* LHS GEMS. *Materials:* Available locally, or from commercial suppliers.

2.21 **Epidemics: Can We Escape Them?** New York Science, Technology and Society Education Project (NYSTEP). Problem-Solving Activities for Middle-Level Science series. Albany, N.Y.: NYSTEP, 1993.

Program Overview The Problem-Solving Activities for Middle-Level Science series consists of 8 stand-alone modules. Each module contains 2 to 6 units focused on technological and/or ethical aspects of issues involving science, technology, and society. The series was designed so that teachers might select modules and units that address local needs and draw on local community resources. A module requires 3 to 8 weeks to complete, depending on the units selected. Supplies and equipment may be required that are not typically part of a school's science inventory.

Teacher's Guide **Recommended grade level: 7-8.** *Epidemics: Can We Escape Them?* introduces students to effects of epidemics in earlier and contemporary societies and to the general scientific principles related to epidemics. During the first of the 2 units in this module, students are introduced to the concept of an epidemic. They develop and conduct a survey to learn about local epidemics in the near or distant past. Then they plot data on the spread of an

epidemic—using actual data from a cholera epidemic in London in the 1840s—as the basis for understanding the concepts of disease transmission, disease identification, and disease control. In the second unit, students use turnip seeds, millet seeds, a common soil plant pathogen, and a variety of procedures to investigate the effects of and to control a common plant disease. In a concluding activity, students try to relate to the problem of disease control what they have learned about epidemics in humans and about a common disease in plants.

Epidemics: Can We Escape Them? is designed to be completed over a 5- to 6-week period. The module's 2 units have a total of 7 activities. Each unit has directions for its activities, a bibliography, interdisciplinary connections (to technology, social studies, language arts, mathematics, health, home and career skills, arts, and foreign languages/cultures), and suggestions for extending classroom activities.

Key to Content Standards: 5-8 (see app. C)

UNIFYING CONCEPTS AND PROCESSES: Evidence, models, and explanation. **SCIENCE AS INQUIRY:** Abilities necessary to do scientific inquiry; understandings about scientific inquiry. **LIFE SCIENCE:** Regulation and behavior. **SCIENCE IN PERSONAL AND SOCIAL PERSPECTIVES:** Risks and benefits; science and technology in society.

Prices: Teacher's guide: In New York State, free with attendance at workshop; outside New York, $7. *Publisher/supplier:* New York Science, Technology and Society Education Project. *Materials:* Available locally, or from commercial suppliers.

2.22 **Food, Energy, and Growth.**
Michigan Science Education
Resources Project. New Directions
Teaching Units. Lansing, Mich.:
Michigan Department of Education,
1992.

Program Overview The New Directions Teaching Units focus on developing scientific literacy and conceptual understanding. They were designed to reflect the ideas about teaching, learning, and curriculum in the Michigan Essential Goals and Objectives for K-12 Science Education, which were developed by the Michigan Science Education Resources Project. Several New Directions Teaching Units can be used with middle school students.

Teacher's Guide **Recommended grade level: 8+.** *Food, Energy, and Growth,* an interdisciplinary unit, helps students understand how our bodies use food for energy, growth, and repair. The unit focuses on the importance of food, considering it at the level of the cell, the system, and the organism. During the unit, students learn what food is made of and why we need it. They explore how the digestive and the circulatory systems work together to distribute food components to the cells. They also look at what goes on inside cells and relate cell respiration and protein synthesis to energy use and growth. Students analyze their diets for nutritional adequacy, and they look at the diets of cultures that do not rely heavily on meat for protein.

In the unit's lab activities, students conduct tests to analyze the composition of foods. They test oatmeal for the presence of sugar and starch, both before and after it has been chewed, to investigate the chemical changes that occur in the mouth as food is mixed with saliva. They make a model representing the small intestine, blood vessels, and cells, and use it in simulating digestion. They also explore how their breathing and pulse rates change with exercise and relate these changes to what is happening when the body uses food for energy.

Food, Energy, and Growth has 15 lessons, which include reading sections, lab activities, and discussion questions. The annotated teacher's edition of the student book contains background information, lab preparation notes, answers to questions posed in the student text, and information about student misconceptions and how to address them. Since the student book has no space for writing answers to questions, this unit works best with the use of student journals.

Key to Content Standards: 5-8 (see app. C)

UNIFYING CONCEPTS AND PROCESSES: Systems, order, and organization; form and function.

SCIENCE AS INQUIRY: Abilities necessary to do scientific inquiry; understandings about scientific inquiry.

PHYSICAL SCIENCE: Properties and changes of properties in matter.

LIFE SCIENCE: Structure and function in living things.

SCIENCE IN PERSONAL AND SOCIAL PERSPECTIVES: Personal health.

Price: $14. Publisher/supplier: Battle Creek Area Math/Science Center. *Materials:* Available locally, or from commercial suppliers.

2.23 **Food from Our Land.** Module 2.5. Foundations and Challenges to Encourage Technology-based Science (FACETS) series. Developed by American Chemical Society (Washington, D.C.). Dubuque, Iowa: Kendall/Hunt, 1996.

Program Overview The Foundations and Challenges to Encourage Technology-based Science (FACETS) program consists of 3 series of 8 modules each for grades 6-8. Each module focuses on a topic in the life, earth, or physical sciences. The time needed to complete FACETS modules varies from 2 to 4 weeks. Each module consists of a student book and a teacher's guide.

Student Edition **Recommended grade level: 7.** In the "mini-farming" module *Food from Our Land,* students investigate the conditions under which crop plants survive and thrive. They learn about the importance of crops as a source of food for people and animals, and they conduct experiments with crops on "modeled soil" that represents farmland.

Among the activities, students conduct research in a local grocery store to determine where locally consumed foods originated. Then they collect information about growing conditions for these crops around the world. Students investigate the basic life requirements of plants—light, carbon dioxide, water, moderate temperature, and nutrients. They set up a series of model farms that have grass or radishes growing on them, to investigate the effects of soil type, water availability, and the spacing of the seeds. In another activity, students conduct a controlled experiment to determine the optimum growing conditions for their grass and radish plants. At the end of the experiment, they "harvest" their crops and determine the yield in terms of "wet mass" and "dry mass." They also research the factors that affect crop yields worldwide. Throughout the module, data collection is important; students depend on the accuracy of one another's data to ensure the validity of the data overall.

Food from Our Land is divided into 6 activities that each take between 2 and 11 class periods to complete. A narrative section at the end of the module provides background information for students on what plants need in order to grow, how plants make food, and how different plant parts are harvested as food.

Teacher's Guide The wraparound teacher's guide includes a unit overview, a time line for completing the module, a materials list, background information, and teaching suggestions.

Key to Content Standards: 5-8 (see app. C)

UNIFYING CONCEPTS AND PROCESSES: Systems, order, and organization. SCIENCE AS INQUIRY: Abilities necessary to do scientific inquiry; understandings about scientific inquiry. LIFE SCIENCE: Structure and function in living systems; populations and ecosystems. SCIENCE IN PERSONAL AND SOCIAL PERSPECTIVES: Populations, resources, and environments; natural hazards.

Prices: Student edition (ISBN 0-7872-1464-7), $7.90. Teacher's guide (ISBN 0-7872-1465-5), $14.90. *Publisher/supplier:* Kendall/Hunt. *Materials:* Available locally, or from commercial suppliers.

2.24 **From Genes to Jeans: An Activity-Based Unit on Genetic Engineering and Agriculture.** John Vogt and Mary Yale. Sacramento, Calif.: California Foundation for Agriculture in the Classroom, 1995.

Program Overview From Genes to Jeans: An Activity-Based Unit on Genetic Engineering and Agriculture is one of many individual instructional units from the California Foundation for Agriculture in the Classroom. This self-contained unit helps students learn about agriculture and its role in American society.

Teacher's Guide **Recommended grade level: 7-8+.** *From Genes to Jeans* introduces students to genetics and genetic engineering. During the unit, students examine and graph personal and family traits. They use Punnett squares to predict possible phenotypic outcomes for a variety of plant breedings. Students also role-play as birds to demonstrate survival of the fittest in a changing environment. In other activities, they build a model of a portion of a DNA molecule from a strawberry and then genetically alter it to produce a hypothetical trait change. They also role-play a design-and-production team as they select an idea for a genetically improved agricultural product and plan how they would market it. Agricultural examples are used throughout the unit.

Divided into 5 sequential lessons, *From Genes to Jeans* takes 20 to 22 class periods to complete. Each lesson includes background information for the teacher, procedures, and reproducible student worksheets. A

short list of resources and references for the teacher is also included.

Key to Content Standards: 5-8 (see app. C)

UNIFYING CONCEPTS AND PROCESSES: Evidence, models, and explanation; evolution and equilibrium. SCIENCE AS INQUIRY: Abilities necessary to do scientific inquiry; understandings about scientific inquiry. LIFE SCIENCE: Structure and function in living systems; reproduction and heredity; diversity and adaptations of organisms. SCIENCE AND TECHNOLOGY: Understandings about science and technology. SCIENCE IN PERSONAL AND SOCIAL PERSPECTIVES: Risks and benefits; science and technology in society.

Price: $8. *Publisher/supplier:* California Foundation for Agriculture in the Classroom. *Materials:* Available locally, or from commercial suppliers.

2.25 **Fungi—Small Wonders.** Delta Science Module (DSM) series. Hudson, N.H.: Delta Education, 1994.

Program Overview The Delta Science Module (DSM) series has 51 life, physical, and earth science units for grades K-8 that emphasize science concepts, science content, and process skills. The series includes 12 modules for grades 5-6 and 8 modules for grades 6-8. Each requires about 3 to 4 weeks to complete and includes a teacher's guide and materials for a class of 32 students.

Teacher's Guide **Recommended grade level: 5-7.** *Fungi—Small Wonders* introduces students to the structure and physiology of fungi. During the module, students identify the structures of seed plants and discuss their functions; they examine a mushroom and some bread mold and compare them to seed plants; and they compare and contrast spores and seeds and make spore prints of mushrooms. Students also compare the growth rate of 2 yeast populations, 1 supplied with food and 1 without; collect and interpret data on mold cultures grown in the classroom; and experiment to observe the effects of temperature on yeast budding.

In other activities, students attempt to extract chlorophyll from seed plants and fungi and confirm that green seed plants contain chlorophyll but fungi do not. They learn about fermentation, and they confirm the presence of carbon dioxide in the gas produced from an actively growing yeast culture. Students also make pretzel dough as an example of how yeast is used in the production of breads, test different substances for their ability to retard fungal growth, and research the problems and uses of fungi.

The 12 activities in *Fungi—Small Wonders* are organized to be completed sequentially over 3 to 4 weeks, and generally take between 30 and 60 minutes each. In addition to directions for activities, the teacher's guide provides a module overview, objectives for each activity, a schedule of activities, background information, materials management and preparation tips, sample answers to discussion questions, teaching suggestions, and reinforcement activities. Reproducible activity sheets for student work and a performance-based assessment are also included. A "connections" feature at the end of each activity provides suggestions for extending or applying the concepts addressed.

Key to Content Standards: 5-8 (see app. C)

UNIFYING CONCEPTS AND PROCESSES: Systems, order, and organization; form and function.
SCIENCE AS INQUIRY: Abilities necessary to do scientific inquiry; understandings about scientific inquiry.

LIFE SCIENCE: Structure and function in living systems; reproduction and heredity; regulation and behavior; populations and ecosystems.
SCIENCE IN PERSONAL AND SOCIAL PERSPECTIVES: Risks and benefits.

Prices: Teacher's guide (ISBN 0-87504-109-4), $27.95. Kit, $249.00. Refill package, $45.00. *Publisher/supplier:* Delta Education. *Materials:* Available locally, from commercial suppliers, or in kit.

2.26 Growing Older. Module 2.2. Foundations and Challenges to Encourage Technology-based Science (FACETS) series. Developed by American Chemical Society (Washington, D.C.). Dubuque, Iowa: Kendall/Hunt, 1996.

Program Overview The Foundations and Challenges to Encourage Technology-based Science (FACETS) program consists of 3 series of 8 modules each for grades 6-8. Each module focuses on a topic in the life, earth, or physical sciences. The time needed to complete FACETS modules varies from 2 to 4 weeks. Each module consists of a student book and a teacher's guide.

Student Edition **Recommended grade level: 7.** In *Growing Older,* students explore some of the biological and sociological issues involved with aging. They learn what happens to human body cells as people grow older, and they find out what effect this change has on the body's senses, mobility, memory, and other macroscopic manifestations of age. Among the activities, for example, students engage in a simulation to see what it is like to have senses such as eyesight and hearing diminished. They examine the attitudes that people can have toward the elderly and

people with disabilities. They play a memory game and think about strategies that people can use to help failing memories. Students also model what happens when arteries become blocked with cholesterol and look at the effects of lifestyles on the risks of getting heart disease.

In the unit's final activity, students develop a public relations piece that provides advice on how people of all ages can prepare for a healthy older life. In many of the activities, students are encouraged to talk with an older person to obtain information. Scenarios are presented that should help students be aware of how they relate to older persons.

Growing Older is a 3-week module divided into 6 activities, which each take between 1 and 5 class periods to complete. A narrative section at the end of the module provides background information for students on cells and aging, how memory works, and society and aging.

Teacher's Guide The wraparound teacher's guide includes a unit overview, a time line for completing the module, a materials list, background information, and teaching suggestions.

Key to Content Standards: 5-8 (see app. C)

UNIFYING CONCEPTS AND PROCESSES: Systems, order, and organization; change, constancy, and measurement.
SCIENCE AS INQUIRY: Abilities necessary to do scientific inquiry; understandings about scientific inquiry.
LIFE SCIENCE: Regulation and behavior.
SCIENCE IN PERSONAL AND SOCIAL PERSPECTIVES: Personal health.

Prices: Student edition (ISBN 0-7872-1470-1), $7.90. Teacher's guide (ISBN 0-7872-1471-X), $14.90. *Publisher/supplier:* Kendall/Hunt. *Materials:* Available locally, or from commercial suppliers.

2.27 How Much Is Too Much? How Little Is Too Little? Factors That Affect Plant Growth. Pamela Emery. Sacramento, Calif.: California Foundation for Agriculture in the Classroom, 1993.

Program Overview *How Much Is Too Much? How Little Is Too Little? Factors That Affect Plant Growth* is one of many individual instructional units from the California Foundation for Agriculture in the Classroom. This self-contained unit helps students learn about agriculture and its role in American society.

Teacher's Guide **Recommended grade level: 6-7.** In this 6- to 8-week unit on factors that affect plant growth, students learn about the nutrients required for plants, where the nutrients come from, and the effects of factors such as soil type and fertilizers on plant growth. During the activities, they learn the 6 basic parts of plants and their functions, they analyze soil samples, and they make a nutrient solution from manure. They also design an experiment to find out if too many nutrients can harm or kill a plant, analyze the contents of fertilizers, and learn to diagnose plant illnesses. Finally, students apply their knowledge to vote on mock ballot propositions that relate to agricultural and urban water issues in a community. Some of the activities require that teachers plant and grow seeds away from the classroom for 2 to 3 weeks.

Divided into 11 lessons, *How Much Is Too Much? How Little Is Too Little?* is composed of both classroom activities and reading and writing exercises. Activities can be completed in a variety of sequences. Each lesson includes background information, a materials list, proce-

dures, reproducible student worksheets, and extensions. A teacher resource section provides management tips, answers to commonly asked questions, additional extension activities, references, and a list of organizations and companies such as agricultural bookstores.

Key to Content Standards: 5-8 (see app. C)

UNIFYING CONCEPTS AND PROCESSES: Systems, order, and organization; form and function.
SCIENCE AS INQUIRY: Abilities necessary to do scientific inquiry; understandings about scientific inquiry.
LIFE SCIENCE: Structure and function in living systems.

Price: $8. *Publisher/supplier:* California Foundation for Agriculture in the Classroom. *Materials:* Available locally.

2.28 The Human Body: How Can I Maintain and Care for Myself? New York Science, Technology and Society Education Project (NYSTEP). Problem-Solving Activities for Middle-Level Science series. Albany, N.Y.: NYSTEP, 1995.

Program Overview The Problem-Solving Activities for Middle-Level Science series consists of 8 stand-alone modules. Each module contains 2 to 6 units focused on technological and/or ethical aspects of issues involving science, technology, and society. The series was designed so that teachers might select modules and units that address local needs and draw on local community resources. A module requires 3 to 8 weeks to complete, depending on the units selected. Supplies and equipment may be required that are not typically part of a school's science inventory.

Teacher's Guide **Recommended grade level: 7-8.** *The Human Body* introduces students to basic human biology and helps them learn how their own informed choices can impact their health and longevity. During the module, students research the structure and systems of the human body, determining which parts and functions can be replaced by technological devices. They work with models of the genetic code and chromosomes to understand how each person is unique. They construct growth curves for themselves and compare them to generalized growth curves. Students also investigate how the number of hours of sleep they get can affect their behavior; design and carry out experiments to see how certain substances protect skin from the harmful effects of sunlight; and participate in a student-run health fair. Several of the activities allow students to design experiments as well as do statistics (mean, median, mode, and range).

Designed to serve either as a starting point or culmination for a study of the body, the unit is built around the idea that each student plans and develops a personal manual of information about caring for his or her body. As students complete the 9 activities in the unit, they gain the information and skills they need to complete their manual.

The Human Body is divided into 3 units; the first and third units are intended to be required, and the second is intended as a set of optional activities. Each unit has directions for its activities, a bibliography, interdisciplinary connections (to technology, social studies, language arts, mathematics, health, home and career skills, arts, and foreign languages/culture), and suggestions for extensions. A list of resources for the study of adolescence and the human body also is provided.

Key to Content Standards: 5-8 (see app. C)

UNIFYING CONCEPTS AND PROCESSES: Systems, order, and organization; change, constancy, and measurement; form and function.

SCIENCE AS INQUIRY: Abilities necessary to do scientific inquiry; understandings about scientific inquiry.

LIFE SCIENCE: Structure and function in living systems; reproduction and heredity; regulation and behavior.

SCIENCE AND TECHNOLOGY: Understandings about science and technology.

SCIENCE IN PERSONAL AND SOCIAL PERSPECTIVES: Personal health; risks and benefits.

Prices: Teacher's guide: In New York State, free with attendance at workshop; outside New York, $7. *Publisher/supplier:* New York Science, Technology and Society Education Project. *Materials:* Available locally, or from commercial suppliers.

2.29 **Hydroponic Instructional Package.** Stephen Butz and Andrew Fagan. Ithaca, N.Y.: Cornell Instructional Materials Service, 1994.

Program Overview The *Hydroponic Instructional Package* introduces students to the history, science, and technology of hydroponics. The unit is intended to be used in conjunction with and as a supplement to textbooks in general science, introductory plant science, and technology for grades 7 through 9.

Teacher's Guide **Recommended grade level: 7-8+.** The *Hydroponic Instructional Package* introduces students to hydroponics—what it is, how it works, and what role it might play in

the future of agricultural production. During the unit, students read about and discuss important points in the history and development of hydroponics. They also review the requirements of plant growth, and they construct a replica of an Aztec chinampas (a floating island) and explain how it works.

In other activities, students construct a wick hydroponic system, build a simple subaeration hydroponic unit, and observe the growth of plants in water with and without nutrients. They prepare a nutrient solution for use in a hydroponic system and monitor the pH and nutrient content of the solution. They also discuss the operation of the 7 basic hydroponic systems (subaeration, wick system, aeroponics, gravity-flow feed, nutrient-flow technique, drip system, aquaponics). They discover the importance of different growing mediums and artificial pollination in a hydroponic system, and they explore the advantages and disadvantages of using a hydroponic system for agricultural production. In the final activity, students design, and may construct, a custom hydroponic system for the classroom.

The complete instructional package for this 11-lesson unit includes a teacher's guide with color overhead transparencies, a student workbook, and a "hydrokit" for building hydroponic gardens in 3 of the lessons. The workbook and hydrokit are also available separately.

Key to Content Standards: 5-8 (see app. C)

UNIFYING CONCEPTS AND PROCESSES: Evidence, models, and explanation; form and function.

SCIENCE AS INQUIRY: Abilities necessary to do scientific inquiry; understandings about scientific inquiry.

LIFE SCIENCE: Structure and function in living systems.

SCIENCE AND TECHNOLOGY: Understandings about science and technology.

SCIENCE IN PERSONAL AND SOCIAL PERSPECTIVES: Science and technology in society.

HISTORY AND NATURE OF SCIENCE: History of science.

Prices: Teacher's guide, $45.00. Student workbook, $5.50. Complete package, $70.00. Hydrokit, $22.50. *Publisher/supplier:* Cornell Instructional Materials Service. *Materials:* Available locally, from commercial suppliers, or in kit.

2.30 **The Interrelationships of Soil, Water and Fertilizers and How They Affect Plant Growth.** Pamela Emery. Sacramento, Calif.: California Foundation for Agriculture in the Classroom, 1993.

Program Overview The *Interrelationships of Soil, Water and Fertilizers and How They Affect Plant Growth* is one of many individual instructional units from the California Foundation for Agriculture in the Classroom. This self-contained unit helps students learn about agriculture and its role in American society.

Teacher's Guide **Recommended grade level: 8+.** In this unit, students learn about soils, nutrient requirements of plants, and the complexity of human interactions with the environment in a community that has limited water resources. Through the unit's experiments, students learn to use the scientific method to find out how water quality, soil quality, fertilizer content, and timing of fertilizer application affect plant growth. In the activities, they learn, for example, how to read a fertilizer label, they become familiar with the meaning of the terms "parts per million" and "parts per billion," and they learn about the mechanics of water-flow and of pollution in groundwater.

The unit's 4 team experiments and 6 other activities, which can be done in a variety of sequences, are designed to be completed in 7 to 9 weeks and to be incorporated into the botany, earth science, or chemistry units of a general science class, or, they can be used in horticulture, earth science, and biology classes.

Each activity and experiment contains a list of materials, background information, procedures, extensions or variations, and reproducible student worksheets, and reading assignments. A teacher resource section provides management tips, answers to commonly asked questions, additional extension activities, references, and a list of organizations and companies such as agricultural bookstores.

Key to Content Standards: 5-8 (see app. C)

UNIFYING CONCEPTS AND PROCESSES: Systems, order, and organization. **SCIENCE AS INQUIRY:** Abilities necessary to do scientific inquiry; understandings about scientific inquiry. **LIFE SCIENCE:** Structure and function in living systems; regulation and behavior; populations and ecosystems. **EARTH AND SPACE SCIENCE:** Structure of the earth system. **SCIENCE AND TECHNOLOGY:** Understandings about science and technology. **SCIENCE IN PERSONAL AND SOCIAL PERSPECTIVES:** Populations, resources, and environments.

Price: $8. *Publisher/supplier:* California Foundation for Agriculture in the Classroom. *Materials:* Available locally.

2.31 **An Introduction to Biotechnology: Book 2.** 2nd ed. Biotechnology series. Developed by Biotechnology Education Project of St. Louis Mathematics and Science Education Center (St. Louis, Mo.). Dubuque, Iowa: Kendall/Hunt, 1995.

Program Overview The Biotechnology series consists of 3 units—1 each for grades 5-6, 7-8, and 9-12. These volumes—*An Introduction to Biotechnology,* Book 1, Book 2, and Book 3—are designed to introduce teachers and students to the science of biotechnology through hands-on activities and analysis.

Teacher's Guide **Recommended grade level: 8+.** *An Introduction to Biotechnology: Book 2* is structured around 5 basic themes: (1) technology, (2) proteins, (3) DNA and protein synthesis, (4) cloning, and (5) social impact. Each lesson teaches a basic concept—such as how DNA works as a code. Among the activities in the unit, students classify objects either as products of technology or as natural objects. They test food samples for the presence of protein. They spool DNA from an aqueous solution of salmon sperm, and they use paper models to transcribe RNA from DNA. Students also analyze problems in fictional situations that involve biotechnology, and, in a final activity, they play a "build-a-bacteria" game during which they review knowledge acquired in previous lessons.

This wire-bound unit includes 16 lessons; each can generally be taught in a 45-minute class period, although 3 lessons may require more class time. The reproducible student pages contain directions for the activities, readings, and laboratory lessons. The teacher's pages contain lesson overviews, an indication of the time

required, lists of materials, student objectives, background information, lesson and laboratory preparation and procedures, extension activities, references and resources, and answer keys to student worksheets. Three appendixes contain additional extension activities, educational strategies and resources, and laboratory resources and notes.

Key to Content Standards: 5-8 (see app. C)

UNIFYING CONCEPTS AND PROCESSES: Evidence, models, and explanation. **SCIENCE AS INQUIRY:** Abilities necessary to do scientific inquiry; understandings about scientific inquiry. **LIFE SCIENCE:** Structure and function in living systems; reproduction and heredity. **SCIENCE AND TECHNOLOGY:** Understandings about science and technology. **SCIENCE IN PERSONAL AND SOCIAL PERSPECTIVES:** Risks and benefits; science and technology in society.

Price: $49.90 (ISBN 0-7872-1639-9). *Publisher/supplier:* Kendall/Hunt. *Materials:* Available locally, or from commercial suppliers.

2.32 **Keeping Fit.** Module 1.1. Foundations and Challenges to Encourage Technology-based Science (FACETS) series. Developed by American Chemical Society (Washington, D.C.). Dubuque, Iowa: Kendall/Hunt, 1996.

Program Overview The Foundations and Challenges to Encourage Technology-based Science (FACETS) program consists of 3 series of 8 modules each for grades 6-8. Each module focuses on a topic in the life, earth, or physical sciences. The time needed to complete FACETS modules varies from 2 to 4 weeks. Each module consists of a student book and a teacher's guide.

Student Edition Recommended grade level: 6. In the 2-week module *Keeping Fit,* students consider the importance of keeping fit by investigating some of the effects that exercise has on their own heart rates and breathing rates and by learning about the human body's circulatory and respiratory systems. The activities include collecting examples of how exercise and fitness are dealt with in the mass media. Students also measure their classmates' heart rates both before and after 4 different kinds of exercises—stair-stepping, jumping rope, sit-ups, and jumping jacks. Then they record their classmates' breathing rates both before and after the same 4 exercises, and they record and then analyze what happens to their heart rates when they repeat an exercise daily for a week. In other activities, students read a research report on the state of fitness in young people, and they survey students in their school about their attitudes and knowledge regarding fitness. At the end of the unit, students communicate the results of their investigations to others.

Keeping Fit is a 3- to 4-week module divided into 8 activities, which each take between 2 and 3 class periods to complete. A narrative section at the end of the module provides brief background information for students on human systems.

Teacher's Guide The wraparound teacher's guide includes a unit overview, a time line for completing the module, a materials list, background information, and teaching suggestions.

Key to Content Standards: 5-8 (see app. C)

UNIFYING CONCEPTS AND PROCESSES: Systems, order, and organization; change, constancy, and measurement.

SCIENCE AS INQUIRY: Abilities necessary to do scientific inquiry; understandings about scientific inquiry.
LIFE SCIENCE: Structure and function in living systems.
SCIENCE IN PERSONAL AND SOCIAL PERSPECTIVES: Personal health.

Prices: Student edition (ISBN 0-7872-1439-6), $7.90. Teacher's guide (ISBN 0-7872-1440-X), $14.90.
Publisher/supplier: Kendall/Hunt.
Materials: Available locally, or from commercial suppliers.

2.33 **Life Changes through Time.** Mary Atwater, Prentice Baptiste, Lucy Daniel, and others. Unit 41. Macmillan/McGraw-Hill Science series. New York, N.Y.: Macmillan/McGraw-Hill School Publishing, 1995.

Program Overview The Macmillan/McGraw-Hill Science series is a comprehensive, activity-based, K-8 science curriculum made up of 42 stand-alone units, 18 of which are designed for grades 6-8. The series is constructed around 7 major themes: (1) systems and interactions, (2) scale and structure, (3) stability, (4) energy, (5) evolution, (6) patterns of change, and (7) models. The subject of each unit—for example, life changes through time—is presented from the perspective of one or more of these themes. One theme is designated as the "major theme" for a unit, and any others are treated as "related themes." For each unit, a wide range of materials, including some optional components, is available for students and teachers.

Student Edition Recommended grade level: 8. *Life Changes through Time* contains 5 lessons that introduce

students to the concept of evolution, with each lesson focusing on a particular aspect of the processes that change organisms over time. While models and examples are regularly provided, the evidence supporting these processes is the main focus of this unit. The organizing themes for the unit are evolution (major theme), patterns of change (related theme), and scale and structure (related theme).

Each of the 5 lessons in the unit typically requires 6 days to complete. During the unit, students learn about inherited characteristics and how these characteristics and their variations are passed from generation to generation. They also observe the differences between mitosis and meiosis, and they learn about DNA structure. Students study natural selection, mutation, adaptation, and speciation; and they learn the different strategies that scientists use to study the evidence and processes of evolution.

Sample activities include predicting and then confirming the ratio of color of kernels (that is, the ratio of purple to white kernels) in corn bred from 2 ears of pure purple corn. Students also conduct a classroom genetics survey to observe and record students' inherited characteristics. They observe the difference between mitosis and meiosis by looking at onion tip cells and lily anther cells. They also build a model of DNA, and they work with imaginary fossils (actually, buttons) to develop a model of evolution.

Each lesson contains narrative information and a series of sequential, hands-on activities—such as an introductory "minds-on" activity, short "try this" activities, and a longer "explore" activity. The unit's 5 "explore activities," which are lab activities, each take a class period to complete. Students use activity logs to record ideas, observations, and results.

Special unit features include curriculum links to language arts, literature, mathematics, music, and art; information about science careers; and narrative sections highlighting science, technology, and society connections.

Teacher's Planning Guide The teacher's planning guide, a spiral-bound, wraparound edition, provides information and strategies for teaching the 5 lessons in the student edition. Each lesson is introduced by a 4-page section that offers background information, a lesson-planning guide, and assessment options. Marginal notes on the lesson pages provide discussion ideas, tips on meeting individual needs, suggestions for addressing misconceptions, assessment ideas, and curriculum connections.

Program Resources and Support Materials A wide range of materials, including some optional components, is available. Examples include consumable and nonconsumable activity materials; audio- and videotapes; interactive videodiscs; color transparencies; assessment materials; a teacher anthology of short stories, poems, fingerplays, and songs; trade books; teacher resource masters; activity cards; activity logs; a staff development package; concept summaries and glossaries for students acquiring English; and software with problem-solving simulations for students.

Key to Content Standards: 5-8 (see app. C)

UNIFYING CONCEPTS AND PROCESSES: Systems, order, and organization; evidence, models, and explanation; evolution and equilibrium; form and function.

SCIENCE AS INQUIRY: Abilities necessary to do scientific inquiry; understandings about scientific inquiry.
LIFE SCIENCE: Structure and function in living systems; reproduction and heredity; diversity and adaptations of organisms.
HISTORY AND NATURE OF SCIENCE: Nature of science; history of science.

Prices: Student edition (ISBN 0-02-276141-1), $7.06. Teacher's planning guide (ISBN 0-02-276089-X), $55.98. Unit package, $115.83. Activity materials kit, $95.00. (Contact publisher/supplier for complete price and ordering information.) *Publisher/supplier:* McGraw-Hill. *Materials:* Available locally, from commercial suppliers, or in kit.

2.34 **The Lives of Plants.** Michigan Science Education Resources Project. New Directions Teaching Units. Lansing, Mich.: Michigan Department of Education, 1993.

Program Overview The New Directions Teaching Units focus on developing scientific literacy and conceptual understanding. They were designed to reflect the ideas about teaching, learning, and curriculum in the Michigan Essential Goals and Objectives for K-12 Science Education, which were developed by the Michigan Science Education Resources Project. Several New Directions Teaching Units can be used with middle school students.

Teacher's Guide Recommended grade level: 5-7. *The Lives of Plants* helps students develop an understanding of how plants transform raw materials and sunlight into food for themselves and for people. In the first cluster of lessons, students explore their prior knowledge of plants, particularly

about how plants obtain the energy and materials they need to grow and live. Students record their ideas about plants and light in a journal; plan and begin projects to observe plants, such as the growth of an amaryllis bulb or a potato; explore a solar-powered device as a model for the energy transformations in a leaf; and attempt to make sugar from water and carbon dioxide, outside of a living plant.

Then, in the second cluster of lessons, students explore the microscopic structure of plants through a radio play about a bean plant and through work with models and microscopes. They perform scenes from the radio play as each lesson begins, and they make drawings of cellular plant structures and write synopses about plants based on scenes in the radio play. They also use hand lenses and microscopes to look at plant leaves; they conduct an experiment to find out if a plant is photosynthesizing under water; and they view *Green Power*—a video about photosynthesis and global warming.

The Lives of Plants has 18 lessons and takes about 35 class sessions to complete. The teacher's guide contains background information; lab preparation notes; answers to questions posed in the unit's separate, reproducible student pages; and information about student misconceptions and how to address them.

An appendix includes lists of resources, information on cooperative learning, instructions for planting seeds and caring for plants, and several optional lessons.

Key to Content Standards: 5-8 (see app. C)

UNIFYING CONCEPTS AND PROCESSES: Systems, order, and organization; form and function.
SCIENCE AS INQUIRY: Abilities necessary to do scientific inquiry; understandings about scientific inquiry.

PHYSICAL SCIENCE: Transfer of energy. **LIFE SCIENCE:** Structure and function in living systems.

Prices: Teacher's guide, $18. Video, $10. *Publisher/supplier:* Battle Creek Area Math/Science Center. *Materials:* Available locally, or from commercial suppliers.

2.35 Lyme Disease: A Sourcebook for Teaching about a Major Environmental Health Problem. Norman D. Anderson and Harriett S. Stubbs. Changes in the Environment Series. Dubuque, Iowa: Kendall/Hunt, 1996.

Program Overview The Changes in the Environment Series was produced as part of the GLOBE-NET Project, a partnership of science teachers and research scientists working on aspects of global change. The scientists make presentations and lead visits to laboratories and field sites, and the teachers use this information to develop activities and instructional materials for grades 4-12.

Teacher's Guide **Recommended grade level: 7-8+.** This sourcebook contains background information, 10 classroom activities, and other resources useful in teaching about Lyme disease, which is caused by a spiral-shaped bacterium transmitted by infected ticks. The activities in *Lyme Disease* employ a number of teaching strategies. For example, students map the incidence of Lyme disease in the United States in 1993. They model natural selection in a population of ticks. They compare the symptoms of Lyme disease with those of more familiar diseases, such as the flu, strep throat, and chicken pox. Students also explore the relationship between Lyme disease and urbanization by examining data from an epidemic that occurred outside a nature preserve in Massachusetts.

Lyme Disease provides basic information needed to minimize the risk of acquiring the disease. Included are questions frequently asked about it, and a Lyme disease time line describing important events in researchers' attempts to understand the disease and its treatment and prevention.

The sourcebook provides a glossary and a conceptual outline for teaching about Lyme disease. Appendixes supply references, teaching resources, assessments, blackline masters for transparencies, and a list of organizations involved in education and research on the disease.

Key to Content Standards: 5-8 (see app. C)

UNIFYING CONCEPTS AND PROCESSES: Evidence, models, and explanation. **SCIENCE AS INQUIRY:** Abilities necessary to do scientific inquiry; understandings about scientific inquiry. **LIFE SCIENCE:** Populations and ecosystems. **HISTORY AND NATURE OF SCIENCE:** Nature of science; history of science.

Price: $22.90 (ISBN 0-7872-1508-2). *Publisher/supplier:* Kendall/Hunt. *Materials:* Available locally.

2.36 Mapping Animal Movements. Reprinted with revisions. Katharine Barrett. Great Explorations in Math and Science (GEMS) series. Berkeley, Calif.: Lawrence Hall of Science, 1992.

Program Overview The Great Explorations in Math and Science (GEMS) series includes more than 50 teacher's guides and handbooks for preschool through grade 10. About 35 of these are appropriate for middle school. The series also includes several assembly presenter's guides and exhibit guides. New guides and handbooks continue to be developed, and current titles are revised frequently. The series is designed to teach key science and mathematics concepts through activity-based learning. The time needed to complete GEMS units varies from about 2 to 10 class sessions.

Teacher's Guide **Recommended grade level: 5-8+.** In *Mapping Animal Movements*, students carry out hands-on experiences with animals such as crickets and hamsters, and learn research techniques used by field biologists to study animal behavior. Students practice a sampling system, using the classroom as a habitat. They use this skill to observe, track, map, graph, and identify patterns in the movements of a variety of animals. Students first observe the animals in an empty container; adding food and shelter to the container, they compare the animals' movements before and after their environment changes.

Mapping Animal Movements includes easy-to-follow lesson plans for each of the 4 activities, which require 30 to 45 minutes each; suggestions for the care and handling of animals; and reproducible student data sheets. Each lesson plan includes an overview, background information, a list of materials, and detailed instructions for preparation and for conducting the activity.

Key to Content Standards: 5-8 (see app. C)

UNIFYING CONCEPTS AND PROCESSES: Systems, order, and organization; change, constancy, and measurement. **SCIENCE AS INQUIRY:** Abilities necessary to do scientific inquiry; understandings about scientific inquiry. **LIFE SCIENCE:** Regulation and behavior. **HISTORY AND NATURE OF SCIENCE:** Nature of science.

Price: $10.50 (ISBN 0-912511-60-5). *Publisher/supplier:* LHS GEMS. *Materials:* Available locally, or from commercial suppliers.

2.37 **Mapping Fish Habitats.** Reprinted with revisions. Katharine Barrett and Cary I. Sneider. Great Explorations in Math and Science (GEMS) series. Berkeley, Calif.: Lawrence Hall of Science, 1992.

Program Overview The Great Explorations in Math and Science (GEMS) series includes more than 50 teacher's guides and handbooks for preschool through grade 10. About 35 of these are appropriate for middle school. The series also includes several assembly presenter's guides and exhibit guides. New guides and handbooks continue to be developed, and current titles are revised frequently. The series is designed to teach key science and mathematics concepts through activity-based learning. The time needed to complete GEMS units varies from about 2 to 10 class sessions.

Teacher's Guide **Recommended grade level: 6-8+.** In *Mapping Fish Habitats*, students discover that fish have behavioral differences that provide clues about what various species need in order to survive and how they interact with each other and their environment. Students set up a fish tank, map fish movements using systematic sampling methods, identify the home range of the fish, and then plan and conduct experiments to determine the effects of an environmental change on the home ranges.

Mapping Fish Habitats includes useful information about setting up an aquarium and interesting facts about fish, as well as specific lesson plans for each of the 4 activities in this unit. Each activity requires a 30- to 45-minute session plus time for daily observations. An overview, a list of materials, and step-by-step instructions for preparing and conducting the lesson are included for each activity.

Key to Content Standards: 5-8 (see app. C)

UNIFYING CONCEPTS AND PROCESSES: Systems, order, and organization; change, constancy, and measurement. **SCIENCE AS INQUIRY:** Abilities necessary to do scientific inquiry; understandings about scientific inquiry. **LIFE SCIENCE:** Regulation and behavior; populations and ecosystems. **HISTORY AND NATURE OF SCIENCE:** Nature of science.

Price: $10.50 (ISBN 0-912511-61-3). *Publisher/supplier:* LHS GEMS. *Materials:* Available locally, or from commercial suppliers.

2.38 **Outbreak!** Field-trial ed. Russell G. Wright. Event-Based Science series. Menlo Park, Calif.: Innovative Learning Publications, 1997.

Program Overview The Event-Based Science series is a program for middle school students in grades 6-9. Each module tells the story of a real event—such as the 1995 outbreak of the Ebola virus in Zaire—through reprinted newspaper articles and personal interviews; sections of background information explain relevant scientific concepts. A central task related to the module's story line leads to a final product that allows students to apply the science they have learned. For each module, a student book, teacher's guide, and videotape and/or videodisc is available.

Student Edition **Recommended grade level: 7-8.** *Outbreak!* uses the 1995 outbreak of the Ebola virus in Zaire as the event on which to base this unit to help students learn about disease prevention and control. Included are topics such as bacteria and viruses, immunity, and epidemiology. Students begin the module by watching television news coverage and reading newspaper accounts about the outbreak of the deadly virus in Kikwit, Zaire. They are told that their major task during the module will be to decide, in 4-member teams, how to prevent the disturbing spread of a very serious illness in a community. The module's 11 activities provide students with the background information and skills they need for this task.

Among the activities, for example, students participate in a discussion on how diseases can be transmitted. They examine food and water samples under a microscope and identify the organisms present, and they investigate the effects of different medicines on pathogens. Students also name bacteria using a dichotomous key, they use patient profiles to track a disease affecting a neighborhood, and they design and construct a table and graphs to show the rapid growth of a single-cell organism and its impact on a community.

The module provides short narratives on communicable diseases, such as tuberculosis, chronic malaria, and viral pneumonia; copies of actual newspaper articles; explanatory graphics; and profiles of professionals—such as a health department investigator, a physician, and a school principal—who might be involved in helping a community protect itself from the spread of a disease. Middle school students who experienced the Ebola outbreak in Zaire tell their stories throughout the module. Other information that students need to complete the task must be obtained from encyclopedias, textbooks, films, magazines, and other sources they can find. The unit culminates with team reports and the selection of a course of action. Teachers may want to supplement or exchange the activities in the unit depending on the latest "real event" in the news.

Teacher's Edition The teacher's guide provides brief overview information on the module's structure and activities. It includes suggestions for guiding specific student activities, a scoring rubric for a performance assessment, and a list of resources.

Key to Content Standards: 5-8 (see app. C)

UNIFYING CONCEPTS AND PROCESSES: Evidence, models, and explanation. **SCIENCE AS INQUIRY:** Abilities necessary to do scientific inquiry; understandings about scientific inquiry. **LIFE SCIENCE:** Structure and function in living systems. **SCIENCE AND TECHNOLOGY:** Understandings about science and technology. **SCIENCE IN PERSONAL AND SOCIAL PERSPECTIVES:** Personal health. **HISTORY AND NATURE OF SCIENCE:** Nature of science.

Prices: Student edition (ISBN 0-201-49750-6), $7.95. Teacher's edition, with video, $18.00. Classroom package, $115.00. *Publisher/supplier:* Addison-Wesley/Longman. *Materials:* Available locally.

2.39 Plants in Our World. Katy Goldner. Delta Science Module (DSM) series. Hudson, N.H.: Delta Education, 1994.

Program Overview The Delta Science Module (DSM) series has 51 life, physical, and earth science units for grades K-8 that emphasize science concepts, science content, and process skills. The series includes 12 modules for grades 5-6 and 8 modules for grades 6-8. Each requires about 3 to 4 weeks to complete and includes a teacher's guide and materials for a class of 32 students.

Teacher's Guide **Recommended grade level: 6-8.** *Plants in Our World* helps students learn what plants need in order to grow, what they produce, and why they are important to life on earth. During the module, students observe microslide images of real plant and animal cells and identify their major parts. They also observe the structure of woody and nonwoody stems and identify the functions of xylem and phloem, compare the growth of seedlings in light and dark and wet and dry conditions, and observe stomata and experiment with transpiration. Students demonstrate that green plants take in carbon dioxide and produce oxygen in the presence of light. They use paper chromatography to separate pigments contained in extracts of anacharis leaves and identify the green pigment as chlorophyll.

In other activities, students use Lugol's solution to demonstrate that plants produce glucose—which is stored as starch—in the presence of light, and demonstrate that glucose is only produced when chlorophyll is present. They use bromthymol blue to show that green plants give off and take in carbon dioxide during the processes of cellular respiration and photosynthesis, respectively. They also investigate the variety of plants that contain carbohydrates, and they explore the variety of ways in which people use plants and plant-based materials, such as clothes, rubber bands, and rope.

The 12 activities in *Plants in Our World* are organized to be completed sequentially over 3 to 4 weeks; they take between 30 and 60 minutes each, and can be done by students working individually or in groups. In addition to directions for activities, the teacher's guide provides a module overview, objectives for each activity, background information, materials management and preparation tips, sample answers to discussion questions, teaching suggestions, and reinforcement activities. Reproducible activity sheets for student work and a performance-based assessment are also included. A "connections" feature at the end of each activity provides suggestions for extending or applying the concepts addressed.

Key to Content Standards: 5-8 (see app. C)

UNIFYING CONCEPTS AND PROCESSES: Systems, order, and organization; form and function. **SCIENCE AS INQUIRY:** Abilities necessary to do scientific inquiry; understandings about scientific inquiry. **PHYSICAL SCIENCE:** Transfer of energy. **LIFE SCIENCE:** Structure and function in living systems.

Prices: Teacher's guide (ISBN 0-87504-170-1), $27.95. Kit, $379.00. Refill package, $115.00. *Publisher/supplier:* Delta Education. *Materials:* Available locally, from commercial suppliers, or in kit.

2.40 Pond Life. Delta Science Module (DSM) series. Hudson, N.H.: Delta Education, 1994.

Program Overview The Delta Science Module (DSM) series has 51 life, physical, and earth science units for grades K-8 that emphasize science concepts, science content, and process skills. The series includes 12 modules for grades 5-6 and 8 modules for grades 6-8. Each requires about 3 to 4 weeks to complete and includes a teacher's guide and materials for a class of 32 students.

Teacher's Guide **Recommended grade level: 4-6.** In *Pond Life*, students visit a pond and investigate water, plant, and animal life. In the classroom, students set up and maintain aquariums containing organisms typically found in a freshwater pond and compare this aquarium ecosystem to the pond ecosystem. Students observe and describe macro- and microscopic organisms in their aquarium ecosystem. They make a hay infusion, comparing the organisms in it with those found in their aquariums. Finally, they examine the food chains that exist in a pond, looking at the relationships between producers and consumers.

Pond Life consists of 12 activities, which require about 20 class sessions to complete. In addition to directions for activities, the teacher's guide provides a module overview, a schedule of activities, objectives for each activity, background information, materials management and preparation tips, sample answers to discussion questions, teaching suggestions, and reinforcement activities. Also included are reproducible activity sheets for student work and a performance-based assessment. A "connections" feature at the end of each activity provides suggestions for extending or applying the concepts addressed.

Key to Content Standards: 5-8 (see app. C)

UNIFYING CONCEPTS AND PROCESSES: Systems, order, and organization; form and function.
SCIENCE AS INQUIRY: Abilities necessary to do scientific inquiry; understandings about scientific inquiry.

LIFE SCIENCE: Regulation and behavior; populations and ecosystems; diversity and adaptations of organisms.

Prices: Teacher's guide (ISBN 0-87504-121-3), $27.95. Kit, $249.00. Refill package, $95.00. *Publisher/supplier:* Delta Education. *Materials:* Available locally, from commercial suppliers, or in kit.

2.41 Power Plants: A Plant-Based Energy Curriculum for Grades 5 through 8. Joy Cohen. Burlington, Vt.: National Gardening Association, 1992.

Program Overview Power Plants contains activities that may be used as a springboard for creating original plant investigations. The unit was developed to complement the plant-based science curriculum *GrowLab: Activities for Growing Minds* (see 2.57), but it may be used alone as well.

Teacher's Guide **Recommended grade level: 5-8.** *Power Plants,* a 6-activity unit, helps students examine how plants and other living things use and transform energy. It teaches them the importance of solar energy and resource conservation.

Among the activities, for example, students conduct an experiment to investigate the relationship between light energy and plant growth and development. They also compare starch production in plants grown in the dark with that of plants grown in light to understand that plants can change light energy to food (chemical) energy through the process of photosynthesis. In another activity, students play a simple business game to simulate how energy becomes less

available at each level in a food chain. They also build and use a simple calorimeter to explore how food energy can be measured in the form of heat energy, explore how energy resources are used in producing food, and analyze their own energy conservation practices.

Power Plants may be used to complement *GrowLab: Activities for Growing Minds* (see 2.57), or it may be used alone. Each activity includes background information for the teacher, procedures, and a materials list.

Key to Content Standards: 5-8 (see app. C)

UNIFYING CONCEPTS AND PROCESSES: Systems, order, and organization; form and function.
SCIENCE AS INQUIRY: Abilities necessary to do scientific inquiry; understandings about scientific inquiry.
PHYSICAL SCIENCE: Transfer of energy.
LIFE SCIENCE: Structure and function in living systems; populations and ecosystems.

Price: $5. (ISBN 0-915873-33-8). *Publisher/supplier:* National Gardening Association. *Materials:* Available locally, or from commercial suppliers.

2.42 Rainforest Researchers. Developed in collaboration with The Arboretum of Harvard University (Boston, Mass.) Watertown, Mass.: Tom Snyder Productions, 1996.

Program Overview Rainforest Researchers is a computer-based program that introduces students to current research efforts on tropical forests and biodiversity. Guided by instructions on the CD-ROM, students work in cooperative teams as they role-play scientific experts investigating 2 ecological "mysteries."

Classroom CD-ROM Program

Recommended grade level: 5-8. The *Rainforest Researchers* unit focuses on plant biology and tropical rainforests as students investigate 2 separate ecological mysteries, called "cases," in the Indonesian rainforest. The first mystery is why cultivated durian trees are not producing much fruit, whereas rainforest trees are producing plenty of fruit. To solve the second mystery, students must identify the source of a cancer-fighting compound obtained from an unknown plant sample purchased at an Indonesian jamu market—a place where people buy and sell traditional medicines, usually as dried plants.

To solve the mysteries, students work together in teams of 4; each member plays the role of a different scientific expert (ecologist, ethnobotanist, chemist, taxonomist). The teams follow a series of guided steps on the CD-ROM to obtain information. Then they share ideas, conduct outside research, and make decisions. While working through the program, students make real-life decisions about conducting tests that might help solve their cases.

Six extension activities and 9 hands-on experiments are included in the unit. Among these, for example, students examine fruits and vegetables to understand the difference between scientific and everyday terms; they look at various fruits and seeds to see how they are adapted for dispersal; and they make an herbal first-aid kit.

Each research case in *Rainforest Researchers* takes 1 to 2 weeks of class time to complete. The program can be used with a single computer and a whole class or with many computers. As many as 8 teams can complete the program at the same time.

Program materials include a CD-ROM, a videotape, a teacher's guide, a classroom set of student books (7 sets of 4 different books) and enough field worksheets for 1 class (worksheets may be reproduced).

Key to Content Standards: 5-8 (see app. C)

UNIFYING CONCEPTS AND PROCESSES: Evidence, models, and explanation. **SCIENCE AS INQUIRY:** Abilities necessary to do scientific inquiry; understandings about scientific inquiry. **LIFE SCIENCE:** Structure and function in living systems; reproduction and heredity; regulation and behavior; populations and ecosystems; diversity and adaptations of organisms. **SCIENCE AND TECHNOLOGY:** Understandings about science and technology. **SCIENCE IN PERSONAL AND SOCIAL PERSPECTIVES:** Populations, resources, and environment; natural hazards. **HISTORY AND NATURE OF SCIENCE:** Science as a human endeavor; nature of science.

Price: Kit, $249.95. **Publisher/supplier:** Tom Snyder. **Materials:** Available in kit.

2.43 **Risk Comparison.** Chemical Education for Public Understanding Program (CEPUP) series. Developed by Lawrence Hall of Science (Berkeley, Calif.). Menlo Park, Calif.: Addison-Wesley, 1990.

Program Overview The Chemical Education for Public Understanding Program (CEPUP) series consists of 12 modules for grades 7-9. The modules focus on chemicals and the interaction of chemicals with people and the environment. The series promotes the use of scientific principles, processes, and evidence in public decision making. The components of a CEPUP module are a teacher's guide and a kit of materials. (SEPUP—the Science Education for Public Understanding Program—is the second phase of the project that began as CEPUP.)

Teacher's Guide **Recommended grade level: 7-8+.** *Risk Comparison* contains 6 activities that introduce students to the concepts of risk, risk management, probability, and epidemiology in a way that relates to students' own lives. During the module, they learn about the ideas of chance and probability as they roll dice and flip coins. They read and react to a story requiring a personal decision about whether or not to be inoculated against an unknown disease. They present, categorize, and discuss pictures showing that all of life involves risk. In other activities, students read and react to the history of inoculations and immunization for smallpox, read the story of John Snow's research on cholera in London and learn about the importance of keeping careful records when analyzing risk, and learn a quantitative approach for comparing risks.

Throughout the module, students are taught to differentiate between fact and emotion. Also, they learn that in making decisions about risks in life, individuals use both mathematical probability and emotional reasoning. Students discuss the risks they take in their own lives and ways of reducing those risks.

The 6 activities in *Risk Comparison* take 6 class periods of 40 to 50 minutes each to complete. Included in this slim, wire-bound book are reproducible student sheets, directions for guiding activities and discussions, suggestions for extensions, and an end-of-unit test.

Key to Content Standards: 5-8 (see app. C)

UNIFYING CONCEPTS AND PROCESSES: Evidence, models, and explanation. **SCIENCE AS INQUIRY:** Abilities necessary to do scientific inquiry; understandings about scientific inquiry. **LIFE SCIENCE:** Structure and function in living systems. **SCIENCE IN PERSONAL AND SOCIAL PERSPECTIVES:** Personal health; risks and benefits. **HISTORY AND NATURE OF SCIENCE:** Nature of science; history of science.

Prices: Teacher's guide (ISBN 0-201-28424-3), $19.99. Module, $29.99. **Publisher/supplier:** Sargent-Welch/VWR Scientific. **Materials:** Available locally, from commercial suppliers, or in kit.

2.44 You and Your Body. Delta Science Module (DSM) series. Hudson, N.H.: Delta Education, 1994.

Program Overview The Delta Science Module (DSM) series has 51 life, physical, and earth science units for grades K-8 that emphasize science concepts, science content, and process skills. The series includes 12 modules for grades 5-6 and 8 modules for grades 6-8. Each requires about 3 to 4 weeks to complete and includes a teacher's guide and materials for a class of 32 students.

Teacher's Guide **Recommended grade level: 5-6.** In *You and Your Body*, students investigate several organ systems of the human body, as well

as foods and nutrition. Activities include constructing models of an arm and a leg to simulate the role of muscles and joints in movement. Students also measure their own reaction times, pulse rate, and lung capacity. They observe and discuss the properties of skin and teeth. They test a variety of foods to determine the relative protein and fat content. Students investigate their senses of smell, touch, hearing, and sight.

You and Your Body includes 14 activities, which require about 17 class sessions. In addition to directions for activities, the teacher's guide provides a module overview, a schedule of activities, objectives for each activity, background information, materials management and preparation tips, sample answers to discussion questions, teaching suggestions, and reinforcement activities. Also included are reproducible activity sheets for student work and a performance-based assessment. A "connections" feature at the end of each activity provides suggestions for extending or applying the concepts addressed.

Key to Content Standards: 5-8 (see app. C)

UNIFYING CONCEPTS AND PROCESSES: Systems, order, and organization; evidence, models, and explanation; change, constancy, and measurement; form and function. **SCIENCE AS INQUIRY:** Abilities necessary to do scientific inquiry; understandings about scientific inquiry. **LIFE SCIENCE:** Structure and function in living systems.

SCIENCE IN PERSONAL AND SOCIAL PERSPECTIVES: Personal health; science and technology in society.

Prices: Teacher's guide (ISBN 0-87504-105-1), $27.95. Kit, $279.00. Refill package, $84.00. **Publisher/supplier:** Delta Education. **Materials:** Available locally, from commercial suppliers, or in kit.

2.45 Zebra Mussel Mania. Robin G. Goettel and Agnes E. Dillon, eds. Urbana, Ill.: Illinois-Indiana Sea Grant Program, 1995.

Program Overview *Zebra Mussel Mania,* developed by the Illinois-Indiana Sea Grant Program, introduces students to zebra mussels and the array of problems associated with these and other exotic species. Students use mathematical skills in many of the unit's 10 activities.

Teacher's Guide **Recommended grade level: 6-7.** The *Zebra Mussel Mania* kit and curriculum guide offer 10 classroom activities that teach students about zebra mussels and the problems associated with these and other exotic species. Working in groups, students record their observations on zebra mussels, classify a group of shells by common characteristics, and distinguish between the life cycles of native mussels and zebra mussels. They measure and graph the length of the ventral side of a sample of zebra mussels to demonstrate that zebra mussels vary in length and size. In other activities, students construct a model to learn how zebra mussels remove nutrients and particles from water, they use sampling techniques to calculate the number of zebra mussels in a given area, and they demonstrate the critical changes that occur in a native river ecosystem after the introduction of zebra mussels.

For each activity, *Zebra Mussel Mania* provides directions for the teacher and reproducible student worksheets. Extensions and simple connections to language, art, and social studies are suggested. The activities are correlated with specific Project 2061 Benchmarks (devel-

oped by the American Association for the Advancement of Science). The unit also includes an assortment of posters, brochures, and other background information on zebra mussels and exotic aquatics gathered from a number of sources.

Key to Content Standards: 5-8 (see app. C)

UNIFYING CONCEPTS AND PROCESSES: Systems, order, and organization; evidence, models, and explanation; form and function.

SCIENCE AS INQUIRY: Abilities necessary to do scientific inquiry; understandings about scientific inquiry.

LIFE SCIENCE: Regulation and behavior; populations and ecosystems.

Prices: Teacher's guide, $80. Kit, $300. ***Publisher/supplier:*** Bob Williams. ***Materials:*** Available locally, from commercial suppliers, or in kit.

Life Science—Science Activity Books

2.46 **Animals Alive! An Ecological Guide to Animal Activities.** Dennis Holley. Niwot, Colo.: Roberts Rinehart, 1994.

Recommended grade level: 6-8+. *Animals Alive!* is designed to help teachers develop activities for studying the animal kingdom. Whenever possible, the live animals used in the activities are collected locally, studied and observed, and then released (unharmed) back into their natural habitats.

Each chapter investigates a major group of animals: the groups are sponges, cnidarians, flatworms, segmented worms, mollusks, arthropods, fish, amphibians, reptiles, birds, and mammals. Sections within the chapters provide detailed information on classification and general phylum characteristics, on the collection of specimens, and on their maintenance in the classroom. The chapter on arthropods, for example, provides background information on the physiology of spiders, centipedes, and mites and tells where to collect these creatures in the wild. It presents 24 pick-and-choose activities that allow students to investigate the habitat, structure, behavior/response, feeding, and reproduction and development of arthropods. It also includes suggestions for activities integrated with subject areas such as art, social studies, and writing.

Each chapter addresses health and safety issues, such as how to handle species; includes observation-based

ABOUT THE ANNOTATIONS IN "LIFE SCIENCE—SCIENCE ACTIVITY BOOKS"

Entry Numbers

Curriculum materials are arranged alphabetically by title in each category (Core Materials, Supplementary Units, and Science Activity Books) in chapters 1 through 5 of this guide.

Each curriculum annotation has a two-part entry number: the chapter number is given before the period; the number after the period locates the entry within that chapter. For example, the first entry number in chapter 1 is 1.1; the second entry in chapter 2 is 2.2; and so on.

The entry numbers within each curriculum chapter run consecutively through Core Materials, Supplementary Units, and Science Activity Books.

Order of Bibliographic Information

Following is the arrangement of the facts of publication in the annotations in this section:

- **Title of publication**
- **Number of edition,** if applicable
- **Authors** (an individual author or authors, an institutional author, or a project or program name under which the material was developed)
- **Series title**
- **Series developer,** if applicable
- **Place of publication, publisher, and date of publication**

Recommended Grade Level

The grade level for each piece of material was recommended by teacher evaluators during the development of this guide. In some instances, the recommended grade level may differ slightly from the publisher's advertised level.

Price and Acquisition Information

Ordering information appears at the end of each entry. Included are—

- **Prices** (of teacher's guides, activity books, and kits or units)
- **Publisher/supplier** (The name of a principal publisher/supplier, although not necessarily the sole source, for the items listed in the price category. Appendix A, "Publishers and Suppliers," provides the address, phone and fax numbers, and electronic ordering information, where available, for each publisher and supplier.)
- **Materials** (various sources from which one might obtain the required materials)

Readers must contact publishers/suppliers for complete and up-to-date ordering information, since prices are subject to change and materials may also change with revised editions. The prices given in this chapter are based on information from publishers and suppliers but are not meant to represent the full range of ordering options.

Indexes of Curriculum Materials

The multiple indexes on pp. 449-78 allow easy access to the information in this guide. Various aspects of the curriculum materials—including titles, topics addressed in each unit, and grade levels—are the focus of seven separate indexes. For example, titles and entry numbers are listed in the "Title Index" on pp. 450-54. The "Index of Authors, Series, and Curriculum Projects," on pp. 455-57, provides entry numbers of any annotated titles in a particular series.

teaching activities; and discusses the release of specimens. Appendixes provide information on commercial suppliers of live animals and lists of state agencies that may provide information on laws or regulations regarding the collection, use, and humane treatment of animals in the classroom.

Price: $29.95 (ISBN 1-879373-58-0). *Publisher/supplier:* Roberts Rinehart. *Materials:* Available locally.

2.47 **Behavioral Research: 7-12 Teacher's Guide.** San Diego, Calif.: Sea World, 1992.

Recommended grade level: 7-8+. *Behavioral Research,* a 20-page resource guide, contains information and guidelines for teaching students how to formally research a readily accessible animal, pose a behavioral question, and then make extensive observations of the animal's behavior. Specifically, the guide explains how to construct an "ethogram"—a detailed chart of behaviors that an animal may exhibit—and how to carry out 6 sampling methods that can be used to study behaviors. The sampling methods are these: (1) ad libitum sampling (for informal observations), (2) focal sampling (for studying 1 animal in a group), (3) all-occurrences-of-some-behaviors sampling (for recording a selected portion of an animal's behavior), (4) sequence sampling (for recording a sequence of events), (5) instantaneous sampling (for recording an animal's activity at preset time intervals), and (6) one/zero sampling (for scoring the occurrence or nonoccurrence of a selected behavior within a set period of time). For each of these methods, a sample of a completed data sheet and a reproducible copy of the blank sheet are provided. The guide includes a description of the scientific method as it applies to conducting behavioral research.

Price: $6. *Publisher/supplier:* Sea World of Florida. *Materials:* Available locally.

2.48 **Biotechnology: The Technology of Life.** 2nd ed. Douglas Dawson, Stacey Hill, and Jill Rulfs, eds. Dubuque, Iowa: Kendall/Hunt, 1995.

Recommended grade level: K-8+. The sourcebook *Biotechnology: The Technology of Life,* developed by the Massachusetts Biotechnology Research Institute, contains about 85 classroom activities, lesson plans, experiments, visual aids, and other reproducible support materials designed to teach science concepts related to biotechnology. ("Biotechnology" is defined in the sourcebook as "the use of organisms and their products for industrial purposes.") Intended to be used in any order and to support a wide variety of lessons, the materials are organized in 12 sections, by subject: (1) what science is, (2) what biotechnology is, (3) the characteristics of living versus nonliving things, (4) biodiversity, (5) cell biology, (6) enzymes, (7) genetics, (8) molecular biology concepts, (9) molecular biology techniques, (10) recombinant DNA, (11) immunology, and (12) bioethics.

Among the activities in *Biotechnology,* for example, students observe the behavior of dissolving sponge-animal capsules under a variety of conditions to learn basic forms of science observation, data collection,

discrimination, and data analysis. They experiment with paper and column chromatography and build an inexpensive agarose gel electrophoresis box to help them understand molecular biology techniques. They participate in a cut-and-paste activity to learn about gene splicing and recombination.

Although the activities and lesson plans are designated according to grade level, they can be modified for use at different grade levels. Information on preparation, materials needed, and topics for discussion are included. Several of the student handouts feature cartoon explanations of phenomena—such as what is inside a cell, how enzymes work, and the process of protein synthesis.

Price: $31.95 (ISBN 0-7872-0565-6). *Publisher/supplier:* Kendall/Hunt. *Materials:* Available locally.

2.49 **Bottle Biology.** Paul H. Williams. Dubuque, Iowa: Kendall/Hunt, 1993.

Recommended grade level: 1-8. *Bottle Biology* offers creative ways to teach science concepts and process skills using the ubiquitous 2-liter plastic soda bottle. Students build, fill, observe, and explore the bottle, which acts as a decomposition column, a fermentation chamber, a sedimentation bottle, a soil column, a fruit fly trap and breeder, a predator-prey column, a TerrAqua column, and an ecocolumn. Suggested activities and experiments are provided for each type of column. Examples of activities include making pH indicators, building a terrarium to house carnivorous plants, building a tropical rainforest ecocolumn, and constructing a bottle microscope. Instructions on using empty 35-mm film canisters in experiments on germination, gravitropism, and phototropism are also included.

Each of *Bottle Biology*'s 10 chapters features background informa-

tion. Detailed instructions and illustrations, activities, and teaching tips are provided. An annotated bibliography is included.

Price: $15.95 (ISBN 0-7872-0132-4). *Publisher/supplier:* Kendall/Hunt. *Materials:* Available locally.

2.50 **Cranial Creations in Life Science: Interdisciplinary and Cooperative Activities.** Charles R. Downing and Owen L. Miller. Walch Reproducible Books. Portland, Maine: Walch, 1990.

Recommended grade level: 7-8. *Cranial Creations* presents 45 cross-disciplinary exercises that encourage the development of students' critical-thinking skills—for example, analysis, synthesis, extrapolation, and interpretation. Designed to be woven into the teaching of life science courses during the year, these activities cover a wide range of subjects: the scientific method, genetics, microbiology, cell biology, zoology, evolutionary patterns, human biology, botany, and ecology.

Among the activities, for example, students write a scientifically accurate essay from the point of view of a bug, they create a cartoon that illustrates the definition of a term used in the field of botany, and they classify a collection of pictures and explain their classification system. Students also research and describe the structures that a goldfish passes through when it is swallowed by a human, and they draw and describe the "perfect" animal for a specific environment.

Each activity in *Cranial Creations in Life Science* includes a reproducible student sheet and directions for the teacher. Most exercises require very few supplies.

Price: $20.95 (ISBN 0-8251-2498-0). *Publisher/supplier:* Walch. *Materials:* Available locally.

2.51 Earthworms. Elaine Pascoe. Nature Close-Up series. Woodbridge, Conn.: Blackbirch Press, 1997.

Recommended grade level: 6-8. This slim hardcover book, illustrated with engaging close-up color photographs, teaches students about earthworms and how they contribute to healthy soil. *Earthworms* offers basic background information about different types of earthworms, their anatomy, and their life cycle. It includes directions for 5 simple experiments. For example, students investigate how earthworms react to light, what they eat, and whether earthworms help plants grow.

Earthworms offers guidelines for collecting earthworms and caring for them in earthworm "hotels" or compost bins. Sources are listed for obtaining the earthworms and other supplies needed for the activities. The experiments in the book have brief directions but no background information; a list of possible results and conclusions for the activities is included.

Price: $16.95 (ISBN 1-56711-177-7). Publisher/supplier: Blackbirch Press. *Materials:* Available locally.

2.52 Exploring Classroom Hydroponics. Growing Ideas series. Burlington, Vt.: National Gardening Association, 1995.

Recommended grade level: 6-8. The booklet *Exploring Classroom Hydroponics* provides basic information on what hydroponics is and how it works. It includes ideas, tips, and procedures for setting up different hydroponic systems and for helping students discover hydroponic concepts on their own. Included are simple diagrams and explanations of 7 hydroponic systems for the classroom (basic wick, milk carton and rock wool, soda bottle, floating Styrofoam raft, basic ebb and flow, simple straw aeration, and Plexiglas

slants). The booklet provides short activities for students to do at "mini-stations" to explore some of the key factors—such as nutrient composition, pH, evaporation, and light—that affect hydroponic setups. Ideas for student investigations are given.

Rather than being a complete "how-to" guide, *Exploring Classroom Hydroponics* synthesizes ideas from teachers who have used hydroponics in the classroom. Teachers may choose to develop further the directions for the activities suggested for classroom use. The booklet provides tips on choosing and nurturing plants, a recipe for a home-made nutrient mix, and a list of resources and suppliers.

Price: $7.95 (ISBN 0-915873-36-2). Publisher/supplier: National Gardening Association. *Materials:* Available locally, or from commercial suppliers.

2.53 Exploring with Wisconsin Fast Plants. Paul H. Williams, Richard P. Green, and Coe M. Williams. Madison, Wis.: University of Wisconsin, 1989.

Recommended grade level: 3-7. Learning about plant growth and development is the focus of *Exploring with Wisconsin Fast Plants*. Wisconsin Fast Plants (specially bred members of the cabbage and mustard families) have a life cycle of 35 to 40 days and can be grown in the classroom under continuous fluorescent light.

The book is organized in 5 sections, which contain (1) basic information for teachers using Fast Plants for the first time, including illustrated growing instructions, tips, troubleshooting suggestions, and ideas for subsequent investigations; (2) explorations pertaining to events and stages of the *Brassica* life cycle; (3) additional explorations in plant physiology and ecology; (4) exten-

sions, stories, modeling ideas, and games; and (5) supplementary materials for teachers. Process skills are embedded throughout the unit. Students are encouraged to generate many of the experimentation ideas.

In *Exploring with Wisconsin Fast Plants*, each experiment follows a science exploration flowchart and includes teaching concepts, background information, and step-by-step illustrated instructions.

Price: $19.95. Publisher/supplier: Carolina Biological Supply. *Materials:* Available locally, from commercial suppliers, or in kit.

2.54 Getting to Know the Whales. Larry Wade. Whales in the Classroom Presents series. Minnetonka, Minn.: Singing Rock Press, 1995.

Recommended grade level: 7-8. *Getting to Know the Whales* includes in-depth information on whales, their characteristics, their evolution, and their status. Many classroom activities are provided. For example, students use a dichotomous key to identify drawings of various whales and dolphins, assemble a flip book that shows lunge feeding, graph the average dive duration of 5 different types of whales, analyze data from a blue whale sighting, and plot migration data on a map.

Getting to Know the Whales has numerous charts, drawings and photographs. Other features of the book include interviews with biologists who study whales and information about whaling and conservation. The book is suitable for students learning about whales for the first time as well as for those who are seriously considering the study of whales as a career. It includes a list of "adopt-a-whale" programs and a bibliography.

Price: $16.95 (ISBN 0-9629395-2-8). Publisher/supplier: Singing Rock Press. *Materials:* Available locally.

2.55 **The Great Bone Mysteries.**
James Robert Taris. Riverview, Fla.:
Idea Factory, 1993.

Recommended grade level: 6-7. *The
Great Bone Mysteries* contains background information and 15 simple
mysteries that help students learn
about the human skeleton. They
learn about bones by first constructing a generic paper skeleton and
reading information about gender,
age, and other factors that account
for visible differences in human
bones. Then, using this knowledge
together with clues that are provided, students try to identify the
sex, height, approximate age, and
cause of death for 15 mystery individuals. Clues consist, for example,
of a description of the bones found at
the scene, information about clothing the victim was wearing, or the
time of death. As students work
through the clues, they discuss them
in class and record their answers on
reproducible sheets.

Tips are provided for discussing
the clues and for maintaining sensi-
tivity to students' feelings and experiences with regard to death (including any experiences they may have
had with the death of a family member). The book has an answer key
and a short bibliography.

Price: $10.95 (ISBN 1-885041-09-8).
Publisher/supplier: Idea Factory.
Materials: Available locally.

2.56 **GrowLab: A Complete Guide
to Gardening in the Classroom.** Eve
Pranis and Jack Hale. Burlington,
Vt.: National Gardening Association,
1988.

Recommended grade level: K-6. *GrowLab:
A Complete Guide to Gardening in
the Classroom* is a resource book
designed to help teachers plan, plant,
and maintain an indoor garden; it can
be used to support a variety of curriculum units on plants (*see also*, 2.57).

This volume provides complete instructions for setting up and cultivat-
ing an indoor garden, maintaining a
healthy environment, tackling pests
and other problems, maintaining
equipment, and building support for
classroom gardening in the school
and the community. It also provides
suggestions—including activities,
lessons, projects, and experiments—
for integrating gardening into all
areas of the curriculum. Students
might, for example, grow an indoor
gift-plant garden; write, illustrate,
and publish a collection of garden
stories; or study the contribution of
foods of Native Americans and of
other cultures in shaping our history
and diet.

The appendixes in *Growlab* offer a
wide range of information, including
instructions and diagrams for building a GrowLab, and a guide to growing and harvesting various crops
indoors. Several reproducible student worksheets, such as a plant
growth chart, are provided. An annotated reference section lists books,
audiovisual materials, organizational
resources, and suppliers of gardening
equipment and seeds.

Prices: Teacher's guide (ISBN 0-
915873-31-1), $19.95. Full-size sup-
ply kit, $139.00. Compact supply kit,
$99.00. *Publisher/supplier:* National
Gardening Association. *Materials:*
Available locally, from commercial
suppliers, or in kit.

2.57 **GrowLab: Activities for
Growing Minds.** Eve Pranis and Joy
Cohen. Burlington, Vt.: National
Gardening Association, 1990.

Recommended grade level: K-6. *Growlab:
Activities for Growing Minds* is a
curriculum guide offering dozens of
ideas and activities relating to plants,
gardening, and the diversity of life;
students can do the activities as they
work on an indoor classroom garden
(*see* 2.56). The *Growlab* activities,
which are presented in 4 chapters,

help students explore plants' basic
needs and structures, learn about
plant life cycles and reproduction,
find out how plants adapt to different
environmental conditions, and learn
how people both use and affect
plants around the world. Among the
activities, for example, students
observe similarities and differences
among plant leaves and consider
why leaves are important for most
plants, conduct classroom studies
about acid rain, and try to simulate
an indoor tropical rainforest. The
book also includes suggestions of
horticultural, conceptual, or topical
themes for organizing plant-based
activities.

Some activities in *Growlab* are
long-term projects; others can be
done sequentially as a series of
shorter science explorations. Each
activity includes background information, step-by-step procedures, a
list showing time and materials
required, cross-curricular connections, and extensions. Appendixes
offer a wide range of information,
including reproducible student activity sheets, an annotated list of
resource books, and suppliers of
seeds.

Prices: Teacher's guide (ISBN 0-
915873-32-X), $24.95. Full-size sup-
ply kit, $139.00. Compact supply kit,
$99.00. *Publisher/supplier:* National
Gardening Association. *Materials:*
Available locally, from commercial
suppliers, or in kit.

2.58 **Living in Water: An Aquatic
Science Curriculum for Grades 5-7.**
3rd ed. National Aquarium in Baltimore. Dubuque, Iowa: Kendall/Hunt,
1997.

Recommended grade level: 5-8. *Living in
Water* is a study of water, water environments, and the plants and animals that live in water—in freshwater, estuarine, and marine habitats.

The unit's 50 activities are in 6 sections on the following subjects: (1) aquatic habitats; (2) substances (such as salts, oxygen, minerals, and pollutants) that dissolve in water; (3) the consequences of temperature changes for plants and animals living in aquatic environments; (4) the physical characteristics of water habitats that determine where plants and animals live; (5) the behavior of light in water and the consequences for the plants and animals that live there; and (6) research projects and programs.

Among the unit's activities, for example, students interpret experimental data about the effect of temperature on the rate at which plants use oxygen, compare temperature changes in water and air, compare the way things float or sink in fresh- and saltwater, and experiment with blue goggles to learn why color patterns that are easy to see in air may be hard to see under water.

In addition to the activities, each section of *Living in Water* provides background information for the teacher, examples of completed student worksheets, and extension activities. Information on preparation of materials and sources of supplies, as well as masters for the reproducible student worksheets, are included.

Price: $10 (ISBN 0-7872-4366-3). *Publisher/supplier:* Kendall/Hunt. *Materials:* Available locally, or from commercial suppliers.

2.59 **Magnificent Microworld Adventures.** Mike Wood. Activities Integrating Mathematics and Science (AIMS) series. Fresno, Calif.: AIMS Education Foundation, 1995.

Recommended grade level: 4-8+. During the 25 activities in *Magnificent Microworld Adventures,* students

develop skills using a microscope and make accurate observations and drawings of animal cells, plant cells, and protozoa. During the first group of activities, students become familiar with a hand lens, looking at mealworms, nightcrawlers, grasshoppers, and sea stars. Then they learn the parts, function, and care of a compound microscope; they prepare wetmount slides; and they make drawings and notes of their observations and measure the field of view of a microscope at various powers of magnification. The microscope-centered activities during the rest of the unit include, for example, observing and drawing the structures in onion cells, seeing how cork cells are different from living plant cells, making a hay infusion and observing the emergence and growth of protozoa over time, looking at the organisms living in a drop of pond water, and observing the circulation of blood through the tail of a goldfish.

Each activity in *Magnificent Microworld Adventures* includes background information for the teacher; procedures, discussion questions, and extensions; and reproducible student pages containing instructions, data sheets, and graphs. Each activity also has a "guiding documents" section, which lists the activity's relevance to specific NCTM (National Council of Teachers of Mathematics) standards and to Project 2061 Benchmarks (developed by the American Association for the Advancement of Science).

Price: Teacher's guide (ISBN 1-881431-53-3), $16.95. *Publisher/supplier:* AIMS Education Foundation. *Materials:* Available locally, or from commercial suppliers.

2.60 **The Microcosmos Curriculum Guide to Exploring Microbial Space.** The Microcosmos Team (Douglas Zook and others). Dubuque, Iowa: Kendall/Hunt, 1992.

Recommended grade level: 4-8+. *The Microcosmos Curriculum Guide to Exploring Microbial Space,* a guide to 29 activities, focuses students' attention on the world of microbes and microbial space. Among the activities, for example, students use inexpensive microscopes to look at different fibers and strands of everyday objects; they go "microfishing" for organisms from a classroom "pond"; and they learn about diatoms (where they are found, what they look like, and how we use them). Students also create a skyscraper of mud, teeming with microbes. They explore fermentation by growing fungal microbes (yeast) and then making root beer.

Designed to be integrated into mainstream life science subjects such as photosynthesis, evolution, or ecology, these wide-ranging activities require no elaborate equipment or materials. The activities in the guide, which is in 3-ring-binder format, can be completed in any order but are presented in a recommended sequence. A glossary and a materials list are included as appendixes.

Price: $31.95 (ISBN 0-7872-0133-2). *Publisher/supplier:* Kendall/Hunt. *Materials:* Available locally, or from commercial suppliers.

2.61 **The Molecular Model of DNA and Its Replication Kit.** Ronkonkoma, N.Y.: Lab-Aids, no date.

Recommended grade level: 8+. This simple kit for 2 activities is designed to help students learn about the structure of DNA and how it replicates. The kit contains 12 packets of colored plastic pieces—students use them to construct a model of a DNA molecule—and 2 student worksheets with background information and instructions. In the first activity, students construct a DNA "ladder." In the second, they unzip their double helix model and complete 2 new DNA helix ladders. A 4-page teacher's guide provides background information and answers to questions on the student worksheets.

Price: $44.50. *Publisher/supplier:* Sargent-Welch. *Materials:* Available in kit.

2.62 **Order and Diversity in the Living World: Teaching Taxonomy and Systematics in Schools.** Jorge V. Crisci, Joseph D. McInerney, and Patricia J. McWethy. Reston, Va.: National Association of Biology Teachers, 1993.

Recommended grade level: 1-8+. *Order and Diversity in the Living World* is a small book that presents a rationale for classroom study of biological diversity and the relationships between different organisms. It also offers a brief review of the current state of diversity and rate of species extinction, identifies standards that should encourage changes in the way systematics is taught in the classroom, and gives directions for 10 sample activities that involve students in "doing" systematics in the classroom rather than simply reading about the nature of this subdiscipline.

Among the activities, for example, students learn about biological classification by classifying music. They design and construct a dichotomous key. They also develop phylogenetic trees to show the evolutionary relatedness of common household hardware "organisms." They use a model of DNA hybridization to investigate the degree of relatedness of 3 organisms (chimpanzee, human, and gorilla). Each activity includes back-

ground information and teaching procedures; some include a list of references.

Price: $10 (ISBN 0-941212-11-4). *Publisher/supplier:* National Association of Biology Teachers. *Materials:* Available locally, or from commercial suppliers.

2.63 **Osmosis and Diffusion Kit.** Ronkonkoma, N.Y.: Lab-Aids, 1995.

Recommended grade level: 7-8. The *Osmosis and Diffusion Kit* allows students to observe the characteristics of a differentially permeable membrane. Students fill a membrane tube with glucose solution and liquid starch, place the tube in a container of water to which Lugol's solution has been added, and then observe any changes in the contents of the tube or the liquid in the container. They also test for the presence of glucose—both at the beginning and at the end of the activity. Completing the activity, students find that some substances will have passed through the membrane, some will not have, and some will have passed through the membrane in both directions simultaneously. Results showing osmosis—the diffusion of water through a membrane—may take more than one class period.

The kit includes student worksheets and materials. A 4-page teacher's guide provides background information and answers to questions on the student worksheets.

Price: $44.20 *Publisher/supplier:* Sargent-Welch. *Materials:* Available in kit.

2.64 **Owl Pellet Study Kit.** Ronkonkoma, N.Y.: Lab-Aids, 1995.

Recommended grade level: 6-8+. The *Owl Pellet Study Kit* contains materials for an activity that can serve as a stimulus for the study of skeletal

systems and food chains. During the activity, students dissect owl pellets and attempt to identify the animals whose skeletons are found in the pellets. Students record data about the kinds and numbers of skeletons they find, and they compare various bones from these skeletons. In an optional activity, students construct a diagram of a food web with the barn owl at the highest trophic level.

The kit includes 15 owl pellets, 15 dissecting needles, and 30 2-page student worksheets. A 6-page teacher's guide provides background information and answers to questions on the student worksheets.

Price: $41.50 *Publisher/supplier:* Sargent-Welch. *Materials:* Available in kit.

2.65 **Plant Biology Science Projects.** David R. Hershey. Best Science Projects for Young Adults series. New York, N.Y. : John Wiley, 1995.

Recommended grade level: 7-8+. *Plant Biology Science Projects*, written for students age 12 and older, provides directions for 21 inexpensive seed-plant experiments. Most of the projects deal with plant physiology, plant ecology, and plant agriculture, featuring such topics as transpiration, photosynthesis, root and stem development, hydroponics, nutrient requirements, and fertilizers. Among the activities, for example, students determine how dicot seedlings are affected by the removal of cotyledons. They investigate the effect of artificial acid rain on plant growth. They also find out whether more expensive houseplant fertilizers make plants grow better.

The introduction to *Plant Biology Science Projects* gives an overview of how to approach a plant biology project. It addresses such topics as standards in plant experiments, choosing a plant for a science project, materials, record keeping, and interpreting and presenting results. Each experiment includes an introduction, statement of purpose, list of materials, procedures, expected results, explanation of results, and suggestions for further investigation. The book's 6 appendixes provide information on preparing plastic soda bottles for the activities, construction of fluorescent lighting systems, hydroponic equipment and nutrient solutions, seedlings and rooted cuttings for hydroponics, suppliers of needed materials, and outdated or inaccurate classroom plant projects to avoid.

Price: $12.95 (ISBN 0-471-04983-2). *Publisher/supplier:* Wiley. *Materials:* Available locally, or from commercial suppliers.

2.66 **Project WILD Aquatic Education Activity Guide.** 2nd ed. Bethesda, Md.: Project WILD, 1992.

Recommended grade level: K-8+. *Project WILD Aquatic Education Activity Guide* is part of an interdisciplinary conservation and environmental education program. The guide's 40 activities are organized in 7 sections: (1) "Awareness and Appreciation"; (2) "Diversity of Values"; (3) "Ecological Principles"; (4) "Management and Conservation"; (5) "People, Culture and Wildlife"; (6) "Trends, Issues and Consequences"; and (7) "Responsible Human Actions."
Examples of activities in the guide include designing a habitat suitable for aquatic wildlife to survive in a zoo or an aquarium, drawing life-size replicas of whales on school grounds, simulating the effects of the changing technology of fishing on fish populations, and producing a newspaper that features aquatic information and issues. A glossary, a conceptual framework, and a guide to the

ecosystem concept are included among the guide's 26 appendixes.

Price: Attendance at Project WILD Workshop. *Publisher/supplier:* Project WILD. *Materials:* Available locally, or from commercial suppliers.

2.67 **Project WILD: K-12 Activity Guide.** 2nd ed. Bethesda, Md.: Project WILD, 1992.

Recommended grade level: K-8+. *Project WILD: K-12 Activity Guide* is part of an interdisciplinary conservation and environmental education program. The guide's 113 activities are organized in 7 sections: (1) "Awareness and Appreciation"; (2) "Diversity of Wildlife Values"; (3) "Ecological Principles"; (4) "Management and Conservation"; (5) "People, Culture and Wildlife"; (6) "Trends, Issues and Consequences"; and (7) "Responsible Human Actions."
Examples of activities in the guide include identifying similarities and differences in the basic needs of ants and humans; forming an interconnected circle of students to demonstrate the components of a habitat; creating murals showing the major stages of pond succession; and working with state highway and vegetative maps to determine relationships between rainfall, vegetation, and animal habitats. A glossary, a conceptual framework, and a guide to the ecosystem concept are included among the guide's 23 appendixes.

Price: Attendance at Project WILD workshop. *Publisher/supplier:* Project WILD. *Materials:* Available locally, or from commercial suppliers.

2.68 **Science Projects about the Human Body.** Robert Gardner. Science Projects series. Hillside, N.J.: Enslow, 1993.

Recommended grade level: 7-8+. *Science Projects about the Human Body,* 1 of

6 books in a series written for students, contains 30 simple activities about the human body and how it functions. Among the activities, for example, students measure the volume of air they breathe in and out in a normal breath; they locate different taste receptors on the tongue; and they test people to see how good their peripheral vision is. In other activities, students compare the strengths of muscle pairs using a spring-type bathroom scale, and they investigate whether people shrink in height during the course of a day.
Designed to be student-directed, many of the stand-alone activities in *Science Projects about the Human Body* could be done at home or as teacher demonstrations, or used as the basis for science fair projects. The activities are narrative in form; the text contains questions to help guide the inquiry. Brief explanations for the results observed in the experiments are provided in the text.

Price: $18.95 (ISBN 0-89490-443-4). *Publisher/supplier:* Enslow. *Materials:* Available locally.

2.69 **Seeds and Seedlings.** Elaine Pascoe. Nature Close-Up series. Woodbridge, Conn.: Blackbirch Press, 1997.

Recommended grade level: 5-7. *Seeds and Seedlings,* illustrated with many close-up color photographs, is designed to teach students about seeds and plant growth. It offers basic background information on how seeds form, grow, and travel; it gives simple guidelines for planting seeds and raising seedlings under different conditions; and it provides directions for 7 experiments or activities that students can do at home or at school. For example, students investigate the effects of water or temperature on seed growth, the importance of cotyledons, and the question of whether plants can grow around obstacles. Brief directions, without background information, are provided for the activities. A list of possible results and conclusions is included.

Price: $16.95 (ISBN 1-56711-178-5). *Publisher/supplier:* Blackbirch Press. *Materials:* Available locally.

2.70 **Sun Awareness for Educating Today's Youth.** Project SAFETY for Middle School Science. Houston, Tex.: University of Texas M. D. Anderson Cancer Center and Texas Cancer Council, 1993.

Recommended grade level: 6-8. *Sun Awareness for Educating Today's Youth* contains 3 50-minute lessons designed to increase students' awareness of the incidence and causes of different types of skin cancer and to inform them of steps they can take to lower their chances of getting the disease. The unit also introduces students to other health risks associated with sun exposure, such as aging, cataracts, and immunosuppression. A variety of optional activities is included. For example, students may develop an advertisement on sun safety, look at a globe and discuss the countries with the highest incidence of skin cancer and their relationship to the Equator, or use sun-sensitive paper to test the effectiveness of sunscreens.

The complete unit in a box includes a teacher's guide, 37 slides with graphic photos of individuals with skin cancer, worksheets and handouts (including a risk assessment instrument), a poster, a 15-minute video of physicians and teenagers discussing sun behavior, and assessment materials (pre- and post-tests).

Price: $69.50. *Publisher/supplier:* University of Texas M. D. Anderson Cancer Center. *Materials:* Available locally, or in kit.

2.71 **What Does DNA Look Like?** EDVO-Kit. West Bethesda, Md.: EDVOTEK, 1995.

Recommended grade level: 8+. *What Does DNA Look Like?* is a kit containing lab materials and instructions for an easy but dramatic DNA spooling activity. Students layer cold isopropanol on top of a buffer solution containing DNA, place the tip of a glass rod in the solution just below the line separating the 2 solutions, and then twist the rod in a circular motion to spool out and collect the DNA. They also stain the spooled DNA with a methylene blue solution.

The kit, which must be stored in a refrigerator, includes concentrated chromosomal DNA and buffer solutions, as well as pipettes, glass rods, and plastic beakers. It provides 2 paragraphs of background information on DNA spooling, student experimental procedures, and guidelines for the teacher. Some additional materials are required, such as graduated cylinders, test tubes, isopropanol, and distilled water. The kit is designed for 30 students working in groups of 2 or 3.

Price: $37. *Publisher/supplier:* Sargent-Welch/VWR Scientific. *Materials:* Available locally, from commercial suppliers, or in kit.

2.72 **What Seed Is It?—A Hands-on Classroom Project.** Newton, Kans.: Young Naturalist, 1990.

Recommended grade level: 6-8. Using *What Seed Is It?,* students explore the importance of tree seeds. During the 7 hands-on activities in this kit, students chart the complete development of a seed and discover the different means of seed dispersal. They observe and record the sprouting of seeds, use a dichotomous seed key to identify unknown seeds that

come in the kit, learn to distinguish between fruits and seeds, and collect and identify seeds from their own neighborhood.

The kit contains 13 identified tree-seed specimens, 26 unidentified tree-seed specimens (2 each of the identified specimens), a seed key for identifying the unknown seeds, a packet of alfalfa seeds, and a teacher's guide. The specimens provided are the actual tree fruits with the seeds enclosed inside the fruit. The types of tree fruits in the kit include nuts, berries, pods, wings, and cones.

Price: $25.95. *Publisher/supplier:* Young Naturalist. *Materials:* Available from Young Naturalist.

2.73 **Whose DNA Was Left Behind?** EDVO-Kit. West Bethesda, Md.: EDVOTEK, 1995.

Recommended grade level: 8+. *Whose DNA Was Left Behind?* is a kit containing lab materials and instructions for an activity that shows students how DNA fingerprinting technology works and how scientists and police use this technology to identify a suspect from evidence left behind at a crime scene. Students load simulated DNA samples (dyes) from a murder scene and simulated DNA samples from 2 suspects into an agarose gel. Then they run the samples through an electrophoresis apparatus and analyze the resulting fragments for particular patterns. When students read and analyze the simulated DNA gel fragments, they are able to determine the correct suspect in a murder case. The objective of the experiment is to demonstrate that each person has a unique pattern within his or her DNA. To do the activity, students need some knowledge of what DNA is and what it does.

This activity takes about 100 minutes (or less, if the buffers and gels are made ahead of time). The kit, which must be stored in a refrigerator, includes background information on DNA fingerprinting; 6 simulated DNA samples (2 from the crime scene and 4 from 2 different suspects); bottles of electrophoresis buffer and agarose; and micropipets. Also included are procedures for student experiments and guidelines for teachers, as well as a document on conducting agarose gel electrophoresis. Some other materials are required, such as an electrophoresis apparatus (M-12 or equivalent), a power supply, and distilled water.

Price: $45. *Publisher/supplier:* Sargent-Welch/VWR Scientific. *Materials:* Available locally, from commercial suppliers, or in kit.

2.74 **Why Do People Look Different?** EDVO-Kit. West Bethesda, Md.: EDVOTEK, 1995.

Recommended grade level: 8+. *Why Do People Look Different?* is a kit containing lab materials and instructions for an activity that shows how DNA fingerprinting can be used to detect the genes inherited by children. Students load simulated DNA samples (dyes) from 2 brown-eyed parents and 4 children into wells in an agarose gel. Then they run the samples through an electrophoresis apparatus and analyze the results using their knowledge of Mendelian genetics. The object of the activity is to detect the alleles (genes) for eye color that are inherited by the children. The same exercise, however,

would also apply if one were testing whether a person had a genetic disease or was a carrier for one.

This activity takes about 100 minutes (or less, if the buffers and gels are made ahead of time). The kit, which must be stored in a refrigerator, includes bottles of electrophoresis buffer and agarose, micropipets, and 6 simulated DNA samples. Also included are background information on DNA fingerprinting, procedures for student experiments, and guidelines for teachers, as well as a document on conducting agarose gel electrophoresis. Some other materials are required, such as an electrophoresis apparatus (M-12 or equivalent), a power supply, and distilled water.

Price: $45. *Publisher/supplier:* Sargent-Welch/VWR Scientific. *Materials:* Available locally, from commercial suppliers, or in kit.

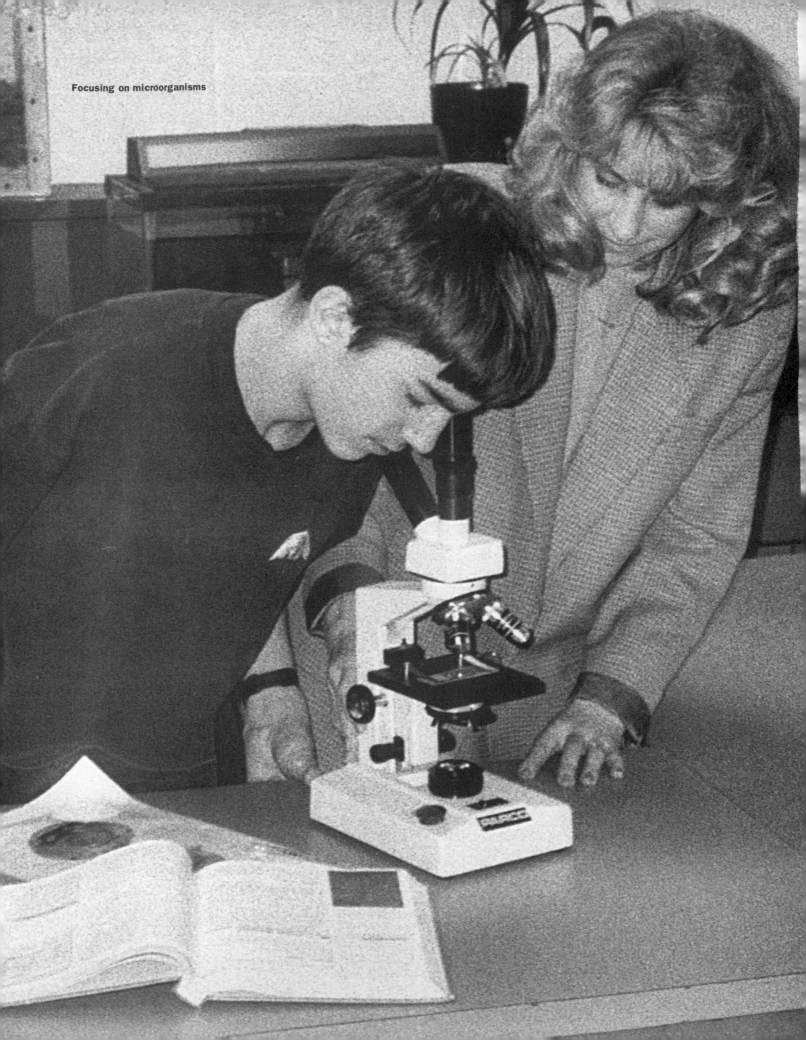

Focusing on microorganisms

CHAPTER 3

ENVIRONMENTAL SCIENCE

Environmental Science—Core Materials

3.1 **Environments.** Full Option Science System (FOSS) series. Developed by Lawrence Hall of Science (Berkeley, Calif.). Hudson, N.H.: Delta Education, 1993.

Program Overview The Full Option Science System (FOSS) program is a K-6 science curriculum consisting of 27 stand-alone modules. The 8 modules for grades 5-6 are organized under topics in the life, physical, and earth sciences and in scientific reasoning and technology. They can be used in any order. The FOSS program is designed to engage students in scientific concepts through multisensory, hands-on laboratory activities. All modules of the program incorporate 5 unifying themes— (1) pattern, (2) structure, (3) interaction, (4) change, and (5) system. The components of a FOSS module are a teacher's guide and a kit of materials.

Teacher's Guide **Recommended grade level: 5-6.** *Environments* introduces students to several basic concepts of environmental biology. Structured investigations in both terrestrial and aquatic systems develop the concepts of environmental factor, tolerance, environmental preference, and environmental range. In this unit, students observe interactions in a terrarium, investigate the environmental preferences of isopods and beetles, determine the water tolerance of seeds and plants, monitor environmental factors in freshwater aquariums, and investigate the salt tolerance of plants and brine shrimp eggs.

Environments consists of 6 activities and requires 8 weeks to complete. The teacher's guide includes a module overview, the 6 individual activity folios, duplication masters (in English and Spanish) for student sheets, and an annotated bibliography.

The module includes science background information, detailed instruc-tions on planning for and conducting each activity, an extensive assessment component, and extensions for integration and enrichment.

Key to Content Standards: 5-8 (see app. C)

UNIFYING CONCEPTS AND PROCESSES: Systems, order, and organization; evidence, models, and explanation.
SCIENCE AS INQUIRY: Abilities necessary to do scientific inquiry; understandings about scientific inquiry.
LIFE SCIENCE: Regulation and behavior; populations and ecosystems.
SCIENCE IN PERSONAL AND SOCIAL PERSPECTIVES: Populations, resources, and environments.

Prices: Teacher's guide (ISBN 0-7826-0070-0), $101. Complete module, $399. ***Publisher/supplier:*** Delta Education. ***Materials:*** Available locally, from commercial suppliers, or in kit.

3.2 Issues, Evidence and You. Science Education for Public Understanding Program (SEPUP) series. Developed by Lawrence Hall of Science (Berkeley, Calif.). Ronkonkoma, N.Y.: Lab-Aids, 1995.

Program Overview The Science Education for Public Understanding Program (SEPUP) series consists of 2 year-long courses—1 for middle and early secondary school (*Issues, Evidence and You*) and 1 for high school (*Science for Citizenship in the 21st Century*). The program focuses on science and technology and on interactions of science and technology with people and the environment. The series promotes the use of scientific principles, processes, and evidence in public decision making. Materials include a teacher's guide, student books, and a kit of materials. (SEPUP is the second phase of a project that began as CEPUP—Chemical Education for Public Understanding Program.)

Teacher's Guide **Recommended grade level: 7-8+. Reading level: middle 10.** *Issues, Evidence and You,* designed to be completed over the course of a year, offers 65 activities that require students to collect and process scientific evidence about real issues of current individual and community interest. Students then use the evidence they accumulate to weigh the advantages and disadvantages of various solutions to the problems being studied. The course has 4 parts: (1) "Water Usage and Safety," (2) "Materials Science," (3) "Energy

ABOUT THE ANNOTATIONS IN "ENVIRONMENTAL SCIENCE—CORE MATERIALS"

Entry Numbers
Curriculum materials are arranged alphabetically by title in each category (Core Materials, Supplementary Units, and Science Activity Books) in chapters 1 through 5 of this guide.

Each curriculum annotation has a two-part entry number: the chapter number is given before the period; the number after the period locates the entry within that chapter. For example, the first entry number in chapter 1 is 1.1; the second entry in chapter 2 is 2.2; and so on.

The entry numbers within each curriculum chapter run consecutively through Core Materials, Supplementary Units, and Science Activity Books.

Order of Bibliographic Information
Following is the arrangement of the facts of publication in the annotations in this section:

- **Title of publication**
- **Number of edition,** if applicable
- **Authors** (an individual author or authors, an institutional author, or a project or program name under which the material was developed)
- **Series title**
- **Series developer,** if applicable
- **Place of publication, publisher, and date of publication**

Recommended Grade Level and Reading Level
The grade level for each piece of material was recommended by teacher evaluators during the development of this guide. In some instances, the recommended grade level may differ slightly from the publisher's advertised level. The Fry Readability Scale was used to determine the approximate reading level of core materials.

Key to Content Standards: 5-8
The key lists the content standards for grades 5-8 from the *National Science Education Standards* (NSES) that are addressed in depth by the item. A key is provided for core materials and supplementary units. (*See* appendix C.)

Price and Acquisition Information
Ordering information appears at the end of each entry. Included are—

- **Prices** (of teacher's guides, student books, lab manuals, and kits or units)
- **Publisher/supplier** (The name of a principal publisher/supplier, although not necessarily the sole source, for the items listed in the price category. Appendix A, "Publishers and Suppliers," provides the address, phone and fax numbers, and electronic ordering information, where available, for each publisher and supplier.)
- **Materials** (various sources from which one might obtain the required materials)

Readers must contact publishers/suppliers for complete and up-to-date listings of the program resources and support materials available for a particular unit. Depending on the developer, these items may be required, optional, or both; they may be offered individually and/or in kits, packages, or boxes. Materials may change with revised editions. The prices given in this chapter for selected resources or materials are based on information from the publishers and suppliers but are not meant to represent the full range of ordering options.

Indexes of Curriculum Materials
The multiple indexes on pp. 449-78 allow easy access to the information in this guide. Various aspects of the curriculum materials—including titles, topics addressed in each unit, grade levels, and standards addressed—are the focus of seven separate indexes. For example, titles and entry numbers are listed in the "Title Index" on pp. 450-54. The "Index of Authors, Series, and Curriculum Projects," on pp. 455-57, provides entry numbers of any annotated titles in a particular series.

Overviews of Core and Supplementary Programs
Appendix D, "Overviews of Core and Supplementary Programs with Titles Annotated in This Guide," on pp. 441-48, lists, by program or series, the individual titles annotated in the sections "Core Materials" and "Supplementary Units" in the five curriculum chapters.

Use," and (4) "Environmental Impact."

In part 1, students are introduced to the problem of waterborne diseases, the problem of biological risks from the water supply, and the use of water treatment processes to control these risks. Students investigate the issue of risks and benefits of chemicals in the environment, and they apply what they have learned about water quality, toxicity, and risk to make a decision about how to clean up groundwater contamination. Among the activities in part 1, students analyze data and information about the 1849 cholera epidemic in London, they perform a simulated investigation of the effect of a potentially toxic substance on a group of rats, and they conduct qualitative and quantitative analyses of water samples.

In part 2, students explore the environmental impacts related to the production, use, and disposal of plastics, metal, and other materials used to make consumer goods. They investigate, for example, the advantages and disadvantages of different approaches to preventing the corrosion of iron, and they observe a simulation of the incineration of hazardous waste.

In part 3, students learn about the availability of different energy sources; they relate what they learn about these energy sources to energy efficiency and to themselves as energy consumers. Among the activities in part 3, students investigate energy conversion through the study of simple electrochemical cells, they use a calorimeter to investigate the heat exchange between hot and cool water, and they examine the costs and trade-offs involved in energy decisions for their school and community.

In part 4, students apply their new learnings to the issue of whether or not to build a factory on an imaginary island within a community. They determine the economic, environmental, and political implications of decisions about obtaining and processing raw materials and about handling transportation and waste disposal issues.

The teacher's guide, in loose-leaf-binder format, provides science background, materials lists, information on advance preparation that is needed, step-by-step teaching summaries and procedures, safety notes, and assessments. Reproducible masters for student worksheets and transparencies are included. Students are required to keep personal journals of their experiences and of the evidence they collect.

Student Books Three student books accompany this 4-part course (the third book contains the investigations for parts 3 and 4). Each activity includes a brief introduction, procedures, and any necessary safety information. Readings expand on the investigation or provide secondary evidence that is not possible or safe to collect directly.

Key to Content Standards: 5-8 (see app. C)

UNIFYING CONCEPTS AND PROCESSES: Systems, order, and organization; evidence, models, and explanation; change, constancy, and measurement.
SCIENCE AS INQUIRY: Abilities necessary to do scientific inquiry; understandings about scientific inquiry.
PHYSICAL SCIENCE: Properties and changes of properties in matter; transfer of energy.
EARTH AND SPACE SCIENCE: Structure of the earth system.

SCIENCE AND TECHNOLOGY: Abilities of technological design; understandings about science and technology.
SCIENCE IN PERSONAL AND SOCIAL PERSPECTIVES: Personal health; populations, resources, and environments; natural hazards; risks and benefits; science and technology in society.
HISTORY AND NATURE OF SCIENCE: Nature of science.

Prices: Teacher's guide (ISBN 1-887725-00-8), $87.59. Set of student books (3 volumes per set) (ISBN 1-887725-06-7), $24.99. Full kit, $3,694.99. *Publisher/supplier:* Sargent-Welch. *Materials:* Available locally, from commercial suppliers, or in kit.

3.3 **There Is No Away.** Insights series. Developed by Education Development Center (EDC). Dubuque, Iowa: Kendall/Hunt, 1997.

Program Overview The Insights program, for grades K-6, consists of 17 modules, several of which are appropriate for middle school. Topics in the program reflect a balance of life, physical, and earth sciences. Insights modules integrate science with the rest of the curriculum, particularly with language arts and mathematics. The activities support cultural, racial, and linguistic diversity. Each module requires about 25 class sessions to complete. The components of an Insights module are a teacher's guide and a kit of materials.

Teacher's Guide **Recommended grade level: 6.** *There Is No Away* introduces students to the subjects of waste production, disposal, and control, and focuses on solid waste disposal and water pollution. The first half of the module develops students' awareness of the amount and variety of trash generated by people. Students collect and analyze a day's waste collected on the school premises and explore the schoolyard for manufactured and natural waste

materials. Then they design and set up controlled experiments to find out what happens to organic and inorganic waste in a sanitary landfill. They examine how the soil in, around, and under a landfill can influence the quality of groundwater. In the second half of the module, students design and construct a model sanitary landfill, investigate the steps involved in purifying water, and develop ideas for alternative packaging and recycling.

There Is No Away is organized in 16 Learning Experiences that can be done in a minimum of 27 class sessions. The teacher's guide includes a unit overview, the 16 Learning Experiences, reproducible masters for student sheets, and annotated lists of suggested readings and audiovisual materials. Science background information, detailed instructions on planning for and conducting each activity, an extensive assessment component, and extensions for integration and enrichment are also included.

Key to Content Standards: 5-8 (see app. C)

UNIFYING CONCEPTS AND PROCESSES: Systems, order, and organization.
SCIENCE AS INQUIRY: Abilities necessary to do scientific inquiry; understandings about scientific inquiry.
EARTH AND SPACE SCIENCE: Structure of the earth system.
SCIENCE AND TECHNOLOGY: Abilities of technological design; understandings about science and technology.
SCIENCE IN PERSONAL AND SOCIAL PERSPECTIVES: Personal health; populations, resources, and environments; natural hazards; risks and benefits; science and technology in society.

Prices: Teacher's guide (ISBN 0-7872-3344-7), $68.90. Materials kit, $272.90. *Publisher/supplier:* Kendall/Hunt. *Materials:* Available locally, from commercial suppliers, or in kit.

Environmental Science—Supplementary Units

3.4 **Acid Rain.** Colin Hocking, Jacqueline Barber, and Jan Coonrod. Reprinted with revisions. Great Explorations in Math and Science (GEMS) series. Berkeley, Calif.: Lawrence Hall of Science, 1994.

Program Overview The Great Explorations in Math and Science (GEMS) series includes more than 50 teacher's guides and handbooks for preschool through grade 10. About 35 of these are appropriate for middle school. The series also includes several assembly presenter's guides and exhibit guides. New guides and handbooks continue to be developed, and current titles are revised frequently. The series is designed to teach key science and mathematics concepts through activity-based learning. The time needed to complete GEMS units varies from about 2 to 10 class sessions.

Teacher's Guide **Recommended grade level: 6-8+.** *Acid Rain* focuses on an important environmental issue, fostering scientific inquiry and critical-thinking skills through varied activity formats. Students develop a working knowledge of the pH scale by measuring the pH of everyday solutions, they make "fake lakes" and determine how the pH changes after an acid-rain storm, and they investigate the effect of buffering to reduce the acidity of lakes. In other activities, students conduct a plant-growth experiment to determine the effect of various dilutions of acid on seed germination, present a play focusing on the effects of acid rain on aquatic life, play a "startling statements" game, and hold a town meeting to discuss possible solutions to the problem of acid rain. The unit provides students with much infor-

mation on acid rain, encourages them to analyze complex environmental issues, and illustrates interrelationships of science, technology, and society.

Each of the 8 activities takes 50 minutes to complete; several activities also involve follow-up homework assignments. The guide includes directions, extensions, brief background information, and reproducible student record sheets.

Key to Content Standards: 5-8 (see app. C)

UNIFYING CONCEPTS AND PROCESSES: Systems, order, and organization; evidence, models, and explanation. **SCIENCE AS INQUIRY:** Abilities necessary to do scientific inquiry; understandings about scientific inquiry. **LIFE SCIENCE:** Populations and ecosystems. **EARTH AND SPACE SCIENCE:** Structure of the earth system. **SCIENCE AND TECHNOLOGY:** Understandings about science and technology. **SCIENCE IN PERSONAL AND SOCIAL PERSPECTIVES:** Personal health; populations, resources, and environments; natural hazards; risks and benefits; science and technology in society. **HISTORY AND NATURE OF SCIENCE:** Nature of science.

Price: $16 (ISBN 0-912511-74-5). *Publisher/supplier:* LHS GEMS. *Materials:* Available locally, or from commercial suppliers.

3.5 **Acid Rain.** Module 2.7. Foundations and Challenges to Encourage Technology-based Science (FACETS) series. Developed by American Chemical Society (Washington, D.C.). Dubuque, Iowa: Kendall/Hunt, 1996.

Program Overview The Foundations and Challenges to Encourage

Technology-based Science (FACETS) program consists of 3 series of 8 modules each for grades 6-8. Each module focuses on a topic in the life, earth, or physical sciences. The time needed to complete FACETS modules varies from 2 to 4 weeks. Each module consists of a student book and a teacher's guide.

Student Edition **Recommended grade level: 7.** In the module *Acid Rain,* students gain an appreciation for the complexity of the issues surrounding acid rain—where it comes from, how it can be studied, what effects it has on the environment, and what is being done about it. Students begin the module by conducting library research to find out as much as possible about acid rain; then they share their information among groups. They work with the pH scale to see how it can be used as a tool for measuring acidity, and they investigate the long-term effects of acid rain on building materials such as steel and limestone. They also simulate the formation of acid rain by dissolving gases in water, which yields acidic solutions. Students then plan and begin to implement a long-term study on acid rain in their area. In the final activity, they present the findings from their study in the form of a poster, a video, or a newsletter that would be helpful and clear to the general public.

Acid Rain, which is divided into 6 activities, requires a minimum of 4 weeks to complete. A narrative section at the end of the module provides background information for students on the global aspects and the chemistry of acid rain.

Teacher's Guide The wraparound teacher's guide includes a unit overview, a time line for completing the module, a materials list, background information, and teaching suggestions.

Key to Content Standards: 5-8 (see app. C)

UNIFYING CONCEPTS AND PROCESSES: Evidence, models, and explanation; change, constancy, and measurement. **SCIENCE AS INQUIRY:** Abilities necessary to do scientific inquiry; understandings about scientific inquiry. **PHYSICAL SCIENCE:** Properties and changes of properties in matter. **SCIENCE AND TECHNOLOGY:** Abilities of technological design; understandings about science and technology. **SCIENCE IN PERSONAL AND SOCIAL PERSPECTIVES:** Populations, resources, and environments; natural hazards; risks and benefits. **HISTORY AND NATURE OF SCIENCE:** Nature of science.

Prices: Student edition (ISBN 0-7872-1445-0), $7.90. Teacher's guide (ISBN 0-7872-1446-9), $14.90. *Publisher/supplier:* Kendall/Hunt. *Materials:* Available locally, or from commercial suppliers.

3.6 **Acid Rain.** National Geographic Kids Network series. Developed by Technical Education Research Centers (TERC) (Cambridge, Mass.). Washington, D.C.: National Geographic Society, 1989.

Program Overview The National Geographic Kids Network series is a telecommunications-based program for grades 3-9 that emphasizes collaborative student research on real-world issues. The series includes 7 units for grades 3-6 and 9 units for grades 6-9. Each unit includes a kit and an 8-week telecommunications package.

ABOUT THE ANNOTATIONS IN "ENVIRONMENTAL SCIENCE—SUPPLEMENTARY UNITS"

Entry Numbers
Curriculum materials are arranged alphabetically by title in each category (Core Materials, Supplementary Units, and Science Activity Books) in chapters 1 through 5 of this guide.

Each curriculum annotation has a two-part entry number: the chapter number is given before the period; the number after the period locates the entry within that chapter. For example, the first entry number in chapter 1 is 1.1; the second entry in chapter 2 is 2.2; and so on.

The entry numbers within each curriculum chapter run consecutively through Core Materials, Supplementary Units, and Science Activity Books.

Order of Bibliographic Information
Following is the arrangement of the facts of publication in the annotations in this section:

- **Title of publication**
- **Number of edition,** if applicable
- **Authors** (an individual author or authors, an institutional author, or a project or program name under which the material was developed)
- **Series title**
- **Series developer,** if applicable
- **Place of publication, publisher, and date of publication**

Recommended Grade Level
The grade level for each piece of material was recommended by teacher evaluators during the development of this guide. In some instances, the recommended grade level may differ slightly from the publisher's advertised level.

Key to Content Standards: 5-8
The key lists the content standards for grades 5-8 from the *National Science Education Standards* (NSES) that are addressed in depth by the item. A key is provided for core materials and supplementary units. (*See* appendix C.)

Price and Acquisition Information

Ordering information appears at the end of each entry. Included are—

- **Prices** (of teacher's guides, student books, lab manuals, and kits or units)
- **Publisher/supplier** (The name of a principal publisher/supplier, although not necessarily the sole source, for the items listed in the price category. Appendix A, "Publishers and Suppliers," provides the address, phone and fax numbers, and electronic ordering information, where available, for each publisher and supplier.)
- **Materials** (various sources from which one might obtain the required materials)

Readers must contact publishers/suppliers for complete and up-to-date listings of the program resources and support materials available for a particular unit. Depending on the developer, these items may be required, optional, or both; they may be offered individually and/or in kits, packages, or boxes. Materials may change with revised editions. The prices given in this chapter for selected resources or materials are based on information from the publishers and suppliers but are not meant to represent the full range of ordering options.

Indexes of Curriculum Materials

The multiple indexes on pp. 449-78 allow easy access to the information in this guide. Various aspects of the curriculum materials—including titles, topics addressed in each unit, grade levels, and standards addressed—are the focus of seven separate indexes. For example, titles and entry numbers are listed in the "Title Index" on pp. 450-54. The "Index of Authors, Series, and Curriculum Projects," on pp. 455-57, provides entry numbers of any annotated titles in a particular series.

Overviews of Core and Supplementary Programs

Appendix D, "Overviews of Core and Supplementary Programs with Titles Annotated in This Guide," on pp. 441-48, lists, by program or series, the individual titles annotated in the sections "Core Materials" and "Supplementary Units" in the five curriculum chapters.

Telecommunications-Based Unit
Recommended grade level: 3-6. In *Acid Rain,* an 8-week telecommunications-based curriculum unit, students explore the issue of acid rain through research and a series of experiments. They learn how to read a pH scale, design and build rain collectors, explore how acid rain forms, examine the effects of acid on nonliving things, and measure the acidity of local rainwater. Then, through the National Geographic Society Kids Network—a computer network that links students around the world doing the same unit—they compare their pH measurements with those taken by students in different parts of the world. As they do so, they look for patterns and make predictions about the geographic distribution of acid rain. In the final week of the unit, students discuss their opinions about acid rain and what should be done about it. Activities incorporate science, geography, social studies, language arts, mathematics, and statistics.

Throughout the unit, students use computers and software (called *NGS Works*) to record information, write letters, make graphs, display maps, and send data to other network participants. They also consult electronically with a scientist about the data they collect.

Acid Rain includes a teacher's guide, reproducible readings and activity sheets, overhead transparencies, posters, wall maps, and a diskette of supplemental information to use with the *NGS Works* software.

Key to Content Standards: 5-8 (see app. C)

UNIFYING CONCEPTS AND PROCESSES: Systems, order, and organization; change, constancy, and measurement.

SCIENCE AS INQUIRY: Abilities necessary to do scientific inquiry; understandings about scientific inquiry.
PHYSICAL SCIENCE: Properties and changes of properties in matter.
EARTH AND SPACE SCIENCE: Structure of the earth system.
SCIENCE AND TECHNOLOGY: Abilities of technological design; understandings about science and technology.
SCIENCE IN PERSONAL AND SOCIAL PERSPECTIVES: Populations, resources, and environments; natural hazards; risks and benefits; science and technology in society.
HISTORY AND NATURE OF SCIENCE: Nature of science.

Prices: Curriculum unit, $149. *NGS Works* software, $199. Acid rain test kit, $150. (Contact NGS regarding membership fees for accessing NGS Kids Network.) *Publisher/supplier:* National Geographic Society. *Materials:* Available from commercial suppliers, or in kit.

3.7 Biology Is Outdoors! A Comprehensive Resource for Studying School Environments. Judith M. Hancock. Walch Reproducible Books. Portland, Maine: Walch, 1991.

Program Overview Biology Is Outdoors! A Comprehensive Resource for Studying School Environments contains investigations that help life science and biology students discover the ecological wealth available in their own schoolyard. The unit can be adapted for various geographic locations and urban or rural settings.

Teacher's Guide **Recommended grade level: 7-8+.** *Biology Is Outdoors!* offers 10 investigations into the familiar world of the schoolgrounds. During these open-ended investigations that focus on data collection and measurement, students first draw a site

map of the school building and grounds. Then they identify and make a list of the plant life on the schoolgrounds, investigate the health of these plants, and conduct a soil analysis. Collecting and observing soil organisms, students look for and identify opportunistic plant and animal species. They also explore the microenvironments found in pavement cracks, in puddles, and on shrubs. Students investigate the effect of the school building itself and that of human activities on the local environment.

Each investigation in *Biology Is Outdoors!* includes a section written for teachers and a section written for students. The teacher's section provides background information, procedures, discussion questions, extensions, a supplies list, and references. The student's section includes reproducible student directions and data sheets, as well as suggestions for further investigations.

Key to Content Standards: 5-8 (see app. C)

UNIFYING CONCEPTS AND PROCESSES: Systems, order, and organization; evidence, models, and explanation; change, constancy, and measurement.
SCIENCE AS INQUIRY: Abilities necessary to do scientific inquiry; understandings about scientific inquiry.
LIFE SCIENCE: Regulation and behavior; populations and ecosystems; diversity and adaptations of organisms.
EARTH AND SPACE SCIENCE: Structure of the earth system.
SCIENCE AND TECHNOLOGY: Abilities of technological design.
SCIENCE IN PERSONAL AND SOCIAL PERSPECTIVES: Populations, resources, and environments; natural hazards.

Price: $21.95 (ISBN 0-8251-1797-6). *Publisher/supplier:* Walch. *Materials:* Available locally.

3.8 Changes in Ecosystems. Mary Atwater, Prentice Baptiste, Lucy Daniel, and others. Unit 38. Macmillan/McGraw-Hill Science series. New York, N.Y.: Macmillan/McGraw-Hill School Publishing, 1995.

Program Overview The Macmillan/McGraw-Hill Science series is a comprehensive, activity-based, K-8 science curriculum made up of 42 stand-alone units, 18 of which are designed for grades 6-8. The series is constructed around 7 major themes: (1) systems and interactions, (2) scale and structure, (3) stability, (4) energy, (5) evolution, (6) patterns of change, and (7) models. The subject of each unit—for example, changes in ecosystems—is presented from the perspective of one or more of these themes. One theme is designated as the "major theme" for a unit, and any others are treated as "related themes." For each unit, a wide range of materials, including some optional components, is available for students and teachers.

Student Edition **Recommended grade level: 7-8.** *Changes in Ecosystems* contains 5 lessons in which students learn about ecosystem changes that occur both naturally and as a result of things people do. All of the lessons stress the importance of interactions among different organisms, and students learn that such interactions keep an ecosystem in balance and allow each organism to survive. Both positive and negative aspects of human interaction with ecosystems are discussed. The organizing themes for this unit are systems and interactions (major theme) and stability (related theme).

Each of the 5 lessons in the unit typically requires 6 days for completion. During the unit, students observe and describe the components of an ecosystem. They learn about factors that shape the environment and about the orderly way in which ecosystems change in ecological succession. They learn the difference between a habitat and a niche. Students also list some of the ways humans influence the environment, evaluate the role of pollution in the degradation of the biosphere, and learn about ways to conserve resources. They also learn about different causes of animal and plant extinctions and study the roles humans have played in such extinctions.

Sample activities include growing and observing a mold garden, and observing and comparing 2 grassy plots over time. Other activities include experimenting with different concentrations of fertilizer to see how a substance that is not a poison can be destructive, and constructing bar graphs of wildlife habitat loss in different countries.

Each lesson contains narrative information and a series of sequential, hands-on activities—such as an introductory "minds-on" activity, short "try this" activities, and a longer "explore" activity. The latter, which are lab activities, each take a class period to complete. Students use activity logs to record ideas, observations, and results.

Special unit features include curriculum links to language arts, literature, mathematics, music, and art; information about science careers; and narrative sections highlighting science, technology, and society connections.

Teacher's Planning Guide The teacher's planning guide, a spiral-bound, wraparound edition, provides information and strategies for teaching the 5 lessons in the student edition. Each lesson is introduced by a 4-page section that offers background information, a lesson-planning guide, and assessment options. Marginal notes on the lesson pages provide discussion ideas, tips on

meeting individual needs, suggestions for addressing misconceptions, assessment ideas, and curriculum connections.

Program Resources and Support Materials A wide range of materials, including some optional components, is available. Examples include consumable and nonconsumable activity materials; audio- and videotapes; interactive videodiscs; color transparencies; assessment materials; a teacher anthology of short stories, poems, fingerplays, and songs; trade books; teacher resource masters; activity cards; activity logs; concept summaries and glossaries for students acquiring English as a second language; and software with problem-solving simulations for students.

Key to Content Standards: 5-8 (see app. C)

UNIFYING CONCEPTS AND PROCESSES: Systems, order, and organization; evidence, models, and explanation; change, constancy, and measurement; evolution and equilibrium.
SCIENCE AS INQUIRY: Abilities necessary to do scientific inquiry; understandings about scientific inquiry.
LIFE SCIENCE: Regulation and behavior; populations and ecosystems; diversity and adaptations of organisms.
SCIENCE AND TECHNOLOGY: Understandings about science and technology.
SCIENCE IN PERSONAL AND SOCIAL PERSPECTIVES: Populations, resources, and environments; natural hazards; risks and benefits; science and technology in society.

Prices: Student edition (ISBN 0-02-276138-1), $7.06. Teacher's planning guide (ISBN 0-02-276086-6), $55.98. Unit package, $115.68. Activity materials kit, $48.00. (Contact publisher/supplier for complete price and ordering information.) *Publisher/supplier:* McGraw-Hill. *Materials:* Available locally, from commercial suppliers, or in kit.

3.9 Chemicals: Choosing Wisely. Developed by E2: Environment and Education (Boulder, Colo.). Environmental Action series. Menlo Park, Calif.: Dale Seymour, 1998.

Program Overview The Environmental Action series consists of 6 stand-alone modules for middle and secondary school students. The series focuses on environmental issues and on the impact of these issues on human health and environmental quality. Each module includes a student edition and a teacher's resource guide.

Student Edition **Recommended grade level: 7-8+.** In *Chemicals: Choosing Wisely,* students investigate the types of materials (for example, various plastics), chemical products, cleaning supplies, and pesticides used in their school. They find out how these materials are used, stored, and disposed of, and what their potential effects are on human health and the environment.

The 15 activities in the module are organized in 4 sections: "Explore the Issues," "Analyze," "Consider Options," and "Take Action." Examples of the activities include the following: learning about the kinds of information on chemical product labels and comparing the relative safety of cleaning products; gathering and recording information on chemical products from expert sources; evaluating the alternatives to using harmful chemical products; weighing costs and benefits; and writing a proposal that includes recommendations for alternatives to current chemical use and practices at the school. About 18 to 20 class sessions are needed to complete the 15 activities in *Chemicals: Choosing Wisely.*

Teacher's Guide The teacher's resource guide includes examples of possible student responses to discussion questions, annotated answers to student activity sheets, and some additional resources and assessment tools. Blackline masters for student activity sheets are also included.

Key to Content Standards: 5-8 (see app. C)

UNIFYING CONCEPTS AND PROCESSES: Evidence, models, and explanation. SCIENCE AS INQUIRY: Abilities necessary to do scientific inquiry; understandings about scientific inquiry. PHYSICAL SCIENCE: Properties and changes of property in matter. SCIENCE AND TECHNOLOGY: Understandings about science and technology. SCIENCE IN PERSONAL AND SOCIAL PERSPECTIVES: Personal health; populations, resources, and environments; natural hazards; risks and benefits; science and technology in society.

Prices: Student edition (ISBN 0-201-49535-X), $5.95. Teacher's guide (ISBN 0-201-49534-1), $13.95. *Publisher/supplier:* Dale Seymour. *Materials:* Available locally, or from commercial suppliers.

3.10 Chemical Survey and Solutions and Pollution. Chemical Education for Public Understanding Program (CEPUP) series. Developed by Lawrence Hall of Science (Berkeley, Calif.). Menlo Park, Calif.: Addison-Wesley, 1990.

Program Overview The Chemical Education for Public Understanding Program (CEPUP) series consists of 12 modules for grades 7-9. The modules focus on chemicals and the interaction of chemicals with people and the environment. The series promotes the use of scientific principles, processes, and evidence in public decision making. The components of a CEPUP module are a teacher's guide and a kit of materials. (SEPUP—the Science Education for Public Understanding Program is the second phase of the project that began as CEPUP.)

Teacher's Guide **Recommended grade level: 7-8+.** This teacher's guide contains 2 modules: *Chemical Survey* and *Solutions and Pollution. Chemical Survey* is a 3-activity introduction to chemicals and their relationship to societal issues. During the activities, students conduct a 5-question class survey of their knowledge and attitudes about chemicals, analyze the data, and explore possible sources of influence on students' ideas about chemicals. Then they compare the class data with data they obtain from their parents using the same survey. The survey addresses such issues as the best definition of the word "chemical," what things are made up of chemicals, and whether chemicals are dangerous.

Solutions and Pollution, a 7-activity module, introduces students to properties of water and to the issue of water pollution. Students explore the solubility of various substances in water and learn the difference in meaning between "dilute" and "concentrated"; they learn about "parts per million" by successively diluting food coloring solutions in water. Students also explore the reactions of an acid, a base, water, and universal indicator when these substances are mixed together in various quantities. They develop an operational definition for acid and base and explore the question of whether dilution is an answer to water pollution. Students are introduced to the concept of acid-base neutralization, and they carry out a quantitative experiment to determine the relative concentration of 2 solutions. They design an experiment to determine the relative concentration of household ammonia when compared to a base solution of known concentration, and they use their acquired knowledge about acids, bases, and relative concentrations to solve a simulated water-pollution problem.

The 3 activities in the *Chemical Survey* module take 3 class periods

of 40 to 50 minutes each to complete. The 7 activities in *Solutions and Pollution* take 12 class periods of 40 to 50 minutes each.

Included in this slim, wire-bound book are reproducible student sheets, directions for guiding activities and discussions, and an end-of-unit test.

Key to Content Standards: 5-8 (see app. C)

UNIFYING CONCEPTS AND PROCESSES: Change, constancy, and measurement. SCIENCE AS INQUIRY: Abilities necessary to do scientific inquiry; understandings about scientific inquiry. PHYSICAL SCIENCE: Properties and changes of properties in matter. SCIENCE AND TECHNOLOGY: Understandings about science and technology. SCIENCE IN PERSONAL AND SOCIAL PERSPECTIVES: Risks and benefits.

Prices: Teacher's guide (ISBN 0-201-28420-0), $19.99; module, $179.99. *Publisher/supplier:* Sargent-Welch/VWR Scientific. *Materials:* Available locally, from commercial suppliers, or in kit.

3.11 Cleaning Water. Module 2.6. Foundations and Challenges to Encourage Technology-based Science (FACETS) series. Developed by American Chemical Society (Washington, D.C.). Dubuque, Iowa: Kendall/Hunt, 1996.

Program Overview The Foundations and Challenges to Encourage Technology-based Science (FACETS) program consists of 3 series of 8 modules each for grades 6-8. Each module focuses on a topic in the life, earth, or physical sciences. The time needed to complete FACETS modules varies from 2 to 4 weeks. Each module consists of a student book and a teacher's guide.

Student Edition **Recommended grade level: 7.** In the module *Cleaning Water,* students investigate some of the contaminants that can get into drinking water, discover how chemical tests can reveal some of the impurities that contaminate the water supply, and learn how some contaminants can be removed by special types of filters. During the module, students role-play the part of marketing employees for a water filter company. They also conduct research on different types of drinking water contaminants. They use map skills and the concept of a watershed to determine where impurities could have entered the water supply. They also test water samples for a variety of impurities and experiment with different types of filtering materials to determine their effect on impure water samples. Students then design, build, and test a filter for the home market. In the final activity, they present a marketing plan for each other's filters.

Cleaning Water is a 3-week module divided into 6 activities, which each take between 2 and 3 class periods to complete. A narrative section at the end of the module provides background information for students on water pollution and water testing.

Teacher's Guide The wraparound teacher's guide includes a unit overview, a time line for completing the module, a materials list, background information, and teaching suggestions.

Key to Content Standards: 5-8 (see app. C)

UNIFYING CONCEPTS AND PROCESSES: Evidence, models, and explanation; change, constancy, and measurement. **SCIENCE AS INQUIRY:** Abilities necessary to do scientific inquiry; understandings about scientific inquiry. **EARTH AND SPACE SCIENCE:** Structure of the earth system.

SCIENCE AND TECHNOLOGY: Understandings about science and technology. **SCIENCE IN PERSONAL AND SOCIAL PERSPECTIVES:** Personal health; populations, resources, and environments; natural hazards; science and technology in society.

Prices: Student edition (ISBN 0-7872-1447-7), $7.90. Teacher's guide (ISBN 0-7872-1448-5), $14.90. *Publisher/supplier:* Kendall/Hunt. *Materials:* Available locally, or from commercial suppliers.

3.12 Earth's Ecosystems. Mary Atwater, Prentice Baptiste, Lucy Daniel, and others. Unit 36. Macmillan/McGraw-Hill Science series. New York, N.Y.: Macmillan/McGraw-Hill Publishing, 1995.

Program Overview The Macmillan/McGraw-Hill Science series is a comprehensive, activity-based, K-8 science curriculum made up of 42 stand-alone units, 18 of which are designed for grades 6-8. The series is constructed around 7 major themes: (1) systems and interactions, (2) scale and structure, (3) stability, (4) energy, (5) evolution, (6) patterns of change, and (7) models. The subject of each unit—for example, earth's ecosystems—is presented from the perspective of one or more of these themes. One theme is designated as the "major theme" for a unit, and any others are treated as "related themes." For each unit, a wide range of materials, including some optional components, is available for students and teachers.

Student Edition **Recommended grade level: 7.** *Earth's Ecosystems* contains 5 lessons that introduce students to interactions among living and nonliving parts of the environment and to the unique roles of humans in their ecosystems. The organizing themes for this unit are systems and interactions (major theme) and stability, evolution, patterns of change, and energy (related themes).

Each of the 5 lessons in the unit typically requires 6 days for completion. During the unit, students learn about the living and nonliving parts of an ecosystem. They examine the water, carbon, oxygen, and nitrogen cycles. They discover 6 major land biomes and 2 aquatic ecosystems on earth and learn how human activities can change these. Students also study populations in ecosystems and factors that limit their growth; they distinguish between a population, a community, and an ecosystem; and they compare and contrast primary and secondary succession.

Sample activities include observing the physical conditions in which brine shrimp grow, noting particularly the effect of light and temperature; and examining the differences in components of various soil samples. Other activities include graphing temperature and precipitation data from different earth regions and making inferences about the climate in those regions; counting the numbers and types of plants in a square-meter plot; observing and identifying animal skulls found in an owl pellet to learn about the owl's niche in its ecosystem; formulating a model of a food web and inferring the effects of changes in the food web; and observing succession in pond water.

Each lesson contains narrative information and a series of sequential, hands-on activities—such as an introductory "minds-on" activity, short "try this" activities, and a longer "explore" activity. The latter, which are lab activities, each take a class period to complete. Students use activity logs to record ideas, observations, and results.

Special unit features include curriculum links to language arts, literature, mathematics, music, and art; information about science careers; and narrative sections highlighting science, technology, and society connections.

Teacher's Planning Guide The teacher's planning guide, a spiral-bound, wraparound edition, provides information and strategies for teaching the 5 lessons in the student edition. Each lesson is introduced by a 4-page section that offers background information, a lesson-planning guide, and assessment options. Marginal notes on the lesson pages provide discussion ideas, tips on meeting individual needs, suggestions for addressing misconceptions, assessment ideas, and curriculum connections.

Program Resources and Support Materials A wide range of materials, including some optional components, is available. Examples include consumable and nonconsumable activity materials; audio- and videotapes; interactive videodiscs; color transparencies; assessment materials; a teacher anthology of short stories, poems, fingerplays, and songs; trade books; teacher resource masters; activity cards; activity logs; concept summaries and glossaries for students acquiring English; and software with problem-solving simulations for students.

Key to Content Standards: 5-8 (see app. C)

UNIFYING CONCEPTS AND PROCESSES: Systems, order, and organization; evidence, models, and explanation; change, constancy, and measurement; evolution and equilibrium.
SCIENCE AS INQUIRY: Abilities necessary to do scientific inquiry; understandings about scientific inquiry.
LIFE SCIENCE: Regulation and behavior; populations and ecosystems; diversity and adaptations of organisms.
EARTH AND SPACE SCIENCE: Structure of the earth system.
SCIENCE IN PERSONAL AND SOCIAL PERSPECTIVES: Populations, resources, and environments; natural hazards; risks and benefits; science and technology in society.

Prices: Student edition (ISBN 0-02-276136-5), $7.06. Teacher's planning guide (ISBN 0-02-276084-9), $55.98. Unit package, $115.83. Activity materials kit, $64.00. (Contact publisher/supplier for complete price and ordering information.) ***Publisher/supplier:*** McGraw-Hill. ***Materials:*** Available locally, from commercial suppliers, or in kit.

3.13 Eco-Inquiry: A Guide to Ecological Learning Experiences for the Upper Elementary/Middle Grades. Kathleen Hogan. Institute of Ecosystem Studies Eco-Inquiry Project. Dubuque, Iowa: Kendall/Hunt, 1994.

Program Overview The modules in *Eco-Inquiry: A Guide to Ecological Learning Experiences for the Upper Elementary/Middle Grades* contain real-world projects and investigations in ecology. The modules build students' understanding of ecological processes in their local environment.

Teacher's Guide **Recommended grade level: 5-8.** Learning practical ecology from a local perspective is the focus of *Eco-Inquiry*. This guide offers 3 modules, each with a different ecological challenge for students. In module 1, students fulfill a request from a local community to survey what is living on a plot of land. They construct a food web from the study site and write environmental impact statements to trace how one change in the site could affect the entire food web. In module 2, students explore decomposition and construct a classroom decomposition chamber. In module 3, they explore nutrient recycling, doing research to test the effects of compost tea on radish growth. The modules can stand alone or can be used in sequence at one or several grade levels.

Each module contains from 7 to 10 lessons and requires from 4 to 7 weeks for completion. (Module 1 takes 4 to 5 weeks, module 2 takes 4 to 5 weeks, and module 3 takes 6 to 7 weeks.) The guide offers numerous tips on how best to use the modules. It includes a variety of assessment strategies.

Key to Content Standards: 5-8 (see app. C)

UNIFYING CONCEPTS AND PROCESSES: Systems, order, and organization; evidence, models, and explanation; change, constancy, and measurement.
SCIENCE AS INQUIRY: Abilities necessary to do scientific inquiry; understandings about scientific inquiry.
LIFE SCIENCE: Regulation and behavior; populations and ecosystems.
EARTH AND SPACE SCIENCE: Structure of the earth system.
SCIENCE AND TECHNOLOGY: Abilities of technological design; understandings about science and technology.
SCIENCE IN PERSONAL AND SOCIAL PERSPECTIVES: Populations, resources, and environments; natural hazards; risks and benefits; science and technology in society.
HISTORY AND NATURE OF SCIENCE: Science as a human endeavor; nature of science.

Price: $36.95 (ISBN 0-7872-0137-5). ***Publisher/supplier:*** Kendall/Hunt. ***Materials:*** Available locally, or from commercial suppliers.

3.14 Ecology Lab. Science Technology and Reading (STAR) series. Developed by Reading Is Fundamental (Washington, D.C.). Dubuque, Iowa: Kendall/Hunt, 1996.

Program Overview Designed for the upper elementary grades, the Science Technology and Reading (STAR) series consists of 8 thematic "labs" in the natural and physical sciences. Each lab focuses both on science activities and on a genre of children's literature, developing correlations between the science process and the process of reading. In addition to a teacher's guide for each of the 8 labs, the STAR program includes a mentor's guide for scientists, engineers, and others assisting in the classroom.

Teacher's Guide **Recommended grade level: 4-6.** In *Ecology Lab*, students become residents of a mythical town—Anytown—whose residents must decide what to do with a large tract of undeveloped land, known as Lakeland. Through a series of hands-on activities, students conduct experiments and gather data to help them decide what to do with the land. Students represent various interest groups—conservationists, recreation advocates, developers, business-growth advocates, and so on—at a town meeting. Then they vote on the plans offered. Students draw up a site plan using the school grounds as the plot of land to be developed. They test air quality and soil permeability and percolation rate, learn about water filtration, conduct a population study and a recreation survey, and use mathematics to interpret employment data for Anytown.

Ecology Lab includes ideas for cross-curricular integration, from writing an "eco haiku" to making a relief map of Lakeland. It also includes a list of resources, including books, computer software, and audiovisual materials. Reproducible pages for students, such as lab procedures, data sheets, and information handouts, are also provided.

Key to Content Standards: 5-8 (see app. C)

UNIFYING CONCEPTS AND PROCESSES: Systems, order, and organization; evidence, models, and explanation; change, constancy, and measurement. **SCIENCE AS INQUIRY:** Abilities necessary to do scientific inquiry; understandings about scientific inquiry. **LIFE SCIENCE:** Populations and ecosystems.

EARTH AND SPACE SCIENCE: Structure of the earth system. **SCIENCE AND TECHNOLOGY:** Abilities of technological design. **SCIENCE IN PERSONAL AND SOCIAL PERSPECTIVES:** Personal health; populations, resources, and environments; natural hazards; risks and benefits. **HISTORY AND NATURE OF SCIENCE:** Nature of science.

Prices: Teacher's guide (ISBN 0-7872-1456-6), $21.90. Mentor's guide, $3.90. *Publisher/supplier:* Kendall/Hunt. *Materials:* Available locally.

3.15 **Energy Conservation.** Developed by E2: Environment and Education (Boulder, Colo.). Environmental Action series. Menlo Park, Calif.: Dale Seymour, 1998.

Program Overview The Environmental Action series consists of 6 stand-alone modules for middle and secondary school students. The series focuses on environmental issues and on the impact of these issues on human health and environmental quality. Each module includes a student edition and a teacher's resource guide.

Student Edition **Recommended grade level: 7-8+.** In *Energy Conservation,* students explore the sources, production, uses, and environmental effects of energy, and they examine ways to improve the energy efficiency of their school and homes.

The 16 activities in the module are organized in 4 sections: "Explore the Issues," "Analyze," "Consider Options," and "Take Action." Examples of the activities include the following: investigating the environmental impact of various fossil fuels; conducting an energy audit of the school; brainstorming ways to reduce waste, increase efficiency, and change personal behavior; and preparing a proposal that includes

recommendations for reducing energy consumption at the school. About 18 to 20 class sessions of 50 minutes each are needed to complete the 16 activities in *Energy Conservation.*

Teacher's Guide The teacher's resource guide includes examples of possible student responses to discussion questions, annotated answers to student activity sheets, and some additional resources and assessment tools. Blackline masters for student activity sheets are also included.

Key to Content Standards: 5-8 (see app. C)

UNIFYING CONCEPTS AND PROCESSES: Evidence, models, and explanation. **SCIENCE AS INQUIRY:** Abilities necessary to do scientific inquiry; understandings about scientific inquiry. **PHYSICAL SCIENCE:** Transfer of energy. **SCIENCE AND TECHNOLOGY:** Understandings about science and technology. **SCIENCE IN PERSONAL AND SOCIAL PERSPECTIVES:** Risks and benefits; science and technology in society.

Prices: Student edition (ISBN 0-201-49529-5), $5.95. Teacher's guide (ISBN 0-201-49528-7), $13.95. *Publisher/supplier:* Dale Seymour. *Materials:* Available locally, or from commercial suppliers.

3.16 **Global Warming and the Greenhouse Effect.** Reprinted with revisions. Colin Hocking, Cary Sneider, John Erickson, and Richard Golden. Great Explorations in Math and Science (GEMS) series. Berkeley, Calif: Lawrence Hall of Science, 1992.

Program Overview The Great Explorations in Math and Science (GEMS) series includes more than 50 teacher's guides and handbooks for preschool through grade 10. About 35 of these are appropriate for middle school. The series also includes several assembly presenter's guides and exhibit guides. New guides and handbooks continue to be developed, and current titles are revised frequently. The series is designed to teach key science and mathematics concepts through activity-based learning. The time needed to complete GEMS units varies from about 2 to 10 class sessions.

Teacher's Guide **Recommended grade level: 7-8+.** *Global Warming and the Greenhouse Effect* uses a variety of hands-on laboratory activities, simulations, and discussions to help students learn about the greenhouse effect and its causes, the uncertainties of global warming theory, and the possible consequences of global warming. At the same time, students improve their understanding of important scientific concepts, such as the molecular model of heat, ways in which energy is transferred, how objects attain a stable temperature, and the structure of the atmosphere.

Among the activities in the unit, students compare the heating of air in an open container with the heating of air in a closed container to develop the concepts of heating and cooling and equilibrium. Students play a board game that simulates what happens to the light energy from the sun when it enters the earth's atmosphere. They also perform a series of experiments in which they compare the relative concentration of carbon dioxide in gas samples from 4 different sources (ambient air, human breath, car exhaust, and a chemical reaction between vinegar and baking soda). Students consider a wide range of impacts that might result from global warming. They role-play people from various countries and interest groups as they participate in a "world conference" to discuss how people might cooperate to decrease the greenhouse effect or how they might cope with the changes it causes.

The unit requires 9 or 10 class periods of 45 to 60 minutes each.

The guide includes directions, extensions, brief background information, and reproducible student record sheets.

Key to Content Standards: 5-8 (see app. C)

UNIFYING CONCEPTS AND PROCESSES: Systems, order, and organization; evidence, models, and explanation; change, constancy, and measurement; evolution and equilibrium. **SCIENCE AS INQUIRY:** Abilities necessary to do scientific inquiry; understandings about scientific inquiry. **PHYSICAL SCIENCE:** Transfer of energy. **EARTH AND SPACE SCIENCE:** Structure of the earth system. **SCIENCE AND TECHNOLOGY:** Understandings about science and technology. **SCIENCE IN PERSONAL AND SOCIAL PERSPECTIVES:** Natural hazards; risks and benefits; science and technology in society. **HISTORY AND NATURE OF SCIENCE:** Nature of science.

Price: $16 (ISBN 0-912511-75-3). *Publisher/supplier:* LHS GEMS. *Materials:* Available locally, or from commercial suppliers.

3.17 **Health Risk: Shadow over Crystal Valley.** Texas Learning Technology Group (TLTG). TLTG Environmental Science Series. Austin, Tex.: TLTG, 1996.

Program Overview The TLTG [Texas Learning Technology Group] Environmental Science Series is a multimedia program for grades 7-12. Designed for the single-computer classroom, the 4 units in this series focus on environmental pollution and health-related issues from a variety of perspectives. For each unit, all video, graphics, and text-based materials—including the teacher's and students' guides—are contained on a CD-ROM.

Computer-Based Classroom Program **Recommended grade level: 7-8.** *Health Risk* is a 1- to 2-week computer-based investigation that involves students in researching and evaluating potential health risks in an imaginary community. The investigation begins as several birds and other animals are discovered with deformities that may be related to environmental pollutants. Assuming the role of a public health investigator in a regional health department, students work in collaborative groups to determine if a toxic agent is present in the environment. They try to identify the source of the toxic agent and to ascertain whether the health of area residents is at risk.

Various computer-based sources of information are available as students work through the investigation. Among them are interviews, medical records, tests of biological and environmental media, and a guide to environmental pollutants. Students learn about pesticide contamination, effects of heavy metals, toxicity of various substances, and nonpoint-source pollution. They also engage in a number of activities—such as creating evidence charts, data tables, and concept maps—that help them learn how to organize, interpret, and present data.

Two text-based support documents—a teacher's guide and a student guide—accompany the CD-ROM. The teacher's guide contains suggestions for classroom management and off-computer activities. The student guide offers research strategies, background information, profiles of people in environmental health careers, skill-building activities or labs, and projects. Both guides are also included on the CD-ROM; they can be viewed and printed out.

Key to Content Standards: 5-8 (see app. C)

UNIFYING CONCEPTS AND PROCESSES: Systems, order, and organization; evidence, models, and explanation; change, constancy, and measurement.

SCIENCE AS INQUIRY: Abilities necessary to do scientific inquiry; understandings about scientific inquiry.

SCIENCE AND TECHNOLOGY: Abilities of technological design; understandings about science and technology.

SCIENCE IN PERSONAL AND SOCIAL PERSPECTIVES: Personal health; populations, resources, and environments; risks and benefits; science and technology in society.

HISTORY AND NATURE OF SCIENCE: Nature of science; history of science.

Prices: Unit, $90.00. Teacher's guide (print) (ISBN 0-9643220-4-8), $10.00. Student guide (print) (ISBN 0-9643228-8-0), $7.50. *Publisher/supplier:* Texas Learning Technology Group. *Materials:* Available locally, or from commercial suppliers.

3.18 **Investigating and Evaluating Environmental Issues and Actions: Skill Development Program.** Harold R. Hungerford, Ralph A. Litherland, R. Ben Peyton, and others. Champaign, Ill.: Stipes, 1996.

Program Overview Investigating and Evaluating Environmental Issues and Actions: Skill Development Program is designed to teach students how to investigate and evaluate science-related social issues. During this one-semester unit, students conduct independent research on environmental issues and follow up on this research with action as responsible citizens.

Teacher's Guide **Recommended grade level: 7-8+.** *Investigating and Evaluating Environmental Issues and Actions* is designed under the assumption that students have a foundation in basic ecological concepts such as energy transfer, population dynamics, homeostatic balance, and community and ecosystem interactions.

Five of the unit's 6 modules are "training" modules. In them, stu-

dents define the term "environment"; analyze a set of environmental interactions in terms of human impact on the environment; and learn to identify the various players, positions, beliefs, and values involved in many environmental issues. Students also learn how to locate, analyze, and use information sources; they learn the difference between first-hand and secondary sources of information; and they identify government or private agencies to which they can write for information. Students write a succinct summary of an article on an environmental topic. They also acquire the skills and strategies useful for collecting data first-hand—for example, doing surveys and using questionnaires—and they discuss techniques for communicating and interpreting data, including both descriptive and graphic methods.

Students apply what they have learned by conducting their own autonomous investigation of an environmental issue. They choose a topic to investigate, formulate a research question, establish the techniques to collect the data that will answer the research questions, and carry out the research. The teacher's tasks during this module are to establish guidelines for the investigation and to serve as a facilitator.

In the final module, students are introduced to the basic elements of environmental action—persuasion, consumerism, political action, and ecomanagement. They also are presented with a list of 14 criteria that comprise a decision-making model relative to responsible citizenship action in the environmental realm.

The unit, which takes about a semester to complete, includes a teacher's guide and student book.

Key to Content Standards: 5-8 (see app. C)

UNIFYING CONCEPTS AND PROCESSES: Systems, order, and organization; evidence, models, and explanation; change, constancy, and measurement.

SCIENCE AS INQUIRY: Abilities necessary to do scientific inquiry; understandings about scientific inquiry.

LIFE SCIENCE: Regulation and behavior; populations and ecosystems; diversity and adaptations of organisms.

SCIENCE AND TECHNOLOGY: Abilities of technological design; understandings about science and technology.

SCIENCE IN PERSONAL AND SOCIAL PERSPECTIVES: Personal health; populations, resources, and environments; natural hazards; risks and benefits; science and technology in society.

HISTORY AND NATURE OF SCIENCE: Science as a human endeavor; nature of science.

Prices: Teacher's edition (ISBN 0-87563-650-0), $24.50. Student edition (ISBN 0-87563-651-9), $12.80. *Publisher/supplier:* Stipes. *Materials:* Available locally, or from commercial suppliers.

3.19 **Investigating Groundwater: The Fruitvale Story.** Chemical Education for Public Understanding Program (CEPUP) series. Developed by Lawrence Hall of Science (Berkeley, Calif.). Menlo Park, Calif.: Addison-Wesley, 1991.

Program Overview The Chemical Education for Public Understanding Program (CEPUP) series consists of 12 modules for grades 7-9. The modules focus on chemicals and the interaction of chemicals with people and the environment. The series promotes the use of scientific principles, processes, and evidence in public decision making. The components of a CEPUP module are a teacher's guide and a kit of materials. (SEPUP—the Science Education for Public Understanding Program—is the second phase of the project that began as CEPUP.)

Teacher's Guide **Recommended grade level: 7-8+.** In *Investigating Groundwater: The Fruitvale Story,* students investigate reports of water contamination in the imaginary town of Fruitvale. Topics discussed during the unit include aquifers and aquitards, concentration and dilution, pollutants, toxicity, and uncertainty in sampling.

Among the activities in this unit, students experiment with the movement of water through materials such as gravel, sand, and clay to learn about factors affecting groundwater movement, and they perform serial dilutions as an introduction to methods of expressing concentration levels in parts per million. Students attempt to locate the source of groundwater contamination in Fruitvale by testing water from various test wells (using simulated samples); they identify the contamination source and plot its distribution; and they role-play a town meeting in which information is presented to the citizens of Fruitvale, who must decide on a plan to clean up the contaminated area.

The 7 sequential activities in *Investigating Groundwater* take 9 class periods of 40 to 50 minutes each to complete. Included in this slim, wire-bound book are reproducible student sheets, directions for guiding activities and discussions, suggestions for extensions, and an end-of-unit test.

Key to Content Standards: 5-8 (see app. C)

UNIFYING CONCEPTS AND PROCESSES: Evidence, models, and explanation; change, constancy, and measurement. SCIENCE AS INQUIRY: Abilities necessary to do scientific inquiry; understandings about scientific inquiry. PHYSICAL SCIENCE: Properties and changes of properties in matter. EARTH AND SPACE SCIENCE: Structure of the earth system. SCIENCE AND TECHNOLOGY: Abilities of technological design; understandings about science and technology.

SCIENCE IN PERSONAL AND SOCIAL PERSPECTIVES: Personal health; populations, resources, and environments; natural hazards; risks and benefits; science and technology in society.

Prices: Teacher's guide (ISBN 0-201-28426-X), $19.99. Module, $159.99. *Publisher/supplier:* Sargent-Welch/VWR Scientific. *Materials:* Available locally, from commercial suppliers, or in kit.

3.20 Investigating Hazardous Materials. Chemical Education for Public Understanding Program (CEPUP) series. Developed by Lawrence Hall of Science (Berkeley, Calif.). Menlo Park, Calif.: Addison-Wesley, 1994.

Program Overview The Chemical Education for Public Understanding Program (CEPUP) series consists of 12 modules for grades 7-9. The modules focus on chemicals and the interaction of chemicals with people and the environment. The series promotes the use of scientific principles, processes, and evidence in public decision making. The components of a CEPUP module are a teacher's guide and a kit of materials. (SEPUP—the Science Education for Public Understanding Program—is the second phase of the project that began as CEPUP.)

Teacher's Guide Recommended grade level: 7-8+. In *Investigating Hazardous Materials,* students participate in a simulation that involves identifying liquid and solid hazardous wastes in a drum found on a lot that is to be developed as the site of a new school. At the beginning of the module, students view a videotape of a hazardous materials team responding to the discovery of a drum of potentially dangerous waste. Students are introduced to the methods and equipment used to identify waste. During the rest of the module, they explore the major categories of haz-

ardous wastes (flammable, corrosive, toxic, reactive), and they develop tests to identify substances belonging to these categories. Students work in groups to plan a separation of a complex mixture of liquids and solids. Then they use these plans to separate the mixture, which represents the contents of the barrel of simulated hazardous waste.

Later in the module, students are asked to consider the costs and risks of disposing of an additional 99 barrels of hazardous materials. They are introduced to decision trees as a system of categorizing or identifying unknown materials quickly. Students also consider the issues involved in the transportation of potentially toxic and hazardous substances through communities, and they discuss trade-offs involved in the transportation, use, and disposal of hazardous substances.

The 5 activities in *Investigating Hazardous Materials* take 9 class periods of 40 to 50 minutes each to complete. Included in this slim, wire-bound book are reproducible student sheets, directions for guiding activities and discussions, suggestions for extensions, and an end-of-unit test.

Key to Content Standards: 5-8 (see app. C)

UNIFYING CONCEPTS AND PROCESSES: Evidence, models, and explanation. SCIENCE AS INQUIRY: Abilities necessary to do scientific inquiry; understandings about scientific inquiry. PHYSICAL SCIENCE: Properties and changes of properties in matter. SCIENCE AND TECHNOLOGY: Understandings about science and technology. SCIENCE IN PERSONAL AND SOCIAL PERSPECTIVES: Natural hazards; risks and benefits; science and technology in society.

Prices: Teacher's guide (ISBN 0-201-45542-0), $19.99. Module, $189.99. *Publisher/supplier:* Sargent-Welch/VWR Scientific. *Materials:* Available locally, from commercial suppliers, or in kit.

3.21 **Living Lightly on the Planet: A Global Environmental Education Guidebook.** Vol. I. Maura O'Connor. Living Lightly series. Milwaukee, Wis.: Schlitz Audubon Center, 1985.

Program Overview The Living Lightly series is a program for grades K-12. Each volume focuses on the environment and on decision making related to environmental issues. The series includes 4 volumes, 1 of which is designed for grades 7-9.

Teacher's Guide **Recommended grade level: 7-8+.** *Living Lightly on the Planet,* an activity and resource guide, contains 29 investigations designed to develop young people's environmental awareness and ability to think about and make decisions for a healthy environment. The investigations are organized in 5 units on the following topics: (1) population growth and carrying capacity, (2) land use patterns and development, (3) the mechanics of groundwater pollution, (4) the interdependence of plants, animals, and the environment, and (5) the advantages and disadvantages of making consumer choices from an environmentalist point of view.

Among the activities in the guide, students graph the past and projected growth of the global human population. They bid for land at a simulated land auction. They create a display depicting the purposes for which average Americans use water each day and how much they use. Students also construct food chains and food webs on the basis of their observations of plants and animals. They determine how their consumer choices would be affected if a natural-resource rationing system were imposed.

Most of the information in the units is background for the teacher and suggestions for carrying out the investigations. Each unit contains resource materials for students— data sheets, readings on environ-

mental concerns, role cards for use in simulations, and a "taking action" page with suggestions for extending concepts and applying them to local situations.

Key to Content Standards: 5-8 (see app. C)

UNIFYING CONCEPTS AND PROCESSES: Systems, order, and organization; evidence, models, and explanation. **SCIENCE AS INQUIRY:** Abilities necessary to do scientific inquiry; understandings about scientific inquiry. **LIFE SCIENCE:** Structure and function in living systems; regulation and behavior; populations and ecosystems. **EARTH AND SPACE SCIENCE:** Structure of the earth system. **SCIENCE AND TECHNOLOGY:** Understandings about science and technology. **SCIENCE IN PERSONAL AND SOCIAL PERSPECTIVES:** Personal health; populations, resources, and environments; natural hazards; risks and benefits; science and technology in society.

Price: $22. Publisher/supplier: Schlitz Audubon Center. *Materials:* Available locally, or from commercial suppliers.

3.22 **Managing Crop Pests.** Module 3.3. Foundations and Challenges to Encourage Technology-based Science (FACETS) series. Developed by American Chemical Society (Washington, D.C.). Dubuque, Iowa: Kendall/Hunt, 1996.

Program Overview The Foundations and Challenges to Encourage Technology-based Science (FACETS) program consists of 3 series of 8 modules each for grades 6-8. Each module focuses on a topic in the life, earth, or physical sciences. The time needed to complete FACETS modules varies from 2 to 4 weeks. Each module consists of a student book and a teacher's guide.

Student Edition **Recommended grade level: 8.** In the module *Managing Crop Pests,* students learn how crop pests such as fungi, rodents, insects, and weeds are managed on farmlands. They explore pesticides and alternative agriculture methods for managing crop pests and examine the trade-offs—such as cost, efficiency, and environmental impact— associated with both methods. During the module, students conduct library research on the types of organisms that can have a detrimental effect on crops. They also make and use a model of groundwater to learn how substances from farm runoff can contaminate the water supply. In other activities, students test local water samples for the presence of nitrates, and they participate in a simulation that shows how pesticide-resistant strains of crop pests can develop. Students also research what is involved in a pest management strategy known as Integrated Pest Management (IPM), and they design an IPM plan for a farm.

Managing Crop Pests is a 3- to 4-week module divided into 6 activities, which each take between 2 and 4 class periods to complete. A narrative section at the end of the module provides background information for students on crop pests and the water cycle.

Teacher's Guide The wraparound teacher's guide includes a unit overview, a time line for completing the module, a materials list, background information, and teaching suggestions.

Key to Content Standards: 5-8 (see app. C)

UNIFYING CONCEPTS AND PROCESSES: Systems, order, and organization; evidence, models, and explanation. **SCIENCE AS INQUIRY:** Abilities necessary to do scientific inquiry; understandings about scientific inquiry. **EARTH AND SPACE SCIENCE:** Structure of the earth system.

SCIENCE IN PERSONAL AND SOCIAL PER-SPECTIVES: Natural hazards; risks and benefits; science and technology in society.

Prices: Student edition (ISBN 0-7872-1474-4), $7.90. Teacher's guide (ISBN 0-7872-1475-2), $14.90. *Publisher/supplier:* Kendall/Hunt. *Materials:* Available locally, or from commercial suppliers.

3.23 **The Monitor's Handbook.** Gayla Campbell and Steve Wildberger. Chestertown, Md.: LaMotte Co., 1992.

Program Overview *The Monitor's Handbook* is a reference booklet containing information about testing water quality. Although not written as a curriculum unit, the guide will support an environmental unit on water quality.

Teacher's Guide **Recommended grade level: 7-8+.** *The Monitor's Handbook,* a 4-chapter reference guide, was developed for people who want to learn more about local waterways and to find out about methods and tests for measuring water quality. Topics covered include the reasons for monitoring water quality, the difference between "good" and "bad" water, the concept of watersheds, where and how to sample water, guidelines for collecting water samples, water-quality factors (such as temperature, turbidity, pH, dissolved oxygen, odor, alkalinity, hardness, nutrients, coliform bacteria, salinity) and their significance, and how to analyze and present data.

An appendix provides basic information on starting a water-quality monitoring program. It explains how to manage people, operate on a budget, and select the right type of equipment. A short but fairly technical bibliography on water-quality

monitoring and data analysis is included.

Key to Content Standards: 5-8 (see app. C)

UNIFYING CONCEPTS AND PROCESSES: Systems, order, and organization; evidence, models, and explanation; change, constancy, and measurement. **SCIENCE AS INQUIRY:** Abilities necessary to do scientific inquiry; understandings about scientific inquiry. **PHYSICAL SCIENCE:** Properties and changes of properties in matter; transfer of energy. **LIFE SCIENCE:** Populations and ecosystems. **EARTH AND SPACE SCIENCE:** Structure of the earth system. **SCIENCE AND TECHNOLOGY:** Understandings about science and technology. **SCIENCE IN PERSONAL AND SOCIAL PER-SPECTIVES:** Populations, resources, and environments; natural hazards; risks and benefits; science and technology in society.

Price: $8.75. *Publisher/supplier:* LaMotte. *Materials:* Available locally, or from commercial suppliers.

3.24 **Oil Spill!** Russell G. Wright. Event-Based Science series. Menlo Park, Calif.: Innovative Learning Publications, 1995.

Program Overview The Event-Based Science series is a program for middle school students in grades 6-9. Each module tells the story of a real event—such as the 1995 outbreak of the Ebola virus in Zaire—through reprinted newspaper articles and personal interviews; sections of background information explain relevant scientific concepts. A central task related to the module's story line leads to a final product that allows students to apply the science they have learned. For each module, a student book, teacher's guide, and videotape and/or videodisc are available.

Student Edition **Recommended grade level: 7-8.** *Oil Spill!* uses the Exxon *Valdez* oil spill as the event on which to base students' study of oceanographic concepts—including tides, currents, marine life, and ocean-floor topography. Students begin the module by watching television news coverage and reading reports from *USA Today* about the 1989 oil spill off the southern coast of Alaska. Then they are told that their major task during the module will be to conduct, in 5-member teams, an in-depth study and analysis of 6 city ports as potential sites for an oil terminal. Team members assume the roles of a harbormaster, a physical oceanographer, a marine biologist, an economist, and a risk planner. The module's 11 activities provide students with the background information and skills for this task.

Among the activities, for example, students use soda bottles and water to investigate how temperature differences in the ocean can cause currents. They use a tide chart as a tool for deciding when a tanker can leave a harbor. They also construct a chart of the major ocean life zones, showing typical life forms found in each. Students design a cost-effective method for using soundings to obtain a profile of a harbor, and they investigate how many gallons an oil tanker can carry and how large an oil spill it could potentially create. Students calculate the accumulation of oil as it passes through a food pyramid.

Oil Spill! also provides short narratives ("discovery files") on oceanographic topics, actual newspaper articles, explanatory graphics, and profiles of professionals who might be involved in conducting such a site analysis. Middle school students who lived near the *Valdez* oil spill tell their stories throughout the module. Other information that students need to complete the task must be obtained from encyclopedias, textbooks, films, and other sources they can find. The unit culminates with team reports and the selection of 1 harbor on the East Coast and 1 on the West Coast for oil terminals.

Teacher's Guide The teacher's guide provides brief overview information on the module's structure and activities. It includes suggestions for guiding specific student activities, a scoring rubric for a performance assessment at the end of the unit, and an annotated bibliography.

Key to Content Standards: 5-8 (see app. C)

UNIFYING CONCEPTS AND PROCESSES: Systems, order, and organization; evidence, models, and explanation; change, constancy, and measurement.
SCIENCE AS INQUIRY: Abilities necessary to do scientific inquiry; understandings about scientific inquiry.
EARTH AND SPACE SCIENCE: Structure of the earth system; earth in the solar system.
SCIENCE AND TECHNOLOGY: Abilities of technological design; understandings about science and technology.
SCIENCE IN PERSONAL AND SOCIAL PERSPECTIVES: Natural hazards; risks and benefits; science and technology in society.
HISTORY AND NATURE OF SCIENCE: Science as a human endeavor; nature of science.

Prices: Student edition (ISBN 0-201-49090-0), $7.95. Teacher's guide (ISBN 0-201-49091-9), with video, $18.00. Classroom package, $115.00. *Publisher/supplier:* Addison Wesley/Longman. *Materials:* Available locally.

3.25 Plastics in Our Lives. Chemical Education for Public Understanding Program (CEPUP) series. Developed by Lawrence Hall of Science (Berkeley, Calif.). Menlo Park, Calif.: Addison-Wesley, 1992.

Program Overview The Chemical Education for Public Understanding Program (CEPUP) series consists of 12 modules for grades 7-9. The modules focus on chemicals and the interaction of chemicals with people and the environment. The series promotes the use of scientific principles, processes, and evidence in public decision making. The components of a CEPUP module are a teacher's guide and a kit of materials. (SEPUP—the Science Education for Public Understanding Program—is the second phase of the project that began as CEPUP.)

Teacher's Guide **Recommended grade level: 7-8.** In *Plastics in Our Lives,* students learn some of the physical and chemical properties of plastics and examine societal issues involved in the use and recycling of plastic materials. Among the activities in the unit, for example, students identify common plastic products and list resources used to produce plastics. They examine the physical properties of 4 common plastics and the advantages and disadvantages of plastic compared with the attributes of natural materials. Students synthesize 2 polymers and compare their properties. They use paper clips to make models of polymer molecules and then describe the behavior of various plastics in terms of molecular structure. They compare the insulating value of popcorn and polystyrene foam "popcorn" and compare the absorbency of cloth diapers and disposable diapers. In other activities, students examine issues related to the disposal of plastics and consider the decision of whether to use plastic or paper bags

in light of the trade-offs that accompany each choice.

The 8 activities in *Plastics in Our Lives* take 12 class periods of 40 to 50 minutes each to complete. Included in this slim, wire-bound book are reproducible student sheets, directions for guiding activities and discussions, suggestions for extensions, and an end-of-unit test.

Key to Content Standards: 5-8 (see app. C)

UNIFYING CONCEPTS AND PROCESSES: Evidence, models, and explanation; form and function.
SCIENCE AS INQUIRY: Abilities necessary to do scientific inquiry; understandings about scientific inquiry.
PHYSICAL SCIENCE: Properties and changes of properties in matter.
SCIENCE AND TECHNOLOGY: Abilities of technological design; understandings about science and technology.
SCIENCE IN PERSONAL AND SOCIAL PERSPECTIVES: Risks and benefits; science and technology in society.

Prices: Teacher's guide (ISBN 0-201-28430-8), $19.99. Module, $220.99. *Publisher/supplier:* Sargent-Welch/VWR Scientific. *Materials:* Available locally, from commercial suppliers, or in kit.

3.26 Pollution. Delta Science Module (DSM) series. Hudson, N.H.: Delta Education, 1994.

Program Overview The Delta Science Module (DSM) series has 51 life, physical, and earth science units for grades K-8 that emphasize science concepts, science content, and process skills. The series includes 12 modules for grades 5-6 and 8 modules for grades 6-8. Each requires about 3 to 4 weeks to complete and includes a teacher's guide and materials for a class of 32 students.

Teacher's Guide **Recommended grade level: 5-6.** *Pollution* introduces students to the concept of pollution—the contamination of the environment caused by the introduction of natural or humanly produced waste or harmful substances. During the unit, students collect, classify, and infer the sources of litter found on school grounds; determine the average volume of paper waste that their class generates on a daily basis; and recycle old newspaper into papier-mâché bowls. They also make a device to measure the concentration of particles in the air at different sites, construct a simple water filtration system and examine the particles that get "filtered out" of several samples, and discover how difficult it is to remove oil from water and from feathers.

In other activities, students determine the relative hardness of water samples, test the pH of 6 different water samples, and investigate the purity of rain water. They also compare the rate of growth among plants that have been watered with tap water, acidic water, and a mixture of both, and infer the reason for the different growth rates. They listen to sounds to develop a definition of noise pollution and take a sound survey of 3 different areas at school. The 12 activities in *Pollution* take from 30 to 60 minutes each, and can be done by students working individually or in groups.

In addition to directions for activities, the teacher's guide provides a module overview, a schedule of activities, objectives for each activity, background information, materials management and preparation tips, sample answers to discussion questions, teaching suggestions, and reinforcement activities. Also included are reproducible activity sheets for student work and a performance-based assessment. A "connections" feature at the end of each activity provides suggestions for extending or applying the concepts addressed.

Key to Content Standards: 5-8 (see app. C)

UNIFYING CONCEPTS AND PROCESSES: Systems, order, and organization; evidence, models, and explanation; change, constancy, and measurement. **SCIENCE AS INQUIRY:** Abilities necessary to do scientific inquiry; understandings about scientific inquiry. **EARTH AND SPACE SCIENCE:** Structure of the earth system. **SCIENCE AND TECHNOLOGY:** Understandings about science and technology. **SCIENCE IN PERSONAL AND SOCIAL PERSPECTIVES:** Populations, resources, and environments; natural hazards; risks and benefits; science and technology in society.

Prices: Teacher's guide (ISBN 0-87504-107-8), $27.95. Kit, $279.00. Refill Package, $75.00. ***Publisher/ supplier:*** Delta Education. ***Materials:*** Available locally, from commercial suppliers, or in kit.

3.27 **The Pondwater Tour.** Developed by LaMotte Co. Chestertown, Md.: LaMotte Co., 1994.

Program Overview *The Pondwater Tour* is an activity kit for carrying out a project that focuses on the quality of surface water—for example, in ponds, streams, or marshes. The chemical and environmental effects of natural and human influences on surface water are studied.

Activity Kit **Recommended grade level: 7-8.** *The Pondwater Tour* engages students in a water-quality testing project. Students collect water samples from a surface-water body and add variables such as plants, fish, and nutrients. Then they experiment with these water samples in class, measuring pH, dissolved oxygen, and nutrient levels over a number of days using colorimetric testing procedures. When the tests are completed, students record their results on bar graphs and discuss the results. (The environmental changes demonstrated in the experiments are more dramatic in freshwater than in saltwater.)

In addition to its experiments, *The Pondwater Tour* provides introductory discussions on water chemistry and several paper-and-pencil activities that lead up to the water-quality tests. Among the activities, for example, students create a large poster showing land uses, activities, and natural features that may affect a surface-water source. Resource information on pH, ammonia, dissolved oxygen, and nitrate is provided to help students interpret the results of their experiments.

The Pondwater Tour includes instructional material for the teacher, chemical tablets for the testing procedures, 6 glass vials for the dissolved oxygen test, and several reproducible student handouts. Some of the other required materials, such as fishbowls for storing water, are not included.

Key to Content Standards: 5-8 (see app. C)

UNIFYING CONCEPTS AND PROCESSES: Systems, order, and organization; evidence, models, and explanation; change, constancy, and measurement. **SCIENCE AS INQUIRY:** Abilities necessary to do scientific inquiry; understandings about scientific inquiry. **PHYSICAL SCIENCE:** Properties and changes of properties in matter. **LIFE SCIENCE:** Populations and ecosystems. **EARTH AND SPACE SCIENCE:** Structure of the earth system. **SCIENCE AND TECHNOLOGY:** Understandings about science and technology.

Prices: Complete kit, $49.00. Replacement kit, $35.70. ***Publisher/ supplier:*** LaMotte. ***Materials:*** Available locally, from commercial suppliers, or in kit.

3.28 Solid Waste: Is There a Solution? New York Science, Technology and Society Education Project (NYSTEP). Problem-Solving Activities for Middle-Level Science series. Albany, N.Y.: NYSTEP, 1992.

Program Overview The Problem-Solving Activities for Middle-Level Science series consists of 8 stand-alone modules. Each module contains 2 to 6 units focused on technological and/or ethical aspects of issues involving science, technology, and society. The series was designed so that teachers can select modules and units that address local needs and draw on local community resources. A module requires 3 to 8 weeks to complete, depending on the units selected. Supplies and equipment may be required that are not typically part of a school's science inventory.

Teacher's Guide **Recommended grade level: 7-8.** *Solid Waste: Is There a Solution?* helps students develop an understanding of the issues related to solid waste and its management. The module's 19 activities address the topics of waste reduction, reuse and recycling, waste-to-energy facilities, landfills, and community involvement in solid waste management decisions. For example, students determine how much solid waste they produce on average each day; they take a field trip to a local landfill. They also design a plan for making experimental minicompost piles in bottles; recycle newspapers in the classroom, creating usable paper; and measure how much heat is released from a burning walnut. In a simulation activity, students decide whether a landfill should be constructed in their community.

Solid Waste: Is There a Solution? is designed to be completed over a 4- to 8-week period. The module is divided into 6 units, each of which has directions for its activities, a bibliography, interdisciplinary connections (to technology, social stud-

ies, language arts, mathematics, health, home and career skills, arts, and foreign languages/culture), and suggestions for extensions.

Key to Content Standards: 5-8 (see app. C)

UNIFYING CONCEPTS AND PROCESSES: Systems, order, and organization; evidence, models, and explanation; change, constancy, and measurement.
SCIENCE AS INQUIRY: Abilities necessary to do scientific inquiry; understandings about scientific inquiry.
PHYSICAL SCIENCE: Properties and changes of properties in matter; transfer of energy.
EARTH AND SPACE SCIENCE: Structure of the earth system.
SCIENCE AND TECHNOLOGY: Abilities of technological design; understandings about science and technology.
SCIENCE IN PERSONAL AND SOCIAL PERSPECTIVES: Populations, resources, and environments; natural hazards; science and technology in society.

Prices: Teacher's guide: In New York State, free with attendance at workshop; outside of New York, $9.
Publisher/supplier: New York Science, Technology and Society Education Project. *Materials:* Available locally, or from commercial suppliers.

3.29 Too Much Trash? National Geographic Kids Network series. Developed by Technical Education Research Centers (TERC) (Cambridge, Mass.). Washington, D.C.: National Geographic Society, 1997.

Program Overview The National Geographic Kids Network series is a telecommunications-based program for grades 3-9 that emphasizes collaborative student research on real-world issues. The series includes 7 units for grades 3-6 and 9 units for grades 6-9. Each unit includes a kit and an 8-week telecommunications package.

Telecommunications-Based Unit
Recommended grade level: 3-6. In *Too Much Trash?,* an 8-week telecommunications-based curriculum unit, students explore the environmental impact of trash while learning data analysis and mathematical skills. Students classify trash, investigate how their school and community manage trash, estimate the total weight of the trash discarded daily by the entire class, and explore ways to reduce the amount of the trash they generate. Then, through the National Geographic Society Kids Network—a computer network that links students around the world doing the same unit—they share data and information on trash generation and disposal with students in different parts of the world. They graph the data and look for patterns and correlations. In a final activity, students develop a presentation to share their findings with an audience outside their classroom. Activities incorporate science, geography, social studies, language arts, mathematics, and statistics.

Throughout the unit, students use computers and software (called *NGS Works*) to record information, write letters, make graphs, display maps, and send data to other network participants. They also consult electronically with a scientist about the data they collect.

Too Much Trash? includes a teacher's guide, reproducible readings and activity sheets, overhead transparencies, posters, wall maps, and a diskette of supplemental information to use with the *NGS Works* software.

Key to Content Standards: 5-8 (see app. C)

UNIFYING CONCEPTS AND PROCESSES: Systems, order, and organization; evidence, models, and explanation; change, constancy, and measurement.
SCIENCE AS INQUIRY: Abilities necessary to do scientific inquiry; understandings about scientific inquiry.

PHYSICAL SCIENCE: Properties and changes of properties in matter.
SCIENCE AND TECHNOLOGY: Abilities of technological design; understandings about science and technology.
SCIENCE IN PERSONAL AND SOCIAL PERSPECTIVES: Populations, resources, and environments; natural hazards; risks and benefits; science and technology in society.
HISTORY AND NATURE OF SCIENCE: Science as a human endeavor; nature of science.

Prices: Curriculum unit (ISBN 0-7922-4072-3), $149. *NGS Works* software, $199. (Contact NGS regarding membership fees for accessing NGS Kids Network.) *Publisher/supplier:* National Geographic Society. *Materials:* Available from commercial suppliers, or in kit.

3.30 **Toxic Waste: A Teaching Simulation.** Chemical Education for Public Understanding Program (CEPUP) series. Developed by Lawrence Hall of Science (Berkeley, Calif.). Menlo Park, Calif.: Addison-Wesley, 1991.

Program Overview The Chemical Education for Public Understanding Program (CEPUP) series consists of 12 modules for grades 7-9. The modules focus on chemicals and the interaction of chemicals with people and the environment. The series promotes the use of scientific principles, processes, and evidence in public decision making. The components of a CEPUP module are a teacher's guide and a kit of materials. (SEPUP—the Science Education for Public Understanding Program—is the second phase of the project that began as CEPUP.)

Teacher's Guide **Recommended grade level: 8+.** In *Toxic Waste,* students are presented with the problem of safe disposal of a toxic copper-plating waste for an imaginary computer chip manufacturer. In the first activ-

ity, they use copper chloride solution to electroplate an object, and in the next 6 activities they test and evaluate various methods of disposing of the used copper chloride solution, which contains a toxic heavy metal. For example, students explore the use of dilution as a strategy, by determining the volume of water needed to dilute 1 liter of a 50,000 parts per million (ppm) solution to produce a legally disposable concentration of 5 ppm. They look at the reclamation of copper using metal replacement reactions, and examine how effective different metals are at removing a toxic metal from solution. They investigate the usefulness of precipitation reactions as a method for removing and securing toxic metal ions under simulated environmental stresses. Students also examine a fixation process that converts a liquid waste containing hazardous metal ions to a solid; then they test the solid's ability to resist leaching of the metal ions by acidic water.

At the end of the module, students review the various processes for disposing of the copper chloride solution. They discuss the advantages and disadvantages of each method in relation to the ultimate fate of the materials; they consider ease of carrying out the process, cost, and general environmental concerns. The discussion emphasizes the importance of source reduction in all waste management decisions.

The 7 activities in *Toxic Waste* generally take 1 or 2 class periods of 40 to 50 minutes each to complete. Included in this slim, wire-bound book are reproducible sheets, directions for guiding activities and discussions, suggestions for extensions, and an end-of-unit test.

Key to Content Standards: 5-8 (see app. C)

UNIFYING CONCEPTS AND PROCESSES: Evidence, models, and explanation.

SCIENCE AS INQUIRY: Abilities necessary to do scientific inquiry; understandings about scientific inquiry.
PHYSICAL SCIENCE: Properties and changes of properties in matter.
SCIENCE AND TECHNOLOGY: Understandings about science and technology.
SCIENCE IN PERSONAL AND SOCIAL PERSPECTIVES: Natural hazards; risks and benefits; science and technology in society.
HISTORY AND NATURE OF SCIENCE: Nature of science.

Prices: Teacher's guide (ISBN 0-201-28422-7), $19.99. Module, $244.99. *Publisher/supplier:* Sargent-Welch/VWR Scientific. *Materials:* Available locally, from commercial suppliers, or in kit.

3.31 **Understanding Basic Ecological Concepts.** Rev. ed. Original ed., by Audrey N. Tomera, revised by Joel Beller. Portland, Maine: Walch, 1989.

Program Overview *Understanding Basic Ecological Concepts* is a combined textbook and workbook that focuses on ecological concepts and the interrelationships of living things and their environments. Students examine current environmental problems such as acid rain, toxic waste, tropical deforestation, and destruction of the ozone layer.

Student Edition **Recommended grade level: 8+.** *Understanding Basic Ecological Concepts* allows students to investigate such ecological concepts as populations, homeostasis, food webs, food chains, succession, and carrying capacity. Organized in 16 pencil-and-paper problems and 4 field laboratories, the workbook asks students to answer questions and complete exercises by using information supplied in the text together with their own knowledge and observations. For example, students list the living and nonliving factors that might interact with a flower shown in a photograph; then they observe a plant in its natural environment every day for 2 weeks and try to identify the interactions that are taking place. They calculate the "student population density" of their classroom. Students also construct a food chain based on an illustration of a redwood forest community, and they investigate how waste is disposed of in their community.

In the laboratory investigations, students conduct a long-term study of a fruit fly population. They watch the fruit fly population increase, observing simultaneous environmental changes. Then they watch the population decline and try to determine the responsible factors. Students investigate the effect of light energy on an aquarium, the effect of automotive exhaust on roadside plants, and the effect of shade on biotic conditions. They observe 2 areas in the community for evidence of succession, and compare these 2 areas in terms of the kinds and numbers of organisms present. Students also monitor the pH of precipitation events in their local area over a period of several months.

Many simple black-and-white photographs illustrate ecological concepts in the volume, helping students make scientific inferences and answer questions. One appendix contains additional worksheets for studying selected resources and environmental problems, such as a sanitary landfill, water consumption, and sewage treatment. Another appendix provides hints and suggestions for answering selected questions and problems in the main text.

Key to Content Standards: 5-8 (see app. C)

UNIFYING CONCEPTS AND PROCESSES: Systems, order, and organization; evidence, models, and explanation; change, constancy, and measurement; evolution and equilibrium; form and function.

SCIENCE AS INQUIRY: Abilities necessary to do scientific inquiry; understandings about scientific inquiry.
LIFE SCIENCE: Regulation and behavior; populations and ecosystems; diversity and adaptations of organisms.
EARTH AND SPACE SCIENCE: Structure of the earth system; earth's history.
SCIENCE AND TECHNOLOGY: Understandings about science and technology.
SCIENCE IN PERSONAL AND SOCIAL PERSPECTIVES: Personal health; populations, resources, and environments; natural hazards; risks and benefits; science and technology in society.

Price: $9.95 (ISBN 0-8251-1622-8). *Publisher/supplier:* Walch. *Materials:* Available locally.

3.32 The Waste Hierarchy: Where Is "Away"? Chemical Education for Public Understanding Program (CEPUP) series. Developed by Lawrence Hall of Science (Berkeley, Calif.). Menlo Park, Calif.: Addison-Wesley, 1993.

Program Overview The Chemical Education for Public Understanding Program (CEPUP) series consists of 12 modules for grades 7-9. The modules focus on chemicals and the interaction of chemicals with people and the environment. The series promotes the use of scientific principles, processes, and evidence in public decision making. The components of a CEPUP module are a teacher's guide and a kit of materials. (SEPUP—the Science Education for Public Understanding Program—is the second phase of the project that began as CEPUP.)

Teacher's Guide **Recommended grade level: 7-8+.** In *The Waste Hierarchy: Where Is "Away"?,* students explore the question of what ultimately happens to the wastes our society gener-

ates. Students consider routes and methods of disposal on the basis of a "waste hierarchy" developed by the U.S. Environmental Protection Agency. This waste hierarchy emphasizes reducing waste at its source, followed by recycling, treatment/incineration, and use of landfills.

Among the activities, for example, students survey the amount and categories of trash they personally discard, and compare their generation of trash to national norms. Students also use a test to examine dilution as a disposal option for solutions containing toxic heavy metals. They investigate the problem of heavy-metal leachates in a simulated landfill. They contrast sanitary landfills with dumps (considering issues such as weight versus volume, contamination of underground aquifers by leachates, methane gas production, and the Not-in-My-Back-Yard syndrome). In other activities, students investigate the pluses and minuses of high-temperature incineration; recycle a plastic and examine data on the recycling of paper, scrap metals, glass and plastics to explore the strengths and limitations of recycling; and examine the advantages and disadvantages of replacing a toxic heavy-metal-based ink with less toxic or nontoxic substitutes as an example of the advantages of source reduction.

In a final, role-playing activity, students are challenged with the problem of the closure of their town's landfill in the near future. They must reconsider the household wastes they generate as a source of both benign and hazardous wastes. Throughout the module, questions are posed for student discussion and for fact-gathering and synthesis of ideas.

The 6 sequential activities in *The Waste Hierarchy* take 16 class periods of 40 to 50 minutes each to complete. Included in this slim, wirebound book are reproducible student sheets, directions for guiding activities and discussions, suggestions for extensions, and an end-of-unit test.

Key to Content Standards: 5-8 (see app. C)

UNIFYING CONCEPTS AND PROCESSES: Evidence, models, and explanation. **SCIENCE AS INQUIRY:** Abilities necessary to do scientific inquiry; understandings about scientific inquiry. **PHYSICAL SCIENCE:** Properties and changes of properties in matter. **SCIENCE AND TECHNOLOGY:** Understandings about science and technology. **SCIENCE IN PERSONAL AND SOCIAL PERSPECTIVES:** Personal health; populations, resources, and environments; natural hazards; risks and benefits; science and technology in society.

Prices: Teacher's guide (ISBN 0-201-29499-0), $19.99. Module, $239.99. *Publisher/supplier:* Sargent-Welch/ VWR Scientific. *Materials:* Available locally, from commercial suppliers, or in kit.

3.33 **Waste Management: Third Module in Bio-Related Technologies Unit.** 4th ed. Integrated Mathematics, Science and Technology (IMaST) Project. IMaST series. Normal, Ill.: Center for Mathematics, Science, and Technology Education, Illinois State University, 1996.

Program Overview The Integrated Mathematics, Science, and Technology (IMaST) series for middle school includes 6 modules. The materials in each are designed to be used by a team of mathematics, science, and technology teachers concurrently over a 9-week period. Each module includes a teacher's guide and a student book.

Student Book **Recommended grade level: 7.** The *Waste Management* module is designed to promote students' active involvement in reducing, reusing, recycling, and rethinking solid waste. Among the activities,

for example, students calculate the surface area and volume of a rectangular prism and then make comparisons of surface area to volume in the context of reducing solid waste. They also conduct a controlled experiment to investigate the variables that influence composting, and they construct and interpret graphs that relate to waste management. Students also design a device that will crush an aluminum can for storage and transportation to recycling centers.

The 23 activities in *Waste Management* are divided in 3 groups, according to their emphasis on mathematics, science, or technology. The activities require both individual and cooperative work. Each activity takes between 2 and 7 class periods to complete.

Teacher's Guide Accompanying the activities in the teacher's guide are brief directions, along with ideas for class discussions and extension activities. Three sections following the activities provide background reading and basic information on waste and waste management, and include discussion questions with sample answers. Guidelines for assessing student performance are provided.

Key to Content Standards: 5-8 (see app. C)

UNIFYING CONCEPTS AND PROCESSES: Systems, order, and organization; evidence, models, and explanation; form and function. **SCIENCE AS INQUIRY:** Abilities necessary to do scientific inquiry; understandings about scientific inquiry. **SCIENCE AND TECHNOLOGY:** Abilities of technological design; understandings about science and technology. **SCIENCE IN PERSONAL AND SOCIAL PERSPECTIVES:** Populations, resources, and environments; science and technology in society.

Prices: Student book, $6.00. Teacher's guide, $12.25. *Publisher/supplier:* Illinois State University. *Materials:* Available locally, or from commercial suppliers.

3.34 **Waste Reduction.** Developed by E2: Environment and Education (Boulder, Colo.). Environmental Action series. Menlo Park, Calif.: Dale Seymour, 1998.

Program Overview The Environmental Action series consists of 6 stand-alone modules for middle and secondary school students. The series focuses on environmental issues and on the impact of these issues on human health and environmental quality. Each module includes a student edition and a teacher's resource guide.

Student Edition **Recommended grade level: 7-8+.** In *Waste Reduction,* students sort and analyze school garbage to identify recyclable and compostable materials. Then they develop a plan to reduce their consumption and waste at school and at home.

The 16 activities in the module are organized in 4 sections: "Explore the Issues," "Analyze," "Consider Options," and "Take Action." Examples of the activities include the following: assessing the pros and cons of using landfills, conducting a waste audit, evaluating the costs and benefits of waste practices that can be used at the audit site, and developing a proposal that includes recommendations for waste management at the audit site. About 18 to 20 class sessions are needed to complete the 16 activities in *Waste Reduction.*

Teacher's Guide The teacher's resource guide includes examples of possible student responses to discussion questions, annotated answers to student activity sheets, and some additional resources and assessment tools. Blackline masters for student activity sheets are also included.

Key to Content Standards: 5-8 (see app. C)

UNIFYING CONCEPTS AND PROCESSES: Evidence, models, and explanation. **SCIENCE AS INQUIRY:** Abilities necessary to do scientific inquiry; understandings about scientific inquiry. **SCIENCE AND TECHNOLOGY:** Understandings about science and technology. **SCIENCE IN PERSONAL AND SOCIAL PERSPECTIVES:** Populations, resources, and environments; natural hazards; risks and benefits; science and technology in society.

Prices: Student edition (ISBN 0-201-49537-6), $5.95. Teacher's guide (ISBN 0-201-49536-8), $13.95. *Publisher/supplier:* Dale Seymour. *Materials:* Available locally, or from commercial suppliers.

3.35 Water: Can We Keep It Fit for Life? New York Science Technology and Society Education Project (NYSTEP). Problem-Solving Activities for Middle-Level Science series. Albany, N.Y.: NYSTEP, 1994.

Program Overview The Problem-Solving Activities for Middle-Level Science series consists of 8 stand-alone modules. Each module contains 2 to 6 units focused on technological and/or ethical aspects of issues involving science, technology, and society. The series was designed so that teachers might select modules and units that address local needs and draw on local community resources. A module requires 3 to 8 weeks to complete, depending on the units selected. Supplies and equipment may be required that are not typically part of a school's science inventory.

Teacher's Guide **Recommended grade level: 7-8+.** *Water: Can We Keep It Fit for Life?* focuses on water for drink-

ing purposes as it introduces students to the properties of water, its importance as a natural resource, and the role students can play in safeguarding water resources. During the module, students carry out tests to compare the properties of water with the properties of corn oil. They also design and implement a plan to prepare a local surface-water sample for everyday human use, and they test water samples for hardness.

In other activities, students map their local water resources and learn about the concept of a watershed. They plan and carry out a field investigation of a local waterworks where water is treated to produce drinking water. They learn what happens to water after it goes down the drain. Students also build models to visualize how little of the earth's water supply exists in groundwater and surface water. They design and implement a household water-monitoring program. They plan and carry out a student-designed action project involving water use or resources in their local community.

Water: Can We Keep It Fit for Life? is designed to be completed over a 4- to 8-week period. The module is divided into 3 units, each of which has directions for its activities, a bibliography, interdisciplinary connections (to technology, social studies, language arts, mathematics, health, home and career skills, arts, and foreign languages/culture), and suggestions for extensions.

Key to Content Standards: 5-8 (see app. C)

UNIFYING CONCEPTS AND PROCESSES: Evidence, models, and explanation. **SCIENCE AS INQUIRY:** Abilities necessary to do scientific inquiry; understandings about scientific inquiry. **PHYSICAL SCIENCE:** Properties and changes of properties in matter. **EARTH AND SPACE SCIENCE:** Structure of the earth system. **SCIENCE AND TECHNOLOGY:** Abilities of technological design; understandings about science and technology.

SCIENCE IN PERSONAL AND SOCIAL PERSPECTIVES: Personal health; populations, resources, and environments; natural hazards; risks and benefits; science and technology in society.

Prices: Teacher's guide: In New York State, free with attendance at workshop; outside of New York, $7. *Publisher/supplier:* New York Science, Technology and Society Education Project. *Materials:* Available locally, or from commercial suppliers.

3.36 What's in Our Water? National Geographic Kids Network series. Developed by Technical Education Research Centers (TERC) (Cambridge, Mass.). Washington, D.C.: National Geographic Society, 1991.

Program Overview The National Geographic Kids Network series is a telecommunications-based program for grades 3-9 that emphasizes collaborative student research on real-world issues. The series includes 7 units for grades 3-6 and 9 units for grades 6-9. Each unit includes a kit and an 8-week telecommunications package.

Telecommunications-Based Unit **Recommended grade level: 3-6.** In *What's in Our Water?,* a 6-week telecommunications-based curriculum unit, students explore the questions of who uses water, where it comes from, and how pollutants get into it. They determine the source of their school's tap water, explore the definition of "pollutants," and test their tap water for nitrates and chlorines. Students set up an experiment with grass seeds and fertilizer to explore the trade-offs between the beneficial effects of a substance (nitrate) and its potentially harmful effects on water quality. Then, through the National Geographic Society Kids Network—a computer network that links students around the world doing the same unit—they compare their nitrate test results with those reported by students in different parts of the world. As they do so, they look for patterns in the data and examine a map of the network data. In the final week of the unit, students focus on international implications of water pollution.

Throughout the unit, students use computers and software (called *NGS Works*) to record information, write letters, make graphs, display maps, and send data to other network participants. They also consult electronically with a scientist about the data they collect.

What's in Our Water? includes a teacher's guide, reproducible readings and activity sheets, overhead transparencies, color posters, wall maps, and a diskette of supplemental information to use with *NGS Works* software.

Key to Content Standards: 5-8 (see app. C)

UNIFYING CONCEPTS AND PROCESSES: Evidence, models, and explanation; change, constancy, and measurement.

SCIENCE AS INQUIRY: Abilities necessary to do scientific inquiry; understandings about scientific inquiry.

EARTH AND SPACE SCIENCE: Structure of the earth system.

SCIENCE AND TECHNOLOGY: Understandings about science and technology.

SCIENCE IN PERSONAL AND SOCIAL PERSPECTIVES: Populations, resources, and environments; natural hazards; risks and benefits; science and technology in society.

HISTORY AND NATURE OF SCIENCE: Nature of science.

Prices: Curriculum unit, $149.00. *NGS Works* software, $199.00. Water nitrate test kit, $49.50. (Contact NGS regarding membership fee for accessing NGS Kids Network.) ***Publisher/supplier:*** National Geographic Society. ***Materials:*** Available from commercial suppliers, or in kit.

3.37 **Wildlife and Humanity: Can We Share the Earth?** New York Science, Technology and Society Education Project (NYSTEP). Problem-Solving Activities for Middle-Level Science series. Albany, N.Y.: NYSTEP, 1993.

Program Overview The Problem-Solving Activities for Middle-Level Science series consists of 8 stand-alone modules. Each module contains 2 to 6 units focused on technological and/or ethical aspects of issues involving science, technology, and society. The series was designed so that teachers might select modules and units that address local needs and draw on local community resources. A module requires 3 to 8 weeks to complete, depending on the units selected. Supplies and equipment may be required that are not typically part of a school's science inventory.

Teacher's Guide **Recommended grade level: 6-8.** *Wildlife and Humanity* is designed to increase students' interest in issues pertaining to wildlife and to encourage their participation in the resolution of local wildlife issues. The guide's 3 units each contain several classroom or outdoor activities; many of these involve reading or research. Students plan and carry out local field walks and investigations, implement a bird feeder project, and visit a zoo or environmental education center.

Through readings, simulations, debates, and reports, students then focus on wildlife and human interactions. They use a simple model, for example, to illustrate resource depletion. They also explore the impact of introduced species, and they gather information on wetlands and relate the effects of habitat destruction to changes in wildlife populations and communities. Finally, students produce case studies on controversial wildlife issues of their choice, and they plan and carry out a project to enhance an outdoor habitat.

Each activity includes suggestions for extensions, evaluations, and interdisciplinary connections. Ideas for long-term studies or for repeating outdoor activities during different seasons of the year are also given. Although the module was produced for use in New York State, it can easily be adapted for use elsewhere. Limited background information is provided.

Key to Content Standards: 5-8 (see app. C)

UNIFYING CONCEPTS AND PROCESSES: Systems, order, and organization; evidence, models, and explanations.

SCIENCE AS INQUIRY: Abilities necessary to do scientific inquiry; understandings about scientific inquiry.

LIFE SCIENCE: Regulation and behavior; populations and ecosystems.

SCIENCE IN PERSONAL AND SOCIAL PERSPECTIVE: Populations, resources, and environments.

Price: Teacher's guide: In New York State, free with attendance at workshop; outside New York, $7. ***Publisher/supplier:*** New York Science, Technology and Society Education Project. ***Materials:*** Available locally, or from commercial suppliers.

Environmental Science—Science Activity Books

3.38 Activities to Teach Mathematics in the Context of Environmental Studies. Barbara Thomson and Martin Hartog. Columbus, Ohio: ERIC Clearinghouse for Science, Mathematics, and Environmental Education, 1993.

Recommended grade level: 5-8. *Activities to Teach Mathematics in the Context of Environmental Studies* contains 35 activities that teach mathematics and problem-solving skills. The activities are designed to respond to the standards of the National Council of Teachers in Mathematics (NCTM) and to promote integrated mathematics and science learning, global awareness, and issue-oriented instruction. Topics covered include energy and natural resources, plants and animals, population growth, solid waste disposal, transportation, water, and weather.

Among the activities, for example, students thin a population of growing plants in several different ways to observe which method promotes the fastest growth of seedlings. They also form number patterns to describe cell populations at successive stages of growth. They develop an understanding of powers of numbers through a problem on population growth. Students also calculate the volume of solid waste produced in their homes in a week. They explore the relationship between geometric shapes and bridge strength by building model bridges. They identify the relationship between the cross-sectional area of a channel and the volume of water passing through the channel. They graph a month's worth of meteorological data for their local area.

Each activity includes brief background information for the teacher, step-by-step procedures, and suggestions for evaluation. Reproducible student worksheets are provided.

Price: $12. *Publisher/supplier:* ERIC Clearinghouse. *Materials:* Available locally, or from commercial suppliers.

3.39 California Smith, Water Investigator: Water Education Program. Los Angeles, Calif.: Metropolitan Water District of Southern California, 1993.

Recommended grade level: 6-7. *California Smith, Water Investigator* is a 10-lesson unit designed to help students learn about water—where it comes from, how much we use, and how to use it wisely. Much of the material involves socioeconomic issues and information specific to California, but with adaptation it could be used in other areas.

During the unit, students identify the sources of water that supply Southern California, and they learn about the steps and processes in a water distribution system. They discuss issues such as overdraft, cost, supply and demand, and water quality, and they identify possible ways to meet future water needs. Students also complete a home water investigation and assess ways they can be wise with water. At the end of each lesson are suggestions for additional activities—for example, collecting and measuring local rainfall, testing the pH of tap water, charting how much water the school uses on a daily, weekly, or monthly basis; building a solar still; testing toilets for leaks; and researching and writing reports and stories on water-related topics. Teacher demonstrations built into the lessons show how a water filtration plant works, how toxic chemicals get into groundwater, and how water can be desalinated.

Students work through the lessons using a 15-page student book. The teacher's guide includes directions for lessons and demonstrations, ideas for additional activities, background information on water in Southern California, an annotated list of educational resources available from the Metropolitan Water District of Southern California, and a list of children's literature.

The complete unit, which is packaged in a cardboard box, includes the teacher's guide, a videotape in Spanish and English, a poster about water in California, multiple copies of the student booklet, pre- and postunit tests, and other related materials.

Prices: Kit, $25; free to teachers in Metropolitan Water District of Southern California. Consumable kit, $10. *Publisher/supplier:* Metropolitan Water District of Southern California. *Materials:* Available locally, or from commercial suppliers.

3.40 Chemicals, Health, Environment, and Me (CHEM 2: Enhanced Program). Science Education for Public Understanding Program (SEPUP) series. Developed by Lawrence Hall of Science (Berkeley, Calif.). Ronkonkoma, N.Y.: Lab-Aids, 1997.

Recommended grade level: 4-7. *Chemicals, Health, Environment, and Me* is a series of 15 units on the nature of chemicals and how they interact with the environment. Students learn to collect, process, and analyze information and to use scientific evidence as a basis for lifestyle-oriented decisions. The units can be used in any order. They focus on (1) the physical and chemical properties of common substances, (2) relationships and interactions between humans and their environment, (3) sound, (4) electricity and magnetism, (5) media techniques and how they are used for different purposes, (6) food additives, (7) sugar and sugar substitutes, (8) the threshold of toxicity, (9) smoking and health, (10) qualitative tests used to identify chemicals in highway spills, (11) the identification and disposal of potentially hazardous chemicals, (12) waste disposal and reduction, (13) the carbon cycle, (14) pharmacology, and (15) water quality.

The *Chemicals, Health, Environment, and Me* program consists of a printed teacher's guide and a complete materials-and-equipment kit. Each of the 15 units contains 2 or more basic activities as well as ideas for curriculum integration. Each activity has a complete lesson plan and focuses on a single concept. Reproducible blackline masters of student activity sheets are included.

Prices: Teacher's guide (ISBN 1-887725-12-1), $24.99. Kit, $249.99. *Publisher/supplier:* Sargent-Welch. *Materials:* Available locally, from commercial suppliers, or in kit.

ABOUT THE ANNOTATIONS IN "ENVIRONMENTAL SCIENCE—SCIENCE ACTIVITY BOOKS"

Entry Numbers

Curriculum materials are arranged alphabetically by title in each category (Core Materials, Supplementary Units, and Science Activity Books) in chapters 1 through 5 of this guide.

Each curriculum annotation has a two-part entry number: the chapter number is given before the period; the number after the period locates the entry within that chapter. For example, the first entry number in chapter 1 is 1.1; the second entry in chapter 2 is 2.2; and so on.

The entry numbers within each curriculum chapter run consecutively through Core Materials, Supplementary Units, and Science Activity Books.

Order of Bibliographic Information

Following is the arrangement of the facts of publication in the annotations in this section:

- **Title of publication**
- **Number of edition,** if applicable
- **Authors** (an individual author or authors, an institutional author, or a project or program name under which the material was developed)
- **Series title**
- **Series developer,** if applicable
- **Place of publication, publisher, and date of publication**

Recommended Grade Level

The grade level for each piece of material was recommended by teacher evaluators during the development of this guide. In some instances, the recommended grade level may differ slightly from the publisher's advertised level.

Price and Acquisition Information

Ordering information appears at the end of each entry. Included are—

- **Prices** (of teacher's guides, activity books, and kits or units)
- **Publisher/supplier** (The name of a principal publisher/supplier, although not necessarily the sole source, for the items listed in the price category. Appendix A, "Publishers and Suppliers," provides the address, phone and fax numbers, and electronic ordering information, where available, for each publisher and supplier.)
- **Materials** (various sources from which one might obtain the required materials)

Readers must contact publishers/suppliers for complete and up-to-date ordering information, since prices are subject to change and materials may also change with revised editions. The prices given in this chapter are based on information from publishers and suppliers but are not meant to represent the full range of ordering options.

Indexes of Curriculum Materials

The multiple indexes on pp. 449-78 allow easy access to the information in this guide. Various aspects of the curriculum materials—including titles, topics addressed in each unit, and grade levels—are the focus of seven separate indexes. For example, titles and entry numbers are listed in the "Title Index" on pp. 450-54. The "Index of Authors, Series, and Curriculum Projects," on pp. 455-57, provides entry numbers of any annotated titles in a particular series.

3.41 Cycling Back to Nature with Biodegradable Polymers. Robert L. Horton, Joe E. Heimlich, and James R. Hollyer. Chevy Chase, Md.: National 4-H Council, 1994.

Recommended grade level: 6-8. *Cycling Back to Nature with Biodegradable Polymers* is a sourcebook of activities addressing the environmental influence of natural products, manufactured products, and by-products of the earth's natural cycles. The guide's 9 chapters focus on (1) earth's 4 natural cycles; (2) interactions among producers, consumers, and decomposers within natural cycles; (3) the production of plastic; (4) the presence of plastics in the environment; (5) biodegradable polymers as an important breakthrough; (6) composting as nature's way of recycling; (7) the need to recycle traditional plastics; (8) the range of possibilities for packaging with biodegradable polymers; and (9) increasing public awareness. Activities in the unit include experimenting with the effects of yeast on food decomposition, taking inventory of the plastic items in the packaging of students' lunches, and experimenting with water-soluble biodegradable polymers. Lessons may be used independently of each other or in sequence.

Appendixes include an earth cycle bio sheet, instructions for making a compost pile, plastic labeling information, a packaging scavenger hunt, and a letter-writing tip sheet.

Price: $5. Publisher/supplier: National 4-H Supply Service. *Materials:* Available locally, or from commercial suppliers.

3.42 **Discovering Deserts.** Nature-Scope series. Washington, D.C.: National Wildlife Federation, 1989.

Recommended grade level: 3-6. The interdisciplinary activities in *Discovering Deserts* introduce students to the ecology of arid lands. Through games, songs, stories, drawings, and drama, students explore the following topics: what a desert is, how deserts form, and the different types of deserts; the ways in which plants and animals have adapted to harsh desert conditions; plant and animal relationships in desert communities; and the ways in which people are changing desert habitats.

Discovering Deserts has 5 chapters (each on a broad theme), a craft section, and an appendix. Teachers may choose from the 23 activities or teach each chapter as a unit. Copycat pages supplement the activities and provide games, puzzles, and worksheets.

Price: $3.98 (ISBN 0-945051-34-4). *Publisher/supplier:* National Wildlife Federation. *Materials:* Available locally, or from commercial suppliers.

3.43 **Endangered Species: Wild and Rare.** NatureScope series. Washington, D.C.: National Wildlife Federation, 1989.

Recommended grade level: K-7. *Endangered Species: Wild and Rare* includes background information and activities that focus on the process of extinction and the role of humans in the destruction or conservation of plants and animals and their habitats. Students participate in classroom and playground activities that integrate science with social studies, mathematics, language arts,

drama, music, and art as they learn about habitat destruction, wildlife trade, pollution, and other factors that put species in danger. The chapters in this module usually begin with primary activities and end with intermediate or advanced activities.

Endangered Species: Wild and Rare contains 17 lessons organized in 4 chapters; a fifth chapter provides art and craft ideas. Teachers may choose single activities or teach each chapter as a unit. Copycat pages supplement the activities and include ready-to-copy games, puzzles, and worksheets.

Price: $12.95 (ISBN 0-07-046508-8). *Publisher/supplier:* McGraw-Hill. *Materials:* Available locally.

3.44 **Environmental Issues: Intermediate.** Pauline Chandler. Hands-on Minds-on Science series. Huntington Beach, Calif.: Teacher Created Materials, 1994.

Recommended grade level: 7-8+. *Environmental Issues: Intermediate* is a teacher's guide with directions for 17 lessons and/or activities that help students explore topics such as environmental awareness, solid waste management, air and water pollution, land use, and the effects that people's everyday actions can have on the environment. Among the activities, for example, students conduct a survey (and tally the results) of people's opinions about the most critical environmental issues facing their community. Students also write letters to preservationist and conservationist agencies to request information. In other activities, they examine how they can reduce the amount of trash they produce in a week, compare the effectiveness of toxic and nontoxic

household products, test products that are advertised to be pH-balanced, and make model greenhouses out of soda bottles to learn about the greenhouse effect.

Most of the activities in this guide involve cooperative learning. Many of them engage students in role-playing or in looking at issues from various perspectives. Students record their observations, thoughts, and experiences in an environmental-issues journal. The guide includes limited background information for the teacher, reproducible student record sheets, and a bibliography.

Price: $11.95 (ISBN 1-55734-638-0). *Publisher/supplier:* Teacher Created Materials. *Materials:* Available locally, or from commercial suppliers.

3.45 **Environmental Resource Guide: Nonpoint Source Pollution Prevention.** Developed by Tennessee Valley Authority Environmental Education Section, for Air & Waste Management Association (A&WMA). Pittsburgh, Pa.: A&WMA, 1992.

Recommended grade level: 6-8. This *Environmental Resource Guide* in 3-ring-binder format offers 15 activities designed to educate students about nonpoint-source water pollution—what it is, where it comes from, and what can be done about it. The activities focus on the 4 major types of water pollutants (sediment, nutrients, bacteria, and toxics) and the best management practices for controlling them. Among the activities, for example, students define water pollution and describe its major sources (urban, agricultural, mining, and forestry activities). They collect samples of surface-water runoff and test them for coliform bacteria. They also observe the effects of fertilizer on algal growth by experimenting with different water sources. In other activities, students construct 2 models of septic tanks with drainfields, simulate and compare different timber-harvesting practices, interview farmers and gardeners to gather data on pesticides used locally, and build models of different landfill liners to see how they work.

Each activity in the *Environmental Resource Guide* contains basic background information, procedures, extensions, and a short list of resources that offer more information. Some activities require the purchase of testing kits and equipment. The guide includes 10 fact sheets on various concepts and issues related to the activities—for example, the connection between land use and water quality, approaches to stopping or preventing water pollution, and steps individuals can take to reduce water pollution.

Prices: $30.50 ($20.50 for A&WMA members). *Publisher/supplier:* Air & Waste Management Association. *Materials:* Available locally, or from commercial suppliers.

3.46 **The Environment: The Science and Politics of Protecting Our Planet.** Decisions, Decisions Series. Watertown, Mass.: Tom Snyder Productions, 1991.

Recommended grade level: 6-8. *The Environment* is a computer-based simulation that plunges students into the middle of a local environmental crisis. As they deal with the crisis, they learn about waste disposal problems, source reduction and recycling, land use conflicts, endangered species, the role of government in achieving environmental quality, and

the greenhouse effect. Acting as the town mayor in the simulation, students must close a local pond because of a fish kill. Some in the community think the source of the pond's pollution is the town dump, where the town's biggest employer—a mining company—dumps its manufacturing waste. With support from 4 advisers—a scientist, a campaign manager, an environmentalist, and an economist—students must evaluate often-conflicting data, facts, and opinions to decide as a group what to do. They also do independent research and reading.

When students decide what action to take, the computer program presents the consequences of the action, which demand further action. Several ideas are given for science experiments that students can perform while they work on the simulation. For example, they can survey all of the species on a plot of land, test the effects of ashes on protists, or construct a model to study leaching.

The program, which requires only one computer, has a mode for small groups and a mode in which the teacher can lead the entire class as a group. The program can take from 2 days to 2 weeks, depending on how it is used.

The teacher's guide that accompanies the simulation provides information on ways to use the program, introductory lessons for use before the simulation, an overview of environmental issues, and reproducible student worksheets. The complete package includes the program disk, the teacher's guide, and sets of student reference booklets.

Price: Classroom kit, $149.95. *Publisher/supplier:* Tom Snyder Productions. *Materials:* Available locally, or from commercial suppliers.

3.47 **Experiments That Explore Recycling.** Martin J. Gutnik. An Investigate! Book. Brookfield, Conn.: Millbrook Press, 1992.

Recommended grade level: 6-8. *Experiments That Explore Recycling,* a small book written for students, contains directions for 10 simple ecology projects for students to do independently or with minimal guidance. Topics explored include the oxygen, carbon, and nitrogen cycles; soil components; recycling of manufactured products; composting; and water pollution. Among the activities, for example, students analyze the trash thrown away each day at their school, collect a soil sample and study the organisms in it, set up an earthworm farm, make a model of a landfill and see which items decompose in it, and build a compost pile.

The procedures for the activities are presented in narrative form for the most part and are interspersed with sections of background information. No materials are provided for the teacher.

Price: $15.40 (ISBN 1-56294-116-X). *Publisher/supplier:* Millbrook Press. *Materials:* Available locally, or from commercial suppliers.

3.48 **Give Water a Hand: Leader Guidebook and Action Guides.** Youth Action Program Promoting Good Water Management Practices at Home and in the Community (Madison, Wis.). Chevy Chase, Md.: National 4-H Council, 1994.

Recommended grade level: 7-8. In the 4-H program called *Give Water a Hand,* students research water-quality and conservation issues at home, on their farm, or in their school or community, and then develop a water-related environmental service project to address the needs they discover. While not attempting to cover all water-related issues, the program helps students investigate selected issues, resources, and answers for themselves.

As they begin the activities, students draw a map of the watershed which includes the project site, such as the schoolyard, that they have chosen to research. They investigate and record water management practices at that site—for example, when and how water is used. Students meet with a local water expert to share their research and learn more about water issues. On the basis of what they have learned, they plan a positive service project, such as landscaping the schoolyard, starting and maintaining a compost pile, or improving soil quality to reduce runoff. Although some project ideas are suggested, students work through a chart and their own discoveries in selecting a workable idea. Then they carry out and document their service project.

Give Water a Hand includes 5 booklets: a leader's guide and 4 student "action" guides, for projects in the community, on a farm, at a school, or at a home. The leader's guide contains guidelines for leading student activities, team-building activities, and tips on reinforcing students' organizational and problem-solving skills.

Price: Free. **Publisher/supplier:** University of Wisconsin-Extension Web site, at http://www.uwex.edu/erc. **Materials:** Available locally, or from commercial suppliers.

3.49 **Global Awareness for Students (GAS): Studies in Climate.** Elisa Passarelli, Tom Arrison, Louise Belnay, and others. Developed in collaboration with National Oceanic and Atmospheric Administration (NOAA), Environmental Research Laboratories, Forecast Systems Laboratory (Boulder, Colo.). Washington, D.C.: U.S. Government Printing Office, 1994.

Recommended grade level: 7-8+. *Global Awareness for Students (GAS): Studies in Climate* is a teacher's guide offering 20 activities—including exercises, labs, and demonstrations—that focus on atmospheric and greenhouse gases and how they may or may not affect earth's climate. Among the activities, students make a model to understand the heating of the earth's atmosphere. They observe air bubbles trapped in ice cubes and compare them to air trapped in a glacier. They test for the presence of carbon dioxide in gas samples by using an indicator, bromthymol blue. Students also design climate models using computer spreadsheets. They examine the social causes of an increase in greenhouse gases by gathering and organizing statistics on population growth, economic development, or natural resources. Other topics addressed in the activities include radiant energy, methane, ozone, and the wide range of impacts that may result from global warming.

The activities in *Global Awareness for Students* were originally developed as part of a summer science institute sponsored by National Oceanic and Atmospheric Administration. Limited background information is provided for some, but not all, of the activities. Some of the activities contain short reading sections for students; many require data analysis and graphing. Each activity includes procedures, sample student record sheets, extensions, and references.

Price: Free. **Publisher/supplier:** Forecast Systems Laboratory. **Materials:** Available locally.

3.50 **Global Warming: Understanding the Forecast: Teacher's Resource Manual.** Carl M. Raab and Jane E. S. Sokolow. New York, N.Y.: American Museum of Natural History, Education Department, 1992.

Recommended grade level: 5-8+. The teacher's resource manual *Global Warming: Understanding the Forecast* was designed to serve as an introduction to an exhibition on the causes and effects of global warming shown in the early 1990s at the American Museum of Natural History in New York City. The exhibition was jointly sponsored by the museum and by the Environmental Defense Fund. This guide offers about 20 activities and much useful information, including a 12-page background section for the teacher, on global warming. It includes simple classroom activities for students in elementary through high school, a demonstration experiment on the greenhouse effect, and a resource list.

Activities for middle school students, for example, include setting up minigreenhouses in mayonnaise jars and comparing the temperature inside and outside the greenhouses over time; reading and interpreting a graph to understand trends in the earth's climate; and demonstrating how solar energy can be used to heat water and spin the blades of a radiometer. Many of the activities intended for high school students—such as reading and interpreting data about greenhouse gases—could also be done at the middle school level. Each activity includes a 1- or 2-paragraph introduction, procedures, and conclusions.

Price: $5. Publisher/supplier: American Museum of Natural History. *Materials:* Available locally, or from commercial suppliers.

3.51 **Hands on Plastics: A Scientific Investigation Kit.** Washington, D.C.: American Plastics Council; and Columbus, Ohio: National Middle Level Science Teachers Association, 1995.

Recommended grade level: 7-8. The kit *Hands on Plastics* contains a series of activities that allow students to explore the world of plastics. The activities are designed to meet 5 of the 12 science literacy goals of Project 2061, developed by the American Association for the Advancement of Science, and to incorporate the learning cycle, cooperative learning, and alternative assessments. Among the activities, for example, students use physical properties to classify containers that have had their plastic codes removed. They perform 4 lab tests (an acetone test, a heat test, an alcohol test, and an oil test) on different plastics, and they compare their lab test results with their initial classification of the plastic materials. Students also conduct an in-depth study of a plastic product, such as kitchen plastic bags, used at home or at school. They view slides to learn about the process for recycling HDPE (high-density polyethylene), and they learn how to set up a school recycling program.

Hands on Plastics takes 8 to 10 class periods to complete if all the activities are used. The kit contains background information for students and teachers on plastics and polymers, activity sheets, recycled plastic resins and labeled plastic items for activities, and a list of state recycling offices.

Price: Kit, $10. *Publisher/supplier:* American Plastics Council. *Materials:* Available locally, or in kit.

3.52 **H₂O Below: An Activity Guide for Groundwater Study.** Bill Henske, Cindy Bidlack, Cathy Fickert, and others. Developed by the Illinois Middle School Groundwater Project. Edwardsville, Ill.: Southern Illinois University, 1997.

Recommended grade level: 6-8. *H₂O Below* contains student activities, teacher demonstrations, and information about groundwater. Topics covered in the guide include water and its importance; the movement of water through the ground; ways in which water becomes polluted; protecting, conserving, and testing groundwater; and recognizing and acting on local groundwater issues. Among the activities, students record how much water they use in a day, observe a model of the water cycle, build a solar still, observe how dissolved surface materials percolate into the ground, and observe water movement through different soils. They also investigate how long it takes for waste materials to decompose, and they construct and use a water filter, construct a model oil spill and test the effectiveness of different cleanup methods, and conduct tests to examine groundwater quality. Students develop a survey or questionnaire to study a local issue. The guide also provides information and suggestions for taking action on groundwater issues.

H₂O Below, developed for middle school students in Illinois, refers to groundwater resources in that state, but many of its activities can be adapted for other locations. Each activity includes background information, a materials list, step-by-step procedures, discussion questions, extensions, suggestions for evaluation, and reproducible student sheets. Appendixes include a glossary, a list of resources on groundwater, a preunit test, and a special case study and activities on karst topography.

Price: Teacher's guide, $12. Groundwater flow model, $145. Kit, $100. *Publisher/supplier:* Southern Illinois University at Edwardsville. *Materials:* Available locally, from commercial suppliers, or in kit.

3.53 **Investigating Your Environment: The MINI Edition.** U.S. Forest Service. Ogden, Utah: U.S. Forest Service, Intermountain Region, 1994.

Recommended grade level: 4-8. *Investigating Your Environment: The MINI Edition,* which takes a multidisciplinary approach to environmental science activities, contains the 11 most popular chapters from the original 21-chapter version of the volume. The first chapter, on developing an environmental investigation, offers teachers suggestions about developing instructional objectives, question sequences, and lesson plans, among other topics. The remaining chapters focus on forests, interpreting the environment, investigating an environmental issue, land use simulation, natural resources in an urban environment, plant relationships, schoolyard activities, soil, water, and wildlife.

Each chapter includes an introduction, a sketch of its activities, suggestions for combining the activities, a section on curriculum relationships, and fully developed lesson plans, including reproducible planning and data sheets.

Price: Free. *Publisher/supplier:* USDA Forest Service Web site, at http://www.fs.fed.us/outdoors/nrce/iye/contents.htm. *Materials:* Available locally.

3.54 Minds-on Science: For Profit, for Planet. Developed by National Museum of American History, Smithsonian Institution (Washington, D.C.). Watertown, Mass.: Tom Snyder Productions, 1995.

Recommended grade level: 7-8. Through the videodisc activity kit *Minds-on Science: For Profit, for Planet,* students take on the role of president of a leading clothing designer and manufacturer. The company needs a breakthrough to keep its leading position in the industry, and the students must decide how to invest the company's resources. To sort out their options and make their decision, students review conflicting data and opinions from 4 advisers—a technologist, a chemist, an environmentalist, and a marketing director. Through video segments and short scientific readings in the student portfolios, students also become familiar with polymers, the use of biotechnology in industry, the environmental aspects of manufacturing, and contributions that science has made to fashion. Short paper-and-pencil activities help students assess how the number of pairs of sneakers they own might affect the environment, design an advertisement for a plastic product, and make their own fashion invention. In 16 extension activities, students examine the role of polymers in sports equipment, compare the biodegradability of various materials, and monitor their behavior as consumers.

Students work cooperatively in teams of 4 as they gather information and do the activities in the kit. At the end of the unit, however, they must reach a consensus and make a decision as a class on what to do with the company. They watch the consequences of their decision on the video, then face a new dilemma and must make a second decision. Including the extension activities, the kit takes approximately 4 to 5 weeks to complete. The complete kit includes the videodisc, student portfolios, and a teacher's guide.

Prices: Videodisc kit, $249.95. Optional software for Macintosh or Windows, $49.95. *Publisher/supplier:* Tom Snyder Productions. *Materials:* Available in kit.

3.55 Our Wonderful World: Solutions for Math + Science. Activities Integrating Mathematics and Science (AIMS) series. Fresno, Calif.: AIMS Education Foundation, 1986.

Recommended grade level: 5-8. The 19 activities in *Our Wonderful World: Solutions for Math + Science* focus on understanding the natural environment. Investigations are organized in 6 topic areas—air, water, transpiration, soil, plants, and animals/insects. Students are involved in activities such as analyzing the volume of snow, comparing habitats, classifying soils and categorizing leaves by their characteristics, exploring natural selection and camouflage, and testing clothes as insulators. Many of the activities are more appropriately done outdoors.

Our Wonderful World provides reproducible student worksheets, including data charts, tables, and graphs. A complete lesson plan is included for each of the 19 activities.

Price: Teacher's guide (ISBN 1-881431-08-8), $16.95. *Publisher/supplier:* AIMS Education Foundation. *Materials:* Available locally, or from commercial suppliers.

3.56 Outlook: The Earth. David V. McCalley. Dubuque, Iowa: Kendall/Hunt, 1994.

Recommended grade level: K-8+. *Outlook: The Earth* contains 140 ideas for interdisciplinary environmental education activities for students in grades K-12. Ideas are grouped by grade level—K-2, 3-5, 6-8, or 9-12—with more than 30 ideas for grades 6-8.

Each activity is a completely self-contained lesson plan. Activities are organized in 11 topical categories: air, community responsibility, heritage, human habitat, land use, mineral resources, natural habitat, population dynamics, production and distribution, soil, and water. Using this guide, teachers could develop activities that would, for example, allow students to contrast past and present air pollutants in their city, create a land use priority list and devise a way to save a wetland area, or investigate bird habitat management.

For each activity, information is included on student learning outcomes, the type of site appropriate for the activity, and the amount of time and the materials needed. The teaching of the activity is then suggested as a 3-phase learning cycle of exploration, concept development, and application. Questions or basic guidelines are given for developing these learning cycles. In addition, follow-up suggestions and resource materials are listed for each activity.

Price: $44.90 (ISBN 0-8403-9280-X). *Publisher/supplier:* Kendall/Hunt. *Materials:* Available locally, or from commercial suppliers.

3.57 Project Learning Tree Environmental Education Activity Guide: Pre K-8. Project Learning Tree. Washington, D.C.: American Forest Foundation, 1996.

Recommended grade level: K-8. The *Project Learning Tree Environmental Education Activity Guide: Pre K-8* provides activities for investigating environmental issues and encourages students to make informed, responsible decisions. The guide has 5 major themes: (1) diversity, (2) interrelationships, (3) systems, (4) structure and scale, and (5) patterns of change. Each theme has activities in the following areas: environment, resource management and technology, and society and culture. The activities integrate the themes within science, language arts, social studies, art, music, and physical education.

Among the activities, for example, students describe how different species of plants and animals are adapted to a particular set of environmental conditions; they examine rotting logs to learn about decomposition, as well as microhabitats and communities; they role-play managers of a tree farm; they learn how land-use decisions and legislation affect wetlands; and they examine the pros and cons of various packaging strategies.

The *Activity Guide* provides a complete lesson plan for each of its nearly 100 activities. The guide also features a glossary and appendixes, including teaching suggestions for controversial issues, multicultural education, working with exceptional students, and teaching outdoors.

Price: Free to teachers who attend a workshop in their own state. *Publisher/supplier:* American Forest Foundation. *Materials:* Available locally, or from commercial suppliers.

3.58 STV: Biodiversity. Interactive Videodiscs. Washington, D.C.: National Geographic Society, 1994.

Recommended grade level: 6-8+. *STV: Biodiversity* is an interactive videodisc program that helps students learn about the destruction and preservation of endangered species and land areas. The disc includes 25 minutes of video featuring a National Geographic film, *The Diversity of Life,* and more than 100 still photographs. Viewers travel from coral reefs to forests to see where human action is destroying habitats, and they see how zoos and botanical gardens are trying to protect plants and animals in artificial environments.

The HyperCard diskette that accompanies the program provides supporting text drawn from National Geographic publications, a glossary, and a feature that allows users to create customized visual presentations. Students can use the software, for example, to arrange video segments and photographs from the videodisc and type in their own narration.

The teacher's guide—*Biodiversity*—includes information on key concepts, preview questions that introduce concepts in the video, and bar codes to allow access to the videodisc with a bar-code reader. The teacher's guide also provides directions for several activities—such as researching the origins of medicine in nature, graphing the population of a nearby city over the past 150 years, or gathering information about environmental organizations for an environmental fair. The videodisc includes a Spanish-language track, and the teacher's guide includes the video script in both English and Spanish.

Prices: Level I kit (includes videodisc), $225. Level III kit (includes videodisc and HyperCard diskette), $325. *Publisher/supplier:* National Geographic Society. *Materials:* Available in kit.

3.59 STV: Water. Interactive Videodiscs. Washington, D.C.: National Geographic Society, 1994.

Recommended grade level: 6-8+. *STV: Water* is an interactive videodisc program that helps students learn about where freshwater comes from, how it is used, and what must be done to conserve it. The disc includes 28 minutes of video featuring a National Geographic film, *Freshwater: Resource at Risk,* and more than 100 still photographs. Viewers travel to the Great Lakes, the Ogallala aquifer, the Colorado River watershed, and south Florida to learn about challenges to water supplies.

The HyperCard diskette that accompanies the program provides supporting text drawn from National Geographic publications, a glossary, and a feature that allows users to create customized visual presentations from the materials. Students can use the software, for example, to arrange video segments and photographs from the videodisc and type in their own narration.

The teacher's guide—*Water*—includes information on key concepts, preview questions that introduce concepts in the video, and bar codes to allow access to the videodisc with a bar-code reader. The teacher's guide also provides directions for several short activities—such as building a model of a wetland or an aquifer, investigating the source of their tap water, or using maps to locate dams on the Colorado River watershed. The videodisc includes a Spanish-language track, and the teacher's guide includes the video script in both English and Spanish.

Prices: Level I kit (including videodisc), $225. Level III kit (including videodisc and HyperCard diskette), $325. *Publisher/supplier:* National Geographic Society. *Materials:* Available in kit.

3.60 **The Tapwater Tour.** LaMotte Co. Chestertown, Md.: LaMotte Co., 1989.

Recommended grade level: 4-8. Students perform a water analysis in *The Tapwater Tour,* which is a test kit and "minicurriculum" for exploring drinking water. The unit is designed to be teacher-directed, but it has hands-on activities throughout. Students determine the pH of various solutions; they test water samples for the presence of chlorine, iron, and copper; and they use a soap solution to determine the "hardness" of water samples. They also summarize results in a water-quality report. Chemical test tablets and plastic bags required for the activities accompany the teacher's guide.

Prices: Complete kit, $44.50. Replacement kit, $35.00. *Publisher/supplier:* LaMotte. *Materials:* Available locally, from commercial suppliers, or in kit.

3.61 **Trash and Garbage: What Happens to Trash and Garbage? An Introduction to the Carbon Cycle.** Lynn Margulis and colleagues. Rochester, N.Y.: Ward's Natural Science Establishment, 1992.

Recommended grade level: 7-8+. *Trash and Garbage: What Happens to Trash and Garbage? An Introduction to the Carbon Cycle* is a kit designed to introduce students to the idea of the cycling of elements in nature. Working in small groups, students learn how refuse, if handled properly, breaks down and is recycled back to a usable form. In the first of 9 activities, they discuss the definitions of trash and garbage and what happens to trash and garbage. In the second activity, they match a series of black-and-white photo-graphs with a series of captions to show what happens to trash and garbage in a real community. During the third activity, students watch a demonstration of fermentation. For the fourth activity, they use a potted plant as a starting point for a discussion of photosynthesis and the carbon cycle. They set up "mold micro-gardens" in jars to observe how small items of trash and garbage break down over time. Students also watch an 18-minute videotape—*Common Fungi*—that allows them to see life histories of common molds, and at the end of the unit they investigate what happens to trash and garbage in their own communities.

Observation of the mold microgarden takes a few minutes a day for 2 to 6 weeks; the other activities take a total of 7 to 9 class periods. Included in the kit are a teacher's guide, photographs and captions for the photo-sorting activity, the videotape, and a poster illustrating the carbon cycle. Other inexpensive materials need to be collected or purchased to complete the unit.

Price: Kit, $149. *Publisher/supplier:* Ward's. *Materials:* Available locally, from commercial suppliers, or in kit.

3.62 **Wading into Wetlands.** Nature-Scope series. Washington, D.C.: National Wildlife Federation, 1989.

Recommended grade level: K-7. *Wading into Wetlands* includes background information and activities for an interdisciplinary introduction to the ecology of wetlands, including salt marshes and mangrove swamps, and freshwater swamps, marshes, and bogs. Students participate in classroom and field experiences, observing flora and fauna. They engage in experiments, games, writing, art, and mathematical activities that demonstrate the unique characteristics of wetlands and their importance to wildlife and humans. Chapters usually begin with primary activities and end with intermediate or advanced activities.

Wading into Wetlands contains 20 lessons organized in 4 chapters; a fifth chapter provides art and craft ideas. Teachers may choose single activities or teach each chapter as a unit. Copycat pages supplement the activities and include ready-to-copy games, puzzles, and worksheets.

Price: $12.95 (ISBN 0-07-046507-X). *Publisher/supplier:* McGraw-Hill Order Services. *Materials:* Available locally, or from commercial suppliers.

3.63 **Water Wisdom: A Curriculum for Grades Four Through Eight.** Carolie Sly, Leslie Comnes, and Sandra Brislain. Hayward, Calif.: Alameda County Office of Education, 1990.

Recommended grade level: 4-8. *Water Wisdom* contains 20 activities through which students explore the subject of water—its importance to biological systems, its use and distribution, and its symbolic role in myth and folklore. The activities are presented in 3 instructional units: a science unit, a social science unit, and a literature unit. In the science unit, for example, students predict how much water they use in a day, keeping a log of their actual water use; they also observe algae and learn how changes in water temperature and nutrient composition can affect algae and other organisms; and they learn about the adaptive characteristics of desert plants. In the social science unit, students conduct a survey to find out peoples' attitudes about water, and they evaluate whether animals or people have more right to water. In the literature unit, students read 2 creation myths and discuss the role that water plays in them. Although the lessons within each unit build on each other sequentially, they can also be recombined within other themes outlined in the unit.

Water Wisdom was designed to supplement the California State Environmental Education Guide, and some activities focus on California water issues. Each activity includes background information, procedures, discussion questions, extension ideas, home learning suggestions, and reproducible student pages.

Price: $15.70 (ISBN 0-88067-002-9). *Publisher/supplier:* Alameda County Office of Education. *Materials:* Available locally, or from commercial suppliers.

Constructing an ecocolumn

EARTH AND SPACE SCIENCE

4.1 **Concepts and Challenges in Earth Science.** 3rd ed., rev. Leonard Bernstein, Martin Schachter, Alan Winkler, and Stanley Wolfe. Concepts and Challenges in Life, Earth, and Physical Science series. Upper Saddle River, N.J.: Globe Fearon, 1998.

Program Overview The series entitled Concepts and Challenges in Life, Earth, and Physical Science consists of 3 textbooks—one in life science, one in earth science, and one in physical science. Each year-long course contains about 20 units. Teaching materials, ancillary student materials, and some optional components are available for each course.

Student Edition **Recommended grade level: 7-8. Reading level: late 6.** *Concepts and Challenges in Earth Science* offers a complete course in earth and space science. This textbook is divided into 18 units, each consisting of 6 to 12 lessons. The following topics are addressed: maps, miner-

als, rocks, weathering, soil, erosion, landforms, volcanoes, earthquakes, plate tectonics, fossils, oceanography, the atmosphere, weather, climate, air and water pollution, energy resources, astronomy, the solar system, the earth-moon system, stars, and galaxies. Basic science concepts and vocabulary are introduced in short paragraphs. A variety of activities or demonstrations require students to extend their learning, model phenomena, or make observations. For example, students look at hard-boiled eggs to model the earth's layers; classify igneous rocks using crystal size; use a container filled with pebbles, sand, soil, and water to demonstrate the settling of ocean sediments; and make a simple wind vane. In other activities, students are asked to design an experiment to find out, for example, if the skeletons of coral contain calcium carbonate, to show

that air is made up of matter, and to demonstrate the law of gravity.

Suggestions for writing exercises and reports are provided. Brief reading features focus on careers in earth science, science connections to everyday life, people in science, technology and society, and looking back in science.

Teacher's Edition The teacher's edition provides unit-by-unit teaching tips and ideas—including suggestions for discussions, class activities, extensions, reinforcements, and bulletin board projects. Answers to in-text questions are provided.

Supplementary Laboratory Manual The laboratory manual contains 48 activities and 8 skills worksheets. Lab activities are directly correlated with lessons in the student textbook. Examples include learning how the difference in arrival time between P and S waves can be used to locate the epicenter of an earthquake, using a psychrometer to determine the relative humidity of air, reading a weather map, and demonstrating how a lunar eclipse occurs. The annotated teacher's edition of the lab manual includes answers to questions in the student manual, materials and equipment lists, and a skills matrix.

Teacher's Resource Book The teacher's resource book contains more than 300 reproducible blackline masters, including lesson review, vocabulary, and enrichment worksheets; unit tests; and a Spanish-language supplement.

Key to Content Standards: 5-8 (see app. C)

UNIFYING CONCEPTS AND PROCESSES: Systems, order, and organization; evidence, models, and explanation; change, constancy, and measurement; evolution and equilibrium; form and function.

SCIENCE AS INQUIRY: Abilities necessary to do scientific inquiry; understandings about scientific inquiry.

PHYSICAL SCIENCE: Properties and changes of properties in matter; transfer of energy.

EARTH AND SPACE SCIENCE: Structure of the earth system; earth's history; earth in the solar system.

SCIENCE IN PERSONAL AND SOCIAL PERSPECTIVES: Natural hazards; science and technology in society.

HISTORY AND NATURE OF SCIENCE: Science as a human endeavor; history of science.

ABOUT THE ANNOTATIONS IN "EARTH AND SPACE SCIENCE—CORE MATERIALS"

Entry Numbers
Curriculum materials are arranged alphabetically by title in each category (Core Materials, Supplementary Units, and Science Activity Books) in chapters 1 through 5 of this guide.

Each curriculum annotation has a two-part entry number: the chapter number is given before the period; the number after the period locates the entry within that chapter. For example, the first entry number in chapter 1 is 1.1; the second entry in chapter 2 is 2.2; and so on.

The entry numbers within each curriculum chapter run consecutively through Core Materials, Supplementary Units, and Science Activity Books.

Order of Bibliographic Information
Following is the arrangement of the facts of publication in the annotations in this section:

- **Title of publication**
- **Number of edition,** if applicable
- **Authors** (an individual author or authors, an institutional author, or a project or program name under which the material was developed)
- **Series title**
- **Series developer,** if applicable
- **Place of publication, publisher, and date of publication**

Recommended Grade Level and Reading Level
The grade level for each piece of material was recommended by teacher evaluators during the development of this guide. In some instances, the recommended grade level may differ slightly from the publisher's advertised level. The Fry Readability Scale was used to determine the approximate reading level of core materials.

Key to Content Standards: 5-8
The key lists the content standards for grades 5-8 from the *National Science Education Standards* (NSES) that are addressed in depth by the item. A key is provided for core materials and supplementary units. (*See* appendix C.)

Price and Acquisition Information

Ordering information appears at the end of each entry. Included are—

* **Prices** (of teacher's guides, student books, lab manuals, and kits or units)
* **Publisher/supplier** (The name of a principal publisher/supplier, although not necessarily the sole source, for the items listed in the price category. Appendix A, "Publishers and Suppliers," provides the address, phone and fax numbers, and electronic ordering information, where available, for each publisher and supplier.)
* **Materials** (various sources from which one might obtain the required materials)

Readers must contact publishers/suppliers for complete and up-to-date listings of the program resources and support materials available for a particular unit. Depending on the developer, these items may be required, optional, or both; they may be offered individually and/or in kits, packages, or boxes. Materials may change with revised editions. The prices given in this chapter for selected resources or materials are based on information from the publishers and suppliers but are not meant to represent the full range of ordering options.

Indexes of Curriculum Materials

The multiple indexes on pp. 449-78 allow easy access to the information in this guide. Various aspects of the curriculum materials—including titles, topics addressed in each unit, grade levels, and standards addressed—are the focus of seven separate indexes. For example, titles and entry numbers are listed in the "Title Index" on pp. 450-54. The "Index of Authors, Series, and Curriculum Projects," on pp. 455-57, provides entry numbers of any annotated titles in a particular series.

Overviews of Core and Supplementary Programs

Appendix D, "Overviews of Core and Supplementary Programs with Titles Annotated in This Guide," on pp. 441-48, lists, by series, the individual titles annotated in the sections "Core Materials" and "Supplementary Units" of the five curriculum chapters.

Prices: Student edition (ISBN 0-835-92241-3), $45.95. Teacher's edition (ISBN 0-835-92245-6), $58.95. Student lab program, $14.95. Teacher's lab program, $22.95. Teacher's resource book, $154.95. *Publisher/supplier:* Globe Fearon. *Materials:* Available locally, or from commercial suppliers.

4.2 Exploring Earth Science. 2nd ed. Anthea Maton, Jean Hopkins, Susan Johnson, and others. Prentice Hall Exploring Life, Earth, and Physical Science series. Upper Saddle River, N.J.: Prentice Hall, 1997.

Program Overview The Prentice Hall Exploring Life, Earth, and Physical Science series is a program for middle school students. Designed to cover all relevant areas of science, this integrated program consists of 3 textbooks (1 for each major discipline) and incorporates 7 science themes—energy, evolution, patterns of change, scale and structure, systems and interactions, unity and diversity, and stability. Each of the 3 year-long courses contains about 6 units. The units are also available, possibly with some modifications, as individual textbooks in the Prentice Hall Science Integrated Learning System series (*see*, e.g., 4.3). For each course, teaching materials, ancillary student materials, and some optional components are available.

Student Edition **Recommended grade level: 7-8+. Reading level: middle 8.** *Exploring Earth Science* offers a complete course in earth science.

The units in this textbook are entitled: (1) "Exploring the Universe," (2) "Exploring Planet Earth," (3) "Dynamic Earth," (4) "Exploring Earth's Weather," (5) "History of the Earth," and (6) "Ecology: Earth's Natural Resources." During the course, students learn about topics in the fields of geology, astronomy, meteorology, and oceanography—for example, stars and galaxies; the solar system; rocks and minerals; the earth's structure, atmosphere, and oceans; weather; erosion; earthquakes and volcanoes; plate tectonics; fossils; geologic time; and the earth's natural resources.

Examples of the lab investigations that students conduct during the 6 units are these: constructing a refracting telescope, determining the porosity of various soils, comparing the decomposition of different types of litter in a landfill, locating patterns of earthquake and volcano distribution, and determining relative humidity using a handmade sling psychrometer.

Each of the 6 units in *Exploring Earth Science* typically has 2 to 6 chapters. Each chapter contains comprehensive reading sections that introduce major science concepts. Also included are suggested skills-oriented activities for discovering, doing, calculating, thinking, and writing about science. The activities range from making a model of the water cycle to calculating shoreline erosion to creating a scrapbook of news items concerning environmental problems. Each chapter includes a laboratory investigation as well as a review and study guide.

Other features of this textbook include problem-solving challenges, science connections to real-world events or issues, and careers in science. A "Science Gazette" feature at the end of each unit profiles prominent scientists—for example, astronomer Ian Shelton, archaeologist

Alan Kalata, and meteorologist Joanne Simpson. An "Activity Bank" at the back of the book provides at least 1 additional laboratory investigation for each chapter. Examples include exploring ways to prevent rusting, measuring the effects of phosphates on plant growth, and building a simple anemometer to measure wind speed.

Teacher's Edition In the teacher's wraparound edition, each chapter begins with a 2-page planning guide and a 2-page preview that summarizes each section within the chapter. The teacher's edition also provides suggestions for teaching, guiding, integrating, and closing lessons, as well as enrichments, extensions, and answers to questions in the student text.

Supplementary Laboratory Manual The supplementary lab manual contains 52 additional investigations directly correlated with the information presented in the student textbook. Examples include investigating how the angle of the sun's rays affects temperature on the earth, creating a model of a density current to observe some of the factors that affect the behavior of deep-sea density currents, preparing a contour map of a landform model, and using a stream table to investigate running water and erosion.

Program Resources and Support Materials A variety of support materials is available, including a box of teaching resources with activities, worksheets, and assessment materials for each chapter. Other available materials are a teacher's desk reference, an integrated science activity book, a computer test bank, videos, videodiscs, transparencies, a class-

room manager guide, and a book of product-testing activities.

Key to Content Standards: 5-8 (see app. C)

UNIFYING CONCEPTS AND PROCESSES: Systems, order, and organization; evidence, models, and explanation; change, constancy, and measurement; evolution and equilibrium; form and function.

SCIENCE AS INQUIRY: Abilities necessary to do scientific inquiry; understandings about scientific inquiry.

PHYSICAL SCIENCE: Properties and changes of properties in matter; motions and forces; transfer of energy.

EARTH AND SPACE SCIENCE: Structure of the earth system; earth's history; earth in the solar system.

SCIENCE AND TECHNOLOGY: Understandings about science and technology.

SCIENCE IN PERSONAL AND SOCIAL PERSPECTIVES: Science and technology in society.

Prices: Student edition (ISBN 0-13-418724-5), $41.47. Teacher's edition (ISBN 0-13-422825-1), $70.40. Lab manual, teacher's edition (1995), $24.47. Teaching resources, $306.47. (Contact publisher/supplier for complete price and ordering information.) *Publisher/supplier:* Prentice Hall. *Materials:* Available locally, or from commercial suppliers.

4.3 Exploring Earth's Weather. 3rd ed. Anthea Maton, Jean Hopkins, Susan Johnson, and others. Prentice Hall Science Integrated Learning System series. Upper Saddle River, N.J.: Prentice Hall, 1997.

Program Overview The Prentice Hall Science Integrated Learning System series is a program for middle school or junior high school students. Designed to cover all relevant areas of science, this program consists of 19 books, each in a particular topic area, such as sound and light, earth's weather, and cells—building blocks of life. Seven science themes are incorporated into the program; the themes are energy, evolution, patterns of change, scale and structure, systems and interactions, unity and diversity, and stability. For each unit, teaching materials, ancillary student materials, and some optional components are available.

Student Edition **Recommended grade level: 6-8. Reading level: late 7.** The textbook *Exploring Earth's Weather,* which helps students investigate the factors that cause weather and climate, is organized in 3 chapters: (1) "What Is Weather?" (2) "What Is Climate?" and (3) "Climate in the United States." During the course, students learn about temperature, air pressure, wind, and humidity. They explore weather patterns and weather forecasting, learn to identify basic types of clouds, and differentiate between weather and climate. They also examine the nature, causes, zones, and changes of climate. Students then explore the climate regions of the United States and identify the 6 major regions on the basis of temperature and precipitation. They also relate land biomes of the United States to their climates.

Each chapter includes a lab investigation. Students use a handmade sling psychrometer to determine relative humidity. They graph temperature and precipitation data to classify the climates of cities in different parts of the world. They also use climate information to determine the biomes of the United States.

Each chapter contains comprehensive reading sections that introduce major science concepts. Suggestions are provided for activities in which students "find out by doing," "find out by reading," and "find out by writing." Other skills-oriented activities are also suggested—for example, using a barometer to forecast the

weather and examining 2 microclimates in a neighborhood.

Other features of the textbook include problem-solving challenges, descriptions of science careers, and science connections to real-world events or issues. The student edition closes with readings on 3 topics: (1) the career of pioneering meteorologist Joanne Simpson, (2) the irrigation of arid lands, and (3) a fictional account of what scientists would expect weather to be like after a nuclear holocaust.

Teacher's Edition In the teacher's wraparound edition, each chapter begins with a 2-page planning guide and a 2-page preview that summarizes each section within the chapter. The teacher's edition also provides suggestions for teaching, guiding, integrating, and closing lessons, as well as enrichments, extensions, and answers to questions in the student text.

Supplementary Laboratory Manual The supplementary lab manual provides 5 additional investigations directly correlated with the information presented in the student textbook. Examples of the investigations include determining how the angle of insolation affects the rate of temperature change of a surface; and constructing a simple barometer, then using it to make observations of changes in atmospheric pressure.

Program Resources and Support Materials A variety of materials, including some optional components, is available. A teacher's resource package contains the student edition and annotated teacher's editions of both the textbook and the lab manual, as well as a test book, an activity book, a review-and-reinforcement guide, and English and Spanish audiotapes for auditory and language learners. Other avail-

able materials include interactive videodiscs, transparencies, assessment materials, English and Spanish guides for language learners, a study guide, a teacher's desk reference, and a booklet of product-testing activities.

Key to Content Standards: 5-8 (see app. C)

UNIFYING CONCEPTS AND PROCESSES: Systems, order, and organization; evidence, models, and explanation; change, constancy, and measurement.
SCIENCE AS INQUIRY: Abilities necessary to do scientific inquiry; understandings about scientific inquiry.
EARTH AND SPACE SCIENCE: Structure of the earth system; earth's history; earth in the solar system.
SCIENCE AND TECHNOLOGY: Understandings about science and technology.
SCIENCE IN PERSONAL AND SOCIAL PERSPECTIVES: Science and technology in society.

Prices: Student edition (ISBN 0-13-423401-4), $9.97. Teacher's edition (ISBN 0-13-423161-9), $22.97. Teacher's resource package, $112.97. (Contact publisher/supplier for complete price and ordering information.)
Publisher/supplier: Prentice Hall.
Materials: Available locally, or from commercial suppliers.

4.4 **Exploring Planet Earth.** 3rd ed. Anthea Maton, Jean Hopkins, Susan Johnson, and others. Prentice Hall Science Integrated Learning System series. Upper Saddle River, N.J.: Prentice Hall, 1997.

Program Overview The Prentice Hall Science Integrated Learning System series is a program for middle school or junior high school students. Designed to cover all relevant areas of science, this program consists of 19 books, each in a particular topic area, such as sound and light, the planet earth, and cells—building blocks of life. Seven science themes are incorporated into the program; the themes are energy, evolution, patterns of change, scale and structure, systems and interactions, unity and diversity, and stability. For each unit, teaching materials, ancillary student materials, and some optional components are available.

Student Edition **Recommended grade level: 7-8. Reading level: early 7.** *Exploring Planet Earth,* which introduces students to the various components and structures of the earth, is organized in 5 chapters: (1) "Earth's Atmosphere," (2) "Earth's Oceans," (3) "Earth's Fresh Water," (4) "Earth's Landmasses," and (5) "Earth's Interior." During the course, students study the composition and layers of the earth's atmosphere and the composition of the magnetosphere. They also learn about the properties, life zones, and motions of the oceans; and they find out how the earth maintains a supply of freshwater. Students study the characteristics of continents, mountains, plains, and plateaus. They discuss the advantages and disadvantages of various types of maps. They also find out about the properties of the earth's layers, and learn how scientists use seismic waves to gather information about the interior of the planet.

Each chapter includes a lab investigation. Students explore whether different types of surfaces gain different amounts of heat in and out of direct sunlight. They determine the effect that different depths of water have on the settling of sediments. They also compare the porosity of various soils, make a topographic map, and simulate the plasticity of the earth's mantle using cornstarch and water.

Each chapter contains comprehensive reading sections that introduce major science concepts. Suggestions are provided for activities in which students "find out by doing," "find

out by reading," and "find out by writing." Other activities are also suggested—for example, constructing a model of the ocean floor and calculating how many earths would have to be lined up in a row to reach the sun.

Other features of the textbook include problem-solving challenges, descriptions of science careers, and science connections to real-world events or issues. The student edition closes with readings on 3 topics: (1) archaeologists who discovered an ancient Bolivian agricultural system that involved canals and raised land, (2) the controversy between conservationists and the timber industry over efforts to save the spotted owl from extinction, and (3) a fictional account of what life might be like in a city under the ocean.

Teacher's Edition In the teacher's wraparound edition, each chapter begins with a 2-page planning guide and a 2-page preview that summarizes each section within the chapter. The teacher's edition also provides suggestions for teaching, guiding, integrating, and closing lessons, as well as enrichments, extensions, and answers to questions in the student text.

Supplementary Laboratory Manual The supplementary lab manual provides 12 additional investigations directly correlated with the information presented in the student textbook. Examples of the investigations include experimenting to determine the relationship of the density of water to the amount of salt dissolved in the water, creating a model of a well system to study the spread of a pollutant, and creating an artificial magma to demonstrate the action of gases in a magma.

Program Resources and Support Materials A variety of materials, including some optional components, is available. A teacher's resource package contains the stu-

dent edition and annotated teacher's editions of both the textbook and the lab manual, as well as a test book, an activity book, a review-and-reinforcement guide, and English and Spanish audiotapes for auditory and language learners. Other available materials include interactive videodiscs, transparencies, assessment materials, English and Spanish guides for language learners, a study guide, a teacher's desk reference, and a booklet of product-testing activities.

Key to Content Standards: 5-8 (see app. C)

UNIFYING CONCEPTS AND PROCESSES: Systems, order, and organization; evidence, models, and explanation; change, constancy, and measurement. **SCIENCE AS INQUIRY:** Abilities necessary to do scientific inquiry; understandings about scientific inquiry. **EARTH AND SPACE SCIENCE:** Structure of the earth system; earth's history. **SCIENCE IN PERSONAL AND SOCIAL PERSPECTIVES:** Populations, resources, and environments; natural hazards; risks and benefits; science and technology in society.

Prices: Student edition (ISBN 0-13-423427-8), $9.97. Teacher's edition (ISBN 0-13-423187-2), $22.97. Teacher's resource package, $112.97. (Contact publisher/supplier for complete price and ordering information.) ***Publisher/supplier:*** Prentice Hall. ***Materials:*** Available locally, or from commercial suppliers.

4.5 **Glencoe Earth Science.** Ralph Feather, Jr., and Susan Leach Snyder. Glencoe Life, Earth, and Physical Science series. New York, N.Y.: Glencoe/McGraw-Hill, 1997.

Program Overview The Glencoe Life, Earth, and Physical Science series includes 3 full-year courses—one in life, one in earth, and one in physical science—for students in grades 8 and above. Four major themes are developed: (1) energy, (2) systems and interactions, (3) scale and structure, and (4) stability and change. An extensive set of materials and resources, including many optional components, is available for students and teachers.

Student Edition **Recommended grade level: 7-8. Reading level: middle 7.** *Glencoe Earth Science* is divided into 7 units: (1) "Earth Materials," (2) "The Changing Surface of Earth," (3) "Earth's Internal Processes," (4) "Change and Earth's History," (5) "Earth's Air and Water," (6) "You and the Environment," and (7) "Astronomy." During this course, students learn about matter and its changes, minerals, rocks, weathering and soil, erosional forces, earthquakes, volcanoes, plate tectonics, geologic time, the earth's atmosphere, water, weather, climate, oceanography, man and the environment, the sun-earth-moon system, the solar system, stars, and galaxies.

Sample lab activities in this textbook include classifying igneous rocks by their characteristics, making a topographic map from a landform model, determining the locations of earthquake epicenters by interpreting data on an earthquake wave-travel-time graph, and making a barometer and observing how it reacts to changes in air pressure. Other lab activities involve observing how water and soil differ in their ability to absorb and release heat, and reading and using a weather map.

Glencoe Earth Science has 24 chapters in its 7 units. Each chapter begins with a self-guided activity in which students make observations and generate questions about chapter concepts and topics. Reading sections on science concepts are then interwoven with various types of activities, including open-ended activities, minilabs (activities that can be done in class or at home), and skill-building or problem-solving activities. In activities for designing their own experiments, students

brainstorm hypotheses, make a decision to investigate a hypothesis that can be tested, plan procedures, and think about why their hypothesis was supported or not.

Special features of the textbook include "connect to" marginal notes that relate basic questions in physics, chemistry, earth science, and life science to one another. The book also provides "science and society" features that invite students to confront real-life problems; profiles of people in science; and reading selections about connections between science, history, literature, and the arts.

Teacher's Edition The wraparound teacher's edition provides information on curriculum integration, assessment, planning, and meeting the diverse needs of students. Each chapter contains a 4-page planning guide; strategies for preparing, teaching, and closing lessons; answers to in-text questions; tips on connecting earth science to other sciences, disciplines, or community resources; and different assessment options.

Supplementary Laboratory Manual The supplementary lab manual offers 1 or more additional labs for each chapter. It has set-up diagrams, data tables, and space for student responses. Examples of investigations include comparing various materials to see which are most suitable for filtering groundwater, constructing a block diagram to illustrate the geologic history of an area, analyzing weather data for patterns, and determining the composition of a star using a simple spectral analyzer.

Program Resources and Support Materials *Glencoe Earth Science* offers an extensive list of support materials and program resources, including the following: activity and reinforcement worksheets, science

integration activities that relate earth and life science to specific physical science chapters, a critical-thinking/problem-solving book, a concept-mapping book, chapter review masters, a study guide, enrichment worksheets, a book on multicultural connections, technology-integration masters, assessments, computer test banks, color transparencies, a Spanish resources book, and interactive CD-ROM and videodisc programs.

Key to Content Standards: 5-8 (see app. C)

UNIFYING CONCEPTS AND PROCESSES: Systems, order, and organization; evidence, models, and explanation; change, constancy, and measurement; evolution and equilibrium; form and function.

SCIENCE AS INQUIRY: Abilities necessary to do scientific inquiry; understandings about scientific inquiry.

PHYSICAL SCIENCE: Properties and changes of properties in matter; transfer of energy.

LIFE SCIENCE: Diversity and adaptations of organisms.

EARTH AND SPACE SCIENCE: Structure of the earth system; earth's history; earth in the solar system.

SCIENCE AND TECHNOLOGY: Understandings about science and technology.

SCIENCE IN PERSONAL AND SOCIAL PERSPECTIVES: Populations, resources, and environments; natural hazards; risks and benefits; science and technology in society.

HISTORY AND NATURE OF SCIENCE: Science as a human endeavor.

Prices: Student edition (ISBN 0-02-827808-9), $41.79. Teacher's edition (ISBN 0-02-827809-7), $57.86. Student lab manual, $8.25. Teacher's lab manual, $14.00. Teacher's classroom resources, $321.87. (Contact publisher/supplier for complete price and ordering information.) *Publisher/supplier:* Glencoe/McGraw-Hill. *Materials:* Available locally, or from commercial suppliers.

4.6 Landforms. Full Option Science System (FOSS) series. Developed by Lawrence Hall of Science (Berkeley, Calif.). Hudson, N.H.: Delta Education, 1993.

Program Overview The Full Option Science System (FOSS) program is a K-6 science curriculum consisting of 27 stand-alone modules. The 8 modules for grades 5-6 are organized under topics in the life, physical, and earth sciences and in scientific reasoning and technology. They can be used in any order. The FOSS program is designed to engage students in scientific concepts through multi-sensory, hands-on laboratory activities. All modules of the program incorporate 5 unifying themes— (1) pattern, (2) structure, (3) interaction, (4) change, and (5) system. The components of a FOSS module are a teacher's guide and a kit of materials.

Teacher's Guide **Recommended grade level: 5-6.** The *Landforms* module introduces students to concepts of physical geography and mapping. Students first create a 3-dimensional model of their school site and transfer information about the locations of landforms and structures in their model to a grid. This allows them to relate physical structures to representations on maps. They use stream tables to simulate the creation of landforms. Students construct a 3-dimensional foam model of an actual mountain, Mount Shasta; then they create a topographic map of the mountain and compare it to a topographic map of the same mountain from the U.S. Geological Survey.

Landforms contains 5 multipart activities, requiring 18 class sessions of 30 to 50 minutes each. The teacher's guide includes a module overview, the 5 individual activity folios, duplication masters (in English and Spanish) for student sheets, and an annotated bibliography. Science background information,

detailed instructions on planning for and conducting each activity, an extensive assessment component, and extensions for integration and enrichment are provided.

Key to Content Standards: 5-8 (see app. C)

UNIFYING CONCEPTS AND PROCESSES: Systems, order, and organization; evidence, models, and explanation; change, constancy, and measurement; evolution and equilibrium; form and function.
SCIENCE AS INQUIRY: Abilities necessary to do scientific inquiry; understandings about scientific inquiry.
EARTH AND SPACE SCIENCE: Structure of the earth system; earth's history.

Prices: Teacher's guide (ISBN 0-7826-0065-4), $101. Complete module, $599. *Publisher/supplier:* Delta Education. *Materials:* Available locally, from commercial suppliers, or in kit.

4.7 Measuring Time. Science and Technology for Children (STC) series. Developed by National Science Resources Center (Washington, D.C.). Burlington, N.C.: Carolina Biological Supply, 1994.

Program Overview The Science and Technology for Children (STC) series consists of 24 inquiry-centered curriculum units for grades 1-6, with 4 units at each grade level. Students learn about topics in the life, earth, and physical sciences. The technological applications of science and the interactions among science, technology, and society are addressed throughout the program. The STC units, each of which takes about 16 class sessions to complete, encourage participatory learning and the integration of science with mathematics, language arts, social studies, and art. The components of an STC

unit are a teacher's guide, a student activity book with simple instructions and illustrations, and a kit of materials.

Teacher's Guide **Recommended grade level: 6. Reading level: 7.** In *Measuring Time,* students explore timekeeping first by observing the natural cycles of the sun and moon and then by building and investigating mechanical devices designed to measure time. Activities include recording the length and position of shadows at different times of day, devising a calendar, and predicting and observing the phases of the moon. In other activities, students construct and experiment with sinking water clocks and pendulums, build and adjust a working clock escapement, and make a 1-minute timer.

Throughout the unit, students are encouraged to develop an appreciation of advances over the centuries in measuring time. They record ideas, questions, and descriptions of their work in notebooks; they organize and report results in charts, tables, and graphs; and they discuss and analyze their experiences in small groups and with the class.

Measuring Time is a 16-lesson unit. The teacher's guide includes a unit overview, the 16 lesson plans, and an annotated bibliography. Science background information, detailed instructions on planning for and conducting each activity, an extensive assessment component, and extensions for integration and enrichment are provided.

Key to Content Standards: 5-8 (see app. C)

UNIFYING CONCEPTS AND PROCESSES: Evidence, models, and explanation; change, constancy, and measurement.
SCIENCE AS INQUIRY: Abilities necessary to do scientific inquiry; understandings about scientific inquiry.
PHYSICAL SCIENCE: Motions and forces.
EARTH AND SPACE SCIENCE: Earth in the solar system.

SCIENCE AND TECHNOLOGY: Abilities of technological design; understandings about science and technology.
SCIENCE IN PERSONAL AND SOCIAL PERSPECTIVES: Science and technology in society.
HISTORY AND NATURE OF SCIENCE: Science as a human endeavor; nature of science; history of science.

Prices: Teacher's guide (ISBN 0-89278-707-4), $24.95. Student activity book, $3.75. Unit, $439.95. *Publisher/supplier:* Carolina Biological Supply. *Materials:* Available locally, from commercial suppliers, or in kit.

4.8 **Project STAR: The Universe in Your Hands.** Harold P. Coyle, Bruce Gregory, William M. Luzader, and others. Project STAR: Science Teaching through Its Astronomical Roots, sponsored by Harvard-Smithsonian Center for Astrophysics. Dubuque, Iowa: Kendall/Hunt, 1993.

Program Overview Project STAR is a full-year course that uses astronomy as a vehicle for teaching students about real-world applications of mathematics and physics. The activities were written for high school students but can be adapted for middle school. The course stresses the importance of measurements, observations, and building models. The program includes a student textbook, a teacher's guide, an activity book, and several kits.

Student Edition **Recommended grade level: 8+. Reading level: late 9.** *Project STAR: The Universe in Your Hands* focuses first on the solar system, then on stars and galaxies beyond the solar system, and finally on a model of the universe as a whole. Subjects covered in this textbook include the day and night sky; dis-

tances, sizes, and angles; the behavior of light; mirrors and lenses; the size and distance relationships of the earth, moon, and sun; paths of the planets; stars; the Milky Way galaxy; and galaxies and the universe.

Each of the 15 chapters in *Project STAR* begins with several questions to test students' preconceptions about the subjects or concepts addressed in the chapter. In several hands-on activities, students then build and use simple but powerful tools to explore those concepts. For example, to answer questions about the position of the sun during the day, students learn how to measure the position of an object in the sky with their hands, plot the sun's apparent daily motion using a plastic hemisphere, and keep a journal of the sun's apparent motion.

Other examples of the lab investigations that students conduct during the course are these: determining the apparent size of an object as an angle measured in degrees; building scale models of the size and distance relations of the earth, moon, and sun to understand how the distances of these objects compare with their sizes; investigating what happens when different colors of the spectrum are projected onto the same place on a white screen; and estimating the size of the Milky Way galaxy and the distances to other galaxies by using the apparent brightness-distance nomogram.

The activities—which include suggestions for homework and extensions—are written at the high school level and employ mathematical skills such as basic arithmetic, algebra, and geometry. However, the activities can be easily adapted for different age groups or for science classes other than astronomy. Appendixes provide a guide to viewing the night sky and descriptive information about the moon and the solar system. A separate activity book—

Where We Are in Space and Time—contains 21 additional hands-on activities.

Teacher's Guide The teacher's guide to using the Project STAR materials and textbook includes a discussion of student preconceptions, tips for teaching each activity, reproducible activity masters, and answers to test questions and homework problems.

Program Resources and Support Materials Individual Project STAR resource kits—for example, the Celestial Sphere Kit; the Refracting Telescope Kit, with Tubes; and the Solar System Scale Model Kit—contain most of the materials required to do an activity.

Key to Content Standards: 5-8 (see app. C)

UNIFYING CONCEPTS AND PROCESSES: Systems, order, and organization; evidence, models, and explanation; change, constancy, and measurement.
SCIENCE AS INQUIRY: Abilities necessary to do scientific inquiry; understandings about scientific inquiry.
PHYSICAL SCIENCE: Transfer of energy.
EARTH AND SPACE SCIENCE: Earth in the solar system.
SCIENCE AND TECHNOLOGY: Understandings about science and technology.
SCIENCE IN PERSONAL AND SOCIAL PERSPECTIVES: Science and technology in society.
HISTORY AND NATURE OF SCIENCE: Science as a human endeavor; nature of science; history of science.

Prices: Student edition (ISBN 0-8403-7715-0), $34.90. Teacher's guide (ISBN 0-8403-7716-9), $99.90. (Contact publisher/supplier for complete price and ordering information for kits.) *Publisher/supplier:* Kendall/Hunt. *Materials:* Available locally, or from commercial suppliers.

4.9 **Solar Energy.** Full Option Science System (FOSS) series. Developed by Lawrence Hall of Science (Berkeley, Calif.). Hudson, N.H.: Delta Education, 1993.

Program Overview The Full Option Science System (FOSS) program is a K-6 science curriculum consisting of 27 stand-alone modules. The 8 modules for grades 5-6 are organized under topics in the life, physical, and earth sciences and in scientific reasoning and technology. They can be used in any order. The FOSS program is designed to engage students in scientific concepts through multisensory, hands-on laboratory activities. All modules of the program incorporate 5 unifying themes— (1) pattern, (2) structure, (3) interaction, (4) change, and (5) system. The components of a FOSS module are a teacher's guide and a kit of materials.

Teacher's Guide **Recommended grade level: 5-6.** This module focuses on solar energy and the variables that affect solar energy transfer. During the unit, students chart changes in the size and position of shadows as the relative position of the sun changes; they investigate temperature changes in equal amounts of water, sand, dry soil, and wet soil when the sun shines on them; and they relate the temperature differences to the properties of the materials. Students then conduct controlled experiments to test the effect of 3 variables on the collection of solar energy by solar water heaters. (The variables are the color of the solar collector, its being covered or uncovered, and its surface area.) Finally, they assemble model solar homes, looking for the most efficient way to heat them. Throughout the unit students organize data on charts and graphs to establish relationships between variables.

Solar Energy contains 4 multipart activities, requiring about 12 class sessions of 30 to 60 minutes each. The teacher's guide includes a module overview, the 4 individual activity folios, duplication masters (in English and Spanish) for student sheets, and an annotated bibliography. Science background information, detailed instructions on planning for and conducting each activity, an extensive assessment component, and extensions for integration and enrichment are provided.

Key to Content Standards: 5-8 (see app. C)

UNIFYING CONCEPTS AND PROCESSES: Systems, order, and organization; evidence, models, and explanation; change, constancy, and measurement. **SCIENCE AS INQUIRY:** Abilities necessary to do scientific inquiry; understandings about scientific inquiry. **PHYSICAL SCIENCE:** Transfer of energy. **EARTH AND SPACE SCIENCE:** Structure of the earth system; earth in the solar system.

SCIENCE AND TECHNOLOGY: Abilities of technological design; understandings about science and technology. **SCIENCE IN PERSONAL AND SOCIAL PERSPECTIVES:** Science and technology in society.

Prices: Teacher's guide (ISBN 0-7826-0087-5), $101. Complete module, $415. *Publisher/supplier:* Delta Education. *Materials:* Available locally, from commercial suppliers, or in kit.

Earth and Space Science—Supplementary Units

4.10 **Asteroid!** Russell G. Wright. Event-Based Science series. Menlo Park, Calif.: Innovative Learning Publications, 1996.

Program Overview The Event-Based Science series is a program for middle school students in grades 6-9. Each module tells the story of a real event—such as the 1995 outbreak of the Ebola virus in Zaire—through reprinted newspaper articles and personal interviews; sections of background information explain relevant scientific concepts. A central task related to the module's story line leads to a final product that allows students to apply the science they have learned. For each module, a student book, teacher's guide, and videotape and/or videodisc are available.

Student Edition **Recommended grade level: 7-8.** The threat of an asteroid hitting the earth is the event on which this study of various topics in astronomy is based. Students begin the module *Asteroid!* by watching television news coverage and reading newspaper articles about objects from space that have hit or just missed hitting the earth. They are told that their major task during the module will be to design, in 5-member teams, a multimedia information campaign to warn people about an asteroid that is on a collision course with the earth. The module's 7 activities provide students with the background information and skills they need for this task.

Among the activities, for example, students work with sand and small objects to investigate how an asteroid's speed and size affect the diameter of an impact crater. They create a time line to see if there is a relationship between mass extinctions and asteroid impacts. They also design and illustrate a scale drawing of the inner planets showing the path of an approaching asteroid, and they construct an "asteroid-smasher" model rocket capable of hitting a target 1 foot in diameter at a distance of at least 30 feet. Students also calculate the time it would take a free-falling object to reach the earth's surface.

The module provides short narratives about astronomical topics, such as the origin of the moon, the solar system, and comets. It includes copies of actual newspaper articles, explanatory graphics, and profiles of professionals—such as public relations managers, planetary scientists, paleontologists, and physicists—who might be involved in a public relations campaign about asteroids. Other information that students need to complete the task must be obtained from encyclopedias, textbooks, films, magazines, and other sources they can find. The unit culminates with the presentation of team multimedia projects.

Teacher's Edition The teacher's guide provides brief overview information on the module's structure and activities. It includes suggestions for guiding specific student activities, and a scoring rubric for a performance assessment.

Key to Content Standards: 5-8 (see app. C)

UNIFYING CONCEPTS AND PROCESSES: Systems, order, and organization; evidence, models, and explanation; change, constancy, and measurement; evolution and equilibrium; form and function.
SCIENCE AS INQUIRY: Abilities necessary to do scientific inquiry; understandings about scientific inquiry.
PHYSICAL SCIENCE: Motions and forces.
EARTH AND SPACE SCIENCE: Earth's history; earth in the solar system.

SCIENCE AND TECHNOLOGY: Abilities of technological design; understandings about science and technology.
SCIENCE IN PERSONAL AND SOCIAL PERSPECTIVES: Natural hazards; risks and benefits; science and technology in society.
HISTORY AND NATURE OF SCIENCE: Science as a human endeavor; nature of science; history of science.

Prices: Student edition (ISBN 0-201-49443-4), $7.95. Teacher's edition (ISBN 0-201-49444-2), with video, $18.00. Classroom package, $115.00. *Publisher/supplier:* Addison-Wesley/Longman. *Materials:* Available locally.

4.11 **Convection: A Current Event.** Reprinted with revisions. Alan Gould. Great Explorations in Math and Science (GEMS) series. Berkeley, Calif.: Lawrence Hall of Science, 1991.

Program Overview The Great Explorations in Math and Science (GEMS) series includes more than 50 teacher's guides and handbooks for preschool through grade 10. About 35 of these are appropriate for middle school. The series also includes several assembly presenter's guides and exhibit guides. New guides and handbooks continue to be developed, and current titles are revised frequently. The series is designed to teach key science and mathematics concepts through activity-based learning. The time needed to complete GEMS units varies from about 2 to 10 class sessions.

Teacher's Guide **Recommended grade level: 6-8+.** Students explore the physical phenomenon of convection and generalize their findings to understand wind patterns in *Convection: A Current Event.* The teacher's guide introduces the concept of convection and then offers 3 sessions: "Observing Convection in Water," "Getting the Whole Picture," and "Convection and Wind." In the first session, students use food coloring to trace convection currents in water. In the second session, they apply their knowledge to guide an imaginary submarine through ocean currents generated near a hot volcanic vent. In the third session, the teacher presents 3 demonstrations to show that convection occurs in gases as well as in liquids, and students apply what they have learned to predict air flow in a room and wind patterns.

Each session in *Convection: A Current Event* requires 30 to 60 minutes and includes a materials list, preparation steps, and directions for activities and discussion. The guide also includes background information, summary outlines for each lesson, and reproducible data sheets.

Key to Content Standards: 5-8 (see app. C)

UNIFYING CONCEPTS AND PROCESSES: Systems, order, and organization; evidence, models, and explanation; change, constancy, and measurement. **SCIENCE AS INQUIRY:** Abilities necessary to do scientific inquiry; understandings about scientific inquiry. **PHYSICAL SCIENCE:** Transfer of energy. **EARTH AND SPACE SCIENCE:** Structure of the earth system; earth in the solar system.

Price: $10.50 (ISBN 0-912511-15-X). *Publisher/supplier:* LHS GEMS. *Materials:* Available locally, or from commercial suppliers.

ABOUT THE ANNOTATIONS IN "EARTH AND SPACE SCIENCE—SUPPLEMENTARY UNITS"

Entry Numbers

Curriculum materials are arranged alphabetically by title in each category (Core Materials, Supplementary Units, and Science Activity Books) in chapters 1 through 5 of this guide.

Each curriculum annotation has a two-part entry number: the chapter number is given before the period; the number after the period locates the entry within that chapter. For example, the first entry number in chapter 1 is 1.1; the second entry in chapter 2 is 2.2; and so on.

The entry numbers within each curriculum chapter run consecutively through Core Materials, Supplementary Units, and Science Activity Books.

Order of Bibliographic Information

Following is the arrangement of the facts of publication in the annotations in this section:

• **Title of publication**
• **Number of edition,** if applicable
• **Authors** (an individual author or authors, an institutional author, or a project or program name under which the material was developed)
• **Series title**
• **Series developer,** if applicable
• **Place of publication, publisher, and date of publication**

Recommended Grade Level

The grade level for each piece of material was recommended by teacher evaluators during the development of this guide. In some instances, the recommended grade level may differ slightly from the publisher's advertised level.

Key to Content Standards: 5-8

The key lists the content standards for grades 5-8 from the *National Science Education Standards* (NSES) that are addressed in depth by the item. A key is provided for core materials and supplementary units. (*See* appendix C.)

Price and Acquisition Information

Ordering information appears at the end of each entry. Included are—

- **Prices** (of teacher's guides, student books, lab manuals, and kits or units)
- **Publisher/supplier** (The name of a principal publisher/supplier, although not necessarily the sole source, for the items listed in the price category. Appendix A, "Publishers and Suppliers," provides the address, phone and fax numbers, and electronic ordering information, where available, for each publisher and supplier.)
- **Materials** (various sources from which one might obtain the required materials)

Readers must contact publishers/suppliers for complete and up-to-date listings of the program resources and support materials available for a particular unit. Depending on the developer, these items may be required, optional, or both; they may be offered individually and/or in kits, packages, or boxes. Materials may change with revised editions. The prices given in this chapter for selected resources or materials are based on information from the publishers and suppliers but are not meant to represent the full range of ordering options.

Indexes of Curriculum Materials

The multiple indexes on pp. 449-78 allow easy access to the information in this guide. Various aspects of the curriculum materials—including titles, topics addressed in each unit, grade levels, and standards addressed—are the focus of seven separate indexes. For example, titles and entry numbers are listed in the "Title Index" on pp. 450-54. The "Index of Authors, Series, and Curriculum Projects," on pp. 455-57, provides entry numbers of any annotated titles in a particular series.

Overviews of Core and Supplementary Programs

Appendix D, "Overviews of Core and Supplementary Programs with Titles Annotated in This Guide," on pp. 441-48, lists, by program or series, the individual titles annotated in the sections "Core Materials" and "Supplementary Units" in the five curriculum chapters.

4.12 Earth and Beyond. Mary Atwater, Prentice Baptiste, Lucy Daniel, and others. Unit 37. Macmillan/McGraw-Hill Science series. New York, N.Y.: Macmillan/McGraw-Hill School Publishing, 1995.

Program Overview The Macmillan/McGraw-Hill Science series is a comprehensive, activity-based, K-8 science curriculum made up of 42 stand-alone units, 18 of which are designed for grades 6-8. The series is constructed around 7 major themes: (1) systems and interactions, (2) scale and structure, (3) stability, (4) energy, (5) evolution, (6) patterns of change, and (7) models. The subject of each unit—for example, earth and beyond—is presented from the perspective of one or more of these themes. One theme is designated as the "major theme" for a unit, and any others are treated as "related themes." For each unit, a wide range of materials, including some optional components, is available for students and teachers.

Student Edition **Recommended grade level: 7-8.** *Earth and Beyond* contains 5 lessons that introduce students to the planet earth, its neighbors in the solar system, the galaxy, and the universe. The organizing themes for the unit are scale and structure (major theme), systems and interactions (related theme), and models (related theme).

Each of the 5 lessons in the unit typically requires 5 days to complete. During the unit, students first examine the earth as part of the sun-moon-earth system and learn that the relative positions of these 3 astronomical objects produce various phenomena—such as seasons, tides, and phases of the moon. Students are introduced to the characteristics of the different planets in the solar system. They find out about star formation and the relationship of a star's color to its evolution. They learn about galaxies, the Big Bang theory of the origin of the universe, and different types of earth- and space-based space exploration.

Sample activities include using a thermometer, foam balls, and black paper to investigate why the earth experiences seasons; constructing a scale model of the solar system; and making and experimenting with a simple spectroscope. Students also use balloons to construct a model that illustrates the Big Bang theory, and communicate how different kinds of technology are used to gather different types of astronomical data.

Each lesson contains narrative information and a series of sequential, hands-on activities—such as an introductory "minds-on" activity, short "try this" activities, and a longer "explore" activity. The unit's 5 "explore activities," which are lab activities, each take a class period to complete. Students use activity logs to record ideas, observations, and results.

Special unit features include curriculum links to language arts, literature, mathematics, music, and art; information about science careers; and narrative sections highlighting science, technology, and society connections.

Teacher's Planning Guide The teacher's planning guide, a spiral-bound, wraparound edition, provides information and strategies for teaching the 5 lessons in the student edition. Each lesson is introduced by a 4-page section that offers background information, a lesson-planning guide, and assessment options. Marginal notes on the lesson pages provide discussion ideas, tips on meeting individual needs, sugges-

tions for addressing misconceptions, assessment ideas, and curriculum connections.

Program Resources and Support Materials A wide range of materials, including some optional components, is available. Examples include consumable and nonconsumable activity materials; audio- and videotapes; interactive videodiscs; color transparencies; assessment materials; a teacher anthology of short stories, poems, fingerplays, and songs; trade books; teacher resource masters; activity cards; activity logs; a staff development package; concept summaries and glossaries for students acquiring English; and software with problem-solving simulations for students.

Key to Content Standards: 5-8 (see app. C)

UNIFYING CONCEPTS AND PROCESSES: Systems, order, and organization; evidence, models, and explanation; change, constancy, and measurement; evolution and equilibrium; form and function.

SCIENCE AS INQUIRY: Abilities necessary to do scientific inquiry; understandings about scientific inquiry.

EARTH AND SPACE SCIENCE: Earth in the solar system.

SCIENCE AND TECHNOLOGY: Understandings about science and technology.

SCIENCE IN PERSONAL AND SOCIAL PERSPECTIVES: Science and technology in society.

HISTORY AND NATURE OF SCIENCE: History of science.

Prices: Student edition (ISBN 0-02-276137-3), $7.06. Teacher's planning guide (ISBN 0-02-276085-7), $55.98. Unit package, $115.98. Activity materials kit, $79.00. (Contact publisher/supplier for complete price and ordering information.) ***Publisher/supplier:*** McGraw-Hill. ***Materials:*** Available locally, from commercial suppliers, or in kit.

4.13 **Earth, Moon, and Stars.** Reprinted with revisions. Cary I. Sneider. Great Explorations in Math and Science (GEMS) series. Berkeley, Calif.: Lawrence Hall of Science, 1994.

Program Overview The Great Explorations in Math and Science (GEMS) series includes more than 50 teacher's guides and handbooks for preschool through grade 10. About 35 of these are appropriate for middle school. The series also includes several assembly presenter's guides and exhibit guides. New guides and handbooks continue to be developed, and current titles are revised frequently. The series is designed to teach key science and mathematics concepts through activity-based learning. The time needed to complete GEMS units varies from about 2 to 10 class sessions.

Teacher's Guide **Recommended grade level: 5-8.** In *Earth, Moon, and Stars*, students investigate ancient models of the universe, the earth's shape, gravity, the moon and its phases, star clocks, and star maps. They compare 4 ancient models of the earth to learn how each one explained common events seen daily in the sky, then they invent their own "ancient models" of the world. They use a questionnaire to launch a discussion about the shape of the earth and about gravity. Students observe the phases of the moon for a month; use a model to explain the moon's monthly cycle of phases and eclipses; make and use star clocks; and learn how to find constellations in the night sky by reading star maps. All of the activities can be done in the classroom or outdoors during the daytime, with a few evening homework assignments.

The 6 activities in *Earth, Moon, and Stars* require 6 sessions of 40 to 45 minutes each, 4 sessions of 20 to 30 minutes each, and 6 sessions of 15 minutes each. The lessons each include a materials list, preparation steps, and directions for activities and discussion. The guide also includes background information, summary outlines for each lesson, reproducible data sheets, and suggestions for related reading.

Key to Content Standards: 5-8 (see app. C)

UNIFYING CONCEPTS AND PROCESSES: Systems, order, and organization; evidence, models, and explanation; change, constancy, and measurement. **SCIENCE AS INQUIRY:** Abilities necessary to do scientific inquiry; understandings about scientific inquiry. **PHYSICAL SCIENCE:** Motions and forces. **EARTH AND SPACE SCIENCE:** Structure of the earth system; earth in the solar system. **SCIENCE IN PERSONAL AND SOCIAL PERSPECTIVES:** Science and technology in society. **HISTORY AND NATURE OF SCIENCE:** Nature of science; history of science.

Price: $10.50 (ISBN 0-912511-18-4). *Publisher/supplier:* LHS GEMS. *Materials:* Available locally, or from commercial suppliers.

4.14 Earth, Moon, and Sun. John G. Radzilowicz and Jan M. Derby. Delta Science Module (DSM) series. Hudson, N.H.: Delta Education, 1994.

Program Overview The Delta Science Module (DSM) series has 51 life, physical, and earth science units for grades K-8 that emphasize science concepts, science content, and process skills. The series includes 12 modules for grades 5-6 and 8 modules for grades 6-8. Each requires about 3 to 4 weeks to complete and includes a teacher's guide and materials for a class of 32 students.

Teacher's Guide **Recommended grade level: 6-8.** *Earth, Moon, and Sun* helps students investigate the properties of and relationships among the

earth, moon, and sun. During the unit, students gather and analyze data on the sun and moon through observation. They make 2- and 3-dimensional scale models of the solar system and the earth-moon system; and they create a real-time model of the earth by rectifying a globe, then use the globe to investigate phenomena such as day, night, sunrise, and sunset.

In other activities, students construct a large, simple horizontal sundial in which they are the gnomon; they model the rotation and revolution of the earth; and they learn how the tilt of the earth is responsible for seasonal changes. Students also model the motions of the moon in relation to the earth and sun; they model solar and lunar eclipses; and they model the positions of the earth, moon, and sun to gain an understanding of the causes and varieties of tides on earth. They also perform some simple techniques of celestial navigation.

The 13 activities in *Earth, Moon, and Sun* are organized to be completed sequentially over 3 to 4 weeks. Each activity takes between 30 and 50 minutes each and can be done by students working individually or in groups.

A "connections" feature at the end of each activity provides suggestions for extending or applying the concepts in the activity. Discussion or activity topics include technology, society, science and careers, language arts, mathematics, the arts, social studies, and health. Follow-up activities that students can do at home or out of the classroom are also provided. For example, a "science and language arts" connection suggests that students read at least the first 6 chapters of Samuel Clemens's *A Connecticut Yankee in King Arthur's Court* and describe how the nineteenth-century hero uses his knowledge of eclipses to impress citizens of the sixth century.

In addition to directions for activities, the teacher's guide provides a

module overview, a schedule of activities, objectives for each activity, background information, materials management and preparation tips, sample answers to discussion questions, teaching suggestions, and reinforcement activities. Also included are reproducible activity sheets for student work and a performance-based assessment.

Key to Content Standards: 5-8 (see app. C)

UNIFYING CONCEPTS AND PROCESSES: Systems, order, and organization; evidence, models, and explanation; change, constancy, and measurement; form and function. **SCIENCE AS INQUIRY:** Abilities necessary to do scientific inquiry; understandings about scientific inquiry. **EARTH AND SPACE SCIENCE:** Earth in the solar system. **SCIENCE AND TECHNOLOGY:** Understandings about science and technology. **SCIENCE IN PERSONAL AND SOCIAL PERSPECTIVES:** Science and technology in society. **HISTORY AND NATURE OF SCIENCE:** History of science.

Prices: Teacher's guide (ISBN 0-87504-166-3), $27.95. Kit, $379.00. Refill package, $67.00. *Publisher/supplier:* Delta Education. *Materials:* Available locally, from commercial suppliers, or in kit.

4.15 Earth Processes. Katy Goldner. Delta Science Module (DSM) series. Hudson, N.H.: Delta Education, 1995.

Program Overview The Delta Science Module (DSM) series has 51 life, physical, and earth science units for grades K-8 that emphasize science concepts, science content, and process skills. The series includes 12 modules for grades 5-6 and 8 modules for grades 6-8. Each requires about 3 to 4 weeks to complete and includes a teacher's guide and materials for a class of 32 students.

Teacher's Guide **Recommended grade level: 6-8.** *Earth Processes* introduces students to the earth processes that shape the world around them. During the unit, students learn about the theory of continental drift, and they use paper cutouts to demonstrate how the continents fit together like pieces of a jigsaw puzzle. They also create a model of the earth and all its layers using a set of concentric spheres; they simulate the chemical and mechanical weathering of rocks; and they compare the formation of sedimentary, igneous, and metamorphic rocks. Students use different-colored layers of clay to model the types of faults in the earth's crust and the mountains created by the faults.

In other activities, students model the energy waves produced by an earthquake; they build a model seismograph and use it to measure the strength of a simulated earthquake; and they map areas of volcanic and seismic activity around the earth. They also investigate isostasy, explore convection currents and the effect they have on the earth's crust, and learn about the theory of plate tectonics.

The 14 activities in *Earth Processes* are organized to be completed sequentially over 3 to 4 weeks. Each activity takes between about 30 and 40 minutes and can be done by students working individually or in groups.

A "connections" feature at the end of each activity provides suggestions for extending or applying the science concepts in the activity. Discussion or activity topics include technology, society, science and careers, language arts, mathematics, the arts, social studies, and health. For example, a "science and social studies" extension suggests that students research the name, location, and height of the tallest mountain on

each continent and locate these mountains on a globe or world map.

In addition to directions for activities, the teacher's guide provides a module overview, a schedule of activities, objectives for each activity, background information, materials management and preparation tips, sample answers to discussion questions, teaching suggestions, and reinforcement activities. Also included are reproducible activity sheets for student work and a performance-based assessment.

Key to Content Standards: 5-8 (see app. C)

UNIFYING CONCEPTS AND PROCESSES: Systems, order, and organization; evidence, models, and explanation; change, constancy, and measurement; form and function.

SCIENCE AS INQUIRY: Abilities necessary to do scientific inquiry; understandings about scientific inquiry.

EARTH AND SPACE SCIENCE: Structure of the earth system; earth's history.

SCIENCE IN PERSONAL AND SOCIAL PERSPECTIVES: Natural hazards; science and technology in society.

HISTORY AND NATURE OF SCIENCE: History of science.

Prices: Teacher's guide (ISBN 0-87504-168-X), $27.95. Kit, $379.00. Refill package, $84.00. **Publisher/ supplier:** Delta Education. **Materials:** Available locally, from commercial suppliers, or in kit.

4.16 Earthquake! Russell G. Wright. Event-Based Science series. Menlo Park, Calif.: Innovative Learning Publications, 1996.

Program Overview The Event-Based Science series is a program for middle school students in grades 6-9. Each module tells the story of a real event—such as the 1995 outbreak of the Ebola virus in Zaire—through

reprinted newspaper articles and personal interviews; sections of background information explain relevant scientific concepts. A central task related to the module's story line leads to a final product that allows students to apply the science they have learned. For each module, a student book, teacher's guide, and videotape and/or videodisc are available.

Student Edition **Recommended grade level: 7-8.** The 1989 Loma Prieta earthquake is the event on which this 5-week study of concepts associated with earthquakes is based. The concepts addressed in *Earthquake!* include faults, earth structure, plate tectonics, liquefaction, and landslides. Students begin the module by watching television news coverage and reading newspaper accounts of the 1989 California earthquake. They are told that their major task during the module will be to design, in 6-member teams, a city for a geographical area with a history of seismic activity.

The module's 8 activities provide students with the background information and skills they need for their task. For example, students identify regions of the earth where earthquakes occur, and they select possible sites for the city-planning project. They investigate conditions that produce liquefaction during an earthquake. They also design and construct a model of an earthquake-resistant building, and they design an experiment to test ways of making a house resist landslides. In another activity, students determine how reliable predictions of major earthquakes have to be before they should be made public.

The module provides short narratives on topics such as tectonic plates, faults, and earthquake preparedness; copies of actual newspaper articles; explanatory graphics; and profiles of professionals involved in site development and planning—for example, geologists, transportation experts, city planners, architects, and civil engineers. Middle school students who experienced the Loma Prieta earthquake tell their stories throughout the module. Other information that students need to complete their task must be obtained from encyclopedias, textbooks, films, magazines, and other sources they can find. The unit culminates with the presentation of student teams' city plans. Teachers may want to supplement or exchange the activities in the unit depending on the latest "real event" in the news.

Teacher's Edition The teacher's guide provides brief overview information on the module's structure and activities. It includes suggestions for guiding specific student activities, a scoring rubric for a performance assessment, and a list of resources.

Key to Content Standards: 5-8 (see app. C)

UNIFYING CONCEPTS AND PROCESSES: Systems, order, and organization; evidence, models, and explanation; change, constancy, and measurement; form and function.
SCIENCE AS INQUIRY: Abilities necessary to do scientific inquiry; understandings about scientific inquiry.
EARTH AND SPACE SCIENCE: Structure of the earth system.
SCIENCE AND TECHNOLOGY: Abilities of technological design; understandings about science and technology.
SCIENCE IN PERSONAL AND SOCIAL PERSPECTIVES: Natural hazards; risks and benefits; science and technology in society.
HISTORY AND NATURE OF SCIENCE: Science as a human endeavor; nature of science.

Prices: Student edition (ISBN 0-201-49092-7), $7.95. Teacher's edition (ISBN 0-201-49093-5), with video, $18.00. Classroom package, $115.00. *Publisher/supplier:* Addison-Wesley/Longman. *Materials:* Available locally.

4.17 Earthquakes. Module 1.6. Foundations and Challenges to Encourage Technology-based Science (FACETS) series. Developed by American Chemical Society (Washington, D.C.). Dubuque, Iowa: Kendall/Hunt, 1996.

Program Overview The Foundations and Challenges to Encourage Technology-based Science (FACETS) program consists of 3 series of 8 modules each for grades 6-8. Each module focuses on a topic in the life, earth, or physical sciences. The time needed to complete FACETS modules varies from 2 to 4 weeks. Each module consists of a student book and a teacher's guide.

Student Edition **Recommended grade level: 6-7.** In *Earthquakes,* students investigate where and why earthquakes happen, what effects they can have on people's lives, and how the risks of injury from earthquakes can be reduced by the careful design of buildings and structures. Throughout the module, students role-play a planning-and-development team in a large construction corporation.

Among the activities in the unit, students use latitude and longitude to find the location of a number of earthquakes and to get a sense of where the major earthquake zones in the world are. They correlate the location of earthquake activity with plate boundaries. They also construct a model with a fish tank and pieces of wood to understand what happens at the edges of plates. Students use coiled springs to investigate different types of waves created during an earthquake. They use the Mercalli scale of earthquake intensity together with information from the library to assess effects of earthquakes. In the unit's final activity, students design, build, and test models of earthquake-resistant buildings or structures.

Earthquakes is a 3-week module divided into 6 activities, which each take between 1 and 6 class periods to complete. A narrative section at the end of the module provides background information for students on detecting earthquakes.

Teacher's Guide The wraparound teacher's guide includes a unit overview, a time line for completing the module, a materials list, background information, and teaching suggestions.

Key to Content Standards: 5-8 (see app. C)

UNIFYING CONCEPTS AND PROCESSES: Systems, order, and organization; evidence, models, and explanation; change, constancy, and measurement; form and function.
SCIENCE AS INQUIRY: Abilities necessary to do scientific inquiry; understandings about scientific inquiry.
EARTH AND SPACE SCIENCE: Structure of the earth system; earth's history.
SCIENCE AND TECHNOLOGY: Abilities of technological design; understandings about science and technology.
SCIENCE IN PERSONAL AND SOCIAL PERSPECTIVES: Natural hazards; risks and benefits.
HISTORY AND NATURE OF SCIENCE: Nature of science.

Prices: Student edition (ISBN 0-7872-1431-0), $7.90. Teacher's guide (ISBN 0-7872-1432-9), $14.90. *Publisher/supplier:* Kendall/Hunt. *Materials:* Available locally, or from commercial suppliers.

4.18 Earth's Solid Crust. Mary Atwater, Prentice Baptiste, Lucy Daniel, and others. Unit 35. Macmillan/McGraw-Hill Science series. New York, N.Y.: Macmillan/McGraw-Hill School Publishing, 1995.

Program Overview The Macmillan/McGraw-Hill Science series is a comprehensive, activity-based, K-8 science curriculum made up of 42 stand-alone units, 18 of which are designed for grades 6-8. The series is constructed around 7 major themes: (1) systems and interactions, (2) scale and structure, (3) stability, (4) energy, (5) evolution, (6) patterns of change, and (7) models. The subject of each unit—for example, earth's solid crust—is presented from the perspective of one or more of these themes. One theme is designated as the "major theme" for a unit, and any others are treated as "related themes." For each unit, a wide range of materials, including some optional components, is available for students and teachers.

Student Edition **Recommended grade level: 7.** *Earth's Solid Crust* contains 4 lessons that introduce students to rocks, minerals, weathering, landforms, and cartography. The organizing themes for the unit are the major theme of scale and structure and 3 related themes—systems and interactions, models, and patterns of change.

Each of the 4 lessons in the unit typically requires 6 days to complete. During the unit, students identify minerals by observing their physical properties; they discover that minerals can be classified as belonging to 1 of 6 crystal systems on the basis of the different angles among their crystal faces. Students also learn about the formation of different types of rocks, they explore erosion and the weathering cycle, and they study different types of maps and their uses.

Sample activities include classifying rocks and minerals, growing salt crystals, and constructing models of sedimentary layers and metamorphic rocks. Students also model the abrasive action of glaciers using sand and ice frozen in milk cartons, they investigate variables that affect wind erosion, and they prepare a basic topographic map of a model landform to scale.

Each lesson contains narrative information and a series of sequential, hands-on activities—such as an introductory "minds-on" activity, short "try this" activities, and a longer "explore" activity. The unit's 4 "explore activities," which are lab activities, each take a class period to complete. Students use activity logs to record ideas, observations, and results.

Special unit features include curriculum links to language arts, literature, mathematics, music, and art; information about science careers; and narrative sections highlighting science, technology, and society connections.

Teacher's Planning Guide The teacher's planning guide, a spiral-bound, wraparound edition, provides information and strategies for teaching the 4 lessons in the student edition. Each lesson is introduced by a 4-page lesson section that offers background information, a lesson-planning guide, and assessment options. Marginal notes on the lesson pages provide discussion ideas, tips on meeting individual needs, suggestions for addressing misconceptions, assessment ideas, and curriculum connections.

Program Resources and Support Materials A wide range of materials, including some optional components, is available. Examples include consumable and nonconsumable activity materials; audio- and video-tapes; interactive videodiscs; color transparencies; assessment materials; a teacher anthology of short stories, poems, fingerplays, and songs; trade books; teacher resource masters; activity cards; activity logs; a staff development package; concept summaries and glossaries for students acquiring English; and software

with problem-solving simulations for students.

Key to Content Standards: 5-8 (see app. C)

UNIFYING CONCEPTS AND PROCESSES: Systems, order, and organization; evidence, models, and explanation; change, constancy, and measurement; evolution and equilibrium; form and function.

SCIENCE AS INQUIRY: Abilities necessary to do scientific inquiry; understandings about scientific inquiry.

PHYSICAL SCIENCE: Properties and changes of properties in matter.

EARTH AND SPACE SCIENCE: Structure of the earth system; earth's history.

SCIENCE AND TECHNOLOGY: Understandings about science and technology.

SCIENCE IN PERSONAL AND SOCIAL PERSPECTIVES: Science and technology in society.

HISTORY AND NATURE OF SCIENCE: History of science.

Prices: Student edition (ISBN 0-02-276135-7), $7.06. Teacher's planning guide (ISBN 0-02-276083-0), $55.98. Unit package, $100.98. Activity materials kit, $93.00. (Contact publisher/supplier for complete price and ordering information.) ***Publisher/supplier:*** McGraw-Hill. ***Materials:*** Available locally, from commercial suppliers, or in kit.

4.19 **Erosion.** Delta Science Module (DSM) series. Hudson, N.H.: Delta Education, 1994.

Program Overview The Delta Science Module (DSM) series has 51 life, physical, and earth science units for grades K-8 that emphasize science concepts, science content, and process skills. The series includes 12 modules for grades 5-6 and 8 modules for grades 6-8. Each requires about 3 to 4 weeks to complete and includes a teacher's guide and materials for a class of 32 students.

Teacher's Guide **Recommended grade level: 5-8.** In *Erosion*, students investigate how wind, glaciers, and especially water cause erosion of the earth's surfaces and how the effects of erosion can be reduced. During the unit, students construct a stream table to test the effects of several variables on the process of erosion. The variables include vegetation, slope, water volume, and type of material being eroded. They compare the erosion and deposition characteristics of several types of earth materials, they simulate the erosive effect of wave action along a shoreline, and they test the effects of wind on sand before and after building a model windbreak.

The 12 activities in *Erosion*, which require approximately 15 class sessions, take between 30 and 60 minutes each and can be done by students working individually or in groups. A "connections" feature at the end of each activity provides suggestions for extending or applying the concepts in the activity. Discussion or activity topics include technology, society, science and careers, language arts, mathematics, the arts, social studies, and health. For example, a "science, technology, and society" extension suggests that students research and report on how glass is made and on its many commercial applications.

In addition to directions for activities, the teacher's guide provides a module overview, a schedule of activities, objectives for each activity, background information, materials management and preparation tips, sample answers to discussion questions, teaching suggestions, and reinforcement activities. Also included are reproducible activity sheets for student work and a performance-based assessment.

Key to Content Standards: 5-8 (see app. C)

UNIFYING CONCEPTS AND PROCESSES: Systems, order, and organization; evidence, models, and explanation; change, constancy, and measurement; form and function.

SCIENCE AS INQUIRY: Abilities necessary to do scientific inquiry; understandings about scientific inquiry.

EARTH AND SPACE SCIENCE: Structure of the earth system; earth's history.

SCIENCE IN PERSONAL AND SOCIAL PERSPECTIVES: Natural hazards; science and technology in society.

HISTORY AND NATURE OF SCIENCE: History of science.

Prices: Teacher's guide (ISBN 0-87504-117-5), $27.95. Kit, $309.00. Refill package, $52.00. *Publisher/supplier:* Delta Education. *Materials:* Available locally, from commercial suppliers, or in kit.

4.20 **The Evolution of a Planetary System.** SETI [Search for Extraterrestrial Intelligence] Academy Planet Project. Life in the Universe Series. Englewood, Colo.: Teacher Ideas Press, 1995.

Program Overview The Life in the Universe Series consists of 6 units, including the 3 volumes in the SETI Academy Planet Project. Each book in the SETI Academy Planet Project is designed to be a complete unit in itself as well as a subunit of a 3-unit course. During the activities in the 3 units, each student plays the role of a "cadet" at the SETI [Search for Extraterrestrial Intelligence] Academy, a fictitious institution. (The SETI Institute is an actual scientific organization.)

Teacher's Guide **Recommended grade level: 5-6.** *The Evolution of a Planetary System* examines one important aspect of the search for intelligent life in the universe: the evolution of stars and planets. During the unit, students discuss their ideas about unidentified flying objects (UFOs)

and extraterrestrials; they make a scale model of the solar system; and they simulate the formation of a planetary system using oatmeal, puffed rice, and tea. Students also use a radiometer to measure infrared radiation coming from the 3 types of "stars." They make a filmstrip showing the breakup of the supercontinent Pangaea, they model interactions of tectonic plates, and they learn about factors that influence climate. At the end of the unit, students use what they have learned to design planetary systems that contain habitable planets, transform their individual planets into life-sustaining worlds, and create continental and climate maps of their planets.

Organized in 14 "missions" or chapters, the activities in *The Evolution of a Planetary System* take about 4 weeks to complete. The guide includes background information, directions for activities, discussion ideas, extensions, and reproducible blackline masters for student logbooks.

Key to Content Standards: 5-8 (see app. C)

UNIFYING CONCEPTS AND PROCESSES: Systems, order, and organization; evidence, models, and explanation; change, constancy, and measurement; evolution and equilibrium.

SCIENCE AS INQUIRY: Abilities necessary to do scientific inquiry; understandings about scientific inquiry.

EARTH AND SPACE SCIENCE: Structure of the earth system; earth's history; earth in the solar system.

SCIENCE AND TECHNOLOGY: Understandings about science and technology.

HISTORY AND NATURE OF SCIENCE: Science as a human endeavor; nature of science.

Price: $25.50 (ISBN 1-56308-324-8). *Publisher/supplier:* Teacher Ideas Press. *Materials:* Available locally, or from commercial suppliers.

4.21 Flood! Russell G. Wright. Event-Based Science series. Menlo Park, Calif.: Innovative Learning Publications, 1996.

Program Overview The Event-Based Science series is a program for middle school students in grades 6-9. Each module tells the story of a real event—such as the 1995 outbreak of the Ebola virus in Zaire—through reprinted newspaper articles and personal interviews; sections of background information explain relevant scientific concepts. A central task related to the module's story line leads to a final product that allows students to apply the science they have learned. For each module, a student book, teacher's guide, and videotape and/or videodisc are available.

Student Edition **Recommended grade level: 7-8.** *Flood!* uses the 1993 flooding of the Mississippi and Missouri Rivers as the event on which to base this 5-week study of streams and rivers and science concepts related to stream dynamics. Students begin the module by watching a videotape of live television news coverage and reading newspaper articles about the power and drama of floods. They are told that their major task during the module will be to design, in 5-member teams, a new national park along the St. Joe River in Idaho to demonstrate the forces and features of a dynamic stream system. The module's 11 activities provide students with the background information and skills they need for this task.

Among the activities, for example, students use a landform model to construct a contour map, and they graph real stream discharge data from the St. Joe River. They also use a stream table to model and observe river dynamics, apply fractals to the meandering of a river, and design and produce a brochure for the park.

The module provides short narratives on topics such as floods and the safety of the water supply, conditions that cause flooding, and satellite surveying; copies of actual newspaper articles; explanatory graphics; and profiles of professionals involved in park design—such as landscape architects, hydrologists, geologists, cartographers, and forest recreation technicians. Middle school students who experienced the 1993 floods tell their stories throughout the module. Other information that students need to complete the task must be obtained from encyclopedias, textbooks, films, magazines, and other sources they can find. At the end of the unit, student teams present their plans and park brochures to the class. Teachers may want to supplement or exchange the activities in the unit depending on the latest "real event" in the news.

Teacher's Edition The teacher's guide provides brief overview information on the module's structure and activities. It includes suggestions for guiding specific student activities, and a scoring rubric for a performance assessment.

Key to Content Standards: 5-8 (see app. C)

UNIFYING CONCEPTS AND PROCESSES: Systems, order, and organization; evidence, models, and explanation; change, constancy, and measurement; form and function.
SCIENCE AS INQUIRY: Abilities necessary to do scientific inquiry; understandings about scientific inquiry.
EARTH AND SPACE SCIENCE: Structure of the earth system; earth's history.
SCIENCE AND TECHNOLOGY: Abilities of technological design; understandings about science and technology.
SCIENCE IN PERSONAL AND SOCIAL PERSPECTIVES: Natural hazards; risks and benefits; science and technology in society.

HISTORY AND NATURE OF SCIENCE: Science as a human endeavor; nature of science.

Prices: Student edition (ISBN 0-201-49438-8), $7.95. Teacher's edition (ISBN 0-201-49439-6), with video, $18.00. Classroom package, $115.00. *Publisher/supplier:* Addison-Wesley/Longman. *Materials:* Available locally.

4.22 Geology Lab. Science Technology and Reading (STAR) series. Developed by Reading Is Fundamental (Washington, D.C.). Dubuque, Iowa: Kendall/Hunt, 1996.

Program Overview Designed for the upper elementary grades, the Science Technology and Reading (STAR) series consists of 8 thematic "labs" in the natural and physical sciences. Each lab focuses both on science activities and on a genre of children's literature, developing correlations between the science process and the process of reading. In addition to a teacher's guide for each of the 8 labs, the STAR program includes a mentor's guide for scientists, engineers, and others assisting in the classroom.

Teacher's Guide **Recommended grade level: 4-6.** In *Geology Lab*, a story about the discovery of a geode by a character in a fictional classroom provides a backdrop and source of background information for a series of geology lab explorations. Students first conduct a rock-hunting expedition around the schoolyard. To identify the rocks, they test them for the presence of carbonates and conduct a streak (color) test. They learn how sedimentary rocks are formed by making artificial sandstone. To simulate core sampling—a technique used by scientists to study the geological history of an area—students make multilayered sandwiches and use straws to extract a "core sample." Students use clay models of folding rock layers to show how movement in the earth's crust creates mountains. They use large blocks of ice to simulate glacial action and its effect on land. Finally students make molds and casts to simulate the process of fossilization.

During the unit, students examine the format and features of nature guides as a model for writing their own geology field guides. Examples of other interdisciplinary activities include developing recipes for a geological cookbook, creating sand paintings, and role-playing specialists in geology-related fields.

The guide provides a list of resources including books, computer software, and audiovisual materials. Reproducible pages for students, such as lab procedures, data sheets, and information handouts, are also provided.

Key to Content Standards: 5-8 (see app. C)

UNIFYING CONCEPTS AND PROCESSES: Systems, order, and organization; evidence, models, and explanation; change, constancy, and measurement.
SCIENCE AS INQUIRY: Abilities necessary to do scientific inquiry; understandings about scientific inquiry.
EARTH AND SPACE SCIENCE: Structure of the earth system; earth's history.

Prices: Teacher's guide (ISBN 0-7872-1460-4), $21.90. Mentor's guide, $3.90. *Publisher/supplier:* Kendall/Hunt. *Materials:* Available locally.

4.23 **Hurricane!** Russell G. Wright. Event-Based Science series. Menlo Park, Calif.: Innovative Learning Publications, 1995.

Program Overview The Event-Based Science series is a program for middle school students in grades 6-9.

Each module tells the story of a real event—such as the 1995 outbreak of the Ebola virus in Zaire—through reprinted newspaper articles and personal interviews; sections of background information explain relevant scientific concepts. A central task related to the module's story line leads to a final product that allows students to apply the science they have learned. For each module, a student book, teacher's guide, and videotape and/or videodisc are available.

Student Edition **Recommended grade level: 7-8.** Hurricane Andrew of 1992 is the event on which this 5-week study of meteorological topics is based. The topics addressed in *Hurricane!* include air pressure, humidity, wind, hurricane formation, and the hydrologic cycle. The module also introduces students to practical ways of preparing for and cleaning up after a major weather event. Students begin the module by watching television news coverage and reading newspaper accounts of the devastation caused by Hurricane Andrew. They are told that their major task during the module will be to design, in 6-member teams, a 3-page newspaper explaining the impact of a hurricane on a community. The module's 10 activities provide students with the background information and skills they need for this task.

Among the activities, for example, students track a hurricane and use various weather features—such as earth wind patterns—to predict its path. They follow the movement of weather across the United States in order to make a forecast. They determine the best location for scientific instruments designed to detect hurricanes that are forming. They also construct a bar graph showing when during the year hurricanes are most likely to occur.

The module provides short narratives on meteorological topics; copies of actual newspaper articles; explanatory graphics; and profiles of professionals who might be involved in publishing a newspaper on a hurricane—for example, an editor, a hurricane specialist, a meteorologist, a natural hazards planner, a reporter, and an environmental scientist. Middle school students who experienced Hurricane Andrew tell their stories throughout the module. Other information that students need to complete the task must be obtained from encyclopedias, textbooks, films, magazines, and other sources they can find. The unit culminates with a display of each team's newspaper. Teachers may want to supplement or exchange the activities in the unit depending on the latest "real event" in the news.

Teacher's Edition The teacher's guide provides brief overview information on the module's structure and activities. It includes suggestions for guiding specific student activities and a scoring rubric for a performance assessment.

Key to Content Standards: 5-8 (see app. C)

UNIFYING CONCEPTS AND PROCESSES: Systems, order, and organization; evidence, models, and explanation; change, constancy, and measurement.
SCIENCE AS INQUIRY: Abilities necessary to do scientific inquiry; understandings about scientific inquiry.
PHYSICAL SCIENCE: Motions and forces; transfer of energy.
EARTH AND SPACE SCIENCE: Structure of the earth system.
SCIENCE AND TECHNOLOGY: Abilities of technological design; understandings about science and technology.
SCIENCE IN PERSONAL AND SOCIAL PERSPECTIVES: Natural hazards; risks and benefits; science and technology in society.

HISTORY AND NATURE OF SCIENCE: Science as a human endeavor; nature of science.

Prices: Student edition (ISBN 0-201-49094-3), $7.95. Teacher's edition (ISBN 0-201-49416-7), with video, $18.00. Classroom package, $115.00. *Publisher/supplier:* Addison-Wesley/Longman. *Materials:* Available locally.

4.24 The Moons of Jupiter. Debra Sutter, Cary Sneider, Alan Gould, and others. Great Explorations in Math and Science (GEMS) series. Berkeley, Calif.: Lawrence Hall of Science, 1993.

Program Overview The Great Explorations in Math and Science (GEMS) series includes more than 50 teacher's guides and handbooks for preschool through grade 10. About 35 of these are appropriate for middle school. The series also includes several assembly presenter's guides and exhibit guides. New guides and handbooks continue to be developed, and current titles are revised frequently. The series is designed to teach key science and mathematics concepts through activity-based learning. The time needed to complete GEMS units varies from about 2 to 10 class sessions.

Teacher's Guide **Recommended grade level: 4-8+.** In this unit, students learn about the exciting world of planets and space exploration by studying Jupiter and its moons. During the unit's 5 activities, students track Jupiter's moons, investigate the creation of craters, create a scale model of the Jupiter system using their schoolyard, go on a tour of the Jupiter system as viewed by the *Voyager* spacecraft, and design and build model space stations. Students are introduced to the work of Galileo and other early astronomers. They have the opportunity to observe photographs of Jupiter and its moons and to discuss and record information; they compare the moons' features with other, more familiar things; and they venture possible ideas, explanations, or conclusions on the basis of what they have seen. In all of the activities, students create and use models of various kinds.

The 5 activities in *The Moons of Jupiter* require about 5 to 7 sessions of 40 to 50 minutes each. Each lesson includes a materials list, preparation steps, and directions for activities and discussion. The guide also includes background information, summary outlines for each lesson, reproducible data sheets, and suggestions for related reading. A set of 23 slides is included with the teacher's guide.

Key to Content Standards: 5-8 (see app. C)

UNIFYING CONCEPTS AND PROCESSES: Systems, order, and organization; evidence, models, and explanation; change, constancy, and measurement; evolution and equilibrium; form and function.
SCIENCE AS INQUIRY: Abilities necessary to do scientific inquiry; understandings about scientific inquiry.
EARTH AND SPACE SCIENCE: Earth in the solar system.
SCIENCE AND TECHNOLOGY: Abilities of technological design; understandings about science and technology.
SCIENCE IN PERSONAL AND SOCIAL PERSPECTIVES: Science and technology in society.
HISTORY AND NATURE OF SCIENCE: Science as a human endeavor; nature of science; history of science.

Prices: $42.00 (ISBN 0-912511-84-2). Slides, $26.50. *Publisher/supplier:* LHS GEMS. *Materials:* Available locally, or from commercial suppliers.

4.25 Project Earth Science: Astronomy. P. Sean Smith. Project Earth Science series. Washington, D.C.: National Science Teachers Association, 1992.

Program Overview The Project Earth Science series consists of 4 volumes for students in middle and junior high school. Each volume focuses on a single area in earth science—astronomy, geology, meteorology, or physical oceanography—and contains a collection of hands-on activities and a series of readings related to the topic area. The central theme of the series is the uniqueness of the earth among the planets in the solar system.

Curriculum Guide **Recommended grade level: 7-8+.** *Project Earth Science: Astronomy* contains 11 hands-on activities and a set of 14 background readings designed to introduce students to planetary astronomy. Many of the activities involve mathematics. They are organized under 3 broad concepts: (1) the placement of earth in relation to the sun and to the other planets, (2) the unique properties of earth, and (3) the reasons for the phases of the moon and the earth's seasons.

Among the activities, students use angular diameters to measure the true diameter of the moon, build a scale model of the planetary distances in the solar system, investigate the effect of distance to the object and baseline on parallax, and use Ping-Pong balls and a light source to understand the cause of the moon's phases.

The set of 14 background readings elaborates on concepts presented in the activities. Included are topics such as scale measurements, the Hubble Space Telescope, and the greenhouse effect. The readings are intended to enhance teacher preparation or to serve as resources for students interested in further study.

Each activity in *Project Earth Science: Astronomy* includes student pages, which can be duplicated, and a teacher's guide. The student pages contain background information, directions, and a set of questions to guide the students as they draw conclusions. The teacher's section contains more detailed background information, preparation tips, and suggestions for interdisciplinary study and extensions. Appendixes provide a master materials list and an annotated bibliography of resources in astronomy.

Key to Content Standards: 5-8 (see app. C)

UNIFYING CONCEPTS AND PROCESSES: Systems, order, and organization; evidence, models, and explanation; change, constancy, and measurement; evolution and equilibrium.
SCIENCE AS INQUIRY: Abilities necessary to do scientific inquiry; understandings about scientific inquiry.
PHYSICAL SCIENCE: Transfer of energy.
EARTH AND SPACE SCIENCE: Structure of the earth system; earth in the solar system.
SCIENCE AND TECHNOLOGY: Understandings about science and technology.

Price: $21.95 (ISBN 0-87355-108-7).
Publisher/supplier: National Science Teachers Association. *Materials:* Available locally, or from commercial suppliers.

4.26 **Project Earth Science: Geology.** Brent A. Ford. Project Earth Science series. Arlington, Va.: National Science Teachers Association, 1996.

Program Overview The Project Earth Science series consists of 4 volumes for students in middle and junior high school. Each volume focuses on a single area in earth science—astronomy, geology, meteo-

rology, or physical oceanography—and contains a collection of hands-on activities and a series of readings related to the topic area. The central theme of the series is the uniqueness of the earth among the planets in the solar system.

Curriculum Guide **Recommended grade level: 6-8+.** *Project Earth Science: Geology* contains 15 hands-on activities and a set of 4 background readings designed to introduce students to the unifying theory of plate tectonics and how this concept can be used to explain the occurrences of volcanoes, earthquakes, and other geologic phenomena. The activities are constructed around 4 basic concepts: (1) the earth's surface is composed of plates that can move independently of one another, (2) tectonic plates move because they "ride" on a rock layer called the asthenosphere, (3) tectonic motion and mechanisms are studied indirectly by investigating a variety of geologic features and events on and near the earth's surface, and (4) rocks and minerals are products of complex geological processes. An understanding of the concept of density is required for several of the activities.

Among the activities in the unit, students use maps and data tables to look for patterns in the frequency and distribution of earthquakes around the world, and they construct paper models that illustrate seafloor spreading. Students also experiment with models of convection cells in water, and they compare the ability of various construction designs to withstand the effects of an earthquake.

The set of 4 background readings— on plate tectonics, volcanoes, earthquakes, and rocks and minerals— elaborates on concepts presented in the activities. The readings are intended to enhance teacher prepa-

ration or to serve as resources for students interested in further study.

Each activity in *Project Earth Science: Geology* includes student pages that can be duplicated and a teacher's guide. The student pages contain background information, directions, and a set of questions to guide the students as they draw conclusions. The teacher's section contains more detailed background information, preparation tips, and suggestions for interdisciplinary study and extensions. Appendixes include a master materials list and an annotated bibliography.

Key to Content Standards: 5-8 (see app. C)

UNIFYING CONCEPTS AND PROCESSES: Systems, order, and organization; evidence, models, and explanation; change, constancy, and measurement.
SCIENCE AS INQUIRY: Abilities necessary to do scientific inquiry; understandings about scientific inquiry.
PHYSICAL SCIENCE: Transfer of energy.
EARTH AND SPACE SCIENCE: Structure of the earth system; earth's history.
SCIENCE AND TECHNOLOGY: Understandings about science and technology.
SCIENCE IN PERSONAL AND SOCIAL PERSPECTIVES: Natural hazards.
HISTORY AND NATURE OF SCIENCE: Nature of science.

Price: $21.95 (ISBN 0-87355-131-1).
Publisher/supplier: National Science Teachers Association. *Materials:* Available locally, or from commercial suppliers.

4.27 **Project Earth Science: Meteorology.** P. Sean Smith and Brent A. Ford. Project Earth Science series. Arlington, Va.: National Science Teachers Association, 1994.

Program Overview The Project Earth Science series consists of 4 volumes for students in middle and junior high school. Each volume focuses on a single area in earth science—astronomy, geology, meteorology, or physical oceanography—and contains a collection of hands-on activities and a series of readings related to the topic area. The central theme of the series is the uniqueness of the earth among the planets in the solar system.

Curriculum Guide **Recommended grade level: 6-8+.** *Project Earth Science: Meteorology* contains 17 hands-on activities, 2 demonstrations, and a set of 10 background readings designed to introduce students to meteorology. The activities are constructed around 3 basic concepts: (1) the origin and composition of the earth's atmosphere, (2) factors that contribute to weather, and (3) the ways air masses interact to produce weather.

Among the activities in the unit, students conduct an experiment to determine the percentage of oxygen in the atmosphere. They also investigate the rates at which different colors of the same surface heat, they use inflated balloons to model how pressure differences create wind, and they investigate some essential factors in the production of hail.

The set of 10 background readings elaborates on concepts presented in the activities. Included are topics such as smog, acid rain, and mechanisms of severe weather. The readings are intended to enhance teacher preparation or to serve as resources for students interested in further study.

Each activity in *Project Earth Science: Meteorology* includes student pages that can be duplicated, and a teacher's guide. The student pages contain background information, directions, and a set of questions to guide the students as they draw conclusions. The teacher's section contains more detailed background information, preparation tips, and suggestions for interdisciplinary

study and extensions. An annotated bibliography is also provided.

Key to Content Standards: 5-8 (see app. C)

UNIFYING CONCEPTS AND PROCESSES: Systems, order, and organization; evidence, models, and explanation; change, constancy, and measurement. **SCIENCE AS INQUIRY:** Abilities necessary to do scientific inquiry; understandings about scientific inquiry. **EARTH AND SPACE SCIENCE:** Structure of the earth system; earth's history; earth in the solar system. **SCIENCE IN PERSONAL AND SOCIAL PERSPECTIVES:** Natural hazards; science and technology in society.

Price: $21.95 (ISBN 0-87355-123-0). ***Publisher/supplier:*** National Science Teachers Association. ***Materials:*** Available locally, or from commercial suppliers.

4.28 **River Cutters.** Reprinted with revisions. Jefferey Kaufmann, Robert C. Knott, and Lincoln Bergman. Great Explorations in Math and Science (GEMS) series. Berkeley, Calif.: Lawrence Hall of Science, 1995.

Program Overview The Great Explorations in Math and Science (GEMS) series includes more than 50 teacher's guides and handbooks for preschool through grade 10. About 35 of these are appropriate for middle school. The series also includes several assembly presenter's guides and exhibit guides. New guides and handbooks continue to be developed, and current titles are revised frequently. The series is designed to teach key science and mathematics concepts through activity-based learning. The time needed to complete GEMS units varies from about 2 to 10 class sessions.

Teacher's Guide **Recommended grade level: 6-8+.** *River Cutters* gives students a sense of events in a river system over time. The unit includes

not only earth science and ecology but social studies. Concepts of erosion, sequencing of geological events, pollution, and human manipulation of rivers are introduced. Students first create their own model rivers, observing and recording information about them. During the first 4 sessions of the unit, they acquire geological terminology and begin to understand rivers as dynamic, ever-changing systems. During 3 optional sessions, students have the opportunity to explore the relationship between the angle of the river models and the events that occur in the developing river, experimenting with dams and modeling problems in toxic waste disposal. Students develop skills such as designing models, experimenting, recording data, communicating, and decision making. It is important that diatomaceous earth—the type used for swimming pool filtration—be used and that teachers make a few trial runs with the river model prior to the class session.

The first 4 sessions in *River Cutters* require about 45 minutes each; the 3 optional sessions require 45 to 60 minutes each. The lesson plan for each session includes an overview, a materials list, and detailed instructions (including diagrams) for preparing and for conducting the activity. The guide also includes background information, summary outlines for each lesson, reproducible data sheets, and suggestions for related reading.

Key to Content Standards: 5-8 (see app. C)

UNIFYING CONCEPTS AND PROCESSES: Systems, order, and organization; evidence, models, and explanation; change, constancy, and measurement; form and function. **SCIENCE AS INQUIRY:** Abilities necessary to do scientific inquiry; understandings about scientific inquiry. **EARTH AND SPACE SCIENCE:** Structure of the earth system; earth's history.

SCIENCE AND TECHNOLOGY: Abilities of technological design.
SCIENCE IN PERSONAL AND SOCIAL PERSPECTIVES: Populations, resources, and environments; natural hazards.
HISTORY AND NATURE OF SCIENCE: Nature of science; history of science.

Price: $16 (ISBN 0-912511-67-2). *Publisher/supplier:* LHS GEMS. *Materials:* Available locally, or from commercial suppliers.

4.29 Rocks and Minerals. Delta Science Module (DSM) series. Hudson, N.H.: Delta Education, 1994.

Program Overview The Delta Science Module (DSM) series has 51 life, physical, and earth science units for grades K-8 that emphasize science concepts, science content, and process skills. The series includes 12 modules for grades 5-6 and 8 modules for grades 6-8. Each requires about 3 to 4 weeks to complete and includes a teacher's guide and materials for a class of 32 students.

Teacher's Guide **Recommended grade level: 5-6.** In this module students investigate the properties and uses of rocks and minerals and learn about some of the methods geologists use to gather data about the materials that make up the earth. Students describe minerals in terms of properties such as luster, hardness, and streak color. They apply their knowledge in inferring some of the mineral constituents of rocks. During the unit, students develop a list of how different rocks and minerals have been used by humans through time. They construct 3-dimensional models of crystals, grow crystals, and take a geological field trip to gather and interpret data on rocks and minerals.

The 12 activities in *Rocks and Minerals* are organized to be completed sequentially over 3 to 4 weeks. Each activity takes about 30 to 50 minutes and can be done by

students working individually or in groups.

A "connections" feature at the end of each activity provides suggestions for extending or applying the concepts in the activity. Discussion or activity topics include technology, society, science and careers, language arts, mathematics, the arts, social studies, and health. For example, a "science and health" extension suggests that students research the causes and sources of acid rain and its effects on plants, wildlife, and people.

In addition to directions for activities, the teacher's guide provides a module overview, a schedule of activities, objectives for each activity, background information, materials management and preparation tips, sample answers to discussion questions, teaching suggestions, and reinforcement activities. Also included are reproducible activity sheets for student work and a performance-based assessment.

Key to Content Standards: 5-8 (see app. C)

UNIFYING CONCEPTS AND PROCESSES: Systems, order, and organization; evidence, models, and explanation; form and function.
SCIENCE AS INQUIRY: Abilities necessary to do scientific inquiry; understandings about scientific inquiry.
EARTH AND SPACE SCIENCE: Structure of the earth system; earth's history.
SCIENCE AND TECHNOLOGY: Understandings about science and technology.
SCIENCE IN PERSONAL AND SOCIAL PERSPECTIVES: Science and technology in society.
HISTORY AND NATURE OF SCIENCE: History of science.

Prices: Teacher's guide (ISBN 0-87504-101-9), $27.95. Kit, $279.00. Refill package, $39.00. *Publisher/supplier:* Delta Education. *Materials*: Available locally, from commercial suppliers, or in kit.

4.30 Shrinking Farmlands. Module 1.8. Foundations and Challenges to Encourage Technology-based Science (FACETS) series. Developed by American Chemical Society (Washington, D.C.). Dubuque, Iowa: Kendall/Hunt, 1996.

Program Overview The Foundations and Challenges to Encourage Technology-based Science (FACETS) program consists of 3 series of 8 modules each for grades 6-8. Each module focuses on a topic in the life, earth, or physical sciences. The time needed to complete FACETS modules varies from 2 to 4 weeks. Each module consists of a student book and a teacher's guide.

Student Edition **Recommended grade level: 6.** In the module *Shrinking Farmlands,* students investigate the effects of wind and water erosion on the world's supply of arable land, and they also examine the issue of equitable distribution of food throughout the world. During the module, students figure out the percentage of land on the planet that is available for farming, and they conduct library research to determine the positive and negative effects of some of the methods farmers use to maximize production and minimize problems with erosion.

In other activities, students make models of farmland to explore the effects of wind and water erosion and to investigate ways in which wind and water erosion can be reduced by planting. Students also participate in a trading simulation (game) to learn why the world food supply gets divided unequally. In the final activity, students design and make a learning center on shrinking farmlands, using the information they have acquired.

Shrinking Farmlands is a 4-week module divided into 6 activities, which each take between 1 and 4 class periods to complete. A narrative section at the end of the module provides background information for students on controlling soil erosion and soil pollution.

Teacher's Guide The wraparound teacher's guide includes a unit overview, a time line for completing the module, a materials list, background information, and teaching suggestions.

Key to Content Standards: 5-8 (see app. C)

UNIFYING CONCEPTS AND PROCESSES: Systems, order, and organization; evidence, models, and explanation; change, constancy, and measurement. **SCIENCE AS INQUIRY:** Abilities necessary to do scientific inquiry; understandings about scientific inquiry. **LIFE SCIENCE:** Populations and ecosystems. **EARTH AND SPACE SCIENCE:** Structure of the earth system. **SCIENCE AND TECHNOLOGY:** Abilities of technological design; understandings about science and technology. **SCIENCE IN PERSONAL AND SOCIAL PERSPECTIVES:** Populations, resources, and environments; natural hazards; risks and benefits; science and technology in society.

Prices: Student edition (ISBN 0-7872-1429-9), $7.90. Teacher's guide (ISBN 0-7872-1430-2), $14.90. *Publisher/supplier:* Kendall/Hunt. *Materials:* Available locally, or from commercial suppliers.

4.31 Solar Energy. Delta Science Module (DSM) series. Hudson, N.H.: Delta Education, 1994.

Program Overview The Delta Science Module (DSM) series has 51 life, physical, and earth science units for grades K-8 that emphasize science concepts, science content, and process skills. The series includes 12 modules for grades 5-6 and 8 modules for grades 6-8. Each requires about 3 to 4 weeks to complete and includes a teacher's guide and materials for a class of 32 students.

Teacher's Guide **Recommended grade level: 5-7.** *Solar Energy* helps students understand what is involved in making use of solar energy. During the unit, students carry out various experiments before designing an optimal solar collector. For example, they plant 2 terrariums, place 1 in a sunny location and 1 in a dark location, and compare the growth rates of their plants. Students investigate the transfer of solar energy and discover that a covered solar collector retains more heat than an uncovered one does. They also measure the change in water temperature in black and white solar collectors, investigate how the same amount of solar energy affects the temperature of different volumes of water, and find out whether exposure time is a determining factor in the amount of solar energy absorbed in a collector.

In other activities, students conduct a controlled experiment—to test the importance of the angle at which the sun's rays strike a solar collector, to learn about the use of a reflector, and to investigate the way in which different types of liquid absorb solar energy. After designing and constructing an efficient solar collector on the basis of what they have learned, students use a solar cell to capture and convert solar energy to electrical energy, they experiment with different insulating materials, and they construct and use solar stills.

The 13 activities in *Solar Energy* are organized to be completed sequentially over 3 to 4 weeks. Each activity takes about 30 to 50 minutes and can be done by students working individually or in groups. Many of the experiments require students to work outdoors.

A "connections" feature at the end of each activity provides suggestions for extending or applying the concepts in the activity. Discussion topics include technology, society, science and careers, language arts, mathematics, the arts, social studies, and health. Other follow-up activities that students can do at home or out of the classroom are also provided. For example, students are encouraged to investigate solar-powered cars and planes that have been built and tested in recent years.

In addition to directions for activities, the teacher's guide provides a module overview, a schedule of activities, objectives for each activity, background information, materials management and preparation tips, sample answers to discussion questions, teaching suggestions, and reinforcement activities. Also included are reproducible activity sheets for student work and a performance-based assessment. The module includes a 15-minute video, *Solar Energy.*

Key to Content Standards: 5-8 (see app. C)

UNIFYING CONCEPTS AND PROCESSES: Systems, order, and organization; evidence, models, and explanation; change, constancy, and measurement. **SCIENCE AS INQUIRY:** Abilities necessary to do scientific inquiry; understandings about scientific inquiry. **PHYSICAL SCIENCE:** Transfer of energy. **EARTH AND SPACE SCIENCE:** Earth in the solar system. **SCIENCE AND TECHNOLOGY:** Abilities of technological design; understandings about science and technology. **SCIENCE IN PERSONAL AND SOCIAL PERSPECTIVES:** Science and technology in society. **HISTORY AND NATURE OF SCIENCE:** Science as a human endeavor; history of science.

Prices: Teacher's guide (ISBN 0-87504-111-6), $27.95. Kit, $279.00. Refill package, $11.00. *Publisher/ supplier:* Delta Education. *Materials:* Available locally, through commercial suppliers, or in kit.

4.32 **Stories in Stone.** Kevin Cuff, with Cary Sneider, Lincoln Bergman, and others. Great Explorations in Math and Science (GEMS) series. Berkeley, Calif.: Lawrence Hall of Science, 1995.

Program Overview The Great Explorations in Math and Science (GEMS) series includes more than 50 teacher's guides and handbooks for preschool through grade 10. About 35 of these are appropriate for middle school. The series also includes several assembly presenter's guides and exhibit guides. New guides and handbooks continue to be developed, and current titles are revised frequently. The series is designed to teach key science and mathematics concepts through activity-based learning. The time needed to complete GEMS units varies from about 2 to 10 class sessions.

Teacher's Guide **Recommended grade level: 5-8+.** In *Stories in Stone,* students closely observe and learn about the properties of rocks and minerals. They also conduct simulations and an experiment to find out about how rocks and minerals are formed. Among the activities of the unit, for example, students examine and describe a class collection of 10 different rocks and minerals, learn to distinguish rocks from minerals, grow sodium chloride crystals, and fold paper templates to make models of crystalline shapes. They also carry out an experiment with phenyl salicylate that simulates the formation of igneous rocks as magma cools and solidifies. They investigate sediments with different grain sizes and then create a model sedimentary rock profile by suspending a mixture of these materials in water and allowing them to settle out. They use clay to model the formation of metamorphic rocks and the rock cycle. In the final session, students apply their new knowledge to classifying the 10 rocks and minerals in the class collection

and to identifying unknown "mystery" rocks.

The 8 sessions in *Stories in Stone* take between 40 and 60 minutes each and require that students work in teams of no more than 4 students. The lesson plan for each session includes an overview, a materials list, and detailed instructions for preparing and for conducting the activity. The guide also includes background information, summary outlines for each lesson, reproducible sheets, and suggestions for related reading. Information on obtaining rock samples for the classroom is included.

Key to Content Standards: 5-8 (see app. C)

UNIFYING CONCEPTS AND PROCESSES: Systems, order, and organization; evidence, models, and explanation; change, constancy, and measurement; evolution and equilibrium.
SCIENCE AS INQUIRY: Abilities necessary to do scientific inquiry; understandings about scientific inquiry.
EARTH AND SPACE SCIENCE: Structure of the earth system; earth's history.
HISTORY AND NATURE OF SCIENCE: Nature of science; history of science.

Price: $16 (ISBN 0-912511-93-1).
Publisher/supplier: LHS GEMS.
Materials: Available locally, or from commercial suppliers.

4.33 **The Universe: Exploring Stars, Constellations, and Galaxies.** Scholastic Science Place series. Developed in cooperation with Houston Museum of Natural Science (Houston, Tex.). New York, N.Y.: Scholastic, 1997.

Program Overview The Scholastic Science Place series is a K-6 program with 42 units, 6 for each grade level. The 6 units for grade 6 are organized under topics in the life, earth, and physical sciences. Three key themes—

(1) scale and structure, (2) systems and interactions, and (3) patterns of change—are incorporated into the program. For each unit, teaching materials, student materials, and some optional components are available.

Student Edition **Recommended grade level: 6-7.** In *The Universe: Exploring Stars, Constellations, and Galaxies,* students learn that the stars and other bodies that make up the universe are constantly changing. The unit's lessons are grouped under 3 subconcepts: (1) Stars can be studied from earth using direct and indirect evidence. (2) Stars have predictable life cycles and exist in groups. (3) The universe is constantly expanding.

In this unit, students use a sampling technique to discover how it is possible to estimate the number of stars in the sky. They observe why constellations change position over a year, investigate how parallax shift is used to measure the distance from earth to the stars, and make a model to show how the universe is expanding.

The Universe is a 17-lesson unit requiring about 22 class sessions of 60 minutes each.

Teacher's Edition The conceptual goals of the unit are presented in the lesson-by-lesson story line in the teacher's guide. Each lesson also includes background information; a complete lesson plan, including suggestions for assessing performance and integrating the curriculum; and a list of the materials required. For each lesson there is also a list of the relevant National Science Education Standards (developed by the National Research Council) and Project 2061 Benchmarks (developed by the American Association for the Advancement of Science).

Key to Content Standards: 5-8 (see app. C)

UNIFYING CONCEPTS AND PROCESSES: Systems, order, and organization; evidence, models, and explanation; change, constancy, and measurement.

CHAPTER 4

CURRICULUM MATERIALS

SCIENCE AS INQUIRY: Abilities necessary to do scientific inquiry; understandings about scientific inquiry.
EARTH AND SPACE SCIENCE: Earth in the solar system.
SCIENCE AND TECHNOLOGY: Understandings about science and technology.
SCIENCE IN PERSONAL AND SOCIAL PERSPECTIVES: Science and technology in society.
HISTORY AND NATURE OF SCIENCE: Science as a human endeavor; history of science.

Prices: Student edition (ISBN 0-590-95535-7), $7.95. Teacher's edition (ISBN 0-590-95462-8), $27.00. Unit, $275.00. Consumable kit, $70.00. *Publisher/supplier:* Scholastic. *Materials:* Available locally, from commercial suppliers, or in kit.

4.34 Using Earth's Resources: What Are the Tradeoffs? New York Science, Technology and Society Education Project (NYSTEP). Problem-Solving Activities for Middle-Level Science series. Albany, N.Y.: NYSTEP, 1992.

Program Overview The Problem-Solving Activities for Middle-Level Science series consists of 8 stand-alone modules. Each module contains 2 to 6 units focused on technological and/or ethical aspects of issues involving science, technology, and society. The series was designed so that teachers can select modules and units that address local needs and draw on local community resources. A module requires 3 to 8 weeks to complete, depending on the units selected. Supplies and equipment may be required that are not typically part of a school's science inventory.

Teacher's Guide **Recommended grade level: 7-8+.** *Using Earth's Resources* introduces students to basic science concepts related to earth's natural

resources and helps them become aware that trade-offs are inherent in the use of these resources. During the 3 units in this module, students construct a comprehensive description of their local area and make a composite map of local land use patterns. They identify and explore various properties of soils and of minerals, and they develop a soil profile. Then they relate the raw materials from soils and mineral resources to manufactured goods, food products, and energy resources.

In other activities, students design and conduct a survey to locate local soil erosion sites. They also participate in a 3-part simulation centered around the decisions that 6 communities in a county must make with respect to a proposed highway. In the simulation activities, students develop community action plans and study the possible impacts—especially on different soils and on water resources—of the proposed siting. They consider the economic, social, and aesthetic benefits and drawbacks of having a highway built through a county.

Using Earth's Resources is designed to be completed over a 3- to 4-week period. The module's 3 units have a total of 11 activities. Each unit has directions for its activities, a bibliography, interdisciplinary connections (to technology, social studies, language arts, mathematics, health, home and career skills, arts, and foreign languages/cultures), and ideas for extending classroom activities. Suggestions for using relational databases in the study of land use, soils, and mineral resources are provided.

Key to Content Standards: 5-8 (see app. C)

UNIFYING CONCEPTS AND PROCESSES: Systems, order, and organization; evidence, models, and explanation;

change, constancy, and measurement.
SCIENCE AS INQUIRY: Abilities necessary to do scientific inquiry; understandings about scientific inquiry.
EARTH AND SPACE SCIENCE: Structure of the earth system.
SCIENCE AND TECHNOLOGY: Abilities of technological design; understandings about science and technology.
SCIENCE IN PERSONAL AND SOCIAL PERSPECTIVES: Populations, resources, and environments; natural hazards; risks and benefits; science and technology in society.

Prices: Teacher's guide: In New York State, free with attendance at workshop; outside of New York, $7. *Publisher/supplier:* New York Science, Technology and Society Education Project. *Materials:* Available locally, or from commercial suppliers.

4.35 Volcano! Russell G. Wright. Event-Based Science series. Menlo Park, Calif.: Innovative Learning Publications, 1997.

Program Overview The Event-Based Science series is a program for middle school students in grades 6-9. Each module tells the story of a real event—such as the 1995 outbreak of the Ebola virus in Zaire—through reprinted newspaper articles and personal interviews; sections of background information explain relevant scientific concepts. A central task related to the module's story line leads to a final product that allows students to apply the science they have learned. For each module, a student book, teacher's guide, and videotape and/or videodisc are available.

Student Edition **Recommended grade level: 7-8.** The 1991 eruption of Mount Pinatubo in the Philippine Islands is the event on which this 6-week unit on earth science concepts is based. The topics addressed in *Volcano!* include, for example, the structure of the earth, plate tectonics, and topographic mapping. Students begin the module by watching television news coverage and reading newspaper reports about the eruption of Mount Pinatubo. They are told that their major task during the module will be to produce, in 5-member teams, a 30-minute television program that will inform middle school students in Seattle, Washington, about volcanoes and the potential hazards of living near Mount Rainier. The module's 10 activities provide students with the background information and skills they need for this task.

Among the activities, for example, students work with a mound of sand to simulate caldera formation. They build a model of Mount Rainier from a topographic map. They also design a lab to test how concentration and temperature affect the viscosity of various liquids. They use distance and rate to calculate the time available to evacuate 3 communities in a valley below Mount Rainier if a mudflow is on its way, and they classify and identify igneous rocks. Students also produce displays that compare cinder cone, shield, and composite volcanoes; and they map volcano locations worldwide.

The module provides short narratives on topics related to volcanoes, such as geysers and smokers, volcano monitoring, and the rock cycle; explanatory graphics; and profiles of professionals who might be involved in producing a program on volcanoes—such as a producer, a special-effects expert, a camera operator, a volcanologist, and a geologist. Middle school students who experienced the eruption of Mount Pinatubo tell their stories throughout the module. Other information that students need to complete the task must be obtained from encyclopedias, textbooks, films, magazines, and other sources they can find.

The unit culminates with the presentation of the television program. Schools without video equipment may consider producing a "live" show without the camera. Teachers may want to supplement or exchange the activities in the unit depending on the latest "real event" in the news.

Teacher's Edition The teacher's guide provides brief overview information on the module's structure and activities. It includes suggestions for guiding specific student activities, and a scoring rubric for a performance assessment.

Key to Content Standards: 5-8 (see app. C)

UNIFYING CONCEPTS AND PROCESSES: Systems, order, and organization; evidence, models, and explanation; change, constancy, and measurement; form and function.
SCIENCE AS INQUIRY: Abilities necessary to do scientific inquiry; understandings about scientific inquiry.
EARTH AND SPACE SCIENCE: Structure of the earth system; earth's history.
SCIENCE AND TECHNOLOGY: Abilities of technological design; understandings about science and technology.
SCIENCE IN PERSONAL AND SOCIAL PERSPECTIVES: Natural hazards; risks and benefits; science and technology in society.
HISTORY AND NATURE OF SCIENCE: Science as a human endeavor; nature of science.

Prices: Student edition (ISBN 0-201-49590-2), $7.95. Teacher's edition (ISBN 0-201-49591-0), with video, $18.00. Classroom package, $115.00. *Publisher/supplier:* Addison-Wesley/Longman. *Materials:* Available locally, or from commercial suppliers.

4.36 Weather and Health. Module 1.4. Foundations and Challenges to Encourage Technology-based Science (FACETS) series. Developed by American Chemical Society (Washington, D.C.). Dubuque, Iowa: Kendall/Hunt, 1996.

Program Overview The Foundations and Challenges to Encourage Technology-based Science (FACETS) program consists of 3 series of 8 modules each for grades 6-8. Each module focuses on a topic in the life, earth, or physical sciences. The time needed to complete FACETS modules varies from 2 to 4 weeks. Each module consists of a student book and a teacher's guide.

Student Edition Recommended grade level: 6. In *Weather and Health,* students working in small groups investigate whether a relationship exists between changing weather patterns and human health and well-being. This topic—called biometeorology—is also used in the module as a vehicle for students to learn about collecting long-term data and about analyzing such data for the patterns and relationships that might exist. For example, students look for possible relationships between 2 data-sets—absentee lists from their school and weather reports over a 2-week period. They also learn about the instruments used to measure weather variables, as well as written instruments used to collect health data. Students collect data on the weather at their school and on the health patterns of themselves and another person for 2 weeks.

In other activities, students work in teams to study and develop a demonstration on a particular aspect of the weather, such as air masses and wind, atmospheric pressure, temperature, or precipitation. In the unit's final activity, they analyze their 2 weeks of data on both the weather and people's health, looking for possible relationships.

Weather and Health is a 3-week module divided into 5 activities, which each take between 1 and 5 class periods to complete. A narrative section at the end of the module provides background information for students on the water cycle, atmospheric pressure, clouds, weather maps, and air masses and winds.

Teacher's Guide The wraparound teacher's guide includes a unit overview, a time line for completing the module, a materials list, background information, and teaching suggestions.

Key to Content Standards: 5-8 (see app. C)

UNIFYING CONCEPTS AND PROCESSES: Systems, order, and organization; evidence, models, and explanation; change, constancy, and measurement.
SCIENCE AS INQUIRY: Abilities necessary to do scientific inquiry; understandings about scientific inquiry.
LIFE SCIENCE: Regulation and behavior.
EARTH AND SPACE SCIENCE: Structure of the earth system.
SCIENCE IN PERSONAL AND SOCIAL PERSPECTIVES: Personal health.

Prices: Student edition (ISBN 0-7872-1441-8), $7.90. Teacher's guide (ISBN 0-7872-1442-6), $14.90. *Publisher/supplier:* Kendall/Hunt. *Materials:* Available locally, or from commercial suppliers.

4.37 **Weather Forecasting.** Delta Science Module (DSM) series. Hudson, N.H.: Delta Education, 1995.

Program Overview The Delta Science Module (DSM) series has 51 life, physical, and earth science units for grades K-8 that emphasize science concepts, science content, and process skills. The series includes 12 modules for grades 5-6 and 8 modules for grades 6-8. Each requires about 3 to 4 weeks to complete and includes a teacher's guide and materials for a class of 32 students.

Teacher's Guide **Recommended grade level: 5-6.** In *Weather Forecasting,* students make weather observations and collect weather-related data and information that they display at a weather station they construct. Students explore how collecting data on temperature, rainfall, and wind helps them forecast the weather. Through participation in the activities in this unit, students are able to relate barometric pressure readings to weather conditions. They learn to code weather information and to plot weather fronts. They discover the usefulness of tracking areas of similar air pressure and temperature on a weather map. Students learn the conditions necessary for clouds to form, and begin to associate specific types of clouds with specific types of weather conditions.

The 12 activities in *Weather Forecasting* are organized to be completed sequentially over 3 to 4 weeks. Each activity takes about 30 to 60 minutes and can be done by students working individually or in groups.

A "connections" feature at the end of each activity provides suggestions for extending or applying the concepts in the activity. Discussion or

activity topics include technology, society, science and careers, language arts, mathematics, the arts, social studies, and health. For example, a "science and health" extension suggests that students find out how the skin helps regulate body temperature.

In addition to directions for activities, the teacher's guide provides a module overview, a schedule of activities, objectives for each activity, background information, materials management and preparation tips, sample answers to discussion questions, teaching suggestions, and reinforcement activities. Also included are reproducible activity sheets for student work and a performance-based assessment.

Key to Content Standards: 5-8 (see app. C)

UNIFYING CONCEPTS AND PROCESSES: Systems, order, and organization; evidence, models, and explanation; change, constancy, and measurement; form and function.
SCIENCE AS INQUIRY: Abilities necessary to do scientific inquiry; understandings about scientific inquiry.
EARTH AND SPACE SCIENCE: Structure of the earth system.
SCIENCE AND TECHNOLOGY: Understandings about science and technology.
SCIENCE IN PERSONAL AND SOCIAL PERSPECTIVES: Science and technology in society.
HISTORY AND NATURE OF SCIENCE: Science as a human endeavor; nature of science.

Prices: Teacher's guide (ISBN 0-87504-123-X), $27.95. Kit, $249.00. Refill package, $64.00. *Publisher/supplier:* Delta Education. *Materials:* Available locally, from commercial suppliers, or in kit.

Earth and Space Science—Science Activity Books

4.38 **Activities for the School Planetarium.** Rev. ed. Gerald L. Mallon. Planetarium Activities for Student Success. Vol. 2. Berkeley, Calif.: Lawrence Hall of Science; Corona Park, N.Y.: New York Hall of Science, 1993.

Recommended grade level: 3-8. *Activities for the School Planetarium* presents ideas for interdisciplinary planetarium activities for elementary and middle school students. Designed both for experienced planetarium professionals and for teachers using a planetarium for the first time, the activities were developed to provide a general introduction to astronomy and space science and to serve as springboards for teachers to create their own or similar activities.

Among the activities, students compare the brightness of a simulated "variable" star with that of surrounding stars of known brightness. They learn how to use a blink comparator—an instrument used to detect a moving object, such as a planet or an asteroid, in a field of stars. They also investigate the reasons for seasons, produce a density map of the Milky Way, and explore some of the navigational tasks that would have been encountered by the characters in the novel *Treasure Island*.

The 16 activities in this volume are categorized by grade level; 7 are intended for use by middle school students. Activities can also be adapted by teachers for various grade levels. Some activities can be done in the classroom; others require a planetarium.

Each activity includes background information, directions for conducting the activities, and reproducible student worksheets. The guide also offers tips on constructing participatory planetarium experiences and provides a framework for thinking about and developing planetarium activities.

Price: $11.50. *Publisher/supplier:* Lawrence Hall of Science. *Materials:* Available locally, or from commercial suppliers.

4.39 **The Amateur Meteorologist: Explorations and Investigations.** H. Michael Mogil and Barbara G. Levine. Amateur Science Series. New York, N.Y.: Franklin Watts, 1993.

Recommended grade level: 4-8. *The Amateur Meteorologist* is an activity and resource book on observing and forecasting weather. Among the activities, for example, students build their own weather instruments—a wind vane, thermometer, barometer, rain gauge, and anemometer—from readily available materials. Other investigations introduce skills needed to identify clouds, to read weather maps, to calculate dew point and relative humidity, and to determine windchill and degree-days. The book includes useful background information on the water cycle, cloud formation, sun and seasons, pressure and wind, and stormy weather. This beginner's guide to meteorology features numerous photographs and charts.

Price: $20.60 (ISBN 0-531-11045-1). *Publisher/supplier:* Grolier. *Materials:* Available locally, or from commercial suppliers.

4.40 **Arid Lands, Sacred Waters.** Marne Potter and Caitlyn Howell, eds. Albuquerque, N.Mex.: New Mexico Museum of Natural History; U.S. Geological Survey; and U.S. Department of Agriculture, Forest Service, 1992.

Recommended grade level: 5-8+. *Arid Lands, Sacred Waters* is a student activity packet designed to accompany an exhibition at the New Mexico Museum of Natural History; the packet can also be used on its own. It provides basic information, games, and introductory activities that allow students to learn about water in the natural environment and to find out about some of the changes that can take place with respect to this natural resource when humans step into the picture. Topics addressed include the water cycle; surface water and groundwater; weather; ecosystems, food chains, and adaptations; wetlands; water pollution; water treatment; and water conservation.

Among the activities, students calculate the flow rate of a river or stream, they make and use a rain gauge, and they investigate how certain plants are adapted to specific water conditions. Students also study maps to discover how water has influenced human settlement in New Mexico from ancient times to the present. They conduct water tests and build a water filter. They evaluate the potential effects on a community's water supply and economy from building a radioactive waste dump nearby.

Each activity in *Arid Lands, Sacred Waters* includes a materials list, brief directions, and limited background information. Some activities emphasize topics particularly relevant to New Mexico and the Southwest, but this does not preclude their use in other geographic regions. The activity packet is also available in Spanish.

Price: $4.95. Publisher/supplier: New Mexico Museum of Natural History. *Materials:* Available locally, or from commercial suppliers.

4.41 Atmospheric Dynamics. Project LEARN [Laboratory Experience in Atmospheric Research at the National Center for Atmospheric Research]. Boulder, Colo.: University Corporation for Atmospheric Dynamics, 1996.

Recommended grade level: 6-8. *Atmospheric Dynamics* offers 35 activities related to weather and the physical processes that create and maintain motion in the atmosphere. Activities focus on topics such as weather measurements and processes; the importance of the sun, radiation, and heat transfer; different types of storms, such as hurricanes, thunderstorms, and cyclones; and the use of weather observations to make forecasts.

Among the activities, for example, students make and use a variety of weather instruments; they use simple materials to demonstrate the differences between conduction, convection, and radiation; and they fly a paper airplane through a carbon dioxide cloud to simulate the effect of microbursts on real aircraft during takeoff and landing.

ABOUT THE ANNOTATIONS IN "EARTH AND SPACE SCIENCE—SCIENCE ACTIVITY BOOKS"

Entry Numbers
Curriculum materials are arranged alphabetically by title in each category (Core Materials, Supplementary Units, and Science Activity Books) in chapters 1 through 5 of this guide.

Each curriculum annotation has a two-part entry number: the chapter number is given before the period; the number after the period locates the entry within that chapter. For example, the first entry number in chapter 1 is 1.1; the second entry in chapter 2 is 2.2; and so on.

The entry numbers within each curriculum chapter run consecutively through Core Materials, Supplementary Units, and Science Activity Books.

Order of Bibliographic Information
Following is the arrangement of the facts of publication in the annotations in this section:

- **Title of publication**
- **Number of edition,** if applicable
- **Authors** (an individual author or authors, an institutional author, or a project or program name under which the material was developed)
- **Series title**
- **Series developer,** if applicable
- **Place of publication, publisher, and date of publication**

Recommended Grade Level
The grade level for each piece of material was recommended by teacher evaluators during the development of this guide. In some instances, the grade-level recommendation may differ slightly from the publisher's advertised level.

Price and Acquisition Information
Ordering information appears at the end of each entry. Included are—

- **Prices** (of teacher's guides, activity books, and kits or units)
- **Publisher/supplier** (The name of a principal publisher/supplier, although not necessarily the sole source, for the items listed in the price category. Appendix A, "Publishers and Suppliers," provides the address, phone and fax numbers, and electronic ordering information, where available, for each publisher and supplier.)
- **Materials** (various sources from which one might obtain the required materials)

Readers must contact publishers/suppliers for complete and up-to-date ordering information, since prices are subject to change and materials may also change with revised editions. The prices given in this chapter are based on information from publishers and suppliers but are not meant to represent the full range of ordering options.

Indexes of Curriculum Materials
The multiple indexes on pp. 449-78 allow easy access to the information in this guide. Various aspects of the curriculum materials—including titles, topics addressed in each unit, and grade levels—are the focus of seven separate indexes. For example, titles and entry numbers are listed in the "Title Index" on pp. 450-54. The "Index of Authors, Series, and Curriculum Projects," on pp. 455-57, provides entry numbers of any annotated titles in a particular series.

The activities include brief directions and background information, and many of them have suggestions for extensions.

Price: $15. *Publisher/supplier:* UCAR LEARN Center. *Materials:* Available locally, or from commercial suppliers.

4.42 **Blue Planet.** Carolyn E. Schmidt. Washington, D.C.: National Air and Space Museum, Office of Education, 1990.

Recommended grade level: 5-8+. Looking at earth from space provides students with a unique perspective in *Blue Planet.* This activity book was designed to be used in conjunction with the IMAX film of the same name, produced by the Smithsonian Institution's National Air and Space Museum. The information, activities, and resources in the book cover many environmental and earth science topics, from earthquakes to groundwater filtration to solar heating. This varied selection offers teachers of students in grades 3 to 12 a wide range of resources from which to choose. Many of the activities are designed to develop students' observational skills, especially with regard to the changing nature of the earth's environment. The guide lists 40 locations where *Blue Planet* can be seen.

Price: Free to educators in response to request on school letterhead. *Publisher/supplier:* National Air and Space Museum. *Materials:* Available locally, or from commercial suppliers.

4.43 Destiny in Space. Carolyn E. Schmidt. Washington, D.C.: National Air and Space Museum, Educational Services Department, 1994.

Recommended grade level: 4-8+. *Destiny in Space* contains 12 activities through which students explore sociological, biological, and technological challenges of living and working in space. For example, they examine reasons for exploring space, such as colonization, curiosity, or the search for life. They experience a sense of weightlessness by exercising with leg and arm weights. They explore how different senses help people keep their balance in earth's gravitational environment.

In other activities, students simulate the problems of communicating in space, and they role-play the programmer of a robot to get a sense of how instructions for a simple task might be sent to a robotic spacecraft. They consider the isolation astronauts might experience on long voyages, and they identify the functions performed by various parts of a space suit.

Each activity includes background information for the teacher, information on the preparation needed, step-by-step procedures, discussion questions, and extensions. The importance of making and recording careful observations is stressed.

The topic of each activity in the book is linked to real-world developments and to scenes in the National Air and Space Museum's IMAX film *Destiny in Space.* A list of teaching materials, books, films and videos, and other materials on space is provided. The guide lists more than 50 locations where *Destiny in Space* can be seen.

Price: Free to educators in response to request on school letterhead. *Publisher/supplier:* National Air and Space Museum. *Materials:* Available locally, or from commercial suppliers.

4.44 Earth at Hand: A Collection of Articles from NSTA's Journals. Washington, D.C.: National Science Teachers Association, 1993.

Recommended grade level: 6-8+. *Earth at Hand* contains 72 articles on earth science published between 1982 and 1991 in the following journals of the National Science Teachers Association (NSTA): *Journal of College Science Teaching, The Science Teacher, Science Scope,* and *Science and Children.* The articles, selected from among hundreds published during the 10-year period, feature teaching ideas and/or hands-on activities that require minimal or no background material and little, if any, further research before being used in the classroom. Other articles provide instructions for making cheap, usable alternatives to expensive equipment.

The articles are organized in 3 broad subject categories: (1) earth's features and properties; (2) water, weather, and the environment; and (3) earth in space. Examples of activities in the volume include developing a 365-day calendar to use as an analogy for earth's 4.5-billion-year history, experimenting with a half-life model in which M&M candies represent radioactive atoms, and participating in an oil spill simulation. In other activities, students build a barometer with an Erlenmeyer flask, watch a demonstration to learn why the sky is blue, and work with a large balloon to see that the earth can look flat even though it is not.

Most articles were originally written for students in a specific age range and may need to be adapted for use at other grade levels. *Earth at Hand* includes a bibliography of all earth science articles published in the NSTA journals between January 1982 and May 1991.

Price: $19.95 (ISBN 0-87355-112-5). *Publisher/supplier:* National Science Teachers Association. *Materials:* Available locally, or from commercial suppliers.

4.45 Earthquakes: A Teacher's Package for K-6. National Science Teachers Association/Federal Emergency Management Agency (NSTA/FEMA) Earthquake Curriculum. Washington, D.C.: U.S. Government Printing Office, 1993.

Recommended grade level: K-6. *Earthquakes: A Teacher's Package for K-6* offers a cross-curricular approach to the study of these events. Copiously illustrated, this teacher's manual contains dozens of activities under 6 unit headings: (1) "Defining an Earthquake," (2) "Why and Where Earthquakes Occur," (3) "Physical Results of Earthquakes," (4) "Measuring Earthquakes," (5) "Recognizing an Earthquake," and (6) "Earthquake Safety and Survival." The units are intended to be used in order. Activities include using a hard-boiled egg to simulate the layers of the earth, constructing models of 3 types of faults, simulating an earthquake using wooden sticks and coffee grounds, and practicing proper reactions to an earthquake.

Each of the first 5 units in *Earthquakes* includes background information, lessons, and activities for each of 3 grade levels: K-2, 3-4, and 5-6, as well as master pages that may be reproduced for transparencies, handouts, and worksheets.

Prices: Single copy free to educators in response to request on school letterhead. *Publisher/supplier:* Federal Emergency Management Agency. *Materials:* Available locally, or from commercial suppliers.

4.46 **Earth Science Investigations.** Margaret A. Oosterman and Mark T. Schmidt, eds. Alexandria, Va.: American Geological Institute, 1990.

Recommended grade level: 7-8+. *Earth Science Investigations* offers 27 activities related to earth science topics including earthquakes, erosion, rocks, weather, tides, the solar system, and mapping skills. The hands-on activities are grouped by general subject. Among the activities, for example, students construct a geologic model that simulates river features and processes. They also visualize how the North Atlantic basin formed and learn how different ages of bedrock reveal the basin's history. They gather data on micro weather patterns, determine the density of soil particles, and prepare and analyze contour maps to determine the flow of contaminated groundwater. In other activities, students determine the approximate circumference of the earth using geometric principles and mathematical proportions, and they look for patterns in the meteorite-impact history of North America.

The activities in *Earth Science Investigations* include step-by-step procedures, basic background information, reproducible student data sheets, a set of questions with an answer key, and a list of additional resources. Many of the activities are paper-and-pencil labs that require the analysis of data provided in the tables and charts.

Price: $34.95 (ISBN 0-922152-07-1). *Publisher/supplier:* American Geological Institute. *Materials:* Available locally, or from commercial suppliers.

4.47 **Earth: The Water Planet.** Rev. ed. Jack E. Gartrell, Jr., Jane Crowder, and Jeffrey C. Callister. Washington, D.C.: National Science Teachers Association, 1992.

Recommended grade level: 6-8+. *Earth: The Water Planet* features 21 activities that investigate various aspects of water: its scarcity or abundance, where it is found, its unique physical properties, how it moves through the atmosphere, and how it reshapes the solid earth. The activities in the book also heighten students' environmental awareness and allow them to see how water affects almost every aspect of life on earth.

Among the activities, for example, students collect data on the rate of water absorption of local soils, use a block of ice containing sand and stones to simulate the abrasive action of a glacier, and use a model of a hillside to investigate how contour farming practices reduce erosion. Students also determine how much water leaks from a faulty plumbing fixture in a year and simulate the major steps in purifying water for human consumption.

This guide includes a collection of 18 readings that provide detailed explanations and additional examples of the concepts explored in the activities. The topics include glaciers, clouds, acid rain, soil erosion, the water cycle, water treatment, water conservation, and seawater. The readings can be used as student handouts or as background information for teachers.

The activities in *Earth: The Water Planet* take between 40 and 60 minutes each and require readily available materials such as paint rollers, toys, plastic bottles, and watering cans. Each activity includes background information, detailed instructions, reproducible students sheets,

extension ideas, and answers when needed. Most of the activities can be adapted for classroom demonstrations. Audiovisual activities are an integral part of some activities.

Price: $18.50 (ISBN 0-87355-083-8). *Publisher/supplier:* National Science Teachers Association. *Materials:* Available locally, or from commercial suppliers.

4.48 **Earthy Things.** Margaret Eidson. Riverview, Fla.: Idea Factory, 1990.

Recommended grade level: 5-8. *Earthy Things*, written by a middle school teacher, offers 87 ideas for basic activities in 4 areas of earth science: astronomy, geology, meteorology, and oceanography. Examples of the activities include making and using a spectroscope, investigating the Doppler effect using a Nerf football, and producing materials that have the characteristics of noncrystalline igneous rocks. In other activities, students construct and use a homemade thermometer or a nephoscope (for observing the direction and velocity of clouds), investigate what happens when a warm air mass meets a cold air mass, prepare a model of an estuary and its natural resources, and investigate a cross-section of a barrier island.

Earthy Things is presented in 3-ring-binder format. Each activity includes a materials list, teacher's notes with basic background information and instructions, and reproducible student pages and record sheets. Appendixes give tips for working with students on slide and filmstrip presentations and for teaching students how to write a lab report.

Price: $24.95 (ISBN 1-885041-11-X). *Publisher/supplier:* Idea Factory. *Materials:* Available locally, or from commercial suppliers.

4.49 Exploring Space: Using Seymour Simon's Astronomy Books in the Classroom. Barbara Bourne and Wendy Saul. New York, N.Y.: Morrow Junior Books, 1994.

Recommended grade level: 5-6. *Exploring Space: Using Seymour Simon's Astronomy Books in the Classroom* contains about 50 space-related activities that build on information in astronomy books by Seymour Simon and other prominent authors of children's nonfiction books. Each activity has a different theme, such as magnetic storms on the sun, black holes, or developing a space quiz. In addition to experiments, this guide for teachers and parents proposes topics for writing assignments and discussions and suggests titles for further reading. Teachers are encouraged to select from among the activities and to encourage their students to amend and refine them. Striking, full-color photographs and useful diagrams appear throughout the guide. Each activity also includes a materials list, step-by-step procedures, and extensions.

Price: $16 (ISBN 0-688-12723-1). *Publisher/supplier:* Morrow Junior Books. *Materials:* Available locally, or from commercial suppliers.

4.50 Finding Your Way: Navigation Activities from the Exploratorium. Peter Weiss and staff of The Exploratorium. San Francisco, Calif.: The Exploratorium, 1992.

Recommended grade level: 4-8. Inspired by an exhibit at The Exploratorium museum in San Francisco celebrating "the amazing human ability to get from here to there," *Finding Your Way* contains sections on finding north, making maps, and orienting oneself on the planet. Among the activities, for example, students use a dial watch and the sun to find true north and then make and use a magnetic compass to find magnetic north. They make a clinometer to measure the height of an object and then use a "shrinking tower" scale to determine how far away the object is. They also measure and map a hill in 3 dimensions, use the North Star and a clinometer to measure latitude, and use a north-south line and a time-zone table to determine longitude.

Each activity includes an objective, a materials list, instructions, and an explanation that provides scientific, technological, and historical context. The book offers helpful illustrations and clear, easy-to-follow directions.

Prices: $5.95 (ISBN 0-943451-35-3). *Publisher/supplier:* The Exploratorium. *Materials:* Available locally, or from commercial suppliers.

4.51 Geothermal Energy. Marilyn Nemzer and Deborah Page. Tiburon, Calif.: Geothermal Education Office, 1994.

Recommended grade level: 5-8. *Geothermal Energy,* designed for use with students in grades 4 to 8, describes geothermal energy in the context of the world's energy needs. The information and activities in this illustrated guide involve students in an in-depth study of geothermal energy, including its geology, history, and many uses. The activities in the 6 sections of the unit include, for example, demonstrating the effects of burning fuels using mirrors and various heat sources, using swirling colored water to show how hot mantle rock moves in convection currents, testing the effects of heat on evaporation, producing electric current in a magnet, and making a model geothermal steam engine.

Science activities are integrated with mathematics, social studies, and language arts in *Geothermal Energy.* Each section of the book has information "For the Teacher." Activities provide an introduction, a materials list, and step-by-step directions. A videotape—*Geothermal Energy: A Down-to-Earth Adventure*—provides an overview of the concepts taught in this unit.

Prices: Teacher's guide, $5. Video, $9. *Publisher/supplier:* Geothermal Education Office. *Materials:* Available locally, or from commercial suppliers.

4.52 Global Climates—Past, Present, and Future: Activities for Integrated Science Education. Sandra Henderson, Steven R. Holman, and Lynn L. Mortensen, eds. Washington, D.C.: U.S. Environmental Protection Agency, Office of Research and Development, 1993.

Recommended grade level: 8+. *Global Climates—Past, Present, and Future,* published by the U.S. Environmental Protection Agency, offers

15 simple activities that focus student attention on global climate change. The curriculum is designed not to convince students that global temperatures are rising at an unprecedented rate but to present the results of research and to encourage students to apply critical-thinking skills to a complex issue. The topics addressed in this guide include weather and climate, the greenhouse effect, the carbon cycle, human activity and the greenhouse effect, and the possible impact of the greenhouse effect on plants and global sea level.

Among the activities in the guide, students collect and graph local weather data, learning about the distinction between weather and climate. They also construct and interpret a 45-foot-long chart of the earth's history. They analyze simulated pollen-sample analogs to replicate the way that scientists gather paleo-data. Students also make model greenhouses, and they investigate the differences between the atmospheres of the planets in our solar system. They plant, care for, and observe the changes in growing plants under conditions of normal (ambient) carbon dioxide (CO_2) and elevated CO_2 levels.

Although most of the activities take 1 or 2 class periods to complete, many could be done over longer periods of time. Each activity in this 3-ring-binder includes a materials list, step-by-step procedures, and separate student pages. A list of 12 articles, books, and reports on climate change is provided.

Price: $31.50. *Publisher/supplier:* National Technical Information Service. *Materials:* Available locally, or from commercial suppliers.

4.53 **The Great Ocean Rescue.** Watertown, Mass.: Tom Snyder Productions, 1993.

Recommended grade level: 5-8. *The Great Ocean Rescue* is a videodisc package designed to engage students in learning about the ocean and related topics in earth science, environmental science, and life science through a cooperative learning experience. The activity (requiring 4 to 12 class periods) consists of 4 rescue missions that take students to trouble spots in the ocean. Students view a videodisc description of the mission, then break into small groups, with each student in the group adopting the role of a different scientist—geologist, marine biologist, oceanographer, or environmental scientist—to analyze the information. Each group reports its recommendations to the class, and the class decides the trouble spot location. Small groups reconvene to come up with possible solutions to the problem, and the class then decides on the best solution. Topics addressed in the rescue missions include habitat selection, pollution, coral reefs, and hydrothermal vent communities.

The videodisc includes a library of short movies that complement and extend the rescue activity. Reproducible masters of student worksheets and a poster-sized map of the ocean floor are included.

Prices: Videodisc kit, $349.95. Software for Macintosh or Windows (optional), $49.95. *Publisher/supplier:* Tom Snyder Productions. *Materials:* Available in kit.

4.54 **The Great Solar System Rescue.** Watertown, Mass.: Tom Snyder Productions, 1992.

Recommended grade level: 4-8. In *The Great Solar System Rescue*, a videodisc-based simulation set in the year 2210, 4 probes are lost in space and the class must rescue them. Students analyze data in order to find the best way of rescuing the probes. They view a videodisc description of the mission, then break into small groups, with each student assuming the role of a specific scientist, such as an astronomer, meteorologist, geologist, or space historian, to analyze the information. Each group reports its recommendations to the class and the class decides where to travel. When the probe is located, the small groups reconvene to develop rescue plans, and the class again decides on the best plan.

The videodiscs include a library of short movies and stills that complement and extend the rescue activity.

Prices: Videodisc kit, $349.95. Software for Macintosh or Windows (optional), $49.95. *Publisher/supplier:* Tom Snyder Productions. *Materials:* Available in kit.

4.55 **Hands-On Geology: K-12 Activities and Resources.** R. Heather Macdonald and Susan G. Stover, eds. Tulsa, Okla.: SEPM [Society for Sedimentary Geology], 1991.

Recommended grade level: 4-8+. *Hands-On Geology* is a collection of 23 stand-alone activities and resources on sedimentary geology. Topics covered include crystals, rocks, fossils, evolution, dinosaurs, global warming, and acid rain. Among the activities, for example, students build a quick-sand model; develop a taxonomic web diagram of cars in a parking lot; learn how fossils are used in paleo-geographic interpretation; investigate the types of stone used for local buildings; and use a geologic map, a soil geochemistry map, and a sediment geochemistry map to locate a copper deposit. Developed by many different geologists and educators, the activities in this volume vary somewhat in approach and detail. Each activity includes background information, a materials list, proce-dures, and a results-and-discussion section. The resources section lists geology suppliers; sources for curric-ula and supplementary materials; state geological surveys; professional geology organizations; and earth science books, films, and periodicals.

Price: $6 (ISBN 0-918985-90-0). *Publisher/supplier:* SEPM. *Materi-als:* Available locally, or from com-mercial suppliers.

4.56 Janice VanCleave's Earth-quakes: Mind-Boggling Experiments You Can Turn into Science Fair Projects. Janice Pratt VanCleave. Spectacular Science Projects. New York, N.Y.: John Wiley, 1993.

Recommended grade level: 4-6. *Janice VanCleave's Earthquakes,* a book written for students, contains 20 simple activities for exploring con-cepts related to earthquakes—such as compression forces, faults, tec-tonic plates, convection currents, seismic waves, and the Richter scale. For each activity, students first com-plete a "cookbook" experiment, such as exploring compression forces by pushing hand towels together to create "folds," using glass jars filled with water at different temperatures

to investigate convection currents, or making a model of a seismograph with a cardboard box. Students then follow suggestions for varying these experiments and for designing their own related experiments on the basis of the models in the book. Some of the related experiments could be developed into science fair projects.

Most of the activities in *Janice VanCleave's Earthquakes* can be done by students working with little supervision. Each activity includes a materials list, step-by-step proce-dures, an explanation of results, and guidelines for further experimenta-tion and research. A glossary of terms is also included.

Price: $10.95 (ISBN 0-471-57107-5). *Publisher/supplier:* Wiley. *Materials:* Available locally.

4.57 Marine Science Activities on a Budget. J. Michael Williamson. Boston, Mass.: Wheelock College, 1993.

Recommended grade level: 8+. *Marine Science Activities on a Budget* is a collection of 18 original experiments, written by a single author, focusing primarily on physical-chemical (rather than biological) oceanogra-phy and designed to be done inex-pensively. Among the activities, for example, students analyze the rates at which different-sized sand parti-cles settle. They also observe and graph a thermocline, and they com-pare the buffering capacities of sam-ples of pondwater and seawater. In other activities, students launch labeled drift bottles to study surface currents, and they observe the effect that temperature has on the meta-

bolic rate of a poikilotherm (cold-blooded organism). The emphasis in these activities is on data collection and analysis and on report-writing ability.

In addition to the 18 activities, ideas and directions are provided for building 12 pieces of marine labora-tory equipment out of inexpensive materials. The equipment includes a core sampler, a hydrometer tube, a sediment-analysis apparatus, and a current-generating apparatus. Each activity in this stapled booklet in-cludes a materials list, preparation instructions, procedures, and sample tables or charts for recording data. No background information is provided.

Price: $13. *Publisher/supplier:* J. Michael Williamson. *Materials:* Available locally, or from commercial suppliers.

4.58 Measuring Earthquakes. Nancy Cook. Real-World Mathemat-ics through Science series. Devel-oped by Washington Mathematics, Engineering, and Science Achieve-ment (MESA) Group (Seattle, Wash.). Menlo Park, Calif: Innovative Learning Publications, 1994.

Recommended grade level: 8+. *Measur-ing Earthquakes* contains 5 class-room activities and 1 home activity that teach students the mathematics underlying the development and use of local-magnitude scales, such as the Richter scale, for measuring earthquakes. Students learn where earthquakes occur and how to mea-sure their size as they explore pow-ers of 10, exponents, rounding num-bers, and scientific notation. The importance of these mathematical concepts to geophysics and seismol-ogy is also emphasized. The book draws largely upon earthquake events in the Pacific Northwest.

Among the activities in *Measuring Earthquakes,* students explore powers of 10, exponents, and logarithmic patterns by comparing and graphing the number of popcorn kernels in 4 prepackaged bags. They also build a simple seismograph and generate "quakes" of 3 magnitudes, and they construct the Richter scale using exponents and logarithmic scales.

In other activities, students calculate the magnitude of selected earthquakes using data from different seismic stations, then use the magnitude of the earthquake to calculate how far the ground actually moved. They also plot the locations of damaging earthquakes in the Pacific Northwest on a geological projection map. In the home activity, students and their families explore the effects of building materials and design on a structure's ability to withstand an earthquake.

Each activity in this book includes an overview, a materials list, background information, procedures, presentation suggestions, assessment strategies, and links to careers, history, and technology.

Price: $18.95 (ISBN 0-201-86122-4). *Publisher/supplier:* Scott Foresman/Addison Wesley. *Materials:* Available locally.

4.59 On the Rocks: Earth Science Activities for Grades 1-8. Susan G. Stover and R. Heather Macdonald, eds. Tulsa, Okla.: SEPM [Society for Sedimentary Geology], 1993.

Recommended grade level: 1-8. *On the Rocks* is a collection of 50 earth science demonstrations, activities, and investigations. The activities are intended for a varied audience—for those new to teaching earth science, for experienced teachers seeking new

ideas or approaches, and for geologists visiting the classroom. The activities are grouped under 7 major topics: (1) rocks and minerals; (2) soils, volcanoes, and earthquakes; (3) water; (4) fossils; (5) maps and map making; (6) science basics; and (7) geology, society, and the environment.

Among the activities in *On the Rocks,* students simulate the formation of sedimentary rocks. They observe how and why ground liquefaction occurs during earthquakes. They create a musical play based on their knowledge of dinosaurs. Students also use a model to see how and why groundwater moves through aquifers; they make a 3-dimensional model of a landscape and relate the model to a topographic map; and they explore the many different ways petroleum is used in modern society, learning about advantages and disadvantages of its use.

Each activity includes a materials list, an indication of time required (which ranges from 15 minutes to several hours), step-by-step procedures, and a results-and-discussion section. Background material is presented with some activities. No student pages are provided.

Price: $9 (ISBN 1-56576-005-0). *Publisher/supplier:* SEPM. *Materials:* Available locally, or from commercial suppliers.

4.60 Project SPICA: A Teacher Resource to Enhance Astronomy Education. Nadine Butcher Ball, Harold P. Coyle, and Irwin I. Shapiro, eds. Project SPICA: Support Program for Instructional Competency in Astronomy, sponsored by Harvard-Smithsonian Center for Astrophysics. Dubuque, Iowa: Kendall/Hunt, 1995.

Recommended grade level: 2-8+. This manual contains 37 stand-alone astronomy activities, selected from

more than 100 activities used nationwide by the Project SPICA teacher network in workshops. These activities are designed to be used by teachers with little or no background in astronomy. The activities cover a wide range of topics, including the earth, moon, and sun; the solar system; stars; our galaxy and other galaxies; and the universe as a whole.

Among the activities, for example, students make and use a moon phase dial and a sundial, and they trace the position of a reflected image (the analemma) of the sun at noon throughout the school year. They also explore "crustal material" from a mystery planet, and they use spectra to identify which of 7 known elements are present in 5 imaginary stars. Students also decode imaginary binary data sent to earth from a spacecraft, and they construct a 3-dimensional model of the Big Dipper inside a box, then observe the constellation from different positions.

The activities in this teacher resource can be adapted for classes from second grade through high school. Most of the activities take 1 class period of 40 to 50 minutes to complete. Some need to be done outside. Each activity lists a key concept and a key question to indicate its focus. Grade-level information, an indication of the time required, background information, procedures, notes on student preconceptions, cross-references to other activities, extensions, and student worksheet masters are provided.

An appendix offers other useful information. For teachers who do not have access to reference materials on astronomy, there are comprehensive background essays on topics relevant to the activities. Also included are tables of information about the planets and the brightest stars, as well as a list of science education equipment suppliers, astronomy organizations, and publications related to astronomy.

Price: $20.95 (ISBN 0-7872-0134-0). *Publisher/supplier:* Kendall/Hunt. *Materials:* Available locally, or from commercial suppliers.

4.61 **Science Experiments: Earth Science.** Science Experiments, Book 2. Tammy K. Williams. Lewistown, Mo.: Mark Twain Media, 1995.

Recommended grade level: 6-8. *Science Experiments: Earth Science* offers 44 stand-alone activities that introduce students to a wide variety of topics in the earth sciences, focusing on geology, oceanography, meteorology, and astronomy. For example, students evaporate the water from a saltwater solution at different rates to observe the crystal sizes, and they investigate how adding salt to water affects the boiling point, freezing point, and rate of temperature change of water. They use P- and S-wave data to plot earthquake epicenters. They investigate which colors absorb more radiant energy, and they practice estimating the altitude of different objects using a "quadrant."

In addition to the earth science activities, 10 laboratory skills activities help strengthen students' familiarity with metric measurements, the scientific method, and classification systems. For example, students use a dichotomous key to give household items nonsense names. They practice using the scientific method while investigating how the height from which a ball is dropped affects how high it bounces. They use a triple-beam balance to measure the mass of different objects.

Each activity in *Science Experiments: Earth Science* is printed on

reproducible, tear-out student sheets. These sheets include a stated objective, directions for the activity, data charts, and questions to guide student work. The book contains an answer key for the astronomy questions, but no teacher pages or background information is provided.

Price: $12.95. *Publisher/supplier:* Carson-Dellosa. *Materials:* Available locally.

4.62 **Science Projects about Weather.** Robert Gardner and David Webster. Science Projects series. Springfield, N.J.: Enslow, 1994.

Recommended grade level: 5-8. *Science Projects about Weather*, 1 of 6 books in the Science Projects series, contains 22 simple experiments or activities that allow students to explore weather and its changes. Topics addressed include the atmosphere, the water cycle, seasons, temperature, weather, and air and wind. Among the activities, for example, students place a ball of steel wool in the bottom of a narrow jar and invert the jar in a pan of water; the next day they determine what fraction of the air—oxygen—originally in the jar reacted with the steel wool. They also make a cloud in a bottle, record and chart temperatures over the course of a day, use a turntable or "lazy Susan" to investigate the Coriolis effect, and make a liquid tornado with 2 plastic soda bottles and colored water. Students may need assistance for some of the experiments.

The last section of the book tells students how to set up their own weather station. Included are instructions for making and using a

wind vane, an anemometer, a rain gauge, and a hygrometer and suggestions about making local weather forecasts.

Designed to be student-directed, many of the stand-alone activities in *Science Projects about Weather* could be done at home or as teacher demonstrations, or used as the basis for science fair projects.

The activities are narrative in form; the text contains questions to help guide inquiry. All of the activities have introductory, student-oriented background readings or explanations. Most activities include suggestions of further investigations for students to conduct on their own. An appendix lists suppliers of materials needed for the experiments.

Price: $18.95 (ISBN 0-89490-533-3). *Publisher/supplier:* Enslow. *Materials:* Available locally, or from commercial suppliers.

4.63 **A Sedimentary Geologists' Guide to Helping K-12 Earth Science Teachers: Hints, Ideas, Activities and Resources.** Molly F. Miller, R. Heather Macdonald, Linda E. Okland, and others, eds. Tulsa, Okla.: SEPM [Society for Sedimentary Geology], 1990.

Recommended grade level: K-8+. *A Sedimentary Geologists' Guide to Helping K-12 Earth Science Teachers* was written to help sedimentary geologists become more involved in earth science education, but it contains many ideas useful for middle school science teachers. Included are 20 classroom activities, suggestions for field trips, hints for successful class visits by professional geologists, and resources.

Classroom activity ideas, which focus on sedimentary geology, include determining the roundness of sedimentary grains, making a quicksand model, identifying the composition of rocks used in local buildings, and modeling geologic time. Several ideas for larger-scale educational activities are also given, such as panning for gold and magnetite or measuring longshore currents.

Gathered from many geologists and educators, the activities in this volume vary somewhat in approach and detail. Each activity includes a specified grade level, a list of materials, procedures, and a section on expected results. The resource section lists suppliers, sources for geology curricula and supplementary materials, and national geology and science organizations.

Price: $5 (ISBN 0-918985-86-2). *Publisher/supplier:* SEPM. *Materials:* Available locally, or from commercial suppliers.

4.64 **Stonehenge: A Program from the Holt Planetarium.** Alan J. Friedman. Planetarium Activities for Student Success, Vol. 12. Berkeley, Calif.: Lawrence Hall of Science; Corona, N.Y.: New York Hall of Science, 1993.

Recommended grade level: 7-8. *Stonehenge* contains guidelines for directing a planetarium show that teaches students what Stonehenge is and how it could have been used as a gigantic astronomical calendar. Through the planetarium program, students learn the basic components of astronomer Gerald Hawkins's theory about Stonehenge's probable functions, and they perform an investigation using the planetarium to test the theory. The key activity involves searching for horizon

events—such as sunset on the winter solstice—and then comparing those events with alignments of the stones at Stonehenge.

The program includes several follow-up classroom activities that allow students to explore apparent solar motion. The activities include creating a horizon sun calendar for a month, building and using a device that accurately models the apparent motion of the sun, and performing a detailed study of the yearly cycle of sunrises. The application of Hawkins's ideas to other ancient archaeological sites is also briefly covered. Each classroom activity has a materials list, cutouts for tools or devices, steps for preparation, procedures, and extensions. Instructions and cutouts for making indicators that show the alignments Hawkins found at Stonehenge are supplied for several types of planetariums.

Price: $11.50. *Publisher/supplier:* Lawrence Hall of Science. *Materials:* Available locally, or from commercial suppliers.

4.65 **Student Activities in Meteorology (SAM).** Version 2. Beverly L. Meier and Elisa Passarelli. Developed in collaboration with National Oceanic and Atmospheric Administration (NOAA), Environmental Research Laboratories, Forecast Systems Laboratory (Boulder, Colo.). Washington, D.C.: U.S. Government Printing Office, 1994.

Recommended grade level: 6-8+. *Student Activities in Meteorology* is a packet of 10 paper-and-pencil activities on meteorology and atmospheric science that give students a sense of the type and form of scientific data with which a meteorologist or an atmospheric scientist might work. All of the activities have strong mathematics and graphing components. They

can be used alone or as a series. The wide range of topics addressed includes Doppler radar, severe weather, windchill, the greenhouse effect, ozone depletion, carbon monoxide pollution, air traffic and weather, and sunspots.

Among the activities in this book, students learn how to track severe weather by looking at a Doppler radar worksheet, they complete a wind chill table, and they plot curves for the occurrence of greenhouse gases over time. Students also calculate the effect that wind speed and direction have on carbon monoxide pollution in Boulder and Denver, Colorado; they examine the type of maps and weather data used by air traffic controllers; and they use techniques similar to those solar observers use to record data based on sunspot observations.

The activities give students the opportunity to manipulate data, look for patterns, and draw conclusions using the data given. Each activity includes background information, procedures, questions to guide students, charts or tables, and a conclusion box to be completed.

Price: Free. *Publisher/supplier:* NOAA/ERL/FSL. *Materials:* Available locally.

4.66 **Thematic Applications: Sciences I.** Technology-Based Solutions series. Developed by Twin Discovery Systems. Freeport, N.Y.: Educational Activities, 1995.

Recommended grade level: 6-8. This CD-ROM offers 47 computer-based activities that allow students to explore 4 topics: dinosaurs, the solar system and space, weather, and inventions.

The activities, which can be completed individually or collaboratively, incorporate computer literacy, mathematics, writing, science, and research, and require students to locate, manipulate, organize, and analyze data. Generally, students use the word processor, database, spreadsheet, or draw/paint program to complete each activity. They are also encouraged to consult research sources such as the Internet, CD-ROM encyclopedias, books, and periodicals.

As they go through the program, students research dinosaurs and input the data into a database; then they use the database to create spreadsheets, graphs, stories, illustrations, and a time line. They research plans for space stations and use a paint program to create their own space station plan. They write a story about what life is like on an imaginary planet. Students also view a short video of the Lunar Rover and then describe it; they interpret an infrared satellite image of the weather, which is on the CD-ROM; and they create a time line of important inventions.

Video clips and clip art illustrations are included on the CD-ROM for students to use as they create documents or reports. A list of relevant Web sites is also provided. The activities are designed to be adapted to different grade levels; thus, they will require varying amounts of time, depending on the level of detail teachers assign.

The CD-ROM uses either Claris-Works (for Macintosh) or Microsoft Works for Windows. Students must know how to use these applications before they can complete the activities. The CD-ROM comes with a teacher's guide that summarizes the goals, skills, and research requirements for each activity.

Price: Unit, $99. ***Publisher/supplier:*** Educational Activities. ***Materials:*** Available locally, from commercial suppliers, or in unit.

4.67 **The Topsoil Tour.** LaMotte Co. Chestertown, Md.: LaMotte Co., 1993.

Recommended grade level: 7-8. The 7 activities in *The Topsoil Tour*—a soil test unit—allow students to examine, discover, and compare the physical and chemical properties of soil samples they gather. During the unit, students also learn about the role of different plant nutrients. Among the activities, they first collect soil samples, and they observe and record information about the soil's texture and appearance on data sheets. Then they make a soil nutrient extract using soda bottle filter funnels; they test the extract for pH, nitrogen, potassium, and phosphorous levels. Students also complete several word games or puzzles that reinforce concepts presented.

The procedures used in *The Topsoil Tour* are simpler versions of procedures used by soil scientists throughout the world. The unit includes a 3-ring binder with information for the teacher, reproducible student data sheets and handouts, and testing reagents in single-unit foil packages.

Prices: Complete kit, $51. Replacement kit, $39. ***Publisher/supplier:*** LaMotte Co. ***Materials:*** Available locally, from commercial suppliers, or in kit.

4.68 **The Universe at Your Fingertips: An Astronomy Activity and Resource Notebook.** Andrew Fraknoi, ed. Developed by Project ASTRO, Astronomical Society of the Pacific. San Francisco, Calif.: Astronomical Society of the Pacific, 1995.

Recommended grade level: 3-8+. *The Universe at Your Fingertips* is an activity and resource guide on astronomy. It contains 87 hands-on classroom activities selected from various sources by a team of teachers and astronomers. The activities are presented in 13 sections, on topics such as moon phases and eclipses, the sun and seasons, planets, the solar system, comets and meteors, and stars and galaxies, as well as less conventional topics such as space exploration, the search for extraterrestrial intelligence, pseudoscience (that is, astrology), and astronomy in different cultures. Ideas for interdisciplinary teaching are given. For example, students use Styrofoam balls to model lunar and solar eclipses; they make a star chart to find constellations in the night sky at any time of year; they construct simple refracting telescopes; and they create lists of songs and other pieces of music that relate in some way to astronomy.

Although activities are arranged within sections by topic and grade level, they can be done in any order. Each section of activities is followed by one or more lists of resources.

This 3-ring binder also contains comprehensive resource lists and bibliographies on topics such as astronomy organizations and suppliers, women in astronomy, the work and lives of astronomers, and astronomy and space software. Background material on astronomical topics and teaching ideas from experienced astronomy educators are also provided.

Price: $29.95 (ISBN 1-886733-00-7). ***Publisher/supplier:*** Astronomical Society of the Pacific. ***Materials:*** Available locally, or from commercial suppliers.

4.69 Water, Stones, and Fossil Bones. Karen K. Lind, ed. CESI Sourcebook VI. Washington, D.C.: National Science Teachers Association and Council for Elementary Science International (CESI), 1991.

Recommended grade level: K-7. *Water, Stones, and Fossil Bones* offers 51 well-illustrated earth science activities from dozens of authors. Activities are grouped within the topics of space, land, water, air, and the earth's past. Activities include making a scale model of the solar system, using Play-Doh to simulate layers of sedimentary rock, creating miniature landfills in a plastic cup, building a solar collector, and making a fossil cast.

Activities vary in length, requiring from 30 minutes to 3 class periods to complete. Each activity includes brief background information, questions to initiate discussion, step-by-step procedures, and suggestions for further investigation.

Price: $16.50 (ISBN 0-87355-101-X).
Publisher/supplier: Council for Elementary Science International.
Materials: Available locally, or from commercial suppliers.

Investigating the technology of papermaking

CHAPTER 5

MULTIDISCIPLINARY AND APPLIED SCIENCE

Multidisciplinary and Applied Science—Core Materials

5.1 **Evolution: Change over Time.** 3rd ed. Anthea Maton, Jean Hopkins, Susan Johnson, and others. Prentice Hall Science Integrated Learning System series. Upper Saddle River, N.J.: Prentice Hall, 1997.

Program Overview The Prentice Hall Science Integrated Learning System series is a program for middle school or junior high school students. Designed to cover all relevant areas of science, this program consists of 19 books, each in a particular topic area, such as sound and light, the planet earth, and evolution—change over time. Seven science themes are incorporated into the program; the themes are energy, evolution, patterns of change, scale and structure, systems and interactions, unity and diversity, and stability. For each unit, teaching materials, ancillary student materials, and some optional components are available.

Student Edition **Recommended grade level: 7-8. Reading level: early 8.** The textbook *Evolution: Change over Time* is organized in 3 chapters: (1) "Earth's History in Fossils," (2) "Changes in Living Things over Time," and (3) "The Path to Modern Humans." During the course, students are introduced to 6 types of fossils and to information on geologic eras and periods. They also learn about the biochemical, anatomical, and fossil evidence of evolution and about natural selection and the effects of overproduction, variation, migration, and isolation on evolutionary change. Students study the general characteristics of the primates and the characteristics that are unique to humans. They also examine some of the fossil and chemical evidence that allows scientists to study human evolution, and

they find out about probable ancestors of humans.

Each chapter includes a lab investigation. Students make casts and molds of 3 small objects and compare the casts with the original objects. They draw a geologic time line to help them visualize the relationships between evolutionary events. They also measure their jaw and thumb indexes and compare them with those of a gorilla and *Australopithecus* to identify changes that occurred among earlier hominids and hominids of today.

Each chapter contains comprehensive reading sections that introduce major science concepts. Suggestions are provided for activities in which students "find out by doing," "find out by calculating," and "find out by writing." Other activities are also suggested—for example, researching the names of several index fossils

(fossils used to identify the age of sedimentary rock layers) or preparing a display of objects that represent a student's culture.

Other features include problem-solving challenges, science career descriptions, and science connections to real-world events or issues. The student edition closes with readings on 3 topics: (1) paleontologist Jack Horner's work on the behavior of dinosaurs, (2) the debate over the cause of the extinction of the great dinosaurs, (3) and a fictional account of the kind of life forms that may have evolved elsewhere in the universe.

Teacher's Edition In the teacher's wraparound edition, each chapter begins with a 2-page planning guide and a 2-page preview that summarizes each section within the chapter. The teacher's edition also provides suggestions for teaching, guiding, integrating, and closing lessons, as well as enrichments, extensions, and answers to questions in the student text.

Supplementary Laboratory Manual The supplementary lab manual provides 8 investigations directly correlated with the information presented in the student textbook. Examples of investigations include developing a model to demonstrate the half-life of a radioactive element; observing variations in kidney beans, pine needles, and maple leaves; and developing a model that illustrates natural selection in deer mice.

Program Resources and Support Materials A variety of materials, including some optional components, is available. A teacher's

ABOUT THE ANNOTATIONS IN "MULTIDISCIPLINARY AND APPLIED SCIENCE—CORE MATERIALS"

Entry Numbers
Curriculum materials are arranged alphabetically by title in each category (Core Materials, Supplementary Units, and Science Activity Books) in chapters 1 through 5 of this guide.

Each curriculum annotation has a two-part entry number: the chapter number is given before the period; the number after the period locates the entry within that chapter. For example, the first entry number in chapter 1 is 1.1; the second entry in chapter 2 is 2.2; and so on.

The entry numbers within each curriculum chapter run consecutively through Core Materials, Supplementary Units, and Science Activity Books.

Order of Bibliographic Information
Following is the arrangement of the facts of publication in the annotations in this section:

- **Title of publication**
- **Number of edition,** if applicable
- **Authors** (an individual author or authors, an institutional author, or a project or program name under which the material was developed)
- **Series title**
- **Series developer,** if applicable
- **Place of publication, publisher, and date of publication**

Recommended Grade Level and Reading Level
The grade level for each piece of material was recommended by teacher evaluators during the development of this guide. In some instances, the recommended grade level may differ slightly from the publisher's advertised level. The Fry Readability Scale was used to determine the approximate reading level of core materials.

Key to Content Standards: 5-8
The key lists the content standards for grades 5-8 from the *National Science Education Standards* (NSES) that are addressed in depth by the item. A key is provided for core materials and supplementary units. (*See* appendix C.)

Price and Acquisition Information

Ordering information appears at the end of each entry. Included are—

- **Prices** (of teacher's guides, student books, lab manuals, and kits or units)
- **Publisher/supplier** (The name of a principal publisher/supplier, although not necessarily the sole source, for the items listed in the price category. Appendix A, "Publishers and Suppliers," provides the address, phone and fax numbers, and electronic ordering information, where available, for each publisher and supplier.)
- **Materials** (various sources from which one might obtain the required materials)

Readers must contact publishers/suppliers for complete and up-to-date listings of the program resources and support materials available for a particular unit. Depending on the developer, these items may be required, optional, or both; they may be offered individually and/or in kits, packages, or boxes. Materials may change with revised editions. The prices given in this chapter for selected resources or materials are based on information from the publishers and suppliers but are not meant to represent the full range of ordering options.

Indexes of Curriculum Materials

The multiple indexes on pp. 449-78 allow easy access to the information in this guide. Various aspects of the curriculum materials—including titles, topics addressed in each unit, grade levels, and standards addressed—are the focus of seven separate indexes. For example, titles and entry numbers are listed in the "Title Index" on pp. 450-54. The "Index of Authors, Series, and Curriculum Projects," on pp. 455-57, provides entry numbers of any annotated titles in a particular series.

Overviews of Core and Supplementary Programs

Appendix D, "Overviews of Core and Supplementary Programs with Titles Annotated in This Guide," on pp. 441-48, lists, by program or series, the individual titles annotated in the sections "Core Materials" and "Supplementary Units" in the five curriculum chapters.

resource package contains the student edition and annotated teacher's editions of both the textbook and the lab manual, as well as a test book, an activity book, a review-and-reinforcement guide, and English and Spanish audiotapes for auditory and language learners. Other available materials include interactive videodiscs, transparencies, assessment materials, English and Spanish guides for language learners, a study guide, a teacher's desk reference, and a booklet of product-testing activities.

Key to Content Standards: 5-8 (see app. C)

UNIFYING CONCEPTS AND PROCESSES: Systems, order, and organization; evidence, models, and explanation; change, constancy, and measurement; evolution and equilibrium; form and function.

SCIENCE AS INQUIRY: Abilities necessary to do scientific inquiry; understandings about scientific inquiry.

LIFE SCIENCE: Diversity and adaptations of organisms.

EARTH AND SPACE SCIENCE: Structure of the earth system; earth's history.

HISTORY AND NATURE OF SCIENCE: Science as a human endeavor; nature of science; history of science.

Prices: Student edition (ISBN 0-13-423450-2), $9.97. Teacher's edition (ISBN 0-13-423211-9), $22.97. Teacher's resource package, $112.97. (Contact publisher/supplier for complete price and ordering information.) *Publisher/supplier:* Prentice Hall. *Materials:* Available locally, or from commercial suppliers.

5.2 Integrated Science: Book One. Alan Fraser, Ian Gilchrist, Tony Partridge, and others. Integrated Science series. Dallas, Tex.: J. M. LeBel, 1994.

Program Overview The Integrated Science series includes 3 full-year courses that integrate chemistry, physics, and the life, earth, and space sciences with environmental issues and emphasize the development of critical-thinking skills. Four major themes are incorporated in the program: energy, changes over time, systems and structures, and environmental interactions. Designed for students of different ability levels, the lessons are graded as "starting off," "going further," or "for the enthusiast." In addition to the student edition and teacher's manual, the program offers a variety of support materials.

Student Edition **Recommended grade level: 6. Reading level: late 7.** *Integrated Science: Book One* is organized in 14 chapters on these subjects: scientific measurements and the processes of science, living things, energy, matter, solvents and solutions, cells and reproduction, electricity, gases, heat, earth sciences, earth in space, and energy and the environment. Each chapter consists of 3 to 5 sections of 3 pages each. Sections begin with a hands-on activity or discussion.

Activities include, for example, calculating the volume of a drop of water, making a tin car racer, building a windmill that can lift a 50-gram mass, measuring the freezing temperature of water, determining the best way to filter muddy water, examining the reproductive parts of a flower, measuring lung capacity, classifying rocks, using weather maps to compare global patterns of winds and air pressures in summer and winter, and extracting metals from their ores.

Teacher's Manual The teacher's manual includes an overview of the organization of the student textbook, safety information, sample lesson plans, information on incorporating cooperative learning techniques, and a summary of the main ideas presented in each chapter of the student textbook. For each section of the student textbook, the teacher's manual includes an estimate of the time required to complete the section, a materials list, information on planning for and conducting activities, and sample answers to student questions.

Program Resources and Support Materials A variety of support materials is available, including a resource pack with additional activities, chapter review tests, a math-and-science process skills program, and transparencies.

Key to Content Standards: 5-8 (see app. C)

UNIFYING CONCEPTS AND PROCESSES: Systems, order, and organization; evidence, models, and explanation; change, constancy, and measurement.

SCIENCE AS INQUIRY: Abilities necessary to do scientific inquiry; understandings about scientific inquiry.

PHYSICAL SCIENCE: Properties and changes of properties in matter; transfer of energy.

LIFE SCIENCE: Structure and function in living systems; reproduction and heredity; populations and ecosystems; diversity and adaptations of organisms.

EARTH AND SPACE SCIENCE: Structure of the earth system; earth's history; earth in the solar system.

SCIENCE AND TECHNOLOGY: Understandings about science and technology.

SCIENCE IN PERSONAL AND SOCIAL PERSPECTIVES: Populations, resources, and environments; science and technology in society.

HISTORY AND NATURE OF SCIENCE: Science as a human endeavor.

Prices: Student edition (ISBN 0-920008-60-7), $37.95. Teacher's manual (ISBN 0-920008-61-5), $19.95. (Contact publisher/supplier for complete price and ordering information.) *Publisher/supplier:* LeBel. *Materials:* Available locally, or from commercial suppliers.

5.3 Integrated Science: Book Two. Alan Fraser, Ian Gilchrist, Tony Partridge, and Harry Herzer III. Integrated Science series. Dallas, Tex.: J. M. LeBel, 1995.

Program Overview The Integrated Science series includes 3 full-year courses that integrate chemistry, physics, and the life, earth, and space sciences with environmental issues and emphasize the development of critical-thinking skills. Four major themes are incorporated in the program: energy, changes over time, systems and structures, and environmental interactions. Designed for students of different ability levels, the lessons are graded as "starting off," "going further," or "for the enthusiast." In addition to the student edition and teacher's manual, the program offers a variety of support materials.

Student Edition **Recommended grade level: 7. Reading level: middle 7.** *Integrated Science: Book Two* is organized in 14 chapters on these subjects: hydrogen, metals, acids, and bases; the senses; forces and movement; the human body; electricity; earth in space; nutrition and health; the periodic table and materials;

electronics; volcanoes, earthquakes, and plate tectonics; weather, atmosphere, and oceans; geologic time; energy; and the environment. Each chapter consists of 1 to 7 sections of 3 pages each. Sections begin with a hands-on activity or discussion.

Activities include, for example, investigating the reactivity series of metals; using an indicator to determine whether substances are acids or bases; experimenting with a newton balance; making an electromagnet; using tide tables to determine the relationship between the position of the moon and the height of the tide; comparing the speed at which microbes grow in different conditions; investigating the qualitative relationships between current, voltage, and resistance; and using a geological time scale chart to correlate fossil layers with geological times.

Teacher's Manual The teacher's manual includes an overview of the organization of the student textbook, safety information, sample lesson plans, information on incorporating cooperative learning techniques, and a summary of the main ideas presented in each chapter of the student textbook. For each section of the student textbook, the teacher's manual includes an estimate of the time required to complete the section, a materials list, information on planning for and conducting activities, and sample answers to student questions.

Program Resources and Support Materials A variety of support materials is available, including a resource pack with additional activities, chapter review tests, a math-and-science process skills program, and transparencies.

Key to Content Standards: 5-8 (see app. C)

UNIFYING CONCEPTS AND PROCESSES: Systems, order, and organization; evidence, models, and explanation;

change, constancy, and measurement; evolution and equilibrium.
SCIENCE AS INQUIRY: Abilities necessary to do scientific inquiry; understandings about scientific inquiry.
PHYSICAL SCIENCE: Properties and changes of properties in matter; motions and forces; transfer of energy.
LIFE SCIENCE: Structure and function in living systems; reproduction and heredity; populations and ecosystems; diversity and adaptations of organisms.
EARTH AND SPACE SCIENCE: Structure of the earth system; earth's history; earth in the solar system.
SCIENCE AND TECHNOLOGY: Understandings about science and technology.
SCIENCE IN PERSONAL AND SOCIAL PERSPECTIVES: Personal health; natural hazards; science and technology in society.
HISTORY AND NATURE OF SCIENCE: Science as a human endeavor; history of science.

Prices: Student edition (ISBN 0-920008-45-6), $37.95. Teacher's manual (ISBN 0-920008-67-4), $19.95. (Contact publisher/supplier for complete price and ordering information.) *Publisher/supplier:* LeBel. *Materials:* Available locally, or from commercial suppliers.

5.4 **Investigating Diversity and Limits.** Middle School Science and Technology series. Developed by Biological Sciences Curriculum Study (BSCS) (Colorado Springs, Colo.). Dubuque, Iowa: Kendall/Hunt, 1994.

Program Overview The Middle School Science and Technology series is a 3-year thematic program that integrates the life, earth, and physical sciences and emphasizes technology as a process for solving problems. The curriculum includes

investigations, simulations, debates, plays, outdoor activities, research projects, and creative-writing projects. The titles of the 3 year-long courses—*Investigating Patterns of Change, Investigating Diversity and Limits,* and *Investigating Systems and Change*—reflect the program's unifying themes. Each course incorporates cooperative learning strategies. Components of the program include the student book, teacher's edition, teacher's resource package, implementation guide, and kit of materials.

Student Edition **Recommended grade level: 7-8. Reading level: early 9.** During the 4 units in *Investigating Diversity and Limits*, students focus on the following questions: (1) What is normal? (2) How does technology account for my limits? (3) Why are things different? and (4) Why are we different? During the course, students learn about the distribution of characteristics in humans and other organisms, about how broad the "normal" range is, and about the diversity of matter and its limits. They explore the concept of setting standards—for example, speed limits based on human reaction time. They find out how technology can help humans overcome their limits.

Students also study the particle theory of matter as an example of the development and use of a scientific model to explain the properties of materials. They study the chromosome theory of inheritance as an explanation for diversity among humans. They examine ethical issues associated with genetic engineering.

Among the activities in the course, for example, students collect data on human limits and diversity by doing investigations about vision and graphing the data to produce normal curves. They also devise tests or methods to determine the best paper towel from among a sampling of brands; this activity introduces them to the concepts of criteria, constraints, and final decisions as they apply to the design of a product. Students also design toy boats and airplanes to explore the design process and product diversity.

Material in the 4 units is presented in 3 formats: readings, investigations, and "connections" sections. The readings explain concepts and ideas underlying the investigations; the investigations, many of which are open-ended, pose a question for students to answer or a problem for them to solve; the connections features, consisting of activities or discussions, allow students to reflect on their work and to make connections between key ideas.

Other text features include "sidelights" and "how to" sections. Sidelights present material such as career descriptions, interesting facts, or historical highlights related to unit topics and themes. Examples include discussions of the limits and diversity of animal senses—such as the poor eyesight of bats and their use of echolocation—or the importance of ergonomics to the design process. "How to" sections explain a particular skill, such as constructing a graph.

Teacher's Edition This wraparound edition includes background information and an overview of each unit, including an overview of the cooperative learning skills emphasized. The guide also provides information on teaching strategies, lesson preparation notes, and materials charts.

Program Resources and Support Materials A combination teacher's guide and resource book offers a 2-week introductory unit for students in cooperative learning. It also includes safety procedures, blackline masters, and other information designed to enhance the teaching of the program. Topics include cooperative learning, learning styles, concept

mapping, assessment strategies, and suggestions for integrating educational technology. A program implementation guide is also available.

Key to Content Standards: 5-8 (see app. C)

UNIFYING CONCEPTS AND PROCESSES: Systems, order, and organization; evidence, models, and explanation; change, constancy, and measurement; form and function.

SCIENCE AS INQUIRY: Abilities necessary to do scientific inquiry; understandings about scientific inquiry.

PHYSICAL SCIENCE: Transfer of energy.

LIFE SCIENCE: Structure and function in living systems; reproduction and heredity; diversity and adaptations of organisms.

SCIENCE AND TECHNOLOGY: Abilities of technological design; understandings about science and technology.

SCIENCE IN PERSONAL AND SOCIAL PERSPECTIVES: Science and technology in society.

HISTORY AND NATURE OF SCIENCE: Science as a human endeavor; nature of science; history of science.

Prices: Student edition (ISBN 0-8403-6678-7), $44.90. Teacher's edition (ISBN 0-8403-6679-5), $89.90. Teacher's resource package, $69.90. Kit, $1,403.90. (Contact publisher/supplier for complete price and ordering information.) ***Publisher/supplier:*** Kendall/Hunt. ***Materials:*** Available locally, or from commercial suppliers.

5.5 **Investigating Patterns of Change.** Middle School Science and Technology series. Developed by Biological Sciences Curriculum Study (BSCS) (Colorado Springs, Colo.). Dubuque, Iowa: Kendall/Hunt, 1994.

Program Overview The Middle School Science and Technology series is a 3-year thematic program that integrates the life, earth, and physical sciences and emphasizes

technology as a process for solving problems. The curriculum includes investigations, simulations, debates, plays, outdoor activities, research projects, and creative-writing projects. The titles of the 3 year-long courses—*Investigating Patterns of Change, Investigating Diversity and Limits,* and *Investigating Systems and Change*—reflect the program's unifying themes. Each course incorporates cooperative learning strategies. Components of the program include the student book, teacher's edition, teacher's resource package, implementation guide, and kit of materials.

Student Edition **Recommended grade level: 6-7. Reading level: early 8.** In *Investigating Patterns of Change,* students learn about a variety of patterns in the natural world and about the relationship between patterns and prediction. The 4 units in the course focus on the following questions: (1) How does my world change? (2) How do we explain patterns of change on earth? (3) How do we adjust to patterns of change? and (4) How can we change patterns?

During the course, students use photographs to search for patterns in nature; they identify factors that can change the patterns in plant growth or in how well a medicine works; and they learn to use patterns to make predictions and to develop scientific explanations. Students also learn how scientists and others have recognized and used patterns to develop explanations of some of the earth's features. They look at the locations of volcanoes and earthquakes and learn about the ages of rocks and the surface features of the ocean floor in order to develop their own explanation for earthquakes and volcanoes. Students learn about patterns that support the theory of plate tectonics, about patterns related to the occurrence of weather, and about patterns such as garbage generation and accumulation associated with the increasing size of human populations.

Examples of investigations include interpreting sales charts from a fast-food company and predicting future sales results, looking at maps to discover patterns on the earth, observing the pattern of air movements in a convection box, testing the wind-resistance of different building shapes, and examining water movement in model landfills to understand how water can move through landfills and become polluted.

Material in the 4 units is presented in 3 formats: readings, investigations, and "connections" sections. The readings explain concepts and ideas underlying the investigations; the investigations, many of which are open-ended, pose a question for students to answer or a problem for them to solve; the connections features, consisting of activities or discussions, allow students to reflect on their work and to make connections between key ideas.

Other text features include "sidelights" and "how to" sections. Sidelights present material such as career descriptions, interesting facts, or historical highlights related to unit topics and themes. Examples include discussions of lodestones and the meaning of the term "in the doldrums." "How to" sections explain a particular skill, such as rounding off numbers or using a balance.

Teacher's Edition This wraparound edition includes background information and an overview of each unit, including an overview of the cooperative learning skills emphasized. The guide also provides teaching strategies, lesson preparation notes, and materials charts.

Program Resources and Support Materials A combination teacher's guide and resource book offers a 2-week introductory unit for students in cooperative learning. It also includes safety procedures, blackline masters, and other information designed to enhance the teaching of the program. Topics include cooperative learning, learning styles, concept mapping, assessment strategies, and suggestions for integrating educational technology. A program implementation guide is also available.

Key to Content Standards: 5-8 (see app. C)

UNIFYING CONCEPTS AND PROCESSES: Systems, order, and organization; evidence, models, and explanation; change, constancy, and measurement; form and function.

SCIENCE AS INQUIRY: Abilities necessary to do scientific inquiry; understandings about scientific inquiry.

EARTH AND SPACE SCIENCE: Structure of the earth system; earth's history; earth in the solar system.

SCIENCE AND TECHNOLOGY: Abilities of technological design; understandings about science and technology.

SCIENCE IN PERSONAL AND SOCIAL PERSPECTIVES: Populations, resources, and environments; natural hazards; risks and benefits; science and technology in society.

HISTORY AND NATURE OF SCIENCE: Science as a human endeavor; nature of science; history of science.

Prices: Student edition (ISBN 0-8403-6676-0), $44.90. Teacher's edition (ISBN 0-8403-6677-9), $89.90. Teacher's resource package, $69.90. Kit, $1,351.90. (Contact publisher/supplier for complete price and ordering information.) ***Publisher/supplier:*** Kendall/Hunt. ***Materials:*** Available locally, or from commercial suppliers.

5.6 Investigating Systems and Change. Middle School Science and Technology series. Developed by Biological Sciences Curriculum Study (BSCS) (Colorado Springs, Colo.). Dubuque, Iowa: Kendall/Hunt, 1994.

Program Overview The Middle School Science and Technology series is a 3-year thematic program that integrates the life, earth, and physical sciences and emphasizes technology as a process for solving problems. The curriculum includes investigations, simulations, debates, plays, outdoor activities, research projects, and creative-writing projects. The titles of the 3 year-long courses—*Investigating Patterns of Change, Investigating Diversity and Limits,* and *Investigating Systems and Change*—reflect the program's unifying themes. Each course incorporates cooperative learning strategies. Components of the program include the student book, teacher's edition, teacher's resource package, implementation guide, and kit of materials.

Student Edition **Recommended grade level: 8+. Reading level: early 11.** During the 4 units in *Investigating Systems and Change*, students focus on the following questions: (1) How much can things change and still remain the same? (2) How do things change? (3) How can we improve our use of energy? and (4) What are the limits to growth? During the course, students learn about systems in and out of balance, including human body processes and how drugs affect those processes. Students are introduced to the theory of evolution as an example of an idea that has changed over time and as a scientific explanation for changes in living organisms. They also learn about the role of technological systems in solving energy problems. Finally, through the study of population systems, students learn about the interrelationships that influence systemwide change.

Examples of activities include investigating chemical balance in the stomach, constructing a scatterplot on the length and width of replicas of fossilized horse teeth to determine how horses have changed over time, designing and constructing a water-heating system, building and using a simple galvanometer as they investigate the benefits and costs of using different energy inputs to generate electricity, and observing the growth of a Daphnia colony.

Material in the 4 units is presented in 3 formats: readings, investigations, and "connections" sections. The readings explain concepts and ideas underlying the investigations; the investigations, many of which are open-ended, pose a question for students to answer or a problem for them to solve; the connections features, consisting of activities or discussions, allow students to reflect on their work and to make connections between key ideas.

Other text features include "sidelights" and "how to" sections. Sidelights present material such as career descriptions, interesting facts, or historical highlights related to unit topics and themes. Examples include discussions of the history of vaccines and ozone depletion. "How to" sections explain a particular skill, such as determining pulse rate or constructing a scatterplot.

Teacher's Edition This wraparound edition includes background information and an overview of each unit, including an overview of the cooperative learning skills emphasized. The guide also provides information on teaching strategies, lesson preparation notes, and materials charts.

Program Resources and Support Materials A combination teacher's guide and resource book offers a 2-week introductory unit for students in cooperative learning. It also includes safety procedures, blackline masters, and other information designed to enhance the teaching of the program. Topics include cooperative learning, learning styles, concept mapping, assessment strategies, and suggestions for integrating educational technology. A program implementation guide is also available.

Key to Content Standards: 5-8 (see app. C)

UNIFYING CONCEPTS AND PROCESSES: Systems, order, and organization; evidence, models, and explanation; change, constancy, and measurement; evolution and equilibrium; form and function.

SCIENCE AS INQUIRY: Abilities necessary to do scientific inquiry; understandings about scientific inquiry.

PHYSICAL SCIENCE: Transfer of energy.

LIFE SCIENCE: Structure and function in living systems; regulation and behavior; populations and ecosystems; diversity and adaptations of organisms.

EARTH AND SPACE SCIENCE: Earth's history.

SCIENCE AND TECHNOLOGY: Abilities of technological design; understandings about science and technology.

SCIENCE IN PERSONAL AND SOCIAL PERSPECTIVES: Personal health; populations, resources, and environments; natural hazards; risks and benefits; science and technology in society.

HISTORY AND NATURE OF SCIENCE: Science as a human endeavor; nature of science; history of science.

Prices: Student edition (ISBN 0-8403-6680-9), $44.90. Teacher's edition (ISBN 0-8403-6681-7), $89.90. Teacher's resource package, $69.90. Kit, $2,495.00. (Contact publisher/supplier for complete price and ordering information.) **Publisher/supplier:** Kendall/Hunt. **Materials:** Available locally, or from commercial suppliers.

5.7 **The Local Environment.** 2nd ed. Francis M. Pottenger III and Donald B. Young. Foundational Approaches in Science Teaching (FAST) series. FAST 1. Honolulu, Hawaii: Curriculum Research and Development Group, 1992.

Program Overview The Foundational Approaches in Science Teaching (FAST) series is an interdisciplinary science program consisting of 3 courses for middle, junior, and senior high school students. Each 1-year course is organized in 3 strands—physical science (chemistry and physics), ecology (biological and earth sciences), and relational study. The ecology and physical science strands, which provide the formal science content, are intended to be presented concurrently by alternating short sequences of investigations from each strand. The relational study strand integrates the sciences, technology, and society. Components of the program include the student book, teacher's guide, several reference booklets for each course, and other optional teacher support materials.

Student Edition Recommended grade level: 7-8. Reading level: late 8. *The Local Environment* is organized in 9 units consisting of 88 lab investigations. In the physical science strand of this textbook, students investigate basic concepts, including mass, volume, and density, as well as the relationships between density and buoyancy. They also investigate the melting, freezing, boiling, and condensing of pure substances and mixtures and use their knowledge of changes of state to identify unknown substances. They invent heat-measuring devices and derive the calorie as a standard unit of heat measurement.

In the ecology strand of the course, students investigate plants, animals, and the physical environment, focusing on interrelationships among them. They learn about plant growth, animal care, the water cycle, soil composition, the atmosphere, weather and climate, field mapping, and population sampling. They investigate the effects of scarification on the germination of seeds, consider the effect of the environment on plant propagation, and build a weather station and analyze the data they collect.

In the relational study strand, students focus on the interrelationships of physical science and ecology by using their knowledge of the environment and of the properties of matter to study air pollution and water resource management issues.

Each lab investigation contains brief background information, directions, and questions to guide student learning. The investigations are designed for small, cooperative groups. An appendix provides information on basic units of metric measurement and directions on how to use measurement devices such as a balance and a graduated cylinder.

Teacher's Guide Keyed to investigations in the student book, this guide contains teaching suggestions, advice on classroom procedures, and detailed discussions of the conceptual and practical progression of the student investigations. It also includes materials and equipment lists, suggested schedules, and other information for using the program.

Program Resources and Support Materials A variety of support materials is available, including 6 student reference booklets—on field mapping, weather instruments, air pollution, plant propagation, animal care, and sampling methods. These booklets describe the use of instruments, suggest experimental designs, outline laboratory techniques, and provide supplemental information

for investigations. A student record book with data tables and space for recording notes and observations is also available.

An instructional guide for teachers explains the philosophy and design of the FAST program and suggests schedules, sequences, and strategies for organizing and managing classes. An evaluation guide includes tests for assessing laboratory skills and understanding of concepts and an inventory of skills and concepts.

Key to Content Standards: 5-8 (see app. C)

UNIFYING CONCEPTS AND PROCESSES: Systems, order, and organization; evidence, models, and explanation; change, constancy, and measurement.
SCIENCE AS INQUIRY: Abilities necessary to do scientific inquiry; understandings about scientific inquiry.
PHYSICAL SCIENCE: Properties and changes of properties in matter; transfer of energy.
LIFE SCIENCE: Structure and function in living systems; regulation and behavior.
EARTH AND SPACE SCIENCE: Structure of the earth system.
SCIENCE AND TECHNOLOGY: Abilities of technological design; understandings about science and technology.
SCIENCE IN PERSONAL AND SOCIAL PERSPECTIVES: Populations, resources, and environments; natural hazards; risks and benefits; science and technology in society.

Prices: Student edition (ISBN 0-937049-67-0), $21.95. Teacher's guide (ISBN 0-937049-68-9), $85.00. (Contact publisher/supplier for complete price and ordering information.)
Publisher/supplier: University of Hawaii at Manoa. ***Materials:*** Available locally, or from commercial suppliers.

5.8 Matter and Energy in the Biosphere. 2nd ed. Francis M. Pottenger III, Donald B. Young, and E. Barbara Klemm. Foundational Approaches in Science Teaching (FAST) series. FAST 2. Honolulu, Hawaii: Curriculum Research and Development Group, 1994.

Program Overview The Foundational Approaches in Science Teaching (FAST) series is an interdisciplinary science program consisting of 3 courses for middle, junior, and senior high school students. Each 1-year course is organized in 3 strands—physical science (chemistry and physics), ecology (biological and earth sciences), and relational study. The ecology and physical science strands, which provide the formal science content, are intended to be presented concurrently by alternating short sequences of investigations from each strand. The relational study strand integrates the sciences, technology, and society. Components of the program include the student book, teacher's guide, several reference booklets for each course, and other optional teacher support materials.

Student Edition **Recommended grade level: 8+. Reading level: middle 8.** *Matter and Energy in the Biosphere* is organized in 8 units consisting of 69 lab investigations and activities designed to teach students about the transfer of matter and energy through ecosystems. In the physical sciences strand of this textbook, students investigate the nature of light and heat, search for evidence of an atomic structure of matter, and explore the kinetic molecular model of matter. In the ecology strand, they investigate the processes of photosynthesis, respiration, and decomposition, and they develop an understanding of the interdependence of all living organisms. In the relational study strand, they engage in decision-making situations that require them to analyze such global problems as shortages of food or of fossil fuel. They also design, create, and maintain a balanced microecosystem and a forced microecosystem, and they measure all inputs and outputs of each system.

Each lab investigation contains brief background information, directions, and questions to guide student learning. The investigations are designed for small, cooperative groups. An appendix provides information on basic units of metric measurement and directions on how to use measurement devices such as a balance and a graduated cylinder.

Teacher's Guide Keyed to investigations in the student book, this guide contains teaching suggestions, advice on classroom procedures, and detailed discussions of the conceptual and practical progression of the student investigations. It also includes materials and equipment lists, suggested schedules, and other information for using the program.

Program Resources and Support Materials A variety of support materials is available, including 6 student reference booklets—on elements and compounds, gases, chromatography, composting, components of biomass, and field productivity. These booklets describe the use of instruments, suggest experimental designs, outline laboratory techniques, and provide additional information.

An instructional guide for teachers explains the philosophy and design of the FAST program and suggests schedules, sequences, and strategies for organizing and managing classes. An evaluation guide includes tests for assessing laboratory skills and

understanding of concepts and an inventory of skills and concepts.

Key to Content Standards: 5-8 (see app. C)

UNIFYING CONCEPTS AND PROCESSES: Systems, order, and organization; evidence, models, and explanation; change, constancy, and measurement.
SCIENCE AS INQUIRY: Abilities necessary to do scientific inquiry; understandings about scientific inquiry.
PHYSICAL SCIENCE: Properties and changes of properties in matter; transfer of energy.
LIFE SCIENCE: Structure and function in living systems; populations and ecosystems.
SCIENCE AND TECHNOLOGY: Abilities of technological design; understandings about science and technology.
SCIENCE IN PERSONAL AND SOCIAL PERSPECTIVES: Populations, resources, and environments; science and technology in society.
HISTORY AND NATURE OF SCIENCE: History of science.

Prices: Student edition (ISBN 0-937049-83-2), $21.95. Teacher's guide (ISBN 0-937049-84-0), $85.00. (Contact publisher/supplier for complete price and ordering information.) *Publisher/supplier:* University of Hawaii at Manoa. *Materials:* Available locally, or from commercial suppliers.

5.9 **Middle Grades Science: A Problem-Solving Approach, Sixth Grade.** Helen M. Parke, Charles R. Coble, and Rita M. Elliott. Middle Grades Science series. Greenville, N.C.: Helen Meriwether Parke, 1996.

Program Overview The Middle Grades Science series is an integrated science program for middle school students (grades 6, 7, and 8). The program uses a "spiral" approach to teaching science content and is designed around an evolving

story line. Each year-long course is based on investigations of a series of questions that focus on scientific concepts and their relationship to the real world. Concepts are drawn from biology, chemistry, earth and space science, and physics. Components of the program include teacher's guides—1 for each grade level, a program handbook, and a technology supplement.

Teacher's Guide Recommended grade level: 6. Reading level: early 7. *Middle Grades Science: A Problem-Solving Approach, Sixth Grade* consists of 5 modules that address the following questions: (1) Where are we in the solar system? (2) How can we tell where we are? (3) How do we interact with our dynamic world? (4) What do we need to survive? and (5) What do we need to do to survive? During the unit, students explore the features and characteristics of the components of our solar system; the relative position and relative motion of the earth with respect to the sun; navigation methods; rocks and soil; properties of air; the composition of the earth's atmosphere; the different forms of water and the location of water on the earth's surface; classification of life forms; and the relationships between populations, communities, and ecosystems.

Among the activities in the module, for example, students make a scale model of the relative sizes of the planets, construct and use a compass, and investigate the relationship between the apparent motion of the sun and shadow movement. They also examine soil samples to determine the composition of soil, design insulators and conductors from different materials, and observe the growth and development of mealworms, pumpkin seeds, and mold.

Investigations in the unit range from hands-on activities to "We-Searches," requiring teams of students to search the literature and the Internet for information. Questions are used throughout the unit to engage students in the investigations, to foster deeper inquiry, or to make connections with other ideas. Also included are suggestions for activities to help students make connections with art, mathematics, social studies, creative writing, and communication skills. Background information for the teacher is presented at the beginning of each lesson. Blackline masters for student handouts and suggestions for homework and student assessment are provided.

Program Resources and Support Materials A teacher's handbook provides an overview of the Middle Grades Science program, an in-depth view of one of the lessons, and information on the alignment of the curriculum content with North Carolina's state science framework, with the National Research Council's National Science Education Standards, and with the Benchmarks of the American Association for the Advancement of Science. A technology supplement provides sample science lessons that incorporate the use of technology; the supplement includes 5 lessons for the sixth-grade course.

Key to Content Standards: 5-8 (see app. C)

UNIFYING CONCEPTS AND PROCESSES: Systems, order, and organization; evidence, models, and explanation; change, constancy, and measurement.
SCIENCE AS INQUIRY: Abilities necessary to do scientific inquiry; understandings about scientific inquiry.
PHYSICAL SCIENCE: Transfer of energy.
LIFE SCIENCE: Structure and function in living systems; populations and ecosystems.
EARTH AND SPACE SCIENCE: Structure of the earth system; earth in the solar system.
SCIENCE AND TECHNOLOGY: Abilities of technological design.

HISTORY AND NATURE OF SCIENCE: Science as a human endeavor; nature of science; history of science.

Prices: Teacher's guide, $40. Handbook, $10. Technology supplement, $30. *Publisher/supplier:* Helen M. Parke. *Materials:* Available locally, or from commercial suppliers.

5.10 Middle Grades Science: A Problem-Solving Approach, Seventh Grade. Helen M. Parke, Charles R. Coble, and Rita M. Elliott. Middle Grades Science series. Greenville, N.C.: Helen Meriwether Parke, 1996.

Program Overview The Middle Grades Science series is an integrated science program for middle school students (grades 6, 7, and 8). The program uses a "spiral" approach to teaching science content and is designed around an evolving story line. Each year-long course is based on investigations of a series of questions that focus on scientific concepts and their relationship to the real world. Concepts are drawn from biology, chemistry, earth and space science, and physics. Components of the program include teacher's guides—1 for each grade level, a program handbook, and a technology supplement.

Teacher's Guide Recommended grade level: 7. Reading level: early 7. *Middle Grades Science: A Problem-Solving Approach, Seventh Grade* consists of 4 modules that address the following questions: (1) What is a system? (2) What causes systems to operate? (3) How are systems connected? and (4) What happens to systems? Topics addressed in the unit include human body systems, the chemical and physical properties of matter, weather, forces and motion, energy transformations, photosynthesis, food as energy, genetics, and the environment.

Among the activities, students compare the automobile "system" to the human body system, determine the density of different metal cubes, and observe chemical reactions. They also collect weather data using weather instruments, they observe the relationship between plant growth and sunlight, and they research different sources and types of pollution.

Investigations in the unit range from hands-on activities to "We-Searches," requiring teams of students to search the literature and the Internet for information. Questions are used throughout the unit to engage students in the investigations, to foster deeper inquiry, or to make connections with other ideas. Also included are suggestions for activities to help students make connections with art, mathematics, social studies, creative writing, and communication skills. Background information for the teacher is presented at the beginning of each lesson. Blackline masters for student handouts and suggestions for homework and student assessment are provided.

Program Resources and Support Materials A teacher's handbook provides an overview of the Middle Grades Science program, an in-depth view of one of the lessons, and information on the alignment of the curriculum content with North Carolina's state science framework, with the National Research Council's National Science Education Standards, and with the Benchmarks of the American Association for the Advancement of Science. A technology supplement provides sample science lessons that incorporate the use of technology; the supplement includes 1 lesson for the seventh-grade course.

Key to Content Standards: 5-8 (see app. C)

UNIFYING CONCEPTS AND PROCESSES: Systems, order, and organization; evidence, models, and explanation; change, constancy, and measurement; form and function.

SCIENCE AS INQUIRY: Abilities necessary to do scientific inquiry; understandings about scientific inquiry.
PHYSICAL SCIENCE: Properties and changes of properties in matter; motions and forces; transfer of energy.
LIFE SCIENCE: Structure and function in living systems; reproduction and heredity; regulation and behavior; populations and ecosystems.
EARTH AND SPACE SCIENCE: Structure of the earth system.
SCIENCE AND TECHNOLOGY: Abilities of technological design; understandings about science and technology.
SCIENCE IN PERSONAL AND SOCIAL PERSPECTIVES: Populations, resources, and environments; natural hazards; risks and benefits; science and technology in society.
HISTORY AND NATURE OF SCIENCE: Science as a human endeavor; nature of science; history of science.

Prices: Teacher's guide, $40. Handbook, $10. Technology supplement, $30. *Publisher/supplier:* Helen M. Parke. *Materials:* Available locally, or from commercial suppliers.

5.11 **Middle Grades Science: A Problem-Solving Approach, Eighth Grade.** Helen M. Parke, Charles R. Coble, and Rita M. Elliott. Middle Grades Science series. Greenville, N.C.: Helen Meriwether Parke, 1996.

Program Overview The Middle Grades Science series is an integrated science program for middle school students (grades 6, 7, and 8). The program uses a "spiral" approach to teaching science content and is designed around an evolving story line. Each year-long course is based on investigations of a series of questions that focus on scientific concepts and their relationship to the real world. Concepts are drawn from biology, chemistry, earth and space science, and physics. Components of the program include teacher's guides—1 for each grade level, a program handbook, and a technology supplement.

Teacher's Guide **Recommended grade level: 8. Reading level: middle 7.** *Middle Grades Science: A Problem-Solving Approach, Eighth Grade* consists of 4 modules that address the following questions: (1) What is the scale of change? (2) How does change occur? (3) What are controlling factors of change? and (4) How do people change their environment? Topics addressed in the unit include geological changes over time, extinction, diversity and natural selection, matter and chemical reactions, energy transformations, electricity and magnetism, and the effect of human choices on changes in the local environment.

Among the activities, students use models to visualize changes in the crust of the earth through continental drift, and they compare limb skeletons of different animals. They also observe chemical reactions, identify materials that act as conductors and insulators of electrical current, and research the environmental impact of road construction.

Investigations in the unit range from hands-on activities to "We-Searches," requiring teams of students to search the literature and the Internet for information. Questions are used throughout the unit to engage students in the investigations, to foster deeper inquiry, or to make connections with other ideas. Also included are suggestions for activities to help students make connections with art, mathematics, social studies, creative writing, and communication skills. Background information for the teacher is presented at the beginning of each lesson. Blackline masters for student handouts and suggestions for homework and student assessment are provided.

Program Resources and Support Materials A teacher's handbook provides an overview of the Middle Grades Science program, an in-depth view of one of the lessons, and information on the alignment of the curriculum content with North Carolina's state science framework, with the National Research Council's National Science Education Standards, and with the Benchmarks of the American Association for the Advancement of Science. A technology supplement provides sample science lessons that incorporate the use of technology; the supplement includes 5 lessons for the eighth-grade course.

Key to Content Standards: 5-8 (see app. C)

UNIFYING CONCEPTS AND PROCESSES: Evidence, models, and explanation; change, constancy, and measurement; evolution and equilibrium.
SCIENCE AS INQUIRY: Abilities necessary to do scientific inquiry; understandings about scientific inquiry.
PHYSICAL SCIENCE: Properties and changes of properties in matter; transfer of energy.
LIFE SCIENCE: Populations and ecosystems; diversity and adaptations of organisms.
EARTH AND SPACE SCIENCE: Structure of the earth system; earth's history.
SCIENCE AND TECHNOLOGY: Abilities of technological design; understandings about science and technology.
SCIENCE IN PERSONAL AND SOCIAL PERSPECTIVES: Populations, resources, and environments; natural hazards; risks and benefits.
HISTORY AND NATURE OF SCIENCE: Science as a human endeavor; nature of science.

Prices: Teacher's guide, $40. Handbook, $10. Technology supplement, $30. *Publisher/supplier:* Helen M. Parke. *Materials:* Available locally, or from commercial suppliers.

5.12 Models and Designs. Full Option Science System (FOSS) series. Developed by Lawrence Hall of Science (Berkeley, Calif.). Hudson, N.H.: Delta Education, 1992.

Program Overview The Full Option Science System (FOSS) program is a K-6 science curriculum consisting of 27 stand-alone modules. The 8 modules for grades 5-6 are organized under topics in the life, physical, and earth sciences and in scientific reasoning and technology. They can be used in any order. The FOSS program is designed to engage students in scientific concepts through multisensory, hands-on laboratory activities. All modules of the program incorporate 5 unifying themes—(1) pattern, (2) structure, (3) interaction, (4) change, and (5) system. The components of a FOSS module are a teacher's guide and a kit of materials.

Teacher's Guide **Recommended grade level: 5-6.** The *Models and Designs* module provides students with experiences that develop the concept of a scientific model and engage them in the processes of design and construction. Students work in cooperative groups to create solutions to a variety of real-world problems as they consider the relationship of structure to function. They use their senses to investigate sealed black boxes, and then they develop conceptual models of the boxes' contents and construct physical models to test their ideas. Students engineer a model that replicates the behavior of another model—a fanciful device called a hum dinger. They construct a self-propelled cart of their own design and modify the cart to perform specific tricks.

Models and Designs consists of 4 activities, requiring about 12 class sessions to complete. The teacher's guide includes a module overview, the 4 individual activity folios, dupli-

cation masters (in English and Spanish) for student sheets, and an annotated bibliography.

This module includes science background information, detailed instructions on planning for and conducting each activity, an extensive assessment component, and extensions for integration and enrichment.

Key to Content Standards: 5-8 (see app. C)

UNIFYING CONCEPTS AND PROCESSES: Systems, order, and organization; evidence, models, and explanation; form and function.
SCIENCE AS INQUIRY: Abilities necessary to do scientific inquiry; understandings about scientific inquiry.
SCIENCE AND TECHNOLOGY: Abilities of technological design; understandings about science and technology.
HISTORY AND NATURE OF SCIENCE: Nature of science.

Prices: Teacher's guide (ISBN 0-7826-0075-1), $101. Complete kit, $495. *Publisher/supplier:* Delta Education. *Materials:* Available locally, from commercial suppliers, or in kit.

5.13 The Nature of Science. 3rd ed. Anthea Maton, Jean Hopkins, Susan Johnson, and others. Prentice Hall Science Integrated Learning System series. Upper Saddle River, N.J.: Prentice Hall, 1997.

Program Overview The Prentice Hall Science Integrated Learning System series is a program for middle school or junior high school students. Designed to cover all relevant areas of science, this program consists of 19 books, each in a particular topic area, such as the nature of science, sound and light, and the planet earth. Seven science themes are incorporated into the program; the themes are energy, evolution, patterns of change, scale and struc-

ture, systems and interactions, unity and diversity, and stability. For each unit, teaching materials, ancillary student materials, and some optional components are available.

Student Edition **Recommended grade level: 7-8. Reading level: middle 7.** *The Nature of Science*, which helps students develop the attitudes and skills necessary for the study of science, is organized in 3 chapters: (1) "What Is Science?," (2) "Measurement and the Sciences," and (3) "Tools and the Sciences." During the course, students use the scientific method of problem solving. They become familiar with the basic rules of lab safety. They learn how to make measurements using the metric system and are introduced to the metric units for length, mass, volume, and temperature and to the tools (such as the metric ruler, triple-beam balance, and Celsius thermometer) for making measurements in those units. Students also learn about the different kinds of microscopes, telescopes, and other scientific instruments that scientists use.

Each chapter includes a lab investigation. Students explore variables that affect the growth of bread mold. They compare measurements of the same objects to discover the uncertainty of measurements. They construct and use a refracting telescope.

Each chapter contains comprehensive reading sections that introduce science methods and skills. Suggestions are provided for activities in which students "find out by doing," "find out by reading," and "find out by writing." Other activities are also suggested—for example, finding out if salt affects plant growth, or creating a measurement system using classroom objects as standards.

Other features include problem-solving challenges, science career descriptions, and science connections to real-world events or issues.

The student edition closes with readings on 3 topics: (1) physicist Stephen Hawking's search for a link between the quantum theory and the force of gravity, (2) efforts to regulate the whaling industry, and (3) a fictional account of space mining.

Teacher's Edition In the teacher's wraparound edition, each chapter begins with a 2-page planning guide and a 2-page preview that summarizes each section within the chapter. The teacher's edition also provides suggestions for teaching, guiding, integrating, and closing lessons, as well as enrichments, extensions, and answers to questions in the student text.

Supplementary Laboratory Manual The supplementary lab manual provides 8 investigations directly correlated with the information presented in the student textbook. Examples of investigations include forming a hypothesis about whether seeds need water to grow, testing the hypothesis, and drawing a conclusion based on the observations; learning how to measure the volume and temperature of a liquid accurately; and observing objects under a microscope.

Program Resources and Support Materials A variety of materials, including some optional components, is available. A teacher's resource package contains the student edition and annotated teacher's editions of both the textbook and the lab manual, as well as a test book, an activity book, a review-and-reinforcement guide, and English and Spanish audiotapes for auditory and language learners. Other available materials include interactive videodiscs, transparencies, assessment materials, English and Spanish guides for language learners, a study guide, a teacher's desk reference,

and a booklet of product-testing activities.

Key to Content Standards: 5-8 (see app. C)

UNIFYING CONCEPTS AND PROCESSES: Evidence, models, and explanation; change, constancy, and measurement. **SCIENCE AS INQUIRY:** Abilities necessary to do scientific inquiry; understandings about scientific inquiry. **SCIENCE AND TECHNOLOGY:** Understandings about science and technology. **SCIENCE IN PERSONAL AND SOCIAL PERSPECTIVES:** Science and technology in society. **HISTORY AND NATURE OF SCIENCE:** Science as a human endeavor; nature of science.

Prices: Student edition (ISBN 0-13-418708-3), $9.97. Teacher's edition (ISBN 0-13-423260-7), $22.97. Teacher's resource package, $112.97. (Contact publisher/supplier for complete price and ordering information.) ***Publisher/supplier:*** Prentice Hall. ***Materials:*** Available locally, or from commercial suppliers.

5.14 **Prime Science: Level A.** Prime Science Education Group. Prime Science series. Dubuque, Iowa: Kendall/Hunt, 1998.

Program Overview The Prime Science series is an interdisciplinary science program for middle and high school students. It consists of 5 textbooks (Levels A, B, and C for grades 6, 7, and 8, respectively, and Levels 1 and 2 for grades 9 and 10). The program uses a "spiral" approach to teaching science content and skills. Concepts from biology, chemistry, earth and space science, and physics, as well as the applications of science, are incorporated throughout the program. Science topics are introduced in personal and social contexts—for example, ideas about speed and motion are presented in the context of travel and road safety.

Each course consists of a student textbook, a teacher's guide, and a test bank on a diskette.

Student Textbook **Recommended grade level: 6. Reading level: middle 6.** *Prime Science: Level A* is organized in 8 chapters that cover a wide range of topics: phase changes of matter; insulators and conductors; the structure of plant and animal cells; how individual animals and plants vary; the growth of trees and the production of paper; the moon, satellites, and space travel; personal hygiene and appearance; electricity, computers, and electronics; and human growth and development. The amount of time devoted to individual topics varies widely, depending on the difficulty of the concepts being presented.

Each chapter begins with an introductory page, which sets the context for the chapter. The bulk of each chapter consists of activity pages. Examples of activities include using litmus paper to test soil acidity, testing the effectiveness of a solvent, comparing rotten wood with wood that has not been attacked by fungi, observing and recording the phases of the moon, assembling simple circuits and drawing conventional diagrams to represent them, and experimenting to find out how shampoo works. Suggestions are given at the end of each unit for further activities, discussions, or reports. An "in brief" section at the end of each chapter provides a summary of the key ideas developed in the chapter. A "things to do" section provides additional ideas for extension activities.

Teacher's Guide The teacher's guide provides detailed guidelines and suggestions for lab work, demonstrations, and writing activities. It also provides chapter overviews, lesson notes, materials lists, safety requirements, blackline masters for student work, answers to student textbook questions, and sample assessment items with answers. A test bank is available on diskette.

Key to Content Standards: 5-8 (see app. C)

UNIFYING CONCEPTS AND PROCESSES: Systems, order, and organization; evidence, models, and explanation; change, constancy, and measurement; form and function.
SCIENCE AS INQUIRY: Abilities necessary to do scientific inquiry; understandings about scientific inquiry.
PHYSICAL SCIENCE: Properties and changes of properties in matter; transfer of energy.
LIFE SCIENCE: Structure and function in living systems; reproduction and heredity; regulation and behavior.
EARTH AND SPACE SCIENCE: Structure of the earth system; earth in the solar system.
SCIENCE AND TECHNOLOGY: Abilities of technological design; understandings about science and technology.
SCIENCE IN PERSONAL AND SOCIAL PERSPECTIVES: Personal health; populations, resources, and environments; natural hazards; risks and benefits; science and technology in society.
HISTORY AND NATURE OF SCIENCE: Science as a human endeavor; nature of science.

Prices: Student textbook (ISBN 0-7872-0357-2), $24.90. Teacher's guide (ISBN 0-7872-0358-0), $99.90. *Publisher/supplier:* Kendall/Hunt. *Materials:* Available locally, or from commercial suppliers.

5.15 Prime Science: Level B. Prime Science Education Group. Prime Science series. Dubuque, Iowa: Kendall/Hunt, 1998.

Program Overview The Prime Science series is an interdisciplinary science program for middle and high school students. It consists of 5 textbooks (Levels A, B, and C for grades 6, 7, and 8, respectively, and Levels 1 and 2 for grades 9 and 10). The program uses a "spiral" approach to teaching science content and skills. Concepts from biology, chemistry, earth and space science, and physics, as well as the applications of science, are incorporated throughout the program. Science topics are introduced in personal and social contexts—for example, ideas about speed and motion are presented in the context of travel and road safety. Each course consists of a student textbook, a teacher's guide, and a test bank on a diskette.

Student Textbook **Recommended grade level: 7. Reading level: middle 6.** *Prime Science: Level B* is organized in 9 chapters that cover a wide range of topics: light, mirrors, and lenses; fruits and vegetables and where they come from; the chemistry of combustion; storing and transferring energy; soil, rocks, and minerals; human health; sound; plant growth; and fabrics. The amount of time devoted to individual topics varies widely, depending on the difficulty of the concepts being presented.

Each chapter begins with an introductory page, which sets the context for the chapter. The bulk of each chapter consists of activity pages. Examples of activities include recording light meter readings at different distances from a bulb, examining flowers and pollen grains under a microscope, exploring the use of binary codes to produce music or control a car, studying the effect of heat on different materials, drawing energy flow diagrams for moving toys, observing the different types of particles present in a soil sample, and investigating the effectiveness of aspirin for prolonging the freshness of cut flowers. An "in brief" section at the end of each chapter provides a summary of the key ideas developed in the chapter. A "things to do" section provides additional ideas for extension activities.

Teacher's Guide The teacher's guide provides detailed guidelines and suggestions for lab work, demonstrations, and writing activities. It also provides chapter overviews, lesson notes, materials lists, safety requirements, blackline masters for student work, answers to student textbook questions, and sample assessment items with answers. A test bank is available on diskette.

Key to Content Standards: 5-8 (see app. C)

UNIFYING CONCEPTS AND PROCESSES: Evidence, models, and explanation; change, constancy, and measurement; form and function.
SCIENCE AS INQUIRY: Abilities necessary to do scientific inquiry; understandings about scientific inquiry.
PHYSICAL SCIENCE: Properties and changes of properties in matter; motions and forces; transfer of energy.
LIFE SCIENCE: Structure and function in living systems; reproduction and heredity; regulation and behavior; populations and ecosystems.
EARTH AND SPACE SCIENCE: Structure of the earth system; earth in the solar system.
SCIENCE AND TECHNOLOGY: Abilities of technological design; understandings about science and technology.
SCIENCE IN PERSONAL AND SOCIAL PERSPECTIVES: Personal health; populations, resources, and environments; risks and benefits; science and technology in society.
HISTORY AND NATURE OF SCIENCE: Science as a human endeavor, history of science.

Prices: Student textbook (ISBN 0-7872-0359-9), $24.90. Teacher's guide (ISBN 0-7872-0360-2), $99.90. *Publisher/supplier:* Kendall/Hunt. *Materials:* Available locally, or from commercial suppliers.

5.16 Prime Science: Level C.
Prime Science Education Group.
Prime Science series. Dubuque,
Iowa: Kendall/Hunt, 1998.

Program Overview The Prime
Science series is an interdisciplinary
science program for middle and high
school students. It consists of 5 textbooks (Levels A, B, and C for grades
6, 7, and 8, respectively, and Levels
1 and 2 for grades 9 and 10). The
program uses a "spiral" approach to
teaching science content and skills.
Concepts from biology, chemistry,
earth and space science, and physics, as well as the applications of
science, are incorporated throughout
the program. Science topics are
introduced in personal and social
contexts—for example, ideas about
speed and motion are presented in
the context of travel and road safety.
Each course consists of a student
textbook, a teacher's guide, and a
test bank on a diskette.

Student Textbook **Recommended grade
level: 8. Reading level: middle 7.** *Prime
Science: Level C* is organized in 10
chapters that cover a wide range of
topics: plants and plant growth, food
chains and food webs, forces, simple
machines, water and the water cycle,
earth and the solar system, color and
light, lenses and mirrors, food, speed
and motion, human growth and
development, properties and uses of
materials, electricity, electromagnets, weather, and pollution.

Each chapter begins with an introductory page, which sets the context
for the chapter. The bulk of each
chapter consists of activity pages.
Examples of activities include investigating how changes in conditions—
such as light—influence the rate of
photosynthesis; making and testing
reinforced beams; making and testing a model backhoe; investigating
the properties of carbonated water;

exploring the refraction of light by
prisms; testing foods for the presence
of starch, sugar, fats, or protein;
investigating the relationship between
speed and braking distance for a
model car; designing an educational
campaign about AIDS; and comparing the physical properties of metals,
ceramics, plastics, and woods. An
"in brief" section at the end of each
chapter provides a summary of the
key ideas developed in the chapter.
A "things to do" section provides
additional ideas for extension
activities.

Teacher's Guide The teacher's
guide provides detailed guidelines
and suggestions for lab work, demonstrations, and writing activities. It
also provides chapter overviews,
lesson notes, materials lists, safety
requirements, blackline masters for
student work, answers to student
textbook questions, and sample
assessment items with answers. A
test bank is available on diskette.

*Key to Content Standards: 5-8
(see app. C)*

UNIFYING CONCEPTS AND PROCESSES:
Systems, order, and organization;
evidence, models, and explanation;
change, constancy, and measurement; form and function.
SCIENCE AS INQUIRY: Abilities necessary
to do scientific inquiry; understandings about scientific inquiry.
PHYSICAL SCIENCE: Properties and
changes of properties in matter;
motions and forces; transfer of
energy.
LIFE SCIENCE: Structure and function
in living organisms; reproduction
and heredity; populations and
ecosystems.
EARTH AND SPACE SCIENCE: Structure of
the earth system; earth in the solar
system.
SCIENCE AND TECHNOLOGY: Abilities of
technological design; understandings
about science and technology.

**SCIENCE IN PERSONAL AND SOCIAL PER-
SPECTIVES:** Personal health; natural
hazards; risks and benefits; science
and technology in society.
HISTORY AND NATURE OF SCIENCE:
History of science.

Prices: Student textbook (ISBN 0-
7872-0361-0), $29.90. Teacher's
guide (ISBN 0-7872-0362-9), $99.90.
Publisher/supplier: Kendall/Hunt.
Materials: Available locally, or from
commercial suppliers.

5.17 Science Interactions: Course 1.
Bill Aldridge, Russell Aiuto, Jack
Ballinger, and others. Science Interactions series. New York, N.Y.: Glen-
coe/McGraw-Hill, 1995.

Program Overview The Science
Interactions series is a complete
program for middle or junior high
school students, consisting of 3 textbooks—*Course 1, Course 2,* and
Course 3. This integrated program is
based on the premise that many
areas of science depend on the fundamentals of physics and chemistry.
During the 3-year program, each
course first introduces basic concepts of physics and chemistry, followed by related topics in life and
earth sciences and further topics in
physics and chemistry. Each course
also incorporates 4 science themes—
energy, systems and interactions,
scale and structure, and stability and
change. In addition, connections are
made among the sciences and with
other subjects such as art and literature. Extensive sets of materials and
resources, including some optional
components, are available.

Student Edition **Recommended grade
level: 6-7. Reading level: middle 6.** *Science Interactions: Course 1* is organized in 5 units: (1) "Observing the
World around You," (2) "Interactions

in the Physical World," (3) "Interactions in the Living World," (4) "Changing Systems," and (5) "Wave Motion." During the course, students use sight and hearing to observe patterns and landforms on earth and in the sky. They identify and classify substances by their physical and chemical properties. They gain an appreciation of the similarities and differences among living organisms. Students also investigate motion and learn how the motion of water, wind, and ice changes the physical appearance of the earth and how it can change the overall ecology of the planet. They study waves, earthquakes, volcanoes, and the interactions between earth and the moon.

Examples of the lab investigations that students conduct during *Course 1* are these: observing how colored lights and pigments affect what we see, determining how the length of an air column affects pitch, investigating the solubility of table sugar in water at different temperatures, determining the effect of water on the speed of seed germination, conducting an experiment to examine factors that affect the period of a pendulum, and plotting the location of active volcanoes and earthquakes.

Each of the 19 chapters in *Course 1* contains a variety of brief reading sections, charts, tables, and graphics. These are interwoven with "explore" activities to introduce students to new concepts; "find out" activities that require students to explore concepts in greater depth and to collect and analyze data; and longer "investigate" activities that encourage students to form hypotheses, manipulate variables, and collect quantitative data. The activities offer a combination of open-ended and structured hands-on experiences.

Special end-of-unit reading shorts feature explanations of how everyday items work; highlight teens in science; and provide science connec-

tions to society, technology, art, history, geography, literature, and other subjects.

Teacher's Edition The wraparound teacher's edition provides information on the conceptual and thematic development of each lesson; includes strategies to motivate, teach, assess, extend, and close each lesson; and provides multicultural perspectives, chapter organizers, ideas for student journal activities, and suggestions for student portfolios.

Supplementary Laboratory Manual The supplementary lab manual provides 39 additional investigations—complete with set-up diagrams, data tables, and space for student responses—directly correlated with the information presented in the student textbook. For example, students construct a sextant and determine approximate latitude in degrees. They also discover what happens when they shine a light through 2 prisms; dissect a preserved cow eye; and investigate the effect of particle size, temperature, and stirring on the dissolving rate of a solute.

In other investigations, students identify acids and bases, observe differences between cyanobacteria and bacteria, and build a condition chamber for pillbugs to determine what environmental conditions pillbugs prefer. They also measure and analyze the flight times of a projectile, graph data on tides and predict future changes in sea level, and compare the velocities of points at different locations on earth as the earth rotates. Extension activities are included with each lab.

Program Resources and Support Materials A full range of resource materials is available, including science discovery activities, activity masters, home activities, a study guide, concept maps for each chap-

ter, critical-thinking and problem-solving exercises, multicultural activities, assessments, color transparencies, Spanish-language resources, and videodisc programs.

Key to Content Standards: 5-8 (see app. C)

UNIFYING CONCEPTS AND PROCESSES: Systems, order, and organization; evidence, models, and explanation; change, constancy, and measurement; evolution and equilibrium; form and function.

SCIENCE AS INQUIRY: Abilities necessary to do scientific inquiry; understandings about scientific inquiry.

PHYSICAL SCIENCE: Properties and changes of properties in matter; motions and forces; transfer of energy.

LIFE SCIENCE: Structure and function in living systems; reproduction and heredity; regulation and behavior; populations and ecosystems; diversity and adaptations of organisms.

EARTH AND SPACE SCIENCE: Structure of the earth system; earth's history; earth in the solar system.

SCIENCE AND TECHNOLOGY: Abilities of technological design; understandings about science and technology.

SCIENCE IN PERSONAL AND SOCIAL PERSPECTIVES: Populations, resources, and environments; natural hazards; risks and benefits; science and technology in society.

HISTORY AND NATURE OF SCIENCE: Science as a human endeavor; nature of science; history of science.

Prices: Student edition (ISBN 0-02-826752-4), $43.45. Teacher's edition (ISBN 0-02-826753-2), $55.62. Teaching resources package, $286.61. (Contact publisher/supplier for complete price and ordering information.) ***Publisher/supplier:*** Glencoe/McGraw-Hill. ***Materials:*** Available locally, or from commercial suppliers.

5.18 Science Interactions: Course 2. Bill Aldridge, Russell Aiuto, Jack Ballinger, and others. Science Interactions series. New York, N.Y.: Glencoe/McGraw-Hill, 1995.

Program Overview The Science Interactions series is a complete program for middle or junior high school students, consisting of 3 textbooks—*Course 1, Course 2,* and *Course 3.* This integrated program is based on the premise that many areas of science depend on the fundamentals of physics and chemistry. During the 3-year program, each course first introduces basic concepts of physics and chemistry, followed by related topics in life and earth sciences and further topics in physics and chemistry. Each course also incorporates 4 science themes— energy, systems and interactions, scale and structure, and stability and change. In addition, connections are made among the sciences and with other subjects such as art and literature. Extensive sets of materials and resources, including some optional components, are available.

Student Edition **Recommended grade level: 7-8. Reading level: early 9.** *Science Interactions: Course 2* is organized in 5 units: (1) "Forces in Action," (2) "Energy at Work," (3) "Earth Materials and Resources," (4) "Air: Molecules in Motion," and (5) "Life at the Cellular Level." During the course, students explore the physical forces that act on moving objects, they learn about the forces that cause earthquakes and volcanoes, and they learn about the forces that cause blood to flow within the blood vessels. Students also learn to compare and contrast metallic and nonmetallic materials, and they learn about the special properties of some minerals. They observe how gases are affected by temperature and pressure as they study gases, atoms, and molecules. They learn about the

structures of different cells and the functions of the structures, and they learn about the basic chemical reactions that occur in cells and why these reactions are essential to life.

Examples of the lab investigations that students conduct during the 5 units are these: predicting and experimentally verifying the effect of mass on acceleration; measuring and comparing an earthworm's pulse with a human pulse; designing an experiment to test reaction time; identifying minerals using different methods; and designing an experiment to observe the effect of exercise on the amount of carbon dioxide exhaled by the lungs.

Each of the 19 chapters in *Course 2* contains a variety of brief reading sections, charts, tables, and graphics. These are interwoven with "explore" activities to introduce students to new concepts; "find out" activities that require students to explore concepts in greater depth and to collect and analyze data; and longer "investigate" activities that encourage students to form hypotheses, manipulate variables, and collect quantitative data. The activities offer a combination of open-ended and structured hands-on experiences.

Special end-of-unit reading shorts feature explanations of how everyday items work; highlight teens in science; and provide science connections to society, technology, art, history, geography, literature, and other subjects.

Teacher's Edition The wraparound teacher's edition provides information on the conceptual and thematic development of each lesson; includes strategies to motivate, teach, assess, extend, and close each lesson; and provides multicultural perspectives, chapter organizers, ideas for student journal activities, and suggestions for student portfolios.

Supplementary Laboratory Manual The supplementary lab manual provides 37 additional investigations— complete with set-up diagrams, data tables, and space for student responses—directly correlated with the information presented in the student textbook. For example, students determine the densities of freshwater, brine, and an egg; they use information from 5 seismograph stations to compute the location of an earthquake's epicenter; and they compare the properties of a single fixed pulley and a block and tackle. They also test foods for protein, construct a wave tank to simulate the action of waves on shorelines, construct a small solar water heater, and build and use a simple device to measure wind speed. Extension activities are included with each lab.

Program Resources and Support Materials A full range of resource materials is available, including science discovery activities, activity masters, home activities, a study guide, concept maps for each chapter, critical-thinking and problem-solving exercises, multicultural activities, assessments, color transparencies, Spanish-language resources, and videodisc programs.

Key to Content Standards: 5-8 (see app. C)

UNIFYING CONCEPTS AND PROCESSES: Systems, order, and organization; evidence, models, and explanation; change, constancy, and measurement; evolution and equilibrium; form and function.

SCIENCE AS INQUIRY: Abilities necessary to do scientific inquiry; understandings about scientific inquiry.

PHYSICAL SCIENCE: Properties and changes of properties in matter; motions and forces; transfer of energy.

LIFE SCIENCE: Structure and function in living systems.

EARTH AND SPACE SCIENCE: Structure of the earth system; earth's history.
SCIENCE AND TECHNOLOGY: Abilities of technological design; understandings about science and technology.
SCIENCE IN PERSONAL AND SOCIAL PERSPECTIVES: Populations, resources, and environments; natural hazards; risks and benefits; science and technology in society.
HISTORY AND NATURE OF SCIENCE: Science as a human endeavor; nature of science; history of science.

Prices: Student edition (ISBN 0-02-826804-0), $43.45. Teacher's edition (ISBN 0-02-826805-9), $55.62. Teaching resources package, $286.61. (Contact publisher/supplier for complete price and ordering information.) *Publisher/supplier:* Glencoe/McGraw-Hill. *Materials:* Available locally, or from commercial suppliers.

5.19 Science Interactions: Course 3. Bill Aldridge, Russell Aiuto, Jack Ballinger, and others. Science Interactions series. New York, N.Y.: Glencoe/McGraw-Hill, 1995.

Program Overview The Science Interactions series is a complete program for middle or junior high school students, consisting of 3 textbooks—*Course 1, Course 2,* and *Course 3.* This integrated program is based on the premise that many areas of science depend on the fundamentals of physics and chemistry. During the 3-year program, each course first introduces basic concepts of physics and chemistry, followed by related topics in life and earth sciences and further topics in physics and chemistry. Each course also incorporates 4 science themes— energy, systems and interactions, scale and structure, and stability and change. In addition, connections are made among the sciences and with other subjects such as art and literature. Extensive sets of materials and resources, including some optional components, are available.

Student Edition **Recommended grade level: 8+. Reading level: middle 9.** *Science Interactions: Course 3* is organized in 5 units: (1) "Electricity and Magnetism," (2) "Atoms and Molecules," (3) "Our Fluid Environment," (4) "Changes in Life and Earth over Time," and (5) "Observing the World around You." During the course, students learn about electricity, magnetism, and electromagnetic waves; they become familiar with the basic structure of matter and its behavior; they learn how the movement of molecules is related to the overall movement of air and water in earth's atmosphere and oceans; and they study about the movement of blood in the human body. Students also learn about the movements of continents and the forces that cause those movements, the fossil record, and the concept of evolution. They learn about fission and fusion reactions and about changes in the solar system and the universe over time.

Examples of the lab activities that students conduct are these: experimenting to determine some of the factors that affect the strength of an electromagnet, and demonstrating the thermal expansion of a solid. Students also make a psychrometer to measure relative humidity, conduct tests to discover if lipids or carbohydrates are present in foods, and model magnetic data to support the hypothesis of seafloor spreading. They also construct a geologic time scale, and they measure the movement of sunspots to estimate the sun's period of rotation.

Each of the 20 chapters in *Course 3* contains a variety of brief reading sections, charts, tables, and graphics. These are interwoven with "explore" activities to introduce students to new concepts; "find out" activities that require students to explore concepts in greater depth and to collect and analyze data; and longer

"investigate" activities that encourage students to form hypotheses, manipulate variables, and collect quantitative data. The activities offer a combination of open-ended and structured hands-on experiences.

Special end-of-unit reading shorts feature explanations of how everyday items work; highlight teens in science; and provide science connections to society, technology, art, history, geography, literature, and other subjects.

Teacher's Edition The wraparound teacher's edition provides information on the conceptual and thematic development of each lesson; includes strategies to motivate, teach, assess, extend, and close each lesson; and provides multicultural perspectives, chapter organizers, ideas for student journal activities, and suggestions for student portfolios.

Supplementary Laboratory Manual The supplementary lab manual provides 41 additional investigations— complete with set-up diagrams, data tables, and space for student responses—directly correlated with the information presented in the student textbook. For example, students construct wet cells and electromagnets; they observe chemical reactions between metals and solutions containing ions of metals and then rank the metals by their activities; and they determine the relationship between reaction rate and temperature for the decomposition of sodium hypochlorite. Students also observe and record weather associated with various types of clouds, determine the relative amounts of vitamin C in different types of orange juice, and examine and compare genetic traits such as the shape of ear lobes. They also build an astronomical telescope, and they photograph the North Star in a time exposure and determine how many degrees the earth rotated during the time exposure. Extension activities are included with each lab.

Program Resources and Support Materials A full range of resource materials is available, including science discovery activities, activity masters, home activities, a study guide, concept maps for each chapter, critical-thinking and problem-solving exercises, multicultural activities, assessments, color transparencies, Spanish-language resources, and videodisc programs.

Key to Content Standards: 5-8 (see app. C)

UNIFYING CONCEPTS AND PROCESSES: Systems, order, and organization; evidence, models, and explanation; change, constancy, and measurement; evolution and equilibrium; form and function.
SCIENCE AS INQUIRY: Abilities necessary to do scientific inquiry; understandings about scientific inquiry.
PHYSICAL SCIENCE: Properties and changes of properties in matter; motions and forces; transfer of energy.
LIFE SCIENCE: Structure and function in living systems; reproduction and heredity; regulation and behavior; diversity and adaptations of organisms.
EARTH AND SPACE SCIENCE: Structure of the earth system; earth's history; earth in the solar system.
SCIENCE AND TECHNOLOGY: Understandings about science and technology.
SCIENCE IN PERSONAL AND SOCIAL PERSPECTIVES: Risks and benefits; science and technology in society.
HISTORY AND NATURE OF SCIENCE: Science as a human endeavor; nature of science; history of science.

Prices: Student edition (ISBN 0-02-826856-3), $43.45. Teacher's edition (ISBN 0-02-826857-1), $55.62. Teaching resources package, $286.61. (Contact publisher/supplier for complete price and ordering information.) ***Publisher/supplier:*** Glencoe/McGraw-Hill. ***Materials:*** Available locally, or from commercial suppliers.

5.20 **SciencePlus Technology and Society: Level Green.** Earl S. Morrison, Alan Moore, Nan Armour, and others. SciencePlus Technology and Society series. Austin, Tex.: Holt, Rinehart and Winston, 1997.

Program Overview The SciencePlus Technology and Society series consists of 3 year-long courses for middle school students. Each of the 3 textbooks—designated Level Green, Level Red, and Level Blue—integrates the life, earth, and physical sciences and incorporates the program's 5 science themes: energy, systems, structures, changes over time, and cycles. Cross-disciplinary connections are emphasized, and the impacts of scientific, technological, and science-related social issues are explored. For each course, an extensive set of materials and resources, including some optional components, is available for students and teachers.

Student Edition **Recommended grade level: 6-7. Reading level: late 8.** *SciencePlus Technology and Society: Level Green* is organized in 8 units: (1) "Science and Technology," (2) "Patterns of Living Things," (3) "It's a Small World," (4) "Investigating Matter," (5) "Chemical Changes," (6) "Energy and You," (7) "Temperature and Heat," and (8) "Our Changing Earth."

The course addresses the following topics: (1) Students learn about the nature of science and what scientists do. (2) They explore the characteristics of living things. (3) They learn about microorganisms and the relationships that exist between people and microorganisms. (4) They discuss matter and its properties. (5) They learn about the chemical nature of substances they encounter in everyday life. (6) They explore the concept of energy and its different forms. (7) They investigate the difference between heat and tempera-

ture. (8) They study how weathering, erosion, and deposition shape the surface of the earth.

Sample lab activities in this textbook include using a microscope to examine onion skin cells and human cheek cells; culturing microorganisms in the classroom, and then examining them under a microscope; and making compost. Students also construct a working thermometer, learn how to handle chemicals safely, observe chemical reactions, and make an acid-base indicator from cabbage leaves. In other activities, they construct a galvanometer, measure rates of energy consumption, test insulating materials, and create a model of tectonic plate movement by convection currents.

The 8 units in *Level Green* contain a total of 26 chapters. Each chapter consists of 2 to 5 lessons on closely related subject matter. At the beginning of each chapter, students describe what they already know about a subject by writing or drawing in a "ScienceLog." Then, through a variety of hands-on activities called "explorations," they observe scientific principles in action and test their misconceptions about specific science concepts. Reading sections on science concepts are interwoven with the activities.

Review sections are included at the end of each chapter and each unit. Special end-of-unit reading sections make connections among science, technology, society, and the arts. Other unit shorts are "weird science"—explanations of unusual creatures or phenomena—and stories about the lives and work of scientists.

The student edition is available with or without the "SourceBook," an in-text science reference that provides additional information which reinforces and extends each unit. Because it is not designed for hands-on exploration, the "SourceBook" lends itself to reading at home or outside the classroom.

Teacher's Edition The wraparound teacher's edition includes a 6-page introductory section for each unit. These sections and the wraparound margins contain information on applying unit themes, using program videodiscs, and managing the program. Planning charts provide suggestions for organizing content, materials, activities, and program resources. Also included are homework options; an assessment planning guide; a resources section; suggestions for creating customized instructional programs; and teaching strategies, exercises, and multicultural extensions.

Program Resource and Support Materials A variety of support materials is available, including 8 teaching resource booklets (1 for each unit) with reproducible worksheets and assessment materials and the student "SourceBook." Other support materials include transparencies; a materials guide; instructions, barcodes, and worksheets for using *Science Discovery,* a videodisc program; audiocassette tapes in English and Spanish for each unit; assessment checklists and rubrics; and a list of test items (test generator software is also available).

Key to Content Standards: 5-8 (see app. C)

UNIFYING CONCEPTS AND PROCESSES: Systems, order, and organization; evidence, models, and explanation; change, constancy, and measurement; form and function.
SCIENCE AS INQUIRY: Abilities necessary to do scientific inquiry; understandings about scientific inquiry.
PHYSICAL SCIENCE: Properties and changes of properties in matter; transfer of energy.
LIFE SCIENCE: Structure and function in living systems; reproduction and heredity; regulation and behavior; diversity and adaptations of organisms.

EARTH AND SPACE SCIENCE: Structure of the earth system; earth's history.
SCIENCE AND TECHNOLOGY: Abilities of technological design; understandings about science and technology.
SCIENCE IN PERSONAL AND SOCIAL PERSPECTIVES: Personal health; risks and benefits; science and technology in society.
HISTORY AND NATURE OF SCIENCE: Science as a human endeavor; nature of science; history of science.

Prices: Student edition (ISBN 0-03-095090-2), $62.50. Teacher's guide (ISBN 0-03-095091-0), $114.50. (Contact publisher/supplier for complete price and ordering information.) *Publisher/supplier:* Harcourt Brace. *Materials:* Available locally, or from commercial suppliers.

5.21 **SciencePlus Technology and Society: Level Red.** Earl S. Morrison, Alan Moore, Nan Armour, and others. SciencePlus Technology and Society series. Austin, Tex.: Holt, Rinehart and Winston, 1997.

Program Overview The SciencePlus Technology and Society series consists of 3 year-long courses for middle school students. Each of the 3 textbooks—designated Level Green, Level Red, and Level Blue—integrates the life, earth, and physical sciences and incorporates the program's 5 science themes: energy, systems, structures, changes over time, and cycles. Cross-disciplinary connections are emphasized, and the impacts of scientific, technological, and science-related social issues are explored. For each course, an extensive set of materials and resources, including some optional components, is available for students and teachers.

Student Edition **Recommended grade level: 7-8. Reading level: middle 8.** *SciencePlus Technology and Society: Level Red* is organized in 8 units: (1) "Interactions," (2) "Diversity of Living

Things," (3) "Solutions," (4) "Force and Motion," (5) "Structures and Design," (6) "The Restless Earth," (7) "Toward the Stars," and (8) "Growing Plants."

The course addresses the following topics: (1) Students identify some of the relationships—such as commensalism, mutualism, and parasitism—that exist among living things, and they investigate the interactions between humans and the environment. (2) They examine the diversity of living things, the possible reasons for diversity, and how scientists make sense of this diversity. (3) They investigate the properties of solutions. (4) They learn about the concepts of force and motion. (5) They explore the integrity of structures and the forces acting on these structures. (6) They study the processes of geological change. (7) They examine the structure of the universe and explore the theories used to explain common astronomical events. (8) They examine the relationship between the environment and plant life.

Sample lab activities in this textbook include studying a woodland, a forest floor, or a pond community in detail; analyzing water-soluble inks using paper chromatography; constructing and using force meters. Students also learn about the formation of igneous rocks by experimenting with stearic acid; they test the strength of different shapes made of different materials; they simulate the life of a star; and they investigate the effects of 5 variables on the growth of 3 types of plants.

The 8 units in *Level Red* contain a total of 25 chapters. Each chapter consists of 2 to 5 lessons on closely related subject matter. At the beginning of each chapter, students describe what they already know about a subject by writing or drawing in a "ScienceLog." Then, through a variety of hands-on activities called "explorations," they observe scientific principles in action and test their misconceptions about specific science concepts. Reading sections on science concepts are interwoven with the activities.

Review sections are included at the end of each chapter and each unit. Special end-of-unit reading sections make connections among science, technology, society, and the arts. Other unit shorts are "weird science"—explanations of unusual creatures or phenomena—and stories about the lives and work of scientists.

The student edition is available with or without the "SourceBook," an in-text science reference that provides additional information, which reinforces and extends each unit. Because it is not designed for hands-on exploration, the "Source-Book" lends itself to reading at home or outside the classroom.

Teacher's Edition The wraparound teacher's edition includes a 6-page introductory section for each unit. These sections and the wraparound margins contain information on applying unit themes, using program videodiscs, and managing the program. Planning charts provide suggestions for organizing content, materials, activities, and program resources. Also included are homework options; an assessment planning guide; a resources section; suggestions for creating customized instructional programs; and teaching strategies, exercises, and multicultural extensions.

Program Resource and Support Materials A variety of support materials is available, including 8 teaching resource booklets (1 for each unit) with reproducible worksheets and assessment materials and the student "SourceBook." Other support materials include transparencies; a materials guide; instruc-

tions, barcodes, and worksheets for using *Science Discovery*, a videodisc program; audiocassette tapes in English and Spanish for each unit; a guide to special activities designed to introduce students to hands-on science; assessment checklists and rubrics; and a list of test items (test generator software is also available).

Key to Content Standards: 5-8 (see app. C)

UNIFYING CONCEPTS AND PROCESSES: Systems, order, and organization; evidence, models, and explanation; change, constancy, and measurement; evolution and equilibrium; form and function.

SCIENCE AS INQUIRY: Abilities necessary to do scientific inquiry; understandings about scientific inquiry.

PHYSICAL SCIENCE: Motions and forces; transfer of energy.

LIFE SCIENCE: Structure and function in living systems; regulation and behavior; populations and ecosystems; diversity and adaptations of organisms.

EARTH AND SPACE SCIENCE: Structure of the earth system; earth's history; earth in the solar system.

SCIENCE AND TECHNOLOGY: Abilities of technological design; understandings about science and technology.

SCIENCE IN PERSONAL AND SOCIAL PERSPECTIVES: Populations, resources, and environments; science and technology in society.

HISTORY AND NATURE OF SCIENCE: Science as a human endeavor; nature of science; history of science.

Prices: Student edition (ISBN 0-03-095093-7), $62.50. Teacher's guide (ISBN 0-03-095094-5), $114.50. (Contact publisher/supplier for complete price and ordering information.) *Publisher/supplier:* Harcourt Brace. *Materials:* Available locally, or from commercial suppliers.

5.22 **SciencePlus Technology and Society: Level Blue.** Earl S. Morrison, Alan Moore, Nan Armour, and others. SciencePlus Technology and Society series. Austin, Tex.: Holt, Rinehart and Winston, 1997.

Program Overview The Science-Plus Technology and Society series consists of 3 year-long courses for middle school students. Each of the 3 textbooks—designated Level Green, Level Red, and Level Blue—integrates the life, earth, and physical sciences and incorporates the program's 5 science themes: energy, systems, structures, changes over time, and cycles. Cross-disciplinary connections are emphasized, and the impacts of scientific, technological, and science-related social issues are explored. For each course, an extensive set of materials and resources, including some optional components, is available for students and teachers.

Student Edition Recommended grade level: 8+. Reading level: middle 8. *SciencePlus Technology and Society: Level Blue* is organized in 8 units. Each unit focuses on 1 major scientific concept, which is developed through a thematic approach. The 8 units are (1) "Life Processes"; (2) "Particles"; (3) "Machines, Work, and Energy"; (4) "Oceans and Climates"; (5) "Electromagetic Systems"; (6) "Sound"; (7) "Light"; and (8) "Continuity of Life."

The course addresses the following topics: (1) Students explore some of the processes of living things, including photosynthesis, diffusion, osmosis, transpiration, and respiration. (2) They examine the particle model of matter. (3) They learn about the concepts of force, energy, work, and power that underlie the operation of machines. (4) They develop an understanding of oceanography, meteorology, and climatology. (5) They explore the relationship between electricity and magnetism. (6) They learn what sound is, how it is created, and how it travels. (7) They examine the fundamental properties of light and its interaction with matter. (8) They study how characteristics are passed from one generation to the next.

Sample lab activities in this textbook include experimenting to determine where the starch in plants comes from and investigating the differences between sugar and starch molecules. Students also construct a model car powered by a rubber band; measure the dew point; and make and calibrate a hydrometer, then use it to measure the density of artificial seawater. They also create weather maps, make chemical cells and test the cells with a galvanometer, investigate the variables that affect the pitch of a stringed instrument, analyze the spectral components of white light, and simulate Mendel's experiments with pea plants.

The 8 units in *Level Blue* contain a total of 23 chapters. Each chapter consists of 2 to 5 lessons on closely related subject matter. At the beginning of each chapter, students describe what they already know about a subject by writing or drawing in a "ScienceLog." Then, through a variety of hands-on activities called "explorations," they observe scientific principles in action and test their misconceptions about specific science concepts. Reading sections on science concepts are interwoven with the activities.

Review sections are included at the end of each chapter and each unit. Special end-of-unit reading sections make connections among science, technology, society, and the arts. Other unit shorts are "weird science"—explanations of unusual creatures or phenomena—and stories about the lives and work of scientists.

The student edition is available with or without the "SourceBook," an in-text science reference that provides additional information which reinforces and extends each unit. Because it is not designed for hands-on exploration, the "Source-Book" lends itself to reading at home or outside the classroom.

Teacher's Edition The wraparound teacher's edition includes a 6-page introductory section for each unit. These sections and the wraparound margins contain information on applying unit themes, using program videodiscs, and managing the program. Planning charts provide suggestions for organizing content, materials, activities, and program resources. Also included are homework options; an assessment planning guide; a resources section; suggestions for creating customized instructional programs; and teaching strategies, exercises, and multicultural extensions.

Program Resource and Support Materials A variety of support materials is available, including 8 teaching resource booklets (1 for each unit) with reproducible worksheets and assessment materials and the student "SourceBook." Other support materials include transparencies; a materials guide; instructions, barcodes, and worksheets for using *Science Discovery*, a videodisc program; audiocassette tapes in English and Spanish for each unit; a guide to special activities designed to introduce students to hands-on science; assessment checklists and rubrics; and a list of test items (test generator software is also available).

Key to Content Standards: 5-8 (see app. C)

UNIFYING CONCEPTS AND PROCESSES: Systems, order, and organization; evidence, models, and explanation; change, constancy, and measurement; form and function.

SCIENCE AS INQUIRY: Abilities necessary to do scientific inquiry; understandings about scientific inquiry.

PHYSICAL SCIENCE: Properties and changes of properties in matter; motions and forces; transfer of energy.

LIFE SCIENCE: Structure and function in living systems; reproduction and heredity; regulation and behavior.

EARTH AND SPACE SCIENCE: Structure of the earth system; earth's history; earth in the solar system.

SCIENCE AND TECHNOLOGY: Understandings about science and technology.

SCIENCE IN PERSONAL AND SOCIAL PERSPECTIVES: Science and technology in society.

HISTORY AND NATURE OF SCIENCE: Science as a human endeavor; nature of science; history of science.

Prices: Student edition (ISBN 0-03-095096-1), $62.50. Teacher's edition (ISBN 0-03-095097-X), $114.50. (Contact publisher/supplier for complete price and ordering information.) *Publisher/supplier:* Harcourt Brace. *Materials:* Available locally, or from commercial suppliers.

5.23 **Science 2000: Grade 6.** Science 2000 series. Developed by Decision Development Corp. San Ramon, Calif.: Decision Development Corp., 1995.

Program Overview The Science 2000 series is an integrated, multimedia science curriculum designed to introduce middle school students (grades 5 through 8) to 6 important themes of science: energy, evolution, patterns of change, scale and structure, stability, and systems and interactions. A separate, year-long course containing 4 units is offered for each grade. Each unit in a course takes from 7 to 9 weeks to complete. Students use videodisc imagery, software simulations, databases, hands-on investigations, and worksheets to explore real-world scientific questions. For each course, an extensive set of materials is available for students and teachers.

Curriculum Resource Guide **Recommended grade level: 6.** The Science 2000 curriculum for sixth-grade students is composed of 4 units: (1) "Earth's Changing Environments," (2) "Growth and Development," (3) "Applying Forces—The Physics of Building," and (4) "Chemistry of Food." Each unit, which has a series of lesson "clusters," requires students to explore general and then more specific investigative questions or problems.

Topics explored during the course include environments and ecosystems, characteristics of living things, climate and weather, interdependence of life, geology, adaptation, oceanography, flow of energy and matter, human growth and development, the physics of motion, simple tools and machines, chemical reactions, metabolism, and nutrition and diet.

Examples of broad questions that students explore include these: "What is an environment and what types of environments occur on Earth?" "How do living things grow and develop?" "How can you use simple tools to design and build a playground?" and "What is food and why do our bodies need it?" To find out how things grow and change, for example, students calculate and plot the average of students' heights and weights, look at images in a database to see what happens when cells undergo mitosis, demonstrate mitosis with rod-shaped balloons on strings, and chart the human life cycle.

Many lessons take more than 50 minutes to complete. All lessons include student investigations—either controlled experiments, field observations, computer simulations, discussions, research projects, presentations, or a combination of these forms of investigation. Instructions for implementing activities are found in the lessons themselves, and text is hot-linked to databases and other files. Students interact with the computer directly or work from lessons

and student activities that are also provided in print form. Teacher information for each lesson, which is accessed separately, includes a list of supplies, background information, procedures, and extensions.

Teacher's Guide Organized in a 3-ring binder, the teacher's guide is designed to familiarize teachers with the Science 2000 program and its components. It provides background information on the Science 2000 curriculum, reviews hardware requirements and procedures for installing the software, explains how to use the Science 2000 software, and offers teaching tips and strategies. It also provides a step-by-step "trial run" chapter for learning how to use the program (including how to plan lessons, print out documents, interact with students, and provide instructions).

Program Resources and Support Materials The course includes blackline masters for student investigations, a set of preprinted lesson plans, and 2 videodiscs. Videodisc audio tracks are provided in both English and Spanish.

Key to Content Standards: 5-8 (see app. C)

UNIFYING CONCEPTS AND PROCESSES: Systems, order, and organization; evidence, models, and explanation; change, constancy, and measurement; evolution and equilibrium; form and function.
SCIENCE AS INQUIRY: Abilities necessary to do scientific inquiry; understandings about scientific inquiry.
PHYSICAL SCIENCE: Properties and changes of properties in matter; motions and forces; transfer of energy.
LIFE SCIENCE: Structure and function in living systems; reproduction and heredity; populations and ecosystems; diversity and adaptations of organisms.

EARTH AND SPACE SCIENCE: Structure of the earth system; earth's history; earth in the solar system.
SCIENCE AND TECHNOLOGY: Abilities of technological design; understandings about science and technology.
SCIENCE IN PERSONAL AND SOCIAL PERSPECTIVES: Personal health; risks and benefits.
HISTORY AND NATURE OF SCIENCE: Science as a human endeavor; nature of science.

Prices: Curriculum resource guide, $350.00. Teacher's guide, $39.95. Videodiscs, $499.00. Site license, $4,500.00. (Contact publisher/supplier for complete price and ordering information.) ***Publisher/supplier:*** Decision Development Corp. ***Materials:*** Available locally, or from commercial suppliers.

5.24 **Science 2000: Science 1 (Grade 7).** Science 2000 series. Developed by Decision Development Corp. San Ramon, Calif.: Decision Development Corp., 1996.

Program Overview The Science 2000 series is an integrated, multimedia science curriculum designed to introduce middle school students (grades 5 through 8) to 6 important themes of science: energy, evolution, patterns of change, scale and structure, stability, and systems and interactions. A separate, year-long course containing 4 units is offered for each grade. Each unit in a course takes from 7 to 9 weeks to complete. Students use videodisc imagery, software simulations, databases, hands-on investigations, and worksheets to explore real-world scientific questions. For each course, an extensive set of materials is available for students and teachers.

Curriculum Resource Guide **Recommended grade level: 7.** The Science 2000 curriculum for seventh-grade students is composed of 4 units: (1) "The Fore People and the Kuru Disease," (2) "Lake Investigation," (3) "Bicycle Investigation," and (4) "Earth's Place in the Universe." Each unit, which has a series of lesson "clusters," requires students to explore general and then more specific investigative questions or problems.

Topics explored during the course include human body systems, nutrition, infectious diseases, genetics, populations and ecosystems, the environment, weather, erosion and siltation, water chemistry, photosynthesis, eutrophication, friction, speed, velocity, gravity, energy resources, space exploration, planetary motion, the solar system, geologic time, and plate tectonics.

Examples of the broad questions that students explore include these: "How do heredity and the environment affect our health and our lives?" "How do we evaluate the health of a lake?" "How does a bicycle move?" "What is weather?" and "How does the earth fit into the universe?" To find out how each member of a lake system is connected, for example, students learn how to read and make topographic maps, draw cross-sections of a lake and its watershed environment showing different habitat zones, view video clips illustrating food chains in aquatic ecosystems, and conduct a week-long experiment to determine the factors that are necessary for photosynthesis to take place.

Many lessons take more than 50 minutes to complete. All lessons include student investigations— either controlled experiments, field observations, computer simulations, discussions, research projects, presentations, or a combination of these forms of investigation. Instructions for implementing activities are found in the lessons themselves, and text is hot-linked to databases and other

files. Students interact with the computer directly or work from lessons and student activities that are also provided in print form. Teacher information for each lesson, which is accessed separately, includes a list of supplies, background information, procedures, and extensions.

Teacher's Guide Organized in a 3-ring binder, the teacher's guide is designed to familiarize teachers with the Science 2000 program and its components. It provides background information on the Science 2000 curriculum, reviews hardware requirements and procedures for installing the software, explains how to use the Science 2000 software, and offers teaching tips and strategies. It also provides a step-by-step "trial run" for learning how to use the program (including how to plan lessons, print out documents, interact with students, and provide instructions).

Program Resources and Support Materials The course includes blackline masters for student investigations, a set of preprinted lesson plans, and 2 videodiscs. Videodisc audio tracks are provided in both English and Spanish.

Key to Content Standards: 5-8 (see app. C)

UNIFYING CONCEPTS AND PROCESSES: Systems, order, and organization; change, constancy, and measurement; evolution and equilibrium; form and function.

SCIENCE AS INQUIRY: Abilities necessary to do scientific inquiry; understandings about scientific inquiry.

PHYSICAL SCIENCE: Properties and changes of properties in matter; motions and forces; transfer of energy.

LIFE SCIENCE: Structure and function in living systems; reproduction and heredity; populations and ecosystems; diversity and adaptations of organisms.

EARTH AND SPACE SCIENCE: Structure of the earth system; earth's history; earth in the solar system.

SCIENCE AND TECHNOLOGY: Abilities of technological design; understandings about science and technology.

SCIENCE IN PERSONAL AND SOCIAL PERSPECTIVES: Personal health; populations, resources, and environments; natural hazards; risks and benefits; science and technology in society.

HISTORY AND NATURE OF SCIENCE: Science as a human endeavor; nature of science.

Prices: Curriculum resource guide, $350.00. Teacher's guide, $39.95. Videodiscs, $499.00. Site license, $4,500.00. (Contact publisher/supplier for complete price and ordering information.) ***Publisher/supplier:*** Decision Development Corp. ***Materials:*** Available locally, or from commercial suppliers.

5.25 **Science 2000: Science 2 (Grade 8).** Science 2000 series. Developed by Decision Development Corp. San Ramon, Calif.: Decision Development Corp., 1995.

Program Overview The Science 2000 series is an integrated, multimedia science curriculum designed to introduce middle school students (grades 5 through 8) to 6 important themes of science: energy, evolution, patterns of change, scale and structure, stability, and systems and interactions. A separate, year-long course containing 4 units is offered for each grade. Each unit in a course takes from 7 to 9 weeks to complete. Students use videodisc imagery, software simulations, databases, hands-on investigations, and worksheets to explore real-world scientific questions. For each course, an extensive set of materials is available for students and teachers.

Curriculum Resource Guide **Recommended grade level: 8+.** The Science 2000 curriculum for eighth-grade students is composed of 4 units: (1) "The Lost Children: Genetics and Heredity," (2) "The Sun and Global Climate Change," (3) "Ears to the Sky: Energy Transformations," and (4) "Natural Disasters." Each unit, which has a series of lesson "clusters," requires students to explore general and then more specific investigative questions or problems.

Topics explored during the course include DNA, heredity, genetic engineering, climate and weather, humans and the environment, oceanography, pollution, electricity, magnetism, communication devices, sound and hearing, light and optics, plate tectonics, natural disasters, nuclear energy, and energy transfer.

Examples of the broad questions that students explore include these: "How can we determine whether two people are biologically related?" "How do the sun and atmosphere shape global climate?" "How do we communicate over long distances?" "Where and how do natural disasters affect land and structures built by man?" To explore sound and communication over distances, for example, students watch a video on dolphin communication and discuss various ways animals communicate; they determine the frequency of a pendulum and examine the relationship between frequency and wavelength; they investigate electricity, current, and voltage by making a wet-cell battery; and they examine how telegraphs and telephones work.

Many lessons take more than 50 minutes to complete. All lessons include student investigations—either controlled experiments, field observations, computer simulations, discussions, research projects, presentations, or a combination of these forms of investigation. Instructions for implementing activities are found in the lessons themselves, and text is hot-linked to databases and other files. Students interact with the computer directly or work from lessons and student activities that are also provided in print form. Teacher information for each lesson, which is accessed separately, includes a list of supplies, background information, procedures, and extensions.

Teacher's Guide Organized in a 3-ring binder, the teacher's guide is designed to familiarize teachers with the Science 2000 program and its components. It provides background information on the Science 2000 curriculum, reviews hardware requirements and procedures for installing the software, explains how to use the Science 2000 software, and offers teaching tips and strategies. It also provides a step-by-step "trial run" for learning how to use the program (including how to plan lessons, print out documents, interact with students, and provide instructions).

Program Resources and Support Materials The course includes blackline masters for student investigations, a set of preprinted lesson plans, and 2 videodiscs. Videodisc audio tracks are provided in both English and Spanish.

Key to Content Standards: 5-8 (see app. C)

UNIFYING CONCEPTS AND PROCESSES: Systems, order, and organization; evidence, models, and explanation; change, constancy, and measurement; evolution and equilibrium; form and function.

SCIENCE AS INQUIRY: Abilities necessary to do scientific inquiry; understandings about scientific inquiry.

PHYSICAL SCIENCE: Properties and changes of properties in matter; motions and forces; transfer of energy.

LIFE SCIENCE: Structure and function in living systems; reproduction and heredity; diversity and adaptations of organisms.

EARTH AND SPACE SCIENCE: Structure of the earth system; earth's history; earth in the solar system.

SCIENCE AND TECHNOLOGY: Abilities of technological design; understandings about science and technology.

SCIENCE IN PERSONAL AND SOCIAL PERSPECTIVES: Natural hazards; risks and benefits; science and technology in society.

HISTORY AND NATURE OF SCIENCE: Science as a human endeavor; nature of science; history of science.

Prices: Curriculum resource guide, $350.00. Teacher's guide, $39.95. Videodiscs, $499.00. Site license, $4,500.00. (Contact publisher/supplier for complete price and ordering information.) ***Publisher/supplier:*** Decision Development Corp. ***Materials:*** Available locally, or from commercial suppliers.

5.26 **Scientific Theories.** Robert C. Knott and Herbert D. Thier. Science Curriculum Improvement Study 3 (SCIS 3) series. Hudson, N.H.: Delta Education, 1993.

Program Overview The Science Curriculum Improvement Study (SCIS) series focuses on the concepts and processes of science for grades K-6. The most current version of the series—SCIS 3—consists of 13 units: a kindergarten unit and 2 sequences of 6 units each in physical-earth science and life-environmental science for grades 1 through 6. Two units are designed for grade 6. The components of a SCIS 3 unit are a teacher's guide and a kit of materials.

Teacher's Guide **Recommended grade level: 6.** In this unit, students are introduced to the meaning of scientific theories through the study of electric circuits, magnets, light, and earthquakes. The unit consists of 25 chapters, organized in 7 sections: (1) "Review," (2) "Scientific Theories," (3) "A Color Theory," (4) "A Magnetic Field Theory," (5) "An Electricity Theory," (6) "A Ray Theory of Light," and (7) "An Earthquake Theory."

During the unit, students have the opportunity to develop and test their own theories to explain their observations. Among the activities, for example, they compare interaction at a distance (between magnets) with touching interaction (electric circuits). They explore the periodic motion of pendulums. They also test their hypotheses concerning their investigation of electric circuit puzzles and a mystery box. Students use prisms and filters to develop their first detailed scientific theory—a theory of colored light.

In other activities, students devise a magnetic field theory to explain magnetic interaction at a distance. They also develop an electricity theory to describe and explain the transfer of electrical energy from a battery to energy receivers in a closed electric circuit. Students use lenses and mirrors to formulate a ray theory of light, and they develop theories to explain the causes and effects of earthquakes.

The unit requires about 45 class sessions to complete. The teacher's guide includes an introduction to the unit, lesson plans for each of the 7 sections, a glossary, and blackline masters for a student journal. Science background information, detailed instructions on planning for and conducting each activity, an extensive assessment component, and extensions for integration and enrichment are provided.

Key to Content Standards: 5-8 (see app. C)

UNIFYING CONCEPTS AND PROCESSES: Systems, order, and organization; evidence, models, and explanation; change, constancy, and measurement.

SCIENCE AS INQUIRY: Abilities necessary to do scientific inquiry; understandings about scientific inquiry.
PHYSICAL SCIENCE: Transfer of energy.
EARTH AND SPACE SCIENCE: Structure of the earth system.
SCIENCE AND TECHNOLOGY: Abilities of technological design.
HISTORY AND NATURE OF SCIENCE: Nature of science.

Prices: Teacher's guide (ISBN 0-87504-941-9), $39.50. Kit, $715.00. *Publisher/supplier:* Delta Education. *Materials:* Available locally, from commercial suppliers, or in kit.

5.27 The Technology of Paper. Science and Technology for Children (STC) series. Developed by National Science Resources Center (Washington, D.C.). Burlington, N.C.: Carolina Biological Supply, 1997.

Program Overview The Science and Technology for Children (STC) series consists of 24 inquiry-centered curriculum units for grades 1-6, with 4 units at each grade level. Students learn about topics in the life, earth, and physical sciences. The technological applications of science and the interactions among science, technology, and society are addressed throughout the program. The STC units, each of which takes about 16 class sessions to complete, encourage participatory learning and the integration of science with mathematics, language arts, social studies, and art. The components of an STC unit are a teacher's guide, a student activity book with simple instructions and illustrations, and a kit of materials.

Teacher's Guide **Recommended grade level: 6. Reading level: 7.** In *The Technology of Paper,* students explore paper and the science of papermaking, as well as the connection between the properties of many forms of paper and the uses of the paper. They also have the opportunity to design their own recycled greeting card, stationery, or postcard.

In the first part of the unit, students explore the nature and properties of paper by collecting different types of paper, examining them under a microscope, and performing a number of tests, such as a smoothness and a tear-resistance test. The tests introduce them to the idea of a "fair test," or controlled experiment. Students then recycle a paper sample, identify the variables that affect its properties (such as the way pulp is prepared, the type of fiber, or kinds of additives in it), and they compare the processes of making paper by hand and by machine. In the final lessons, students work through 4 steps in a technological design process as they develop and evaluate their own paper product.

The Technology of Paper is a 17-lesson unit. The teacher's guide includes a unit overview, the 17 lesson plans, an annotated bibliography, and reproducible masters. The module includes science background information, detailed instructions on planning for and conducting each activity, an extensive assessment component, and extensions for integration and enrichment.

Appendixes in the teacher's guide include directions for setting up a school paper-recycling center and provide a list of organizations, paper companies, and individuals that can be used as resources for the unit. The student activity book that accompanies this unit provides reading selections, helpful illustrations, and directions for completing activities.

Key to Content Standards: 5-8 (see app. C)

UNIFYING CONCEPTS AND PROCESSES: Evidence, models, and explanation; change, constancy, and measurement; form and function.

SCIENCE AS INQUIRY: Abilities necessary to do scientific inquiry; understandings about scientific inquiry. **PHYSICAL SCIENCE:** Properties and changes of properties in matter. **SCIENCE AND TECHNOLOGY:** Abilities of technological design; understandings about science and technology. **SCIENCE IN PERSONAL AND SOCIAL PERSPECTIVES:** Natural hazards; science and technology in society. **HISTORY AND NATURE OF SCIENCE:** Science as a human endeavor; nature of science; history of science.

Prices: Teacher's guide (ISBN 0-89278-684-1), $24.95. Student activity book (ISBN 0-89278-685-X), $3.50. Kit, $689.95. *Publisher/supplier:* Carolina Biological Supply. *Materials:* Available locally, from commercial suppliers, or in kit.

5.28 **Variables.** Full Option Science System (FOSS) series. Developed by Lawrence Hall of Science (Berkeley, Calif.). Hudson, N.H.: Delta Education, 1993.

Program Overview The Full Option Science System (FOSS) program is a K-6 science curriculum consisting of 27 stand-alone modules. The 8 modules for grades 5-6 are organized under topics in the life, physical, and earth sciences and in scientific reasoning and technology. They can be used in any order.

The FOSS program is designed to engage students in scientific concepts through multisensory, hands-on laboratory activities. All modules of the program incorporate 5 unifying themes—(1) pattern, (2) structure, (3) interaction, (4) change, and (5) system. The components of a FOSS module are a teacher's guide and a kit of materials.

Teacher's Guide **Recommended grade level: 5-6.** In *Variables,* students investigate the concept "variable" as they design and conduct their own experiments with pendulums, airplanes, boats, and catapults. They systematically investigate weight, release position, and length of pendulums to find out which of these variables affects the number of swings completed in a given period of time. They make paper boats of various heights and determine how many pennies each boat can hold before sinking. They build windup airplanes to fly along a string, and then they control variables such as the number of times the propeller is wound, the weight of the plane, and the slope of the string in measuring how far the planes will fly. They catapult objects of various sizes and weights to investigate the variables

that contribute to the highest and longest flips.

Variables consists of 4 major activities, requiring a total of about 20 class sessions. The teacher's guide includes a module overview, the 4 activity folios, duplication masters (in English and Spanish) for the student sheets, and an annotated bibliography.

This module includes science background information, detailed instructions on planning for and conducting each activity, an extensive assessment component, and extensions for integration and enrichment.

Key to Content Standards: 5-8 (see app. C)

UNIFYING CONCEPTS AND PROCESSES: Systems, order, and organization; evidence, models, and explanation; change, constancy, and measurement. **SCIENCE AS INQUIRY:** Abilities necessary to do scientific inquiry; understandings about scientific inquiry. **PHYSICAL SCIENCE:** Motions and forces. **SCIENCE AND TECHNOLOGY:** Abilities of technological design. **HISTORY AND NATURE OF SCIENCE:** Nature of science.

Prices: Teacher's guide (ISBN 0-7826-0052-2), $101. Kit, $319. *Publisher/supplier:* Delta Education. *Materials:* Available locally, from commercial suppliers, or in kit.

Multidisciplinary and Applied Science—Supplementary Units

5.29 Chemicals in Foods: Additives. Chemical Education for Public Understanding Program (CEPUP) series. Developed by Lawrence Hall of Science (Berkeley, Calif.). Menlo Park, Calif.: Addison-Wesley, 1993.

Program Overview The Chemical Education for Public Understanding Program (CEPUP) series consists of 12 modules for grades 7-9. The modules focus on chemicals and the interaction of chemicals with people and the environment. The series promotes the use of scientific principles, processes, and evidence in public decision making. The components of a CEPUP module are a teacher's guide and a kit of materials. (SEPUP—the Science Education for Public Understanding Program—is the second phase of the project that began as CEPUP.)

Teacher's Guide **Recommended grade level: 7-8+.** *Chemicals in Foods: Additives* consists of 8 activities during which students examine food additives and their effect on food quality. Among the activities, for example, students investigate the effects of selected natural and synthetic substances on the rate of apple browning. They examine food labels from home to determine what additives are present in their own diets. They also investigate the chemical and physical properties of 3 common food additives—citric acid, modified food starch, and guar gum.

In other activities, students investigate the role microorganisms play in food spoilage, and they learn how chemical food preservatives are used to increase the safety of the food supply. They also design an experiment to investigate the effect of selected variables on the growth of active yeast cultures. They conduct a simulated test for the presence of pesticide residues in samples of black-eyed peas, and they rate the risks of eating foods prepared or stored in different ways.

The 8 activities in *Chemicals in Foods: Additives* each take 1 to 2 class periods of 40 to 50 minutes. Included in the slim, wire-bound book are reproducible student sheets, directions for guiding activities and discussions, and an end-of-unit assessment.

Key to Content Standards: 5-8 (see app. C)

UNIFYING CONCEPTS AND PROCESSES: Systems, order, and organization; evidence, models, and explanation. **SCIENCE AS INQUIRY:** Abilities necessary to do scientific inquiry; understandings about scientific inquiry. **PHYSICAL SCIENCE:** Properties and changes of properties in matter. **LIFE SCIENCE:** Structure and function in living systems. **SCIENCE AND TECHNOLOGY:** Understandings about science and technology. **SCIENCE IN PERSONAL AND SOCIAL PERSPECTIVES:** Personal health; risks and benefits; science and technology in society. **HISTORY AND NATURE OF SCIENCE:** Nature of science.

Prices: Teacher's guide (ISBN 0-201-29489-3), $19.99. Kit, $239.99. *Publisher/supplier:* Sargent-Welch/ VWR Scientific. *Materials:* Available locally, from commercial suppliers, or in kit.

5.30 Classifying Fingerprints. Nancy Cook. Real-World Mathematics through Science series. Developed by Washington Mathematics, Engineering, Science Achievement (MESA) Group (Seattle, Wash.). Menlo Park, Calif.: Innovative Learning Publications, 1995.

Program Overview The Real-World Mathematics through Science series consists of 10 units for grades 6-8. Each unit combines pre-algebra topics with science explorations to motivate students in both areas of study. Students work in cooperative groups to solve open-ended problems and make connections between real-world mathematics and science.

Teacher's Guide **Recommended grade level: 6-8.** *Classifying Fingerprints* contains 6 activities that teach students about the different types of fingerprint patterns, methods of classifying and filing fingerprints, and some of the mathematics involved with fingerprint analysis. The unit allows students to study a real-world use of a number system other than the decimal system, since the most widely used method of classifying fingerprints is a binary system.

During the unit, students make a full set of prints and analyze the prints of their right index finger. They learn about several binary systems of fingerprint classification and file their prints according to one of the systems. They also analyze and graph class data on the distribution of their prints' loops, arches, and whorls, and they investigate family prints to see if whorl patterns might be inherited.

Each activity includes an overview, background information, teaching procedures, discussion and assessment questions, and reproducible student sheets. In addition to the activities, which each require 2 periods of 40 to 50 minutes, *Classifying Fingerprints* includes links to careers, history, technology, and writing. Students are asked, for example, to write a short essay presenting their own ideas for uses of fingerprinting and to learn what FBI agents do. Real-life examples are used throughout the unit, and students are required to collect and analyze evidence.

Key to Content Standards: 5-8 (see app. C)

UNIFYING CONCEPTS AND PROCESSES: Systems, order, and organization; evidence, models, and explanation.
SCIENCE AS INQUIRY: Abilities necessary to do scientific inquiry; understandings about scientific inquiry.
SCIENCE AND TECHNOLOGY: Abilities of technological design; understandings about science and technology.
SCIENCE IN PERSONAL AND SOCIAL PERSPECTIVES: Science and technology in society.
HISTORY AND NATURE OF SCIENCE: Nature of science; history of science.

Price: $18.95 (ISBN 0-201-49310-1).
Publisher/supplier: Addison-Wesley/Longman. *Materials:* Available locally, or from commercial suppliers.

ABOUT THE ANNOTATIONS IN "MULTIDISCIPLINARY AND APPLIED SCIENCE—SUPPLEMENTARY UNITS"

Entry Numbers

Curriculum materials are arranged alphabetically by title in each category (Core Materials, Supplementary Units, and Science Activity Books) in chapters 1 through 5 of this guide.

Each curriculum annotation has a two-part entry number: the chapter number is given before the period; the number after the period locates the entry within that chapter. For example, the first entry number in chapter 1 is 1.1; the second entry in chapter 2 is 2.2; and so on.

The entry numbers within each curriculum chapter run consecutively through Core Materials, Supplementary Units, and Science Activity Books.

Order of Bibliographic Information

Following is the arrangement of the facts of publication in the annotations in this section:

- **Title of publication**
- **Number of edition,** if applicable
- **Authors** (an individual author or authors, an institutional author, or a project or program name under which the material was developed)
- **Series title**
- **Series developer,** if applicable
- **Place of publication, publisher, and date of publication**

Recommended Grade Level

The grade level for each piece of material was recommended by teacher evaluators during the development of this guide. In some instances, the recommended grade level may differ slightly from the publisher's advertised level.

Key to Content Standards: 5-8

The key lists the content standards for grades 5-8 from the *National Science Education Standards* (NSES) that are addressed in depth by the item. A key is provided for core materials and supplementary units. (*See* appendix C.)

Price and Acquisition Information

Ordering information appears at the end of each entry. Included are—

- **Prices** (of teacher's guides, student books, lab manuals, and kits or units)
- **Publisher/supplier** (The name of a principal publisher/supplier, although not necessarily the sole source, for the items listed in the price category. Appendix A, "Publishers and Suppliers," provides the address, phone and fax numbers, and electronic ordering information, where available, for each publisher and supplier.)
- **Materials** (various sources from which one might obtain the required materials)

Readers must contact publishers/suppliers for complete and up-to-date listings of the program resources and support materials available for a particular unit. Depending on the developer, these items may be required, optional, or both; they may be offered individually and/or in kits, packages, or boxes. Materials may change with revised editions. The prices given in this chapter for selected resources or materials are based on information from the publishers and suppliers but are not meant to represent the full range of ordering options.

Indexes of Curriculum Materials

The multiple indexes on pp. 449-78 allow easy access to the information in this guide. Various aspects of the curriculum materials—including titles, topics addressed in each unit, grade levels, and standards addressed—are the focus of seven separate indexes. For example, titles and entry numbers are listed in the "Title Index" on pp. 450-54. The "Index of Authors, Series, and Curriculum Projects," on pp. 455-57, provides entry numbers of any annotated titles in a particular series.

Overviews of Core and Supplementary Programs

Appendix D, "Overviews of Core and Supplementary Programs with Titles Annotated in This Guide," on pp. 441-48, lists, by program or series, the individual titles annotated in the sections "Core Materials" and "Supplementary Units" in the five curriculum chapters.

5.31 **Climate and Farming.** Module 3.5. Foundations and Challenges to Encourage Technology-based Science (FACETS) series. Developed by American Chemical Society (Washington, D.C.). Dubuque, Iowa: Kendall/Hunt, 1996.

Program Overview The Foundations and Challenges to Encourage Technology-based Science (FACETS) program consists of 3 series of 8 modules each for grades 6-8. Each module focuses on a topic in the life, earth, or physical sciences. The time needed to complete FACETS modules varies from 2 to 4 weeks. Each module consists of a student book and a teacher's guide.

Student Edition **Recommended grade level: 8.** In the module *Climate and Farming,* students learn how climatic conditions are analyzed and matched with the crop plants best suited to those conditions. The module emphasizes responding to climate changes rather than possible causes of climate change such as global warming. Students learn what climate is and what factors affect it. They analyze a series of data sets on temperature and rainfall, set up a long-term investigation of the effects of temperature on seed germination and plant growth, and make climatograms of various cities in the United States. Next, students look at how the characteristics that make up biomes have an effect on what actually lives in their environment, and they work with elementary genetics to get a sense of how crop plants can be bred to withstand certain climatic conditions. In the final activity, students draw on their research in climate and farming to plan a garden with plants especially suited to the local climate.

Climate and Farming is divided into 6 activities that each take between 1 and 3 class periods to complete. Two short reading sections at the end of the module provide limited background information on biomes and on global warming.

Teacher's Guide The wraparound teacher's guide includes a unit overview, a time line for completing the module, a materials list, background information, and teaching suggestions.

Key to Content Standards: 5-8 (see app. C)

UNIFYING CONCEPTS AND PROCESSES: Change, constancy, and measurement. **SCIENCE AS INQUIRY:** Abilities necessary to do scientific inquiry; understandings about scientific inquiry. **LIFE SCIENCE:** Reproduction and heredity; populations and ecosystems. **EARTH AND SPACE SCIENCE:** Structure of the earth system. **SCIENCE AND TECHNOLOGY:** Understandings about science and technology. **SCIENCE IN PERSONAL AND SOCIAL PERSPECTIVES:** Populations, resources, and environments.

Prices: Student edition (ISBN 0-7872-1476-0), $7.90. Teacher's guide (ISBN 0-7872-1477-9), $14.90. *Publisher/supplier:* Kendall/Hunt. *Materials:* Available locally, or from commercial suppliers.

5.32 Determining Threshold Limits. Chemical Education for Public Understanding Program (CEPUP) series. Developed by Lawrence Hall of Science (Berkeley, Calif.). Menlo Park, Calif.: Addison-Wesley, 1990.

Program Overview The Chemical Education for Public Understanding Program (CEPUP) series consists of 12 modules for grades 7-9. The modules focus on chemicals and the interaction of chemicals with people and the environment. The series promotes the use of scientific principles, processes, and evidence in public decision making. The components of a CEPUP module are a teacher's guide and a kit of materials. (SEPUP—the Science Education for Public Understanding Program—is the second phase of the project that began as CEPUP.)

Teacher's Guide **Recommended grade level: 7-8+.** *Determining Threshold Limits* contains 6 activities that introduce students to ways in which scientists test products for the presence and amount of potentially toxic substances. During the activities, students determine their taste threshold for salt in water solutions by tasting drops of saltwater of known concentrations. They experiment with 2 reagents and 4 known solutions to discover the identity of unknown solutions (both single and combination solutions). They learn how to determine the concentration of an unknown salt solution quantitatively (in parts per million). They also simulate 2 controlled animal experiments in which they explore the effect of a potentially toxic substance (silver nitrate) on "rats" (salt solution and potassium chromate). Using given experimental data, they explore the difference between acute and chronic toxicity. They also learn about how real-life animal experiments are conducted and about the problems involved in trying to extrapolate data from animal studies to human tolerances.

The 6 activities in *Determining Threshold Limits* each take 1 or 2 periods of 40 to 50 minutes. Included in the slim, wire-bound book are reproducible student sheets, directions and information for guiding activities and discussions, and an end-of-unit test.

Key to Content Standards: 5-8 (see app. C)

UNIFYING CONCEPTS AND PROCESSES: Evidence, models, and explanation. **SCIENCE AS INQUIRY:** Abilities necessary to do scientific inquiry; understandings about scientific inquiry. **PHYSICAL SCIENCE:** Properties and changes of properties in matter. **SCIENCE AND TECHNOLOGY:** Abilities of technological design; understandings about science and technology. **SCIENCE IN PERSONAL AND SOCIAL PERSPECTIVES:** Risks and benefits. **HISTORY AND NATURE OF SCIENCE:** Nature of science.

Prices: Teacher's guide (ISBN 0-201-28418-9), $19.99. Kit, $144.99. *Publisher/supplier:* Sargent-Welch/VWR Scientific. *Materials:* Available locally, from commercial suppliers, or in kit.

5.33 Energy Transformations: Fourth Module in Bio-Related Technologies Unit. 4th ed. Integrated Mathematics, Science, and Technology (IMaST) Project. IMaST series. Normal, Ill.: Center for Mathematics, Science, and Technology Education, Illinois State University, 1996.

Program Overview The Integrated Mathematics, Science, and Technology (IMaST) series for middle school includes 6 modules. The materials in each are designed to be used by a team of mathematics, science, and technology teachers concurrently over a 9-week period. Each module includes a teacher's guide and a student book.

Student Book **Recommended grade level: 7-8.** The *Energy Transformations* module ties together energy transformations relating to wellness, food production, and waste management. Over the course of the module, students collect and display data (using tables, graphs, and spreadsheets) about types of foods that fuel their bodies. They calculate the cost per gram and determine the number of calories per gram of various food items. They also work with figures relating to energy usage to develop skills with scientific notation and exponents.

In other activities, students examine the flow of energy through a food chain. They experiment to determine the factors that affect the amount of heat energy absorbed by a calorimeter, and they use the calorimeter to measure and compare the energy stored in food and in fuels. Students design, build, and test a solar car. They also build and test a model wind turbine that transfers wind energy into mechanical energy, and then into electrical energy.

The 10 activities in *Energy Transformations* are organized in 3 groups, according to their emphasis on mathematics, science, or technology. Three sections following the activities provide background reading and basic information on relevant energy topics.

Teacher's Guide Accompanying the activities in the teacher's guide are brief directions, along with ideas for class discussions, and extension activities. Guidelines for assessing student performance are provided.

Key to Content Standards: 5-8 (see app. C)

UNIFYING CONCEPTS AND PROCESSES: Systems, order, and organization; evidence, models, and explanation; change, constancy, and measurement.

SCIENCE AS INQUIRY: Abilities necessary to do scientific inquiry; understandings about scientific inquiry.
PHYSICAL SCIENCE: Transfer of energy.
LIFE SCIENCE: Populations and ecosystems.
SCIENCE AND TECHNOLOGY: Abilities of technological design; understandings about science and technology.
SCIENCE IN PERSONAL AND SOCIAL PERSPECTIVES: Science and technology in society.

Prices: Student book, $5.50. Teacher's guide, $10.00. *Publisher/supplier:* Illinois State University. *Materials:* Available locally, or from commercial suppliers.

5.34 **Food Production: Second Module in Bio-Related Technologies Unit.** 4th ed. Integrated Mathematics, Science and Technology (IMaST) Project. IMaST series. Normal, Ill.: Center for Mathematics, Science, and Technology Education, Illinois State University, 1996.

Program Overview The Integrated Mathematics, Science, and Technology (IMaST) series for middle school includes 6 modules. The materials in each are designed to be used by a team of mathematics, science, and technology teachers concurrently over a 9-week period. Each module includes a teacher's guide and a student book.

Student Book **Recommended grade level: 7-8.** The *Food Production* module involves students in activities that focus primarily on the appropriate use of materials and technology to produce food. A simulation game that allows students to explore food and hunger issues is suggested as an introductory activity. Among the 18 activities in the unit, students learn data collection methods by conducting a survey on preferred summer farm jobs; they interpret graphs of world grain production, population, and meat consumption; and they develop checkbook recordkeeping

skills for an imaginary farm enterprise. Students also design and conduct controlled experiments with plants over 5 weeks to identify the variables that affect a crop; they examine and test the characteristics of soil to discover what type is best for plants; they identify the parts of a seed and the conditions needed for seeds to germinate; and they design, build, and test a hydroponics system.

The 18 activities in *Food Production* are organized in 3 groups, according to their emphasis on mathematics, science, or technology. Three sections following the activities provide background reading and basic information on topics related to food production.

Teacher's Guide Accompanying the activities in the teacher's guide are brief directions, along with ideas for class discussions, and extension activities. Guidelines for assessing student performance are provided.

Key to Content Standards: 5-8 (see app. C)

UNIFYING CONCEPTS AND PROCESSES: Systems, order, and organization; evidence, models, and explanation; change, constancy, and measurement.
SCIENCE AS INQUIRY: Abilities necessary to do scientific inquiry; understandings about scientific inquiry.
LIFE SCIENCE: Structure and function in living systems; populations and ecosystems.
EARTH AND SPACE SCIENCE: Structure of the earth system.
SCIENCE AND TECHNOLOGY: Abilities of technological design; understandings about science and technology.
SCIENCE IN PERSONAL AND SOCIAL PERSPECTIVES: Populations, resources, and environments; science and technology in society.
HISTORY AND NATURE OF SCIENCE: Science as a human endeavor; nature of science.

Prices: Student book, $11.00. Teacher's guide, $19.50. *Publisher/supplier:* Illinois State University. *Materials:* Available locally, or from commercial suppliers.

5.35 **Forecasting: Discovering, Simplifying, and Applying Patterns.** 4th ed. Integrated Mathematics, Science and Technology (IMaST) Project. IMaST series. Normal, Ill.: Center for Mathematics, Science, and Technology Education, Illinois State University, 1996.

Program Overview The Integrated Mathematics, Science, and Technology (IMaST) series for middle school includes 6 modules. The materials in each are designed to be used by a team of mathematics, science, and technology teachers concurrently over a 9-week period. Each module includes a teacher's guide and a student book.

Student Book **Recommended grade level: 8+.** The module *Forecasting: Discovering, Simplifying, and Applying Patterns* involves students in discovering, collecting, and manipulating data about patterns found in the natural and manufactured worlds—particularly patterns related to airplanes and flight. The module also shows students how the ability to recognize and express patterns algebraically—in graphs, for example—leads to the ability to predict future trends. Throughout the module, students develop, graph, and solve linear equations verbally, tabularly, graphically, and symbolically.

Among the activities, students communicate the landing positions of different counters by naming points on a coordinate grid using ordered pairs. They also translate an English expression into an algebraic expression using a variable; they examine the relationship between distance, speed, and time through experiments with launchers (for model planes) built by the class; and they solve equations using the balance method. Students also deter-

mine the effect of changing 1 variable in a pendulum system; they investigate and graph information about the behavior of elastic devices, which is an important factor in certain airplane components; and they use the principle of center of mass to balance prototype planes. In other activities, students use ordered pairs to define the shape of an airplane, as is done with computer numerical controlled (CNC) machines. They design, evaluate, and analyze a working prototype airplane.

The 19 activities in *Forecasting* are organized in 3 groups, according to their emphasis on mathematics, science, or technology. Three sections following the activities provide background reading and basic information on patterns, their context, and their social application.

Teacher's Guide Accompanying the activities in the teacher's guide are brief directions, along with ideas for class discussions, and extension activities. Guidelines for assessing student performance are provided.

Key to Content Standards: 5-8 (see app. C)

UNIFYING CONCEPTS AND PROCESSES: Evidence, models, and explanation; change, constancy, and measurement; form and function.
SCIENCE AS INQUIRY: Abilities necessary to do scientific inquiry; understandings about scientific inquiry.
PHYSICAL SCIENCE: Motions and forces.
SCIENCE AND TECHNOLOGY: Abilities of technological design; understandings about science and technology.
SCIENCE IN PERSONAL AND SOCIAL PER-SPECTIVES: Science and technology in society.
HISTORY AND NATURE OF SCIENCE: Nature of science.

Prices: Student book, $13.50. Teacher's guide, $24.50. *Publisher/supplier:* Illinois State University. *Materials:* Available locally, or from commercial suppliers.

5.36 **Handling Information.** Module 3.8. Foundations and Challenges to Encourage Technology-based Science (FACETS) series. Developed by American Chemical Society (Washington, D.C.). Dubuque, Iowa: Kendall/Hunt, 1996.

Program Overview The Foundations and Challenges to Encourage Technology-based Science (FACETS) program consists of 3 series of 8 modules each for grades 6-8. Each module focuses on a topic in the life, earth, or physical sciences. The time needed to complete FACETS modules varies from 2 to 4 weeks. Each module consists of a student book and a teacher's guide.

Student Edition **Recommended grade level: 8.** In the module *Handling Information,* students are introduced to the concept of systems—and in particular to communication networks as systems on which people rely constantly—as they investigate how information is handled and transmitted both in their school and in the world at large. Students first play a game to help them understand the importance of the encoding, transmission, and decoding processes. Then they analyze how information gets into, out of, and around their school. They compare different methods of acquiring information—such as by telephone, regular mail, World Wide Web, and fax—in terms of cost, efficiency, and other factors. They investigate some of the simpler science and technology behind commonly used communication methods—voice, paper and ink, and electrical transmissions. In the final activity, students design a communications plan for their school building and present their plan to an audience of students and teachers.

Handling Information is divided into 6 activities that each take between 1 and 4 class periods to complete. Two short reading sections at the end of the module provide limited background information on how language is used to communicate and on how information is sometimes used as a control measure.

Teacher's Guide The wraparound teacher's guide includes a unit overview, a time line for completing the module, a materials list, background information, and teaching suggestions.

Key to Content Standards: 5-8 (see app. C)

UNIFYING CONCEPTS AND PROCESSES: Systems, order, and organization.
SCIENCE AS INQUIRY: Abilities necessary to do scientific inquiry; understandings about scientific inquiry.
PHYSICAL SCIENCE: Transfer of energy.
SCIENCE AND TECHNOLOGY: Understandings about science and technology.
SCIENCE IN PERSONAL AND SOCIAL PERSPECTIVES: Science and technology in society.
HISTORY AND NATURE OF SCIENCE: Nature of science.

Prices: Student edition (ISBN 0-7872-1486-8), $7.90. Teacher's guide (ISBN 0-7872-1487-6), $14.90. *Publisher/supplier:* Kendall/Hunt. *Materials:* Available locally, or from commercial suppliers.

5.37 **Height-O-Meters.** Reprinted with revisions. Cary I. Sneider. Great Explorations in Math and Science (GEMS) series. Berkeley, Calif: Lawrence Hall of Science, 1991.

Program Overview The Great Explorations in Math and Science (GEMS) series includes more than 50 teacher's guides and handbooks for preschool through grade 10. About 35 of these are appropriate for middle school. The series also

includes several assembly presenter's guides and exhibit guides. New guides and handbooks continue to be developed, and current titles are revised frequently. The series is designed to teach key science and mathematics concepts through activity-based learning. The time needed to complete GEMS units varies from about 2 to 10 class sessions.

Teacher's Guide Recommended grade level: 6-8+. The booklet *Height-O-Meters* helps students construct a simple cardboard device called a Height-O-Meter (technically, a clinometer), which can be used to measure the angular height of an object in degrees. Students construct and calibrate their Height-O-Meters to read zero degrees when they are pointed horizontally. They learn how to use their instruments to determine the height of the school flagpole. They also perform an experiment to compare how high a styrofoam ball and a rubber ball can be thrown.

The teacher's guide includes background information and step-by-step directions for the activities (which require 4 sessions of 45 to 50 minutes each). An extension section suggests activities that clarify the relationship between angular and linear height, illustrate how forest rangers use triangulation to spot fires, introduce the tangent function, and explain how astronomers measure the distance to stars. After completing this unit, students can use their Height-O-Meters to track the altitudes of model rockets as described in the GEMS teacher's guide, *Experimenting with Model Rockets* (see 1.28).

Key to Content Standards: 5-8 (see app. C)

UNIFYING CONCEPTS AND PROCESSES: Systems, order, and organization; evidence, models, and explanation; change, constancy, and measurement.

SCIENCE AS INQUIRY: Abilities necessary to do scientific inquiry; understandings about scientific inquiry.
SCIENCE AND TECHNOLOGY: Understandings about science and technology.

Price: $10.50 (ISBN 0-912511-22-2). *Publisher/supplier:* LHS GEMS. *Materials:* Available locally, or from commercial suppliers.

5.38 **Hot Water and Warm Homes from Sunlight.** Reprinted with revisions. Alan Gould. Great Explorations in Math and Science (GEMS) series. Berkeley, Calif.: Lawrence Hall of Science, 1995.

Program Overview The Great Explorations in Math and Science (GEMS) series includes more than 50 teacher's guides and handbooks for preschool through grade 10. About 35 of these are appropriate for middle school. The series also includes several assembly presenter's guides and exhibit guides. New guides and handbooks continue to be developed, and current titles are revised frequently. The series is designed to teach key science and mathematics concepts through activity-based learning. The time needed to complete GEMS units varies from about 2 to 10 class sessions.

Teacher's Guide Recommended grade level: 5-8. In *Hot Water and Warm Homes from Sunlight,* students perform experiments with model houses and water heating to investigate solar power. An introductory activity on the experimental design and results of a plant-growth study introduces students to the concept and essential elements of a controlled experiment. Students then build model houses to determine how windows affect passive solar heating of the house. They use aluminum pie pans as model water heaters to investigate the effect of clear covers on water-heating efficiency. Students relate their findings to the greenhouse effect and play a game to simulate the greenhouse effect.

Each of the 5 lesson plans (requiring a total of 5 or 6 class sessions of 45 minutes each) includes an overview, a list of materials, suggestions for preparation, directions for the activity, and extensions. Reproducible masters of patterns and student data sheets are included in the teacher's guide.

Key to Content Standards: 5-8 (see app. C)

UNIFYING CONCEPTS AND PROCESSES: Systems, order, and organization; evidence, models, and explanation; change, constancy, and measurement. **SCIENCE AS INQUIRY:** Abilities necessary to do scientific inquiry; understandings about scientific inquiry. **PHYSICAL SCIENCE:** Transfer of energy. **SCIENCE AND TECHNOLOGY:** Abilities of technological design; understandings about science and technology. **SCIENCE IN PERSONAL AND SOCIAL PERSPECTIVES:** Science and technology in society.

Price: $13.50 (ISBN 0-912511-24-9). ***Publisher/supplier:*** LHS GEMS. ***Materials:*** Available locally, or from commercial suppliers.

5.39 How Might Life Evolve on Other Worlds? SETI [Search for Extraterrestrial Intelligence] Academy Planet Project. Life in the Universe Series. Englewood, Colo.: Teacher Ideas Press, 1995.

Program Overview The Life in the Universe Series consists of 6 units, including the 3 volumes in the SETI Academy Planet Project. Each book in the SETI Academy Planet Project is designed to be a complete unit in

itself as well as a subunit of a 3-unit course. During the activities in the 3 units, each student plays the role of a "cadet" at the SETI [Search for Extraterrestrial Intelligence] Academy, a fictitious institution. (The SETI Institute is an actual scientific organization.)

Teacher's Guide **Recommended grade level: 7-8+.** *How Might Life Evolve on Other Worlds?* engages students in interdisciplinary activities related to the evolution of life on earth and asks them to apply their knowledge of this topic to the search for life on planets beyond our solar system. Within this context, the book deals primarily with the evolution of the atmosphere and the biosphere on earth.

During the unit, students use microscopes to observe bacteria, cyanobacteria, green algae, and planaria—some of the descendants of ancient organisms; they also conduct an experiment to see which of these organisms give off oxygen. Students make a "fossil jar" showing how sedimentary rock layers form with fossils inside. They play a game to learn about the process of natural selection, watch a video that describes the later stages of evolution on earth, and construct a record sheet showing geologic periods. Students learn how a dichotomous classification key works. They also design an extraterrestrial life form using some of the characteristics that distinguish life forms on earth.

Organized in 12 "missions," or chapters, the activities in *How Might Life Evolve on Other Worlds?* take 4 weeks to complete. The guide includes background information, directions for activities, discussion ideas, extensions, and reproducible blackline masters for student logbooks.

Program Resources and Support Materials A video—*History of Earth*—and a poster are available for use with this unit.

Key to Content Standards: 5-8 (see app. C)

UNIFYING CONCEPTS AND PROCESSES: Systems, order, and organization; evidence, models, and explanation; evolution and equilibrium. **SCIENCE AS INQUIRY:** Abilities necessary to do scientific inquiry; understandings about scientific inquiry. **LIFE SCIENCE:** Structure and function in living systems; diversity and adaptations of organisms. **EARTH AND SPACE SCIENCE:** Earth's history. **SCIENCE AND TECHNOLOGY:** Understandings about science and technology. **HISTORY AND NATURE OF SCIENCE:** Science as a human endeavor; nature of science.

Prices: Teacher's guide (ISBN 1-56308-325-6), $27.50. Videotape, $30.50. ***Publisher/supplier:*** Teacher Ideas Press. ***Materials:*** Available locally, or from commercial suppliers.

5.40 How Telecommunication Works: How People Use Energy to Communicate. Scholastic Science Place series. Developed in cooperation with Ann Arbor Hands-on Museum. New York, N.Y.: Scholastic, 1997.

Program Overview The Scholastic Science Place series is a K-6 program with 42 units, 6 for each grade level. The 6 units for grade 6 are organized under topics in the life, earth, and physical sciences. Three key themes—(1) scale and structure, (2) systems and interactions, and (3) patterns of change—are incorporated into the program. For each unit, teaching materials, student materials, and some optional components are available.

Student Edition **Recommended grade level: 6-8.** Through the activities in *How Telecommunication Works,* students explore what telecommunication is, how it works, and how it relates to sound and energy. Among the activities, for example, students observe how sound moves through different materials, they compare sound energy at varying distances from a sound source, and they use a spring to observe the characteristics of a compression wave. They also make models of a microphone, build a speaker to observe how it converts electric signals back into sound, and model digital recording by using a graph.

In other activities, students send a code using light, build a model of a radio tuner, and make models of the interface between a camera and a television set. At the end of the unit, they design and build a model of an interactive menu that can understand and respond to spoken words.

How Telecommunication Works is a 17-lesson unit consisting of approximately 18 class sessions, typically 60 to 90 minutes in duration.

Teacher's Edition The conceptual goals of the unit are presented in the lesson-by-lesson story line in the teacher's guide. Each lesson also includes background information; a complete lesson plan, including suggestions for assessing performance and integrating the curriculum; and a list of the materials required. For each lesson there is also a list of the relevant National Science Education Standards (developed by the National Research Council) and Project 2061 Benchmarks (developed by the American Association for the Advancement of Science).

Key to Content Standards: 5-8 (see app. C)

UNIFYING CONCEPTS AND PROCESSES: Systems, order, and organization; evidence, models, and explanation; change, constancy, and measurement.

SCIENCE AS INQUIRY: Abilities necessary to do scientific inquiry; understandings about scientific inquiry.
PHYSICAL SCIENCE: Transfer of energy.
SCIENCE AND TECHNOLOGY: Abilities of technological design; understandings about science and technology.
SCIENCE IN PERSONAL AND SOCIAL PERSPECTIVES: Science and technology in society.

Prices: Student edition (ISBN 0-590-95538-1), $7.95. Teacher's edition, (ISBN 0-590-95465-2), $27.00. Unit, $275.00. Consumable kit, $89.00. *Publisher/supplier:* Scholastic. *Materials:* Available locally, from commercial suppliers, or in kit.

5.41 **If Shipwrecks Could Talk.** R. Duncan Mathewson III. Delta Science Module (DSM) II series. Hudson, N.H.: Delta Education, 1995.

Program Overview The Delta Science Module (DSM) series has 51 life, physical, and earth science units for grades K-8 that emphasize science concepts, science content, and process skills. The series includes 12 modules for grades 5-6 and 8 modules for grades 6-8. Each requires about 3 to 4 weeks to complete and includes a teacher's guide and materials for a class of 32 students.

Teacher's Guide **Recommended grade level: 6-8.** *If Shipwrecks Could Talk* introduces students to the subjects of shipwrecks and marine archeology. On a map, students identify the continents and oceans of the world, labeling the principal surface currents of the Atlantic and Pacific Oceans. They probe an ocean-floor model and interpret the data to create a series of depth profiles. They also plot major sixteenth- to nineteenth-century maritime shipping routes in the Americas and locate some historic shipwreck sites.

In other activities, students experiment with objects that sink or float in water and apply what they learn

to the design of model cargo ships. They construct and calibrate a floating compass and then plot the course of a historic voyage using a modern magnetic compass. Students also assemble a model quadrant and use it to determine their position as they "navigate" around the classroom. They discover that water pressure increases with depth and speculate about the effect of this pressure on an underwater diver. They also observe the effects of water pressure on a volume of confined air and relate what they learn to a diver's ability to breathe under water. Students examine a variety of everyday objects, learning to view them as artifacts of contemporary life; they map a shipwreck site and examine and interpret the pattern of artifacts found there; and they examine the conflicting interests of shipwreck salvagers and archaeologists.

The 11 activities in *If Shipwrecks Could Talk* generally take 1 or 2 class sessions of 30 to 60 minutes each. They can be done by students working individually or in groups.

In addition to directions for activities, the teacher's guide provides a module overview, a schedule of activities, objectives for each activity, background information, materials management and preparation tips, sample answers to discussion questions, teaching suggestions, and reinforcement activities. Also included are reproducible activity sheets for student work and a performance-based assessment. A "connections" feature at the end of each activity provides suggestions for extending or applying the concepts in the activity.

Key to Content Standards: 5-8 (see app. C)

UNIFYING CONCEPTS AND PROCESSES: Systems, order, and organization; evidence, models, and explanation; change, constancy, and measurement.

SCIENCE AS INQUIRY: Abilities necessary to do scientific inquiry; understandings about scientific inquiry.
PHYSICAL SCIENCE: Properties and changes of properties in matter.
EARTH AND SPACE SCIENCE: Structure of the earth system.
SCIENCE AND TECHNOLOGY: Understandings about science and technology.
SCIENCE IN PERSONAL AND SOCIAL PERSPECTIVES: Science and technology in society.
HISTORY AND NATURE OF SCIENCE: Nature of science; history of science.

Prices: Teacher's guide (ISBN 0-87504-164-7), $27.95. Kit, $379.00. Refill package, $75.00. *Publisher/ supplier:* Delta Education. *Materials:* Available locally, from commercial suppliers, or in kit.

5.42 **Investigating and Evaluating STS Issues and Solutions: A Worktext for STS Education.** John M. Ramsey, Trudi L. Volk, and Harold R. Hungerford. Champaign, Ill.: Stipes, 1997.

Program Overview *Investigating and Evaluating STS [science-technology-society] Issues and Solutions: A Worktext for STS Education* is a semester-long skill-development program designed for middle school students. The program focuses on science and technology and on how science and technology interact with society. It emphasizes the processes needed by students as they investigate, evaluate, and take action on STS issues.

Student Edition **Recommended grade level: 6-8+.** Emphasizing the importance of responsible citizen action, the 7 chapters in *Investigating and Evaluating STS Issues and Solutions* begin with an overview of the nature of science and technology, their relationship to one another, and how they interact with society.

Students are then introduced to issue analysis and the roles of human beliefs and values in negotiating science and technology issues. They classify issues in terms of the type of investigation (primary or secondary) that would produce the best information on those issues, and they learn how to use different information sources (government agencies, periodicals, and knowledgeable people in the community).

Students are also introduced to ways of using surveys, questionnaires, and other data-gathering techniques, and they learn how to interpret and communicate data using graphs and tables. Students then choose and investigate a topic independently, using the techniques and skills they have acquired. Finally, they find out about specific ways of taking responsible action on issues, such as letter writing, changing consumer habits, and political action.

Teacher's Edition The teacher's edition includes a supplementary section with background information on teaching the program, detailed teaching notes for each chapter, and additional data sheets.

Key to Content Standards: 5-8 (see app. C)

UNIFYING CONCEPTS AND PROCESSES: Systems, order, and organization; evidence, models, and explanation; change, constancy, and measurement.
SCIENCE AS INQUIRY: Abilities necessary to do scientific inquiry; understandings about scientific inquiry.
SCIENCE AND TECHNOLOGY: Abilities of technological design; understandings about science and technology.
SCIENCE IN PERSONAL AND SOCIAL PERSPECTIVES: Personal health; populations, resources, and environments; natural hazards; risks and benefits; science and technology in society.

HISTORY AND NATURE OF SCIENCE: Science as a human endeavor; nature of science; history of science.

Prices: Student edition (ISBN 0-87563-717-5), $12.60. Teacher's edition (ISBN 0-87563-718-3), $24.20. *Publisher/ supplier:* Stipes. *Materials:* Available locally.

5.43 **Investigating Chemical Processes: Your Island Factory.** Chemical Education for Public Understanding Program (CEPUP) series. Developed by Lawrence Hall of Science (Berkeley, Calif.). Menlo Park, Calif.: Addison-Wesley, 1992.

Program Overview The Chemical Education for Public Understanding Program (CEPUP) series consists of 12 modules for grades 7-9. The modules focus on chemicals and the interaction of chemicals with people and the environment. The series promotes the use of scientific principles, processes, and evidence in public decision making. The components of a CEPUP module are a teacher's guide and a kit of materials. (SEPUP—the Science Education for Public Understanding Program—is the second phase of the project that began as CEPUP.)

Teacher's Guide **Recommended grade level: 7-8+.** *Investigating Chemical Processes: Your Island Factory* contains 6 activities during which students explore the role of chemicals and chemical processes in manufacturing industries and the effect of such chemicals on people and their environment—in this case, on an island community. During the activities, students examine their attitudes toward and knowledge about 4 different industries—computers, food processing, chemical manufacturing, and oil refining. They read brief descriptions of the chemical processes involved in these industries. They learn the meaning of such concepts as reactant, product, and by-product by investigating a simple reaction in which a mixture of vinegar and salt is used to remove oxidation from copper pennies.

In other activities, students imagine they live on an island that has large deposits of limestone and marble, which leads to their developing a plan to produce gypsum. Students synthesize gypsum in the lab in a 2-step procedure. Next, they design a plan for an island factory (for large-scale production), taking into account the availability of raw materials, disposal of wastes, energy management, and labor.

The 6 activities in *Investigating Chemical Processes* each take 1 or 2 periods of 40 to 50 minutes. Included in the slim, wire-bound book are reproducible student sheets, directions for guiding activities and discussions, and an end-of-unit test.

Key to Content Standards: 5-8 (see app. C)

UNIFYING CONCEPTS AND PROCESSES: Systems, order, and organization; evidence, models, and explanation.
SCIENCE AS INQUIRY: Abilities necessary to do scientific inquiry; understandings about scientific inquiry.
PHYSICAL SCIENCE: Properties and changes of properties in matter.
SCIENCE AND TECHNOLOGY: Understandings about science and technology.
SCIENCE IN PERSONAL AND SOCIAL PERSPECTIVES: Risks and benefits; science and technology in society.
HISTORY AND NATURE OF SCIENCE: Nature of science.

Prices: Teacher's guide (ISBN 0-201-28432-4), $19.99. Kit, $174.99.
Publisher/supplier: Sargent-Welch/VWR Scientific. *Materials:* Available locally, from commercial suppliers, or in kit.

5.44 **JASON IV Curriculum: Baja California Sur.** JASON Project series. Developed by National Science Teachers Association (NSTA). Washington, D.C.: NSTA, 1992.

Program Overview Each year, the JASON Project—administered by the JASON Foundation for Education—embarks on a 2-week scientific expedition to a remote location. The project develops a science and technology curriculum module to prepare students to participate in the expedition using interactive telecommunication. The JASON Project series currently consists of 9 such modules.

Teacher's Guide **Recommended grade level: 6-8+.** The *JASON IV Curriculum: Baja California Sur* contains 21 lessons and more than 70 activities that prepared students for live satellite participation in a March 1993 expedition to Baja California Sur to study whales in the San Ignacio Lagoon and hydrothermal vent communities in the Guaymas Basin of the Sea of Cortez. During the module, students learn about past JASON Projects and about the goals of the JASON IV expedition. They also find out about the technological innovations that make such expeditions work—for example, robotics, sonar technology, and fiber optics. They learn about the science involved in the expedition—tectonic geological processes, photosynthesis, chemosynthesis, and the physiology, behavior, and migration pattern of gray whales—as well as about the social and cultural history of Baja California and the pros and cons of whaling.

Among the activities, students build models of some of the devices that JASON scientists used to collect and retrieve samples from the ocean floor. They plot points from soundings of the Guaymas Basin and draw a profile of the seafloor. They also locate and describe geological features above and below the ocean

surface, build a model of a hydrothermal vent community, piece together a model of a gray whale's skeleton, and experiment with using whalelike sounds for communication.

Each activity includes objectives, step-by-step teaching procedures, and a materials list. Most of the activities were developed for middle school students, but suggestions are included for adapting the activities for use with older or younger students. In addition to the activities, the module contains background materials for the teacher, reproducible student worksheets and readings, resource lists, and a glossary.

Program Resources and Support Materials The module also contains a poster, a large map of the ocean floor, several small maps, and complete materials for several games and simulations. A videotape—*Sea of Cortez Highlights*—is also available.

Key to Content Standards: 5-8 (see app. C)

UNIFYING CONCEPTS AND PROCESSES: Systems, order, and organization; evidence, models, and explanation; change, constancy, and measurement; evolution and equilibrium; form and function.
SCIENCE AS INQUIRY: Abilities necessary to do scientific inquiry; understandings about scientific inquiry.
PHYSICAL SCIENCE: Properties and changes of properties in matter; transfer of energy.
LIFE SCIENCE: Structure and function in living systems; regulation and behavior; populations and ecosystems; diversity and adaptations of organisms.
EARTH AND SPACE SCIENCE: Structure of the earth system; earth's history.
SCIENCE AND TECHNOLOGY: Abilities of technological design; understandings about science and technology.
SCIENCE IN PERSONAL AND SOCIAL PERSPECTIVES: Science and technology in society.

HISTORY AND NATURE OF SCIENCE: Science as a human endeavor; nature of science; history of science.

Price: Teacher's guide, $15. (Contact publisher/supplier for complete price and ordering information.) *Publisher/supplier:* JASON Foundation for Education. *Materials:* Available locally, or from commercial suppliers.

5.45 **JASON VI: Island Earth, Hawai'i Expedition Curriculum.** JASON Foundation for Education. JASON Project series. Waltham, Mass.: JASON Foundation for Education, 1994.

Program Overview Each year, the JASON Project—administered by the JASON Foundation for Education—embarks on a 2-week scientific expedition to a remote location. The project develops a science and technology curriculum module to prepare students to participate in the expedition using interactive telecommunication. The JASON Project series currently consists of 9 such modules.

Teacher's Guide **Recommended grade level: 4-8.** *JASON VI: Island Earth, Hawai'i Expedition Curriculum* contains 17 lessons, 31 activities, and more than 100 exercises that prepared students for live satellite participation in a 1995 research expedition to Hawaii to study volcanoes and what they reveal about the formation of the earth and the solar system. During the module, students learn about the organization of our solar system and about island ecology. They also learn about the technological innovations, such as planetary probes, robots, satellites, remote sensing, aerial photography, fiber optics, and computer communications, that accompany many of today's expeditions. They study about geoscience concepts—plate tectonics, terrestrial volcanic activity, and planetary volcanism—as well as life

science concepts relevant to the expedition—animal migration, island biogeography, and adaptation. They are introduced to the history, culture, and people of Hawaii both before and after the arrival of Captain James Cook, the first documented European to reach the Islands.

Among the activities, students simulate the formation of an island chain, design and build a particulate trap, collect seismic data using the Internet, and predict the morphological characteristics of Hawaiian honeycreeper birds. They investigate how data are transmitted from a probe back to earth, simulate a volcanic eruption, examine causes of volcanism on other planets, compare the colonization of the Galapagos and the Hawaiian Islands, and display Hawaiian *'ohana* (family) values through a pantomime.

Each activity includes objectives, step-by-step teaching procedures, a materials list, and suggestions for adapting the activities to use with older or younger students. In addition to the activities, the module contains background materials for the teacher, reproducible student worksheets and readings, resource lists, and a glossary.

Program Resources and Support Materials The module also contains a poster and a topographic map of Hawaii. A network of distributed resources is available on the Internet through the JASON Online Systems. JASON Discovery Kits, which contain materials and instructions for conducting a selection of curriculum experiments in the fields of astronomy, geology, and technology, are also available.

Key to Content Standards: 5-8 (see app. C)

UNIFYING CONCEPTS AND PROCESSES: Systems, order, and organization; evidence, models, and explanation; change, constancy, and measurement; evolution and equilibrium; form and function.

SCIENCE AS INQUIRY: Abilities necessary to do scientific inquiry; understandings about scientific inquiry.
PHYSICAL SCIENCE: Transfer of energy.
LIFE SCIENCE: Reproduction and heredity; regulation and behavior; populations and ecosystems; diversity and adaptations of organisms.
EARTH AND SPACE SCIENCE: Structure of the earth system; earth's history; earth in the solar system.
SCIENCE AND TECHNOLOGY: Abilities of technological design; understandings about science and technology.
SCIENCE IN PERSONAL AND SOCIAL PERSPECTIVES: Populations, resources, and environments; natural hazards; science and technology in society.
HISTORY AND NATURE OF SCIENCE: Science as a human endeavor; nature of science.

Price: Teacher's guide, $28. (Contact publisher/supplier for complete price and ordering information.) *Publisher/supplier:* JASON Foundation for Education. *Materials:* Available locally, or from commercial suppliers.

5.46 **Life: Here? There? Elsewhere? The Search for Life on Venus and Mars.** SETI [Search for Extraterrestrial Intelligence] Institute. Life in the Universe Series. Englewood, Colo.: Teacher Ideas Press, 1996.

Program Overview The Life in the Universe Series consists of 6 units, including the 3 volumes in the SETI Academy Planet Project. Each book in the SETI Academy Planet Project is designed to be a complete unit in itself as well as a subunit of a 3-unit course. During the activities in the 3 units, each student plays the role of a "cadet" at the SETI [Search for Extraterrestrial Intelligence] Academy, a fictitious institution. (The SETI Institute is an actual scientific organization.)

Teacher's Guide **Recommended grade level: 7-8+.** *Life: Here? There? Else-*

where? engages students in activities designed to explore the possibility of life on Venus or Mars and to find out about methods used to detect life in the atmosphere and soil of earth. Comparative planetology and exobiology (the study of life outside or beyond the earth) are used to help students discover that life is not always intelligent, nor always easy to recognize.

During the unit, students construct an orbital model of earth, Mars, Venus, and the sun, and they learn about conditions on the 3 planets and why the search for life in the solar system is focused on these planets. They also learn about scale and powers of 10. They culture a microscopic organism and see whether it can grow under simulated Martian conditions. They design a spacecraft-lander system to search for life at a specific site on Mars or Venus. Students also "discover" life (dormant brine shrimp eggs) in apparently lifeless soil, they test soils for the presence of carbohydrates and proteins, and they build "life traps" (nutrient gelatin dishes) to capture microbial life present in earth's atmosphere and figure out how they could use these traps on Venus or Mars. Finally, they analyze simulated data from a Viking mission to decide if life is present on Mars.

Organized in 14 sequential "missions," or chapters, the activities can take 4 to 6 weeks to complete. The guide includes background information, directions for activities, discussion ideas, extensions, and reproducible blackline masters.

Program Resources and Support Materials Powers-of-10 cards, a poster, and a videotape—*Voyages to Earth, Mars, and Venus*—accompany the teacher's guide.

Key to Content Standards: 5-8 (see app. C)

UNIFYING CONCEPTS AND PROCESSES: Systems, order, and organization; evidence, models, and explanation; evolution and equilibrium.

SCIENCE AS INQUIRY: Abilities necessary to do scientific inquiry; understandings about scientific inquiry.
LIFE SCIENCE: Diversity and adaptations of organisms.
EARTH AND SPACE SCIENCE: Earth in the solar system.
SCIENCE AND TECHNOLOGY: Understandings about science and technology.
SCIENCE IN PERSONAL AND SOCIAL PERSPECTIVES: Science and technology in society.

Price: Kit, $90. ***Publisher/supplier:*** Teacher Ideas Press. ***Materials:*** Available locally, or from commercial suppliers.

5.47 Manufacturing. 4th ed. Integrated Mathematics, Science and Technology (IMaST) Project. IMaST series. Normal, Ill.: Center for Mathematics, Science, and Technology Education, Illinois State University, 1996.

Program Overview The Integrated Mathematics, Science, and Technology (IMaST) series for middle school includes 6 modules. The materials in each are designed to be used by a team of mathematics, science, and technology teachers concurrently over a 9-week period. Each module includes a teacher's guide and a student book.

Student Book **Recommended grade level: 7-8+.** The module *Manufacturing* engages students in activities related to contemporary manufacturing and engineering processes and helps them develop an understanding of the importance of manufacturing to society. The module begins with 2 optional introductory activities in which students design and manufacture a custom book cover and investigate the operations of a manufacturing plant.

Then, during the unit's 32 activities, students learn to measure for precision using metric or standard measure; they work with geoboards to find the area of triangles and parallelograms; and they examine the mathematics involved with scaling work. Students also examine the qualities of a box of new pencils to develop an understanding of the manufacturing term "tolerance interval," used for levels of acceptable standards. They classify sample materials used in manufacturing according to 4 categories—polymers, metals, ceramics, and composites; and they investigate the physical and chemical properties of different materials.

In other activities, students test materials for strength, flammability, porosity, resistance to scratches, or adhesive nature. They identify the impact manufacturing materials might have on living organisms. They also design, build, and use jigs and fixtures to control a tool or a work piece during manufacturing processing, and they design and build a prototype of a product.

The 32 activities in *Manufacturing* are organized in 3 groups, according to their emphasis on mathematics, science, or technology. Three sections following the activities provide background reading on manufacturing and its impact on people and societies.

Teacher's Guide Accompanying the activities in the teacher's guide are brief directions, ideas for class discussions, and extension activities. Guidelines for assessing student performance are provided.

Key to Content Standards: 5-8 (see app. C)

UNIFYING CONCEPTS AND PROCESSES: Systems, order, and organization; evidence, models, and explanation; change, constancy, and measurement.
SCIENCE AS INQUIRY: Abilities necessary to do scientific inquiry; understandings about scientific inquiry.

PHYSICAL SCIENCE: Properties and changes of properties in matter. **LIFE SCIENCE:** Regulation and behavior. **SCIENCE AND TECHNOLOGY:** Abilities of technological design; understandings about science and technology. **SCIENCE IN PERSONAL AND SOCIAL PERSPECTIVES:** Populations, resources, and environments; science and technology in society. **HISTORY AND NATURE OF SCIENCE:** Nature of science.

Prices: Student book, $13.50. Teacher's guide, $24.50. *Publisher/supplier:* Illinois State University. *Materials:* Available locally, or from commercial suppliers.

5.48 **Packaging.** Module 1.3. Foundations and Challenges to Encourage Technology-based Science (FACETS) series. Developed by American Chemical Society (Washington, D.C.). Dubuque, Iowa: Kendall/Hunt, 1996.

Program Overview The Foundations and Challenges to Encourage Technology-based Science (FACETS) program consists of 3 series of 8 modules each for grades 6-8. Each module focuses on a topic in the life, earth, or physical sciences. The time needed to complete FACETS modules varies from 2 to 4 weeks. Each module consists of a student book and a teacher's guide.

Student Edition **Recommended grade level: 6.** In the module *Packaging,* students investigate packaging materials and their assembly and learn about some of the science and technology involved in packaging. Students first investigate how packaging shapes are made—from flat pieces with fold lines, forming a package of a particular shape. They analyze the pluses and minuses of different packaging shapes, and they design and make models of a package for shipping glass olive oil bottles.

Students also investigate the properties—strength, elasticity, ability to be shaped, tearability, and water repulsion—of different packaging materials. They take a field trip to a grocery store to observe different types of packaging, and they gather data on the "environmental friendliness" of packages they see; then they write to manufacturers that they think could use more ecologically friendly packaging for certain products. In the final activity, students design a single serving package for a "designer" cookie. The package meets certain specifications for size, appearance, and performance.

Packaging is divided into 5 activities, which each take between 1 and 4 class periods to complete. Four short reading sections at the end of the module provide limited background information on how packages are shaped to contain their products and to be stacked, on some of the basic science behind the most commonly used polymers in packaging, and on what is meant by "environmentally friendly" packaging.

Teacher's Guide The wraparound teacher's guide includes a unit overview, a time line for completing the module, a materials list, background information, and teaching suggestions.

Key to Content Standards: 5-8 (see app. C)

UNIFYING CONCEPTS AND PROCESSES: Form and function. **SCIENCE AS INQUIRY:** Abilities necessary to do scientific inquiry; understandings about scientific inquiry. **SCIENCE AND TECHNOLOGY:** Abilities of technological design; understandings about science and technology. **HISTORY AND NATURE OF SCIENCE:** Nature of science.

Prices: Student edition (ISBN 0-7872-1435-3), $7.90. Teacher's guide (ISBN 0-7872-1436-1), $14.90. *Publisher/supplier:* Kendall/Hunt. *Materials:* Available locally, or from commercial suppliers.

5.49 **Paper Towel Testing.** Reprinted with revisions. Cary I. Sneider and Jacqueline Barber. Great Explorations in Math and Science (GEMS) series. Berkeley, Calif.: Lawrence Hall of Science, 1990.

Program Overview The Great Explorations in Math and Science (GEMS) series includes more than 50 teacher's guides and handbooks for preschool through grade 10. About 35 of these are appropriate for middle school. The series also includes several assembly presenter's guides and exhibit guides. New guides and handbooks continue to be developed, and current titles are revised frequently. The series is designed to teach key science and mathematics concepts through activity-based learning. The time needed to complete GEMS units varies from about 2 to 10 class sessions.

Teacher's Guide **Recommended grade level: 5-7.** In *Paper Towel Testing,* students design and conduct scientific tests to compare the qualities of several brands of paper towels. Teams of students plan and conduct controlled experiments to determine which brand is most absorbent and which has the greatest wet strength. They discuss their results and plan and conduct follow-up experiments. Results are averaged and compared. After calculating the unit cost of each brand of paper towel, students reexamine their findings and discuss which brand is the best buy.

The teacher's guide includes background information, detailed instructions for conducting the activities, and summary outlines of the 4 sessions, which require 30 to 35 minutes each. Reproducible masters of student data sheets are included.

Key to Content Standards: 5-8 (see app. C)

UNIFYING CONCEPTS AND PROCESSES: Systems, order, and organization; change, constancy, and measurement.

SCIENCE AS INQUIRY: Abilities necessary to do scientific inquiry; understandings about scientific inquiry.
SCIENCE AND TECHNOLOGY: Abilities of technological design.
HISTORY AND NATURE OF SCIENCE: Nature of science.

Price: $9 (ISBN 0-912511-65-6).
Publisher/supplier: LHS GEMS.
Materials: Available locally, or from commercial suppliers.

5.50 Steamed Up! Michigan Science Education Resources Project. New Directions Teaching Units. Lansing, Mich.: Michigan Department of Education, 1993.

Program Overview The New Directions Teaching Units focus on developing scientific literacy and conceptual understanding. They were designed to reflect the ideas about teaching, learning, and curriculum in the Michigan Essential Goals and Objectives for K-12 Science Education, which were developed by the Michigan Science Education Resources Project. Several New Directions Teaching Units can be used with middle school students.

Teacher's Guide **Recommended grade level: 5-7.** *Steamed Up!* helps students understand how evaporation and condensation work at the molecular and macroscopic levels. The unit also helps students develop familiarity with the scientific approach to experimentation and with ways in which results of such experiments can be applied to real-world problems.

During the first cluster of lessons, students review their prior knowledge of water and evaporation. Working cooperatively and individually, they explain what they think happens when a shirt dries. Then they design, set up, and carry out experiments to test factors such as heat, light, and moving air that affect the rate of evaporation.

In the second cluster of lessons, students read a "fog" story containing several situations that involve condensation. Then they construct a closed system and manipulate conditions within the system to cause evaporation and condensation to occur. They also develop an explanation for one of the condensation situations in the "fog" story and draw a cartoon strip illustrating it. In the final activity students use the information they have learned in the unit to design and/or explain a real-world device such as a hair dryer, humidifier, or steam iron that employs the principles of evaporation and condensation to perform its function.

Steamed Up! has 13 lessons and takes about 22 class sessions to complete. The teacher's guide contains background information, lab preparation notes, answers to questions posed in the unit's separate reproducible student pages, and information about student misconceptions and how to address them.

Key to Content Standards: 5-8 (see app. C)

UNIFYING CONCEPTS AND PROCESSES: Evidence, models, and explanation.
SCIENCE AS INQUIRY: Abilities necessary to do scientific inquiry; understandings about scientific inquiry.
PHYSICAL SCIENCE: Properties and changes of properties in matter.
EARTH AND SPACE SCIENCE: Structure of the earth system.
SCIENCE AND TECHNOLOGY: Abilities of technological design; understandings about science and technology.
SCIENCE IN PERSONAL AND SOCIAL PERSPECTIVES: Science and technology in society.
HISTORY AND NATURE OF SCIENCE: Science as a human endeavor; nature of science.

Price: $18. *Publisher/supplier:* Battle Creek Area Math/Science Center. *Materials:* Available locally, or from commercial suppliers.

5.51 A Sunken Ship. Module 2.8. Foundations and Challenges to Encourage Technology-based Science (FACETS) series. Developed by American Chemical Society (Washington, D.C.). Dubuque, Iowa: Kendall/Hunt, 1996.

Program Overview The Foundations and Challenges to Encourage Technology-based Science (FACETS) program consists of 3 series of 8 modules each for grades 6-8. Each module focuses on a topic in the life, earth, or physical sciences. The time needed to complete FACETS modules varies from 2 to 4 weeks. Each module consists of a student book and a teacher's guide.

Student Edition **Recommended grade level: 7.** In the module *A Sunken Ship,* students are involved in a simulation about salvaging the cargo on board a mythical ship that sank in the Atlantic Ocean 50 years ago. In the process, they work with several science concepts, including the solubility of sodium chloride, the effect of saltwater on certain metals, the noncompressibility of liquids, and the conservation of matter.

Students first use plastic soda bottles to make models of the ocean where the ship sank. They investigate the compressibility of gases and the noncompressibility of liquids to determine the fate of fuel barrels that were on board the ship. They observe the effect of immersion in saltwater on copper, steel, and silver. They refer to the financial pages from a newspaper to calculate the value of the gold, silver, and platinum that were on board the ship. Finally, they prepare a brief proposal for a salvage operation to a funding agency.

In addition to the science in the module, students use map skills (identifying latitude and longitude; reading depth levels; working with scale); mathematics (calculating the total cost of a salvage venture, setting up a budget, making a model to scale); and language arts skills (writing a proposal to a funding agency).

A Sunken Ship is divided into 6 activities that each take between 1 and 3 class periods to complete. Three short reading sections at the end of the module provide limited background information on how a ship is structured, the chemistry of corrosion, and the technology used in undersea explorations.

Teacher's Guide The wraparound teacher's guide includes a unit overview, a time line for completing the module, a materials list, background information, and teaching suggestions.

Key to Content Standards: 5-8 (see app. C)

UNIFYING CONCEPTS AND PROCESSES: Evidence, models, and explanation; change, constancy, and measurement. **SCIENCE AS INQUIRY:** Abilities necessary to do scientific inquiry; understandings about scientific inquiry. **PHYSICAL SCIENCE:** Properties and changes of properties in matter. **SCIENCE AND TECHNOLOGY:** Abilities of technological design; understandings about science and technology. **SCIENCE IN PERSONAL AND SOCIAL PERSPECTIVES:** Risks and benefits; science and technology in society.

Prices: Student edition (ISBN 0-7872-1443-4), $7.90. Teacher's guide (ISBN 0-7872-1444-2), $14.90. ***Publisher/ supplier:*** Kendall/Hunt. ***Materials:*** Available locally, or from commercial suppliers.

5.52 Threads. Module 3.1. Foundations and Challenges to Encourage Technology-based Science (FACETS) series. Developed by American Chemical Society (Washington, D.C.). Dubuque, Iowa: Kendall/Hunt, 1996.

Program Overview The Foundations and Challenges to Encourage Technology-based Science (FACETS) program consists of 3 series of 8 modules each for grades 6-8. Each module focuses on a topic in the life, earth, or physical sciences. The time needed to complete FACETS modules varies from 2 to 4 weeks. Each module consists of a student book and a teacher's guide.

Student Edition **Recommended grade level: 8.** In the module *Threads*, students investigate the physical and chemical properties of a variety of natural and synthetic fibers. During these investigations, they gain firsthand experience with problems of experimental design, conducting experiments, interpreting data, and forming conclusions.

Students first conduct a survey of the types of fibers used in garments. They examine fibers under a microscope using several levels of magnification. They also watch a demonstration led by the teacher that illustrates how flame tests can be used to identify fibers. Students design a way of testing fibers for tensile strength. They investigate how well soiled fabrics can be cleaned using water at various temperatures and different cleaning agents. In the last activity, students draw on their research on fabrics and fibers to design a school-related garment that uses the best possible fabrics and fibers for the purposes of the garment.

Threads is divided into 6 activities that each take between 1 and 4 class periods to complete. Three short reading sections at the end of the module provide limited background information on using a microscope

and on the composition of fibers, as well as their characteristics.

Teacher's Guide The wraparound teacher's guide includes a unit overview, a time line for completing the module, a materials list, background information, and teaching suggestions.

Key to Content Standards: 5-8 (see app. C)

UNIFYING CONCEPTS AND PROCESSES: Evidence, models, and explanation. **SCIENCE AS INQUIRY:** Abilities necessary to do scientific inquiry; understandings about scientific inquiry. **SCIENCE AND TECHNOLOGY:** Abilities of technological design; understandings about science and technology. **SCIENCE IN PERSONAL AND SOCIAL PERSPECTIVES:** Science and technology in society. **HISTORY AND NATURE OF SCIENCE:** Nature of science.

Prices: Student edition (ISBN 0-7872-1482-5), $7.90. Teacher's guide (ISBN 0-7872-1483-3), $14.90. ***Publisher/ supplier:*** Kendall/Hunt. ***Materials:*** Available locally, or from commercial suppliers.

5.53 Wellness: First Module in Bio-Related Technologies Unit. 4th ed. Integrated Mathematics, Science and Technology (IMaST) Project. IMaST series. Normal, Ill.: Center for Mathematics, Science, and Technology Education, Illinois State University, 1996.

Program Overview The Integrated Mathematics, Science, and Technology (IMaST) series for middle school includes 6 modules. The materials in each are designed to be used by a team of mathematics, science, and technology teachers concurrently over a 9-week period. Each module includes a teacher's guide and a student book.

Student Book **Recommended grade level: 7.** The module *Wellness* engages students in activities related to nutrition, exercise, and communicable diseases. Many of the activities are relevant to students' lifestyles, encouraging them to think about their eating and exercise habits. In an optional introductory activity, students conduct a "wellness fair" to evaluate their level of fitness. Then, during the 13 activities in the module, they calculate "golden" ratios from measurements they take of each other's bodies; they build and use a paper protractor to measure the range of motion in their wrists, thumbs, and fingers; and they calculate their base metabolic rate and plan a diet or menu based on that rate.

In other activities, students investigate how bones, joints, and muscles make motion possible. They use a calorimeter to measure the amount of energy per gram released during the burning of food samples; and they design, build, and test a prosthetic hand. They also learn how a communicable disease spreads through a population, and they plan and produce an educational wellness video.

The 13 activities in *Wellness* are organized in 3 groups, according to their emphasis on mathematics, science, or technology. Three sections following the activities provide background reading and basic information on health topics related to the module.

Teacher's Guide Accompanying the activities in the teacher's guide are brief directions, along with ideas for class discussions, and extension activities. Guidelines for assessing student performance are provided.

Key to Content Standards: 5-8 (see app. C)

UNIFYING CONCEPTS AND PROCESSES: Evidence, models, and explanation; change, constancy, and measurement; form and function.
SCIENCE AS INQUIRY: Abilities necessary to do scientific inquiry; understandings about scientific inquiry.

LIFE SCIENCE: Structure and function in living systems.
SCIENCE AND TECHNOLOGY: Understandings about science and technology.
SCIENCE IN PERSONAL AND SOCIAL PERSPECTIVES: Personal health; risks and benefits; science and technology in society.
HISTORY AND NATURE OF SCIENCE: Nature of science.

Prices: Student book, $7.50. Teacher's guide, $15.75. *Publisher/supplier:* Illinois State University. *Materials:* Available locally, or from commercial suppliers.

5.54 **A World in Motion II: The Design Experience, Challenge 2.** A World in Motion II: The Design Experience series. Developed by Education Development Center (Newton, Mass.) for Society of Automotive Engineers, International, and the SAE Foundation. Pittsburgh, Pa.: SAE International, 1996.

Program Overview: A World in Motion II: the Design Experience series consists of 3 units on using science, mathematics, and technology to explore the process of design. Each unit engages students in a problem-solving context for which they must create a design or solution to address a particular need or problem. The active participation of volunteers in the classroom is a distinguishing feature of this series.

Teacher's Guide **Recommended grade level: 7.** In *A World in Motion II: The Design Experience, Challenge 2,* students respond to a request for proposals from a fictitious toy company to develop designs for new motorized, gear-driven toys that meet a specific set of requirements. Students work in design teams to develop a proposal and a prototype for a toy of their own design. To

participate in this program, a teacher must form a partnership with a business or organization willing to provide voluntary support for the classroom.

Science and mathematics concepts examined in the unit include force and friction, simple machines, levers and gears, torque, and the relationship between gear ratios and the radius of a wheel. During the activities in this 8-week unit, students identify the target market; gather and synthesize information; predict a plausible solution; design, develop, and test a prototype or potential design; and prepare for a presentation of their design ideas.

Program Resources and Support Materials The teacher's guide is available separately or as part of a teacher's kit. The teacher's kit also includes posters, 4 implementation videotapes, and a CD-ROM resource disc. Kits with hands-on laboratory materials for constructing prototypes are also available.

Key to Content Standards: 5-8 (see app. C)

UNIFYING CONCEPTS AND PROCESSES: Evidence, models, and explanation; change, constancy, and measurement; form and function.
SCIENCE AS INQUIRY: Abilities necessary to do scientific inquiry; understandings about scientific inquiry.
PHYSICAL SCIENCE: Motions and forces.
SCIENCE AND TECHNOLOGY: Abilities of technological design; understandings about science and technology.
SCIENCE IN PERSONAL AND SOCIAL PERSPECTIVES: Science and technology in society.
HISTORY AND NATURE OF SCIENCE: Science as a human endeavor; nature of science.

Prices: Free upon establishment of partnership with local business or organization. *Publisher/supplier:* SAE International. *Materials:* Available locally, from commercial suppliers, or in kit.

Multidisciplinary and Applied Science—Science Activity Books

5.55 The Art and Science Connection: Hands-on Activities for Intermediate Students. Kimberley Tolley. Menlo Park, Calif.: Innovative Learning, 1994.

Recommended grade level: 4-8. *The Art and Science Connection* for intermediate students is a sourcebook of creative art activities that integrate art and science concepts and processes. The 30 lessons are organized around 3 conceptual themes of science: structure, interactions, and energy. Activities include the following art forms: drawing, painting, sculpture, bas-relief, printmaking, collage, graphic arts, textiles, and mixed media.

Each lesson includes an overview, student objectives, a list of materials, step-by-step teaching instructions, extension ideas, and suggested resources. Blackline masters for activity sheets, tips for classroom management and working with art and science materials, safety precautions, and a glossary are included.

Price: $19.95 (ISBN 0-201-45545-5). *Publisher/supplier:* Addison-Wesley/Longman. *Materials:* Available locally, or from commercial suppliers.

ABOUT THE ANNOTATIONS IN "MULTIDISCIPLINARY AND APPLIED SCIENCE—SCIENCE ACTIVITY BOOKS"

Entry Numbers

Curriculum materials are arranged alphabetically by title in each category (Core Materials, Supplementary Units, and Science Activity Books) in chapters 1 through 5 of this guide.

Each curriculum annotation has a two-part entry number: the chapter number is given before the period; the number after the period locates the entry within that chapter. For example, the first entry number in chapter 1 is 1.1; the second entry in chapter 2 is 2.2; and so on.

The entry numbers within each curriculum chapter run consecutively through Core Materials, Supplementary Units, and Science Activity Books.

Order of Bibliographic Information

Following is the arrangement of the facts of publication in the annotations in this section:

- **Title of publication**
- **Number of edition,** if applicable
- **Authors** (an individual author or authors, an institutional author, or a project or program name under which the material was developed)
- **Series title**
- **Series developer,** if applicable
- **Place of publication, publisher, and date of publication**

Recommended Grade Level

The grade level for each piece of material was recommended by teacher evaluators during the development of this guide. In some instances, the recommended grade level may differ slightly from the publisher's advertised level.

Price and Acquisition Information

Ordering information appears at the end of each entry. Included are—

- **Prices** (of teacher's guides, activity books, and kits or units)
- **Publisher/supplier** (The name of a principal publisher/supplier, although not necessarily the sole source, for the items listed in the price category. Appendix A, "Publishers and Suppliers," provides the address, phone and fax numbers, and electronic ordering information, where available, for each publisher and supplier.)
- **Materials** (various sources from which one might obtain the required materials)

Readers must contact publishers/suppliers for complete and up-to-date ordering information, since prices are subject to change and materials may also change with revised editions. The prices given in this chapter are based on information from publishers and suppliers but are not meant to represent the full range of ordering options.

Indexes of Curriculum Materials

The multiple indexes on pp. 449-78 allow easy access to the information in this guide. Various aspects of the curriculum materials—including titles, topics addressed in each unit, and grade levels—are the focus of seven separate indexes. For example, titles and entry numbers are listed in the "Title Index" on pp. 450-54. The "Index of Authors, Series, and Curriculum Projects," on pp. 455-57, provides entry numbers of any annotated titles in a particular series.

5.56 **The Ben Franklin Book of Easy and Incredible Experiments: Activities, Projects, and Science Fun.** A Franklin Institute Science Museum Book. New York, N.Y.: John Wiley, 1995.

Recommended grade level: 4-8. This book contains more than 60 activities related to 6 subjects that interested Benjamin Franklin: (1) observation and experimentation, (2) meteorology, (3) electricity, (4) sound and music, (5) paper and printing, and (6) lenses and vision. Among the activities, for example, students play an observation game, make a weather station, experiment with static electricity, build their own printing press, and make and use a kaleidoscope. They also create an orchestra with handmade flutes, water chimes, and a shoe-box guitar.

Each of the 6 chapters in the book begins with entertaining historical anecdotes about Franklin, his inventions, or the experiments he did; entries from his journals or letters are often included. Each activity includes a list of materials, scientific background or explanations, step-by-step procedures, illustrations, and suggestions for extensions. All of the activities use inexpensive, readily available materials and can be done in any order.

Price: $12.95 (ISBN 0-471-07638-4). *Publisher/supplier:* Wiley. *Materials:* Available locally.

5.57 Classroom 2061: Activity-Based Assessments in Science Integrated with Mathematics and Language Arts. Elizabeth Hammerman and Diann Musial. Palatine, Ill.: IRI/Skylight Training and Publishing, 1995.

Recommended grade level: 4-8. *Classroom 2061: Activity-Based Assessments in Science Integrated with Mathematics and Language Arts* includes performance assessments and practical guidelines for developing such assessments. This teacher's guide is organized in 2 sections. The first focuses on "the new visions" for science, mathematics, and language arts education and provides guidelines for developing meaningful, integrated performance assessments.

The second section includes a set of 10 performance assessments linked to national standards. The assessments incorporate a variety of ways to assess students' concept understanding, process-skill acquisition, habits of mind, and ability to make real-world connections. Most of the assessments include more than one activity, a writing prompt, and a set of criterion-referenced questions that can be used in conjunction with the activities. Reproducible student masters are included.

Price: $22.95 (ISBN 1-57517-004-3). *Publisher/supplier:* IRI/Skylight. *Materials:* Available locally, or from commercial suppliers.

5.58 Critical Issues in Today's World: A Module for Grades 4-7. Marilyn Bodourian and Louis A. Iozzi. Science-Technology-Society: Preparing for Tomorrow's World series. Longmont, Colo.: Sopris West, 1993.

Recommended grade level: 6-8. *Critical Issues in Today's World* contains 10 activity modules designed to help students explore and consider solutions to current science and technology problems or issues. The emphasis is on increasing students' ability to analyze issues that arise in a technological society and on enhancing their awareness of their own role in the process of technological change. The 10 modules examine (1) decision making, (2) technology, (3) inventions, (4) artificial intelligence, (5) energy, (6) transportation, (7) environmental concerns, (8) oceans, (9) endangered species, and (10) conservation.

Among the activities, for example, students examine a model for making decisions, discuss whether inventions are always good, and analyze what dangerous or boring tasks currently done by people could be done by robots in the future. Students also prepare a transportation plan for a new city, participate in a simulation to decide if an amendment should be added to the Clean Air Act, and think about what would happen if all birds became extinct.

Each module begins with background readings and discussion questions and is meant to stand alone, as are most of the exercises or activities. Designed to develop analytical skills, the activities include writing exercises, scenario discussions, and informal and formal debates. Most of them are paper-and-pencil exercises; many combine science and social studies. This 3-ring-binder includes student pages, teaching guidelines for each activity, and background information on the program.

Price: $60 (ISBN 0-944584-80-2). *Publisher/supplier:* Sopris West. *Materials:* Available locally.

5.59 Earth and Physical Science: Content and Learning Strategies. Mary Ann Christison and Sharron Bassano. Science Through Active Reading (STAR) series. Reading, Mass.: Addison-Wesley, 1992.

Recommended grade level: 6-8+. *Earth and Physical Science: Content and Learning Strategies* is a specialized text for middle school and secondary ESL (English as a Second Language) students or for students experiencing difficulty using a traditional science textbook. One of 4 books in the Science Through Active Reading (STAR) series, it is designed to help students with limited English proficiency develop the science vocabulary, critical-thinking skills, and learning strategies needed for higher-level schoolwork. Largely a reading text, this book integrates exercises in reading comprehension, vocabulary, and learning strategies with hands-on science activities in 6 areas of science: meteorology, topography, oceanography, astronomy, and physics and chemistry. Topics covered include the difference between weather and climate, the water cycle, drainage basins, rocks, ocean movement, properties of matter, and Newton's laws of motion. In the hands-on activities, for example, students work together to compare and contrast different soils, model ocean currents, or play with a ball to explore inertia.

Each chapter features a very brief introduction to a science topic, to be read by the teacher and students together. This introduction is followed by critical-thinking activities, directions for simple hands-on group experiments, prereading focus questions to help students read selectively, reading sections, self-evaluation activities, and extension activities. Each chapter also includes diagrams and charts to help students' comprehension and learning. All of the activities emphasize cooperative groups and peer-tutoring. The teacher's edition includes an answer key for the prereading focus questions.

Prices: Teacher's edition (ISBN 0-8013-0986-7), $12.84. Student edition (ISBN 0-8013-0348-6), $11.12. *Publisher/supplier:* Addison-Wesley/Longman. *Materials:* Available locally.

5.60 **Everyday Science: Real-Life Activities.** John M. Scott. Portland, Maine: Walch, 1988.

Recommended grade level: 5-8. *Everyday Science* offers more than 300 ideas for short activities and simple demonstrations designed to heighten students' interest in science. The activities are organized in 16 chapters by topic. The wide range of topics includes motion and forces, space travel, weather, oceanography, matter, energy, senses, photosynthesis, electricity, and astronomy.

Among the activities, for example, students explore the pressure-volume relationship of a gas using a basting tube and a glass of water; they see how convection currents work by heating a glass coffeepot filled with sawdust and water; and they make a compass galvanometer out of a cardboard cylinder, insulated wire, and a small compass.

Each chapter begins with several pages of stories, examples, applications, or "believe-it-or-not" anecdotes illustrating how science principles operate in everyday situations or events. Examples include explanations of why golf balls are dimpled or of how Newton's laws operate when a car is being driven. Simple directions are then given for carrying out related activities at home or in the classroom. The activities require simple equipment and ordinary household items. Some activities are open-ended; others are solved for students.

Price: $17.95 (ISBN 0-8251-2705-X). *Publisher/supplier:* Walch. *Materials:* Available locally.

5.61 **Exciting Science and Engineering: A Series of Problem Solving Tasks for Seven to Fourteen Year Olds.** Heslington, York, England: Chemical Industry Education Centre, 1995.

Recommended grade level: 6-8. *Exciting Science and Engineering* contains 9 units for 11- to 14-year-olds. Most units include 2 or 3 lessons or activities. In each unit, students are involved in problem solving as they investigate real-life situations or stories such as being snowbound, constructing Stonehenge, or getting rid of dampness in an apartment building. The book is designed to help students see that the science they learn in school can be used to solve real-world problems.

Topics addressed include noise pollution, the use of dynamos for bicycle lights, industrial problems involving the transportation and dissolving of salt, the scientific principles involved in floating and sinking (a shipwreck is analyzed), coastline erosion, and the properties of hydrocarbons in pipelines. In the unit on condensation, for example, students explore the causes of condensation, design a simple dehumidifier, and evaluate commercial anti-condensation systems. In the unit on Stonehenge, they consider the scale of Stonehenge and the kinds of problems involved in its construction; they investigate how simple machines, such as levers or ramps, must have been used by Neolithic people to move the enormous rocks at the site; and they try to figure how the lintels could have been raised. Throughout the activities, students must apply integrated scientific principles to find solutions. Each activity has suggestions for involving a local engineer or scientist in the classroom as an adviser or as a contributor to discussions.

Each unit provides background information, teaching notes, a brief description of possible roles in the unit for an engineer, and student

sheets, where appropriate. Because the guide is published in Great Britain, some words may need to be Americanized (for example, "flats" or "petrol" may be unfamiliar to students).

Price: $70. *Publisher/supplier:* Chemical Industry Education Centre. *Materials:* Available locally, or from commercial suppliers.

5.62 **Fingerprinting.** Reprinted with revisions. Jeremy John Ahouse and Jacqueline Barber. Great Explorations in Math and Science (GEMS) series. Berkeley, Calif.: Lawrence Hall of Science, 1993.

Recommended grade level: 4-7. In the unit *Fingerprinting*, students explore the similarities and variations of fingerprints. They take their own fingerprints, devise a scheme for classifying fingerprints, and apply their classification skills to solve a crime. In session 1 students use pencils, paper, and tape to take their fingerprints. In session 2 they group 10 different fingerprints according to the way they look. Students are then introduced to the standard arch-loop-whorl system of fingerprint classification. In the final session, they apply their knowledge of fingerprints to determine which of 5 suspects robbed a safe. The mystery scenario, "Who Robbed the Safe?" includes plot and character sketches. Examples of extension activities include fingerprint art, an introduction to genetics, and role-playing news reporters covering the crime scene.

Fingerprinting includes 3 or 4 sessions of 30 to 60 minutes each. The lesson plan for each session includes an overview, a list of materials, blackline masters of student worksheets, and complete instructions for planning and conducting the activity. This teacher's guide also includes answers to typical student questions, summary outlines for the 3 sessions, literature connections, and assessment suggestions for fifth-grade students.

Price: $9 (ISBN 0-912511-21-4). *Publisher/supplier:* LHS GEMS. *Materials:* Available locally, or from commercial suppliers.

5.63 **Forecasting the Future: Exploring Evidence for Global Climate Change.** Education Department, Stephen Birch Aquarium-Museum, in collaboration with Center for Clouds, Chemistry and Climate at Scripps Institution of Oceanography. Arlington, Va.: National Science Teachers Association, 1996.

Recommended grade level: 8+. *Forecasting the Future* is designed to help students understand the science behind climate and global climate change. The first section of the guide includes a detailed narrative of scientific background, which may need to be interpreted or adapted for student use. The section explains the clues that scientists study to find out about climate in the past and where they find them, how scientists measure the earth's temperature, the importance of water in climate change, how living organisms contribute or respond to climate change, and the role human beings can play in limiting greenhouse gases.

The second section of the guide offers 14 stand-alone activities that explore various aspects of climate and cover a range of disciplines: plant and animal biology, chemistry, geology, meteorology, and physics. For example, students study fish scales to identify changes in environmental conditions experienced by a fish. They create a simulated sediment bed with pollen grains and take core samples and analyze them. They also expose soil samples to sunlight to study the relationship between heat, evaporation, and ero-

sion. In other activities, they examine tree rings, and they observe phase changes in water due to heating and cooling and relate these changes to climate zones. Several activities promote the concept of change over time. Reproducible student pages and teacher's pages are included for each activity.

The third section of the guide includes tips on designing science lessons that employ scientific inquiry and 40 ideas for extension activities. The last section includes a geological time line; a glossary; and an annotated bibliography of resources, including books, teacher's guides, and Internet resources that deal with climate change.

Price: $21.95 (ISBN 0-87355-139-7). *Publisher/supplier:* National Science Teachers Association. *Materials:* Available locally, or from commercial suppliers.

5.64 **Great Moments in Science: Experiments and Readers Theatre.** Kendall Haven. Englewood, Colo.: Teacher Ideas Press, 1996.

Recommended grade level: 5-8. *Great Moments in Science* contains 12 stories about historic moments in the development of Western science. Included are stories about the work and discoveries of Archimedes, Galileo, Franklin, Newton, Pasteur, Mendel, and Goddard, among others. Topics addressed include levers, gravity, air pressure, electricity, heat, comets, microorganisms, heredity, rocketry, radioactivity, and the discovery of penicillin.

The stories are presented in the form of scripts for reading aloud; each script includes 4 to 6 roles. Several simple experiments after each story allow students to replicate or learn more about the "science moment" described in the story. For example, students investigate levers

and beams as Archimedes did. They observe the swinging of a pendulum as Galileo did. They also study the growth of common bread molds as Pasteur did. The experiments, mostly done in small groups, allow students many opportunities to investigate sources of error in scientific research and to revise the design, conduct, and materials of their experiments. Each story and experiment has brief scientific background information, step-by-step instructions, and a list of references for further reading.

Price: $24.50 (ISBN 1-56308-355-8). *Publisher/supplier:* Teacher Ideas Press. *Materials:* Available locally, or from commercial suppliers.

5.65 **Historical Connections in Mathematics: Resources for Using History of Mathematics in the Classroom. Vol I.** Wilbert Reimer and Luetta Reimer. Historical Connections in Mathematics series. Fresno, Calif.: AIMS Education Foundation, 1992.

Recommended grade level: 5-8. Volume I of *Historical Connections in Mathematics* is a collection of resources designed to help teachers integrate the history of mathematics into their teaching. The book emphasizes how people have discovered and developed mathematics, and it stresses that the process of problem solving is as important as the solution.

Organized in 10 chapters, each on a famous mathematician, the book provides portraits, concise biographical information, and interesting anecdotal stories—on Pythagoras, Archimedes, Napier, Galileo, Fermat, Pascal, Newton, Euler, Germain, and Gauss. Also included are reproducible puzzles, crosswords, skits, games, and other activities that allow students to make connections with social studies, language arts, and science.

Not all of the activities replicate the exact problems worked on by the famous mathematicians, but they do represent the areas of interest of those mathematicians. For example, students use a technique that Archimedes used to calculate how many kernels of popcorn it would take to fill their classroom. They complete a table to discover Fermat's Two-Square Theorem. They also solve the same mathematical problem given to Gauss when he was 10 years old. Complete solutions and suggestions for using the activities are included.

Price: Teacher's guide (ISBN 1-881431-35-5), $16.95. *Publisher/supplier:* AIMS Education Foundation. *Materials:* Available locally.

5.66 **Historical Connections in Mathematics: Resources for Using History of Mathematics in the Classroom. Vol. III.** Wilbert Reimer and Luetta Reimer. Historical Connections in Mathematics series. Fresno, Calif.: AIMS Education Foundation, 1995.

Recommended grade level: 5-8. Volume III of *Historical Connections in Mathematics* is a collection of resources designed to help teachers integrate the history of mathematics into their teaching. The book emphasizes how people have discovered and developed mathematics, and it stresses that the process of problem solving is as important as the solution. Organized in 10 chapters, each on a famous mathematician, the book provides portraits, concise biographical information, and interesting anecdotal stories—on Eratosthenes, Fibonacci, Descartes, Agnesi, Lagrange, Somerville, Dodgson, Venn, Noether, and Polya. Also included are reproducible puzzles, crosswords, skits, games, and other activities that allow students to make connections with social studies, language arts, and science.

Not all of the activities replicate the exact problems worked on by the

famous mathematicians, but they do represent the areas of interest of those mathematicians. For example, students use a method developed by Eratosthenes to find all the prime numbers between 1 and 100. They create Fibonacci-like mathematical sequences. They also solve the puzzles called doublets that Charles Dodgson (also known as Lewis Carroll) invented.

Complete solutions and suggestions for using the activities are provided at the back of the book. An appendix includes a collection of programs for the TI-82 graphic calculator. The programs may be modified for use with other programmable calculators.

Price: Teacher's guide (ISBN 1-881431-49-5), $16.95. *Publisher/supplier:* AIMS Education Foundation. *Materials:* Available locally.

5.67 **Investigating Apples.** Christine V. Johnson. Real-World Mathematics through Science series. Developed by Washington Mathematics, Engineering, Science Achievement (MESA) Group (Seattle, Wash.). Menlo Park, Calif.: Innovative Learning Publications, 1995.

Recommended grade level: 6-8. *Investigating Apples* contains 6 activities that teach students the basics of statistical analysis by having them collect, organize, and interpret data related to apples. Students also learn how apples are cultivated and sized. Working in cooperative groups, they measure the masses of different varieties of size-80 apples, and they organize their data by preparing and analyzing line plots. They also explore stem plots and box plots as additional methods for displaying and analyzing data. They investigate the relationship between an apple's height and mass and its diameter and mass by constructing and analyzing scatter plots. At the end of the unit, they conduct and analyze a survey

with their families on the texture and flavor of 3 varieties of apples.

During the unit, students discuss the uncertainty of measurement, the importance of statistical reasoning, and the advantages and disadvantages of different methods of organizing data. Short readings introduce them to careers in pomology (the science of growing fruit) and statistics and to the role of statistics in improving and monitoring apple-storage procedures.

Each activity requires 1 or 2 class sessions of 40 to 50 minutes and includes an overview, a materials list, background information, teaching procedures, discussion and assessment questions, and reproducible student record sheets.

Price: $18.95 (ISBN 0-201-49040-4). *Publisher/supplier:* Addison-Wesley/Longman. *Materials:* Available locally.

5.68 **Learning about Learning.** Jacqueline Barber, Katharine Barrett, Kevin Beals, and others. Great Explorations in Math and Science (GEMS) series. Berkeley, Calif.: Lawrence Hall of Science, 1996.

Recommended grade level: 6-8. *Learning about Learning* contains 10 activities that allow students to explore questions of how individual humans and animals learn, of how learning helps humans survive, and of how the brain changes with learning. Students consider these questions as they explore the human organism, animal behavior, health and safety, product testing, the ethics of experimentation, and what scientists do. The activities include simulations, a play, stories, hands-on investigations, and discussions.

Among the activities, for example, students make tactile mazes and test the mazes on a blindfolded partner to investigate how limiting sensory information makes learning more challenging. They attempt to solve 2 health-related mysteries that are based on true stories of how scientists learn. They also investigate how animals and humans learn what is safe to eat and why there is a need for regulations applying to food, drugs, and cosmetics.

In other activities, students read and discuss "Genie," the true story about a girl raised in isolation. They measure and compare diagrams of brain cells from rats raised in "impoverished" environments and those raised in "enriched" environments. They engage in a dialogue about the benefits and costs of learning from conducting research with humans or animals.

Each activity in this unit takes 45 to 60 minutes to complete. The guide includes background information for the teacher, summary outlines for each activity, extensions, assessments activities, and reproducible student pages.

Price: $25.50 (ISBN 0-912511-95-8). *Publisher/supplier:* LHS GEMS. *Materials:* Available locally, or from commercial suppliers.

5.69 Minds-on Science: For the Sake of the Nation. Minds-on Science series. Developed by National Museum of American History, Smithsonian Institution (Washington, D.C.). Watertown, Mass.: Tom Snyder Productions, 1995.

Recommended grade level: 7-8+. During the activities in *Minds-on Science: For the Sake of the Nation,* a videodisc activity kit, students role-play the science adviser to the President of the United States. The scenario is that the nation is facing both urgent and long-term problems, and students must make a decision about the nation's scientific policy: Should the federal government focus its money and energy on biotechnology, space exploration, or the environment?

To help make their decision, students review conflicting data and opinions from 4 advisers—a congressional representative, an engineer, a scientist, and an economist. Through video segments and short scientific readings in their student portfolios, they also become familiar with "big science" projects—such as the Manhattan Project, the Space Program, and the Human Genome Project—and how these projects have affected people's lives. In short paper-and-pencil activities, students look at how science pervades their everyday lives, calculate how they can reduce their contribution to pollution, think about items they would take on a space trip, and consider how a genetically engineered item differs from the original. Eight extension activities are also suggested. They include conducting an experiment that illustrates the greenhouse effect, modeling the process of DNA profiling, or interviewing adults about scientific changes they have witnessed in their lifetime.

Students work cooperatively in teams of 4 as they gather information and do the activities. At the end of the unit, they must reach a consensus and decide as a class what direction scientific research should take. They watch the consequences of their decision on the video, then face a new dilemma and must make a second decision.

Including the extensions, the activities in *Minds-on Science: For the Sake of the Nation* take about 4 to 5 weeks to complete. The kit includes the videodisc, 28 student portfolios, and a teacher's guide.

Prices: Videodisc kit, $245.95. Software for Macintosh or Windows (optional), $49.50. *Publisher/supplier:* Tom Snyder Productions. *Materials:* Available in kit.

5.70 Minds-on Science: The Impact of Discovery. Minds-on Science series. Developed by National Museum of American History, Smithsonian Institution (Washington, D.C.). Watertown, Mass.: Tom Snyder Productions, 1995.

Recommended grade level: 7-8. During the activities in *Minds-on Science: The Impact of Discovery,* a videodisc activity kit, students role-play a research scientist who has just discovered a compound that improves memory in laboratory rats. Students must decide what to do next: Should they publish the results, hold a press conference to announce the discovery to the world, or start a company to sell the compound?

To help make their decision, students review conflicting data and opinions from 4 advisers—a scientist, a friend, a doctor, and a businessperson. Through video segments and short scientific readings in their student portfolios, they also develop an understanding of the brain, memory, the scientific method, and the process of turning a scientific discovery into a new product or medicine. In short paper-and-pencil activities, students conduct a memory experiment, look at safety problems with food and drugs, and consider the pros and cons of animal testing. Seven extension activities are suggested. They include designing and carrying out a memory experiment, tracking science in the news, or interviewing adults about scientific developments they have witnessed in their lifetime.

Students work cooperatively in teams of 4 as they gather information and do the activities. At the end of the unit, they must reach a consensus and make a decision as a class on what to do with the company. Students watch the consequences of their decision on the video, then face a new dilemma and must make a second decision.

Including the extensions, the activities in *Minds-on Science: The Impact of Discovery* take about 4 to

5 weeks to complete. The kit includes the videodisc, 28 student portfolios, and a teacher's guide.

Prices: Videodisc kit, $249.95. Software for Macintosh or Windows (optional), $49.95. *Publisher/supplier:* Tom Snyder Productions. *Materials:* Available in kit.

5.71 **Multiculturalism in Mathematics, Science, and Technology: Readings and Activities.** Menlo Park, Calif.: Addison-Wesley, 1993.

Recommended grade level: 8+. *Multiculturalism in Mathematics, Science, and Technology* is designed to help teachers infuse multicultural education into their science and mathematics classes. Divided into 37 short stand-alone units, the book features more than 50 activities and readings that highlight the achievements of a broad spectrum of individuals and cultures—from the Zuni, to Omar Khayyam, to the ancient Egyptians.

Among the activities, for example, students use the ancient Egyptian method of multiplication to calculate 11 x 33. They also test young corn and potato plants in ways that parallel the experiments of Native-American agriculturalists, and they simulate the method the Celts used to make butter.

Each unit begins with a 1-page reading on the achievements of the individual or the culture highlighted in the unit. Critical-thinking questions then encourage learning and reflection, and 1 or 2 activities give students an idea of the mathematical or scientific reasoning used by the subject of the unit. The book contains many paper-and-pencil activities that require analysis or interpretation of collected data. Knowledge of algebra and geometry is required for some activities. Although the activities in each unit may be used independently of the readings, it is recommended that units be treated as a whole.

Teaching notes are provided for each unit. They include specific suggestions for using the readings and activities, limited background information, preparation tips, and extension ideas.

Price: $22.20 (ISBN 0-201-29417-6). *Publisher/supplier:* Addison-Wesley/ Longman. *Materials:* Available locally.

5.72 **Multicultural Science and Math Connections: Middle School Projects and Activities.** Beatrice Lumpkin and Dorothy Strong. Walch Reproducible Books. Portland, Maine: Walch, 1995.

Recommended grade level: 5-8+. *Multicultural Science and Math Connections* is organized in 2 parts, each containing units that feature a culture or an individual. The book includes more than 80 science and mathematics activities and projects that introduce students to brilliant discoveries of 17 cultures from Africa to the Arctic. Also featured are contributions of 10 outstanding scientists and mathematicians—for example, Lewis Latimer, Leon Roddy, and Mae Jemison.

Among the activities, for example, students learn about and make an Egyptian carpenter's level. They make a model planetarium of an ancient observatory in Kenya. They also build and use an Inca abacus, and they study Native American teepee designs.

Each unit includes an introductory classroom activity and background information presented through a short reading about the experiences of young people from the time and culture of interest or about events in the life of the scientist or mathematician. Critical-thinking questions follow, and additional science, mathematics, or class research or experimentation projects are suggested.

The units are designed to be used as a whole but can also be used individually. The materials are inexpensive and readily available. Answers to the critical-thinking questions are provided.

Price: $24.95 (ISBN 0-8251-2659-2). *Publisher/supplier:* Walch. *Materials:* Available locally.

5.73 **Science and Technology by Design: 3.** Colin Webb. Sydney, Australia: Harcourt Brace Jovanovich, 1992.

Recommended grade level: 5-6. The activities in *Science and Technology by Design: 3* involve investigating, designing, making, and using technology. The nearly 100 activities are organized in 10 units. Students (1) design and calibrate simple measuring instruments; (2) use the activity of microorganisms in practical ways such as making bread, cottage cheese, and yogurt; (3) investigate structures built by animals, by various civilizations, and by contemporary society; (4) investigate space; (5) explore concepts related to the muscular and skeletal systems, body movement, circulation, respiration, diet, reactions and learning; (6) investigate the use of levers, wheels, gears, and pulleys performing design tasks; (7) investigate the various forms of energy and the ways people use energy in their homes, for transport, and as food; (8) look at a variety of testing procedures, such as market research surveys; (9) investigate things that are used for entertainment; and (10) examine aspects of packaging.

Science and Technology by Design: 3 provides an introduction for each unit. The 2-page activities consist of a reproducible student page that presents the challenge and notes for the teacher explaining the scientific concept involved, along with ideas to stimulate discussion.

Prices: Aust. $51.95 (ISBN 0-7295-2854-5). *Publisher/supplier:* Harcourt Brace, Australia. *Materials:* Available locally, or from commercial suppliers.

5.74 **Science Experiments and Projects for Students.** Julia H. Cothron, Ronald N. Giese, and Richard J. Rezba. Dubuque, Iowa: Kendall/Hunt, 1996.

Recommended grade level: 7-8+. Using *Science Experiments and Projects for Students*, students can practice the skills they need to create and conduct their own original experiments and assess their work. Written for students, the guide is designed to teach the fundamentals of planning and conducting science experiments using the scientific method—that is, generating experimental ideas, developing an experimental design, collecting and presenting data, conducting statistical analysis, using library resources, and writing about and presenting scientific findings in the classroom or in a competition.

The 14 chapters in the book could be used individually but are sequenced to be treated as a whole. Each chapter addresses an aspect of the scientific method in detail through a structured sequence of readings, skill-building exercises, activities, practice problems, and self-assessments. In the chapter on analyzing experimental data, for example, students learn to distinguish among quantitative, qualitative, ratio, interval, ordinal, and nominal data. They also select the appropriate measures of central tendency and variation for a given set of data, describe 3 ways to find the central value of a set of data, describe 4 ways to report the variation in a set of data, construct a data table and graph for sets of quantitative and qualitative data, and use a checklist to evaluate data tables and graphs and to identify needed improvements.

Science Experiments and Projects for Students is the student version of *Students and Research: Practical Strategies for Science Classrooms and Competitions.* (*See* 1.106.)

Price: $18.95 (ISBN 0-7872-2826-5). *Publisher/supplier:* Kendall/Hunt. *Materials:* Available locally, or from commercial suppliers.

5.75 **Science Is . . .** 2nd ed. Susan V. Bosak. Richmond Hill, Ontario, Canada: Scholastic Canada; and Markham, Ontario, Canada: The Communication Project, 1991.

Recommended grade level: 1-8. *Science Is . . .* is a comprehensive collection of more than 450 activities, experiments, projects, games, puzzles, and stories organized by type of activity, by subject area, and by topic. The 3 types of activities are as follows: (1) "Quickies" are short activities that require few or no materials and can be done on the spur of the moment. They might be used to introduce basic concepts in a subject area. (2) "Make Time" activities require a little planning, some readily available and inexpensive materials, and at least 30 minutes to complete. These activities often deal with key subject area concepts in depth. (3) "One Leads to Another"—activities within a subject area that build upon one another—emphasize a key theme for the subject area or result in a completed project and require some planning.

Within each type, activities are organized in 10 subject areas: (1) discovering science, (2) matter and energy, (3) humans, (4) the environment, (5) rocks, (6) plants, (7) living creatures, (8) weather, (9) the heavens, and (10) applying science. In addition to the 10 subject areas, activities are organized in 40 topics that interrelate activities within and between subject areas. A master chart shows where items on the 40 topics can be found in the 10 subject areas.

Each activity in *Science Is . . .* includes a 2-line introduction, a materials list, and procedures, as well as appropriate background information and other fact-filled boxes. This sourcebook also includes a section for teachers on how to use the book, an extensive list of resources, and an index.

Price: $29.95 (ISBN 0-590-74070-9). *Publisher/supplier:* Idea Factory. *Materials:* Available locally, or from commercial suppliers.

5.76 **Science on a Shoestring.** 2nd ed. Kara Strongin and Gloria Strongin. Menlo Park, Calif.: Addison-Wesley, 1991.

Recommended grade level: K-8. This second edition of *Science on a Shoestring* includes 62 investigations grouped under 3 themes—matter, change, and energy. Students investigate how matter behaves, interacts, and how it can change; they become aware of the changes occurring in themselves and in their environment; and they become more aware of the effects of gravity, magnetism, electricity, sound, and light upon them and their environment. Most investigations may be introduced without regard to sequence.

Each lesson in *Science on a Shoestring* includes a suggested grade level; a list of required materials (all inexpensive and easily obtainable); a short vocabulary list; a brief overview of the activity, including an explanation of the concepts involved; and step-by-step procedures for conducting the activity. Most lessons offer ideas for home investigations, and questions for discussion and/or evaluation. A master list of materials is included.

Price: Teacher's guide (ISBN 0-201-25760-2), $18.95. *Publisher/supplier:* Addison-Wesley/Longman. *Materials:* Available locally, or from commercial suppliers.

5.77 **Science Projects in Renewable Energy and Energy Efficiency: A Guide for Elementary and Secondary School Teachers.** National Renewable Energy Laboratory. Boulder, Colo.: American Solar Energy Society, 1991.

Recommended grade level: 6-8+. *Science Projects in Renewable Energy and Energy Efficiency* is a resource book with suggestions and information for developing experimental and nonexperimental projects related to solar energy, renewable energy technologies, and other related areas such as superconductivity and energy storage. Rather than being an instruction book with complete directions and answers for projects or experiments, this idea book is designed to help teachers and students develop and conduct their own experiments or science-fair projects.

The book has 4 sections: (1) an outline of ways teachers can help students during an experimental project; (2) a review of how to do a science project—that is, the steps in the scientific method; (3) more than 100 ideas for projects in energy efficiency and sources of information or tips relevant to that topic; and (4) an excellent annotated list of resources, many of which are free, including books, articles, films, slide presentations, and software packages related to solar and renewable energy.

Included in the section on project ideas is a short introduction to each topic, hints on how to set up and conduct possible experiments, bibliographic references, a list of special equipment required, and schematics for setups.

Price: $10. *Publisher/supplier:* National Energy Foundation. *Materials:* Available locally, or from commercial suppliers.

5.78 **Sciencewise, Book 2: Discovering Scientific Process through Problem Solving.** Dennis Holley. Pacific Grove, Calif.: Critical Thinking Books and Software, 1996.

Recommended grade level: 5-8. *Sciencewise, Book 2* is a resource guide containing 54 demonstrations and activities designed to develop students' creative-thinking, problem-solving, and "inventioneering" skills. Specific principles or concepts are demonstrated in the exercises, but the emphasis is on active involvement of the students in learning science process skills. The guide features 2 types of exercises: "Dynamic Demos" and "Creative Challenges."

In the first type, the 36 teacher-led demonstration activities, students do the thinking and the teacher does the doing. The teacher sets up and presents a problem situation ("What will happen if . . . " or "Why did that happen?"). Using guided questions and manipulating apparatus and equipment, the teacher helps the student understand the problem, make accurate observations and reasonable predictions, and arrive at a conclusion or answer to the problem. The activities include, for example, investigating whether a jar of sand will roll as far as a jar of water (and why or why not), or thinking of ways to blow up a balloon that is inside a container—without touching the balloon or removing the stopper from the container that holds the balloon.

With the 18 Creative Challenges, students are asked to develop a solution to a problem (given a particular set of rules) using the scientific process skills shown by the teacher in the demonstrations. For example, they are asked to invent a new use for a wire coat hanger; to design and build a device that will float as many pennies as possible; or to construct a

maze that will take a marble from the top of a shoebox to the bottom of the box in 30 seconds.

Each demonstration activity includes a teacher section that lists materials needed, step-by-step procedures, outcomes and explanations, extensions, and ways the activity can be continued at home. A student record sheet is also provided. Each challenge activity includes a student page and a teacher's page.

Price: $21.95 (ISBN 0-89455-648-7). *Publisher/supplier:* Critical Thinking Books. *Materials:* Available locally, or from commercial suppliers.

5.79 **Super Science Activities: Favorite Lessons from Master Teachers.** Rob Beattie, Diane Bredt, Janet Graeber, and others. Palo Alto, Calif.: Dale Seymour Publications, 1988.

Recommended grade level: 5-8+. *Super Science Activities* includes 25 lessons in the physical, earth, and life sciences from the repertoires of 8 science teachers. Topics include plate tectonics, earthquakes, genetics, ecology, electricity, and chromatography. Examples of activities include inventing a seismograph, using chromatography to identify the author of a mystery note, building a working battery, and creating a balanced ecosystem in an aquarium.

Super Science Activities contains 6 units, each with 3 to 5 lessons and a bibliography. Each lesson has background information, vocabulary, a list of materials, classroom management suggestions, step-by-step procedures, and enrichment activities.

Price: $18.95 (ISBN 0-86651-445-7). *Publisher/supplier:* Dale Seymour. *Materials:* Available locally, or from commercial suppliers.

5.80 **The Teaching Tank Discovery Book.** Vol. 1. Paul J. Reinbold and David R. Burgess. Nashua, N.H.: Captivation, 1996.

Recommended grade level: 5-8. Volume 1 of *The Teaching Tank Discovery Book* contains directions for 50 activities meant to be done with a simple device called a "teaching tank"—a 2-sided Plexiglas container. The activities, many of which are demonstrations, cover a wide range of topics in the life, earth, and physical sciences. For example, students use the tank for observing root growth, for growing stalactites and stalagmites, or for predicting and observing the effect of wind on evaporation rate. They also use it to observe the work of enzymes in the digestion of foods, to observe a model of the internal gaseous forces within a volcano, or to measure the mass of various solids.

Each lesson includes a list of objectives, a materials list, a reference diagram showing how the tank is used, step-by-step procedures, thought-provoking questions for students, and brief teaching notes or explanations of results.

Price: Teacher's guide (ISBN 0-9633907-0-8), $21.95. Teaching tank, $32.95. *Publisher/supplier:* Captivation. *Materials:* Available locally, or from commercial suppliers.

5.81 **The Teaching Tank Discovery Book.** Vol. 2. Gordon Corbett and David R. Burgess. Nashua, N.H.: Captivation, 1996.

Recommended grade level: 5-8. Volume 2 of *The Teaching Tank Discovery Book* contains directions for 50 activities meant to be done with a simple device called a "teaching tank"—a 2-sided Plexiglas container. The activities, many of which are demonstrations, cover a wide range of topics in the life, earth, and physical sciences. For example, students use the tank for determining that

displacement is essential to the functioning of a submarine, for observing the influence of temperature on the action of yeast, or for demonstrating that surface tension of water can be broken by soap or detergent. They also use it for observing the separation of plant pigments using paper chromatography or for creating a model of a thermocline.

Each lesson includes a list of objectives, a materials list, a reference diagram showing how the tank is used, step-by-step procedures, thought-provoking questions for students, and brief teaching notes or explanations of results.

Price: Teacher's guide (ISBN 0-9633907-1-6), $21.95. Teaching tank, $32.95. *Publisher/supplier:* Captivation. *Materials:* Available locally, or from commercial suppliers.

5.82 **Technology Science Mathematics Connection Activities.** James LaPorte and Mark Sanders. Developed by TSM [Technology Science Mathematics] Integration Project, Virginia Polytechnic Institute and State University (Blacksburg, Va.). New York, N.Y.: Glencoe/McGraw-Hill, 1996.

Recommended grade level: 7-8+. This unit, in a 3-ring-binder format, contains 6 problem-solving activities designed to facilitate team teaching among technology, science, and mathematics teachers. (The activities are for 3-teacher teams, but implementation suggestions are given for pairs or individual teachers.) During the unit, students must simultaneously apply the concepts, principles, and skills they learn in 3 subject areas—science, mathematics, and technology—to design, construct, and evaluate solutions to stated problems. They are asked to design, construct, and evaluate a working model of a self-propelled toy power boat, a composite beam made from 2 or more recyclable materials, an insulation panel, a magnetically levitated

vehicle, a model hydroponic farming system, and a model rocket.

A typical activity requires several days to a week in science and mathematics classes and 1 to 3 weeks in a technology laboratory. Each activity has an introductory overview that provides a general idea of the activity and its goal, followed by the technology, science, and mathematics components. In developing a working model of a toy powerboat, for example, students design, construct, and test their boat hulls and propulsion systems in technology class; they study Newton's laws of motion, as well as buoyancy and conservation of energy in science class; and they study symmetry, balance, volume, and surface area in mathematics class.

Each activity includes a suggested sequence of instruction, background information, resources, teaching notes for the different components, questions to guide student discussion and thinking, reproducible student sheets, and links to standards of the National Council of Teachers of Mathematics. Each activity is also correlated with Glencoe textbooks in technology, science, and mathematics.

Price: Teacher's resource binder (ISBN 0-02-636947-8), $64.46. *Publisher/supplier:* Glencoe/McGraw-Hill. *Materials:* Available locally, or from commercial suppliers.

5.83 **Thematic Applications: Sciences II.** Technology-Based Solutions series. Developed by Twin Discovery Systems. Freeport, N.Y.: Educational Activities, 1995.

Recommended grade level: 6-8. *Thematic Applications: Sciences II* is a CD-ROM with 67 computer-based activities that allow students to learn about topics in environmental, life, earth, and physical science. The activities, which can be completed individually or collaboratively, incorporate computer literacy, mathematics, writing, science, social studies, art, and research. They require students to locate, manipulate, organize, and analyze data. Generally, students use the word processor, database, spreadsheet, or draw/paint program to complete each activity. For example, they make a graph from a spreadsheet showing the number of endangered and threatened animal and plant species, they create an illustration of the food chain in a tropical rainforest using a paint or draw program, and they write an environmental newsletter using desktop publishing. They also identify and collect information on the 10 highest active volcanoes in the world, and they research and write a report on the superconducting supercollider.

The CD-ROM uses either ClarisWorks for Macintosh or Microsoft Works for Windows. Students must know how to use these applications before they can complete the activities. All of the activities are designed so that students can conduct their research on the computer using an electronic encyclopedia or other reference source. Full-video clips and clip art illustrations are included on the CD-ROM for students to use as they create documents or reports. A list of relevant Web sites for obtaining information is provided. Students are encouraged to consult research sources such as the Internet, CD-ROM encyclopedias, books, and periodicals.

The CD-ROM comes with a teacher's guide that summarizes the goals, skills, and research requirements for each activity. The activities can be tailored for different grade levels; the time they require depends on the level of detail teachers assign.

Price: Unit, $99. (Contact publisher/supplier for complete price and ordering information.) ***Publisher/supplier:*** Educational Activities. ***Materials:*** Available locally, or from commercial suppliers.

5.84 **Transformations: Science, Technology and Society.** Developed by American Institute of Mining, Metallurgical and Petroleum Engineers [AIME] (New York, N.Y.). New York, N.Y.: AIME, 1991.

Recommended grade level: 7-8. *Transformations* is a series of 8 videotapes of 15 minutes each, with companion teacher's guides, designed to motivate learning and enhance science instruction in middle school classrooms. Hosted by 4 high school members of a rock-'n'-roll band, each video unit explores a major theme through a set of specific topics and connections. The videotapes are on (1) problem solving, (2) geology and mapping, (3) energy resources and the environment, (4) electronics and computers, (5) heat and electrical power, (6) microbes and mining, (7) recycling, and (8) technology and values.

Each video features a site visit to a place where young engineers and technicians explain how science and technology relate to their everyday problems. In the video on recycling, for example, the band finds itself overwhelmed by trash while trying to practice at a band member's house. The band makes 2 visits to recycling facilities, where they are hosted by a young recycling supervisor, and the band also investigates the value of recycling. Among the activities, students calculate how much solid waste they generate every year, examine different types of packaging, and construct a model landfill.

The video programs maintain a rapid visual pace, and the band members perform songs with lyrics that underscore questions raised in the unit. Each videotape comes with a 16-page teacher's guide that presents background material, summarizes key concepts, offers short follow-up classroom activities and

project ideas, and lists research topics and resources such as recent book titles and organizations. Reproducible activity masters are also included.

Price: Teacher's guides, with set of 8 videos, $125. ***Publisher/supplier:*** Karol Media. ***Materials:*** Available locally.

5.85 **The Whole Cosmos Catalog of Science Activities.** 2nd ed. Joe Abruscato and Jack Hassard. Glenview, Ill.: Good Year Books, 1991.

Recommended grade level: 5-8. *The Whole Cosmos Catalog of Science Activities* is an oversized book containing a collection of more than 275 stand-alone science activities, puzzles, board games, biographies, and creative arts activities that cover topics in life, earth, physical, and aerospace science, along with science and technology subjects such as computers and biomaterials. Among the activities, for example, students make spore prints, grow brine shrimp from fertilized eggs, build a sand sculpture, play pendulum games, or build a small spectroscope.

Each idea or activity includes a very brief introduction to concepts, directions for experiments or activities, and black-and-white illustrations or diagrams to guide student work. Some of the activities are abstracted or adapted from various curriculum projects, including the Science Curriculum Improvement Study (SCIS), Science—A Process Approach (SAPA), and the Earth Science Curriculum Project (ESCP), among others. All of the activities can be done with inexpensive and readily available materials.

Price: $14.95 (ISBN 0-673-16753-4). ***Publisher/supplier:*** Scott Foresman/Addison-Wesley. ***Materials:*** Available locally, or from commercial suppliers.

Researching with software

CHAPTER 6

SOURCES OF INFORMATION ON EDUCATIONAL SOFTWARE AND MULTIMEDIA PROGRAMS

6.1 The American Biology Teacher

The American Biology Teacher (*see* 9.3) includes regular departments entitled "AV Reviews" and "Computer Center" that feature reviews of films, videos, laserdiscs, and software programs. Software reviews included in this journal provide a general description of the software's purpose and information on ease of operation.

Issues/price: 8 per year; $48 per year for National Association of Biology Teacher members; $60 per year for nonmembers. *Available from:* National Association of Biology Teachers.

6.2 Astronomy

The "New Products" department of *Astronomy* magazine (*see* 9.6) sometimes includes reviews of software.

Product reviews and buying guides that include software are also available on the Internet at http://www.kalmbach.com/astro/astronomy.html.

Issues/price: 12 per year; $34.95 per year. *Available from:* Kalmbach.

6.3 Booklist

The "Audiovisual Media" section of *Booklist* magazine recommends materials for all age groups, from preschool through adult. Each year this section reviews more than 1,000 items for school, public library, and home use. Among the items reviewed are curriculum-related videos, audio materials, audiobooks, videodiscs, microcomputer software, and CD-ROMs. A selection of reviews is available on the Internet at http://www.ala.org/booklist.

Issues/price: 22 per year; $69.50 per year. *Available from:* American Library Association.

6.4 California Instructional Technology Clearinghouse, 801 County Center III Court, Modesto, CA 95355-4490 (209) 525-4979 http://www.clearinghouse.k12.ca.us

The California Instructional Technology Clearinghouse evaluates instructional technology resources—programs that use a computer, a VCR or a laserdisc player, a network or the Internet, or any combination of these—for use in California schools. The California Technology in the Curriculum Evaluations Database—on all types of instructional technology resources—is available on the Internet at http://www.clearinghouse.k12.ca.us. Databases are also available in print and on CD-ROM at the Clearinghouse's Software Resource Centers located in California county offices of education. A Clearinghouse publication entitled *Guidelines for the Evaluation of Instructional Technology Resources for California Schools,* contains the evaluation criteria used for reviews.

ABOUT THE ANNOTATIONS IN CHAPTER 6

The annotations in chapter 6 include publications and organizations that specialize in reviewing computer software and other multimedia instructional materials appropriate for middle school science classrooms. The listing is not meant to be exhaustive but to serve as a research tool that readers can reference for locating diverse sources of information on this topic.

The annotations are arranged in one alphabetical listing. Some annotations contain cross-references to fuller descriptions of the same titles in other chapters. For example, *The American Biology Teacher* is also annotated in chapter 9, "Periodicals."

The prices given for books and other publications in chapter 6 do not include costs for shipping and handling. Before placing an order, readers are advised to contact the publishers of these items for current ordering information, including shipping charges. In some cases, discounts or special rates may be available to schools and educators.

Publishers' names are cited in the bibliographic data for books. The name of the place to contact for ordering a periodical is given immediately after its annotation. Publishers' addresses and telephone and fax numbers, as well as e-mail addresses, when available, are listed in appendix A, "Publishers and Suppliers."

6.5 Children's Software Revue

Children's Software Revue provides parents, schools, and libraries with reviews and other information to help them use computers effectively with children between the ages of 2 and 15. Each issue of the magazine includes more than 120 software reviews, comparisons of programs for each school subject area, and information about useful Internet sites. The *Children's Software Revue* database of nearly 3,000 titles is available on the Internet at http://www. childrenssoftware.com.

Issues/price: 6 per year; $29 per year. *Available from:* Active Learning Associates.

6.6 Eisenhower National Clearinghouse for Mathematics and Science Education (ENC), The Ohio State University, 1929 Kenny Rd., Columbus, OH 43210-1079 (614) 292-7784; (800) 621-5785 http://www.enc.org

The Eisenhower National Clearinghouse for Mathematics and Science Education (ENC), which is funded by the U.S. Department of Education, is a clearinghouse for science and mathematics education information for grades K-12. The clearinghouse maintains a collection of curriculum resources in many formats (print, audio, multimedia, video, kits, games). *ENC Resource Finder,* a detailed catalog of these resources, is available at the ENC Web site ENC Online, which is accessible via World Wide Web [http://www.enc.org], modem [1-800-362-4448 or 1-614-292-9040], and Telnet [enc.org].

Although ENC does not evaluate materials, the catalog cites reviews and evaluations by other organizations.

ENC products and services are available in print and electronic format. They include newsletters (such as *ENC Update*), topical catalogs (such as *ENC Focus*), CD-ROMs, and a database of federal programs.

6.7 Electronic Learning

Electronic Learning, a magazine on technology and school change, offers in-depth reviews of hardware and educational software. Special sections focus on evaluation and selection of software and on new and emerging technologies. One section provides a listing of new products available to educators, including software, hardware, CD-ROMs, and videodiscs. Software reviews are also available on the Internet at http://www. scholastic.com/el.

Issues/price: 6 per year; $23.95 per year. *Available from:* Electronic Learning.

6.8 International Society for Technology in Education (ISTE), University of Oregon, 1787 Agate St., Eugene, OR 97403-1923 (800) 336-5191 http://www.iste.org

The International Society for Technology in Education (ISTE) is a nonprofit professional organization dedicated to improving all levels of education through the use of computer-based technology. ISTE serves as a clearinghouse on the use of technology in education. The society publishes 2 journals (*Learning and Leading with Technology* [see 6.9] and *Journal of Research on Computing in Education*), a newsletter (*ISTE Update*), and a guide (*ISTE Resources and Services for Technology-Using Educators*).

6.9 Learning and Leading with Technology

Learning and Leading with Technology, published by the International Society for Technology in Education (ISTE) (*see* 6.8 and 9.24), focuses on curriculum development and on practical ideas for using technology in the classroom. Each issue of this journal contains articles by teachers; features; and software reviews that address language arts, mathematics, science, social studies, integrated curricula, and special needs. Other topics in an issue might include multimedia materials, telecommunications, computer science, networking, library and information technology, the single-computer classroom, staff development, and technology planning.

Issues/price: 8 per year; $58 per year for members of International Society for Technology in Education; $65 per year for nonmembers. *Available from:* International Society for Technology in Education.

6.10 Media & Methods

Media & Methods is a resource magazine for K-12 educators involved with instructional technologies. Feature articles focus on the creative use of media and technologies in education. Multimedia product reviews cover CD-ROMs, computer software, databases, laserdiscs, videos, peripherals, and presentation equipment. Reviews are available on the Internet at http://www.media-methods.com.

Issues/price: 6 per year; $33.50 per year. *Available from:* American Society of Educators.

6.11 Multimedia Schools

Multimedia Schools is a "how-to" magazine focusing on the needs of school practitioners. Articles, reviews, and columns address issues associated with using electronic information resources in schools. The column "Product Reviews-in-Brief" reviews CD-ROMs, videodiscs, magnetic media, and Web sites that relate to K-12 curricula. Reviews are grouped in 3 categories: elementary school, middle/high school, and general interest. Reviews are available on the Internet at http://www.infotoday.com.

Issues/price: 5 per year; $38 per year. *Available from:* Information Today.

6.12 NSTA Science Education Suppliers 1998. National Science Teachers Association (NSTA). Arlington, Va.: NSTA, 1998. 165 pp.

Price: $5.00

NSTA Science Education Suppliers provides lists of firms that produce computer hardware and software. It also includes lists of manufacturers and distributors of audiovisual materials and other media such as CD-ROMs and videodiscs. Addresses and telephone and fax numbers are provided, as well as e-mail and World Wide Web addresses, where available. This annual directory can be purchased separately, and it is also distributed in conjunction with the January or February issue of the following NSTA periodicals: *Science & Children, The Science Teacher, Science Scope,* and the *Journal of College Science Teaching*.

6.13 1997 Educational Software Preview Guide. Judi Mathis Johnson, ed. Developed by Educational Software Preview Guide Consortium. Eugene, Oreg.: International Society for Technology in Education, 1997. 128 pp.

Price: $14.95 (ISBN 1-56484-125-1)

The *1997 Educational Software Preview Guide* was developed by the Educational Software Preview Guide Consortium, which represents 16 organizations involved in evaluating educational software and other technology resources throughout North America. The guide is designed to assist educators in locating software for preview. It lists more than 700 titles of favorably reviewed software for K-12 classroom use; 133 science titles are included. The guide is organized by subject and application and includes computer type, grade level, instructional mode, a brief description of each product, and publisher/developer contact information.

6.14 Only the Best: The Annual Guide to the Highest-Rated Educational Software and Multimedia 1997-1998. Alexandria, Va.: Association for Supervision and Curriculum Development, 1997. 143 pp.

Price: $29.00 (ISSN 1053-4326); on CD-ROM: $150.00

Only the Best is an annual review guide of highly rated educational software and multimedia programs, compiled from the findings of top software and multimedia evaluators. Although software programs on a wide variety of topics are reviewed, science and social studies programs predominate. Each entry includes a program description, cost, grade level, hardware requirements, references for further information, and user tips. The guide, organized by subject area, also includes titles and tips for diverse learners, and a directory of software publishers. *Only the Best* is also available on CD-ROM and on the Internet at http://www.ascd.org.

6.15 School Library Journal

School Library Journal is written for children's librarians, young adults' librarians, and school librarians. In addition to feature articles and book reviews, it includes reviews of CD-ROMs, computer software, and audiovisual materials.

Issues/price: 12 per year; $87.50 per year. *Available from:* School Library Journal.

6.16 School Science & Mathematics

School Science & Mathematics is an international journal emphasizing issues, concerns, and lessons within and between the disciplines of science and mathematics in the classroom. The regular column "Technology Reviews" provides information on new and current technology and software. The reviews include a description and rating of the software or technology and tips on its successful use in the classroom.

Issues/price: 8 per year; $35 per year. *Available from:* School Science and Mathematics Association.

6.17 Science & Children

Science & Children (*see* 9.38) is a journal on teaching elementary and middle school science. It features "Software Reviews," a regular department that includes reviews of newly available software resources.

Issues/price: 8 per year; $55 per year for members of National Science Teachers Association. *Available from:* National Science Teachers Association.

6.18 Science Books & Films

Science Books & Films (*see* 9.39)—produced by the American Association for the Advancement of Science—is a journal of critical reviews devoted exclusively to print and nonprint materials in all of the sciences and for all age groups. Each issue contains some 100 evaluations of books, audiovisual materials, and software—for general audiences, professionals, teachers, and students from kindergarten through college. Sample reviews are available on the Internet at http://ehr.aaas.org/ehr/6_0_0.html.

Issues/price: 9 per year; $40 per year. *Available from:* Science Books & Films.

6.19 The Science Teacher

The Science Teacher (*see* 9.44) provides articles by science educators on innovations in science teaching, current developments in science, and classroom projects and experiments. Each issue includes reviews of books, software, and audiovisual materials relevant to teaching science in middle and high schools.

Issues/price: 9 per year; $56 per year for members of National Science Teachers Association. *Available from:* National Science Teachers Association.

6.20 Technology & Learning

Technology & Learning is a leading publication in educational technology, written for K-12 school administrators, teachers, and technology coordinators. The magazine provides product information and guidance in improving and expanding the use of technology in schools. Regularly featured departments include reviews and comparisons of software, with an annual software awards contest; technology updates, featuring a different hardware category or trend each month; and product and program announcements. A searchable database of software reviews is available on the Internet at http://www.techlearning.com.

Issues/price: 10 per year; $24 per year. *Available from:* Miller Freeman.

6.21 Technology Connection

Technology Connection provides a professional forum for school media and technology specialists as they organize and facilitate access to electronic resources. This magazine includes reviews of new products, tips and pointers, and information on emerging technologies and training opportunities. Electronic products reviewed include videodiscs, CD-ROMs, and computer software. Reviews are available on the Internet at http://www.linworth.com.

Issues/price: 9 per year; $43 per year. *Available from:* Linworth Publishing.

6.22 The Technology Teacher

The Technology Teacher is a journal on technology education published by the International Technology Education Association—an affiliate of the American Association for the Advancement of Science. A section called "Product News" includes information on software, CD-ROMs, and Internet resources.

Issues/price: 8 per year; $65 per year. *Available from:* International Technology Education Association.

6.23 TESS: The Educational Software Selector CD-ROM. 1996 ed. Hampton Bays, N.Y.: Educational Products Information Exchange (EPIE) Institute, 1996.

Price: $82.50 (Updates $32.50)

TESS: The Educational Software Selector CD-ROM (*see* 8.34) provides an annotated listing of essential information on 18,000 educational software programs for preschool through college from more than 1,300 software publishers. Nearly 4,000 science titles are included. The detailed entries include a program description and software requirements. Search parameters include computer type, grade, price, program type, software title, review score (where available), subject, and supplier.

PART 3

REFERENCE
MATERIALS

OVERVIEW

CHAPTER 7
BOOKS ON TEACHING SCIENCE

CHAPTER 8
SCIENCE BOOK LISTS AND
RESOURCE GUIDES

CHAPTER 9
PERIODICALS

Reviewing resources

Part 3, "Reference Materials," consists of annotated lists of reference books and periodicals to which the middle school science teacher can turn for assistance in teaching hands-on, inquiry-centered science. The lists are as follows: "Books on Teaching Science," chapter 7; "Science Book Lists and Resource Guides," chapter 8; and "Periodicals," chapter 9.

Chapter 7, "Books on Teaching Science," includes almost 50 titles that offer guidance in learning theory and pedagogical techniques. The reference materials selected for this chapter vary in length, style, purpose, and approach. A few of the many topics that they address include these:

- science standards, their implementation in the classroom, and their implications in terms of the special educational needs of students with disabilities;
- the theory and practice of activity-based, inquiry-centered science learning and teaching;
- assessment in science education for early adolescents, the role of assessment in science education reform, performance-based assessment strategies, and the improvement of techniques for measuring and evaluating outcomes of science instruction in the classroom;
- practical issues, such as organizing barrier-free classrooms, assuring laboratory safety in grades 6 through 12, and keeping small animals in the classroom;

- strategies for helping middle school science teachers incorporate cooperative learning effectively and develop lessons and activities that encourage problem-solving and higher-level thinking skills; and
- professional development needs and opportunities for middle school science teachers.

Chapter 8, "Science Book Lists and Resource Guides," focuses on almost 40 directories and guides produced by organizations as diverse in their expertise as the World Wildlife Fund, the Smithsonian Office of Education, the American Library Association, the California Foundation for Agriculture in the Classroom, and the Mississippi-Alabama Sea Grant Consortium. The authoritative reference works annotated in chapter 8 provide teachers with titles, reviews, and recommendations for books, materials, and other resources, as well as information on how to select and obtain what they need for teaching middle school science.

Among the directories annotated in the chapter are—

- bibliographies and reviews of publications and films for middle school students, including lists of trade books highly recommended to satisfy the interests and academic needs of students in grades 6 through 8 in science and mathematics;
- guides to science equipment and material resources;
- guides to resources in electronic formats, including a comprehensive directory of computer software for preschool through college;
- a directory of Internet resources, including science resources suitable for K-12 students;
- directories of key personnel at various organizations, including educational research centers, environmental organizations and conservation agencies, and state and federal agencies of interest to those in middle school science.

A final category of reference materials is presented in chapter 9, "Periodicals." This chapter contains annotations for almost 60 magazines. It includes titles not only for middle school science teachers but for their students as well. The annotations indicate the grade level for which each title is recommended.

The periodicals annotated in chapter 9 were chosen for their excellence as instructional tools, for the quality of their articles and stories on scientific topics, for their appeal to young adolescents, and for their adaptability to classroom use. They offer current information in the sciences, ideas and activities for science teaching, and engaging reading matter for students. The variety of periodicals annotated in chapter 9 includes, for example—

- magazines for middle school science teachers that include features on "big ideas" in mathematics and science education; a periodical containing articles by teachers about hands-on learning, problem solving, and a multidisciplinary approach to teaching science and mathematics;

- an international journal of research in science education; a journal designed to further understanding of intermediate education and the implementation of effective practices at the middle school level; a periodical on innovations in science teaching, current developments in science, and classroom projects and experiments; a journal that addresses the needs of both new and veteran middle school teachers;

- publications by science educators and scientists that cover news, research, and issues related to specific disciplines or fields, such as aerospace, astronomy, biology, chemistry, physics, and earth sciences;

- publications on electronic learning that focus on educational technology, including in-depth reviews of software and hardware, information on new products available to educators, coverage of all aspects of precollege educational technology such as telecommunications/distance learning, computer literacy, and hypermedia/multimedia;

- student periodicals that cover a wide range of topics—from science news, science careers, and competitions and experiments to natural history, marine biology, the environment, wildlife, space travel, technology, and achievements of young people and adults.

The listings in chapters 7 through 9 are not exhaustive. Teachers are encouraged to keep their eyes open for new or other publications for their own lists of references. The absence of any volume or periodical from these lists is not intended as a comment on its quality or usefulness.

Insofar as possible, the most current edition of a publication is annotated in part 3. However, later editions of some volumes, particularly annual or biannual directories, may have appeared after the text of *Resources for Teaching Middle School Science* was completed.

Ordering Information

Prices for the books and periodicals in chapters 7 through 9 are given in the annotations. Costs for shipping and handling are not included. The addresses, telephone and fax numbers, and e-mail addresses, when available, for publishers of these materials are in appendix A, "Publishers and Suppliers."

Every effort was made to provide accurate, up-to-date ordering information. However, because of frequent changes in company names, addresses, and telephone and fax numbers, readers may wish to consult annually updated directories, such as *NSTA Science Education Suppliers* (see 8.22), or standard reference directories such as *Books in Print* from their local libraries or bookstores.

Likewise, because prices and availability may change, readers should check the prices of publications or supplies listed before placing an order. They are encouraged to contact publishers directly for current ordering information (including shipping charges). In some cases, discounts or special rates may be available to schools and educators.

CHAPTER 7

BOOKS ON TEACHING SCIENCE

7.1 David C. Kramer. **Animals in the Classroom: Selection, Care, and Observations.** Menlo Park, Calif.: Addison-Wesley, 1989. 234 pp.

Price: $19.95 (ISBN 0-201-20679-X)

Animals in the Classroom: Selection, Care, and Observations is for elementary and middle school teachers interested in keeping small animals such as earthworms, praying mantises, frogs, and hamsters in the classroom. The book focuses on 28 individual creatures that represent various levels of the animal kingdom, from worms through mammals. A section on each animal combines text and illustrations to describe where and how the animal lives in nature, how to obtain it, and how to care for it with classroom-tested techniques. The book encourages teachers to stimulate student curiosity and interest in learning about animals. It helps teachers select appropriate animals and care for them humanely, and supplies back-

ground information to help answer students' questions and provide meaningful learning experiences with the animals. Suggestions for student observations and activities are given.

7.2 Margaret Jorgensen. **Assessing Habits of Mind: Performance-Based Assessment in Science and Mathematics.** Columbus, Ohio: ERIC Clearinghouse for Science, Mathematics, and Environmental Education, 1994. 112 pp.

Price: $16.75 (ERIC Accession No. SE 054 513)

This book is designed to provide K-12 science and mathematics teachers with strategies for identifying, developing, and using performance-based assessment in the classroom. In 7 chapters, the book defines performance-based assessment, discusses why it should be used in the classroom, presents a structure for designing performance-based assessments, describes the process of

developing scoring rubrics, and suggests guidelines for reviewing commercially developed assessments as well as those developed by colleagues or available in the public domain. The book closes with a list of important but as yet unanswered questions on this subject—questions about equity, fairness, consequences of use, and concerns shared by theoreticians and practitioners about the value and appropriateness of performance-based assessment.

7.3 Senta A. Raizen, Joan B. Baron, Audrey B. Champagne, and others. **Assessment in Science Education: The Middle Years.** Washington, D.C.: National Center for Improving Science Education, 1990. 129 pp. (Available from Learning Innovations; *see* app. A.)

Price: $18.00

Assessment in Science Education: The Middle Years is 1 in a series of 5 reports on science and mathematics

Facilitating student discussion

ORDERING INFORMATION FOR PUBLICATIONS IN CHAPTER 7

The prices given for books and other publications in chapter 7 do not include the costs of shipping and handling. Before placing an order, readers are advised to contact the publishers of these items for current ordering information, including shipping charges. In some cases, discounts or special rates may be available to schools and educators.

Publishers' names are cited in the bibliographic data of the annotations. Their addresses and telephone and fax numbers, as well as e-mail addresses, when available, are listed in appendix A, "Publishers and Suppliers."

for young adults (ages 10 to 14) from the National Center for Improving Science Education. This 8-chapter report addresses the role of assessment in early adolescents' science learning. It first reviews the capabilities and interests of early adolescents and considers the nature of an education, especially in science and technology, that can build on these assets. It discusses what is known about the cognitive and social development of 10- to 14-year-old students, and reviews the nature of science programs and the middle school environment. The core of the report then explains assessment and instruction in the service of science learning as viewed by the National Center for Improving Science Education, and it points out opportunities for assessment presented by the growing cognitive abilities of early adolescents. Examples show how scientific inquiry itself can provide assessment opportunities and how teachers can weave assessment into their science teaching. Finally, the report discusses assessment for broad policy purposes. It suggests 6 principles for science assessments at the middle level and recommends steps for achieving these principles.

7.4 American Association for the Advancement of Science (AAAS). **Barrier-Free in Brief: Laboratories and Classrooms in Science and Engineering.** Washington, D.C.: AAAS, 1991. 36 pp.

Price: Free (ISBN 0-87168-421-6)

Barrier-Free in Brief was prepared by the American Association for the Advancement of Science's Project on Science, Technology, and Disability. The booklet is a guide for university research laboratories, but it addresses meeting the needs of students with disabilities in the science classroom in any educational institution. A barrier-free classroom is defined as being fully accessible to people with disabilities. The booklet offers specific suggestions about organizing a barrier-free classroom and teaching students with disabilities. It presents related material such as a building access checklist and a list of organizations to contact for information on helping students with particular disabilities.

7.5 American Association for the Advancement of Science (AAAS). **Benchmarks for Science Literacy.** New York, N.Y.: Oxford University Press, 1993. 418 pp.

Price: $22.95 (ISBN 0-19-508986-3)

Benchmarks for Science Literacy on Disk [text and companion software version]

Price: $24.95

Created in close consultation with teachers, administrators, and scientists, *Benchmarks for Science Literacy* and its companion *Benchmarks for Science Literacy on Disk* suggest guidelines for what all students should know and be able to do in science and mathematics by the end of specific grade levels. *Benchmarks* is part of the Project 2061 initiative of AAAS. The volume outlines ways of achieving the standards for science literacy recommended in the 1989 AAAS publication *Science for All Americans.* Rather than being a proposed curriculum or a plan for one, *Benchmarks* is a compendium of specific goals that educators and policymakers can use to build new curricula. The software version allows users to browse, assemble, and print benchmarks in various formats, examine conceptual strands, use cross-reference features to identify conceptual connections, and brainstorm activities to address random sets of benchmarks from one grade span.

7.6 National Center for Improving Science Education. **Building Scientific Literacy: A Blueprint for Science in the Middle Years.** Washington, D.C.: National Center for Improving Science Education, 1992. 73 pp. (Available from Learning Innovations; *see* app. A.)

Price: $8.40

Building Scientific Literacy is 1 in a series of 5 reports on science and mathematics for young adults (ages 10 to 14) from the National Center for Improving Science Education. This report is a blueprint for the creation of an effective national program of science education for students in America's middle-grade schools. It is designed as a "briefing" for those who have a concern with and responsibility for education in public schools—middle-level teachers and principals, science specialists, curriculum directors, assessment personnel, staff development leaders, school district superintendents and administrators, and state and federal education officials. The report first surveys what is known about middle-level curriculum instruction, assessment, and teacher development, and then proposes ideal goals for science education in the middle years. Included are specific recommendations on what the federal government, state agencies, institutions of higher education, building and district administrators, and teachers should do to promote changes in policies and practices in the science curriculum.

7.7 Sally Berman. **Catch Them Thinking in Science: A Handbook of Classroom Strategies.** Palatine, Ill.: IRI/Skylight Publishing, 1993. 127 pp.

Price: $22.95 (ISBN 0-932935-55-9)

Catch Them Thinking in Science is designed to help middle and high school teachers create activities and lessons that emphasize and teach higher-level thinking skills in science. Featured activity topics include, for example, salamanders and frogs, planets, fungi, and elements and compounds. The activities require cooperative learning while using discipline-crossing strategies such as think-pair-share, Venn diagrams, prediction guides, learning logs, wraparounds, webs, and metacognitive questioning methods. The 21 chapters or lessons are grouped in 3 parts: part I focuses on information-gathering activities, part II on activities that involve organizing and making sense of information, and part III on activities that combine critical and creative thinking and transfer. Some lessons can be used exactly as they appear; others can serve as models for lessons that fit into any curriculum, lecture, or textbook assignment. Each lesson includes background information and suggestions for guiding discussion. Blackline masters are also provided.

7.8 Joseph L. Accongio and Rodney L. Doran. **Classroom Assessment: Key to Reform in Secondary Science Education.** Columbus, Ohio: ERIC Clearinghouse for Science, Mathematics, and Environmental Education, 1993. 207 pp.

Price: $16.75

Classroom Assessment: Key to Reform in Secondary Science Education discusses how teachers can improve assessment techniques for measuring and evaluating outcomes of science instruction in their classrooms. This monograph was undertaken with the idea that the improvement of assessment practices directly relates to the improvement of instruction and achievement in science. Its 5 chapters address these topics: (1) Assessing Science Achievement in Middle and High Schools; (2) A Framework for Teaching and Assessing Science: The Nature of Science and the Nature of the Learner; (3) Assessing Levels of Cognition in the Content Areas of Science; (4) Assessing Process Skills: Scientific Thinking, Inquiry and Problem Solving; and (5) Authentic Assessment in Science: Performing Like a Scientist. Appendixes include concrete examples of items that can be used to assess learning in the cognitive domain. They also present items for assessing planning, performing, and reasoning in scientific problem solving. Other appendixes offer proficiency profiles and a rate sheet for science process skills, and examples of authentic assessment tasks.

7.9 Robert J. Stahl, ed. **Cooperative Learning in Science: A Handbook for Teachers.** Menlo Park, Calif.: Addison-Wesley, Innovative Learning Publications, 1996. 445 pp. (Available from Addison-Wesley/Longman; *see* app. A.)

Price: $22.95 (ISBN 0-201-49422-1)

This *Handbook for Teachers* contains 16 essays by teachers and leaders in the cooperative learning movement. It describes cooperative learning strategies that can be used effectively in the classroom. One essay, for example, gives step-by-step directions for using Jigsaw—a learning strategy that involves team learning. Another essay offers suggestions on how to implement cooperative learning in classrooms with students of different achievement levels and cultures. Other entries in the volume present an approach to learning that requires students to "compete" in games and tournaments; guidelines for structuring successful academic controversy within the classroom; and procedures for helping students complete research papers within a cooperative learning context. Many of the strategies are appropriate for any science content area and can be used with all levels of students—from elementary through high school—as well as in teacher training and professional staff development workshops. Some essays provide classroom examples and scenarios; others include sample lesson plans, resource materials, generic checklists, and forms.

7.10 Alfred De Vito. **Creative Wellsprings for Science Teaching.** 2nd ed. West Lafayette, Ind.: Creative Ventures, 1989. 348 pp.

Price: $18.95 (ISBN 0-942034-06-6)

This lighthearted but useful book stresses methods for creative teaching to improve the quality of science education for children. *Creative Wellsprings for Science Teaching* presents 3 approaches to teaching science—morphological, process, and ideation-generation—and outlines classroom activities for each approach. The book addresses the following topics: educating the gifted in science; science instruction and its enhancement through provocative question asking; the skill of building models; and peripheral enhancements to use in the classroom, such as discrepant events, puzzlers, problems, and tenacious "think abouts." *Creative Wellsprings* emphasizes ways that teachers can expand basic classroom activities into multiple activities and experiments that stimulate thinking and foster a challenging atmosphere.

7.11 Imogene Forte and Sandra Schurr. **The Definitive Middle School Guide: A Handbook for Success.** Nashville, Tenn.: Incentive Publications, 1993. 351 pp.

Price: $29.95 (ISBN 0-86530-270-7)

The Definitive Middle School Guide is a handbook for teachers and administrators about middle school

education and its essential program components. The book features 7 self-contained modules designed to help readers think about what makes an effective middle school. The topics addressed are (1) the needs and characteristics of young adolescents and basic elements of the exemplary middle school, including facility requirements and classroom management tips; (2) ways of forming interdisciplinary teams; (3) characteristics of successful advisory programs and advisory activities; (4) methods for implementing cooperative student learning; (5) suggestions for fostering creative and critical-thinking skills; (6) assessment strategies; and (7) guidelines for designing and implementing an interdisciplinary curriculum. Each module includes a short overview, important questions about its topic, a glossary, findings from the published literature, "need-to-know" information about the topic in a "Top Ten" list format, and activities at each level of Bloom's Taxonomy. A comprehensive index and bibliography are also provided.

7.12 Susan Loucks-Horsley, Jackie Grennon Brooks, Maura O. Carlson, and others. **Developing and Supporting Teachers for Science Education in the Middle Years.** Washington, D.C.: National Center for Improving Science Education, 1990. 94 pp. (Available from Learning Innovations; *see* app. A.)

Price: $18.00

Developing and Supporting Teachers for Science Education in the Middle Years is 1 in a series of 5 reports on science and mathematics for young adults (ages 10 to 14) from the National Center for Improving Science Education. It addresses issues of improving middle-grade science education, with an emphasis on the importance of the

teacher as learner and facilitator. Written from the perspective that science education reform depends on helping individual teachers change their practices and beliefs, the report considers what teachers need to know, believe, and be able to do to meet the science and other learning needs of young adolescents. It also looks at what development opportunities and organizational features and structures teachers need in order to change or refine the knowledge, beliefs, practices, and classroom environments which current research says are critical to middle-grade science learning. Also addressed is the question of how prospective science teachers can best be prepared to participate fully in good programs for middle-grade students. Finally, the report provides specific recommendations for implementing changes pertaining to the development and support of teachers.

7.13 Committee on Goals 2000 and the Inclusion of Students with Disabilities, Board on Testing and Assessment, Commission on Behavioral and Social Sciences and Education, National Research Council. **Educating One and All: Students with Disabilities and Standards-Based Reform.** Washington, D.C.: National Academy Press, 1997. 302 pp.

Price: $42.95 (ISBN 0-309-05789-2)

In *Educating One and All,* an expert committee makes recommendations to states and communities that have adopted standards-based reform and that are trying to make these reforms consistent with current policies and practices in special education. *Educating One and All* explores the ideas, implementation issues, and legislative initiatives behind the tradition of special education for students with disabilities. It also investigates the policy and practice implications of the current reform movement toward high educational standards for all students. In addition, the report describes the diverse population of students with disabilities and the variation in their school experiences and educational needs. It examines the assumptions about curriculum and instruction that are embodied in standards-based reform and also examines the curricula, instruction, and postschool outcomes of special education; points of alignment between these assumptions and outcomes are identified. The report also analyzes technical and policy issues involved in increasing the participation of students with disabilities in assessments and accountability systems. Finally, it addresses some legal and resource implications of standards-based reforms.

7.14 Lars J. Helgeson and William C. Bohnsack. **Flinn Scientific Science Safety Lecture Series: Secondary.** Batavia, Ill.: Flinn Scientific, 1996. 500 pp.

Price: $99.95 (ISBN 1-877991-41-4)

This series of 9 lectures is designed to provide a short course in laboratory safety for secondary teachers (grades 6-12). Topics discussed include the legal aspects of laboratory safety, chemical hazards, proper storage and disposal of chemicals, biological safety, personal protective and emergency equipment, ventilation of science laboratories, and teaching techniques to reduce hazards. Each lecture includes activities that require participants to think critically about important safety-related ideas. Transparency masters and tests are provided for each lecture, and a generic chemical hygiene plan for high school laboratories is included in an appendix.

7.15 National Environmental Education and Training Foundation. **Getting Started: A Guide to Bringing Environmental Education into Your Classroom.** David Bones, ed. Ann Arbor, Mich.: National Consortium for Environmental Education and Training, 1994. 138 pp. (Available from Kendall/Hunt; *see* app. A.)

Price: $15.95 (ISBN 0-7872219-1-0)

This volume is a collection of real stories about teachers in grades K-12 who started environmental programs in their classrooms. *Getting Started* contains brief, helpful suggestions, resources, and ideas on bringing environmental education into the classroom. The first section provides a brief overview of the scope, history, and value of environmental education. The second offers suggestions for instructional materials, funding, workshops, courses, and in-service opportunities in environmental education. The third section includes information on networking with other environmental educators; securing grants; managing a growing environmental project; and locating awards, scholarships, and stipends. Rather than outlining a comprehensive program, the guide offers stories and information to inspire teachers and help them creatively find resources to meet their own unique needs.

7.16 Maria Sosa, Estrella M. Triana, Valerie L. Worthington, and Mary C. Chobot, eds. **Great Explorations: Discovering Science in the Library.** Washington, D.C.: American Association for the Advancement of Science, 1994. 187 pp.

Price: $14.95 (ISBN 0-87168-537-X)

Great Explorations addresses the role that librarians and media specialists can play in science, mathematics, and technology education

reform. This volume is the result of a project that brought together 28 school and public librarians from the Washington, D.C., area. In its 12 chapters, the book offers information on selecting good science resources for a library and on disseminating new science and mathematics education projects, products, techniques, and practices. Topics addressed include creating hands-on and interdisciplinary activities in a library (directions for 13 activities are included); technology in the library; teaching science in a multicultural context; fundraising for a media center; and forming partnerships with teachers, administrators, parents, and community leaders to promote education reform. Many chapters have lists of resources, networks, or references. One chapter describes events, activities, and exhibits conducted by project participants to implement science, mathematics, and technology reform at their schools.

7.17 David Jarmul, ed. **Headline News, Science Views II.** Washington, D.C.: National Academy Press, 1993. 256 pp.

Price: $19.95 (ISBN 0-309-04834-6)

Headline News, a book of 75 previously published articles, is designed to help teachers and students make sense of some of today's most important issues involving science, technology, and health care. Written by scientific and technical experts and distributed by the National Academy Op-Ed Service, the short, readable articles appeared originally on the editorial and opinion pages of 250 daily newspapers. They are organized in 10 chapters by subject: science and society, education, the environment, health care, diet and nutrition, technology and transportation, the economy, international affairs, looking to the future, and the scientific enterprise. Topics discussed include global warming, health care reform, traffic jams, foods in our future, science and animals, computers, the brain, gene therapy, and toxic waste sites. The book also includes an essay that tells readers how to write and publish their own op-ed articles.

7.18 Robert J. Swartz and Sandra Parks. **Infusing Critical and Creative Thinking into Content Instruction: A Lesson Design Handbook for the Elementary Grades.** Pacific Grove, Calif.: Critical Thinking Press and Software, 1994. 549 pp.

Price: Teacher's Handbook, $42.95 (ISBN 0-89455-481-6); Macintosh or Windows Masters, $19.95

This handbook presents a teacher-oriented approach to improving student thinking that infuses critical and creative thinking into content instruction. The thinking skills and processes featured in the book include generating, clarifying, and assessing the reasonableness of ideas, and decision making and problem solving. Sample lessons in core content areas, together with activity sheets, are provided to help teachers construct their own infused lessons. The book also includes a variety of examples for the science classroom.

7.19 John W. Layman, George Ochoa, and Henry Heikkinen. **Inquiry and Learning: Realizing Science Standards in the Classroom.** New York, N.Y.: College Entrance Examination Board, 1996. 71 pp.

Price: $12.00 (ISBN 0-87447-547-3)

Inquiry and Learning addresses the central question of how science instruction based on national stan-

dards should look and feel in the classroom. The book also considers 2 issues related to that question: how teachers can cultivate the quality of scientific thinking and understanding defined by standards, and how they can verify that students have actually attained the level of learning envisioned by the standards. Specific examples of productive classroom practice are highlighted. Recent research findings and advances in the understanding of student cognition and learning then provide the framework for generalizing from those practices. The teaching and assessment standards from the *National Science Education Standards* (*see* 7.27) help frame the book's discussion of content standards in the classroom.

7.20 Merrill Harmin. **Inspiring Active Learning: A Handbook for Teachers.** Alexandria, Va.: Association for Supervision and Curriculum Development, 1994. 208 pp.

Price: $14.95 (ISBN 0-87120-228-X)

Inspiring Active Learning is a handbook of instructional strategies for teachers to use in helping students become active, responsible learners. These strategies are centered on teachers' and students' mutual respect, collaboration, and commitment to learning. The description of each strategy is followed by examples of how it can be used, at any grade level and in any subject specialty. The strategies are grouped in broad categories. In addition to basic instructional strategies, the categories include raising student motivation; organizing the classroom; handling homework, testing, and grading; and producing meaningful learning. An indexed glossary provides quick access to all the strategies.

7.21 Robin Fogarty and Judy Stoehr. **Integrating Curricula with Multiple Intelligences: Teams, Themes, and Threads.** Palatine, Ill.: IRI/Skylight Publishing, 1995. 221 pp.

Price: $35.95 (ISBN 0-932935-81-8)

"Multiple intelligences theory," pioneered by Howard Gardner, holds that each person receives and expresses ideas in a myriad of ways—verbal, logical, musical, visual, bodily, interpersonal, and intrapersonal. *Integrating Curricula with Multiple Intelligences* offers ideas for translating multiple intelligences theory into classroom activities that meet a variety of integrated curriculum models and assessment needs. The first of 4 chapters reviews Gardner's theory and discusses 10 different ways (fragmented, connected, nested, sequenced, shared, webbed, threaded, integrated, immersed, and networked) of integrating curricula in a classroom. The second chapter explores the concept of developing teacher teams to implement holistic, integrated, and interdisciplinary approaches to curriculum. The third chapter presents a 6-step process for developing thematic learning units that focus on thinking, decision making, and problem solving. The final chapter highlights ways of threading specific skills into subject-matter content. An endnote describes assessment issues that arise when using integrated curricula and holistic instruction with multiple intelligences.

7.22 Diane C. Cantrell and Patricia A. Barron, eds. **Integrating Environmental Education and Science: Using and Developing Learning Episodes.** Newark, Ohio: Environmental Education Council of Ohio, 1994. 182 pp. (Available from ERIC Clearinghouse for Science, Mathematics, and Environmental Education; *see* app. A.)

Price: $16.75

Integrating Environmental Education and Science is designed to encourage environmental literacy and responsible environmental behavior, and to assist developers and teachers in designing curriculum. The first of the book's 3 main sections discusses goals of environmental and science education, identifies key content elements, and suggests various ways to organize the curriculum. The second section defines and exemplifies the term "learning episode." The last section offers general guidelines for developing learning episodes. The volume's appendixes include an outline of Ohio's Model Competency-Based Science Program; guidelines for environmental education activities; helpful lists, samples, and tips; curricular and professional resources; an overview of the learning episodes included in the book; linkages to ninth-grade proficiency test outcomes; and blank forms for models and webs.

7.23 Michael J. Caduto and Joseph Bruchac. **Keepers of Life: Discovering Plants Through Native American Stories and Earth Activities for Children.** Golden, Colo.: Fulcrum Publishing, 1994. 265 pp.

Price: $26.95 (ISBN 1-55591-186-2)

This book, about learning to understand, live with, and care for plants, draws on Native American history and culture and uses an interdisciplinary approach. Eighteen carefully selected Native North American stories are combined with imaginative hands-on activities to promote children's understanding of, appreciation for, empathy with, and stewardship of plants. The indoor and outdoor activities in the 15 chapters cover a wide range of concepts: botany, plant ecology, environmental and stewardship issues that are important to plants, and the natural history of North American plants and plantlike organisms. Children are introduced to the greenhouse effect, global warming, ozone depletion, acid rain, endangered species, and extinction. Each chapter includes extensive background information, suggested discussion questions, and extensions. The book emphasizes the complex and interconnected nature of all living things. An index of activities arranged by subject describes the specific lessons taught by each activity. A teacher's guide is available; it lists books, guides to environmental and outdoor education, and interdisciplinary studies.

7.24 Michael J. Caduto and Joseph Bruchac. **Keepers of the Animals: Native American Stories and Wildlife Activities for Children.** Golden, Colo.: Fulcrum Publishing, 1991. 286 pp.

Price: $26.95 (ISBN 1-55591-088-2)

This volume is about learning to understand, live with, and care for animals. Combining 24 carefully selected Native American animal stories with interdisciplinary activities, it guides students through a study of the concepts and topics of wildlife ecology; issues in environmental stewardship that are particularly important to animals; and the natural history and habitat of North American animals, from mollusk to mammal. The activities are designed to provoke curiosity and facilitate discovery of animals and their environments. They involve students in creative arts, theater, reading, writing, listening, science, social studies, mathematics, and sensory awareness. Each chapter includes extensive science background information, discussion questions, and extensions. An index of activities arranged by subject describes the specific lessons taught by each activity. A companion teacher's guide that discusses the nature of Native North American stories and cultures is available. That volume provides lists of books for further reading and suggests guides to environmental and outdoor education.

7.25 Francis X. Sutman, Virginia French Allen, and Francis Shoemaker. **Learning English through Science: A Guide to Collaboration for Science Teachers, English Teachers, and Teachers of English as a Second Language.** Washington, D.C.: National Science Teachers Association, 1986. 43 pp.

Price: $4.00 (ISBN 0-87355-061-7)

This 7-chapter booklet, written by English teachers and a science education specialist, suggests teaching procedures that can help students learn the English language and science together. The opening chapters describe general strategies, such as visual materials and student notebooks, for teaching in multilingual settings; specific methods, such as improving nontechnical vocabulary and comprehension of sentence structure, to prepare limited-English-proficient (LEP) students for reading science materials; activities, such as dialogues, cloze exercises, crossword puzzles, group activities, and hands-on activities, that are particularly effective for teaching science concepts to LEP students; and samples of 3 science lessons that teach both

English language and science content. A closing chapter presents a model that teachers can use to develop and conduct their own lessons to stress science comprehension and English-language learning.

7.26 Paul S. George, Chris Stevenson, Julia Thomason, and James Beane. **The Middle School—and Beyond.** Alexandria, Va.: Association for Supervision and Curriculum Development, 1992. 172 pp.

Price: $17.95 (ISBN 0-87120-190-9)

This book describes how middle schools across the nation are focusing on students' needs, accommodating diversity, integrating the curriculum, emphasizing a close-knit school community, and creating the kinds of learning experiences that promote excellence. *The Middle School—and Beyond* is organized in 7 chapters that address the middle school concept (grades 6-8), the traits of positive student-teacher relationships, the organization of effective middle schools, new visions of the middle school curriculum, leadership in middle schools, and the impact of the middle school movement on some elementary and high schools.

7.27 National Research Council. **National Science Education Standards.** Washington, D.C.: National Academy Press, 1996. 272 pp.

Price: $19.95 (ISBN 0-309-05326-9)

In an effort to guide the science education system in the United States, this document offers a vision of what it means to be scientifically literate and describes what students nationwide should know and be able to do in science as a result of their learning experiences. The volume is the result of a 3-year effort that involved thousands of teachers, parents, scientists, and others. The standards address what students should be able to do and understand at different grade levels, exemplary practices of science teaching and teacher training, criteria for assessing and analyzing learning, the nature and design of the school and district science program, and the support and resources needed to provide all students with the opportunity to learn science. The standards suggested in this document reflect the principles that learning science should be an inquiry-based process, that science in schools should reflect the intellectual trends of contemporary science, and that all Americans have a role in science education reform.

7.28 Richard F. Brinckerhoff. **One-Minute Readings: Issues in Science, Technology, and Society.** Menlo Park, Calif.: Addison-Wesley, 1992. 142 pp.

Prices: Student book, $10.95 (ISBN 0-201-23157-3); Teacher's guide, $7.95 (ISBN 0-201-23159-X)

One-Minute Readings offers 80 succinct readings—1- or 2-page issue descriptions, interwoven with questions—designed to provoke student thinking about real-world problems related to science, technology, and society. The readings touch upon social and ethical aspects of many topics in chemistry, physics, biology, and social science. They include current questions or dilemmas in medicine, environmental science, bioethics, space science, and computers. Readers, for example, are asked to consider whether parents should be able to learn—or choose—the sex of their unborn child (and what rights such a fetus may have); whether there is a moral difference between an athlete's taking energy-giving glucose pills and taking an anabolic steroid; and whether there is a distinction between an individual who flushes polluting material down a drain and an oil company whose tanker causes an oil spill. Teachers can use the readings for several purposes: to add debate about science topics to any course, to promote the integration of science content and social issues in the classroom, to expose students to the applications of science, and to offer problem-solving practice for decision making as an adult.

7.29 David L. Haury and Peter Rillero. **Perspectives of Hands-On Science Teaching.** Columbus, Ohio: ERIC Clearinghouse for Science, Mathematics, and Environmental Education, 1994. 156 pp.

Price: $14.50 (ERIC Accession No. SE 054 205)

In question-and-answer format, this book addresses frequently asked questions about hands-on approaches to science teaching and learning. The volume was intended to be a ready reference for making the case for an activity-based, inquiry-oriented, hands-on approach to teaching and learning in the science classroom. To present a range of perspectives, the book offers the views of three groups of individuals: teachers, curriculum developers, and science education scholars. Topics discussed include these: what hands-on learning is; how a hands-on science approach fits into a textbook-centered science program; how practicing teachers can gain experience with hands-on methods; how the use of hands-on materials should, or should not, vary with students' ages; where to find resources or materials to develop hands-on activities; and how hands-on learning can be evaluated. An appendix provides a list of selected materials that support an activity-based approach to science teaching; included are curriculum guides, supplementary materials, program frameworks, and planning resources.

7.30 John W. Jewett, Jr. **Physics Begins with an *M* . . . Mysteries, Magic, and Myth.** Boston, Mass.: Allyn and Bacon, 1994. 432 pp.

Price: $29.95 (ISBN 0-205-15133-7)

This resource book presents some thought-provoking questions (mysteries), activities (magic tricks), and misconceptions (myths) that challenge students to explore the application of physics to everyday life. Although the material was prepared for high school and college students, many of the activities and concepts can be adapted for middle school. Students, for example, are asked to use their knowledge of physics to figure out why it is a myth that a vacuum cleaner "sucks up" dirt. Or why, mysteriously, scraps of paper put in a metal kitchen strainer and then held over a candle flame do not burn. The mysteries, magic tricks, and myths are organized in 29 chapters by topics often found in introductory physics books. Examples include vectors, Newton's laws, friction, equilibrium, gravity, energy, momentum, pressure, fluids, heat, simple harmonic motion, electric fields and forces, reflection and refraction, and polarization. At the end of each chapter is a discussion section containing comments on the mysteries, magic, and myths in that chapter. Each chapter also contains a brief outline of relevant physics principles. References and a subject index are included.

7.31 Stanley L. Helgeson. **Problem Solving Research in Middle/Junior High School Science Education.** Columbus, Ohio: ERIC Clearinghouse for Science, Mathematics, and Environmental Education, 1992. 97 pp.

Price: $14.00

Drawing on 145 papers published over the past 30 years, this resource summarizes various aspects of research on the importance of problem-solving skills in school science. Although the book's primary concern is with science in the middle grades, some studies that are referenced extend into the elementary grades and high school years. Subjects of research reviewed in the summary include these: instruments used to assess problem-solving skills or abilities; strategies or behaviors exhibited by students as they engage in problem solving; students' cognitive styles or preferences in relationship to problem solving; various aspects of reasoning ability and its relationship to cognitive development; the effects of various aspects of instruction on students' problem-solving abilities; and the effects of certain types of curricula on problem-solving skills.

7.32 Rodger W. Bybee and Joseph D. McInerney, eds. **Redesigning the Science Curriculum: A Report on the Implications of Standards and Benchmarks for Science Education.** Colorado Springs, Colo.: Biological Sciences Curriculum Study, 1995. 152 pp.

Price: $10.00

Redesigning the Science Curriculum is a compilation of background papers and recommendations directed to those responsible for curriculum reform. Largely a response to the first complete draft of the *National Science Education Standards* (see 7.27), the book grew

out of a 1993 conference on "Rethinking the Science Curriculum." Recognizing the need for new science curricula based on standards, it presents the ideas of 20 authorities on science education in brief papers. The papers address questions such as these: How will curriculum development change in an era of standards-based science education? Can curriculum-development groups maintain their integrity and unique approaches to science education and still develop materials that will help science teachers achieve national and local standards? Should those responsible for curriculum development also provide leadership training and technical assistance for school districts developing their own science programs? To what degree can local school districts develop science programs that will achieve local, state, and national standards? Although most papers focus on issues raised by the publication of the *National Science Education Standards*, other curriculum reform projects, such as Project 2061 and Scope, Sequence, and Coordination, are also discussed.

7.33 Clair G. Wood. **Safety in School Science Labs.** Natick, Mass.: James A. Kaufman & Associates, 1995. 149 pp.

Price: $19.95 (ISBN 0-9647512-0-8)

Safety in School Science Labs is a "survival guide" on how to teach science at a time of complex federal legislation on hazardous materials ("right-to-know" laws) and in an era when teachers face increasing risk of becoming defendants in lawsuits brought by students. In plain language the book's 13 chapters discuss the limits of teachers' liabilities in the laboratory; present guidelines for conducting safe experiments; indicate what constitutes a hazardous material; tell what teachers need to know to comply with federal laws about labeling, storing, and using hazardous materials; and explain how to avoid accidents. Some chapters focus on hazards unique to the chemistry, physics, or biology lab, and the art studio. Since science teachers are frequently called upon to serve as safety training officers for their school districts, a chapter on employee safety training is also included.

7.34 National Science Teachers Association (NSTA). **Science and Math Events: Connecting and Competing.** Washington, D.C.: NSTA, 1990. 192 pp.

Price: $4.00 (ISBN 0-87355-090-0)

Science and Math Events lists and analyzes opportunities for teenagers to participate in organized science and math activities both in and outside the classroom. The activities discussed include clubs, interest groups, and fairs at the school or local level; national competitions; and international olympiads or other contests. Part I of *Science and Math Events* presents the views of four high school teachers on what inspires students to join science fairs or to participate in competitions, and on the benefits students derive from such activities. Part II provides nuts-and-bolts information about starting programs or activities. Included are directions for organizing science interest groups and clubs; a sample science club constitution; tips on planning a successful science fair, invention fair, poster project, or research project; and detailed information about 28 science and 4 math competitions, many of which are open to middle school students. Part III contains the results of an NSTA poll of 164 U.S. Nobel and Medal of Science winners about their experiences with organized science and mathematics events and how such events influenced their careers.

7.35 Rodger W. Bybee, C. Edward Buchwald, Sally Crissman, and others. **Science and Technology Education for the Middle Years: Frameworks for Curriculum and Instruction.** Washington, D.C.: National Center for Improving Science Education, 1990. 152 pp. (Available from Learning Innovations; *see* app. A.)

Price: $18.00

Science and Technology Education for the Middle Years is 1 in a series of 5 reports on science and mathematics for young adults (ages 10 to 14) from the National Center for Improving Science Education. Synthesized from findings, recommendations, and perspectives in recent studies, this report is a set of policy recommendations for science curriculum and instruction in middle-level schools. The beginning chapters describe characteristics of the early adolescent learner, review the history of education at the middle level, and review middle-level science programs from the 1970s through the 1990s. Subsequent chapters present a conception of science and technology appropriate for the development of middle-level curriculum and instructional strategies, suggest educational goals and major organizing concepts for programs, and highlight appropriate instruction and learning environments for the early adolescent. Each chapter includes a set of specific recommendations. The report features an annotated bibliography on science and technology education.

7.36 Gerald Kulm and Shirley M. Malcom, eds. **Science Assessment in the Service of Reform.** Washington, D.C.: American Association for the Advancement of Science, 1991. 410 pp. (Available from Lawrence Erlbaum; *see* app. A.)

Price: $36.00 (ISBN 0-887168-426-5)

This volume presents papers by 36 experts—assessment and curriculum specialists, psychologists, researchers, and teachers—on the role of assessment in science education reform. Part I looks at why assessment has assumed such prominence in the debate about the purpose, shape, and control of American education. Part II considers the relationship between science assessment and curriculum reform. It also includes information on existing assessment systems, efforts by some states to develop and test performance assessments, and performance assessments being used in England and Wales. Part III reviews some of the alternative modes of assessment being explored by researchers and practitioners. The central message of this book is that, whatever system of assessment is used, it should meet the following guidelines: (1) It should be free of bias. (2) It should reflect what is being taught and give information to improve classroom instruction, to diagnose problems, and to identify student misconceptions. (3) It should provide a measurement of the effectiveness of a teacher or curriculum. (4) It should reflect the values and content of science teaching. An appendix to the volume provides concrete examples of current assessment practices and innovations in school and university science classrooms.

7.37 National Science Resources Center. **Science for All Children: A Guide to Improving Elementary Science Education in Your School District.** Washington, D.C.: National Academy Press, 1997. 239 pp.

Price: $19.95 (ISBN 0-309-05297-1)

Science for All Children presents the strategic planning model of the National Science Resources Center for bringing about districtwide elementary science reform. The model, which is also appropriate for middle school science reform, is based on research and practice. It consists of 5 elements: a research-based, inquiry-centered curriculum; professional development; materials support; appropriate assessment strategies; and community and administrative support. Part 1 of the book's 3 parts explains the rationale for inquiry-centered science and provides some basic tools for planning such a program. Part 2 explains how to implement an inquiry-centered science program by focusing on the 5 elements of the NSRC model. Part 3 presents 8 case studies that show how the model is being implemented in school districts nationwide. Two appendixes provide additional resources. The first describes a number of professional associations and government agencies involved in science education reform. The second describes some exemplary elementary science curriculum materials.

7.38 National Science Teachers Association (NSTA). **Science for All Cultures: A Collection of Articles from NSTA's Journals.** Arlington, Va.: NSTA, 1993. 72 pp.

Price: $16.50 (ISBN 0-87355-122-2)

The articles in this collection, written by individuals of culturally diverse backgrounds, discuss the issue of multicultural science education, its scope, its implications for teacher education and for individual and national well-being, and suggestions for using such an approach as an instructional process. The articles had been published between 1988 and 1993 in NSTA journals—*The Science Teacher, Science & Children, Science Scope,* and *The Journal of College Science Teaching.* Topics addressed in the articles include the historical contribution of non-European cultures to the advancement of science, the participation rate of female and minority students in science, the relevance of science to everyday life, and the need for culturally relevant assessments. Most of the articles conclude with a list of references.

7.39 Leroy W. Dubeck, Suzanne E. Moshier, and Judith E. Boss. **Science in Cinema: Teaching Science Fact through Science Fiction Films.** New York, N.Y.: Teachers College Press, 1988. 205 pp.

Price: $17.95 (ISBN 0-8077-2915-9)

Science in Cinema, written by science and English professors, shows how teachers can use young people's attraction to science fiction films to foster appreciation for real science and its interactions in the world. The real or not-so-real science of 10 popular science fiction films—including *Forbidden Planet, The Day the Earth Stood Still,* and *The Andromeda Strain*—is analyzed in depth. By identifying scientific principles portrayed accurately and inaccurately in the films, students can enhance their understanding of these principles and develop an interest in relationships among science, technology, and society. The following is provided for each film: a plot summary; a discussion of relevant scientific principles (such as energy, momentum, gravity); a scientific commentary keyed to the film's sequence of events; classroom activities, such as exercises and discussion topics, to stimulate student thinking; a literary commentary on the sources for the film; and bibliographic information. The book also includes abbreviated information—credits, 1- or 2-paragraph plot summaries, and sequential scientific commentary—about 24 additional films, including *The Time Machine* and *Close Encounters of the Third Kind.*

7.40 Victor J. Mayer and Rosanne W. Fortner, eds. **Science Is a Study of Earth: A Resource Guide for Science Curriculum Restructure.** Columbus, Ohio: The Ohio State University, 1995. 252 pp.

Price: $20.00 ($5.00, with teacher request on school letterhead)

This resource guide for Earth Systems Education (ESE) was developed by staff and participants in the Program for Leadership in Earth Systems Education (PLESE) conducted at the Ohio State University and the University of Northern Colorado from 1990 to 1994. The guide consists of several independent sections that focus on the following topics: the philosophy and approach of ESE; the current national climate for science education reform and how ESE meshes with other efforts; several successful efforts by teachers to implement ESE curricula in their schools and districts; steps and ideas that teachers have found useful in their own efforts at curriculum restructure using the ESE model; the type of classroom climate that should typify an ESE classroom; ideas about sources of materials and information successfully used by teachers in developing ESE curricula; teacher-developed and -tested approaches to conducting short ESE workshops; syllabi that provide ideas for the scope and sequence of topics in model ESE curricula; and samples of ESE units developed by teachers for the elementary and middle school levels.

7.41 Mike Watts. **The Science of Problem-Solving: A Practical Guide for Science Teachers.** Portsmouth, N.H.: Heinemann, 1991. 170 pp. (Available from Greenwood Heinemann; *see* app. A.)

Price: $23.00 (ISBN 0-435-08314-7)

The Science of Problem-Solving was written for science teachers in middle and secondary schools who want to know more about problem solving as a strategy for classroom teaching and learning. The book first explores the language of problem solving and justifies the usefulness of problem solving in a student's curriculum. It then considers the skills, processes, and methods involved in problem solving, how such skills can be learned or taught, and whether they can be transferred from one context to another. Later chapters look at the factors that affect learning in individuals and groups as they solve problems; ways in which the often-noisy dynamics of problem-solving exercises can be managed in the classroom; and ways of incorporating problem-solving opportunities into a curriculum. Although much of the book functions as a background reader and is therefore somewhat theoretical, many practical tips for using, thinking about, or engaging in problem-solving activities are given, as well as problems that could contribute to a problem bank or list.

7.42 Robert A. Weisgerber. **Science Success for Students with Disabilities.** Menlo Park, Calif.: Addison-Wesley, Innovative Learning Publications, 1995. 168 pp. (Available from Addison-Wesley/Longman; *see* app. A.)

Price: $16.95 (ISBN 0-201-49089-7)

This comprehensive guide for K-12 teachers suggests classroom-tested techniques for helping intellectually able students with disabilities realize their potential in science. The outcome of 2 research and development studies, it is concerned with individuals with physical, visual, and hearing impairments, as well as with emotional disorders, speech impairments, and learning disabilities. The 5-chapter book provides disability-specific guidelines for making information more accessible in the classroom, laboratory, or field. It provides ideas for avoiding and minimizing the negative effect of attitudinal, personal, or environmental barriers. It also offers strategies, with case examples, for increasing the participation of students in teacher-centered instruction, student-centered activities, or group activities. Specific topics addressed include structuring lessons and activities, gaining students' attention, giving directions, making assignments, evaluating student accomplishments, obtaining and using equipment or materials, and using computers. Also included is a list of sourcebooks, periodicals, computer database sources, software, and organizations concerned with disabilities. Guidelines are given for turning the information in the volume into an in-service workshop.

7.43 Helen H. Voris, Maija Sedzielarz, and Carolyn P. Blackmon. **Teach the Mind, Touch the Spirit: A Guide to Focused Field Trips.** Chicago, Ill.: Field Museum of Natural History, Department of Education, 1986. 88 pp.

Price: $10.00 (ISBN 0-914868-09-8)

Based on the experiences of more than 400 teachers at the Field Museum of Natural History, this guide helps K-12 educators become familiar with the unique characteristics of museums as teaching-learning environments. It also helps them develop skill in object-based teaching strategies. The first section of the book describes the philosophy, strategies, and techniques of museum teaching. Tips are given on analyzing a museum exhibit, learning from objects, and using what one knows to ask questions that engage and motivate students. The second section describes an overall structure for field trips, and includes ideas for activities, such as collages, theme boxes, or observation exercises, to be done before, during, and after the trip. The third section provides a general orientation to the Field Museum of Natural History in Chicago, including information about its resources for teachers and some ideas for field trip experiences. Many of these ideas focus on science themes, such as prehistoric animals, the structure and history of the earth, and rocks and minerals, and can be easily adapted for use in other natural history museums, zoos, aquariums, and even art and history museums. The fourth section of the publication offers a checklist for planning a field trip and a short bibliography for more information about museum and object-based learning.

7.44 Helen Ross Russell. **Ten-Minute Field Trips: A Teacher's Guide to Using the School Grounds for Environmental Studies.** 2nd ed. Washington, D.C.: National Science Teachers Association, 1990. 175 pp.

Price: $16.95 (ISBN 0-87355-098-6)

Ten-Minute Field Trips is based on the concept that a school site and its surrounding neighborhood can serve as an environmental studies laboratory where elementary and middle school teachers and students can actively investigate natural and built environs. The ideas for school-ground field trips listed in the book are many and varied; such trips provide a resource for relating classroom learning to everyday life and for understanding relationships that tie the world together. The guide covers such subjects as animals (birds, insects, earthworms, and others); weather and weather prediction; seasonal changes (leaf coloration, sun and shadows); building materials, rocks, and soil formation; water and its effects; and recycling and natural decomposition. Each subject is introduced with a page or 2 of background information, followed by related classroom activities, a section on teacher preparation, and a list of suggested field trips. Specific directions for conducting field trips are not provided.

7.45 Carnegie Council on Adolescent Development. **Turning Points: Preparing American Youth for the 21st Century.** New York, N.Y.: Carnegie Corporation of New York, Carnegie Council on Adolescent Development, 1989. 106 pp.

Price: $9.95 (ISBN 0-9623154-1-9)

This report on preparing American youth for the twenty-first century has 2 parts. The first part examines the condition of America's young adolescents and how well middle-grade schools presently serve them. The second part presents a series of recommendations for a fundamental transformation in middle-grade schools and in relations among parents, schools, and communities. Among the recommendations for transforming middle schools are these: creating a community for learning, teaching a core of common knowledge, ensuring success for all students, empowering teachers and administrators, preparing teachers for the middle grades, improving academic performance through better health and fitness, re-engaging families in the education of young adolescents, and connecting schools with communities. The specific steps or structures needed to achieve these changes are outlined, and case studies from innovative middle schools provided. Several of these case studies address science and mathematics learning.

7.46 David Macaulay. **The Way Things Work.** Boston, Mass.: Houghton Mifflin, 1988. 384 pp.

Price: $29.95 (ISBN 0-395-42857-2)

This illustrated guide to how machines and other technologies work is divided in 4 sections—the mechanics of movement, harnessing the elements, working with waves, and electricity and automation. Large, hand-drawn illustrations and brief explanations provide an overview of all the key inventions that shape our lives today. The book brings potentially difficult concepts into the context of everyday life. *The Way Things Work* demonstrates how machines, from the simplest lever to the most sophisticated computer, do what they do. It also shows how the concept behind 1 invention is linked to the concept behind another. The scientific principles that govern the action of different machines are also explained (for example, how gears make work easier, why jumbo jets are able to fly, what the computer actually does); readers can see why a plow and a zipper are actually similar devices. Some of the hundreds of machines and devices in *The Way Things Work* include holograms, hang gliders, airliners, telephones, parking meters, robots, televisions, can openers, and compact discs. The book also catalogs the origins or invention of nearly 100 machines, and provides a dictionary of technical terms.

SCIENCE BOOK LISTS AND RESOURCE GUIDES

8.1 **ASTC/CIMUSET Directory and Statistics 1996.** Washington, D.C.: Association of Science-Technology Centers, 1996. 180 pp.

Price: $40.00 (ISBN 0-944040-49-7)

This directory lists the addresses, telephone and fax numbers, e-mail addresses, and names of key staff members at more than 400 institutions. Included are science-technology centers, nature centers, aquariums, planetariums, space theaters, natural history museums, children's museums, and other multidisciplinary museums. The organizations listed in the directory belong to ASTC (the Association of Science-Technology Centers) or to CIMUSET (the International Committee of Science and Technology Museums, a branch of the International Council of Museums). The statistics in the volume provide information about more than 100 of these institutions. The directory is updated annually.

8.2 H. Robert Malinowsky. **Best Science and Technology Reference Books for Young People.** Phoenix, Ariz.: Oryx Press, 1991. 227 pp.

Price: $24.95 (ISBN 0-89774-580-9)

This book provides brief summary information—including bibliographic data, a 1-paragraph description of contents, and sources of book reviews—for 669 science and technology reference books for readers in grades 3-12. A grade-level index identifies 231 of these titles as being appropriate for students in grades 6-8. The titles are arranged by broad subjects in 12 chapters: General Science, Astronomy, Mathematics/Computer Science, Physics, Chemistry, Earth Sciences, General Biology, Botany, Zoology, Technology/Engineering, Energy/Environment/Ecology, and Medical Sciences. Within chapters, the entries are organized by type of publication—for example, atlases, bibliographies, dictionaries, encyclopedias, field books, guides, and handbooks. *Best Science and Technology*

Reference Books for Young People can be used by students who are seeking science resources, as well as by teachers and librarians who may need collections development and assessment guides. In addition to the grade-level index, title, author, and subject indexes are provided.

8.3 Sandra Finley, Marilyn Fowler, Mary Jo Powell, and Barbara Salyer. **Directory of Science-Rich Resources in the Southwest.** Austin, Tex.: Southwest Educational Development Laboratory, 1996. 77 pp.

Price: $7.50

This directory of organizations that offer opportunities to enhance science teaching and learning is a product of the project SCIMAST—the Eisenhower Southwest Consortium for the Improvement of Mathematics and Science Teaching. Most of the resources listed in the directory are located in Arkansas, Louisiana, New

Evaluating science materials

ORDERING INFORMATION FOR PUBLICATIONS IN
CHAPTER 8

The prices given for books and other publications in chapter 8 do not include the costs of shipping and handling. Before placing an order, readers are advised to contact the publishers of these references for current ordering information, including shipping charges. In some cases, discounts or special rates may be available to schools and educators.

Publishers' names are cited in the bibliographic data of the annotations. Their addresses and telephone and fax numbers, as well as e-mail addresses, when available, are listed in appendix A, "Publishers and Suppliers."

Mexico, Oklahoma, and Texas. National resources that might be of interest to science educators in this 5-state region are also included. The organizations are arranged by state, with entries organized by category, including aquariums, botanical gardens, and zoos; educational organizations; museums and science centers; nature and environmental centers; professional organizations; state agencies; state-based federal programs; and university affiliates. A separate section is devoted to the national organizations.

8.4 Maeve A. Boland and Leanne Wiberg Milton, eds. **Earth-Science Education Resource Directory.** Alexandria, Va.: American Geological Institute, 1994. 150 pp.

Price: $19.95 (ISBN 0-922152-21-7)

This loose-leaf notebook provides a convenient list of diverse educational resources and materials on the subject of earth science. It lists 179

organizations and more than 550 individual products. These resources, which can be used for school groups and other audiences, include traditional items such as books, classroom materials, posters, activity kits, and computer and audiovisual aids, as well as workshops, training courses, networks, and special-interest organizations. Each organization's entry provides a short summary of scope and purpose, together with contact information, including addresses and telephone and fax numbers. The description of the organization is followed by information on its individual products. Each item is described briefly; supplementary information lists the general subject matter of the material, grade level, cost, and ordering information. The volume is indexed by organization, general subject matter combined with grade level, and medium of the product.

8.5 Will Snyder and the 1994 National 4-H Energy Education Review Team. **Educating Young People about Energy for Environmental Stewardship: A Guide to Resources for Curriculum Development with an Emphasis on Youth-Led, Community-Based Learning.** Chevy Chase, Md.: National 4-H Council, Environmental Stewardship Program, 1994. 47 pp.

Price: $5.00

Educating Young People about Energy for Environmental Stewardship is a resource guide for educators who wish to develop energy and environmental curricula and programs. The booklet includes descriptions of important criteria for choosing or evaluating such curricula. It also provides general and age-specific suggestions for developing programs and program formats; an annotated list of materials and resource organizations that focus on environmental and energy issues; information on accessing the 4-H electronic Energy Education Resources Database; and an overview chart of resources or organizations for teaching, learning, and program planning.

8.6 **Educators Guide to Free Science Materials.** 38th ed. Randolph, Wis.: Educators Progress Service, 1997. 255 pp.

Price: $29.95 (ISBN 0-87708-301-0)

The *Educators Guide to Free Science Materials* is an annual annotated listing of selected free, mixed-media science materials. It is designed to provide an up-to-date means of identifying currently available materials. This 38th edition classifies and provides descriptions of content, as well as complete source and availability information, for a total of more than 1,300 films, film strips, sets of slides, videotapes, and printed items. The book is divided in sections by media format and is organized by subject within each section. Entries are indexed by title and subject. The guide's source and availability index provides the names and addresses of organizations from which materials may be obtained.

8.7 Patti K. Sinclair. **E for Environment: An Annotated Bibliography of Children's Books with Environmental Themes.** New Providence, N.J.: R. R. Bowker, 1992. 292 pp.

Price: $42.00 (ISBN 0-8352-3028-7)

E for Environment in an annotated guide to 517 children's books with environmental themes. Selections cover a wide range of subjects and are organized in 5 major areas: fostering positive attitudes about the environment; ecology; environmental issues; people and nature; and learning activities. Titles include fiction and nonfiction books for children from preschool age to 14; a few titles for adults who work with children are included. An appendix lists environmental classics and titles reflecting environmental issues and "ecophilosophy." Entries are indexed by author, title, and subject.

8.8 National Energy Information Center. **Energy Education Resources: Kindergarten through 12th Grade.** Washington, D.C.: U.S. Department of Energy, National Energy Information Center, 1997. 130 pp.

Price: Free

Energy Education Resources, published annually by the U.S. Department of Energy, lists organizations that provide free or low-cost energy-related educational materials to students and educators. The organizations represented range from non-profit educational organizations to utilities, trade associations, publishers, and federal agencies. Each entry includes a short description of the organization, its address, and notes on relevant energy materials. Entries are broadly indexed by subject.

8.9 Richard J. Wilke, ed. **Environmental Education Teacher Resource Handbook: A Practical Guide for K-12 Environmental Education.** Millwood, N.Y.: Kraus International Publications, 1993. 459 pp. (Available from Corwin Press; *see* app. A.)

Price: $29.95 (ISBN 0-8039-6370-X)

This resource guide provides information on the historical background of environmental education curriculum and presents current, comprehensive information on useful publications, standards, and special materials for implementing a K-12 environmental education program. Topics covered in the first half of the book include creating or revising an environmental education program or curriculum, funding curriculum projects, developing assessment programs, and conducting special projects. Later chapters include an annotated bibliography of children's trade books (organized by subject); addresses and information on publishers and producers of curriculum materials; and an index of recently published reviews of environmental education software, videos, and curriculum guides.

8.10 Wendy Saul. **Find It! Science.** McHenry, Ill.: Follett Software, 1995.

Price: $189.00 ($75.00 for each additional CD-ROM)

This multimedia CD-ROM is designed to guide teachers, media specialists, and children in selecting appropriate literature to support science education in grades K-8. Featuring a user-friendly, playful interface for elementary and middle school learners, the application contains textual annotations and images of book covers for approximately 2,500 current books. The books were chosen from award-winning lists and recommendations made by librarians and science teachers nationwide. Reviews from journals are included for each book. Minimum hardware and software requirements for using this guide are a 68020 Macintosh with at least 4 MB of RAM, a hard drive with at least 4 to 5 MB of free space, a CD-ROM drive, System 6.0.7, and QuickTimes 1.5.

8.11 Eisenhower National Clearinghouse for Mathematics and Science Education. **The Guidebook of Federal Resources for K-12 Mathematics and Science.** Columbus, Ohio: Eisenhower National Clearinghouse, 1996. 424 pp. (Available from Superintendent of Documents, U.S. Government Printing Office; *see* app. A.)

Price: $25.00

The Guidebook of Federal Resources for K-12 Mathematics and Science is a directory of federal offices, programs, and facilities concerned with education in mathematics and science in grades K-12. The volume contains background information on 16 federal departments and agencies, descriptive information about federal offices and programs for mathematics and science education at the national and regional levels, and state-by-state contacts for many of these resources. Although the book does not list all federally funded education programs, it provides contacts for additional information.

8.12 Barbara Walthall, ed. **IDEAAAS: Sourcebook for Science, Mathematics and Technology Education**. Washington, D.C.: American Association for the Advancement of Science; Armonk, N.Y.: The Learning Team, 1995. 252 pp. (Available from The Learning Team.)

Price: $24.95 (ISBN 0-87168-545-0)

IDEAAAS is a reference work designed to foster communication, connections, and ideas among individuals involved in science, mathematics, and technology education. Included are the following: 3 detailed guides that can help locate sources of approximately 10,000 activities, materials, and programs within 80 different categories and 7 disciplines; a state-by-state listing of information about resources; a section that details organizations with a national constituency; and a publications and media section. The book lists scientific professional societies, state science societies, state science academies, state and federal agencies, community-based organizations, zoos, planetariums, nature centers, and many other informal or formal places of science. Two indexes are provided: an organization index and a name index of project directors, education directors, curators, or those responsible for science, mathematics, or technology education.

8.13 Donna F. Berlin. **Integrating Science and Mathematics in Teaching and Learning: A Bibliography**. Columbus, Ohio: ERIC Clearinghouse for Science, Mathematics, and Environmental Education, 1991. 54 pp.

Price: $7.50

Current literature related to reform in science and mathematics education endorses the integration of science and mathematics teaching and learning as a means of improving achievement and attitudes within both disciplines. This bibliography identifies and categorizes literature related to such integration. It is intended for classroom teachers, teacher educators, curriculum specialists, and researchers. The bibliography includes more than 550 citations, which are organized in 5 sections: (1) Curriculum, (2) Instruction, (3) Research, (4) Curriculum—Instruction, and (5) Curriculum—Evaluation. The fourth and fifth sections classify curriculum programs that include instructional activities and evaluation of curriculum programs.

8.14 Carol M. Butzow and John W. Butzow. **Intermediate Science through Children's Literature: Over Land and Sea**. Englewood, Colo.: Teacher Ideas Press, 1994. 218 pp.

Price: $23.00 (ISBN 0-87287-946-1)

Intermediate Science through Children's Literature contains ideas and directions for earth and environmental science activities that can be linked to 14 popular children's novels, such as *Julie of the Wolves,* by Jean Craighead George; *The Cay,* by Theodore Taylor; and *Island of the Blue Dolphins,* by Scott O'Dell. The hands-on activities, which can be done in any order or can stand alone, include field trips, simple craft projects, library research, and collateral reading and writing. The first half of the guide combines novels with activities about land: students learn about the American prairie, tornadoes, weather, the Arctic, woods, the Rocky Mountains, and fossils. The second half of the guide connects books and activities that draw upon the environment of the sea: students learn about coral reefs, tropical lagoons, coastal islands, the ocean, wetlands, and whales.

8.15 Elizabeth B. Miller. **The Internet Resource Directory for K-12 Teachers and Librarians: 96/97 Edition**. Englewood, Colo.: Libraries Unlimited, 1997. 235 pp.

Price: $25.00 (ISBN 1-56308-506-2)

This annual directory identifies more than 900 Internet resources for school library media specialists, educators, and students. Resources are presented in chapters according to broad curricular areas. The chapter on science lists 176 resources in the following categories: general science, earth science, biology, human anatomy, animals, botany, chemistry, crystals, environment and ecology, physics, space and astronomy, space flight and space stations and exploration, and weather. Each entry includes the name of the resource, tells how it is accessed, and provides address, path, log-in, or other instructions. The name of a contact person associated with the resource is sometimes given. A descriptive annotation provides an overview of the resource and, in some cases, a brief list of contents. All sites included in the directory were screened for their suitability for K-12 education.

8.16 Library of Congress. **LC Science Tracer Bullet Series**. Washington, D.C.: Library of Congress, Science and Technology Division, Science Reference Section, various years.

Price: Free upon receipt of self-addressed mailing label

The *LC Science Tracer Bullet* is an informal series of literature guides—each on a specific subject—designed to help locate published materials on that subject for readers who have only general knowledge. Examples of subjects in the series include pesticides and foods, environmental science projects, human diet and nutrition, and the brain. Among the major features of these brief guides are a weighted list of subject headings to be used in searching a card, book, or electronic catalog; lists of basic texts, bibliographies, state-of-the-art reports, conference proceedings, or government publications; a list of abstracting and indexing services useful in finding journal articles and technical reports; and the names and addresses of organizations to contact for additional information. New titles in the series are announced in the *Library of Congress Information Bulletin,* distributed to many libraries.

8.17 Isabel Schon. **"Libros de Ciencias en Español."** (A selection of recent science trade books in Spanish.) *Science & Children*, Vol. 34, No. 6 (March 1997): 37-39. (Available from National Science Teachers Association; *see* app. A.)

"Libros de Ciencias en Español" is a short bibliography, published in the National Science Teachers Association journal *Science & Children,* annotating recent science trade books in Spanish. (The annotations are in English.) The books are grouped by subject and within each section are arranged alphabetically by title. The following subject areas are represented: biology, ecology, general science, and technology. A list of U.S. dealers of books in Spanish for children and young adults is provided.

8.18 Science and Environmental Education Unit, California Department of Education. **Literature for Science and Mathematics: Kindergarten through Grade Twelve.** Sacramento, Calif.: California Department of Education, 1993. 144 pp.

Price: $11.00 (ISBN 0-8011-1066-1)

Literature for Science and Mathematics was compiled by a statewide committee in California composed of science and mathematics teachers, curriculum planners, and librarians employed in schools and public libraries. The volume contains more than 1,000 annotated entries on science- and mathematics-related literature for grades K-12. It is divided into 4 sections—on the physical, earth, and life sciences and mathematics. Within each section, entries are listed alphabetically by author. Each entry includes information to help educators choose and locate supplemental reading for their students. Appendix A offers concrete suggestions for incorporating literature into the science curriculum. Appendix B extends the listings in the main text to include selected resources, references, and field guides. Subject, author, and title indexes are provided.

8.19 **Marine Education: A Bibliography of Educational Materials Available from the Nation's Sea Grant College Programs.** Ocean Springs, Miss.: Mississippi-Alabama Sea Grant Consortium, 1994. 54 pp.

Price: $2.00

This bibliography of more than 500 titles is a tool for teachers and other individuals interested in helping students explore and understand the world's oceans and the Great Lakes. The materials annotated in *Marine*

Education are available from the Sea Grant college program or institution that developed them. Listings are arranged alphabetically by the universities sponsoring Sea Grant college programs. The annotations include title, ordering instructions, cost, and a brief summary of the resource.

8.20 Rue E. Gordon, ed. **1997 Conservation Directory.** 42nd ed. Vienna, Va.: National Wildlife Federation, 1997. 318 pp.

Price: $55.00 (ISBN 0-945051-60-3)

The *Conservation Directory* is a complete annual reference guide to organizations, agencies, and officials concerned with environmental conservation, education, and natural resource use and management. Entries include names, addresses, telephone numbers, descriptions of program areas, sizes of membership (where appropriate), principal publications, and senior staff by name and responsibility. A subject index lists organizations by special areas of interest.

8.21 **1997 Teacher Resource Guide: A Guide to Educational Materials about Agriculture.** Sacramento, Calif.: California Foundation for Agriculture in the Classroom, 1997. 59 pp.

Price: $5.00

The California Foundation for Agriculture in the Classroom is dedicated to helping teachers integrate agriculture into mathematics, history and social studies, language arts, and science. This *Teacher Resource Guide* is designed to help educators in grades K-12 locate high-quality resources, instructional materials, and activities on agriculture. It provides a list of resources typically available in the local community; a resource book list; recommended agricultural readings for history and social sciences; and a listing by subject of various videos, booklets, guides, posters, brochures, and other agriculture-related materials available free or at minimal charge.

8.22 National Science Teachers Association (NSTA). **NSTA Science Education Suppliers 1998.** Arlington, Va.: NSTA, 1998. 165 pp.

Price: $5.00

NSTA Science Education Suppliers is published annually and distributed in conjunction with the January or February issue of the following NSTA periodicals: *Science & Children, The Science Teacher, Science Scope,* and the *Journal of College Science Teaching.* The directory can also be purchased separately. This yearly publication includes lists of suppliers and school science laboratory equipment; lists of firms producing computer hardware and software; manufacturers and distributors of audiovisual materials and other media; and textbook, resource materials, and trade book publishers. Addresses and telephone and fax numbers are provided, as well as e-mail and World Wide Web addresses, where available.

8.23 **Only the Best: The Annual Guide to the Highest-Rated Educational Software and Multimedia 1997-1998.** Alexandria, Va.: Association for Supervision and Curriculum Development, 1997. 143 pp.

Price: $29.00 (ISSN 1053-4326); on CD-ROM: $150.00

Only the Best is an annual review guide of highly rated educational software and multimedia programs, compiled from the findings of top software and multimedia evaluators. Although software programs on a wide variety of topics are reviewed, science and social studies programs predominate. Each entry includes a program description, cost, grade level, hardware requirements, references for further information, and user tips. The guide, which is organized by subject area, also includes titles and tips for diverse learners, and a directory of software publishers. *Only the Best* is also available on CD-ROM and at the World Wide Web site of the Association for Supervision and Curriculum Development (*see* 11.27).

8.24 **"Outstanding Science Trade Books for Children for 1997."** *Science & Children,* Vol. 34, No. 6 (March 1997). 6 pp. (Available from Children's Book Council; *see* app. A.)

Price: $2.00 for a single copy of the 6-page reprint when accompanied by a stamped, self-addressed envelope

"Outstanding Science Trade Books for Children for 1997" (published in the National Science Teachers Association [NSTA] journal *Science & Children*) is an annotated bibliography of approximately 50 children's science trade books published in 1996. The books, intended primarily for students in grades K-8, were evaluated by a book review panel appointed by the NSTA and assembled in cooperation with the Children's Book Council. Selection for inclusion was based on a book's accuracy of information, readability, and format and illustrations. The books are grouped by subject, and within each section are arranged alphabetically by title. The following subject areas are represented in this edition: anthropology and paleontology, biography, earth science, environment and ecology, integrated science, life science, and physical science. The content standards from the *National Science Education Standards* (*see* 7.27) to which each book relates are indicated at the end of each annotation.

8.25 **Polystyrene Packaging and the Environment: Classroom Activities Sourcebook.** Washington, D.C.: The Polystyrene Packaging Council, no date. 7 pp.

Price: Free

This sourcebook is a compendium of information and educational resources designed to help teachers educate students about polystyrene packaging and the environment. It is a useful reference tool for teachers in grades K-12 who lack the time or resources to review the large numbers of materials available on this subject. The sourcebook contains a listing of curriculum materials available from several industry and independent sources. Materials are categorized by grade level; information is provided on their content; cost and ordering information are provided. The sourcebook also contains classroom activities designed to provide students with hands-on experiences with polystyrene packaging and other materials.

8.26 Michelle Wolfson. **Resources for Teaching Astronomy and Space Science.** John Hewitt, ed. Planetarium Activities for Student Success. Vol. 3. Berkeley, Calif.: Lawrence Hall of Science; Flushing Meadows, Corona Park, N.Y.: New York Hall of Science, 1993. 76 pp.

Price: $11.50

Resources for Teaching Astronomy and Space Science is a volume in a series designed for the experienced planetarium professional as well as for the teacher using a planetarium for the first time. This annotated resource guide covers the wide spectrum of resources available for teaching astronomy and space science in elementary and middle schools. It includes school curricula, books, periodicals, films, videos, slides, software, professional organizations, planetariums, and telescopes. The guide has listings such as camps for students, computer bulletin boards, opportunities for stargazing, and teacher institutes and workshops.

8.27 Maria Sosa and Shirley M. Malcom, eds. *Science Books & Films' Best Books for Children 1988-91.* Mahwah, N.J.: Lawrence Erlbaum Associates, 1994. 317 pp.

Price: $19.95 (ISBN 0-8058-1879-0)

Science Books & Films' Best Books for Children 1988-91 (see also 8.28) is a guide to recommended children's books and resource materials gathered from reviews published previously in *Science Books & Films,* the review journal of the American Association for the Advancement of Science (*see* 11.2). Subjects covered include the life and physical sciences, mathematics, engineering and technology, medicine, the social and behavioral sciences, and science/language arts connections. Some sections also contain a separate listing of hands-on science books. Entries are arranged alphabetically within broad subject areas, which are then further subdivided into smaller topics. The guide is indexed by author and title.

8.28 Tracy Gath and Maria Sosa, eds. *Science Books & Films' Best Books for Children 1992-1995.* Washington, D.C.: American Association for the Advancement of Science, Directorate for Education and Human Resources, 1996. 301 pp.

Price: $24.00 (ISBN 0-87168-586-8)

Science Books & Films' Best Books for Children 1992-95 (see also 8.27) is a guide to recommended children's books and resource materials gathered from reviews published previously in *Science Books & Films,* the review journal of the American Association for the Advancement of Science (*see* 11.2). Subjects covered include the life and physical sciences, mathematics, engineering and technology, medicine, and the social and behavioral sciences. Some sections also contain a separate listing of hands-on science books. Entries are arranged alphabetically within broad subject areas, which are then further subdivided into smaller topics. The guide is indexed by reviewer, author, and title.

8.29 Carolyn Phelan. **Science Books for Young People.** Chicago, Ill.: American Library Association, Booklist Publications, 1996. 80 pp.

Price: $9.95 (ISBN 0-8389-7837-1)

Science Books for Young People is an annotated bibliography of more than 500 science books for students in grades K-8 published from 1990 to 1995. Most of the entries are based on reviews that appeared in *Booklist,* the reviewing journal of the American Library Association. The books listed are generally limited to pure science. They are organized by subject—for example, astronomy, life science, plants, reptiles, and mammals. Reference books and books of science experiments appear within subject areas.

8.30 **Science Curriculum Resource Handbook: A Practical Guide for K-12 Science Curriculum.** Millwood, N.Y.: Kraus International Publications, 1992. 384 pp. (Available from Corwin Press; *see* app. A.)

Price: $29.95 (ISBN 0-803-96373-4)

This resource book provides basic information on the background of science curriculum design. It presents current information on trends in science teaching and curriculum development in grades K-12 and includes a step-by-step guide to creating or revising curriculum, information on grants for program development, exemplary science curriculum guides, comparisons of state requirements, and sources of ideas and materials for special projects. Rather than prescribing any particular form of curriculum, the handbook gives a sense of the available options and is a practical reference for curriculum developers, teachers, and administrators. It includes an annotated source list for materials, publishers, and project ideas, and provides an index to reviews of science textbooks, videos, software, and support materials.

8.31 Mary Budd Rowe. **Science Helper K-8: Version 3.0.** Armonk, N.Y.: The Learning Team, 1993.

Price: $195.00

Science Helper is a CD-ROM produced by the Knowledge Utilization Project in Science. It contains plans for 919 elementary science and mathematics lessons and 2,000 activities, compiled from 7 elementary science curriculum projects funded by the National Science Foundation during the 1960s, 1970s, and 1980s. Lessons are included from the following projects: Conceptually Oriented Program in Elementary Science (COPES), Elementary Science Study (ESS), Elementary School Science Project (Astronomy) (ESSP), Minnesota Mathematics and Science Teaching Project (MINNEMAST), Science: A Process Approach (SAPA), Science Curriculum Improvement Study (SCIS), and Unified Science and Mathematics for Elementary Schools (USMES). Lesson plans or activities can be located on the CD-ROM using the following criteria (alone or in combination): grade level, subject, process skills, keywords, content themes, and programs. Each lesson plan has a detailed abstract that can be viewed on the screen, printed out, and used to find other, related lessons. Background information on each lesson is available, including an introduction, a listing of responsible authors, and the book's original table of contents. All lessons can be printed and copied as often as needed. *Science Helper* can operate on either the PC or the Macintosh platform.

8.32 Smithsonian Resource Guide for Teachers 1997/98. Washington, D.C.: Smithsonian Office of Education, 1997. 81 pp.

Price: $5.00

The *Smithsonian Resource Guide for Teachers 1997/98* is an annotated listing of educational materials and resources available from the Smithsonian Institution. Science materials are included in the following subject areas: anthropology/human life, astronomy/space sciences, botany/plant life, general science/ecology, geology/minerals/paleontology, and zoology/animal life. Materials are grouped by subject, and within each section are arranged alphabetically by title. The booklet also lists catalogs, visitor guides, periodicals, and information on electronic access to the Smithsonian Institution.

8.33 Project WILD and the World Wildlife Fund. **Taking Action: An Educator's Guide to Involving Students in Environmental Action Projects.** Bethesda, Md.: Project WILD, 1995. 74 pp.

Price: $7.00

The purpose of *Taking Action* is to inspire ideas and provide models for conducting effective environmental action projects that engage students from start to finish. The book begins with nuts-and-bolts information on the whats, whys, and hows of action projects. It also presents a summary of the specifics of planning, implementing, and evaluating effective environmental action projects. It analyzes more than 30 actual projects from elementary, middle, and high schools around the country. The themes of such projects include adopting species in need, using agriculture on the schoolgrounds, protecting coastal and ocean habitats, conserving energy, and influencing lawmakers. Following each group of success stories is a list of ideas for similar projects and additional resources. Finally, the guide lists national student organizations, telecommunications networks, fundraising programs, and other resources to help teachers incorporate environmental action into their activities.

8.34 TESS: The Educational Software Selector CD-ROM. 1996 ed. Hampton Bays, N.Y.: Educational Products Information Exchange (EPIE) Institute, 1996.

Price: $82.50 (Updates $32.50)

This CD-ROM provides an annotated listing of essential information on 18,000 educational software programs for preschool through college from more than 1,300 software pub-

lishers. Nearly 4,000 science titles are included. Subjects covered by the science-oriented programs include anatomy and physiology, astronomy, biology, chemistry, earth science, oceanography, ecology and environment, general science, geology, horticulture, meteorology, natural history, physical science, physics, scientific measurement, technology education, and zoology. The detailed entries include a program description and software requirements. Search parameters include computer type, grade, price, program type, software title, review score (where available), subject, and supplier.

8.35 Phyllis J. Perry. **The World of Water: Linking Fiction to Nonfiction.** Literature Bridges to Science series. Englewood, Colo.: Teacher Ideas Press, 1995. 165 pp.

Price: $21.50 (ISBN 1-56308-321-3)

The World of Water is designed to help teachers plan a middle-grade integrated unit of study involving oceans, rivers, and lakes. The first 4 parts of the book are on (1) Ships, Diving, and Treasure; (2) Animals and Plants Living in and around the Sea; (3) Understanding, Exploring, and Surviving; and (4) Environmental Concerns. Each of these parts contains detailed summaries of fiction books, with discussion starters for each book, summaries of related nonfiction books of various lengths and levels of difficulty, and ideas for multidisciplinary activities based on both types of books. Between the fiction and nonfiction books listed in each section is the summary of a book or video that combines factual information with fiction to enable readers to make an easy transition from one type of material to another. The fifth part of the book contains information on additional resources and linkages. All books suggested in this volume were published after 1980 and are easily available. The titles were selected from a large number of books recommended by children's librarians with special expertise in books for young adults.

8.36 Phyllis J. Perry. **The World's Regions and Weather: Linking Fiction to Nonfiction.** Literature Bridges to Science series. Englewood, Colo.: Teacher Ideas Press, 1996. 173 pp.

Price: $22.00 (ISBN 1-56308-338-8)

The World's Regions and Weather is designed to help teachers plan a middle-grade integrated unit of study involving regions of the world and weather. The first 4 parts of the book are on (1) Snow, Hail, and Ice; (2) Drought, Dust, and Dunes; (3) Clouds, Rain, and Floods; and (4) Winds: Hurricanes, Tornadoes, and Typhoons. Each of these parts provides detailed summaries of fic-

tion books, with discussion starters for each book, summaries of related nonfiction books of various lengths and levels of difficulty, and ideas for multidisciplinary activities based on both types of books. Between the fiction and nonfiction books listed in each section is the summary of a book or video that combines factual information with fiction to enable readers to make an easy transition from one type of material to another. The fifth part of the book provides information on additional resources and linkages. All books suggested in this volume were published after 1980 and are readily available. The titles were selected from a large number of books recommended by children's librarians with special expertise in books for young adults.

8.37 World Resources Institute. **World Resources 1996-1997.** New York, N.Y.: Oxford University Press, 1996. 384 pp.

Price: $24.95 (ISBN 0-19-521161-8)

World Resources 1996-1997 reports on conditions and trends in the world's natural resources and in the

global environment. It provides data, presented in tables, maps, and graphs, for almost every country in the world. Part I, on the urban environment, includes a comparison of urban conditions and trends throughout the developing and developed world; information on the impacts of urban environmental conditions on health and productivity; an analysis of how urban transportation systems are contributing to, or reducing, environmental problems; and strategies for improving the urban environment based on case studies from cities and communities across the globe. Part II is a collection of global statistics and trend reports that cover basic economic indicators, population and human development, food and agriculture, forests, biodiversity, energy and materials, water and fisheries, and atmosphere and climate. Extensive source references and technical notes are included.

Using magazines to develop ideas for student projects

CHAPTER 9

PERIODICALS

9.1 AIMS Magazine

Level: Teachers of grades 3-8+ *AIMS Magazine* is a teacher resource of ready-to-use science and mathematics activities for the primary, middle, and upper grades. Each issue has 3 sections—features, departments, and activities. The features section is dedicated to the "big ideas" in mathematics and science education. The departments section includes "Mind Bogglers" (for example, discrepant events), "Puzzle Corner" (to develop problem-solving strategies), "Tinkering, Toys and Teaching" (directions for building devices that can be used as instructional aids), "Maximizing Math" (open-ended, problem-solving situations), and "Side Talk" (dialogue about the processes and thinking involved in problem solving). Each activity includes background information, step-by-step procedures, and blackline student pages. Many of the ideas in this periodical can be adapted to other curriculum programs besides AIMS (Activities Integrating Mathematics and Science), for which the activities were developed.

Issues/price: 10 per year; $30 per year. *Available from:* AIMS Education Foundation.

9.2 Air & Space/Smithsonian

Teacher resource *Air & Space/Smithsonian* is the world's largest aerospace magazine and the official publication of the National Air and Space Museum of the Smithsonian Institution (*see* 10.270). Written especially for audiences interested in the history and technology of aerospace, the articles in this publication convey the adventure of flight and space travel. Readers learn how the U.S. military destroys its surplus B-52 bombers, take a look at the pioneering science fiction series *Tom Corbett,* or consider the great gamma ray mystery (an intriguing puzzle from the cosmos). Middle school teachers will find *Air & Space/ Smithsonian* a source of instructive background information, enhanced by illustrations and photographs.

Issues/price: 6 per year; $20 per year. *Available from:* Air & Space/ Smithsonian.

9.3 The American Biology Teacher

Teacher resource Providing background reading for middle school teachers, *The American Biology Teacher* presents nonfiction articles that report on the results of research on teaching alternatives; discuss the social and ethical implications of biology; provide specific how-to suggestions for laboratory, field activities, or interdisciplinary programs; and present imaginative views of the future and suggestions for coping with changes. The articles, by science educators, are accompanied by statistical graphs and tables and are fully referenced. Each issue includes a software review (which gives a general description of the software's purpose and information on ease of operation) and several reviews of recent books on biology.

Issues/price: 8 per year; $48 per year for National Association of Biology Teachers members; $60 per year for nonmembers. *Available from:* National Association of Biology Teachers.

9.4 Appraisal: Science Books for Young People

Level: Teachers of grades PreK, K, 1-8+ *Appraisal* reviews science trade books written for young people from age 3 to 17. Each issue begins with a feature article, such as "Wanted: An Electronic Librarian to Find Science Trade Books," or "Bringing Constructivity to the Classroom." The feature is followed by approximately 100 book reviews written by children's librarians and subject specialists; reviewers' names and affiliations are provided in each issue. Complete bibliographic information and a recommended reading level are included for each title. A rating is also provided—excellent, very good,

good, fair, or unacceptable. This journal does not have an index.

Issues/price: 4 per year; $45 per year. *Available from:* Appraisal.

9.5 Art to Zoo: Teaching with the Power of Objects

Level: Teachers of grades 3-8 *Art to Zoo*—renamed *Smithsonian in Your Classroom*—brings exhibit-based lessons and activities from the Smithsonian Institution to science, social studies, and art teachers. Each issue focuses on a different topic—such as "Oceans and Weather," or "Visions of the Future: Technology and American Society"—and contains background information, lesson plans, classroom activities, activity sheets, and resource lists. An English/Spanish "Take-Home Page" can be duplicated for student use. Current and selected back issues of *Art to Zoo* are available in print and online [http://educate.si.edu/art-to-zoo/azindex.htm].

Issues/price: 4 per year; free. *Available from:* Smithsonian Office of Education.

9.6 Astronomy

Teacher resource *Astronomy* was developed to make the complex field of astronomy understandable and enjoyable for a broad audience. It covers all aspects of astronomy and reports on the latest astronomical news. Articles focus on topics such as the exploration of Mars, using gravitational lenses to probe the universe, and the birth of black holes. The "Sky Almanac" feature in each issue tells where and when to look so that one can see planets, spot constellations, or catch a shower of shooting stars. This colorfully illustrated magazine also reviews new products, such as telescopes, binoculars, and books, and software. It provides amateur astronomers with information on upcoming events and meetings.

Issues/price: 12 per year; $34.95 per year. *Available from:* Kalmbach.

9.7 Audubon

Teacher resource This bimonthly magazine from the National Audubon Society (*see* 11.71) focuses on the environment, wildlife, and protection of wildlife habitat. Illustrated with full-color photographs, *Audubon* includes features on topics such as wetlands preservation, the reintroduction of endangered species to their natural habitats, and the behavior of Arctic wolves in the wild. Each issue includes regular columns such as "Reports" (short explanations of recent scientific events and discoveries) and "Inside Audubon" (on people, places, and issues of interest to readers). Other articles in each issue present a wide range of news and feature material on natural history and the environment. Also included is a section of letters to the editor, "Other Voices, Other Views."

Issues/price: 6 per year; $20 per year. *Available from:* National Audubon Society.

9.8 Chem Matters

Teacher resource *Chem Matters* is a magazine written for high school students that is also a useful source for keeping middle school teachers up to date on recent chemical advances. Nonfiction articles covering such issues as nicotine patches, biodegradable bags, insect arsenals, and the chemistry of ink help relate chemistry to everyday life. Each issue contains puzzles, cartoons, and descriptions of real-life mysteries solved through chemistry. The *Chem Matters Classroom Guide* for teachers offers additional facts and background information for each article, as well as high-school-level chemistry demonstrations, laboratory experiments, and questions for students to answer.

Issues/price: 4 per year; $8 per year. *Chem Matters Classroom Guide:* 4 per year; $3 per year. ***Available from:*** American Chemical Society.

9.9 Connect

Level: Teachers of grades K-8 *Connect* is a bimonthly newsletter published throughout the school year. It offers practical articles, written by teachers, to support hands-on learning, problem solving, and multidisciplinary approaches to the teaching of science and mathematics. Each 20-page issue focuses on a key theme, such as investigating water, wetlands, energy, or variation and classification, and includes photographs and illustrations. Regular features include science and technology news (specifically, current news stories chosen because of the teaching opportunities they offer) and resource reviews (theme-related items selected for their high quality and immediate usefulness).

Issues/price: 5 per year; $20 per year. *Available from:* Teacher's Laboratory.

9.10 Discover: The World of Science

Level: Students, grades 7-8+, teachers *Discover* is a general-interest magazine devoted to increasing understanding in all areas of science, from archeology to ecology, technology to medicine, and astronomy to physics. This monthly magazine includes articles on the latest breakthroughs in major subjects of interest to a wide readership—for example, the origins of life, the evolution of the universe, the inner workings of the brain, and the mass extinction of the dinosaurs. The articles are written in a clear, engaging style, and are accessible to readers with varying levels of science background.

Educators who enroll in the *Discover Magazine School Science Program* receive a free monthly, 6-page teaching aid that includes innovative techniques for using *Discover* in the classroom. This guide provides article summaries, objectives, vocabulary words, quizzes, and hands-on activities, as well as a list of national educational resources.

Issues/price: Discover: 12 per year; $24.95 per year. *Discover Magazine School Science Program* (*Discover* magazine and educator's guide): 12 per year; $17.49. ***Available from:*** Discover.

9.11 Dolphin Log

Level: Students, grades 2-8 Each issue of *Dolphin Log* presents a variety of nonfiction articles on science, natural history, marine biology, ecology, and the environment as they relate to the global water system. The articles have colorful and instructive photographs. Features cover such subjects as sharks, making recycled paper, survivors of ancient seas, and the comeback of the California grey whale. Regular features include "Nature News," "Did You Know?"

(interesting facts), "Creature Feature" (a focused exploration of one animal), and the "Cousteau Adventure" cartoon series. The magazine has games, puzzles, and hands-on activities for students.

Issues/price: 6 per year; $15 per year. *Available from:* Cousteau Society.

9.12 Dragonfly

Level: Students, grades 3-6; teachers *Dragonfly* is a magazine for young investigators issued 5 times per school year by the National Science Teachers Association (*see* 11.89). Each issue focuses on a central theme—such as trees, communication, or ice and snow—and includes several articles written by student investigators describing experiments on that theme which they have conducted individually or with their class. Each issue also contains poetry, autobiographies, natural history essays, humor, artwork, and other creative expressions by children and scientists. Additionally, in some articles, "challenges" are issued by scientists; students can join with these scientists in carrying out investigations—for example, by gathering simple data as explained in the magazine. *Dragonfly* also allows students, teachers, and parents to exchange data, to learn about various scientific careers, and to have science questions answered by experts. Supplemental student activities for each issue are available on DragonflyNet [http://www.MUOhio.edu/Dragonfly].

Dragonfly Teacher's Companion, available with each issue, is a 16-page handbook that offers useful ideas, discussion, and concrete recommendations for guiding student investigation. Detailed guidelines cover process skills, writing, cooperative learning, and self-assessment (allowing students to move through several stages of learning and investigation). A pull-out *Dragonfly Home*

Companion suggests ways for parents to broaden family participation in children's science explorations.

Issues/prices: 5 per school year; $18.95 per year for teachers (with *Dragonfly Teacher's Companion,* and *Dragonfly Home Companion*); $12.95 per year for individuals (with *Dragonfly Home Companion*); $39.95 per year for libraries (including 3 teacher subscriptions); and $6.00 per year for each subscription for classrooms (20 or more individual subscriptions and 1 *Dragonfly Teacher's Companion*). *Available from:* National Science Teachers Association.

9.13 Earth: The Science of Our Planet

Level: Students, grades 6-8+; teachers
This magazine takes middle school teachers and students on journeys from Antarctica to Amazonia, from the giant crystal at the planet's center to the atmosphere's outer limits, and from earth's earliest moments to its future. *Earth* presents the latest scientific discoveries about the land, oceans, atmosphere, biosphere, and history of life. A "Reports" section discusses the science behind critical issues of the day, such as global environmental change. *Earth*'s in-depth articles, explanatory illustrations, and photographs provide teachers and students with an important source for research, for understanding the world, and for appreciating its wonders.

Issues/price: 6 per year; $19.95 per year. *Available from:* Kalmbach.

9.14 Electronic Learning

Teacher resource Educational technology, industry news, and conference and research reports are regularly featured subjects in *Electronic Learning*, a magazine on technology and school change. This periodical offers in-depth reviews of hardware and software. One major section provides articles on "Curriculum and Instruction." Another section, "Technology," focuses on evaluation and selection of software and on new and emerging technologies. An "Update" section provides a listing of new products available to educators, including software, hardware, books, CD-ROMs, and videodiscs.

Issues/price: 6 per year; $23.95 per year. *Available from:* Electronic Learning.

9.15 Exploring

Level: Students, grades 6-8+; teachers
Exploring is a magazine of science, art, and human perception from The Exploratorium (*see* 10.62), one of the world's major hands-on museums, in San Francisco. Through articles, illustrations, and activities, *Exploring* communicates ideas that museum exhibits cannot easily demonstrate. Each issue examines a single topic from a variety of viewpoints. The focus on 1 topic per issue allows investigation and discussion of interconnections between apparently unrelated phenomena, revealing the essential unity of nature. For example, in *Exploring Gardening,* readers learn about techniques for double-digging garden beds, composting, gardening for birds and butterflies—and find out what the American yard says about our culture. Examples of topics include gardening, visual illusions, oceans, and sound.

Issues/price: 4 per year; $18 per year for individuals; $24 per year for institutions. *Available from:* The Exploratorium.

9.16 The Helix

Level: Students, grades 5-8+; teachers *The Helix* is the official magazine of an Australian science club for students ages 10 and up—the Double Helix Science Club of the Commonwealth Science and Industrial Research Organization (CSIRO). The magazine contains information about competitions and experiments, as well as members' contributions and feature articles. In *The Helix*, students can learn about science careers, and teachers can gather ideas for classroom activities and discover new ways to approach current science topics. Although written for an Australian audience, *The Helix* contains much useful material for other student populations as well.

Issues/price: 6 per year; A$15 per year (within Australia) for CSIRO members; A$25 per year (outside Australia). *Available from:* CSIRO's Double Helix Science Club.

9.17 International Wildlife

Level: Students, grades 6-8+; teachers
International Wildlife features in-depth nonfiction articles exploring wildlife topics from around the world and global environmental issues. A representative sampling from an issue might include articles on the Fennec fox in the Algerian Sahara, disappearing forests in Canada, the earth's top 10 environmental problems, the Bahama Parrot, and the diversity of life in Borneo's Mount Kinabalu. Articles are accompanied by excellent photographs. This magazine is a useful tool for both teacher and student research on nature worldwide and is a natural supplement to the classroom library.

Issues/price: 6 per year; $16 per year. *Available from:* National Wildlife Federation.

9.18 Issues in Science and Technology

Teacher resource *Issues in Science and Technology* is a journal of the National Academy of Sciences (NAS), the National Academy of Engineering (NAE), the Institute of Medicine (IOM), and the Cecil and Ida Green Center for the Study of Science and Society at the University of Texas at Dallas. *Issues* is intended to inform public opinion and to raise the quality of private and public decision making by providing a forum for discussion and debate. Each issue includes feature articles on topics such as overcoming barriers to medical innovation and technology policy for a global economy. Regular columns include "Perspectives" (articles by scientists and academics) and book reviews. Middle school teachers will find this title a good resource on major new or controversial developments in the areas of science, technology, and health.

Issues/price: 4 per year; $43.50 per year. *Available from:* Issues in Science and Technology.

9.19 Journal of Chemical Education

Teacher resource The *Journal of Chemical Education* includes articles of interest to those who teach chemistry at all levels from high school through graduate courses. Published by the American Chemical Society's Division of Chemical Education, this "living textbook of chemistry" helps teachers stay current with research advances as well as with new ideas in teaching methodologies and course organization. Articles include reviews of developing areas of chemistry, methods for teaching difficult concepts, discus-

sions of learning theory, lecture demonstrations, computer programs, course outlines, and laboratory experiments.

Issues/price: 12 per year; $34 per year for individuals; $70 per year for libraries, institutions, and companies. *Available from:* Journal of Chemical Education.

9.20 Journal of Geoscience Education

Teacher resource The *Journal of Geoscience Education* (formerly, *Journal of Geological Education*) is published by the National Association of Geoscience Teachers (*see* 11.70). The journal fosters improvement in the teaching of earth sciences at all levels of formal and informal instruction. Its articles emphasize the cultural and environmental significance of this scientific field. Middle school science teachers will find it an important source of information on innovations and other aspects of teaching the earth sciences.

Issues/price: 5 per year; $33 per year. *Available from:* Journal of Geoscience Education.

9.21 Journal of Research in Science Teaching

Teacher resource The *Journal of Research in Science Teaching* is the official journal of the National Association for Research in Science Teaching (NARST) (*see* 11.68). Its scholarly articles discuss investigations employing various research approaches—such as experimental, qualitative, ethnographic, historical, survey, philosophical, and case study. Position papers, policy perspectives, and critical reviews of the literature are also presented. In the section "Comments and Criti-

cism," readers express their views relating to articles in previous issues or to matters of interest to science educators.

Issues/price: 10 per year; $450 per year; $77 per year for NARST members. *Available from:* NARST.

9.22 Kansas School Naturalist

Level: Teachers of grades 3-8+ The *Kansas School Naturalist* is a 16-page magazine distributed twice a year to teachers, school administrators, youth leaders, librarians, conservationists, and others interested in natural history and nature education. Each issue focuses on a single topic. Examples include snowflies (flies that survive in the snow), the surface mining of coal, and the collection and maintenance of ants. Clearly written text is supported by helpful illustrations and graphs. Suggestions for simple student research projects and classroom and field activities are provided. Also featured are tips on data collection techniques and methods of experimental design.

Issues/price: Typically 2 per year; free. *Available from:* Emporia State University.

9.23 Kids Discover

Level: Students, grades 1-8 *Kids Discover* helps students explore the wonder of the world around them. Each issue focuses on a key theme, such as oceans, rain forests, fire, weather, light, volcanoes, or space. Easy-to-read text is accompanied by excellent color photographs and illustrations. The magazine poses challenging questions to students, and includes puzzles, additional resources for students and teachers on the issue's theme, and instructions for related hands-on activities.

Issues/price: 10 per year; $19.95 per year. *Available from:* Kids Discover.

9.24 Learning and Leading with Technology

Level: Teachers of grades K-8+ *Learning and Leading with Technology* focuses on curriculum development and practical ideas for using technology in the classroom. It emphasizes integrating technology where it can make a difference—for example, by easing the teacher's job; saving time; motivating students; helping students with varying learning styles, abilities, and backgrounds; and creating learning environments that are new or unique or that would be impossible without technology. Each issue contains articles by teachers, features, and software reviews that address language arts, mathematics, science, social studies, integrated curricula, and special needs. Other topics in an issue might include multimedia materials, telecommunications, computer science, networking, library and information technology, the single-computer classroom, staff development, and technology planning. Many articles include sample lesson plans, extensive resource lists, and reproducible work sheets for students and teachers.

Issues/price: 8 per year; $65 per year; $58 per year for members of International Society for Technology in Education. *Available from:* International Society for Technology in Education.

9.25 Middle School Journal

Teacher resource *Middle School Journal* provides a forum for ideas and opinions among middle-level educators. It is designed to further the

understanding of intermediate education and the implementation of effective practices. The journal includes information on current trends and research as well as innovative ideas for the classroom. Each issue contains more than 15 articles on topics as varied as advisory programs, curriculum and instruction, portfolios, integrated studies, teacher certification, and family and community involvement.

Issues/price: 5 per year; $35 per year; $50 per year for members of National Middle School Association. *Available from:* National Middle School Association.

9.26 Muse

Level: Students, grades 1-8+ This richly illustrated, 52-page magazine for students ages 6 to 14 is from the publishers of *Smithsonian* magazine (*see* 9.50) and *Cricket* (a literary magazine for elementary school students). *Muse* brings the Smithsonian's many areas of interest to life for young readers through themes such as geography, architecture, biology, music, paleontology, physics, and theater. A sampling of topics includes space travel, travel to foreign countries, mummies, genetics, lasers, rainforests, computers, and ancient world history. The magazine presents long and short articles, photo essays, narratives, biographies, excerpts from letters and diaries, cartoons, jokes, and experiments.

Issues/price: 6 per year; $24 per year. *Available from:* Muse.

9.27 NASA Technology Today

Level: Teachers of grades 6-8+ *NASA Techology Today* is a resource for teachers on technology, science, and mathematics. It is published by Associated Business Publications

International in cooperation with the National Aeronautics and Space Administration (NASA) (*see* 11.66) and the International Technology Education Association. Articles focus on topics such as space exploration, software applications, design challenges, and the role of technology in public safety. Examples of featured subjects include technologies that enable pilots to detect and react to severe weather conditions, the adaptation of space simulation software by garment makers for designing apparel production lines, and how scientists are using data collected by NASA's Small Explorer Project to better understand the phenomenon of the northern and southern lights. Each colorfully illustrated article provides suggested student activities. The magazine also has regular sections on careers in the aerospace and aeronautical fields, aerospace spinoffs, and "techbits."

Issues/price: 6 per year; $17.95 per year. *Available from:* Associated Business Publications International.

9.28 National Geographic World

Level: Students, grades 3-8+; teachers A goal of *National Geographic World* is to instill curiosity about the world in young readers and to encourage geographic awareness. Each issue offers 5 or 6 nonfiction articles on science, geography, the environment, natural history, sports, and achievements of young people and adults. Articles are accompanied by excellent color photographs and illustrations, and children's art and writing are often included. The magazine features puzzles, maps, games, posters, hands-on projects, and contests to spark interest and encourage interactivity. *National Geographic World* is a useful teaching aid for a variety of curriculum goals.

Issues/price: 12 per year; $17.95 per year. *Available from:* National Geographic Society.

9.29 National Wildlife

Teacher resource *National Wildlife* features in-depth nonfiction articles about nature, wildlife, and important environmental trends and issues. A representative sampling from an issue might include articles on dolphins, recycling, beavers, Alaskan grizzlies, and the effects of flooding in the Midwest. Articles are accompanied by excellent photographs. This magazine is useful for both teacher and student research on nature. It is a natural supplement to the classroom library.

Issues/price: 6 per year; $16 per year. *Available from:* National Wildlife Federation.

9.30 Natural History

Teacher resource *Natural History* is the monthly magazine of the American Museum of Natural History (*see* 10.287 and 10.288), an institution dedicated to understanding and preserving biological and cultural diversity. Reflecting this broad mission, the magazine's contents range widely—including features and news articles in various fields, such as paleontology, evolution, natural selection and species diversity, ecology and the environment, animal behavior, botany, astronomy, and anthropology. Some of the articles and regular columns focus on research, exhibits, and events at the museum. Also included are reviews of recent books, CD-ROMs, and Internet Web sites.

Issues/price: 12 per year; $30 per year. *Available from:* Natural History.

9.31 NOVA Teacher's Guide

Level: Students, grades 6-8+; teachers
NOVA Teacher's Guide, published in conjunction with the Public Broadcasting System (PBS) series of *NOVA* educational science programs, helps teachers use the *NOVA* series with their classes. The guide includes 1-page lesson plans for many of the programs. Each lesson identifies a teaching focus and gives a brief program overview. The lesson plans suggest activities and discussions to conduct before and after viewing the *NOVA* programs. A reproducible student activity page accompanies each lesson to help students develop useful critical-thinking skills. (Teachers may tape *NOVA* programs for classroom use within 7 days of broadcast, or they may purchase videocasettes for $19.95 each.)

Issues/price: 2 per year; free. *Available from:* WGBH Boston.

9.32 Oceanus

Teacher resource *Oceanus* magazine is a semiannual report on research at the Woods Hole Oceanographic Institute (WHOI). Written by WHOI scientists and their colleagues, the 32-page publication includes full-color photographs and illustrations. Each issue provides several articles on a single theme, such as biodiversity, Atlantic Ocean circulation, or research in the Arctic. Middle school teachers will find this magazine a useful source of information on the environment of the oceans and marine resources.

Issues/price: 2 per year; $15 per year. *Available from:* WHOI Publication Services.

9.33 Odyssey

Level: Students, grades 4-8 *Odyssey* presents nonfiction information related to astronomy. Each issue focuses on a main theme, such as technology from the space program, the moon, or superstition and science. Regular features include "Activity to Discover" (suggestions for do-it-yourself activities related to the issue's featured topic), "Backyard Observations" (tips on astronomical occurrences children can watch for the month), "Future Forum" (children's written thoughts on a proposed subject of interest), and "Ask Ely" (a question-and-answer column). *Odyssey* is enhanced by color photographs and illustrations.

Issues/price: 9 per year; $26.95 per year. *Available from:* Cobblestone.

9.34 Popular Science

Level: Students, grades 7-8+; teachers
Popular Science presents current news and features on research in science and technology and on new products resulting from such research. Examples of the topics covered in the magazine include WEBTV and how it works, testing the purity of drinking water, a potential design for a new space launcher, and the effectiveness of braking and traction control systems in automobiles. *Popular Science* also includes useful background information for middle school teachers and students on recent discoveries, such as signs of life on Mars as determined by fossils found in a meteorite in Antarctica.

Issues/price: 12 per year; $17.94 per year. *Available from:* Popular Science.

9.35 Quantum

Teacher resource *Quantum,* a magazine about mathematics and science, is published by the National Science Teachers Association (*see* 11.89) and the Quantum Bureau of the Russian Academy of Sciences in conjunction with the American Association of Physics Teachers (*see* 11.3) and the National Council of Teachers of Mathematics. It contains authorized

English-language translations from *Kvant*, a physics and mathematics magazine of the Quantum Bureau, as well as original material in English. *Kvant* is noted for its serious—yet whimsical—approach. This approach is retained in *Quantum*, which engages readers in some of the breadth, wonder, and excitement of mathematics and the quantitative sciences.

Issues/price: 6 per year; $15 per year for students; $20 per year for nonstudents; $34 per year for institutions. *Available from:* Springer-Verlag New York.

9.36 Ranger Rick

Level: Students, grades 1-6 *Ranger Rick* helps students learn about animals and their habitats, about how to help endangered species, and about what other young people are doing to protect the environment. Each issue contains readable nonfiction text with excellent color photographs and drawings. Regular features include fictional stories about wildlife, "Dear Ranger Rick" (letters to the editor from students), puzzles, hands-on activities, and jokes and riddles.

Issues/price: 12 per year; $15 per year. *Available from:* National Wildlife Federation.

9.37 Science Activities

Level: Teachers of grades 1-8 *Science Activities* is a source of experiments, explorations, and projects for the classroom science teacher. Written by science educators, each issue contains a cross-section of activities for all ages, from the young child to the advanced high school student. Each issue focuses on a key theme, such as exploring the earth inside and out, natural science activities

indoors and out, and ecology at the mall and in the classroom. A sampling of topics from *Science Activities* includes fun with fungi, science through drama, discovering wildlife, and electrical conductivity. Regular features include news notes, computer news, book reviews, and information about new products available to the classroom teacher.

Issues/price: 4 per year; $14.50 for single copy; $32.00 per year for individuals; $58.00 per year for institutions. *Available from:* Heldref.

9.38 Science & Children

Level: Teachers of grades PreK, K-8 *Science & Children* is a journal on teaching elementary and middle school science. It contains articles by educators for educators on how to teach specific science activities, as well as articles on more general aspects of science teaching, such as how to improve children's observational skills and reasoning abilities. Each article concludes with a list of topic-related resources. Regular features include "In the News" (science news items from around the country), "Teaching Teachers" (practical teaching methods for pre-service and in-service teachers), and reviews of newly available print and software resources.

Issues/price: 8 per year; $55 per year for members of National Science Teachers Association. *Available from:* National Science Teachers Association.

9.39 Science Books & Films

Level: Teachers of grades PreK, K-8+ *Science Books & Films* is produced by the American Association for the Advancement of Science (*see* 11.2) for science teachers, librarians,

media specialists, curriculum supervisors, and others responsible for recommending or purchasing science materials. It provides critical reviews of the scientific accuracy and presentation of print, audiovisual, and electronic resources intended for use in science, technology, and mathematics education. Reviews include descriptions of the merits and demerits of a book or film and any accompanying supplements; the content, technical quality, and instructional value; the audience(s) for which the material is most appropriate and why; and how the material could be used for collateral reading or viewing, reference, or classroom use. Each issue includes a feature article, reviews by young readers, audiovisual notes about educational or professional materials and programs, an index of books and films, and a selection of the reviewers' favorite titles from that issue.

Issues/price: 9 per year; $40 per year. *Available from:* Science Books & Films.

9.40 Science Education

Teacher resource *Science Education* is an international journal of research. A "General" section presents descriptive articles and research reports that deal with areas such as science curricula and instructional programs, science tests and assessment instruments, and the history of science education. Another section—"Science Teacher Education"—focuses on empirical research studies related to the instruction and preparation of teachers in science; the organization and operation of science teacher education programs; and the effectiveness and effects of particular practices, procedures, and programs of teacher education in science. The section entitled "Learning" reports on empirical research studies and offers interpretative articles related to psychological aspects of learning science. In another section, "Issues and Trends," analytical, interpretative, and persuasive essays discuss current education, social, or philosophical issues and trends relevant to science teaching. The "International Science Education" section reports on comparative studies of science teaching across several countries, describing or interpreting science education programs and practices in countries other than the United States and Canada. *Science Education* also has a "Comments and Criticism" section.

Issues/price: 6 per year; $386 per year. *Available from:* John Wiley.

9.41 Science Is Elementary

Level: Teachers of grades K-6 *Science Is Elementary* is a resource magazine for teachers, produced by the Museum Institute for Teaching Science (*see* 11.64) to help further the teaching of science, mathematics, and technology through participatory, inquiry-based methods. Each issue focuses on a single theme—for example, color and light, toys and tools, or populations—and includes a variety of hands-on activities. Background information, extensions and integrations, and assessment suggestions are provided. Sections on "Book Looking" and "Knowledge Unbound" identify useful books, as well as audiovisual and other resources. "Good Things Cheap" lists free or inexpensive classroom materials, and "In the Know," "Trade Secrets," and "Doing Science" provide additional activities and background information.

Issues/price: 4 per year; $24 per year. *Available from:* Museum Institute for Teaching Science.

9.42 Science News

Level: Teachers of grades 6-8+ Though written primarily for scientists and university professors, *Science News* can be used by teachers at all levels to keep abreast of the latest developments in science, engineering, medicine, and mathematics. Each issue contains a lengthy article on a current subject of interest, such as the human genome, biodiversity, or erosion, as well as brief news items on such topics as biomedicine, chemistry, space science, and the environment.

Issues/price: Published weekly; $49.50 per year. *Available from:* Science Service.

9.43 Science Scope

Level: Teachers of grades 6-8 Written specifically for middle-level science teachers, *Science Scope* addresses the needs of both new and veteran teachers. Each issue presents nonfiction articles by science educators on the life, physical, and earth sciences and on science and society. The magazine provides science teachers with ideas for creative, well-designed, and safe hands-on activities and demonstrations. Each issue features "scoops" (news items on recent scientific discoveries or investigations); information on helpful science resources; short, practical, how-to tips on lessons and teaching methods; and a colorful science poster related to a key article in the issue.

Issues/price: 8 per year; $55 per year for members of National Science Teachers Association. *Available from:* National Science Teachers Association.

9.44 The Science Teacher

Level: Teachers of grades 7-8+ *The Science Teacher* provides nonfiction articles by science educators on innovations in science teaching, current developments in science, and classroom projects and experiments. Each issue contains brief news items on recent scientific discoveries, an idea bank of hands-on activities, and reviews of books and software relevant to teaching science. Though targeted for high school teachers, librarians, principals, and supervisors, this magazine is a useful source of background information for middle school science teachers as well.

Issues/price: 9 per year; $56 per year for members of National Science Teachers Association. *Available from:* National Science Teachers Association.

9.45 The Science Times

Level: Teachers of grades 5-7 (elementary edition) and grades 8+ (junior secondary edition) *The Science Times* consists of short articles summarizing science stories from the news that involve life science, physical science, technology, and the environment. The magazine provides quizzes, word searches, crosswords, and discussion questions to use with students. *The Science Times* is available in 3 editions—elementary, junior secondary, and senior secondary. When placing an order, teachers choose the edition that best suits their needs. Topics and activities are similar in all the editions but are adjusted for age level and reading ability.

Issues/price: 10 per year; $50 per year for elementary edition; $50 per year for junior secondary edition. *Available from:* ZED Consulting.

9.46 Science World

Level: Students, grades 6-8+; teachers
Each issue of *Science World*, a magazine for students, explores 3 major areas of the science curriculum—life science/health, earth science/astronomy, and physical science/technology. Topics in these areas are approached by way of the scientific principles involved in occurrences ranging from high-interest news events and to everyday activities. The teacher's edition includes an 8-page guide with lesson plans and activities.

Issues/price: 18 per year; $7.50 per year (with a minimum of 10 subscriptions). *Available from:* Scholastic.

9.47 Scientific American

Teacher resource This monthly journal features articles on a variety of scientific topics and research trends. Examples include brain-scanning technologies, microchips that can modify their own hardwired circuits as they run, trends in animal research, biological weapons, global climate change on Mars, and microbes deep inside the earth. In addition to feature articles, *Scientific American* includes regular sections of "News and Analysis" and "Reviews and Commentaries." The former includes articles on new discoveries, science and the citizen, profiles of scientists and their work, and angles on cyperspace. The latter presents book reviews and commentaries, including, in each December issue, the *Scientific American* Young Readers Book Awards for the year's best children's science books. On occasion, an entire issue is devoted to a single topic.

Issues/price: 12 per year; $36 per year. *Available from:* Scientific American.

9.48 Scientific American Frontiers

Level: Teachers of grades 7-8+ *Scientific American Frontiers* is a teacher's guide published in connection with the Public Broadcasting System (PBS) series by the same name. The monthly PBS series tracks stories on technology, medicine, biology, physics, geology, and chemistry. The 15-page teacher's guide helps educators use the television series in the classroom. Lessons focus on science concepts presented in the program, and may include hands-on activities and games, as well as interactive options and resources on the Internet (such as e-mailing questions to scientists) and curriculum links. Videotapes of past shows are available for purchase. Educators may photocopy materials from the guides for classroom use.

Issues/price: 5 per year; free. *Available from:* Scientific American Frontiers School Program.

9.49 Sky and Telescope

Level: Teachers of grades 6-8+ *Sky and Telescope* features a variety of news and feature stories on astronomy and space science. Its 3 sections— "Features," "Departments," and "Columns"—include (1) articles by leading professionals on topics such as the exploration of Mars and a solar theory to explain global warming; (2) stories on activities of amateur astronomers, reviews of books and films, descriptions of new products such as binoculars and telescopes, and current sky events; and (3) other interesting tidbits and background information, such as reviews of Web sites and updates on the space program.

Issues/price: 12 per year; $36 per year. *Available from:* Sky and Telescope.

9.50 Smithsonian

Teacher resource *Smithsonian* magazine reflects the diversity of the sciences, humanities, and arts featured in the Smithsonian museums. It also draws upon research performed by museum staff. Each issue presents 8 extensive, richly illustrated feature articles. Examples of the science-related topics addressed in these features include toxins in food, the use of connoisseurship and science to recognize authentic Rembrandt paintings, and experiments in the language and behavior of orangutans. Among the regular departments in the magazine are the commentary by the Secretary of the Smithsonian Institution; highlights of Smithsonian exhibits, activities, and events; and book reviews.

Issues/price: 12 per year; $24 per year for Smithsonian Associates. *Available from:* Smithsonian Institution.

9.51 StarDate

Level: Students, grades 7-8+; teachers *StarDate* is an astronomy magazine published by the McDonald Observatory Public Information Office, University of Texas at Austin. Astonomy news, features, and history are presented with full-color illustrations and photographs. *StarDate* also includes star charts; a solar system "orrery" showing the positions of planets each month; and a step-by-step observing calendar highlighting eclipses, meteor showers, and other events.

Issues/price: 6 per year; $18 per year. *Available from:* StarDate.

9.52 SuperScience Blue

Level: Students, grades 4-6 *SuperScience Blue* provides science material that fits into all areas of the curriculum and helps students see the science connections around them. Containing in-depth nonfiction articles and related hands-on activities, each issue explores one key topic, such as hurricanes, endangered animals, or the physics and chemistry of construction. Accompanying each issue (at additional cost) is a teacher's guide, *SuperScience Blue Teacher,* outlining article topics, related curriculum areas, relevant process skills, learning objectives, general background, suggestions on introducing subject matter, questions for discussion, and lab tips. A resource section cites related books for teachers and children. Regular features of *SuperScience Blue* include an "Ask the Experts" question-and-answer column, a "We Dare You" problem-solving challenge, and a colorful, instructive, foldout poster relating to the issue topic.

Issues/price: 8 per year; $5.95 per year for magazine only (free teacher's guide comes with 10 or more magazine subscriptions); $27.80 per year for teacher's guide and 1 student subscription. *Available from:* Scholastic.

9.53 3-2-1 Contact

Level: Students, grades 3-8 *3-2-1 Contact* explores nature, science, and technology through short nonfiction articles accompanied by lively, colorful photographs and drawings. Examples of topics covered include animal-tracking satellites, the world of snowboarders, peculiar pets, and a journey through a rainforest. Each issue also provides games, puzzles, contests, and suggestions for hands-on activities. Regular features include "News Blasts" (brief items about enjoyable or exciting science stories), thought-provoking questions and answers, reviews of video and computer games, "Future File" (about scientific developments coming our way), and "Basic Training" (a set of hands-on computer instructions challenging students to solve a particular problem).

Issues/price: 10 per year; $19.90 per year. *Available from:* 3-2-1 Contact Magazine.

9.54 Weatherwise

Teacher resource *Weatherwise* is published by the Helen Dwight Reid Educational Foundation in association with the American Meteorological Society (*see* 11.14). This magazine includes well-illustrated articles on topics such as radar images of the internal structure and motion of clouds, the costliest thunderstorm in the history of the United States, and photographing tornadoes. Regular departments include "Front and Center" (on people, places, and projects); "Weather Queries" (answers to questions posed by readers); "Reviews and Resources" (reviews of books, videos, and other resources); and "Weatherwatch" (monthly maps and a discussion of each month's weather).

Issues/price: 6 per year; $9.75 per issue; $29.00 per year for individuals; $58.00 per year for institutions. *Available from:* Heldref.

9.55 WonderScience

Level: Students, grades 6-7; teachers *Wonder Science* is published as a joint effort of the American Chemical Society (*see* 11.7) and the American Institute of Physics (*see* 11.13). Each issue focuses on a particular topic, such as optical illusions, weather measurements, magnifiers, or physics on the playground. Several hands-on activities related to this topic are included. Each activity is accompanied by a list of the materials needed and step-by-step instructions for teachers and students to follow. A 4-page teacher's guide with reproducible student work sheets is available for each issue.

Issues/price: 8 per year (4 issues each in October and January); $9.50 per year (teacher's guide with orders of 2 or more subscriptions). *Available from:* American Chemical Society.

9.56 Your World/Our World

Level: Students, grades 7-8+; teachers *Your World/Our World* is a semi-annual magazine of biotechnology applications in health care, agriculture, the environment, and industry. Designed to capture student interest and to explain difficult information in an easily understandable way, articles begin with basic information and slowly progress to clearly defined, more complex issues. Laboratory activities are provided. Feature articles include photographs of actual processes and structures related to the subject matter. Each issue is accompanied by a teacher's guide.

Issues/price: 2 per year; $13 per year. *Available from:* Pennsylvania Biotechnology Association.

Arts and Industries Building of the
Smithsonian Institution in
Washington, D.C.—home of the
National Science Resources Center

PART 4

ANCILLARY
RESOURCES

OVERVIEW

CHAPTER 10
MUSEUMS AND OTHER PLACES
TO VISIT

CHAPTER 11
PROFESSIONAL ASSOCIATIONS AND
U.S. GOVERNMENT ORGANIZATIONS

P

art 4, "Ancillary Resources," provides information about resources that are available from hundreds of institutions—including museums, zoos, science centers, and professional and government organizations—to enrich the experiences of teaching and learning inquiry-centered middle school science. Such resources are "ancillary" in that they are available from sources other than the school or the classroom and they are used to support an existing science curriculum.

Although such resources vary widely, it is convenient for purposes of this guide to describe them in three general categories: (1) programs for students, such as exhibits and guided tours; (2) materials and publications, such as teacher's guides and kits of hands-on materials available for loan to science classes; and (3) education and support for teachers, such as workshops, in-service training, and databases of scientists and engineers committed to enhancing science education.

For the middle school teacher to incorporate such resources into the curriculum first requires the time to research them. Which organizations offer such support? What is available locally? Where would one call for further information about such programs and services? This part of the guide provides a quick reference source that answers these initial questions.

Teachers can become acquainted with the kinds of resources and programs available throughout the country as well as in their own local areas by leafing through this part of the guide. They may want to focus on specific annotations—which highlight resources available at the individual facilities and organizations. The annotations provide addresses, telephone numbers, and World Wide Web addresses, where available, for obtaining more detailed information about particular resources.

Part 4 contains two chapters: chapter 10, "Museums and Other Places to Visit," and chapter 11, "Professional Associations and U.S. Government Organizations." Together these chapters refer readers to a total of almost 700 institutions. Most of them are in the United States; several are in Canada.

All of the facilities and organizations included in these chapters actively support hands-on, inquiry-centered middle school science education through their programs, services, or materials. Following are brief descriptions of the two chapters.

"Museums and Other Places to Visit"

Chapter 10 focuses on ancillary resources at museums and other local "places to visit," including zoos, science centers, aquariums, planetariums, and botanical gardens. The facilities are diverse in terms of size, areas of emphasis, and types of materials and support offered. Large and small institutions, some known only locally and others world-renowned, are included to help meet the needs of middle school science classes.

The information in the chapter is based on responses to a national survey conducted by the National Science Resources Center (NSRC). Facilities were selected for inclusion on the basis of the following criteria:

- They offer resources that can help middle school teachers teach science more effectively.
- They provide interactive science experiences that can complement students' classroom experiences.
- They are sites that science classes can visit.

Chapter 10 opens with a section called the "Complete Regional Listing." This section identifies—by name, city, and state—about 550 facilities in the United States and several in Canada. The institutions whose names appear in boldface type—approximately 300—are featured in the second section of the chapter—the "Select Annotated Listing."

This annotated listing focuses on facilities that are making a particularly significant effort to help teachers teach science more effectively. The annotations provide a brief description of each facility, together with a listing of the specific types of support and resources they offer for middle school science.

As explained in more detail by the boxed information and map at the beginning of chapter 10 (see page 312), the regional and annotated lists are arranged by geographical regions. Within each region the states are listed alphabetically. The name of each institution appears alphabetically within its state listing.

"Professional Associations and U.S. Government Organizations"

Many groups of professional scientists and educators engage in active efforts to improve pre-college science education and to offer assistance relevant to middle school science. Chapter 11 highlights about 130 such professional associations, societies, and U.S. government organizations. They represent a variety of scientific fields, including physics, biology, chemistry, geology, astronomy, entomology, and others. The annotations in the chapter list programs, services, publications, and materials that are available to schools and teachers from these sources. This information is based on the results of a formal survey conducted by the NSRC.

Each annotation in chapter 11 first provides a brief description of the organization and then lists its resources in two general categories. In the first category—"Programs/services"—are items such as conferences, seminars, and in-service workshops for teachers; information hotlines; and databases of experts available for teacher-scientist partnerships, classroom presentations, and student mentoring. Also mentioned (and highlighted in boldface type) are formal programs such as the National Science Foundation's Teacher Enhancement Program and Comprehensive Partnerships for Mathematics and Science Achievement Program. The second category of resources—"Publications/materials"—includes, for example, periodicals, curriculum units and guidelines, catalogs, and audiovisual and computer-based materials.

Some annotations include several sources, such as field centers, regional resource centers, and networks of affiliated organizations. For any organization that does not have a fixed address, the name and address of an appropriate person, such as the executive director, is provided.

Starting Points

Because some of the detailed information presented here will change with time, chapters 10 and 11 should be treated as starting points for gathering further details. Teachers will want to contact the organizations listed to arrange for class visits and to obtain specific information, such as dates and duration of classes, workshops, and other programs; any costs involved; exact descriptions of items listed here in somewhat generic categories—"teacher's guide," "field trip," and so on. By following up on information in these chapters, individual teachers, schools, or school systems might significantly enhance the effectiveness of their science education efforts.

Finally, it should be noted that the absence of any facility or organization from chapters 10 and 11 is not intended as a reflection on the quality of its programs or on their possible value for middle school science teaching. Readers are encouraged to use what is offered here and to seek out additional sources suitable to meeting their needs for professional development and for assistance in the classroom.

MUSEUMS AND OTHER PLACES TO VISIT

Complete Regional Listing

PACIFIC REGION

10.1 Alaska

The Imaginarium: A Science Discovery Center (Anchorage)

Pratt Museum (Homer)

University of Alaska Museum (Fairbanks)

10.2 California

Cabrillo Marine Aquarium (San Pedro)

California Academy of Sciences (San Francisco)

California Museum of Science and Industry (Los Angeles)

Carter House Natural Science Museum (Redding)

Chabot Observatory and Science Center (Oakland)

Chaffee Zoological Garden (Fresno)

Chula Vista Nature Center (Chula Vista)

Coyote Point Museum for Environmental Education (San Mateo)

Discovery Museum Learning Center (Sacramento)

Elkhorn Slough National Estuarine Research Reserve (Watsonville)

The Exploratorium (San Francisco)

¡Explorit! Science Center (Davis)

Fresno Metropolitan Museum (Fresno)

Hall of Health (Berkeley)

Hi-Desert Nature Museum (Yucca Valley)

Lawrence Hall of Science, University of California (Berkeley)

Lawrence Livermore National Laboratory (Livermore)

Lindsay Wildlife Museum (Walnut Creek)

The Living Desert (Palm Desert)

Lori Brock Children's Discovery Center (Bakersfield)

Los Angeles Zoo (Los Angeles)

Marine World–Africa USA (Vallejo)

Maturango Museum of the Indian Wells Valley (Ridgecrest)

Monterey Bay Aquarium (Monterey)

Museum of Paleontology, University of California (Berkeley)

Natural History Museum of Los Angeles County (Los Angeles)

Oakland Museum of California (Oakland)

Pacific Grove Museum of Natural History (Pacific Grove)

Palm Springs Desert Museum (Palm Springs)

Rancho Santa Ana Botanic Garden, Claremont Colleges (Claremont)

Randall Museum (San Francisco)

Reuben H. Fleet Space Theater and Science Center (San Diego)

Sacramento Zoo (Sacramento)

Sanborn Discovery Center (Youth Science Institute) (Saratoga)

San Diego Aerospace Museum (San Diego)

Engaging in hands-on inquiry at a museum

ABOUT THE "COMPLETE REGIONAL LISTING"

The "Complete Regional Listing" provides the names and locations (city and state) of about 550 facilities in the United States and several in Canada. The "Part 4 Overview" lists the criteria used in the selection of these facilities (*see* p. 307).

The "Complete Regional Listing" is arranged as follows:

- It is divided into nine geographical regions, arranged in a roughly west-to-east array, as shown on the map in this box.
- The states within each region are listed alphabetically; each state in the "Complete Regional Listing" has an entry number—e.g., 10.1 for Alaska.
- The facilities in each state are arranged alphabetically.
- Facilities whose names appear in boldface type in the "Complete Regional Listing" are annotated in the second section of chapter 10—the "Select Annotated Listing," on pages 320-71.

Following is a list of the nine regions and the states in each. The entry number for each state is given in parentheses after its name.

- **Pacific Region**
  Alaska (10.1)
  California (10.2)
  Hawaii (10.3)
  Oregon (10.4)
  Washington (10.5)
- **Mountain Region**
  Arizona (10.6)
  Colorado (10.7)
  Idaho (10.8)
  Montana (10.9)
  Nevada (10.10)
  New Mexico (10.11)
  Utah (10.12)
  Wyoming (10.13)
- **Great Plains/Midwest Region**
  Iowa (10.14)
  Kansas (10.15)
  Minnesota (10.16)
  Missouri (10.17)
  Nebraska (10.18)
  North Dakota (10.19)
  South Dakota (10.20)
- **South Central Region**
  Arkansas (10.21)
  Louisiana (10.22)
  Oklahoma (10.23)
  Texas (10.24)

- **Great Lakes Region**
  Illinois (10.25)
  Indiana (10.26)
  Michigan (10.27)
  Ohio (10.28)
  Wisconsin (10.29)
- **Southeast Region**
  Alabama (10.30)
  Florida (10.31)
  Georgia (10.32)
  Kentucky (10.33)
  Mississippi (10.34)
  North Carolina (10.35)
  South Carolina (10.36)
  Tennessee (10.37)
  Virginia (10.38)
  West Virginia (10.39)

- **Middle Atlantic Region**
  Delaware (10.40)
  District of Columbia (10.41)
  Maryland (10.42)
  New Jersey (10.43)
  New York (10.44)
  Pennsylvania (10.45)
- **New England Region**
  Connecticut (10.46)
  Maine (10.47)
  Massachusetts (10.48)
  New Hampshire (10.49)
  Rhode Island (10.50)
  Vermont (10.51)
- **Canada**
  Canadian Provinces (10.52)

Readers will note that the series of entry numbers in the "Complete Regional Listing" continues without interruption into the "Select Annotated Listing," where each institution has its own entry number.

10.2 California (continued)

San Diego Natural History Museum (San Diego)

San Diego Zoo and Wild Animal Park (San Diego)

San Francisco Bay Model Visitor Center, U.S. Army Corps of Engineers (Sausalito)

San Francisco Zoological Gardens (San Francisco)

Santa Ana Zoo (Santa Ana)

Santa Barbara Botanic Garden (Santa Barbara)

Santa Barbara Museum of Natural History (Santa Barbara)

Sea World of California (San Diego)

Stephen Birch Aquarium-Museum, Scripps Institution of Oceanography (La Jolla)

Tech Museum of Innovation (San Jose)

Vasona Discovery Center (Youth Science Institute) (Los Gatos)

10.3 Hawaii

Bishop Museum (Honolulu)

Harold L. Lyon Arboretum, University of Hawaii at Manoa (Honolulu)

Hawaii Volcanoes National Park (Island of Hawaii)

Sea Life Park Hawaii (Waimanalo)

Waikiki Aquarium, University of Hawaii at Manoa (Honolulu)

10.4 Oregon

Douglas County Museum of History and Natural History (Roseburg)

High Desert Museum (Bend)

Mark O. Hatfield Marine Science Center Aquarium (Newport)

Metro Washington Park Zoo (Portland)

Oregon Museum of Science and Industry (Portland)

Pacific Northwest Museum of Natural History (Ashland)

Wildlife Safari (Winston)

Willamette Science and Technology Center (Eugene)

World Forestry Center (Portland)

10.5 Washington

The Burke Museum (Seattle)

Columbia River Exhibition of History, Science, and Technology (Richland)

LifeTrek—Northwest Museum of Health and Science (Spokane)

Marine Science Society of the Pacific Northwest (Poulsbo)

Mt. Rainier National Park (Ashford)

Museum of Flight (Seattle)

North Cascades Institute (Sedro-Woolley)

Northwest Trek Wildlife Park (Eatonville)

Pacific Science Center (Seattle)

Seattle Aquarium (Seattle)

Woodland Park Zoological Gardens (Seattle)

MOUNTAIN REGION

10.6 Arizona

Arizona Science Center (Phoenix)

Arizona-Sonora Desert Museum (Tucson)

Desert Botanical Garden (Phoenix)

Flandrau Science Center and Planetarium, University of Arizona (Tucson)

Kitt Peak Museum (Tucson)

Lowell Observatory (Flagstaff)

Phoenix Zoo (Phoenix)

Pima Air and Space Museum (Tucson)

10.7 Colorado

Cheyenne Mountain Zoological Park (Colorado Springs)

Children's Museum of Denver (Denver)

Colorado School of Mines Geology Museum (Golden)

Denver Botanic Gardens (Denver)

Denver Museum of Natural History (Denver)

Denver Zoological Gardens (Denver)

Florissant Fossil Beds National Monument (Florissant)

Hall of Life (Denver)

May Natural History Museum and Museum of Space Exploration (Colorado Springs)

Museum of Western Colorado (Grand Junction)

National Center for Atmospheric Research (Boulder)

National Renewable Energy Laboratory (Golden)

Pueblo Zoo (Pueblo)

Rocky Mountain National Park (Estes Park)

University of Colorado Museum (Boulder)

10.8 Idaho

Discovery Center of Idaho (Boise)

Idaho Museum of Natural History, Idaho State University (Pocatello)

10.9 Montana

Glacier National Park (West Glacier)

Museum of the Rockies, Montana State University (Bozeman)

10.10 Nevada

Fleischmann Planetarium (Reno)

Great Basin National Park (Baker)

Lied Discovery Children's Museum (Las Vegas)

10.11 New Mexico

Bradbury Science Museum (Los Alamos)

¡Explora! Science Center (Albuquerque)

Las Cruces Museum of Natural History (Las Cruces)

New Mexico Bureau of Mines Mineral Museum (Socorro)

New Mexico Museum of Natural History and Science (Albuquerque)

Rio Grande Zoological Park (Albuquerque)

Santa Fe Children's Museum (Santa Fe)

The Space Center (Alamogordo)

10.12 Utah

Canyonlands Field Institute (Moab)
College of Eastern Utah Prehistoric Museum (Price)
Hansen Planetarium (Salt Lake City)
Hogle Zoological Garden (Salt Lake City)
Monte L. Bean Life Science Museum, Brigham Young University (Provo)
Utah Museum of Natural History, University of Utah (Salt Lake City)

10.13 Wyoming

Greybull Museum (Greybull)

GREAT PLAINS/ MIDWEST REGION

10.14 Iowa

Bluedorn Science Imaginarium, Grout Museums (Waterloo)
Science Center of Iowa (Des Moines)
Science Station (Cedar Rapids)
University of Iowa Museum of Natural History (Iowa City)

10.15 Kansas

Kansas Cosmosphere and Space Center (Hutchinson)
Kansas Learning Center for Health (Halstead)
Kauffman Museum, Bethel College (North Newton)
KU Natural History Museum, University of Kansas (Lawrence)
Lake Afton Public Observatory, Wichita State University (Wichita)
Lee Richardson Zoo (Garden City)
Pratt Wildlife Center and Aquarium (Pratt)
Topeka Zoological Park (Topeka)

10.16 Minnesota

The Bakken: A Library and Museum of Electricity in Life (Minneapolis)
Bell Museum of Natural History (*See* James Ford Bell Museum of Natural History)
Headwaters Science Center (Bemidji)
James Ford Bell Museum of Natural History (Minneapolis)
Minnesota Zoological Garden (Apple Valley)
Science Museum of Minnesota (St. Paul)

10.17 Missouri

Dickerson Park Zoo (Springfield)
Discovery Center (Springfield)
Kansas City Museum (Kansas City)
Kansas City Zoological Gardens (Kansas City)
The Magic House, St. Louis Children's Museum (St. Louis)
Missouri Botanical Garden (St. Louis)
St. Louis Science Center (St. Louis)
St. Louis Zoological Park (St. Louis)
U.S. Army Engineer Museum (Fort Leonard Wood)

10.18 Nebraska

Folsom Children's Zoo and Botanical Garden (Lincoln)
Hastings Museum (Hastings)
Henry Doorly Zoo (Omaha)
Neale Woods Nature Center (Omaha)
Omaha Children's Museum (Omaha)
Pioneers Park Nature Center (Lincoln)
University of Nebraska State Museum (Lincoln)

10.19 North Dakota

Dakota Zoo (Bismarck)
Gateway to Science Center (Bismarck)
Roosevelt Park Zoo (Minot)

10.20 South Dakota

Badlands National Park (Interior)
South Dakota Discovery Center and Aquarium (Pierre)
Wind Cave National Park (Hot Springs)

SOUTH CENTRAL REGION

10.21 Arkansas

Arkansas Museum of Science and History (Little Rock)
Little Rock Zoological Gardens (Little Rock)
Logoly State Park (McNeil)
Mid-America Museum (Hot Springs)

10.22 Louisiana

Alexandria Zoological Park (Alexandria)
Aquarium of the Americas (New Orleans)
Audubon Zoological Garden (New Orleans)
Children's Museum of Lake Charles (Lake Charles)
Greater Baton Rouge Zoo (Baker)
Louisiana Arts and Science Center (Baton Rouge)
Louisiana Nature Center (New Orleans)
Sci-Port Discovery Center (Shreveport)
Walter B. Jacobs Memorial Nature Park (Shreveport)

10.23 Oklahoma

Harmon Science Center (Tulsa)
Kirkpatrick Science and Air Space Museum of Omniplex (Oklahoma City)
Oklahoma City Zoo (Oklahoma City)
Oklahoma Museum of Natural History, University of Oklahoma (Norman)
Tulsa Zoological Park (Tulsa)

10.24 Texas

Abilene Zoological Gardens (Abilene)
Armand Bayou Nature Center (Houston)
Big Thicket National Preserve (Beaumont)
Caldwell Zoo (Tyler)
Centennial Museum, University of Texas at El Paso (El Paso)
Children's Museum of Houston (Houston)
Corpus Christi Museum of Science and History (Corpus Christi)
Dallas Aquarium (Dallas)
Dallas Museum of Natural History (Dallas)
Dallas Zoo (Dallas)
Don Harrington Discovery Center (Amarillo)
El Paso Zoo (El Paso)
Environmental Science Center (Houston)
Fort Worth Museum of Science and History (Fort Worth)
Fort Worth Zoological Park (Fort Worth)
Fossil Rim Wildlife Center (Glen Rose)
Heard Natural Science Museum and Wildlife Sanctuary (McKinney)
Houston Museum of Natural Science (Houston)
Houston Zoological Gardens (Houston)
Insights—El Paso Science Center (El Paso)
McAllen International Museum (McAllen)
McDonald Observatory Visitors Center (Fort Davis)
Museum of the Southwest (Midland)
National Wildflower Research Center (Austin)
San Antonio Botanical Center (San Antonio)
San Antonio Zoological Gardens and Aquarium (San Antonio)
The Science Place, Southwest Museum of Science and Technology (Dallas)
Science Spectrum (Lubbock)
Sea World of Texas (San Antonio)
Space Center Houston (Houston)
Strecker Museum (Waco)
Texas Energy Museum (Beaumont)
Welder Wildlife Foundation (Sinton)
Witte Museum (San Antonio)

GREAT LAKES REGION

10.25 Illinois

Adler Planetarium and Astronomy Museum (Chicago)
Brookfield Zoo (*See* Chicago Zoological Park)
Chicago Botanic Garden (Glencoe)
Chicago Children's Museum (Chicago)
Chicago Zoological Park (Brookfield Zoo) (Brookfield)
Discovery Center Museum (Rockford)
Fermilab Lederman Science Education Center (Batavia)
The Field Museum (Chicago)
Henson Robinson Zoo (Springfield)
Illinois State Museum (Springfield)
International Museum of Surgical Science (Chicago)
John G. Shedd Aquarium (Chicago)
Jurica Nature Museum (Lisle)
Kampsville Archaeological Museum (Kampsville)
Lakeview Museum of Arts and Sciences (Peoria)
Lincoln Park Zoological Gardens (Chicago)
Morton Arboretum (Lisle)
Museum of Science and Industry (Chicago)
Nature Museum, Chicago Academy of Sciences (Chicago)
SciTech—Science and Technology Interactive Center (Aurora)
Shedd Aquarium (*See* John G. Shedd Aquarium)

10.26 Indiana

Children's Museum of Indianapolis (Indianapolis)
Evansville Museum of Arts and Science (Evansville)
Fort Wayne Children's Zoo (Fort Wayne)
Indianapolis Zoo (Indianapolis)
Mesker Park Zoo (Evansville)
Potawatomi Zoo (South Bend)

10.27 Michigan

Abrams Planetarium, Michigan State University (East Lansing)
Ann Arbor Hands-On Museum (Ann Arbor)
Belle Isle Nature Center (Detroit)
Binder Park Zoo (Battle Creek)
Chippewa Nature Center (Midland)
Cranbrook Institute of Science (Bloomfield Hills)
Detroit Zoo (Royal Oak)
Fernwood Botanic Garden (Niles)
Gerald E. Eddy Geology Center (Chelsea)
Hall of Ideas, Midland Center for the Arts (Midland)
Impression 5 Science Center (Lansing)
John Ball Zoological Garden (Grand Rapids)
Kalamazoo Valley Museum (Kalamazoo)
Kingman Museum of Natural History (Battle Creek)
Michigan Space and Science Center, Jackson Community College (Jackson)
Michigan State University Museum (East Lansing)
Muskegon County Museum (Muskegon)
Nichols Arboretum (Ann Arbor)
Oakwoods Metropark Nature Center (Flat Rock)
Potter Park Zoo (Lansing)
Robert T. Longway Planetarium (Flint)
Sarett Nature Center (Benton Harbor)
Sloan Museum (Flint)
Southwestern Michigan College Museum (Dowagiac)

10.28 Ohio

Akron Zoological Park (Akron)

Aullwood Audubon Center and Farm (Dayton)

Cincinnati Museum of Natural History and Planetarium (Cincinnati)

Cincinnati Zoo and Botanical Garden (Cincinnati)

Cleveland Botanical Garden (Cleveland)

Cleveland Metroparks Outdoor Education Division (Garfield Heights)

Cleveland Metroparks Zoo (Cleveland)

Cleveland Museum of Natural History (Cleveland)

Columbus Zoological Park (Powell)

COSI/Columbus—Ohio's Center Of Science and Industry (Columbus)

COSI Toledo (Toledo)

Dayton Museum of Discovery (Dayton)

Great Lakes Science Center (Cleveland)

Holden Arboretum (Kirtland)

Lake Erie Nature and Science Center (Bay Village)

McKinley Museum of History, Science and Industry (Canton)

Orton Geological Museum, Ohio State University (Columbus)

Rainbow Children's Museum (Cleveland)

Sea World of Ohio (Aurora)

Shaker Lakes Regional Nature Center (Cleveland)

Trailside Nature Center and Museum (Cincinnati)

University of Toledo SciMaTEC (Toledo)

Wilderness Center (Wilmot)

10.29 Wisconsin

Discovery World (Milwaukee)

International Crane Foundation (Baraboo)

Madison Children's Museum (Madison)

Milwaukee County Zoo (Milwaukee)

Milwaukee Public Museum (Milwaukee)

Museum of Natural History (Stevens Point)

University of Wisconsin-Madison Arboretum (Madison)

SOUTHEAST REGION

10.30 Alabama

Alabama Mining Museum (Dora)

Alabama Museum of Natural History, University of Alabama (Tuscaloosa)

Anniston Museum of Natural History (Anniston)

Birmingham Botanical Gardens (Birmingham)

Birmingham Zoo (Birmingham)

Children's Hands-On Museum (Tuscaloosa)

Exploreum Museum of Science (Mobile)

George Washington Carver Museum (Tuskegee Institute)

Iron and Steel Museum of Alabama (McCalla)

McWane Center (Birmingham)

U.S. Space and Rocket Center (Huntsville)

10.31 Florida

Astronaut Memorial Space Science Center (Cocoa)

Biscayne National Park (Homestead)

Brevard Museum (Cocoa)

Children's Science Center (Cape Coral)

Discovery Science Center (Ocala)

Dolphin Research Center (Grassy Key)

Florida Aquarium (Tampa)

Florida Museum of Natural History, University of Florida (Gainesville)

Imaginarium Hands-On Museum and Aquarium (Fort Myers)

Great Explorations, The Hands On Museum (St. Petersburg)

Gulf Coast World of Science (Sarasota)

Gulf Islands National Seashore (Gulf Breeze)

Miami Museum of Science and Space Transit Planetarium (Miami)

Mote Marine Laboratory/Aquarium (Sarasota)

Museum of Arts and Sciences (Daytona Beach)

Museum of Discovery and Science (Fort Lauderdale)

Museum of Natural History of the Florida Keys (Marathon)

Museum of Science and History of Jacksonville (Jacksonville)

Museum of Science and Industry (Tampa)

Orlando Science Center (Orlando)

Science Center of Pinellas County (St. Petersburg)

Sea World of Florida (Orlando)

Silver River Museum and Environmental Education Center (Ocala)

South Florida Science Museum (West Palm Beach)

10.32 Georgia

Fernbank Museum of Natural History (Atlanta)

Fernbank Science Center (Atlanta)

Georgia Southern University Museum (Statesboro)

Museum of Arts and Sciences (Macon)

National Science Center (Fort Gordon)

Oatland Island Education Center (Savannah)

Savannah Science Museum (Savannah)

SciTrek—The Science and Technology Museum of Atlanta (Atlanta)

University of Georgia Museum of Natural History (Athens)

Zoo Atlanta (Atlanta)

10.33 Kentucky

Hardin Planetarium (Bowling Green)
John James Audubon Museum (Henderson)
Living Arts and Science Center (Lexington)
Louisville Science Center (Louisville)
Louisville Zoological Garden (Louisville)

10.34 Mississippi

J. L. Scott Marine Education Center and Aquarium (Biloxi)
Mississippi Museum of Natural Science (Jackson)
Russell C. Davis Planetarium (Jackson)
University Museums, The University of Mississippi (University)

10.35 North Carolina

Arts and Science Center (Statesville)
Catawba Science Center (Hickory)
Colburn Gem and Mineral Museum (Asheville)
Discovery Place (Charlotte)
Harris Visitors Center, Carolina Power and Light Company (New Hill)
The Health Adventure (Asheville)
Imagination Station (Wilson)
Morehead Planetarium, University of North Carolina at Chapel Hill (Chapel Hill)
Natural Science Center of Greensboro (Greensboro)
North Carolina Aquarium at Fort Fisher (Kure Beach)
North Carolina Aquarium at Pine Knoll Shores (Atlantic Beach)
North Carolina Aquarium on Roanoke Island (Manteo)
North Carolina Maritime Museum (Beaufort)
North Carolina Museum of Life and Science (Durham)

North Carolina State Museum of Natural Sciences (Raleigh)
North Carolina Zoological Park (Asheboro)
Piedmont Environmental Center (High Point)
Reed Gold Mine State Historic Site (Stanfield)
Rocky Mount Children's Museum (Rocky Mount)
Schiele Museum of Natural History and Planetarium (Gastonia)
SciWorks—The Science Center and Environmental Park of Forsyth County (Winston-Salem)
Western North Carolina Nature Center (Asheville)

10.36 South Carolina

Charleston Museum (Charleston)
Greenville Zoo (Greenville)
Museum of York County (Rock Hill)
Riverbanks Zoological Park (Columbia)
Roper Mountain Science Center (Greenville)
South Carolina Botanical Garden (Clemson)
South Carolina State Museum (Columbia)
The World of Energy at Keowee-Toxaway (Seneca)

10.37 Tennessee

American Museum of Science and Energy (Oak Ridge)
Cumberland Science Museum (Nashville)
Grassmere Wildlife Park (Nashville)
Hands On! Regional Museum (Johnson City)
Knoxville Zoological Gardens (Knoxville)
Lichterman Nature Center (Memphis)
Memphis Museum System (Memphis)
Memphis Zoo and Aquarium (Memphis)

10.38 Virginia

D. Ralph Hostetter Museum of Natural History (Harrisonburg)
Leander J. McCormick Observatory (Charlottesville)
M. T. Brackbill Planetarium (Harrisonburg)
Norfolk Botanical Garden (Norfolk)
Orland E. White Arboretum (Boyce)
Science Museum of Virginia (Richmond)
Science Museum of Western Virginia (Roanoke)
Virginia Air and Space Center and Hampton Roads History Center (Hampton)
Virginia Living Museum (Newport News)
Virginia Marine Science Museum (Virginia Beach)
Virginia Museum of Natural History (Martinsville)
Virginia Museum of Transportation (Roanoke)
Virginia Zoological Park (Norfolk)

10.39 West Virginia

Good Children's Zoo (Wheeling)
Sunrise Museum (Charleston)

MIDDLE ATLANTIC REGION

10.40 Delaware

Brandywine Zoo (Wilmington)
Delaware Museum of Natural History (Wilmington)
Hagley Museum and Library (Wilmington)

10.41 District of Columbia

Capital Children's Museum (Washington, D.C.)
Explorers Hall, National Geographic Society (Washington, D.C.)
National Air and Space Museum, Smithsonian Institution (Washington, D.C.)
National Aquarium (Washington, D.C.)

10.41 District of Columbia (continued)

National Museum of American History, Smithsonian Institution (Washington, D.C.)

National Museum of Health and Medicine (Washington, D.C.)

National Museum of Natural History, Smithsonian Institution (Washington, D.C.)

National Zoological Park, Smithsonian Institution (Washington, D.C.)

10.42 Maryland

Baltimore Zoo (Baltimore)

Brookside Gardens (Wheaton)

Calvert Marine Museum (Solomons)

Carrie Weedon Natural Science Museum (Annapolis)

Chesapeake Beach Railway Museum (Chesapeake Beach)

Columbus Center (Baltimore)

Historical Electronics Museum (Baltimore)

Howard B. Owens Science Center (Lanham)

Maryland Science Center (Baltimore)

National Aquarium in Baltimore (Baltimore)

Smithsonian Environmental Research Center (Edgewater)

30th Street Nature Center (Mt. Rainier)

Watkins Nature Center (Upper Marlboro)

10.43 New Jersey

Bergen County Zoological Park (Paramus)

Invention Factory Science Center (Trenton)

Liberty Science Center (Jersey City)

Monmouth Museum (Lincroft)

Morris Museum (Morristown)

Newark Museum (Newark)

New Jersey State Aquarium at Camden (Camden)

New Jersey State Museum (Trenton)

Reeves-Reed Arboretum (Summit)

Trailside Nature and Science Center (Mountainside)

Wetlands Institute (Stone Harbor)

10.44 New York

Alley Pond Environmental Center (Douglaston)

American Museum of Natural History (New York City)

American Museum of Natural History—Hayden Planetarium (New York City)

Aquarium for Wildlife Conservation (Brooklyn)

Aquarium of Niagara (Niagara Falls)

Brookhaven National Laboratory Science Museum (Upton)

Brooklyn Botanic Garden (Brooklyn)

Brooklyn Children's Museum (Brooklyn)

Bronx Zoo/Wildlife Conservation Park (Bronx)

Buffalo Museum of Science (Buffalo)

Central Park Wildlife Center (New York City)

Children's Museum of Manhattan (New York City)

Corning Museum of Glass (Corning)

DNA Learning Center (Cold Spring Harbor)

George Landis Arboretum (Esperance)

Greenburgh Nature Center (Scarsdale)

Hayden Planetarium (See American Museum of Natural History—Hayden Planetarium)

Hicksville Gregory Museum (Hicksville)

Hudson River Museum of Westchester (Yonkers)

Institute of Ecosystem Studies (Millbrook)

Intrepid Sea–Air–Space Museum (New York City)

Kopernik Space Education Center (See Roberson Museum and Science Center)

Milton J. Rubenstein Museum of Science and Technology (Syracuse)

Museum of the Hudson Highlands (Cornwall-on-Hudson)

New York Botanical Garden (Bronx)

New York Hall of Science (Corona Park)

New York State Museum (Albany)

New York Transit Museum (Brooklyn)

North Wind Undersea Institute (Bronx)

Old Westbury Gardens (Old Westbury, Long Island)

Paleontological Research Institution (Ithaca)

Pember Museum of Natural History (Granville)

Queens Botanical Garden (Queens)

Roberson Museum and Science Center (Binghamton) and Kopernik Space Education Center (Vestal)

Rochester Museum and Science Center (Rochester)

Ross Park Zoo (Binghamton)

Schenectady Museum and Planetarium (Schenectady)

Schoellkopf Geological Museum (Niagara Falls)

Science Discovery Center of Oneonta (Oneonta)

Science Museum of Long Island (Manhasset)

Sciencenter (Ithaca)

Seneca Park Zoo (Rochester)

South Street Seaport Museum (New York City)

Staten Island Children's Museum (Staten Island)

Staten Island Institute of Arts and Sciences (Staten Island)

Staten Island Zoo (Staten Island)

Utica Zoo (Utica)

Vanderbilt Museum (Centerport)

Westmoreland Sanctuary (Mount Kisco)

10.45 Pennsylvania

Academy of Natural Sciences of Philadelphia (Philadelphia)

Carnegie Museum of Natural History (Pittsburgh)

Carnegie Science Center (Pittsburgh)

Discovery Center of Science and Technology (Bethlehem)

Erie Zoo (Erie)
Franklin Institute Science Museum
(Philadelphia)
Museum of Scientific Discovery
(Harrisburg)
National Aviary in Pittsburgh
(Pittsburgh)
North Museum of Natural History
and Science, Franklin and
Marshall College (Lancaster)
Philadelphia Zoological Garden
(Philadelphia)
Pittsburgh Zoo (Pittsburgh)
Railroad Museum of Pennsylvania
(Strasburg)
Schuylkill Center for Environ-
mental Education (Philadelphia)
Stroud Water Research Center,
Academy of Natural Sciences of
Philadelphia (Avondale)
Wagner Free Institute of Science
(Philadelphia)
ZOOAMERICA North American
Wildlife Park (Hershey)

NEW ENGLAND REGION

10.46 Connecticut
Beardsley Zoo (Bridgeport)
Bruce Museum (Greenwich)
Connecticut State Museum of
Natural History (Storrs)
Dinosaur State Park (Rocky Hill)
Discovery Museum (Bridgeport)
Eli Whitney Museum (Hamden)
Maritime Center at Norwalk
(Norwalk)
Mystic Marinelife Aquarium
(Mystic)
Nature Center for Environmental
Activities (Westport)
Science Center of Connecticut
(West Hartford)
Stamford Museum and Nature
Center (Stamford)

10.47 Maine
Children's Museum of Maine
(Portland)
L. C. Bates Museum (Hinckley)
Maine State Museum (Augusta)
Mount Desert Oceanarium
(Southwest Harbor)
Owls Head Transportation Museum
(Owls Head)

10.48 Massachusetts
Aquarium of the National Marine
Fisheries Service (Woods Hole)
Berkshire Botanical Garden
(Stockbridge)
Berkshire Museum (Pittsfield)
Cape Cod Museum of Natural
History (Brewster)
Children's Museum (Boston)
Children's Museum at Holyoke
(Holyoke)
Computer Museum (Boston)
Discovery Museums (Acton)
Harvard Museums of Cultural and
Natural History (Cambridge)
Laughing Brook Education Center
and Wildlife Sanctuary
(Hampden)
Museum of Science (Boston)
National Plastics Center and
Museum (Leominster)
New England Aquarium (Boston)
New England Science Center
(Worcester)
Springfield Science Museum
(Springfield)
Woods Hole Oceanographic
Institution (Woods Hole)

10.49 New Hampshire
Audubon Society of New
Hampshire (Concord)
Children's Museum of Portsmouth
(Portsmouth)
Science Center of New Hampshire
(Holderness)
Seacoast Science Center (Rye)
SEE Science Center (Manchester)

10.50 Rhode Island
Audubon Society of Rhode Island
(Smithfield)
Museum of Natural History
(Providence)
Roger Williams Park Zoo
(Providence)
Slater Mill Historic Site
(Pawtucket)
Thames Science Center (Newport)

10.51 Vermont
Discovery Museum (Essex
Junction)
Fairbanks Museum and
Planetarium (St. Johnsbury)
Montshire Museum of Science
(Norwich)

CANADA

10.52 Canadian Provinces
Aitken Bicentennial Exhibition
Centre (St. John, New
Brunswick)
Calgary Science Centre (Calgary,
Alberta)
Calgary Zoo, Botanical Garden and
Prehistoric Park (Calgary, Alberta)
Canadian Museum of Nature
(Ottawa, Ontario)
Discovery Centre (Halifax, Nova
Scotia)
Metropolitan Toronto Zoo
(Toronto, Ontario)
National Aviation Museum
(Ottawa, Ontario)
National Museum of Science and
Technology (Ottawa, Ontario)
Ontario Science Centre
(Don Mills, Ontario)
Saskatchewan Science Centre
(Regina, Saskatchewan)
Science North (Sudbury, Ontario)
SCIENCE WORLD British
Columbia (Vancouver, British
Columbia)
Vancouver Aquarium, Canada's
Pacific National Aquarium
(Vancouver, British Columbia)

Select Annotated Listing

ABOUT THE "SELECT ANNOTATED LISTING"

The "Select Annotated Listing" provides annotations for approximately 300 facilities, which appear in boldface type in the "Complete Regional Listing," on pages 310-19. The "Part 4 Overview" lists the criteria used in the selection of these facilities (*see* p. 307).

The "Select Annotated Listing" is arranged the same way as the "Complete Regional Listing"—

- in nine regions (see the map on page 312),
- by states arranged alphabetically within regions, and
- by facilities arranged alphabetically within the states where they are located.

The series of entry numbers in the "Complete Regional Listing" continues without interruption into the "Select Annotated Listing," where each institution has its own entry number. Following is a list of the nine regions, their states, and the range of entry numbers for the facilities in each state.

- **Pacific Region**
  Alaska (10.53-10.54)
  California (10.55-10.85)
  Hawaii (10.86-10.88)
  Oregon (10.89-10.93)
  Washington (10.94-10.100)
- **Mountain Region**
  Arizona (10.101-10.108)
  Colorado (10.109-10.114)
  Idaho (10.115-10.116)
  Montana (10.117)
  Nevada (10.118)
  New Mexico (10.119-10.121)
  Utah (10.122-10.124)
- **Great Plains/Midwest Region**
  Iowa (10.125)
  Kansas (10.126-10.128)
  Minnesota (10.129-10.133)
  Missouri (10.134-10.139)
  Nebraska (10.140-10.142)
  North Dakota (10.143-10.144)
  South Dakota (10.145)

- **South Central Region**
  Arkansas (10.146)
  Louisiana (10.147-10.152)
  Oklahoma (10.153-10.155)
  Texas (10.156-10.169)
- **Great Lakes Region**
  Illinois (10.170-10.182)
  Indiana (10.183-10.185)
  Michigan (10.186-10.195)
  Ohio (10.196-10.207)
  Wisconsin (10.208-10.209)
- **Southeast Region**
  Alabama (10.210-10.216)
  Florida (10.217-10.230)
  Georgia (10.231-10.236)
  Kentucky (10.237-10.239)
  Mississippi (10.240-10.242)
  North Carolina (10.243-10.255)
  South Carolina (10.256-10.259)
  Tennessee (10.260-10.263)
  Virginia (10.264-10.269)

- **Middle Atlantic Region**
  District of Columbia
    (10.270-10.273)
  Maryland (10.274-10.280)
  New Jersey (10.281-10.286)
  New York (10.287-10.310)
  Pennsylvania (10.311-10.321)
- **New England Region**
  Connecticut (10.322-10.325)
  Maine (10.326-10.328)
  Massachusetts (10.329-10.335)
  New Hampshire (10.336-10.337)
  Rhode Island (10.338-10.341)
  Vermont (10.342-10.344)
- **Canada**
  Canadian Provinces
    (10.345-10.351)

PACIFIC REGION

Alaska

10.53 The Imaginarium: A Science Discovery Center, 737 W. Fifth Ave., Suite 140, Anchorage, AK 99501
(907) 276-3179

Regional discovery center with a planetarium and a marine-life touch tank; focused on life, earth, and physical sciences, with special emphasis on the animals and ecology of Alaska. *Programs for students:* At the Imaginarium: classes; guided tours; hands-on exhibits; field trips. At schools: statewide outreach programs; traveling exhibits. *Materials:* Curriculum materials; teacher's guides; audiovisual and computer-based materials. *Education and support for teachers:* In-service education on science content and hands-on learning.

10.54 Pratt Museum, 3779 Bartlett St., Homer, AK 99603
(907) 235-8635
http://www.alaska.net/~pratt

Natural history museum with a botanical garden, forest ecology trail, marine aquarium, and reference library; focused on regional natural and cultural history and on marine biology, with emphasis on conservation. *Programs for students:* At the museum: programs for school groups; guided/self-guided tours; hands-on exhibits.

At schools: outreach programs that include visiting scientists, scholars, and Native tradition bearers; traveling exhibits. *Materials:* Lending kits for grades K-8; audiovisual materials; interactive murals available for loan (topics include biodiversity, oil spill prevention, and shorebirds). *Education and support for teachers:* In-service education on natural history and hands-on learning.

California

10.55 Cabrillo Marine Aquarium, 3720 Stephen White Dr., San Pedro, CA 90731
(310) 548-7562

Combined museum and aquarium, housing 35 aquariums and exhibits, located on the shore adjacent to sandy beaches, salt marsh, and rocky shore habitats; focused on the marine life of southern California. *Programs for students:* At the aquarium: wet lab/field workshops; guided tours; hands-on exhibits; whale-watching boat trips. At schools: outreach programs. *Materials:* Teacher's guides. *Education and support for teachers:* In-service workshops on marine and environmental topics and on hands-on learning; resource library.

10.56 California Academy of Sciences, Golden Gate Park, San Francisco, CA 94118-4599
(415) 221-5100

Research-based institution that includes a natural history museum, aquarium, and planetarium; focused on life sciences, natural history and evolution, astronomy, physics, and chemistry. *Programs for students:* At the academy: planetarium programs; guided tours; field trips; hands-on exhibits; after-school and Saturday classes. At schools: outreach vans. *Materials:* Activity books; kits with curriculum guides and audiocassettes; lending boxes of hands-on materials; teacher's guides. *Education and support for teachers:* In-service education on science content and hands-on learning; library resource center; newsletter.

10.57 California Museum of Science and Industry, 700 State Dr., Los Angeles, CA 90037
(213) 744-7444

Extensive science and technology museum, with an IMAX theater; focused on physical sciences, human biology and health, aerospace, technology, the environment, and the relationship of science to the arts and humanities. *Programs for students:* At the museum: participatory exhibits; guided tours; science literature and theater presentations; demonstrations; science workshops. At schools: outreach programs, including science theater and science clubs. *Materials:* Teacher's guides; *Science Explorers* activity sheets; posters. *Education and support for teachers:* In-service workshops on science content and hands-on learning; leadership conferences.

10.58 Carter House Natural Science Museum, 48 Quartz Hill Rd., Redding, CA 96003 (*Mailing address: P.O. Box 990185, Redding, CA 96099*)
(916) 243-5457

Science museum and nature center focused on local ecosystems. *Programs for students:* At the museum: hands-on exhibits; outdoor laboratory classes; teen volunteer/naturalist program; field trips; museum-based charter school in the natural sciences. At schools:

outreach programs. *Materials:* Hands-on activity books; teacher's guides; hands-on curriculum materials featuring local plants, animals, and habitats; catalog of materials. *Education and support for teachers:* In-service education on science content and hands-on learning; classes; newsletter.

10.59 Chabot Observatory and Science Center, 4917 Mountain Blvd., Oakland, CA 94619-3014 (510) 530-3480

A 113-year-old observatory, a science center with a theater and a planetarium, and an outdoor environmental facility; emphasis on astronomy and earth, life, and environmental sciences. *Programs for students:* At the observatory and science center: workshops on the observatory and the telescopes; planetarium shows; hands-on exhibits. At schools: portable planetarium; traveling exhibits; environmental education programs. *Materials:* Hands-on activity books; curriculum units with hands-on materials; teacher's guides; audiovisual and computer-based materials; catalog of materials. *Education and support for teachers:* In-service education on science content and hands-on learning; on-line information and resources (e-mail: chabot@astro.berkeley.edu); newsletter.

10.60 Coyote Point Museum for Environmental Education, 1651 Coyote Point Dr., San Mateo, CA 94401 (415) 342-7755

Nature center with an environmental hall, wildlife habitats, and a curriculum library; emphasis on life sciences and the environment.

Programs for students: At the museum: hands-on exhibits; guided tours; field studies. At schools: outreach programs. *Materials:* Curriculum units and supplemental activities, developed upon request; audiovisual materials. *Education and support for teachers:* In-service workshops on science content and hands-on learning; newsletter.

10.61 Discovery Museum Learning Center, 3615 Auburn Blvd., Sacramento, CA 95628 (916) 277-6181

Science center with a discovery trail and a planetarium; focused on astronomy, botany, earth sciences, life science and the human body, matter and energy, and robotics. *Programs for students:* At the center: hands-on exhibits; docent-led tours; planetarium shows; programs with live animals. At schools: outreach programs, including assembly programs and traveling Star Dome. *Materials:* Teacher's guides. *Education and support for teachers:* In-service education on science content and hands-on learning, including workshops on several national curriculum projects.

10.62 The Exploratorium, 3601 Lyon St., San Francisco, CA 94123 (415) 563-7337 http://www.exploratorium.edu

One of the world's major hands-on museums, with a center for teaching and learning; focused on science, art, and human perception. *Programs for students:* At the museum: programs for school groups; guided/self-guided tours; 650 interactive exhibits; field trips. At schools: outreach programs. *Materials:* Hands-on activity books; curriculum materials; teacher's guides; lending boxes of hands-on materials; audiovisual

and computer-based materials; catalog of materials. *Education and support for teachers:* At the center: summer institute (has more than 2,000 graduates) for teachers of grades K-12, concentrating on science content, hands-on learning, and innovative approaches to teaching discovery-based science; quarterly magazine *Exploring*.

10.63 ¡Explorit! Science Center, 3141 5th St., Davis, CA 95616 *(Mailing address: P.O. Box 1288, Davis, CA 95617-1288)* (916) 756-0191 http://www.dcn.davis.ca.us/go/explorit

Science center focused on integrated, interactive science experiences. *Programs for students:* At the center: hands-on exhibits; classes; guided/self-guided tours; Saturday lectures; demonstrations; field trips; special-interest clubs. At schools: outreach programs; traveling exhibits. *Materials:* Hands-on activity books; teacher's guides; resource packets; audiovisual materials; loans of science equipment and specimens; posters. *Education and support for teachers:* In-service education on science content and hands-on learning; lectures; newsletter.

10.64 Lawrence Hall of Science, University of California, Centennial Drive, Berkeley, CA 94720 (510) 642-5133

Science museum and leading center for research and curriculum development in science and mathematics education; develops and disseminates model programs; facilities include a participatory planetarium and discovery-oriented physics, biology, and computer labs. *Programs for students:* At Lawrence Hall: classes; hands-on

CHAPTER 10

MUSEUMS AND OTHER PLACES TO VISIT / PACIFIC REGION

exhibits; field trips. At schools: outreach programs; traveling exhibits. *Materials:* Activity books; curriculum units; lending boxes of hands-on materials; audiovisual and computer-based materials; catalogs of materials. ***Education and support for teachers:*** In-service education on science content and hands-on learning for more than 30 programs; extensive library of science education and curriculum materials; newsletter.

10.65 **Lawrence Livermore National Laboratory,** Visitors Center, 7000 East Ave., Livermore, CA 94550 *(Mailing address: P.O. Box 808, L-793, Livermore, CA 94550)*
(510) 424-0576

National laboratory with an active educational program for grades K-12, focused on physics. ***Programs for students:*** At schools: science and technology presentations with about 20 scientific demonstrations, including light and laser experiments, by Science Presentation Volunteers. *Materials:* Teacher's guides. ***Education and support for teachers:*** In-service education on science content.

10.66 **The Living Desert,** 47-900 Portola Ave., Palm Desert, CA 92260
(619) 346-5694

Botanical garden and wildlife park, including 200 acres of gardens and live-animal exhibits representing various desert ecosystems of the world; 1,000 acres of wilderness preserve and hiking trails; and a discovery room. ***Programs for students:*** At the park: guided/self-guided tours; hands-on exhibits. At schools: outreach programs. *Materials:* Teacher's guides; audiovisual and computer-based materials. ***Education and support for teachers:*** Workshops.

10.67 **Los Angeles Zoo,** 5333 Zoo Dr., Los Angeles, CA 90027
(213) 666-4650
http://www.lazoo.org

Zoo, with educational programs that emphasize an understanding of and appreciation for wildlife and conservation. ***Programs for students:*** At the zoo: workshops; interactive exhibits; guided/self-guided tours. At schools: outreach programs. *Materials:* Curriculum materials and activities for school classes; lending boxes of hands-on materials. ***Education and support for teachers:*** Workshops on science content and hands-on learning, for the classroom and for zoo visits.

10.68 **Monterey Bay Aquarium,** 886 Cannery Row, Monterey, CA 93940-1085
(408) 648-4850
http://www.mbayaq.org

Regional aquarium and marine research and conservation institution, with hands-on discovery labs and a touch pool; focused on marine biology, ecology, geology, meteorology, oceanography of central California, and on the methods and processes of science. ***Programs for students:*** At the aquarium: guided/self-guided tours; hands-on discovery labs. In the community: community conservation partnerships; student oceanography club. *Materials:* Pre-/postvisit activities and information; videotapes; regional natural history book; catalog of materials. ***Education and support for teachers:*** In-service workshops, symposia, and institutes for central California educators on science content and hands-on learning, including field, exhibit, lab, and classroom experiences.

10.69 **Museum of Paleontology, University of California,** 1101 Valley Life Sciences Bldg., Berkeley, CA 94720 *(Mailing address: Museum of Paleontology, Valley Life Sciences Bldg., University of California, Berkeley, CA 94720-4780)*
(510) 642-1821
http://www.ucmp.berkeley.edu

Research-based paleontology museum housing one of the largest collections of fossils in North America, as well as collections of modern vertebrate skeletal elements and invertebrates; focused on fossils, evolution, biogeography, and how paleontology serves society. ***Programs for students:*** At the museum: young people's lecture series; community fossil dig; guided tours. *Materials:* World Wide Web site providing virtual museum, with information about the museum, collections, catalogs, and exhibits. ***Education and support for teachers:*** In-service courses and workshops on science content; lecture series; newsletter.

10.70 **Natural History Museum of Los Angeles County,** 900 Exposition Blvd., Los Angeles, CA 90007
(213) 744-3466
http://www.lam.mus.ca.us/lacmnh

Museum comprising the original museum on Exposition Boulevard, Page Museum of La Brea Discoveries, Petersen Automotive Museum, and the William S. Hart Museum in Newhall, Calif.; facilities include hands-on discovery centers and an insect zoo; emphasis on earth and life sciences, history, and anthropology. ***Programs for students:*** At the museums: classes; workshops; field trips; guided/self-guided tours; hands-on exhibits. At schools: outreach programs; traveling exhibits.

Materials: Hands-on activity books; curriculum materials; lending boxes with science specimens; teacher's guides; computer-based materials. *Education and support for teachers:* Courses in natural history; lectures; library.

10.71 **The Oakland Museum of California,** 1000 Oak St., Oakland, CA 94607
(510) 238-3818
http://www.museumca.org

Museum featuring California art and focusing on the state's history and ecology, with emphasis on the natural sciences. *Programs for students:* At the museum: classes; guided tours. *Materials:* Lending boxes of hands-on materials; curriculum packets; teacher's guides; catalog of materials.

10.72 **Rancho Santa Ana Botanic Garden,** 1500 N. College Ave., Claremont, CA 91711
(909) 625-8767
http://www.cgs.edu/inst/rsa

Botanic garden, affiliated with the Claremont Colleges, featuring an 86-acre display of California native plants; focused on research and education in botany and on conservation and cultivation of native plants. *Programs for students:* At the garden: hands-on learning centers; guided tours; field studies. At schools: outreach programs. *Materials:* Loans of hands-on materials and live specimens; pre-/postvisit teacher's packets; curriculum and audiovisual materials. *Education and support for teachers:* Workshops to review national and California curricula in biological and environmental sciences.

10.73 **Randall Museum,** 199 Museum Way, San Francisco, CA 94114
(415) 554-9600

Children's museum on 16 acres, with live animals, a petting corral, and a hiking trail; emphasis on physical, life, earth, and environmental sciences. *Programs for students:* At the museum: hands-on exhibits; classes for school groups; guided tours. *Materials:* Curriculum materials. *Education and support for teachers:* In-service workshops on science content and hands-on learning, including national curriculum projects; newsletter.

10.74 **Reuben H. Fleet Space Theater and Science Center,** 1875 El Prado, Balboa Park, San Diego, CA 92101 *(Mailing address: P.O. Box 33303, San Diego, CA 92163)*
(619) 238-1233
http://www.rhfleet.org

Science center, with a planetarium, Omnimax theater, and Challenger Learning Center, focused on physical and space sciences and astronomy. *Programs for students:* At the center: hands-on exhibits; self-guided tours; presentations; after-school and summer classes. At the Challenger Center: programs and simulated space missions for classes; behind-the-scenes tours at Palomar Observatory; lectures; sky shows. At schools: outreach programs; traveling exhibits. *Materials:* Hands-on activity books; teacher materials and resource guides with many student activities. *Education and support for teachers:* In-service workshops on science content and hands-on learning.

10.75 **Sacramento Zoo,** 3930 W. Land Park, Sacramento, CA 95822-1123
(916) 264-5889

Zoo on 15 acres with a botanical garden, focused on wildlife conservation. *Programs for students:* At the zoo: programs for school groups; guided/self-guided tours; hands-on exhibits. At schools: outreach programs with live animals; slide shows. *Materials:* Lending boxes of hands-on materials; biological artifacts for loan; audiovisual materials; fact sheets. *Education and support for teachers:* In-service workshops on science content and hands-on learning; reference library.

10.76 **San Diego Aerospace Museum,** 2001 Pan American Plaza, Balboa Park, San Diego, CA 92101
(619) 234-8291
http://www.aerospacemuseum.org

Aviation and space museum, emphasizing the technology of aviation and space flight and the historical and cultural impact of the aerospace experience. *Programs for students:* At the museum: classes; programs for school groups; guided/self-guided tours; field studies. At schools: outreach programs; traveling exhibits. *Materials:* Curriculum units with hands-on materials; teacher's guides; audiovisual materials; newsletter for students. *Education and support for teachers:* In-service education on science content and hands-on learning; newsletter.

10.77 **San Diego Natural History Museum,** 1788 El Prado, Balboa Park, San Diego, CA 92101 *(Mailing address: P.O. Box 1390, San Diego, CA 92112)*
(619) 232-3821

Regional research and educational museum, with desert and earth science discovery labs, and (under development) an Environmental Science Education Center; focused on life and earth sciences and the environment, but also emphasizing interdisciplinary fields that combine science with society and the arts and humanities. *Programs for students:* At the museum: ecology field walks; guided/self-guided tours; hands-on exhibits; junior docent and internship program. At schools: outreach presentations. *Materials:* Specimens and videos for loan; curriculum materials (in English and Spanish) to accompany museum visits; teacher's guides. *Education and support for teachers:* In-service education including workshops, classes, field trips, and expeditions; resource lending library.

10.78 **San Diego Zoo and Wild Animal Park,** 2920 Zoo Dr., San Diego, CA 92103 *(Mailing address: P.O. Box 551, San Diego, CA 92112-0551)*
(619) 231-1515
http://www.sandiegozoo.org

World-renowned zoo on 100 acres and wild animal park on 1,800 acres, operated by Zoological Society of San Diego. *Programs for students:* At the zoo: classes; guided/self-guided tours. At schools: outreach programs. *Materials:* Interdisciplinary curriculum packets on various topics (e.g., rain forests, panda habitats); lending boxes of hands-on materials; pre-/postvisit materials; fact sheets.

Education and support for teachers: In-service workshops on science content and hands-on learning; newsletter.

10.79 **San Francisco Bay Model Visitor Center,** U.S. Army Corps of Engineers, 2100 Bridgeway, Sausalito, CA 94965
(415) 332-3871

Visitor center featuring a 1 1/2-acre working tidal hydraulic model built in 1956 to study the effects of water projects on the San Francisco Bay and Sacramento-San Joaquin Delta estuarine systems; emphasis on oceanography, ecology, and environmental issues. *Programs for students:* At the visitor center: hands-on exhibits; guided/self-guided tours; classes. At schools: outreach programs. *Materials:* Teacher's guides; audiovisual materials. *Education and support for teachers:* In-service education on science content and hands-on learning; environmental education resource library; audiovisual library; workshops.

10.80 **San Francisco Zoological Gardens,** Sloat Boulevard at the Pacific Ocean, San Francisco, CA 94132 *(Mailing address: One Zoo Rd., San Francisco, CA 94312-1098)*
(415) 753-7073

Zoo, with nature trail, emphasizing conservation biology and ecology. *Programs for students:* At the zoo: classes; lectures; guided tours. At schools: ZooMobile outreach programs. *Materials:* Lending boxes of hands-on materials; audiovisual materials. *Education and support for teachers:* In-service education on science content and hands-on learning; speakers bureau.

10.81 **Santa Ana Zoo,** 1801 E. Chestnut Ave., Santa Ana, CA 92701
(714) 836-4000
http://www.santaanazoo.org

Zoo, featuring South American wildlife and an extensive primate collection, focused on conservation education. *Programs for students:* At the zoo: classes and programs; guided/self-guided tours. At schools: zoomobile outreach programs. *Materials:* Teacher's guides; loan of nonliving artifacts. *Education and support for teachers:* In-service workshops on science content and hands-on learning.

10.82 **Santa Barbara Museum of Natural History,** 2559 Puesta del Sol Rd., Santa Barbara, CA 93105
(805) 682-4711

Natural history museum, including a planetarium, with a satellite marine museum (The Sea Center) on Stearns Wharf featuring a touch tank; emphasis on natural history and marine science. *Programs for students:* At the museums: presentations and guided programs for school groups; hands-on exhibits. At schools: outreach programs; traveling exhibits. *Materials:* Curriculum units; natural objects and kits for loan; catalog of materials.

10.83 **Sea World of California,** 1720 S. Shores Rd., San Diego, CA 92109-7995
(619) 226-3834; (800) 23-SHAMU for marine life information
http://www.bev.net/education/SeaWorld

Aquarium, oceanarium, and marine museum; focused on marine science, with emphasis on ecology and conservation. *Programs for students:* At Sea World: classes; guided/self-guided tours; hands-on exhibits. At schools throughout the western United States: assembly programs; live, interactive television programs via satellite, cable, and Public Broadcasting System. *Materials:* Teacher's guides; audiovisual and computer-based materials; catalog of materials. *Education and support for teachers:* In-service education on science content and hands-on learning, including courses for college credit.

10.84 **Stephen Birch Aquarium-Museum,** Scripps Institution of Oceanography, 2300 Expedition Way, La Jolla, CA 92037 *(Mailing address: UCSD-0207, 9500 Gilman Dr., La Jolla, CA 92093-0207)* (619) 534-FISH http://aqua.ucsd.edu

Aquarium and museum of ocean science serving as the public education center for the Scripps Institution of Oceanography at the University of California, San Diego; focused on the oceans and global science. *Programs for students:* At the aquarium-museum: classes; guided/self-guided tours; hands-on exhibits; field activities. At schools: outreach programs. *Materials:* Hands-on activity books; teacher's guides; curriculum materials; discovery kits; audiovisual and computer-based materials; ocean science journal. *Education and support for teachers:* In-service workshops on science content and hands-on learning; summer institute on ocean science techniques, global change, and field methods; magazine, *Explorations.*

10.85 **The Tech Museum of Innovation,** 145 W. San Carlos St., San Jose, CA 95113 (408) 279-7182 http://www.thetech.org

Interactive museum and learning center, with emphasis on learning about science and technology

through active involvement. *Programs for students:* At the museum: classes and programs (grades 4-6); hands-on exhibits; guided tours. At schools: outreach programs (limited); traveling exhibits. *Materials:* Hands-on activity books; teacher's guides; audiovisual and computer-based materials; catalog of materials. *Education and support for teachers:* In-service workshops on science content and hands-on learning; newsletter.

Hawaii

10.86 **Bishop Museum,** 1525 Bernice St., Honolulu, HI 96817 *(Mailing address: P.O. Box 19000-A, Honolulu, HI 96817-0916)* (808) 847-3511

Cultural and natural history museum, with a planetarium and an observatory; emphasizes zoology, botany, and archaeology. *Programs for students:* At the museum: classes; guided tours; hands-on exhibits; field trips. At schools: outreach programs. *Materials:* Hands-on activity books; lending boxes of hands-on materials; teacher's guides; audiovisual and computer-based materials. *Education and support for teachers:* In-service workshops on science content.

10.87 **Sea Life Park Hawaii,** Makapuu Point, Waimanalo, HI 96795 *(Mailing address: 41-202 Kalanianaole Hwy., Suite 7, Waimanalo, HI 96795)* (808) 259-7933

Oceanarium with an education center, on the island of Oahu, focused on marine science and marine conservation. *Programs for*

students: At the oceanarium: programs; hands-on exhibits; guided tours. At schools: outreach programs; traveling exhibits. *Materials:* Hands-on activity books; teacher's guides; audiovisual materials. *Education and support for teachers:* In-service workshops on science content and hands-on learning; teacher resource library.

10.88 **Waikiki Aquarium,** 2777 Kalakaua Ave., Honolulu, HI 96815 (808) 923-9741

Research-based marine aquarium of the University of Hawaii at Manoa, emphasizing ecology, habitats, adaptations for survival, and conservation of Hawaiian and Pacific marine life. *Programs for students:* At the aquarium: guided/self-guided tours; hands-on exhibits. At outer district schools: outreach programs (grades 3-6). *Materials:* Teacher's guides; audiovisual and pre-/postvisit materials; catalog of materials. *Education and support for teachers:* In-service workshops on science content and hands-on learning.

Oregon

10.89 **The High Desert Museum,** 59800 S. Hwy. 97, Bend, OR 97702-7963 (541) 382-4754 http://www.highdesert.org

Regional, participation-oriented, "living" museum focused on the natural history of the arid Intermountain West. *Programs for students:* At the museum: field trip programs; hands-on exhibits; self-guided tours; junior volunteer program. At schools within 150-mile radius of the museum: outreach programs. *Materials:* Science resource kits for rural outreach. *Education and support for teachers:* In-service education on science content and hands-on learning in life and earth sciences; newsletter.

10.90 **Metro Washington Park Zoo,** 4001 S.W. Canyon Rd., Portland, OR 97221
(503) 226-1561

Regional zoo with special emphasis on endangered-wildlife issues at the local, regional, and international levels. *Programs for students:* At the zoo: classes; hands-on exhibits; guided/self-guided tours; youth volunteer program. At schools: zoomobile with outreach programs. *Materials:* Hands-on activity books; field guides for nature trail; lending boxes of hands-on materials; teacher's guides; pre-/postvisit and audiovisual materials; catalog of materials. *Education and support for teachers:* In-service workshops on science content and hands-on learning; newsletter.

10.91 **Oregon Museum of Science and Industry,** 1945 S.E. Water Ave., Portland, OR 97214-3354
(503) 797-4000
http://www.omsi.edu

Science and technology museum, with a planetarium, Omnimax theater, botanical garden, environmental center, and education resource center. *Programs for students:* At the museum: many hands-on classes and exhibits; week-long day camps at sites from beach to desert; guided tours; field trips. At schools in Oregon, Alaska, California, Colorado, Idaho, and Washington: outreach assemblies and classroom programs with hands-on activities; interactive demonstrations (some with live animals); portable planetarium. *Materials:* Hands-on activity books; teacher's guides; audiovisual and computer-based materials; catalog of materials. *Education*

and support for teachers: In-service workshops and courses on science content and hands-on learning, both at the museum and at schools anywhere in the Pacific Northwest; newsletter.

10.92 **Pacific Northwest Museum of Natural History,** 1500 E. Main St., Ashland, OR 97520
(541) 488-1084
http://www.projecta.com/nwmuseum

Natural history museum, with a discovery center and realistic, multisensory exhibits reflecting 6 ecosystems of the Pacific Northwest; focused on the physical, life, earth, and environmental sciences. *Programs for students:* At the museum: hands-on exhibits (many with computer interactions); classes; self-guided tours; presentations with live animals. *Materials:* Hands-on activity books; supplemental materials; magazine for students. *Education and support for teachers:* Workshops on science content and hands-on learning.

10.93 **World Forestry Center,** 4033 S.W. Canyon Rd., Portland, OR 97221
(503) 228-1367

Forestry center with a museum, an information institute, and a 70-acre working tree farm and outdoor education site in Wilsonville, Oreg.; focused on the study and conservation of global forests and forest resources. *Programs for students:* At the museum and tree farm: guided tours; learning lab presentations. At the museum: hands-on activity stations. At schools: outreach programs. *Materials:* Hands-on activity kits; curriculum units with hands-on materials and teacher's guides. *Education and support for teachers:* International information network on forest resources; newsletter.

Washington

10.94 **The Burke Museum,** University of Washington, 45th Street and 17th Avenue, N.E., Seattle, WA 98195 *(Mailing address: Box 353010, University of Washington, Seattle, WA 98195-3010)*
(206) 543-5591
http://www.washington.edu/ burkemuseum

University-based natural history and anthropology museum, focusing on biology, marine biology, geology, paleontology, and cultural anthropology. *Programs for students*: At the museum: programs for school groups; hands-on exhibits; guided/self-guided tours. *Materials:* Lending kits of museum specimens; previsit materials; annual guide to educational resources. *Education and support for teachers:* Workshops and classes; newsletter.

10.95 **Marine Science Society of the Pacific Northwest,** Marine Science Center, 18743 Front St., N.E., Poulsbo, WA 98370 *(Mailing address: P.O. Box 2079, Poulsbo, WA 98370-0942)*
(206) 779-5549

Small marine facility on the shore of Puget Sound, focusing on the marine environment. *Programs for students:* At the facility: hands-on instruction; guided tours; hands-on exhibits. At schools: outreach programs (including field studies). *Materials:* Hands-on activity books; science kits of hands-on materials and live animals for loan; teacher's guides; audiovisual and computer-based materials. *Education and support for teachers:* In-service workshops on science content and hands-on learning.

10.96 Museum of Flight, 9404 E. Marginal Way S., Seattle, WA 98108 (206) 764-5720

Aeronautics and science museum with a Challenger Learning Center and resource centers for teachers; emphasis on physical sciences, earth and space sciences, and the history of aviation and space technology. *Programs for students:* At the museum: guided/self-guided tours; hands-on exhibits; programs for school groups. At schools: outreach programs; traveling exhibits. *Materials:* Hands-on activity books; teacher's guides; computer-based materials; posters; glider designs. *Education and support for teachers:* In-service education on science content and hands-on learning; Challenger workshops; Federal Aviation Administration (FAA) Aviation Education Resource Center; National Aeronautics and Space Administration (NASA) Teacher Resource Center; newsletter.

10.97 North Cascades Institute, 2105 State Rte. 20, Sedro-Woolley, WA 98284 (360) 856-5700, ext. 209 http://www.ncascades.org/nci

Institute focusing on field-based, experiential, environmental education in the North Cascades ecosystem, including North Cascades National Park, Puget Sound, and the Columbia River Basin. *Programs for students:* In North Cascades National Park: 3-day mountain school (grades 4-8, with teachers and parents). At schools: outreach programs (field and classroom) on watershed education. *Materials:* Hands-on activity books; curriculum and resource materials; catalog of field seminars; newsletter for students. *Education and support for teachers:* In-service workshops and field seminars focused on watersheds, natural history, and experiential teaching.

10.98 Pacific Science Center, 200 Second Ave., N., Seattle, WA 98109-4895 (206) 443-2001

Science and technology center with an IMAX theater, a planetarium, and an extensive science education program. *Programs for students:* At the center: more than 200 hands-on exhibits; classes; demonstrations; laser light shows; peer-teaching workshops; field-study programs at summer camps. At schools in a majority of school districts in Washington State: 7 traveling vans bringing interactive assemblies, hands-on classes, and hands-on exhibits. *Materials:* Materials and, where appropriate, lesson plans for Science Center education programs; audiovisual and computer-based materials. *Education and support for teachers:* Hands-on workshops for teams (a teacher and 5 students); teacher institutes on science content and hands-on learning; newsletter.

10.99 The Seattle Aquarium, Pier 59, Waterfront Park, Seattle, WA 98101 (206) 386-4300 http://www.seattleaquarium.org

Regionally focused marine science institution, with a discovery lab and tide pool; provides outdoor environmental education programs for both students and teachers. *Programs for students:* At the aquarium: hands-on exhibits; self-guided tours; field studies; hands-on classes, with live animals. At schools: interactive programs. *Materials:* Lending boxes of hands-on materials; teacher's guides; pre-/postvisit and audiovisual materials. *Education and support for teachers:* In-service workshops on science content and hands-on learning.

10.100 Woodland Park Zoological Gardens, 5500 Phinney Ave. N., Seattle, WA 98103 (206) 684-4800

Zoo featuring naturalistic exhibits and an education center with a discovery room; focus includes major ecosystems of the world and wildlife conservation. *Programs for students:* At the zoo: hands-on exhibits; programs for school groups; guided tours. At schools: outreach programs. *Materials:* Hands-on activity books; curriculum packets; loan kits; slide programs; videos; catalog of materials. *Education and support for teachers:* In-service workshops, lectures, and classes on science content and hands-on learning; newsletter.

MOUNTAIN REGION

Arizona

10.101 **Arizona Science Center,** 600 E. Washington St., Phoenix, AZ 85004
(602) 716-2000

Science and technology center, with demonstration areas, a planetarium, theater, and labs; focused on energy, light, life science, physics, weather, geology, aerospace, technology, and psychology. *Programs for students:* At the center: classes; interactive exhibits; self-guided tours; planetarium shows. At schools: outreach programs, including family telescope nights. *Materials:* Hands-on activity books; teacher's guides; network resources link. *Education and support for teachers:* In-service workshops on science content and hands-on learning; newsletter.

10.102 **Arizona-Sonora Desert Museum,** 2021 N. Kinney Rd., Tucson, AZ 85743-8918
(520) 883-1380

Natural history museum focusing on the ecology of the Sonoran Desert region; most exhibits outdoors, consisting of living representations of plant and animal communities; educational programs emphasize conservation. *Programs for students:* At the museum: programs for school groups; self-guided tours; summer classes; internships. At schools: junior naturalist and

junior docent outreach programs. *Materials:* Kits on ecological subjects for loan; audiovisual materials. *Education and support for teachers:* In-service workshops on desert ecology; field trips; hikes.

10.103 **Desert Botanical Garden,** 1201 N. Galvin Pkwy., Phoenix, AZ 85008
(602) 941-1225

Botanical garden and research facility, with plants representing more than 4,000 species; focused on arid-land plants of the world, with special emphasis on succulents and native plants of the southwestern United States. *Programs for students:* At the garden: guided/self-guided tours with hands-on demonstrations; interactive investigation stations; field studies. At schools: outreach programs. *Materials:* Teacher's guides and information packets; resource notebook; audiovisual materials. *Education and support for teachers:* In-service education on science content and hands-on learning; field-test site for curriculum materials.

10.104 **Flandrau Science Center and Planetarium,** University of Arizona, Tucson, AZ 85721
(520) 621-4515
http://www.seds.org/flandrau

University-based science center, with a domed theater and interactive exhibit halls; focused on astronomy, physics, and computers. *Programs for students:* At the center: planetarium programs; self-guided tours; hands-on exhibits; demonstrations; field studies. At schools: outreach programs (limited). *Materials:* Curriculum materials; teacher's guides; audiovisual materials. *Education and support for teachers:* In-service education on science content and hands-on

learning; National Aeronautics and Space Administration (NASA) Regional Teacher Resource Center.

10.105 **Kitt Peak Museum,** Kitt Peak National Observatory, State Rte. 86/Rte. 386, Tucson, AZ 85726 *(Mailing address: P.O. Box 26732, Tucson, AZ 85726-6732)*
(602) 322-3426

Education-oriented, astronomy-based museum, focused on astronomical research and the activities of Kitt Peak National Observatory; exhibits also emphasize aspects of the Native American culture and natural history of the surrounding desert. *Programs for students:* At the museum: guided tours and "star-party" activities featuring a hands-on approach to telescopes and sky-object identification. At schools: audiovisual and lecture-format outreach programs; traveling exhibits. *Materials:* Teacher's guides; audiovisual and computer-based materials. *Education and support for teachers:* In-service education on science content.

10.106 **Lowell Observatory,** 1400 W. Mars Hill Rd., Flagstaff, AZ 86001
(520) 774-2096
http://www.lowell.edu

Research observatory, with a Visitor Center featuring many instruments modified for interactive display; emphasis on astronomy and physical and earth sciences. *Programs for students:* At the observatory: interactive displays; programs and workshops on various astronomical topics; guided/self-guided tours. At schools: outreach programs; traveling exhibits. *Materials:* Workshop materials; fact sheets; audiovisual and computer-based materials. *Education and support for teachers:* Visitor Center (including 24-inch Clark telescope and 16-inch reflector) that can be reserved for teacher workshops.

10.107 Phoenix Zoo, 455 N. Galvin Pkwy., Phoenix, AZ 85008-3431
(602) 273-1341
http://aztec.asu.edu/phxzoo

Zoo, with educational programs that emphasize wildlife and conservation. *Programs for students:* At the zoo: programs for school groups; guided/self-guided tours; hands-on exhibits; field trips. At schools: outreach programs, with live animals. *Materials:* Lending boxes of hands-on materials; curriculum materials; teacher-orientation packet; fact sheets. *Education and support for teachers:* Workshops; letter-answering service; newsletter.

10.108 Pima Air and Space Museum, 6000 E. Valencia Rd., Tucson, AZ 85706
(520) 574-0462

Aeronautics and space museum featuring 220 aircraft and aviation-related artifacts; emphasis on physical science, earth and space sciences, and technology. *Programs for students:* At the museum: classes; guided/self-guided tours; hands-on exhibits. At schools: outreach programs; traveling exhibits. *Materials:* Hands-on activity books; teacher's guides; catalog of exhibits; informational pamphlets; audiovisual materials. *Education and support for teachers:* Special tours; information hotline; newsletter.

Colorado

10.109 The Children's Museum of Denver, 2121 Children's Museum Dr., Denver, CO 80211
(303) 433-7444
http://www.artstozoo.org/cmd

Children's museum, with hands-on experiences in ScienceLAB (biological and physical sciences), EarthLAB (weather and earth science), and CompuLAB (computers and communications). *Programs for students:* At the museum: experiences in the hands-on labs and other programs for classes, including Discovery Digs (fossils) and StarLAB demonstrations. At schools: outreach programs; traveling exhibits. *Materials:* Hands-on activity books; lending boxes of hands-on materials; teacher's guides. *Education and support for teachers*: In-service education on science content and hands-on learning.

10.110 Colorado School of Mines Geology Museum, 16th and Maple, Golden, CO 80401 *(Mailing address: 1500 Illinois, Golden, CO 80401-1887)*
(303) 273-3815

Small, university museum in the geosciences, with considerable collections of minerals, rocks, fossils, gems, and mining artifacts. *Programs for students:* At the museum: guided/self-guided tours (including local geology); hands-on exhibits. *Materials:* Teaching trunks and fossil kits of hands-on materials for loan; excess mineral and fossil material (not in the collection) available upon request.

10.111 Denver Museum of Natural History, 2001 Colorado Blvd., in City Park, Denver, CO 80205
(303) 370-6387

Museum with an IMAX theater and a planetarium, focused on earth, life, environmental, anthropological, and health sciences and planetarium studies. *Programs for students:* At the museum: classes; guided tours; hands-on exhibits. At schools: outreach programs; traveling exhibits. *Education and support for teachers:* In-service education on science content and hands-on learning.

10.112 Denver Zoological Gardens, City Park, 2300 Steele St., Denver, CO 80205
(303) 331-4100
http://www.denverzoo.org

Zoo with several naturalistic displays, including Bird World, Northern Shores (the Arctic), Tropical Discovery, and Primate Panorama. *Programs for students:* At the zoo: topical guided tours; self-guided tours. At schools: outreach van with school programs on reptiles (grades 5-7); speakers bureau. *Materials:* Previsit teacher packets for trips to zoo and outreach programs; lending boxes of hands-on materials (Suitcase for Survival program). *Education and support for teachers:* In-service workshops; newsletter.

10.113 National Center for Atmospheric Research, 1850 Table Mesa Dr., Boulder, CO 80303 *(Mailing address: P.O. Box 3000, Boulder, CO 80307-3000)*
(303) 497-1000
http://www.ucar.edu

Research-based center focused on atmospheric sciences. *Programs for students:* At the center:

classes; guided/self-guided tours; hands-on exhibits. At schools: outreach programs. *Materials:* Project LEARN teaching modules on atmospheric dynamics, ozone, and cycles on earth and in the atmosphere; Digital Media Catalog of visual images on World Wide Web. *Education and support for teachers:* In-service education on science content and hands-on learning; teacher resource area; newsletter.

10.114 National Renewable Energy Laboratory, 1617 Cole Blvd., Golden, CO 80401-3393 (303) 275-3044

Science center located at the U.S. Department of Energy's national laboratory for research and development in renewable energy and energy efficiency; emphasis on physical sciences, mathematics, and technology. *Programs for students:* At the center: classes; guided tours; hands-on exhibits. At schools: outreach programs. *Materials:* Audiovisual materials; catalog of materials. *Education and support for teachers:* In-service education on science content and hands-on learning; information hotline; resource center.

Idaho

10.115 The Discovery Center of Idaho, 131 Myrtle St., Boise, ID 83702 *(Mailing address: P.O. Box 192, Boise, ID 83701)* (208) 343-9895

Participatory science museum, with more than 150 hands-on exhibits. *Programs for students:* At the center: grade-specific demonstrations; classes; hands-on exhibits. At schools: portable planetarium shows. *Materials:* Hands-on activity books; curriculum

materials; audiovisual and computer-based materials; newsletter for students. *Education and support for teachers:* In-service workshops on science content and hands-on learning; extensive training program in astronomy; teacher resource center and National Aeronautics and Space Administration (NASA) materials viewing center; newsletter.

10.116 Idaho Museum of Natural History, Fifth and Dillon, Pocatello, ID 83209 *(Mailing address: Idaho State University, P.O. Box 8096, Pocatello, ID 83209-8096)* (208) 236-2195 http://www.isu.edu/departments/museum

Natural history museum of Idaho State University; focused on several physical and biological sciences in addition to natural history fields (paleontology, geology, botany, archaeology, and ethnography). *Programs for students:* At the museum: classes; hands-on exhibits; guided/self-guided tours. At schools: outreach programs on fossils, geologic time, dinosaurs, and endangered animals. *Materials:* Teacher's guides; discovery boxes and other educational resources for loan; audiovisual and computer-based materials; catalog of resource materials. *Education and support for teachers:* Newsletter.

Montana

10.117 Museum of the Rockies, 600 W. Kagy Blvd., Bozeman, MT 59717 (406) 994-5283

Museum at Montana State University, focused on the natural and cultural history of the Northern Rocky Mountain region; emphasizes archaeology, geology, ethnology, paleontology, and astronomy.

Programs for students: At the museum: hands-on exhibits; programs for school groups; guided/self-guided tours; field studies. At schools: outreach programs, including a portable planetarium and traveling trunks; Science-by-Mail (national student/scientist pen pal program for grades 4-9). *Materials:* Hands-on activity books; curriculum materials; teacher's guides; lending boxes of hands-on materials; audiovisual and computer-based materials. *Education and support for teachers:* In-service workshops on science content and hands-on learning; newsletter.

Nevada

10.118 Lied Discovery Children's Museum, 833 Las Vegas Blvd., N., Las Vegas, NV 89101 (702) 382-3445

Children's museum, with more than 100 hands-on exhibits and an in-house radio station. *Programs for students:* At the museum: educational programs; guided/self-guided tours; hands-on exhibits. At schools: outreach programs. *Materials:* Packets, provided before guided tours; newsletter for students. *Education and support for teachers:* In-service workshops on science content and hands-on learning; newsletter.

New Mexico

10.119 ¡Explora! Science Center, 40 First Plaza, Suite 68, Albuquerque, NM 87102 (505) 842-6188

Science and technology center focused on physical science concepts (including air pressure, fluids, sound, motion, light, and electricity) and health. *Programs for students:* At the center: hands-on exhibits; demonstrations; classes. At schools: outreach program combining science and art; traveling exhibits. *Materials:* Teacher's guides; previsit materials. *Education and support for teachers:* Workshops; newsletter.

10.120 **New Mexico Museum of Natural History and Science,** 1801 Mountain Rd., N.W., Albuquerque, NM 87104-1375
(505) 841-2800
http://www.nmmnh-abq.mus.nm.us

Natural history museum focusing on earth and life sciences, with special emphasis on strengthening science education in rural schools. *Programs for students:* At the museum: large-format film theater; self-guided tours; hands-on exhibits; summer science camps. At schools: outreach programs; satellite broadcasts on ecology of the Southwest. *Materials:* Hands-on bilingual activity books; lending boxes of specimens; teacher's guides; lending equipment for student research in ecology. *Education and support for teachers:* Statewide in-service education programs on science content and hands-on learning; newsletter.

10.121 **The Space Center,** Top of New Mexico Highway 2001, Alamogordo, NM 88310 *(Mailing address: P.O. Box 533, Alamogordo, NM 88311)*
(505) 437-2840

Space center complex with a 4-story museum, space theater (planetarium and Omnimax), and air

and space park. *Programs for students:* At the center: guided/self-guided tours; numerous classes; planetarium shows. At schools in Arizona, Texas, and Colorado: outreach programs with grade-specific, hands-on learning experiences; traveling exhibits. *Materials:* Hands-on activity books; lending boxes of hands-on materials; teacher's guides; audiovisual and computer-based materials; catalog of materials. *Education and support for teachers:* In-service workshops at schools on science content and hands-on learning, using national curricular materials; resource library.

Utah

10.122 **Canyonlands Field Institute,** 1320 S. Hwy. 191, Moab, UT 84532 *(Mailing address: P.O. Box 68, Moab, UT 84532)*
(800) 860-5262

Educational institute situated in and using as its classroom the canyons of southeastern Utah (including Arches National Park, Canyonlands National Park, and several Bureau of Land Management Wilderness Study Areas); focused on physical, earth, and life sciences, and on public lands issues; also emphasizes scientific, recreational, and social aspects of the environment. *Programs for students:* At the institute: multidisciplinary program for school groups. At schools: outreach programs. *Materials:* River study programs on the Colorado, Green, San Juan, and Dolores rivers. *Education and support for teachers:* Programs; workshops; graduate residency program.

10.123 **Hansen Planetarium,** 15 S. State St., Salt Lake City, UT 84111
(801) 531-4940

Planetarium and space science museum, emphasizing astronomy and astrophysics, space science, physics, and chemistry. *Programs for students:* At the planetarium: planetarium shows; discussions on space topics; science demonstrations; hands-on exhibits; telescope observing sessions. At schools: assemblies; classroom visits; exhibits; portable planetarium. *Materials:* Lending boxes with hands-on materials; teacher's guides; computer-based materials.

10.124 **Utah Museum of Natural History,** University of Utah, President's Circle, 200 S. University St., Salt Lake City, UT 84112 *(Mailing address: University of Utah, Salt Lake City, UT 84112)*
(801) 581-4887

University-based natural history museum focusing on physical, life, and earth sciences. *Programs for students:* At the museum: classes; guided/self-guided tours; hands-on exhibits. At schools: outreach classes. *Materials:* Teaching kits with hands-on materials for loan. *Education and support for teachers:* In-service classes on science content and hands-on learning; field trips.

GREAT PLAINS/MIDWEST REGION

Iowa

10.125 **Science Center of Iowa,** 4500 Grand Ave., Greenwood Park, Des Moines, IA 50312-2499 (515) 274-6868 http://www.sciowa.org

Science center with a Challenger Learning Center and planetarium, emphasizing the life, physical, and space sciences, astronomy, and mathematics. *Programs for students:* At the center: classes; hands-on exhibits; field trips. At schools: outreach programs. *Education and support for teachers:* In-service workshops on science content and hands-on learning.

Kansas

10.126 **Kansas Cosmosphere and Space Center,** 1100 N. Plum, Hutchinson, KS 67501-1499 (316) 662-2305 http://www.cosmo.org

Space center, with a planetarium, Omnimax theater, and Hall of Space Museum; focused on physical, earth, and space sciences. *Programs for students:* At the center: Discovery workshops; classes; hands-on exhibits; guided/self-guided tours; field trips to Johnson Space Center; Future Astronaut Training Program (space science camp for students in grades 7-9). *Materials:* Curriculum units with hands-on materials; teacher's guides; audiovisual and computer-based materials. *Education and support for teachers:* Teachers and Space in-service workshops on science content and hands-on learning, onsite/offsite; National Aeronautics and Space Administration (NASA) Regional Teacher Resource Center; newsletter.

10.127 **KU Natural History Museum,** University of Kansas, Dyche Hall, Lawrence, KS 66045-2454 (913) 864-4540

Research-based natural history museum with collections of more than 5 million specimens; focused on vertebrate and invertebrate fossils, on modern insects, plants, and vertebrates, and on astronomy. *Programs for students:* At the museum: exhibits; workshops; field trips. At schools: outreach programs. *Materials:* Traveling kits of museum specimens with curriculum materials; audiovisual materials. *Education and support for teachers:* In-service workshops on science content.

10.128 **Lake Afton Public Observatory,** 25000 W. 39th St. S., Wichita, KS 67052 *(Mailing address: 1845 Fairmont, Wichita, KS 67260-0032)* (316) 689-3191

Small observatory and astronomy museum affiliated with Wichita State University. *Programs for students:* At the observatory: programs; hands-on exhibits. At schools: classroom presentations; portable learning centers. *Materials:* Astronomy activity books; curriculum guidelines; videotape programs; instructional games. *Education and support for teachers:* In-service workshops on science content and hands-on learning.

Minnesota

10.129 **The Bakken: A Library and Museum of Electricity in Life,** 3537 Zenith Ave. S., Minneapolis, MN 55416 (612) 927-6508 http://www.bakkenmuseum.org

Museum and library, with books, instruments, and archival materials focused on the history, cultural context, and applications of electricity and magnetism in medicine and the life sciences. *Programs for students:* At the museum: hands-on workshops; guided tours. *Materials:* Hands-on activity books; audiovisual materials; kits; teacher's guide. *Education and support for teachers:* In-service education on science content and hands-on learning, including courses for college credit; summer institutes; newsletter.

10.130 **James Ford Bell Museum of Natural History,** University of Minnesota, 10 Church St., S.E., Minneapolis, MN 55455-0140 (612) 624-7083 http://www.umn.edu/bellmuse

University museum of natural history serving as a regional center for the JASON Project and Bell LIVE!, with a Touch and See Room; focused on life sciences, life history, and the environment. *Programs for students:* At the museum: hands-on exhibits (especially in Touch and See Room); classes; guided tours; field trips. At schools: outreach programs (by special arrangement). *Materials:* Hands-on activity books; Bell LIVE! curriculum; Bell Museum Learning Kits with hands-on specimens and activity guides. *Education and support for teachers:* In-service workshops on science content and hands-on learning; wildlife information service; newsletter.

10.131 **Headwaters Science Center,** 413 Beltrami, Bemidji, MN 56601 (*Mailing address: P.O. Box 1176, Bemidji, MN 56601*)
(218) 751-1110

Science and environmental learning center; emphasis on the physical, life, earth, space, and environmental sciences. *Programs for students:* At the museum: programs; hands-on exhibits; guided tours; nature field trips. At schools: outreach programs, including a portable planetarium. *Materials:* Hands-on activity books; curriculum units with hands-on materials; supplemental activities; audiovisual and computer-based materials; magazines for students; catalog of materials. *Education and support for teachers:* In-service education on science content; workshops on hands-on learning; teacher resource room.

10.132 **Minnesota Zoological Garden,** 13000 Zoo Blvd., Apple Valley, MN 55124
(612) 432-9000
http://www.wcco.com/community/mnzoo

State zoological garden (480 acres, more than 2,000 animals), with trails exhibiting animals in natural settings, and Zoolab; focused on wildlife, environmental issues, and conservation. *Programs for students:* At the zoo: wildlife quest classes; guided/self-guided tours; hands-on exhibits; field trips. At schools: zoomobile with programs; speakers bureau; theater-in-the-wild performances. *Materials:* Curriculum units; teacher's guides; lending boxes of hands-on materials; audiovisual and computer-based materials; catalog of materials. *Education and support for teachers:* In-service workshops on science content and hands-on learning.

10.133 **Science Museum of Minnesota,** 30 E. 10th St., St. Paul, MN 55101
(612) 221-9488
http://www.sci.mus.mn.us

Renowned science museum with a nature center and an Omnitheater; emphasizes a broad range of sciences with varied object- and activity-centered programs. *Programs for students:* At the museum: hands-on exhibits; classes; demonstrations; field trips. At schools: assembly programs; week-long resident programs. *Materials:* Exhibit guides; lending trunks of hands-on materials; teacher's guides; audiovisual and computer-based materials; catalog of materials. *Education and support for teachers:* In-service workshops on science content and hands-on learning; teacher conferences, field trips, and institutes; on-line newsletter.

Missouri

10.134 **Kansas City Museum,** 3218 Gladstone Blvd., Kansas City, MO 64123-1199
(816) 483-8300
http://www.kcmuseum.com

Museum of history, science, technology, and natural history, with a planetarium and a Challenger Learning Center; emphasis on space science, weather, astronomy, nineteenth-century regional history, and multicultural folklore. *Programs for students:* At the museum: classes; hands-on exhibits; self-guided tours; space flight simulations; planetarium shows. At schools: outreach programs, including a portable planetarium; participatory theater; Science-in-a-Sack; classroom workshops. *Materials:* Teacher packet and student activity sheet.

Education and support for teachers: In-service education on science content and hands-on learning.

10.135 **Kansas City Zoological Gardens,** 6700 Zoo Dr., Kansas City, MO 64132
(816) 871-5700
http://www.kansascity.com/zoo

Zoo, including natural areas representing Australian and African habitats and farm habitats; emphasis on wildlife conservation and environmental education. *Programs for students:* At the zoo: hands-on exhibits; guided/self-guided tours; theater programs (seasonal). At schools: outreach programs. *Materials:* Lending boxes of hands-on materials; teacher's guides; audiovisual and computer-based materials. *Education and support for teachers:* In-service education on science content and hands-on learning; lectures; newsletter.

10.136 **The Magic House, St. Louis Children's Museum,** 516 S. Kirkwood Rd., St. Louis, MO 63122
(314) 822-8900

Children's museum devoted to providing hands-on learning experiences; emphasis in exhibits and outreach programs on water, magnets, air, simple machines, and much more. *Programs for students:* At the museum: guided/self-guided tours; more than 50 curriculum-related hands-on exhibits; Piaget-based Expericenter (hands-on learning laboratory). At schools: assembly and hands-on learning programs. *Materials:* Activity books; child-oriented guide to each exhibit.

10.137 Missouri Botanical Garden, 4344 Shaw Ave., St. Louis, MO 63110
(314) 577-5140
http://www.mobat.org

Renowned botanical garden, with numerous specialized gardens and greenhouses; additional sites include 2,400-acre Shaw Arboretum, a nature preserve at Gray Summit, and Litzsinger Road Ecology Center in Ladue, Mo. *Programs for students:* At the garden, arboretum, and ecology center: classes; field studies. At the garden and arboretum: guided/self-guided tours; interpretive exhibits. At schools: outreach programs. *Materials:* Hands-on activity books; Suitcase Science Kits (contain information and supplies needed to teach a full unit on physical or life science) for loan locally; teacher's guides; audiovisual and computer-based materials. *Education and support for teachers:* In-service education on science content and hands-on learning, including summer workshops and travel-study programs; teacher resource center.

10.138 St. Louis Science Center, 5050 Oakland Ave., St. Louis, MO 63110
(314) 289-4444
http://www.slsc.org

Science center, including a planetarium, Omnimax theater, and a discovery room, and featuring more than 600 hands-on exhibits on technology, human society, ecology and the environment, and space science. *Programs for students:* At the museum: interactive demonstrations (grades 3-8); hands-on rooms; planetarium and laser light shows. At schools: Outreach Van, with demonstrations, dynamic activities; portable planetarium

programs; science festivals. *Materials:* Teacher's guides; extensive pre-/postvisit materials; lending boxes of hands-on materials; audiovisual materials. *Education and support for teachers:* In-service education on hands-on learning; previsit briefings; newsletter.

10.139 St. Louis Zoological Park, Forest Park, St. Louis, MO 63110
(314) 768-5466

Zoo with more than 4,300 animals, and featuring a Classroom of the Future. *Programs for students:* At the zoo: classes with live-animal demonstrations; docent-led tours; hands-on exhibits; self-guided scavenger hunts. At schools: outreach programs; traveling exhibits. *Materials:* Hands-on activity books; lending boxes of hands-on materials (Zoocase Science Kits); 6-week science curriculum units; teacher's guides; audiovisual and computer-based materials; catalog of materials. *Education and support for teachers:* In-service workshops on science content and hands-on learning; library and teacher resource center; newsletter.

Nebraska

10.140 Hastings Museum, 1330 N. Burlington, Hastings, NE 68901 *(Mailing address: P.O. Box 1286, Hastings, NE 68902-1286)*
(402) 461-4629

General and natural history museum, with a planetarium, an IMAX theater, and a Discovery Center; focused on astronomy, biology, zoology, geology, paleontology, archaeology, and space science. *Programs for students:* At the museum: hands-on exhibits; presentations for school groups; planetarium shows; IMAX films; orientation and self-guided tours. *Materials:* Information packets

including suggested activities; teacher's manuals for films. *Education and support for teachers:* In-service workshops on hands-on learning; film previews.

10.141 Henry Doorly Zoo, 3701 S. 10th St., Omaha, NE 68107-2200
(402) 733-8401

Zoological park featuring more than 2,000 animals, with emphasis on wildlife conservation. *Programs for students:* At the zoo: hands-on exhibits; guided/self-guided tours; classroom programs. At schools: zoomobile visits; speakers bureau. *Materials:* Teacher's guides; activity guides; audiovisual materials. *Education and support for teachers:* In-service workshops on science content; newsletter.

10.142 University of Nebraska State Museum, 307 Morrill Hall, 14th and U Sts., Lincoln, NE 68588-0338
(402) 472-2637
http://www.museum.unl.edu

Natural science museum, with a planetarium and a discovery room; emphasizes life science, earth science and paleontology, and space science. *Programs for students:* At the museum: Encounter Center (discovery) programs; planetarium and laser light shows; guided tours; hands-on gallery programs; field trips. At schools: outreach programs; traveling exhibits. *Materials:* Lending boxes of hands-on materials; lesson plans; audiovisual and computer-based materials; catalog of materials. *Education and support for teachers:* In-service workshops and programs on science content and hands-on learning; National Aeronautics and Space Administration (NASA) Teacher Resource Center; newsletter.

North Dakota

10.143 Gateway to Science Center, 2700 State St., Gateway Mall, Bismarck, ND 58501
(701) 258-1975

Science center focused on the physical, life, earth, and atmospheric sciences and engineering. *Programs for students:* At the center: hands-on exhibits; programs for school groups; guided/self-guided tours. *Materials:* Activity questionnaires; instructional materials; posters; newsletter for students. *Education and support for teachers:* In-service workshops on science content and hands-on learning; newsletter.

10.144 Roosevelt Park Zoo, 1219 Burdick Expressway, E., Minot, ND 58701 *(Mailing address: P.O. Box 538, Minot, ND 58702)*
(701) 857-4166

Zoo and regional center for wildlife education, featuring approximately 200 mammals, birds, and reptiles, with a children's zoo and a zoo education center. *Programs for students:* At the zoo: classes; guided tours. At the center: exhibit area for hands-on, interactive activities. At schools: outreach programs; traveling exhibits. *Materials:* Teacher's guides; audiovisual materials. *Education and support for teachers:* Reference center (at the zoo education center) with wildlife books and magazines.

South Dakota

10.145 South Dakota Discovery Center and Aquarium, 805 W. Sioux Ave., Pierre, SD 57501 *(Mailing address: P.O. Box 1054, Pierre, SD 57501)*
(605) 224-8295

Discovery center and aquarium, with a planetarium, and Discovery Island (150 meters away in the Missouri River). *Programs for students:* At the center: hands-on exhibits; planetarium shows; laboratory activities; guided tours. On Discovery Island: wetlands ecology field site. At schools in South Dakota, Nebraska, and North Dakota: outreach programs; traveling exhibits; portable planetarium. *Materials:* Lending kits.

SOUTH CENTRAL REGION

Arkansas

10.146 **Arkansas Museum of Science and History,** MacArthur Park, Little Rock, AR 72202
(501) 324-9231

Science and history museum concentrating on natural sciences, life sciences, and geology. *Programs for students:* At the museum: classes with some live animals; hands-on exhibits. At schools: outreach programs with live animals; 6-week series of summer classes traveling the state to rural areas. *Materials:* Loans of kits; teacher's guides; audiovisual materials; catalog of materials. *Education and support for teachers:* In-service education on science content and hands-on learning.

Louisiana

10.147 **Aquarium of the Americas,** Audubon Institute, One Canal St., New Orleans, LA 70178 *(Mailing address: Education Department, 111 Iberville St., Suite 500, New Orleans, LA 70130)*
(504) 565-3033

Internationally known aquarium, with an IMAX theater; exhibits about 8,000 animals from the waters in and around North, Central, and South America in 5 galleries, each focused on a different habitat. *Programs for students:* At the aquarium: hands-on touch-pool

exhibits; workshops; participatory shows. At schools: outreach programs. *Materials:* Hands-on activity books; lending boxes of hands-on materials; teacher's guides; audiovisual materials. *Education and support for teachers:* In-service workshops on science content, hands-on learning, and regional and national curriculum projects; newsletter.

10.148 **Audubon Zoological Garden,** Audubon Institute, 6500 Magazine St., Audubon Park, New Orleans, LA 70118 *(Mailing address: P.O. Box 4327, New Orleans, LA 70178)*
(504) 861-2537

Zoological garden with more than 1,400 animals representing 360 species; located within a 365-acre urban park with more than 1,200 kinds of exotic and indigenous flora. *Programs for students:* At the zoo: presentations; hands-on exhibits. At schools: outreach programs. *Materials:* Hands-on activity books; teacher's guides; lending boxes of hands-on materials; audiovisual materials. *Education and support for teachers:* In-service workshops on science content and hands-on learning in several areas of natural history; some workshops on national curriculum projects; newsletter.

10.149 **Greater Baton Rouge Zoo,** 3601 Thomas Rd., Baton Rouge, LA 70807 *(Mailing address: P.O. Box 60, Baker, LA 70704)*
(504) 775-3877

Municipal zoo; emphasis in educational programs on conservation, natural history, environmental awareness, and global environmental issues. *Programs for students:* At the zoo: hands-on exhibits; programs for school groups; guided/self-guided tours. At schools: out-

reach programs with slide shows and live animals. *Materials:* Audiovisual materials. *Education and support for teachers:* Workshops on hands-on learning.

10.150 **Louisiana Arts and Science Center,** 100 S. River Rd., Baton Rouge, LA 70802 *(Mailing address: P.O. Box 3373, Baton Rouge, LA 70821)*
(504) 344-5272

Arts and science center with a Challenger Learning Center and Science Station—a hands-on physical science gallery primarily designed for grades 3-9; exhibits focus on light and color, sound, electricity and magnetism, and simple machines. *Programs for students:* At the center: National Aeronautics and Space Administration (NASA) flight simulations (in the Challenger Learning Center); hands-on exhibits; guided tours; weekend and summer workshops. At schools: outreach programs. *Materials:* Teacher's guides. *Education and support for teachers:* In-service workshops on science content and hands-on learning.

10.151 **Louisiana Nature Center,** Joe W. Brown Memorial Park, Nature Center Drive, New Orleans, LA 70127 *(Mailing address: P.O. Box 870610, New Orleans, LA 70187-0610)*
(504) 246-5672

Nature center with a planetarium and greenhouse located in the New Orleans metropolitan area, and having direct access to an urban forest and wetlands area that includes wildflower and butterfly gardens and hiking trails. *Programs for students:* At the center: classes, guided/self-guided tours;

hands-on exhibits; field trips. At schools: outreach programs. *Materials:* Teacher's guides; lending boxes of hands-on materials; audio-visual materials. *Education and support for teachers:* In-service workshops on science content and hands-on learning; newsletter.

10.152 Sci-Port Discovery Center, 101 Milam St., Shreveport, LA 71101
(318) 424-3466

Science center actively involved with the Louisiana Statewide Systemic Initiative (LSSI) in teacher training and support; emphasis on the physical, life, space, and some earth sciences. *Programs for students:* At the center: workshops; summer science series with activities and materials. At schools: outreach programs; traveling exhibits. *Materials:* Teacher's packets, including hands-on experiments related to exhibits. *Education and support for teachers:* In-service education on science content.

Oklahoma

10.153 Harmon Science Center, 5707 E. 41st St., Tulsa, OK 74135 *(Mailing address: P.O. Box 52568, Tulsa, OK 74152-0568)*
(918) 622-5000
http://hsc.tulsa.k12.ok.us

Interactive science center with emphasis on chemistry, geology, geophysics, and applied mathematics. *Programs for students:* At the center: classes; field trips; hands-on exhibits. At schools: outreach programs. *Materials:* Curriculum units with hands-on materials; portable planetarium. *Education and support for teachers:* In-service education on science content and hands-on learning.

10.154 Kirkpatrick Science and Air Space Museum of Omniplex, 2100 N.E. 52nd St., Oklahoma City, OK 73111-7198
(405) 424-5545

Science and technology museum, featuring more than 300 hands-on exhibits and about 100 science and planetarium programs; focused on geology, astronomy, paleontology, and the physical and life sciences; part of the larger Kirkpatrick Center Museum Complex. *Programs for students:* At the museum: hands-on exhibits; science and planetarium programs. *Materials:* Teacher's guides; loans of equipment; catalog of materials. *Education and support for teachers:* In-service workshops on science content and hands-on learning; telephone support and conferences.

10.155 Oklahoma City Zoo, 2101 N.E. 50th St., Oklahoma City, OK 73111
(405) 424-3344

Zoo with an aquarium and an exotic horticultural collection. *Programs for students:* At the zoo: guided tours; hands-on classes and labs on animals. At schools: outreach programs. *Materials:* Hands-on activity books; loan of Suitcase for Survival (containing endangered-animal artifacts). *Education and support for teachers:* Workshops.

Texas

10.156 Dallas Museum of Natural History, First Avenue and Grand in Fair Park, Dallas, TX 75226 *(Mailing address: P.O. Box 150349, Fair Park Station, Dallas, TX 75315)*
(214) 670-8466

Museum with a discovery center, focusing on the native plants and animals of Texas, including fossils. *Programs for students:* At the museum: classes; guided tours;

hands-on exhibits. At schools: outreach programs; traveling exhibits. *Materials:* Lending boxes of hands-on materials; teacher's guides; pre-/postvisit and audiovisual materials; catalog of materials. *Education and support for teachers:* In-service workshops on science content and hands-on learning, including Project Wild (environmental education program emphasizing wildlife); teacher resource center; newsletter.

10.157 Don Harrington Discovery Center, 1200 Streit Dr., Amarillo, TX 79106
(806) 355-9547

Discovery center with a planetarium, focused on the physical, life, earth, space, and environmental sciences. *Programs for students:* At the center: hands-on exhibits; classes on science and health; planetarium shows; guided tours. At schools: traveling exhibits. *Materials:* Previsit materials. *Education and support for teachers:* In-service education on hands-on learning; newsletter.

10.158 Environmental Science Center, 8856 Westview Dr., Houston, TX 77055
(713) 465-9628

Science center, with a 5-acre arboretum, botanical garden, and outdoor classroom; focused on wildlife, botany, natural history, geology, and oceanography. *Programs for students:* At the center: hands-on programs for school classes. At schools: outreach programs; traveling exhibits. *Materials:* Hands-on activity books; loans of specimens, kits, and audiovisual materials; posters; catalog of materials; newsletter for students. *Education and support for teachers:* In-service education on science content and hands-on learning; newsletter.

10.159 Fort Worth Museum of Science and History, 1501 Montgomery St., Fort Worth, TX 76107-3079
(817) 732-1631

Museum founded in 1941 in an elementary school, with a planetarium and Omni theater; focused on paleontology, astronomy, and natural history. *Programs for students:* At the museum: programs for school groups; guided tours; hands-on exhibits. *Materials:* Lending boxes of hands-on materials; teacher's guides. *Education and support for teachers:* Workshops on science content, with field trips and hands-on activities; preview events for Omni films and planetarium programs.

10.160 Fort Worth Zoological Park, 1989 Colonial Pkwy., Fort Worth, TX 76110
(817) 871-7000

Zoo, including education center with classrooms and a library; emphasis on wildlife and habitat conservation. *Programs for students:* At the zoo: classes; programs for school groups. At schools: outreach programs. *Materials:* Hands-on activity books; lending boxes of hands-on materials; teacher's guides. *Education and support for teachers:* In-service education on science content and hands-on learning; workshops.

10.161 Heard Natural Science Museum and Wildlife Sanctuary, One Nature Place, McKinney, TX 75069-8840
(214) 562-5566

Natural science museum, located on a 274-acre wildlife sanctuary with nature trails; emphasis on natural science, ecology, and the environment. *Programs for students:* At the museum: programs for school groups; labs; guided/self-guided tours; field studies. At schools: outreach programs. *Education and support for teachers:* In-service education on science content and hands-on learning.

10.162 Houston Museum of Natural Science, One Hermann Circle Dr., Houston, TX 77030
(713) 639-4600
http://www.hmns.mus.tx.us/hmns/home.html

Natural science museum with a planetarium, IMAX theater, Challenger Space Science Center, and off-site observatory; emphasis on physical, space, earth, and life sciences. *Programs for students:* At the museum: exploratorium of hands-on exhibits; guided tours; classes; field trips. At schools: outreach programs; traveling exhibits. *Materials:* Hands-on activity books; lending boxes of hands-on materials and living things; teacher's guides; audiovisual and computer-based materials; catalog of materials. *Education and support for teachers:* In-service workshops on science content and hands-on learning; newsletter.

10.163 Houston Zoological Gardens, Hermann Park, 1513 N. MacGregor, Houston, TX 77030
(713) 520-3200
http://keck.tamu.edu/HoustonZoo

Zoological garden, including children's zoo, aquarium, mammal marina, and education center; emphasis on wildlife conservation. *Programs for students:* At the zoo: classes; hands-on exhibits; self-guided tours. At schools: outreach programs with zoomobile. *Materials:* Packet of pre-/postvisit activi-ties. *Education and support for teachers:* In-service education on science content and hands-on learning.

10.164 Insights—El Paso Science Center, 505 N. Santa Fe, El Paso, TX 79901
(915) 542-2990

Participatory science museum serving large sections of Texas, New Mexico, and the Mexican State of Chihuahua; focusing on perceptions in energy, physical science, motion, earth science, microcomputers, and human anatomy. *Programs for students:* At the museum: classes; guided/self-guided tours; more than 180 interactive exhibits; field trips. At schools: outreach programs; traveling exhibits. *Materials:* Hands-on activity books; teacher's guides; audiovisual and computer-based materials. *Education and support for teachers:* In-service workshops on science content and hands-on learning; field trips; newsletter.

10.165 National Wildflower Research Center, 4801 La Crosse Ave., Austin, TX 78739
(512) 292-4200

Botanical garden and nature center with a research library, focused on preservation and reestablishment of North American native plants. *Programs for students:* At the center: classes; guided/self-guided tours; hands-on exhibits. At schools: outreach programs. *Materials:* Curriculum materials for prekindergarten through grade 6; teacher's guides; regional audiovisual materials; posters; catalog of materials. *Education and support for teachers:* In-service workshops on science content and hands-on learning; information hotline; speaker series.

10.166 The Science Place, Southwest Museum of Science and Technology, 1318 Second Ave. in Fair Park, Dallas, TX 75210 (*Mailing address: P.O. Box 151469, Dallas, TX 75315-1469*)
(214) 428-7200

Science center with a planetarium, emphasizing physics, chemistry, biology, astronomy, health, dinosaurs, and mathematics. *Programs for students:* At the center: classes; guided tours; planetarium shows; hands-on exhibits; field trips. At schools: outreach programs; traveling exhibits. *Materials:* Lending boxes of hands-on materials; teacher's guides; audiovisual materials; catalog of materials. *Education and support for teachers:* In-service workshops on science content and hands-on learning; newsletter.

10.167 Sea World of Texas, 10500 Sea World Dr., San Antonio, TX 78251
(210) 523-3606
http://www.bev.net/education/SeaWorld

Marine zoological park with living learning centers, focused on marine and environmental science. *Programs for students:* At Sea World: guided/self-guided tours; presentations with animals; field trips; classes. At schools: outreach programs. *Materials:* Teacher's guides; audiovisual materials; posters; catalog of materials. *Education and support for teachers:* Workshops.

10.168 Space Center Houston, 1601 NASA Road One, Houston, TX 77058 (*Mailing address: P.O. Box 580653, Houston, TX 77258-0653*)
(713) 244-2105

Space center, designed for both education and entertainment, providing a variety of space experiences and serving as the visitor complex for the Johnson Space Center of the National Aeronautics and Space Administration (NASA).

Programs for students: At the center: self-guided class visits; hands-on exhibits, including computer simulators. *Materials:* Classroom activities; hands-on activity books and accompanying teacher's guides on space exhibits and attractions at the center. *Education and support for teachers:* Briefings on space science topics; newsletter.

10.169 The Witte Museum, 3801 Broadway, San Antonio, TX 78209-6396
(210) 820-2181

General history and natural science museum with a science education center, focusing on science and the humanities. *Programs for students:* At the museum: demonstrations and live science theater presentations; hands-on exhibits. At schools: outreach programs. *Materials:* Teacher's guides; audiovisual materials. *Education and support for teachers:* In-service workshops on science content and hands-on learning; evenings for educators; internships for preservice teachers; newsletter.

GREAT LAKES REGION

Illinois

10.170 **The Adler Planetarium and Astronomy Museum**, 1300 S. Lake Shore Dr., Chicago, IL 60605
(312) 922-STAR
http://astro.uchicago.edu/adler

Planetarium and science museum focusing on astronomy, astrophysics, and the history of science; 1 of a constellation of 3 lakeside museums, along with the Field Museum and the John G. Shedd Aquarium. *Programs for students:* At the planetarium: classes; hands-on exhibits. At schools: outreach programs, including portable planetarium visits. *Materials:* Hands-on previsit materials; curriculum materials. *Education and support for teachers:* In-service workshops on science content; library with curriculum materials.

10.171 **Chicago Botanic Garden**, 1000 Lake-Cook Rd., Glencoe, IL 60022 *(Mailing address: P.O. Box 400, Glencoe, IL 60022-0400)*
(847) 835-5440

Living museum on 380 acres, with special emphasis on native plant communities—woodlands, prairies, and wetlands—and including an education center. *Programs for students:* At the garden: guided tours; hands-on exhibits; field trips; programs designed to complement school curriculum. At schools:

outreach programs throughout the Chicago area. *Materials:* Lending boxes of hands-on materials; curriculum materials; teacher's guides. *Education and support for teachers:* In-service workshops on science content and hands-on learning; newsletter.

10.172 **Chicago Zoological Park (Brookfield Zoo)**, 8400 W. 31st St., Brookfield, IL 60513 *(Mailing address: 3300 Golf Rd., Brookfield, IL 60513)*
(708) 485-0263

Chicago's major zoo, with more than 2,000 animals representing more than 400 species, many in naturalistic habitats; emphasis on conservation. *Programs for students:* At the zoo: hands-on exhibits; classes; guided/self-guided tours. *Materials:* Hands-on activity books; teacher's guides; pre-/post-visit materials developed in collaboration with teachers to enhance classroom studies; audiovisual materials; brochure of programs and materials. *Education and support for teachers:* In-service education on science content and hands-on learning; newsletter.

10.173 **Discovery Center Museum**, 711 N. Main St., Rockford, IL 61103
(815) 963-6769

Science center with a planetarium and an outdoor science park, focused on astronomy and physical sciences. *Programs for students:* At the museum: classes; guided tours; hands-on exhibits; summer programs for middle school girls. At schools: outreach programs; traveling exhibits. *Materials:* Hands-on activity books; teacher's guides. *Education and support for teachers:* Workshops and classes on science content and hands-on learning; newsletter.

10.174 **Fermilab Lederman Science Education Center**, Batavia, IL 60510 *(Mailing address: P.O. Box 500, MS777, Batavia, IL 60510)*
General information: (630) 840-8258
Teacher Resource Center: (630) 840-3094
http://www-ed.fnal.gov

Fermilab, a world-famous high-energy physics laboratory that offers an extensive science education program; emphasizes physics, physical science, technology, and prairie-related topics. *Programs for students:* At Fermilab: curriculum-related field trips; interactive teaching/learning stations; informal classes emphasizing hands-on learning and process skills. At schools: hands-on exhibits and previsit activities. *Materials:* Curriculum units; audiovisual and computer-based materials; catalog of materials. *Education and support for teachers:* In-service workshops on science content, pedagogy, technology, and integration; teacher resource center for previewing extensive collection of science education materials; directory of regional science resources; newsletter.

10.175 **The Field Museum**, Roosevelt Road at Lake Shore Drive, Chicago, IL 60605-2496
(312) 922-9410
http://www.bvis.uic.edu/museum

World-renowned research institution and museum focused on evolutionary biology and the environment and on cultural understanding and change, with more than 21 million specimens and artifacts in anthropology, botany, geology, and zoology; 1 of a constellation of 3 lakeside museums, along with the Adler Planetarium and Astronomy Museum and the John G. Shedd

Aquarium. *Programs for students:* At the museum: classes; guided tours; hands-on exhibits. At schools: traveling exhibits. *Materials:* Hands-on activity books; lending boxes/kits; teacher's guides; audiovisual materials; catalog of materials. *Education and support for teachers:* In-service workshops on science content and hands-on learning; training for teaching in urban neighborhoods; newsletter.

10.176 Illinois State Museum, Spring and Edwards Streets, Springfield, IL 62706
(217) 782-5993
http://www.museum.state.il.us

Museum, with a discovery room, focused on the natural history, culture, and art of Illinois; emphasis on botany, geology, zoology, and anthropology. *Programs for students:* At the museum: programs for school groups; guided/self-guided tours; hands-on exhibits. *Materials:* Lesson plans; curriculum materials; computer-based materials; catalog of materials; magazine for students. *Education and support for teachers:* In-service workshops on science content and hands-on learning.

10.177 John G. Shedd Aquarium, 1200 S. Lake Shore Dr., Chicago, IL 60605
(312) 939-2426

Aquarium and oceanarium, including an aquatic science center, with more than 6,000 aquatic animals representing every region of the world; 1 of a constellation of 3 lakeside museums (along with the Field Museum and the Adler Planetarium and Astronomy Museum).

Programs for students: At the aquarium: workshops and classes for student groups; hands-on exhibits; self-guided tours; local field trips. *Materials:* Lending boxes/kits; teacher's guides. *Education and support for teachers:* In-service education on science content and hands-on learning; teacher resource center; field trips.

10.178 Lincoln Park Zoological Gardens, 2200 N. Cannon Dr., Chicago, IL 60614
(312) 294-4649
http://www.lpzoo.com

City zoo on 35 acres of parkland, including a children's zoo with a conservation station and hands-on farm area. *Programs for students:* At the zoo: programs and classes for students; guided/self-guided tours; exhibit-based learning stations. At schools: outreach programs; animals-in-the-classroom programs. *Materials:* Hands-on activity books; teacher's guides; audiovisual and computer-based materials. *Education and support for teachers:* School-based programs, in collaboration with museum partners and university.

10.179 The Morton Arboretum, Rte. 53, Lisle, IL 60532
(708) 719-2462
http://www.mortonarb.org

Arboretum on 1,700 acres, with a library and research center, focused on natural history, botany, and regional ecology. *Programs for students:* At the arboretum: classes; guided/self-guided tours. *Materials:* Hands-on activity books; activity sheets. *Education and support for teachers:* In-service education on science content and hands-on learning; workshops and classes.

10.180 Museum of Science and Industry, 57th Street and Lake Shore Drive, Chicago, IL 60637
(312) 684-1414

World-renowned, interactive museum, with more than 2,000 exhibits in 71 exhibit zones, and featuring learning laboratories embedded within museum exhibits for grades 5-8; emphasis on science, technology, and industry. *Programs for students:* At the museum: programs for school groups; interactive exhibits; guided tours; workshops; live demonstrations and interpretation. At schools: outreach programs, including Science Club Network. *Materials:* Hands-on activity books; teacher's guides; pre-/postvisit and audiovisual materials. *Education and support for teachers:* In-service education and teacher-parent workshops on science content, curriculum planning, and hands-on learning; newsletter.

10.181 The Nature Museum, Chicago Academy of Sciences, 435 E. Illinois St., at Lake Shore Drive, Chicago, IL 60614 *(Mailing address: 2060 N. Clark St., Chicago, IL 60614)*
(773) 549-0606
http://www.chias.org

Natural science museum with a children's gallery, in the Chicago Academy of Sciences, focused on natural history. *Programs for students:* At the museum: science lab activities; field studies; guided/self-guided tours; hands-on exhibits. At schools: outreach programs. *Materials:* Teacher's guides. *Education and support for teachers:* In-service workshops on science content and hands-on learning.

10.182 SciTech—Science and Technology Interactive Center, 18 W. Benton, Aurora, IL 60506 (630) 859-8112 http://town.hall.org/places/SciTech

Science and technology center, emphasizing the physical sciences, mathematics, and developing technologies, and featuring more than 200 hands-on exhibits and a solar telescope. *Programs for students:* At the center: classes; guided tours; hands-on exhibits; field trips; demonstrations. At schools: outreach classes with hands-on exhibits (grades 4-8); science demonstrations. *Materials:* Hands-on materials for outreach programs. *Education and support for teachers:* In-service education on science content and hands-on learning linked to outreach programs.

Indiana

10.183 The Children's Museum of Indianapolis, 3000 N. Meridian St., Indianapolis, IN 46208 *(Mailing address: P.O. Box 3000, Indianapolis, IN 46206)* (317) 924-5431 http://www.a1.com/children/home.html

World's largest children's museum, with a 310-seat, large-format, domed theater; state-of-the-art science gallery; and nature preserve; focused on natural and physical sciences, history, art, and cultural studies. *Programs for students:* At the museum: classes; guided tours; hands-on exhibits; lending library; apprentice opportunities. At the nature preserve: outdoor education. *Materials:* Loans of materials, including kits, science mounts and specimens, and artifacts; pre-/postvisit materials. *Education and support for teachers:* In-service education on science content; resource center; community resource database.

10.184 Fort Wayne Children's Zoo, 3411 Sherman Blvd., Fort Wayne, IN 46808 (219) 427-6800

Zoo on 40 acres, with more than 1,000 animals and 3 hands-on exhibit centers. *Programs for students:* At the zoo: miniclasses; in-depth exploration programs; hands-on exhibits. At schools: outreach programs. *Materials:* Lending boxes of hands-on materials; teacher's guides; audiovisual materials; grade-specific packets for teachers with suggestions for pre-/postvisit activities; catalog of materials. *Education and support for teachers:* In-service education on science content and hands-on learning; newsletter.

10.185 Indianapolis Zoo, 1200 W. Washington St., Indianapolis, IN 46222 *(Mailing address: P.O. Box 22309, Indianapolis, IN 46222-0309)* (317) 630-2040 http://www.indyzoo.com

Zoo designed around habitats, with animals in simulated natural environments; emphasis on preservation of species diversity. *Programs for students:* At the zoo: educational programs; hands-on exhibits; long-distance learning program. At schools: outreach programs. *Materials:* Lending boxes of hands-on materials; teacher's guides; audiovisual materials. *Education and support for teachers:* In-service workshops on hands-on learning; newsletter.

Michigan

10.186 Ann Arbor Hands-On Museum, 219 E. Huron St., Ann Arbor, MI 48104 (313) 995-5439

Science and technology center with more than 200 interactive exhibits, a computer room, a discovery room, and a greenhouse; emphasis on physics, biology, human perception, and geology. *Programs for students:* At the museum: guided tours; hands-on exhibits; classes; field trips. At schools: outreach programs; traveling exhibits. *Materials:* Hands-on activity books; computer-based materials; catalog of materials. *Education and support for teachers:* Newsletter.

10.187 Cranbrook Institute of Science, 1221 N. Woodward Ave., Bloomfield Hills, MI 48303 *(Mailing address: P.O. Box 801, Bloomfield Hills, MI 48303-0801)* (313) 645-3230

Science center, with a planetarium, observatory, participatory physics hall, natural history exhibits, and a nature center with a discovery room and 315 acres of grounds. *Programs for students:* At the institute: programs for student groups; hands-on exhibit. At schools in southeast Michigan: outreach programs. *Education and support for teachers:* In-service workshops on science content and hands-on learning.

10.188 Fernwood Botanic Garden, 13988 Range Line Rd., Niles, MI 49120-9042 (616) 683-8653

Botanic garden and nature preserve, with emphasis on botany and horticulture; on ecological issues concerning water, wildlife, and native and rare flora and fauna; and on the arts. *Programs for students:* At the garden and preserve: classes; hands-on exhibits; guided/self-guided tours; field programs. At schools: programs with naturalists. *Materials:* Hands-on activity books; curriculum units; teacher's guides; audiovisual materials; posters. *Education and support for teachers:* In-service education on science content and hands-on learning; resource library; newsletter.

10.189 Gerald E. Eddy Geology Center, 17030 Bush Rd., Chelsea, MI 48118 *(Mailing address: 16345 McClure Rd., Chelsea, MI 48118)* (313) 475-3170 http://www.eecs.umich.edu/ mathscience/exploringsci/ tourlisting/eddyinfo.html

Geology museum and visitor center for 20,000-acre Waterloo Recreation Area, featuring Michigan rocks, minerals, fossils, crystals, and glacial information; focused on geology and natural science. *Programs for students:* At the center: programs for school groups; guided/self-guided tours; hands-on exhibits. At schools: outreach programs. *Materials:* Audiovisual materials; posters. *Education and support for teachers:* Lectures.

10.190 Hall of Ideas, Midland Center for the Arts, 1801 W. Saint Andrews Rd., Midland, MI 48640 (517) 631-5930

Science, art, and history museum within a performing arts center; focused on geology and the environment and the relationship of science to the arts and humanities. *Programs for students:* At the museum: classes; guided tours; hands-on exhibits. At schools: outreach programs; traveling exhibits. *Materials:* Teacher's guides; audiovisual and computer-based materials; catalog of materials. *Education and support for teachers:* In-service education on science content and hands-on learning; workshops; newsletter.

10.191 Impression 5 Science Center, 200 Museum Dr., Lansing, MI 48933-1922 (517) 485-8116

Science and technology center focused on chemistry, physics, and the environmental and biological sciences. *Programs for students:* At the museum: demonstrations; workshops; hands-on exhibits; summer science camp. At schools: outreach programs. *Materials:* Newsletter for students. *Education and support for teachers:* In-service workshops on science content and hands-on learning.

10.192 Kalamazoo Valley Museum, 230 N. Rose St., Kalamazoo, MI 49003 *(Mailing address: P.O. Box 4070, Kalamazoo, MI 49003-4070)* (616) 373-7990

Museum of history and science and technology, with a Digistar II planetarium and Challenger Learning Center. *Programs for students:* At the museum: hands-on exhibits; planetarium shows; space mission simulations. At schools: outreach programs. *Materials:* Curriculum materials; teacher's guides; lending boxes of hands-on materials; audiovisual materials. *Education and support for teachers:* Workshops; newsletter.

10.193 Kingman Museum of Natural History, West Michigan Avenue at 20th Street, Battle Creek, MI 49017 (616) 965-5117 http://www.quikpage.com/K/ kingmuseum

Natural history museum with a planetarium, located in the Leila Arboretum; focused on earth and natural history, astronomy, and the human body. *Programs for students:* At the museum: classes;

guided/self-guided tours; hands-on exhibits. At schools: outreach programs; traveling exhibits. *Materials:* Hands-on activity books; Discovery Kits; teacher's guide; catalog of materials; newsletter for students. *Education and support for teachers:* In-service workshops on science content; library; newsletter.

10.194 Michigan Space and Science Center, Jackson Community College, 2111 Emmons Rd., Jackson, MI 49201 (517) 787-4425 http://www.jackson.cc.mi.us/ centers/michigan_space_center/ default.html

Space museum and educational center for the space sciences; exhibits focus on space exploration, astronomy, physics, geology, mathematics, electronics, and biology. *Programs for students:* At the museum: self-guided tours; hands-on exhibits; films in Astro Theatre. *Materials:* Kits with materials and instructions; previsit and audiovisual materials. *Education and support for teachers:* In-service education on science content.

10.195 Michigan State University Museum, West Circle Drive, East Lansing, MI 48224 (517) 355-2373

Natural and cultural history museum, with emphasis on life and earth sciences and the environment. *Programs for students:* At the museum: guided tours; classes. At schools: outreach programs. *Materials:* Lending boxes of hands-on materials; teacher's guides; audiovisual and computer-based materials. *Education and support for teachers:* In-service education on science content; workshops; newsletter.

Ohio

10.196 Aullwood Audubon Center and Farm, 1000 Aullwood Rd., Dayton, OH 45414
(513) 890-7360

Regional environmental education center of the National Audubon Society for the 7-state Great Lakes region, with a 350-acre sanctuary including a working educational farm. *Programs for students:* At the center: classes; guided/self-guided tours; hands-on exhibits. At schools: occasional programs. *Materials:* Hands-on activity books; curriculum units with hands-on materials; teacher's guides; pre-/postvisit materials; audiovisual materials; magazine for students, *Audubon Adventures*. *Education and support for teachers:* In-service workshops and courses on science content and hands-on learning; field trips; newsletters; magazine, *Audubon*.

10.197 Cincinnati Museum of Natural History and Planetarium, Museum Center at Union Terminal, 1301 Western Ave., Cincinnati, OH 45203
(513) 287-7020
http://www.cincymuseum.org

Research-based museum with a highly interactive children's discovery center. *Programs for students:* At the museum: classes; demonstrations; field trips; hands-on exhibits. At schools: outreach programs. *Materials:* Teacher's guides. *Education and support for teachers:* In-service workshops on science content; newsletter.

10.198 Cleveland Botanical Garden, 11030 East Boulevard, Cleveland, OH 44106
(216) 721-1600

Botanical garden with a reference library, emphasizing hands-on science through garden activities.

Programs for students: At the garden: classes; guided/self-guided tours; hands-on exhibits. At schools: outreach programs, including home gardening/seed distribution program and school/community gardens. *Materials:* Teacher's guides; horticultural supplies; audiovisual materials; children's gardening resource directory. *Education and support for teachers:* In-service workshops on science content and hands-on learning; newsletter.

10.199 Cleveland Metroparks Zoo, 3900 Brookside Park Dr., Cleveland, OH 44109
(216) 661-6500
http://www.clemetzoo.com

One of America's oldest zoos, on 165 acres in the heart of the city, with an education center and wide-ranging programs in conservation education. *Programs for students:* At the zoo: classes; programs; guided/self-guided tours; hands-on exhibits; field studies. At schools: outreach programs; traveling exhibits. *Materials:* Lending boxes of hands-on materials; teacher's guides; videos; newsletter for students. *Education and support for teachers:* In-service workshops on science content and hands-on learning; newsletter.

10.200 The Cleveland Museum of Natural History, One Wade Oval Dr., University Circle, Cleveland, OH 44106-1767
(216) 231-4600; (800) 317-9155
http://www.cmnh.org

Major research-based natural history museum, with an observatory, a planetarium, and natural areas. *Programs for students:* At the museum: gallery programs; self-guided tours; presentations with live animals; hands-on programs; obser-

vatory/planetarium programs; field studies. At schools: outreach programs, with live animals; portable planetarium. *Materials:* Extensive loan program (including portable dioramas, teaching kits, curriculum units, activity guides, slide sets, and videos); catalog of materials. *Education and support for teachers:* In-service workshops on science content and hands-on learning; extensive science resource center; travel/study trips; newsletter.

10.201 COSI/Columbus—Ohio's Center Of Science and Industry, 280 E. Broad St., Columbus, OH 43215-3773
(614) 228-2674
http://cosi.org

Hands-on science center with a planetarium and featured-exhibition area; emphasis on learning opportunities in physical sciences and technology, history, earth sciences, health, and life science. *Programs for students:* At the center: hundreds of interactive exhibits, classes, shows, and demonstrations. At schools throughout Ohio and in parts of Kentucky, Michigan, Pennsylvania, and West Virginia: extensive outreach programs, with assemblies and hands-on classes. *Materials:* Catalog of Fun in Science kits. *Education and support for teachers*: In-service workshops on science content and hands-on learning.

10.202 Dayton Museum of Discovery, 2600 DeWeese Pkwy., Dayton, OH 45414
(513) 275-7431

Museum consisting of Caryl D. Philips Space Theater (Digistar planetarium), Dayton Science Center (physical sciences), Wild Ohio Exhibit (indoor zoo with animals native to Ohio), Bieser Discovery Center (hands-on life and earth science gallery), and exhibit galleries. *Programs for students:* At the museum: planetarium shows; hands-on natural and cultural history and physical science programs; guided/self-guided tours. At schools: talks, with live animals. *Materials:* Geology loan kits; previsit activity packet for field trip programs. *Education and support for teachers:* In-service workshops on hands-on learning.

10.203 Great Lakes Science Center, 601 Erieside Ave., Cleveland, OH 44114
(216) 694-2000

Science center with an Omnimax theater and a mathematics and science resource center; focused on regional and global environmental concerns and on the interdependence of science, the environment, and technology. *Programs for students:* At the center: hands-on exhibits; guided tours; classes; field trips; demonstrations. At schools: outreach programs. *Education and support for teachers:* In-service workshops on science content and hands-on learning.

10.204 The Holden Arboretum, 9500 Sperry Rd., Kirtland, OH 44094-5172
(216) 256-1110

Largest U.S. arboretum, on 3,100 acres, with a horticultural science center. *Programs for students:* At the arboretum: extensive guided field trip programs and self-guided tours. At schools: outreach programs (limited). *Materials:* Materials for visits; lending boxes of hands-on materials; audiovisual materials for loan. *Education and support for teachers:* In-service workshops and classes on science content and hands-on learning; summer teacher-in-residence program for K-12 teachers to develop

and test a science program; reference library; newsletter.

10.205 Sea World of Ohio, 1100 Sea World Dr., Aurora, OH 44202
(216) 562-8101

Marine-life park, focused on underwater and overwater animals in the park's varied marine environments and on marine ecology. *Programs for students:* At the park: programs for school groups; guided tours; hands-on exhibits; summer classes. At schools: hands-on, interactive assembly programs; traveling exhibits. *Materials:* Activity books; teacher's guides; catalog of materials. *Education and support for teachers:* In-service workshops on science content and hands-on learning.

10.206 University of Toledo Sci-MaTEC, 2801 W. Bancroft St., Toledo, OH 43606
(419) 530-8456

Regional science, mathematics, and technology center, emphasizing physical, life, earth, and space sciences. *Programs for students:* At the center: workshops; field trips; guided tours. At schools: outreach programs. *Materials:* Lending kits of hands-on materials; teacher's guides; audiovisual and computer-based materials; newsletter for students. *Education and support for teachers:* In-service workshops on science content and hands-on learning; information hotline; software library; newsletter.

10.207 The Wilderness Center, 9877 Alabama Ave., S.W., Wilmot, OH 44689 *(Mailing address: P.O. Box 202, Wilmot, OH 44689-0202)*
(330) 359-5235

Nature center, with a planetarium, an observation room, and hiking

trails, emphasizing wildlife conservation, astronomy, and environmental education. *Programs for students:* At the center: programs for school groups; guided/self-guided tours; hands-on exhibits. At schools: outreach programs. *Education and support for teachers:* Workshops; newsletter.

Wisconsin

10.208 Milwaukee County Zoo, 10005 W. Bluemound Rd., Milwaukee, WI 53226
(414) 771-3040

Zoo with an education center, focused on animal science and environmental issues. *Programs for students:* At the zoo: classes; workshops; presentations; guided/self-guided tours; hands-on exhibits. *Materials:* Activity books; pre-/postvisit activities; teacher's guides. *Education and support for teachers:* In-service workshops on science content.

10.209 University of Wisconsin-Madison Arboretum, 1207 Seminole Hwy., Madison, WI 53711
(608) 262-2746

Research-based, university arboretum, with an Earth Partnership Program (EPP) emphasizing prairie restoration. *Programs for students:* At the arboretum: guided tours of 1,100 acres of restored prairies, woodlands, and wetlands; EPP classes. At schools: presentations by naturalists; student-EPP research collaborations. *Materials:* Hands-on activity books; teacher's guides. *Education and support for teachers:* EPP workshops, meetings, and conferences, and EPP summer institutes, all on prairie restoration and hands-on learning, with materials and a newsletter.

SOUTHEAST REGION

Alabama

10.210 **Alabama Museum of Natural History,** Smith Hall, University of Alabama, Tuscaloosa, AL 35487 *(Mailing address: Box 870340, Tuscaloosa, AL 35487-0340)* (205) 348-7550

Natural history museum (headquarters at Smith Hall) and anthropological park (Moundville Archaeological Park), with a paleontological site (Harrell Station Paleontological Site); focused on field studies in geology, archaeology, and natural science. *Programs for students:* At the museum: classes; guided tours; field studies. At schools: outreach programs. *Materials:* Lending boxes of hands-on materials; teacher's guides; audiovisual materials. *Education and support for teachers:* In-service education on science content and hands-on learning.

10.211 **Anniston Museum of Natural History,** 800 Museum Dr., Anniston, AL 36202 *(Mailing address: P.O. Box 1587, Anniston, AL 36202)* (205) 237-6766 http://www.anniston.org

Regional natural history museum and cultural center with nature trails and a wildlife garden, focused on biology, zoology, and the environment. *Programs for students:* At the museum: classes and work-shops; programs with live animals; guided/self-guided tours; hands-on exhibits. At schools: outreach programs with live animals and hands-on objects. *Materials:* Traveling trunks for loan; teacher's guides; audiovisual materials. *Education and support for teachers:* In-service education in science content and hands-on learning; newsletter.

10.212 **Birmingham Botanical Gardens,** 2612 Lane Park Rd., Birmingham, AL 35223 (205) 879-1227

Botanical gardens and bird sanctuary on 67 acres, representing multiple ecosystems; focused on biology, botany, horticulture, and the environment. *Programs for students:* At the gardens: workshops; guided tours. *Materials:* Resource materials; audiovisual materials; 2 Grow Labs (for indoor classroom gardening) for 1- to 2-year loan to schools; catalog of materials. *Education and support for teachers:* Workshops; horticultural library.

10.213 **Birmingham Zoo,** 2630 Cahaba Rd., Birmingham, AL 35223 (205) 871-9447 http://www.bhm.tis.net/zoo

Zoo with a library, focused on wildlife conservation. *Programs for students:* At the zoo: programs and wildlife shows for school groups; self-guided tours. At schools: outreach programs. *Materials*: Loans of biological artifacts; computer-based materials; posters; magazine, *Animal Tracks*. *Education and support for teachers:* In-service workshops on science content and hands-on learning; letter-answering service.

10.214 **The Exploreum Museum of Science,** 1906 Springhill Ave., Mobile, AL 36607 (334) 471-5923

Science museum with programs focusing on the physical and natural sciences; principal exhibitor of national traveling exhibits in the region. *Programs for students:* At the museum: classes; hands-on exhibits; guided/self-guided tours. At schools: outreach programs. *Materials:* Teacher's guides; lending boxes of hands-on materials; audiovisual materials. *Education and support for teachers:* In-service education on hands-on learning; workshops; newsletter.

10.215 **McWane Center,** 1320 22nd St. S., Birmingham, AL 35205 (205) 558-2000

Science and technology center (scheduled to open in 1998), with an Omnimax theater, Challenger Learning Center, and hands-on exhibits; focused on physical science, oceanography, paleontology, the environment, and technology. *Programs for students:* At the center: programs for school groups; self-guided tours; hands-on exhibits. At schools: outreach programs; traveling exhibits. *Materials*: Hands-on activity books; curriculum materials. *Education and support for teachers:* In-service education on science content and hands-on learning; workshops.

10.216 **U.S. Space and Rocket Center,** One Tranquility Base, Huntsville, AL 35805 (800) 63SPACE

Space center with rocket and shuttle parks, a spacedome theater, and a space museum; offers bus tours of the Marshall Space Flight Center of the National Aeronautics and Space

Administration (NASA). *Programs for students:* At the center: classes; hands-on exhibits; 5- to 8-day programs (including U.S. Space Camp, Academy, and Aviation Challenge programs) in aviation and space flight (grades 4-12); field trips. *Materials:* Field trip guide. *Education and support for teachers:* In-service workshops on science content and hands-on learning; NASA Teacher Resource Center.

Florida

10.217 **Discovery Science Center,** 50 S. Magnolia Ave., Ocala, FL 34474
(904) 620-2555

Science center with a weather center and a NOAA (National Oceanic and Atmospheric Administration) weather satellite ground station; focused on physics, astronomy, meteorology, and human physiology. *Programs for students:* At the center: hands-on exhibits and demonstrations. At schools in 14 surrounding counties: portable planetarium programs. *Materials:* Pre-/postvisit materials. *Education and support for teachers:* In-service education on science content and hands-on learning; newsletter.

10.218 **The Florida Aquarium,** 701 Channelside Dr., Tampa, FL 33602
(813) 273-4000

Aquarium with areas devoted to Florida's wetlands, bays and beaches, coral reefs, and offshore waters, and with staffed teaching wet labs in 3 major galleries. *Programs for students:* At the aquarium: auditorium presentations; aqua-class teaching lab and customized wetlab programs; field trips; guided/self-guided tours; hands-on exhibits. At schools: out-

reach programs; traveling exhibits. *Materials:* Curriculum units with hands-on materials; teacher's guides; audiovisual materials; magazine for students. *Education and support for teachers:* In-service workshops on science content and hands-on learning; information hotline; newsletter.

10.219 **Florida Museum of Natural History,** University of Florida, Museum Road, Gainesville, FL 32611 *(Mailing address: P.O. Box 117800, Gainesville, FL 32611-7800)*
(904) 392-1721

Both a university research-and-teaching museum and the state museum of natural history; focused on the natural history, archaeology, and ethnography of the state and region. *Programs for students:* At the museum: classes; guided tours; hands-on discovery area. At schools: programs on requested topics; suitcase exhibits. *Materials:* Educational packets; curriculum guidelines on exhibit topics; teacher's guides; videocassettes; previsit materials. *Education and support for teachers:* Statewide teacher workshops on science content and hands-on learning; educational tours.

10.220 **Imaginarium Hands-On Museum and Aquarium,** 2000 Cranford St., Fort Myers, FL 33901 *(Mailing address: P.O. Box 2217 Fort Myers, FL 33902)*
(941) 337-3332

Science museum with an aquarium and a resource library; emphasizing physical, life, and earth sciences and the connections between science and the arts and humanities. *Programs for students:* At the museum: Saturday workshops; lectures; demonstrations; field trips; guided tours; hands-on exhibits. At

schools: outreach programs. *Materials:* Lending boxes of hands-on materials; teacher's guides; computer-based materials. *Education and support for teachers:* Workshops on hands-on learning.

10.221 **Great Explorations, The Hands On Museum,** 1120 Fourth St. S., St. Petersburg, FL 33701
(813) 821-8992

Hands-on museum with 5 pavilions for permanent exhibits and 1 for changing exhibits; focused on arts, sciences, and health. *Programs for students:* At the museum: programs for school groups. At schools: auditorium and classroom programs; shows with a portable planetarium; traveling hands-on exhibits. *Materials:* Hands-on activity books; loans of live animals and plants; teacher's guide. *Education and support for teachers:* In-service workshops on science content and hands-on learning.

10.222 **Miami Museum of Science and Space Transit Planetarium,** 3280 S. Miami Ave., Miami, FL 33129
(305) 854-4247

Science museum, with a natural history collection, a wildlife center, an aviary, and Space Transit Planetarium. *Programs for students:* At the museum: classes; guided tours; demonstrations; hands-on exhibits; field trips. At the planetarium: multimedia astronomy and laser shows. At schools: outreach programs. *Materials:* Hands-on activity books; audiovisual and computer-based materials. *Education and support for teachers:* In-service education on science content and hands-on learning; Technology Training Center; teacher resource library; newsletter.

10.223 Mote Marine Laboratory/Aquarium, 1600 Ken Thompson Pkwy., Sarasota, FL 34236
(941) 388-4441
http://www.marinelab.sarasota.fl.us

Aquarium and marine research laboratory, with a touch tank and more than 200 varieties of fish and invertebrates; emphasis on marine biology, oceanography, and environmental sciences. *Programs for students:* At the aquarium: classes; guided/self-guided tours; hands-on exhibits; field trips. At schools: outreach programs; traveling exhibits. *Materials:* Curriculum guides; fact sheets; audiovisual and computer-based materials. *Education and support for teachers:* In-service workshops on science content and hands-on learning; lectures.

10.224 Museum of Arts and Sciences, 1040 Museum Blvd., Daytona Beach, FL 32114
(904) 255-0285

Museum featuring a planetarium, a hands-on science section, and the use of adjacent Tuscawilla Park Preserve and 150-acre Spruce Creek Preserve/Environmental Education Center; emphasis on the arts, sciences, and history. *Programs for students:* At the museum: guided/self-guided tours; hands-on exhibits; Summer Science Institute in life and environmental sciences, marine biology, zoology, and archaeology. At the planetarium: curriculum-related, grade-specific programs; field trips. At the museum and education center: environmental programs. *Materials:* Curriculum materials; teacher's guides; lending boxes of hands-on materials; audiovisual materials; catalog of materials. *Education and support for teachers:* In-service workshops on science content and hands-on learning; newsletter.

10.225 Museum of Discovery and Science, 401 S.W. Second St., Fort Lauderdale, FL 33312-1707
(305) 467-6637

Science museum with an IMAX theater and several science labs, focusing on science, technology, and mathematics. *Programs for students:* At the museum: hands-on exhibits; programs; guided/self-guided tours. At schools: outreach programs; traveling exhibits. *Materials:* Teacher's guides.

10.226 Museum of Science and History of Jacksonville, 1025 Museum Circle, Jacksonville, FL 32207-9053
(904) 396-7062

Science and history museum with a planetarium, a live-animal area with an aviary, and a native plant garden; emphasis on the natural, physical, and medical sciences. *Programs for students:* At the museum: planetarium shows; demonstrations; guided tours; science camps. At schools: outreach programs; traveling exhibits. *Materials:* Hands-on activity books; lending boxes with teacher's guides; loans of live animals and plants; audiovisual materials; catalog of materials. *Education and support for teachers:* In-service education on science content and hands-on learning; newsletter.

10.227 Museum of Science and Industry, 4801 E. Fowler Ave., Tampa, FL 33617-2099
(813) 987-6324

Science center, with a planetarium, an IMAX theater, and a Challenger Learning Center; emphasizes physical, earth, space, life, and environmental sciences and archaeology. *Programs for students:* At the center: hands-on exhibits; self-guided tours; hands-on classes; planetarium and IMAX shows; telescope viewing; fossil-finding and archaeological field trips. At schools: outreach programs, including portable planetarium. *Materials:* Curriculum units with hands-on materials to accompany program topics. *Education and support for teachers:* Workshops and seminars for teachers on science content and hands-on learning; newsletter.

10.228 Orlando Science Center, 777 E. Princeton St., Orlando, FL 32803
(407) 514-2000
http://www.osc.org

Science center, with a CineDome (large-format Iwerks theater combined with a planetarium), an observatory, and 10 exhibition halls, including more than 380 interactive exhibits and 5 Discovery Labs; focused on natural and physical sciences, mathematics, and applied technologies. *Programs for students:* At the center: classes; interactive exhibits; Discovery Labs; field trips. At schools: outreach programs; traveling exhibits. *Materials:* Teacher's guides; lending boxes of hands-on materials; audiovisual and computer-based materials; catalog of materials. *Education and support for teachers:* Preservice and in-service education on science content and hands-on learning; teacher resource center; distance learning center.

10.229 Sea World of Florida, 7007 World Dr., Orlando, FL 32821
(407) 351-3600
http://www.bev.net/education/SeaWorld

Marine park, focused on marine animals and the park's diverse marine environments. *Programs for students:* At the park: programs for school groups; guided tours; hands-on exhibits. *Materials:* Curriculum materials; teacher's guides; audiovisual and computer-based materials; catalog of materials. *Education and support for teachers:* In-service workshops on science content and hands-on learning.

10.230 **Silver River Museum and Environmental Education Center,** 7189 N.E. 7th St., Ocala, FL 34470 (904) 236-5401

History and natural history museum and environmental education center, operated by the Marion County Public School System, with interpretive nature trails, a 600-foot boardwalk, and river access; focused on natural history, the history of Florida, geology, archeology, paleontology, and ecology. *Programs for students:* At the center: programs for school groups; guided/ self-guided tours; hands-on exhibits. At schools: outreach programs; traveling exhibits. *Materials:* Hands-on activity books; teacher's guides; lending boxes of hands-on materials. *Education and support for teachers:* In-service education on science content and hands-on learning; workshops.

Georgia

10.231 **Fernbank Museum of Natural History,** 767 Clifton Rd., N.E., Atlanta, GA 30307-1221 (404) 378-0127 http://www.fernbank.edu/museum/ fmnhfr.html

Natural history museum, closely linked with the Fernbank Science Center, featuring an IMAX theater and a hands-on Naturalist Center; emphasis on chemistry, earth science, geology, and archaeology.

Programs for students: At the museum: classes; hands-on exhibits; archaeology field studies. At schools: outreach programs (limited). *Materials:* Supplemental materials for all programs and exhibits; posters. *Education and support for teachers:* Archaeology programs; newletter.

10.232 **Fernbank Science Center,** 156 Heaton Park Dr., N.E., Atlanta, GA 30307-1398 (404) 378-4311 http://www.fernbank.edu/fsc2.html

Science center of DeKalb County School System, closely linked with Fernbank Museum of Natural History; includes a planetarium, observatory, a 65-acre forest, greenhouses, gardens, and laboratories. *Programs for students:* At the center: exhibits; planetarium shows; programs for school groups. At schools: outreach programs; traveling exhibits. *Materials:* Lending kits; audiovisual materials; children's newsletter. *Education and support for teachers:* In-service workshops on science content and hands-on learning; magazine, *Fernbank Quarterly.*

10.233 **National Science Center,** Bldg. 25722 (Discovery Center 29727), Fort Gordon, GA 30905 *(Mailing address: ATTN: ATZH-NSC-DT, Fort Gordon, GA 30905-5689)* (706) 791-2009 http://www.nsc.gordon.army.mil

Science center (authorized by an act of Congress in 1985), with an exhibit center (Fort Discovery) in Augusta, Ga., that operates a national outreach program; focused on mathematical and physical science concepts basic to communications, electronics, computers, and other technologies, with material and technical support from a pri-

vate, nonprofit group and the U.S. Army. *Programs for students:* At the center: field trips; workshops; demonstrations; planetarium shows; video broadcasts. At schools: outreach programs with mobile vans; portable planetarium; science and mathematics demonstrations. *Materials:* Activity kits; videotapes; lesson plans; computer software. *Education and support for teachers:* In-service workshops on hands-on science and mathematics materials; teacher resource center; video broadcasts; electronic bulletin board; newsletter.

10.234 **Savannah Science Museum,** 4405 Paulsen St., Savannah, GA 31405 (912) 355-6705

Science museum, with a planetarium, hands-on discovery room and exhibit hall, a tower with a Foucault pendulum, and live reptiles and amphibians on display; emphasis on natural and physical sciences pertaining to coastal environment. *Programs for students:* At the museum: classes; planetarium programs. At schools: outreach programs. *Materials:* Teacher's guides; lending boxes of hands-on materials. *Education and support for teachers:* Opportunity for involvement in summer-long research project on the loggerhead sea turtle.

10.235 **SciTrek—The Science and Technology Museum of Atlanta,** 395 Piedmont Ave., N.E., Atlanta, GA 30308 (404) 522-5500

Science and technology center, with live science demonstrations, hands-on science and mathematics activities in 6 permanent halls, and a working research laboratory behind glass; focused principally on the physical sciences and technology. *Programs for students:* At the center: workshops; hands-on exhibits. *Materials:* Hands-on activity books; exhibit guides. *Education and support for teachers:* In-service education on science content and hands-on learning.

10.236 **Zoo Atlanta,** 800 Cherokee Ave., S.E., Atlanta, GA 30315
(404) 624-5600
http://www.netdepot.com/~zooatl

Zoo with extensive educational activities and a strong focus on wildlife conservation, featuring an Environmental Resource Center and a Conservation Action Resource Center. *Programs for students:* At the zoo: guided tours; programs for school groups; field studies; hands-on exhibits. At schools: zoomobile visits. *Materials:* Curriculum materials; activity boxes; teacher's guides; videotapes; curriculum supplements; pre-/postvisit activities. *Education and support for teachers:* Workshops on science content and hands-on learning; teacher resource center; newsletter.

Kentucky

10.237 **The Living Arts and Science Center,** 362 N. Martin Luther King Blvd., Lexington, KY 40508
(606) 252-5222

Center with art galleries and science exhibits; emphasis on science education outreach. *Programs for students:* At the center: classes; guided tours; hands-on exhibits. At schools: workshops; presentations; traveling exhibits. *Materials:* Traveling kits; teacher's guides; audiovisual and computer-based materials. *Education and support for teachers:* In-service workshops on science content and hands-on learning; newsletter.

10.238 **Louisville Science Center,** 727 W. Main St., Louisville, KY 40202
(502) 561-6103

Science and technology center, with an IMAX theater, a videoconferencing center, and 6 modern science classrooms; focused on health, physical science, earth science, geology, paleontology, and applied science. *Programs for students:* At the center: discovery lab; classes; demonstrations; hands-on exhibits. *Materials:* Hands-on activity books; teacher's guides. *Education and support for teachers:* In-service education on science content and hands-on learning; institutes and workshops; newsletter.

10.239 **Louisville Zoological Garden,** 1100 Trevilian Way, Louisville, KY 40213 *(Mailing address: P.O. Box 37250, Louisville, KY 40233)*
(502) 459-2181
http://www.iglou.com/louzoo

Zoo on 133 acres in a park setting, with 1,100 animals in more than 60 environmental exhibits, and including Metazoo Education Center and a HerpÁquarium with arid, water, and forest habitats. *Programs for students:* At the zoo: programs and classes for school groups; guided/self-guided tours; hands-on exhibits. At the center: live-animal exhibits; microscope stations; "biofact" exhibits. At schools: outreach programs. *Materials:* Hands-on activity books; teacher's guides; program kits for teacher-guided class visits. *Education and support for teachers:* In-service workshops on science content and hands-on learning; newsletter.

Mississippi

10.240 **Mississippi Museum of Natural Science,** 111 N. Jefferson St., Jackson, MS 39202
(601) 354-7303

State of Mississippi's biological and natural science museum, focusing on the state's natural history; massive aquarium system and indoor garden. *Programs for students:* At the museum: presentations and hands-on exhibits. At schools: exhibits and interactive programs. *Materials:* Object kits; teacher's guides; pre-/postvisit and audiovisual materials; museum artifact kits, some for loan (requiring teacher to attend hands-on workshop). *Education and support for teachers:* In-service workshops on hands-on learning; natural science library (available by appointment); newsletter.

10.241 **Russell C. Davis Planetarium,** 201 E. Pascagoula St., Jackson, MS 39201 *(Mailing address: P.O. Box 22826, Jackson, MS 39225-2826)*
(601) 960-1550

Planetarium, with a space theater and full-scale space station simulator; focused on life, physical, and space sciences, astronomy, and space travel. *Programs for students:* At the planetarium: programs for school groups; Student Space Station summer residencies for students of ability (ages 12-15), featuring 14 days of laboratory research and a 96-hour space flight simulation. At schools: career day presentations. *Materials:* Curriculum materials; teacher's guides. *Education and support for teachers:* Teacher workshops and in-service education featuring hands-on astronomy and space science.

10.242 University Museums, The University of Mississippi, University, MS 38677
(601) 232-7073
http://www.olemiss.edu/depts/u_museum

Two small university museums—the Mary Buie Museum and the Kate Skipwith Teaching Museum; science programs focused on physics and on life, space, and earth sciences, including ecology and natural history. *Programs for students:* At the museum: physics tours; summer science camp. At schools: outreach programs. *Materials:* Hands-on activity books; lending trunks of hands-on materials; teacher's guides; instructional materials on environmental education; audiovisual materials. *Education and support for teachers:* Newsletter.

North Carolina

10.243 Catawba Science Center, 243 Third Ave., N.E., Hickory, NC 28603 *(Mailing address: P.O. Box 2431, Hickory, NC 28603)*
(704) 322-8169
http://www.sohodev.com/catawba.htm

Science and technology center focused on physical, life, and earth and space sciences. *Programs for students:* At the center: science and environmental education programs for school groups; field trips; guided tours. At schools: outreach programs. *Education and support for teachers:* In-service workshops on process skills; resource center; newsletter.

10.244 Colburn Gem and Mineral Museum, Pack Place Education, Arts and Science Center, 2 S. Pack Sq., Asheville, NC 28801 *(Mailing address: P.O. Box 1617, Asheville, NC 28802)*
(704) 254-7162; (800) 935-0204
http://main.nc.us/colburn

Museum focusing on earth sciences, mineralogy, gemology, and paleontology. *Programs for students:* At the museum: classes; guided/self-guided tours; mineral shows; hands-on exhibits. At schools: outreach programs, including portable planetarium and gem mine. *Materials:* Curriculum units with suggested activities; teacher's guides; audiovisual materials for loan; postvisit materials. *Education and support for teachers:* In-service workshops on hands-on learning; newsletter.

10.245 Discovery Place, 301 N. Tryon St., Charlotte, NC 28202
(704) 372-6261

A science and technology center with a planetarium, aquarium, rain forest, Omnimax theater, and Challenger Learning Center; programs focused on astronomy and on the physical, chemical, health, natural, environmental, and space sciences and on computer science. *Programs for students:* At the museum: demonstrations; classes; hands-on exhibits. At schools: outreach programs. *Materials:* Lending boxes of hands-on materials; audiovisual materials. *Education and support for teachers:* In-service workshops on science content and hands-on learning.

10.246 Imagination Station, 224 E. Nash St., Wilson, NC 27893 *(Mailing address: P.O. Box 2127, Wilson, NC 27893)*
(919) 291-5113
http://www2.coastalnet.com/~h4k8k4wl

Science and mathematics learning center, with 80 hands-on exhibits covering basic physical and life science principles. *Programs for students:* At the center: live science programs (on chemistry, cryogenics, flight, electricity, and sound); guided tours; workshops. At schools: Science on Wheels (outreach programs). *Materials:* Hands-on activity books; traveling science trunks; teacher's guides; audiovisual and resource materials; catalog of materials. *Education and support for teachers:* In-service workshops on science content and hands-on learning; newsletter.

10.247 Morehead Planetarium, East Franklin Street, Chapel Hill, NC 27599 *(Mailing address: CB #3480, University of North Carolina at Chapel Hill, Chapel Hill, NC 27599-3480)*
(919) 962-1236
http://www.unc.edu/depts/mhplanet

Planetarium of the University of North Carolina at Chapel Hill (UNC-CH), working closely with the Center for Mathematics and Science Education of UNC-CH School of Education, and drawing students from 3 states; emphasis on astronomy and space science education. *Programs for students:* At the planetarium: shows, tied to state curricula, where possible; Saturday morning classes. *Materials:* Curriculum guides; catalogs of materials from other resource agencies. *Education and support for teachers:* In-service workshops on science content and hands-on learning; information service.

10.248 The Natural Science Center of Greensboro, 4301 Lawndale Dr., Greensboro, NC 27455
(919) 288-3769

Science education complex featuring a museum, zoo, and planetarium, with traditional natural history exhibits, modern interactive and technological exhibits, and discovery labs. *Programs for students:* At the center: demonstrations; classes; hands-on exhibits; field trips. At schools: outreach programs. *Materials:* Lending boxes of hands-on materials. *Education and support for teachers:* In-service education on science content and hands-on learning.

10.249 North Carolina Maritime Museum, 315 Front St., Beaufort, NC 28516
(919) 728-7317
http://www.agr.state.nc.us/maritime/index.htm

State museum with dual focus: (1) boats, boat building, and maritime history; and (2) marine sciences as part of coastal natural history. *Programs for students:* At the museum: audiovisual programs; programs with live animals; guided/self-guided tours; hands-on exhibits; field trips to coastal habitats. At schools: outreach programs; traveling exhibits. *Materials:* Lending boxes of hands-on materials; "Educational Services Guide"; audiovisual materials; staff-authored field guides to local habitats; catalog of materials. *Education and support for teachers:* In-service workshops on science content and hands-on learning; newsletter.

10.250 North Carolina Museum of Life and Science, 433 Murray Ave., Durham, NC 27704 *(Mailing address: P.O. Box 15190, Durham, NC 27704)*
(919) 220-5429

Regional science and technology center, with learning labs and 2 discovery rooms; emphasis on aerospace, the human body, physical science, animals, geology, and weather. *Programs for students:* At the museum: hands-on indoor and outdoor exhibits; classes. At schools: outreach programs, including a portable planetarium, neighborhood ecology program, and programs with live animals. *Materials:* Science loan kits; *Sharing Science with Children*—guides for teachers, parents, scientists, and engineers, to promote involvement in science education; postvisit activities. *Education and support for teachers:* In-service workshops on science content and hands-on learning; science resource center; newsletter.

10.251 North Carolina State Museum of Natural Sciences, 102 N. Salisbury St., Raleigh, NC 27603 *(Mailing address: P.O. Box 29555, Raleigh, NC 27626-0555)*
(919) 733-7450
http://www.nando.net/links/museum

Research-based natural history museum, with a discovery room, exhibit halls, and a working laboratory of paleontology; focused on North Carolina's biological diversity. *Programs for students:* At the museum: hands-on exhibits; classes; field trips; self-guided tours. At schools: statewide outreach programs. *Materials:* Lending boxes of hands-on materials; teacher's guides. *Education and support for teachers:* 1- and 3-day field trips led by a naturalist, emphasizing both science content and hands-on learning; newsletter.

10.252 North Carolina Zoological Park, 4401 Zoo Pkwy., Asheboro, NC 27203-9416
(910) 879-7000

Zoo on 500 acres, with natural habitats for more than 15,000 plant and 950 animal species from Africa and North America; focused on ecological systems and environmental conservation. *Programs for students:* At the zoo: informational scavenger hunts; "smart carts"; interaction with zoo educators. *Materials:* Teacher activity packet; videotape. *Education and support for teachers:* Workshops.

10.253 Piedmont Environmental Center, 1220 Penny Rd., High Point, NC 27265
(910) 883-8531

Environmental education center and wildlife refuge on 376 acres, with 11 miles of hiking/nature trails; focused on natural history, ecology, and environmental education. *Programs for students:* At the center: hands-on classes emphasizing field studies and data manipulation; field trips; guided tours. *Education and support for teachers:* Hands-on workshops; newsletter.

10.254 Schiele Museum of Natural History and Planetarium, 1500 E. Garrison Blvd., Gastonia, NC 28054 *(Mailing address: P.O. Box 953, Gastonia, NC 28053-0953)*
(704) 866-6900

Natural history museum and planetarium, with a theater, an arboretum, and an earth-space center; emphasis on natural history, earth and life sciences, ethnology, and environmental education. *Programs for students:* At the museum: hands-on exhibits;

classes; guided/self-guided tours; field trips. At schools in more than 20 counties: outreach programs; traveling exhibits. *Materials:* Hands-on activity books; lending boxes of hands-on materials; teacher's guides; audiovisual and computer-based materials; catalog of materials. *Education and support for teachers:* In-service workshops on science content and hands-on learning; newsletter.

10.255 SciWorks—The Science Center and Environmental Park of Forsyth County, 400 W. Hanes Mill Rd., Winston-Salem, NC 27105 (910) 767-6730

Science center with a planetarium and a 15-acre environmental park; emphasizes life, physical, earth, space, and environmental sciences. *Programs for students:* At the center: hands-on exhibits; classes; programs for school groups; planetarium programs; guided tours. At schools in 22 regional districts: outreach programs. *Materials:* Pre-/postvisit materials; teacher's guides. *Education and support for teachers:* In-service workshops on science content and hands-on learning; newsletter.

South Carolina

10.256 Museum of York County, 4621 Mount Gallant Rd., Rock Hill, SC 29732-9905 (803) 329-2121 http://www.cetlink.net/commercial/myco/mycohome.html

General museum, with a nature trail and a planetarium; emphasizes natural history, astronomy, and physical science. *Programs for students:* At the museum: classes; guided/self-guided tours; hands-on exhibits. At schools: outreach programs (including traveling trunks).

Materials: Lending boxes of self-contained curriculum units with resource materials; videos as a previsit package. *Education and support for teachers:* In-service education on science content and hands-on learning, including Project Wild (environmental education program emphasizing wildlife); weekend and week-long "Learning Expeditions"; newsletter.

10.257 Roper Mountain Science Center, 504 Roper Mountain Rd., Greenville, SC 29615 (803) 281-1188

Multifaceted science center, on 62 acres, operated by the local school system as a local resource and also for teachers statewide; features the following: a planetarium, observatory, living-history farm, arboretum, sea-life room with aquariums and a touch tank, health education center, chemistry and physics labs, and discovery room. *Programs for students:* At the center: classes; planetarium shows; guided tours; hands-on exhibits. At schools: outreach programs; traveling exhibits. *Materials:* Hands-on activity books; lending boxes of hands-on materials; teacher's guides; loans of live animals; audiovisual and computer-based materials; previsit activities; catalog of materials. *Education and support for teachers:* In-service courses and workshops on science content and hands-on learning; natural science institute.

10.258 South Carolina State Museum, 301 Gervais St., Columbia, SC 29201 (*Mailing address: P.O. Box 100107, Columbia, SC 29202*) (803) 737-4999

General museum, with a Science Discovery Theatre for science demonstrations, and NatureSpace,

a hands-on area featuring natural history. *Programs for students:* At the museum: hands-on thematic science and natural history lessons and programs; demonstration programs. *Materials:* Teacher's handbook of programs; audiovisual materials for classroom use; lists of suggested previsit activities and a bibliography. *Education and support for teachers:* In-service workshops on science content and hands-on learning.

10.259 The World of Energy at Keowee-Toxaway, 7812 Rochester Hwy., Seneca, SC 29672 (864) 885-4600

Science museum and visitor center, located adjacent to Oconee Nuclear Station, with a simulated control room for a nuclear power plant; emphasis on energy and electricity generation and environmental stewardship. *Programs for students:* At the center: classes; hands-on exhibits. At schools: outreach programs (within 10 miles of the center). *Materials:* Curriculum materials; scavenger hunt sheets. *Education and support for teachers:* In-service education on science content and hands-on learning.

Tennessee

10.260 American Museum of Science and Energy, 300 S. Tulane Dr., Oak Ridge, TN 37830 (423) 576-3200 http://www.korrnet.org/amse

Science and technology museum sponsored by the U.S. Department of Energy, with more than 200 interactive exhibits; focused on physical sciences and on energy forms and their uses. *Programs for students:* At the museum: classes; self-guided tours; demonstrations;

hands-on exhibits. *Materials:* Catalog of materials. *Education and support for teachers:* In-service education on hands-on learning.

10.261 **Cumberland Science Museum,** 800 Fort Negley Blvd., Nashville, TN 32703
(615) 862-5160
http://www.infi.net/~csmnet

Natural science and technology museum with a planetarium; focused on physical, earth, and life sciences. *Programs for students:* At the museum: live-animal programs; planetarium programs; guided tours; field trips; hands-on exhibits; science camps. At schools: outreach programs; traveling exhibits. *Materials:* Teacher's guides; audiovisual materials; catalog of materials. *Education and support for teachers:* In-service education on hands-on learning; workshops; newsletter.

10.262 **Hands On! Regional Museum,** 315 E. Main St., Johnson City, TN 37601
(423) 928-6508
http://www.thewebcorp.com/handson/handson.htm

Children's museum with an aquarium, featuring exhibits, programs, and materials on the physical, life, earth, and environmental sciences. *Programs for students:* At the museum: guided tours; hands-on exhibits. At schools: outreach programs. *Materials:* Lending boxes with hands-on materials; teacher's guides; audiovisual and computer-based materials. *Education and support for teachers:* In-service education on science content; newsletter.

10.263 **Memphis Museum System,** 3050 Central Ave., Memphis, TN 38111-3399
(901) 320-6369

Museum and planetarium, with an IMAX theater; museum also operates the Coon Creek Science Center, a renowned, upper-Cretaceous fossil site located in McNairy County; exhibits focus on natural and cultural history of the region. *Programs for students:* At the museum: laboratory, demonstration, and science theater experiences. At the planetarium: live presentations; recorded shows; field trips. At schools: outreach programs. *Materials:* Lending boxes of hands-on materials with teacher's guides. *Education and support for teachers:* In-service workshops on science content and hands-on learning.

Virginia

10.264 **Science Museum of Virginia,** 2500 W. Broad St., Richmond, VA 23220
(804) 367-1013
http://www.smv.mus.va.us

Science and technology museum and education center, with a planetarium and space theater; Omnimax theater; demonstration laboratories; 250 interactive exhibits in the areas of aerospace, electricity and power, physics, chemistry, astronomy, and crystallography, and other programs in the life sciences. *Programs for students:* At the museum: planetarium shows; films; hands-on exhibits. At schools: outreach programs. *Materials:* Hands-on activity books; teacher's guides for all exhibits; lending boxes of hands-on materials. *Education and support for teachers:* In-service workshops on science content and hands-on learning.

10.265 **Science Museum of Western Virginia,** One Market Square, Roanoke, VA 24011
(703) 342-5710

Science museum with a planetarium; emphasizes a wide range of sciences, including energy, natural history, and physical and earth sciences. *Programs for students:* At the museum: labs; guided tours; hands-on exhibits; planetarium shows. *Materials:* Catalog of materials. *Education and support for teachers:* Teacher resource center, featuring curriculum materials and science fair components for grades K-12; newsletter.

10.266 **Virginia Air and Space Center and Hampton Roads History Center,** 600 Settlers Landing Rd., Hampton, VA 23669
(804) 727-0800
http://seastar.vasc.mus.va.us/vasc
http://seastar.vasc.va.us (Teacher Resource Center)

Center for aerospace education with an IMAX theater, serving as the visitors center for Langley Research Center of the National Aeronautics and Space Administration (NASA); focused primarily on the science, history, and technology of aviation and space. *Programs for students:* At the center: guided/self-guided tours; demonstrations; classroom experiences; hands-on exhibits; field activities. At schools: outreach programs. *Materials:* Hands-on activity books; teacher's guides; previsit packets; audiovisual and computer-based materials. *Education and support for teachers:* In-service education on science content and hands-on learning; NASA Teacher Resource Center.

10.267 Virginia Living Museum, 524 J. Clyde Morris Blvd., Newport News, VA 23601 (757) 595-1900

Living museum, featuring native animals and plants, an aviary, a nature trail, a planetarium and observatory, and a discovery center; focused on the life and earth sciences. *Programs for students:* At the museum: planetarium programs; science survey classes; environmental science laboratories; guided/self-guided tours; hands-on exhibits. At schools: participatory assembly programs; classes, with live animals. *Materials:* Discovery boxes with teacher resource packets for loan; catalog of materials. *Education and support for teachers:* In-service science seminars and field trips; courses on hands-on learning; reference library.

10.268 Virginia Marine Science Museum, 717 General Booth Blvd., Virginia Beach, VA 23451 (757) 437-4949 http://www.whro.org/vmsm

Marine science museum and aquarium; focus includes sea turtle conservation and bottlenose dolphin research. *Programs for students:* At the museum: programs for school groups; hands-on exhibits. Through the museum: whale-watch, dolphin-watch, and ocean collection boat trips (grades 4 and above). At schools: outreach programs; traveling exhibits. *Materials:* Curriculum guides. *Education and support for teachers:* In-service workshops on science content and hands-on learning; newsletter.

10.269 Virginia Museum of Natural History, 1001 Douglas Ave., Martinsville, VA 24112 (703) 666-8600 http://www.bev.net/education/ museum/vmnhmvl/vmnh.html

Center for statewide research and outreach on the natural history of Virginia. *Programs for students:* At the museum: classes; hands-on exhibits; guided tours. At schools throughout the state: inquiry-based, participatory programs; traveling exhibits. *Materials:* Hands-on activity books; educational resource kits for loan; teacher's manuals; audiovisual materials; catalog of materials. *Education and support for teachers:* In-service workshops on science content and hands-on learning throughout the state; newsletter; magazine, *Virginia Explorer.*

MIDDLE ATLANTIC REGION

District of Columbia

10.270 **National Air and Space Museum, Smithsonian Institution,** 6th St. and Independence Ave., S.W., Washington, DC 20560
(202) 357-1400
http://www.nasm.edu

National museum focusing on the technology, science, and history of aviation, rocketry, and space exploration; featuring many historic air- and spacecraft, an IMAX theater, and a planetarium. *Programs for students:* At the museum: programs for school groups; guided tours; hands-on exhibits. *Materials:* Hands-on activity books. *Education and support for teachers:* In-service workshops on science content and hands-on learning.

10.271 **National Museum of American History, Smithsonian Institution,** 14th St. and Constitution Ave., N.W., Washington, DC 20560 *(Mailing address: Smithsonian Institution, Washington, DC 20560)*
(202) 357-2700

National museum focusing on American culture, science, and technology; includes Science in American Life exhibition that examines the relationship between science and society from 1876 to the present, and features a Hands-

On Science Center. *Programs for students:* At the museum: classes; guided tours; hands-on exhibits. *Materials:* Curriculum units on science-society issues; audiovisual materials. *Education and support for teachers:* Teacher resource area in Hands-On Science Center.

10.272 **National Museum of Natural History, Smithsonian Institution,** 10th St. and Constitution Ave., N.W., Washington, DC 20560
(202) 357-2747
http://www.nmnh.si.edu

National museum with an insect zoo, discovery room, the Living Marine Ecosystem, and (for grades 6 and up) the Naturalist Center, where students can experience hands-on research. *Programs for students:* At the museum: lesson tours; hands-on exhibits; classroom programs. *Materials:* Teacher's guides; previsit materials. *Education and support for teachers:* In-service education on science content and hands-on learning; workshops and summer institutes.

10.273 **National Zoological Park, Smithsonian Institution,** 3000 Connecticut Ave., N.W., Washington, DC 20008-2598
(202) 673-4717

National zoo, with focus extending beyond traditional zoology to botany, anthropology, ethology, ecology, and paleontology, and with numerous interactive learning opportunities such as Amazonia, the Reptile Discovery Center, Invertebrate Exhibit, and Think Tank. *Programs for students:* At the zoo: self-guided tours; hands-on exhibits. *Materials:* Outreach kit; teacher's guides; curriculum guides; audiovisual materials; catalog of materials. *Education and support for teachers:* In-service workshops on science content and hands-on learning.

Maryland

10.274 **Baltimore Zoo,** Druid Hill Park, Baltimore, MD 21217
(410) 396-7102

Zoo with state-of-the-art exhibits (e.g., Maryland Wilderness and African Watering Hole). *Programs for students:* At the zoo: guided tours; classroom programs featuring live animals. At schools: outreach programs with a zoomobile. *Materials:* Lending boxes of hands-on materials; teacher's guides; catalog of materials. *Education and support for teachers:* In-service workshops on science content and hands-on learning; newsletter.

10.275 **Calvert Marine Museum,** 14150 Solomons Island Rd., Rte. 2, Solomons, MD 20688 *(Mailing address: P.O. Box 97, Solomons, MD 20688)*
(410) 326-2042

Marine museum with a 15-tank estuarium, a touch tank, a marine biology laboratory, and various outdoor environments; focused on the paleontology of Calvert Cliffs, estuarine life of the Patuxent River and Chesapeake Bay, and local maritime history. *Programs for students:* At the museum: hands-on exhibits; guided tours; classes; nature walks through salt- and freshwater marshes; fossil field experience. *Education and support for teachers:* In-service education on science content and hands-on learning.

10.276 **Columbus Center,** Piers 5 and 6 at Inner Harbor, Baltimore, MD 21202 *(Mailing address: 111 Market Place, Suite 300, Baltimore, MD 21202)*
(410) 547-5741
http://www.columbuscenter.org

Science and technology center, including the Hall of Exploration, Science and Technology (SciTEC) Education Center, and Center of Marine Biotechnology (COMB) research facility, with an interactive exhibit hall, student research laboratories, and a 32-station Silicon Graphic Indy computer facility; emphasis on marine biology, biotechnology, and technology. *Programs for students:* At the education center: 3-hour Exploration programs integrating inquiry-based wet lab investigations with World Wide Web research; interactive research program with COMB scientists. At the exhibit hall: interactive video programs and media presentations; hands-on lab demonstrations; live specimens; large-scale simulations. At schools: outreach programs. *Materials:* Computer-based materials using World Wide Web access. *Education and support for teachers:* In-service education on science content, inquiry-based learning, and bioscience career awareness; on-line information service.

10.277 **Howard B. Owens Science Center,** 9601 Greenbelt Rd., Lanham, MD 20706
(301) 918-8750
http://www.gsfc.nasa.gov/hbowens/agu_poster.html

Science center that includes a planetarium and a Challenger Learning Center, serving public schools in Prince George's County, Maryland. *Programs for students:* At the center: classes and programs for school groups; guided tours (limited); hands-on exhibits; docent programs for students in grades 4-6 to share science with younger students. *Materials:* Pre-/postvisit materials; teacher's guides; catalog of programs. *Education and support for teachers:* In-service workshops on science content and hands-on learning; newsletter.

10.278 **Maryland Science Center,** 601 Light St., Baltimore, MD 21230
(410) 685-2370

Science center, with a planetarium and an IMAX theater; focused on the environmental, physical, life, and space sciences, and mathematics. *Programs for students:* At the museum: hands-on exhibits; planetarium and IMAX shows; field trips. At schools: participatory demonstration programs; portable planetarium classes. *Materials:* Teacher's guides. *Education and support for teachers:* In-service workshops on science content and hands-on learning.

10.279 **National Aquarium in Baltimore,** Pier 3, 501 E. Pratt St., Baltimore, MD 21202-3194
(410) 576-3800

State-of-the-art aquatic institution with a diverse collection of more than 9,000 aquatic animals, dedicated to encouraging lifelong learning and participation in the conservation of the environment. *Programs for students:* At the aquarium: classes and programs for school groups; hands-on exhibits. At schools: outreach programs. *Materials:* Hands-on activity books; teacher's guide; audiovisual materials; catalog of materials. *Education and support for teachers:* In-service workshops on science content and hands-on learning.

10.280 **Smithsonian Environmental Research Center,** Contees Wharf Road, Edgewater, MD 21037
(410) 798-4424
http://www.serc.si.edu

Research-based environmental education center on 2,700 acres along the Chesapeake Bay and Rhode River, offering nature trails, canoeing through wetlands, and an opportunity to see the center's scientists at work. *Programs for students:* At the center: group outdoor activities involving marsh, forest, and river. *Materials:* Audiovisual and computer-based materials; posters. *Education and support for teachers:* In-service workshops on hands-on learning; teacher resource library; newsletter.

New Jersey

10.281 **Invention Factory Science Center,** 650 S. Broad St., Trenton, NJ 08611-1822
(609) 396-2002

Regional science and technology center, with emphasis on telecommunications and distance learning, located in an 1890 machine shop; exhibits and programs focused on biotechnology, energy, the environment, materials science, telecommunications, and transportation. *Programs for students:* At the center: programs for school groups; guided tours; hands-on exhibits. At schools: outreach programs, with an emphasis on distance learning. *Materials:* Science to Go (lending kits of hands-on materials); computer-based materials, including Pathways to Science and Technology, a learning system to facilitate access to offerings in the center and around the region. *Education and support for teachers:* In-service workshops on hands-on learning; teacher resource center; Teacher Pathways, an on-line information service; newsletter.

10.282 Liberty Science Center, Liberty State Park, 251 Phillip St., Jersey City, NJ 07305-4699
(201) 451-0006
http://www.lsc.org

Science center with more than 250 interactive exhibits in science and technology, an Omnimax theater, and a science theater. *Programs for students:* At the center: courses; films; presentations; hands-on exhibits. At schools: assembly programs and demonstrations. *Materials:* Hands-on activity books; previsit materials; teacher's guides. *Education and support for teachers:* In-service workshops on science content and hands-on learning; newsletter.

10.283 The Newark Museum, 49 Washington St., Newark, NJ 07101 *(Mailing address: P.O. Box 540, Newark, NJ 07101-0540)*
(201) 596-6550

General museum with a planetarium and a small zoo, emphasizing astronomy and the life and earth sciences. *Programs for students:* At the museum: hands-on exhibits; planetarium shows; guided tours. At schools: outreach programs, including a portable planetarium. *Materials:* Extensive lending collections of science objects (charts; models; and plant, geological, and animal specimens); teacher's guides.

10.284 The New Jersey State Aquarium at Camden, One Riverside Dr., Camden, NJ 08103-1060
(609) 365-3300

Aquarium with a 760,000-gallon open-ocean exhibit and an outdoor exhibit of seals; emphasis on marine and aquatic life. *Programs for students:* At the aquarium:

classroom, amphitheater, and auditorium programs; hands-on exhibits. At schools: classroom and auditorium programs with live animals. *Materials:* Teacher's guides. *Education and support for teachers:* In-service workshops on science content and hands-on learning; newsletter.

10.285 Reeves-Reed Arboretum, 165 Hobart Ave., Summit, NJ 07901-2908
(908) 273-8787

Arboretum and botanical garden on 12.5 acres, with wet and dry woodlands, glacial kettle holes, fields, lawns, and formal gardens; emphasis on botany, geology, and ecology. *Programs for students:* At the arboretum: guided tours; field studies for student groups. *Materials:* Curriculum units with hands-on materials; curriculum guidelines; teacher's guides.

10.286 The Wetlands Institute, 1075 Stone Harbor Blvd., Stone Harbor, NJ 08247-1424
(609) 368-1211

Scientific research and public education institute, with an aquarium, a salt marsh trail, and a discovery room; concerned with environmental sciences, intertidal salt marshes, and coastal ecosystems. *Programs for students:* At the institute: classes; guided tours. At schools: outreach programs. *Materials:* Hands-on activity booklets complementing school programs at the institute; pre-/postvisit materials. *Education and support for teachers:* Workshops on marine sciences and estuarine ecosystems; teacher resource center; newsletter.

New York

10.287 American Museum of Natural History, Central Park West at 79th Street, New York, NY 10024
(212) 769-5300

World-renowned, research-driven museum with an education department founded in 1884, a separate planetarium (Hayden Planetarium), Naturemax theater (IMAX), a discovery room, and a natural science center; emphasis on anthropology, astronomy, paleontology, many branches of zoology, and mineral sciences. *Programs for students:* At the museum: education programs; guided tours; field trips. At schools: outreach programs; traveling exhibits. *Materials:* Hands-on activity books; lending boxes of hands-on materials; teacher's guides; audiovisual and computer-based materials. *Education and support for teachers:* In-service workshops on science content and hands-on learning.

10.288 American Museum of Natural History—Hayden Planetarium, 81st Street and Central Park West, New York, NY 10024
(212) 769-5920

Renowned planetarium, with a sky theater (for planetarium), a space theater (with 22 screens), and several museum halls, focused on astronomy, meteorology, and space science. *Programs for students:* At the planetarium: planetarium shows. *Materials:* Lists of recommended hands-on activity books and of audiovisual and computer-based materials. *Education and support for teachers:* In-service workshops in astronomy and space science; occasional student/teacher workshops; extensive course program in astronomy, meteorology, aviation, and celestial navigation.

10.289 **Aquarium for Wildlife Conservation,** Boardwalk and West 8th Street, Brooklyn, NY 11224 (718) 265-3448

Indoor/outdoor facility on 13 acres, with more than 3,400 live specimens (including beluga whales, dolphins, walruses, fish, sharks, and thousands of invertebrates), and featuring Discovery Cove, an award-winning building with a touch-it tank, devoted to hands-on science education; emphasis on coastal habitats and adaptations for survival. *Programs for students:* At the aquarium: classes; guided/self-guided tours; workshops; interactive exhibits. At schools: outreach programs. *Materials:* Hands-on activity books and sheets; teacher's guides; kits with curriculum units, resources, and bibliographies. *Education and support for teachers:* Pre-/in-service workshops on science content and hands-on learning, with an interdisciplinary approach.

10.290 **Aquarium of Niagara,** 701 Whirlpool St., Niagara Falls, NY 14301 (716) 285-3575; (800) 500-4609

Aquarium with a touch tank and more than 1,500 specimens of aquatic life in about 40 exhibits; emphasis on marine biology and the ecology of the Great Lakes. *Programs for students:* At the aquarium: classes; hands-on exhibits. At schools: outreach programs; traveling exhibits. *Materials:* Hands-on activity books; teacher's guides; audiovisual materials. *Education and support for teachers:* In-service education on science content and hands-on learning; workshops; newsletter.

10.291 **Bronx Zoo/Wildlife Conservation Park,** Bronx River Parkway at Fordham Road, Bronx, NY 10460 *(Mailing address: 2300 Southern Blvd., Bronx, NY 10460)* (718) 220-5100 http://www.wcs.org

Zoo, with a wide range of teacher-training and hands-on student programs, focused on animals, habitats, adaptations, and conservation. *Programs for students:* At the zoo: hands-on exhibits; classes; guided/self-guided tours. *Materials:* Hands-on activity books; lending boxes of hands-on materials; teacher's guides; curriculum and audiovisual materials; catalog of materials; magazine for students. *Education and support for teachers:* In-service workshops and seminars on science content and hands-on learning; newsletter; magazine, *Wildlife Conservation.*

10.292 **Brooklyn Botanic Garden,** 1000 Washington Ave., Brooklyn, NY 11225-1099 (718) 622-4433

Research-based botanic garden with a museum, conservatory, herbarium, teaching greenhouses, and a children's discovery center and garden; leader in formal and informal science education for 80 years. *Programs for students:* At the garden: workshops; garden explorations; guided tours; field trips. At schools: indoor gardening facilities; hands-on science curricula. *Materials:* Hands-on activity books; teacher's guides; previsit and audiovisual materials; catalog of materials. *Education and support for teachers:* In-service workshops on science content and hands-on learning; newsletter.

10.293 **The Brooklyn Children's Museum,** 145 Brooklyn Ave., Brooklyn, NY 11213 (718) 735-4400

World's first children's museum, now housed in a modern, underground building, with a resource library and greenhouse; emphasizes natural science, culture, and history. *Programs for students:* At the museum: programs for school groups; hands-on exhibits; guided tours; field trips. *Materials:* Lending boxes of hands-on materials; teacher's guides; loans of objects from natural history collection. *Education and support for teachers:* In-service education on science content and hands-on learning.

10.294 **Buffalo Museum of Science,** 1020 Humboldt Pkwy., Buffalo, NY 14211-1293 (716) 896-5200

Natural history museum, with an observatory, a solar observatory, a 260-acre nature preserve, a science magnet school, and a hands-on discovery room; focused on botany, zoology, geology, paleontology, astronomy, and the environment. *Programs for students:* At the museum: classes, hands-on exhibits, guided tours. At schools: outreach programs. *Materials:* Object-based teaching kits and live plants and animals for loan; teacher's guides; audiovisual materials. *Education and support for teachers:* Exhibit-related, in-service workshops on hands-on learning, offered by the museum's Center for Science Education; teacher-support program; newsletter.

10.295 The Corning Museum of Glass, One Museum Way, Corning, NY 14830-2253
(607) 937-5371, ext. 231
http://www.pennynet.org/glmuseum/corningm.htm

Museum focused on the history, art, science, and technology of glass. *Programs for students:* At the museum: classes; field trips; guided/self-guided tours; hands-on exhibits. At schools: outreach programs. *Materials:* Curriculum units with hands-on materials; fact sheets; audiovisual and computer-based materials. *Education and support for teachers:* Workshops.

10.296 DNA Learning Center, Cold Spring Harbor Laboratory, One Bungtown Rd., Cold Spring Harbor, NY 11724-2219
(516) 367-7240

Science center, at the site of a leading genetics research laboratory, focused on molecular genetics and biotechnology. *Programs for students:* At the center: classes; field trips; hands-on exhibits; summer workshops on genetics and biochemistry for students in grades 5-8. At schools: outreach programs. *Materials:* Curriculum units with hands-on materials. *Education and support for teachers:* In-service education on science content and hands-on learning; lectures; instructional materials.

10.297 The Hicksville Gregory Museum, Heitz Place, Hicksville, NY 11801 *(Mailing address: Heitz Place and Bay Avenue, Hicksville, NY 11801)*
(516) 822-7505

Long Island's earth science center, with a primary collection of minerals and fossils, augmented by exhibits on local geology and water resources. *Programs for students:* At the museum: classes; guided tours. At schools: outreach programs. *Materials:* Postvisit materials; rocks and minerals kits and narrated slide sets for loan. *Education and support for teachers:* In-service education on earth science topics and the local environment; newsletter.

10.298 Institute of Ecosystem Studies, Rte. 44A, Millbrook, NY 12545 *(Mailing address: Box R, Millbrook, NY 12545-0178)*
(914) 677-5343

Research and education institute with outdoor trails and exhibits, focusing on ecology and environmental science. *Programs for students:* At the institute and at schools: programs teaching ecology through direct investigations. *Materials:* Curriculum guides on ecological inquiry. *Education and support for teachers:* In-service workshops on schoolyard ecology and on learning through inquiry; newsletter.

10.299 Milton J. Rubenstein Museum of Science and Technology, 500 S. Franklin St., Syracuse, NY 13202-1245
(315) 425-9068
http://www.rway.com/most

Science and technology museum with a planetarium, an IMAX theater, and a teacher resource center. *Programs for students:* At the center: hands-on exhibits; interactive planetarium presentations; curriculum-related workshops. At schools: traveling science program; portable planetarium shows. *Materials:* Hands-on activity books; loan kits; teacher's guides; audiovisual and computer-based materials. *Education and support for teachers:* In-service workshops on science content and hands-on learning.

10.300 The New York Botanical Garden, 200th Street and Southern Boulevard, Bronx, NY 10458
(718) 817-8700

Research-based, 250-acre botanical garden and arboretum with a conservatory; focused on plant development, plant-and-animal relationships, and the study of ecology and habitats. *Programs for students:* At the garden: workshops; guided/self-guided tours. At schools: outreach programs. *Education and support for teachers:* In-service workshops on science content and hands-on learning.

10.301 New York Hall of Science, 47-01 111th St., Flushing Meadows, Corona Park, NY 11368
(718) 699-0005

Science center, with more than 150 interactive exhibits emphasizing physical and life sciences. *Programs for students:* At the center: student workshops; guided tours; hands-on exhibits. At schools: outreach programs. *Materials:* Hands-on activity books; lending boxes of hands-on materials; teacher's guides; audiovisual and computer-based materials. *Education and support for teachers:* In-service workshops on science content and hands-on learning; multimedia reference library; newsletter.

10.302 New York State Museum, Rm. 3099, Cultural Education Center, Empire State Plaza, Albany, NY 12230 *(Mailing address: Rm. 3099 CEC, Albany, NY 12230)* (518) 474-5877

Oldest and largest state museum in the country, focusing on the geology, biology, anthropology, and history of New York State. *Programs for students:* At the museum: classes; hands-on exhibits; guided tours. At schools: outreach programs, including alliance with local magnet school. *Materials:* Lending boxes with hands-on materials; teacher's guides; pre-/postvisit suggestions. *Education and support for teachers:* In-service workshops on science content and hands-on learning; newsletter.

10.303 Roberson Museum and Science Center, 30 Front St., Binghamton, NY 13905, and **Kopernik Space Education Center,** 698 Underwood Rd., Vestal, NY 13850 Roberson Museum: (607) 772-0660 Kopernik Center: (607) 748-3685 http://www.kopernik.org

General and science museum with Link Planetarium (including 50 hands-on exhibits) and, nearby, Kopernik Center (Roberson's public observatory, with 3 observatories and 5 science labs, designed for young people); focused on astronomy, earth and physical sciences, technology, and computers. *Programs for students:* At the museum and center: hands-on exhibits; classes; guided tours; field trips. At schools: outreach programs; traveling exhibits. *Materials:* Hands-on activity books; lending boxes of hands-on materials; teacher's guides; audiovisual and computer-

based materials. *Education and support for teachers:* In-service workshops on science content and hands-on learning; newsletter.

10.304 Rochester Museum and Science Center, 657 East Ave., Rochester, NY 14603 *(Mailing address: P.O. Box 1480, Rochester, NY 14603-1480)* (716) 271-4320

Large center, composed of the Rochester Museum, Strasenburgh Planetarium, Gannett School of Science and Man, and nearby Cumming Nature Center; focused on astronomy, botany, and the earth, space, and environmental sciences. *Programs for students:* At the museum and nature center: programs and classes for school groups; self-guided tours. At the Gannett School: classes; workshops; expeditions. At the planetarium: shows. At the nature center: classes for school groups. *Materials:* Curriculum units with hands-on materials; audiovisual materials. *Education and support for teachers:* In-service workshops on hands-on learning.

10.305 Schenectady Museum and Planetarium, Nott Terrace Heights, Schenectady, NY 12308 (518) 382-7890

General museum with a planetarium, and a 90-acre nature preserve in nearby Niskayuna, N.Y.; emphasis on physics, chemistry, human perception, space, geology, health, animals, and plants. *Programs for students:* At the museum and nature center: hands-on exhibits; classes; planetarium programs. At schools: outreach programs. *Materials:* Lending trunks of hands-on materials; audiovisual materials. *Education and support for teachers:* Teacher workshops.

10.306 Schoellkopf Geological Museum, New York State Parks, Niagara Region, Robert Moses State Parkway, near Man Street, Niagara Falls, NY 14303 *(Mailing address: New York State Parks, Western District, Niagara Region, Niagara Reservation, P.O. Box 1132, Niagara Falls, NY 14303-0132)* (716) 278-1780

Geology museum located in a state park on the site of a former hydroelectric-generating complex; emphasis on local geology and the history of Niagara Falls. *Programs for students:* At the museum: classes; guided tours. *Education and support for teachers:* Letter-answering service.

10.307 Science Museum of Long Island, Leeds Pond Preserve, 1526 N. Plandome Rd., Manhasset, NY 11030 *(Mailing address: P.O. Box 908, Plandome, NY 11030)* (516) 627-9400

Regional science activity center and nature center on a 36-acre wildlife preserve; focused on a broad range of life, physical, and earth sciences and on natural history, ecology, mathematics, and technology. *Programs for students:* At the center: hands-on classes and exhibits; demonstrations; guided/self-guided tours; field trips; field studies. At schools: hands-on classes; demonstrations for large audiences; science-on-wheels van. *Materials:* Loan of live animals and plants. *Education and support for teachers:* In-service workshops on science content and hands-on learning; expeditions.

10.308 Staten Island Children's Museum, 1000 Richmond Terrace at Snug Harbor, Staten Island, NY 10301
(718) 273-2060

General museum for children, with emphasis on integrating the performing, visual, literary, and musical arts to teach science content. *Programs for students:* At the museum: classes; guided tours; hands-on exhibits. At schools: outreach programs; traveling exhibits. *Materials:* Hands-on activity books; lending boxes of hands-on materials; teacher's guides; pre-/postvisit materials. *Education and support for teachers:* In-service workshops on science content and hands-on learning.

10.309 Staten Island Institute of Arts and Sciences, 75 Stuyvesant Pl., Staten Island, NY 10301-1998
(718) 727-1135

General museum, with science focus on the life and earth sciences. *Programs for students:* At the museum: classes; guided/self-guided tours; field trips; hands-on exhibits. At Staten Island schools: outreach programs. *Materials:* Hands-on activity books; teacher's guides; pre-/postvisit materials; lending boxes of hands-on materials; audiovisual materials. *Education and support for teachers:* Workshops on environmental education.

10.310 Staten Island Zoo, 614 Broadway, Staten Island, NY 10310
(718) 442-3100
http://www.earthcom.net/~sizoo

Zoo, with a noted reptile collection, an aquarium, tropical forest and African savannah exhibits, and a children's center with domestic farm animals. *Programs for students:* At the zoo: programs for school groups; field studies. At schools: Traveling Zoo. *Materials:* Hands-on activity books; teacher's guides and instructional materials; audiovisual materials. *Education and support for teachers:* Workshops on science content and hands-on learning; internships for recent graduates.

Pennsylvania

10.311 The Academy of Natural Sciences of Philadelphia, 1900 Benjamin Franklin Pkwy., Philadelphia, PA 19103-1195
(215) 299-1000
http://www.acnatsci.org

Research-based natural history museum, focused on biology, zoology, earth science, geology, paleontology, natural history, and ecology. *Programs for students:* At the museum: classes; guided tours; hands-on exhibits. At schools: outreach programs with live animals. *Materials:* Hands-on activity books; curriculum units on ecologial topics with hands-on materials; education handbooks. *Education and support for teachers:* In-service workshops and miniconferences on science content and hands-on learning; *Environmental Education Resource Manual* (for Philadelphia teachers); safari overnights in museum.

10.312 Carnegie Museum of Natural History, 4400 Forbes Ave., Pittsburgh, PA 15213-4080
(412) 622-3131
http://www.clpgh.org/cmnh

Research-based natural history museum, with a discovery room and an educational loan collection of more than 4,000 specimens and artifacts, including thematic kits; emphasis on paleontology, geology, life sciences, archaeology, and anthropology. *Programs for students:* At the museum: classes; guided interpretive tours; hands-on exhibits. At schools: outreach programs. *Materials:* Hands-on activity books; thematic kits; curriculum materials; natural history publications; catalog of materials. *Education and support for teachers:* In-service courses on science content and hands-on learning; workshops.

10.313 Carnegie Science Center, One Allegheny Ave., Pittsburgh, PA 15212-5850
(412) 237-3400
http://www.csc.clpgh.org

Science and technology center, with more than 250 hands-on exhibits, a planetarium, a submarine, an Omnimax theater, and Sciquest—an exhibit designed specifically for the middle school audience. *Programs for students:* At the center: hands-on exhibits; discovery labs for further explorations; demonstrations. At schools: outreach programs for assembly or classroom-sized groups. *Materials:* Hands-on activity books to supplement field trips; teacher's guides. *Education and support for teachers:* Workshops to enhance science and mathematics education.

10.314 Erie Zoo, Erie Zoological Society, 423 W. 38th St., Erie, PA 16508 *(Mailing address: P.O. Box 3268, Erie, PA 16508-0268)*
(814) 864-4091

Zoological park and botanical garden with more than 300 animals and over 450 species of plants, with a children's zoo. *Programs for students:* At the zoo: guided/self-guided tours; presentations; classes. *Materials:* Lending boxes with thematic units, materials, and activities; audiovisual materials; "tour totes" for self-guided tours. *Education and support for teachers:* In-service workshops on science content and hands-on learning.

10.315 The Franklin Institute Science Museum, 20th Street and The Benjamin Franklin Parkway, Philadelphia, PA 19103 *(Mailing address: 222 N. 20th St., Philadelphia, PA 19130)*
(215) 448-1200
http://www.fi.edu
http://www.sln.org (Science Learning Network)

World-renowned science and technology museum, with a planetarium and Omniverse theater; covers a broad range of sciences, technology, and mathematics. *Programs for students:* At the museum: interactive exhibits; self-guided tours; Omniverse films; theater presentations; demonstrations; workshops; Internet exploration; summer science camp. At schools: assembly programs. *Materials:* Science activity kits; teacher's guides; materials for self-guided tours. *Education and support for teachers:* In-service workshops on science content, telecomputing, and hands-on learning; leadership programs.

10.316 The Museum of Scientific Discovery, Strawberry Square, Third and Walnut, Harrisburg, PA 17108 *(Mailing address: P.O. Box 934, Harrisburg, PA 17108)*
(717) 233-7969

Science and technology center, with discovery labs and a discovery bar for interactive demonstrations; emphasizes physics, earth sciences, biology, health, mathematics, and technology. *Programs for students:* At the center: discovery lab workshops (enhanced field trip workshops); more than 100 participatory presentations and demonstrations; more than 100 interactive exhibits. At schools: outreach assembly programs; hands-on workshops; portable planetarium; Pennsylvania chapter of Science-by-Mail (national student/scientist pen pal program for grades 4-9). *Materials:* Hands-on activity books; teacher's guides; pre-/postvisit materials. *Education and support for teachers:* In-service workshops on science content and hands-on learning; newsletter.

10.317 National Aviary in Pittsburgh, Allegheny Commons West Park, Pittsburgh, PA 15212
(412) 323-7235

A zoo for birds—more than 450, representing 225 species—with 5 discovery stations and a botanical garden. *Programs for students:* At the aviary: guided/self-guided tours; classes; discovery workshops; bird shows; hands-on exhibits. *Materials:* Hands-on activity books; curriculum units with hands-on materials; teacher's guides; pre-/postvisit materials; newsletter for students. *Education and support for teachers:* Environmental discovery workshops and in-service workshops on science content and hands-on learning; newsletter.

10.318 The North Museum of Natural History and Science, Franklin and Marshall College, 400 College Ave., Lancaster, PA 17604 *(Mailing address: P.O. Box 3003, Lancaster, PA 17604-3003)*
(717) 291-3941

Museum of natural history and science, with a planetarium, herpetarium, and hands-on discovery room. *Programs for students:* At the museum: interactive tours; hands-on exhibits; planetarium shows; field trips; 8-week, award-winning summer science program. At schools: outreach programs. *Materials:* Hands-on activity books; teacher's guides; lending boxes of hands-on materials. *Education and support for teachers:* Newsletter.

10.319 Philadelphia Zoological Garden, 3400 W. Girard Ave., Philadelphia, PA 19104-1196
(215) 243-1100
http://www.phillyzoo.org

Zoo and botanical collection on 42 acres, with 1,600 animals representing 500 species. *Programs for students:* At the zoo: classes; guided tours; field trips; animal demonstrations; hands-on exhibits. At schools: outreach programs; traveling exhibits. *Materials:* Teacher's guides; audiovisual and computer-based materials. *Education and support for teachers:* In-service workshops on science content and hands-on learning; newsletter.

10.320 **Stroud Water Research Center,** The Academy of Natural Sciences of Phildelphia, 970 Spencer Rd., Avondale, PA 19311 (610) 268-2153

Stream research laboratory of the Academy of Natural Sciences of Philadelphia, focusing on watersheds and the conservation of water resources. ***Programs for students***: At the center: programs for school groups; field studies. At schools: outreach programs; traveling exhibits. ***Materials:*** Leaf Pack Experiment (curriculum packet on streamside forests and stream ecology). ***Education and support for teachers:*** In-service workshops and institutes on science content and hands-on learning; speakers bureau.

10.321 **Wagner Free Institute of Science,** 1700 W. Montgomery Ave., Philadelphia, PA 19121 (215) 763-6529

Historic museum, focused primarily on natural history, geology, and paleontology. ***Programs for students:*** At the museum: hands-on classes; guided tours; lectures. ***Materials:*** Exhibit worksheets. ***Education and support for teachers:*** Courses, lectures, and workshops on science content; newsletter.

NEW ENGLAND REGION

Connecticut

10.322 **The Discovery Museum,** 4450 Park Ave., Bridgeport, CT 06604
(203) 372-3521

Museum focusing on the physical sciences and the arts, with a planetarium and a Challenger Learning Center. *Programs for students:* At the museum: hands-on exhibits; classes for school groups. At schools: participatory programs. *Materials:* Hands-on activity books; teacher's guides; audiovisual and computer-based materials. *Education and support for teachers:* In-service workshops on science content and hands-on learning; newsletter.

10.323 **The Maritime Aquarium at Norwalk,** 10 N. Water St., Norwalk, CT 06854
(203) 852-0700

Aquarium and maritime history museum with an IMAX theater; a primary participant in the JASON Project and The Voyage of the *Mimi* (oceanography curriculums); focused on marine and environmental sciences and ecology. *Programs for students:* At the center: hands-on exhibits; classes; JASON- and *Mimi*-related programs; guided/self-guided tours; marine biology and ecology cruises; coastal field programs. At schools: outreach programs with hands-on

activities. *Materials:* Curriculum units with hands-on materials; audiovisual and supplemental materials; teacher's guides. *Education and support for teachers:* In-service workshops on science content and hands-on learning; teacher resource room; newsletter.

10.324 **Mystic Marinelife Aquarium,** 55 Coogan Blvd., Mystic, CT 06355 *(Mailing address: 55 Coogan Blvd., Mystic, CT 06355-1997)*
(860) 572-5955

Aquarium and marine-life museum with a marine theater. *Programs for students:* At the aquarium: programs for school groups; hands-on exhibits; interpretation of exhibits. At the aquarium and at schools within a 75-mile radius: workshops for students from prekindergarten through college. At field sites (salt marshes and estuary): field study programs. *Materials:* Hands-on activity books; teacher's guides; pre-/during-/postvisit activity kits; fact sheets and research updates. *Education and support for teachers:* In-service education on science content and hands-on learning, at the aquarium, at schools, and in the field.

10.325 **Science Center of Connecticut,** 950 Trout Brook Dr., West Hartford, CT 06119
(860) 231-2824

Science and technology center, with a planetarium, a center with live animals and a touch tank, a computer laboratory, interactive mathematics exhibits, and an affiliated nature center focused on environmental education and outdoor learning experiences. *Programs for students:* At the center: more than 50 hands-on programs for school groups; summer and school

vacation science sessions; hands-on exhibits; exhibit scavenger hunts. At schools: outreach programs, including the Wizard's Lab traveling science show. *Materials:* Curriculum activities. *Education and support for teachers:* In-service workshops on integration of hands-on science activities in the classroom; Internet training sessions; curriculum design consultation.

Maine

10.326 **The Children's Museum of Maine,** 142 Free St., Portland, ME 04101 *(Mailing address: P.O. Box 4041, Portland, ME 04101)*
(207) 828-1234

Children's museum with a computer lab and a hands-on science bar, for children ages 1-14, with an interdisciplinary approach to the sciences, arts, and humanities, and special emphasis on science. *Programs for students:* At the museum: hands-on exhibits; demonstrations; after-school curriculum program; guided/self-guided tours. At schools: outreach programs; traveling exhibits. *Materials:* Curriculum units with hands-on materials; supplemental activities. *Education and support for teachers:* In-service workshops on science content and hands-on learning; newsletter.

10.327 **Maine State Museum,** Library-Museum-Archives Building, State House Complex, Augusta, ME 04333 *(Mailing address: State House Station 83, Augusta, ME 04333)*
(207) 287-2301

State museum serving as a repository for the historic and prehistoric evidence of Maine's past, with science programs and exhibits emphasizing natural history, prehistory, engineering, and technology. *Programs for students:* At the museum: formal education classes, including hands-on gallery programs and guided tours. *Materials:* Loans of archaeological artifacts; exhibit guides; resource kit of materials, slides, and teacher's guide to natural fibers; video production on Maine's only mammoth. *Education and support for teachers:* Annual 1-week field school in archaeology; upon request, additional information on science-related topics of museum exhibits.

10.328 **Mount Desert Oceanarium**, 172 Clark Point Rd., Southwest Harbor, ME 04679 *(Mailing address: P.O. Box 696, Southwest Harbor, ME 04679)* (207) 244-7330

Oceanarium, lobster museum, lobster hatchery and marsh walk, located at 2 sites near each other, emphasizing marine life, natural history, aquaculture, and commercial fishing in Maine. *Programs for students:* At the sites: programs for school groups, featuring live animals; guided/self-guided tours; hands-on exhibits. At schools: outreach programs; traveling exhibits. **Education and support for teachers:** In-service workshops on science content and hands-on learning.

Massachusetts

10.329 **Cape Cod Museum of Natural History**, Rte. 6A, Brewster, MA 02631 *(Mailing address: P.O. Box 1710, Brewster, MA 02631)* (508) 896-3867

Museum with aquariums; interactive exhibits; and a trail system traversing woodlands, salt marsh, beach, and tidal estuaries; emphasis on natural history, with a strong Cape

Cod focus. *Programs for students:* At the museum: simulated archaeological dig; guided/self-guided tours; off-site field studies; marine science cruises. At schools: programs during and after school. *Materials:* Loans of science-enrichment kits; teacher's guides; audiovisual materials. *Education and support for teachers:* In-service workshops on natural history topics and hands-on learning; teacher resource library; newsletter.

10.330 **The Children's Museum**, Museum Wharf, 300 Congress St., Boston, MA 02210-1034 (617) 426-6500

Children's museum with strong physical and life science components; produces exhibits that travel to other science/discovery museums, demonstrating principles of physical science with everyday objects. *Programs for students:* At the museum: self-guided tours; visits guided by museum educators; hands-on exhibits. At schools: outreach programs. *Materials:* Hands-on activity books; multimedia rental kits on more than 25 topics in natural history and physical science; teacher's guides; audiovisual materials; catalog of materials. *Education and support for teachers:* In-service workshops on science content and hands-on learning; resource center.

10.331 **Harvard Museums of Cultural and Natural History,** Harvard University, 26 Oxford St., Cambridge, MA 02138 (617) 495-2341

Four university museums of international renown: Museum of Comparative Zoology, Peabody Museum of Archaeology and Ethnology, Botanical Museum, and Mineralogical Museum. *Programs for students:* At the museums: guided

tours; hands-on exhibits; hour-long programs for school groups on themes suggested by exhibited materials. *Education and support for teachers:* At a school's request: in-service workshops on science content and hands-on learning.

10.332 **Museum of Science,** Science Park, Boston, MA 02114-1099 (617) 723-2500 http://www.mos.org

Renowned museum, housing 400 permanent exhibits on the process of science and on natural history and the physical sciences, with 3 staffed discovery spaces, a planetarium, an OMNI theater, and the world's largest air-insulated Van de Graaff generator. *Programs for students:* At the museum: hands-on exhibits; demonstrations; more than 25 programs for school groups; field studies; science theater presentations; Science-by-Mail (national student/scientist pen pal program for grades 4-9). At schools: outreach programs. *Materials:* Science kits on 16 topics; audiovisual materials; catalog of materials. *Education and support for teachers:* In-service workshops on science content, hands-on learning, and the Internet.

10.333 **New England Aquarium,** Central Wharf, Boston, MA 02110-3399 (617) 973-5200 http://www.neaq.org

Aquarium with an education center featuring 2 learning studios, a wet lab, and an aquarium library; focused on aquatic education and conservation. *Programs for students:* At the aquarium: guided tours; demonstrations; whale-watch trips and exploration of local marine life by boat. At schools: assemblies; class programs; traveling exhibits. *Materials:* Hands-on activity books; audiovisual, computer-based, and supplemental materials; teaching kits; catalog of materials. *Education and support for teachers:* In-service education on science content and hands-on learning; information service; teacher resource center; newsletter.

10.334 New England Science Center, 222 Harrington Way, Worcester, MA 01604
(508) 791-9211

Museum and wildlife center focused on environmental science, earth systems, and global change, with an observatory, a planetarium/omnisphere, a telecommunications center, a children's discovery room, and more than 100 animals (27 species) and 60 acres that include nature trails, streams, ponds, and wetland areas. *Programs for students:* At the center: classes; guided tours; hands-on exhibits. At schools: outreach programs, including semester or year-long collaborative programs. *Materials:* Teacher's guides. *Education and support for teachers:* In-service workshops on science content and hands-on learning; library.

10.335 Springfield Science Museum, 236 State St., Springfield, MA 01103
(413) 733-1194

Regional museum with 10 exhibit halls, including an exploration center; focused on natural history, physical science, and anthropology. *Programs for students:* At the museum: hands-on exhibits; participatory daytrip programs; guided tours. At schools: outreach programs. *Materials:* Activity kits for rent; catalog of

materials. *Education and support for teachers:* In-service seminars and workshops on science content and hands-on learning.

New Hampshire

10.336 Audubon Society of New Hampshire, 3 Silk Farm Rd., Concord, NH 03301-8200
(603) 224-9909

Organization that operates the following: Concord Audubon Center in Concord, N.H.; Paradise Point Nature Center in Hebron, N.H.; Loon Preservation Center in Moultonboro, N.H.; Seacoast Science Center in Rye, N.H.; Massabesic Audubon Center in Auburn, N.H.; and more than 50 other wildlife sanctuaries, critical habitat areas, and easements throughout the state. *Programs for students:* At the centers: hands-on exhibits; programs; guided/self-guided tours; field trips. At schools: extensive, participatory, environmental education programs. *Materials:* Hands-on activity books; curriculum units with hands-on materials; teacher's guides; audiovisual materials for loan. *Education and support for teachers:* In-service workshops on hands-on learning, some on national programs, some at teachers' schools, many in summer; newsletter.

10.337 Seacoast Science Center, Rte. 1A, at Odiorne Point State Park, Rye, NH 03870 *(Mailing address: 570 Ocean Blvd., Rye, NH 03870)*
(603) 436-8043

Aquarium and environmental education center at a 300-acre park featuring 7 distinct habitats; focused on marine and coastal biology, natural sciences, and cultural history. *Programs for students:* At the center: outdoor classes;

guided/self-guided tours. At schools: outreach programs, with live animals. *Materials:* Hands-on activity books; teacher's guides with activities for classes at the center; pre-/postvisit activities. *Education and support for teachers:* Seasonal workshops; newsletter.

Rhode Island

10.338 Audubon Society of Rhode Island, 12 Sanderson Rd., Smithfield, RI 02917
(401) 949-5454

Headquarters for a 78-acre habitat area and other wildlife refuges, and location of the Teacher Resource Center, a statewide lending library of environmental materials. *Programs for students:* At refuges and at schools: field trip programs led by Audubon educators. At schools: hands-on outreach programs. *Materials:* Lending boxes; hands-on activity books; curriculum units with hands-on materials; teacher's guides. *Education and support for teachers:* In-service workshops on science content and hands-on learning.

10.339 Museum of Natural History, Roger Williams Park, Providence, RI 02905
(401) 785-9450
http://ids.net/~cormack_pl/museum.html

Natural history museum, with a planetarium, an education center, and teacher resource center; focused on environmental, life, earth and space sciences, and material culture. *Programs for students:* At the museum: interactive, discovery-based science workshops. *Materials:* Loan kits of natural history objects. *Education and support for teachers:* In-service education on the teaching and learning of science.

10.340 Roger Williams Park Zoo, 1000 Elmwood Ave., Providence, RI 02907-3600
(401) 785-3510

One of America's first zoos, with more than 900 animals on 42 acres in naturalistic settings, arranged in geographical sections including the Plains of Africa, Tropical America, Madagascar, Australasia, and the Marco Polo Trail. *Programs for students:* At the zoo: programs for school groups; guided/self-guided tours. At schools: outreach programs. *Materials:* Hands-on activity books; lending kits. *Education and support for teachers:* In-service workshops on science content and hands-on learning; summer institutes; individual consulting; newsletter.

10.341 Thames Science Center, 77 Long Wharf, Newport, RI 02840 *(Mailing address: P.O. Box 194, Newport, RI 02840)*
(401) 849-6966

Regional science museum, with a marine touch tank, emphasizing biological, physical, and applied sciences. *Programs for students:* At the museum: programs for school groups; hands-on exhibits; guided tours; scientist inventors program. At schools: outreach programs. *Materials:* Curriculum materials. *Education and support for teachers:* In-service workshops on science content and hands-on learning.

Vermont

10.342 The Discovery Museum, 51 Park St., Essex Junction, VT 05452
(802) 878-8687

Science museum for grades K-12, with a planetarium and a 1950s-style diner in which students participate in hands-on experiments; emphasis on the physical, natural, and environmental sciences. *Programs for students:* At the museum: participatory exhibits; classes and workshops; guided tours; planetarium shows; field trips. At schools: classroom workshops and experiments. *Materials:* Lending kits with hands-on materials; supplemental activities; catalog of materials. *Education and support for teachers:* Teacher training sessions; newsletter.

10.343 Fairbanks Museum and Planetarium, Main and Prospect, St. Johnsbury, VT 05819
(802) 748-2372
http://www.genghis.com/fairbanks/museum.htm

General museum and planetarium, also including the Northern New England Weather Center, offering instructional programs in biology, ecology, meteorology, astronomy, geology, and physics. *Programs for students:* At the museum: hands-on natural history exhibits; classes. At field study sites: programs. At schools: outreach programs. *Materials:* Curriculum materials; audio-visual materials; catalog of materials. *Education and support for teachers:* In-service workshops on science content and hands-on learning; lending library of science materials.

10.344 Montshire Museum of Science, Montshire Road, Norwich, VT 05055 *(Mailing address: P.O. Box 770, Norwich, VT 05055)*
(802) 649-2200

Science museum and education center, with 100 acres of woodland and trails along the Connecticut River; focused on the natural and physical sciences, ecology, and technology. *Programs for students:* At the museum: workshops; classes; self-guided tours; field trips; hands-on exhibits and demonstrations. At schools: hands-on exhibits; portable planetarium; "rent-a-scientist" programs. *Materials:* Teacher's guides; catalog of materials. *Education and support for teachers:* In-service workshops and courses on science content and hands-on learning.

CANADA

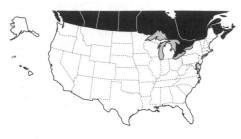

10.345 The Calgary Science Centre, 701 11th St., S.W., Calgary, Alberta, Canada T2P 2M5 *(Mailing address: Box 2100, Stn. M, Loc. Code #73, Calgary, Alberta, Canada T2P 2M5)* (403) 221-3701

Science center, including a multi-media science theater with Digistar projector, exhibit hall, and a science demonstration area. ***Programs for students:*** At the center: programs for school groups; science demonstrations; hands-on exhibits; science theater presentations; multimedia shows; science and technology competitions. At schools: inflatable planetarium. ***Materials:*** Teacher's guides; pre-/postvisit materials. ***Education and support for teachers:*** Professional development program associated with a 1-week class experience at the science center for grades 4-6 (teacher-directed program with guidance from campus coordinator and volunteer experts).

10.346 National Museum of Science and Technology, 1867 St. Laurent Blvd., Ottawa, Ontario, Canada K1G 5A3 *(Mailing address: P.O. Box 9724, Ottawa Terminal, Ottawa, Ontario, Canada K1G 5A3)* (613) 991-3044

Science and technology museum, emphasizing physical and space sciences, computers, and technol-ogy. ***Programs for students:*** At the museum: hands-on exhibits; guided tours; programs for school groups. ***Materials:*** Teacher's guides; audio-visual materials; pre-/postvisit materials and activity sheets available to program participants; catalog of materials. ***Education and support for teachers:*** In-service workshops on hands-on learning; newsletter.

10.347 Ontario Science Centre, 770 Don Mills Rd., Don Mills, Ontario, Canada M3C 1T3 (416) 429-4100 http://www.osc.on.ca

Renowned science center, with a Challenger Learning Center, an Omnimax theater, and numerous hands-on exhibits focused on the life, physical, earth, and space sciences. ***Programs for students:*** At the center: hands-on participatory workshops; presentations to school groups; programs to accompany films; hands-on exhibits. At schools: outreach programs. ***Materials:*** Hands-on activity books; teacher's guides; pre-/postvisit materials. ***Education and support for teachers:*** Workshops.

10.348 Saskatchewan Science Centre, Winnipeg Street and Wascana Drive, Regina, Saskatchewan, Canada S4P 3M3 *(Mailing address: P.O. Box 5071, Regina, Saskatchewan, Canada S4P 3M3)* (306) 791-7900 http://www.sciencecentre.saskweb.com

Science center in 2 facilities: an IMAX theater and a Powerhouse of Discovery with more than 80 hands-on exhibits; emphasis on the physical, life, and environmental sciences. ***Programs for students:*** At the center: shows; demonstrations; programs for school groups; table-top science experiences; workshops. At schools: outreach programs. ***Materials:*** Hands-on activity books; lending boxes of hands-on materials; teacher's guides. ***Education and support for teachers:*** In-service workshops on science content and hands-on learning; newsletter.

10.349 Science North, 100 Ramsey Lake Rd., Sudbury, Ontario, Canada P3E 5S9 (705) 522-3701 http://sciencenorth.on.ca

Northern Ontario's original science center, with an IMAX theater, nickel mine, fossil lab, and solar telescope; focused on the physical, life, earth, space, environmental, and information sciences, and technology. ***Programs for students:*** At the center: classes; interactive workshops; hands-on exhibits; field trips. At schools: outreach programs; traveling exhibits. ***Materials:*** Hands-on activity books; teacher's guide. ***Education and support for teachers:*** In-service workshops on science content and hands-on learning; newsletter.

10.350 SCIENCE WORLD British Columbia, 1455 Quebec St., Vancouver, British Columbia, Canada V6A 3Z7 (604) 443-7440 http://www.scienceworld.bc.ca

Science center with an Omnimax theater, emphasizing all the sciences, technology, and mathematics. ***Programs for students:*** At the center: interactive displays; shows; demonstrations; workshops. At schools throughout British Columbia: science presentations and hands-on displays. *Materials:* Hands-on activity books; teacher's guides; pre-/postvisit and computer-based materials. ***Education and support for teachers:*** In-service education on science content and hands-on learning; lecture series; newsletter.

10.351 **Vancouver Aquarium, Canada's Pacific National Aquarium,** in Stanley Park, Vancouver, British Columbia, Canada V6B 3X8 *(Mailing address: P.O. Box 3232, Vancouver, British Columbia, Canada V6B 3X8)* (604) 685-3364 http://www.vancouver-aquarium.org

Canada's Pacific National Aquarium, dedicated to effecting the conservation of aquatic life through display and interpretation, education, research, and direct action. ***Programs for students:*** At the aquarium: self-guided tours; hands-on exhibits; field trips; curriculum-based school programs; overnight programs. At schools: aquavan; aquakits; speakers bureau. ***Materials:*** Hands-on activity books; teacher resource manual and pre-/postvisit materials with each formal on-site program; fact sheets. ***Education and support for teachers:*** Pre-/in-service workshops on hands-on, curriculum-based activities for teaching life sciences in the classroom; newsletter.

CHAPTER 11

PROFESSIONAL ASSOCIATIONS AND U.S. GOVERNMENT ORGANIZATIONS

11.1 **Amateur Astronomers Association**, 1010 Park Ave., New York, NY 10028
(212) 535-2922
http://www.aaa.org

Association of 500 career and amateur astronomers. ***Programs/services:*** Classes; lectures; constellation study; outdoor observing; telescope making; trips to observatories; speakers panel; reference library. ***Publications/materials:*** *Sky and Telescope* (magazine).

11.2 **American Association for the Advancement of Science**, 1200 New York Ave., N.W., Washington, DC 20005
(202) 326-6400
http://www.aaas.org/ehr
http://www.aaas.org/project2061
http://www.kineticcity.com

U.S. science organization that embraces all the sciences, with membership of 140,000 individuals and nearly 300 science societies and organizations. ***Programs/services:***

- Extensive programs and materials produced by the association's Directorate for Education and Human Resources include the following: **Annual Forum for School Science; Collaboration for Equity in Science; Minority Women in Science;** radio programs *Science Update* and *Kinetic City Super Crew* (the latter with teacher's guide, home activities, and call-in); senior scientists to collaborate with individual teachers; database of scientists who are available to help teachers; project **SLIC** (Science Linkages in the Community) to train people to teach science. ***Publications/materials:*** Books in many fields of science and science education, including *IDEAAAS: Sourcebook for Science, Mathematics and Technology Education*; *Science Books & Films* (review magazine); *Science Books & Films' Best Books for Children 1992-95*; videos focused on out-of-school programs for minorities, girls, and disabled students; *Earth Explorer*—comprehensive resource on environmental issues for students in grades 5-9; posters.

- **Project 2061:** a long-term science education reform initiative (grades K-12), seeking science literacy for all high school graduates. ***Publications/materials:*** *Science for All Americans*—on science literacy; *Benchmarks for Science Literacy*—curriculum-design tool defining expectations for science knowledge for grades 2, 5, 8, and 12; *Resources for Science Literacy: Professional Development*; other books and computer-based materials on curriculum design, exemplary resources, and research.

Educators participating in a hands-on workshop

ABOUT THE ANNOTATIONS IN CHAPTER 11

General information about chapter 11, "Professional Associations and U.S. Government Organizations," is contained in the "Part 4 Overview," on pages 306-309.

The annotations in this chapter are arranged alphabetically by organization names. The annotations provide addresses, telephone and fax numbers, and Web site addresses, where available. The name and address of an appropriate person, such as an executive director, is provided for any organization that does not have a fixed address.

11.3 American Association of Physics Teachers, American Center for Physics, One Physics Ellipse, College Park, MD 20740
(301) 209-3300
http://www.aapt.org

Professional association of more than 11,000 college-level physicists, high school physics teachers, and others interested in the quality of physics education. *Programs/services:* Cooperates with American Physical Society (*see* 11.17) in **Teacher-Scientist Alliance Institute** to mobilize scientists in support of systemic reform of science education. *Publications/materials: The Physics Teacher* (journal).

11.4 American Astronomical Society, Education Office, c/o Adler Planetarium, 1300 S. Lake Shore Dr., Chicago, IL 60605
(312) 294-0340
http://www.aas.org

Professional society of more than 6,000 astronomers, physicists, and other scientists in related fields. *Programs/services:* Teacher workshops at society meetings; Bok Prize for Astronomy, at Intel International Science and Engineering Fair. *Publications/materials: A New Universe to Explore: Careers in Astronomy* (brochure).

11.5 American Ceramic Society, 735 Ceramic Pl., P.O. Box 6136, Westerville, OH 43081-6136
(614) 890-4700
http://www.acers.org

Professional society of 10,000 scientists, engineers, educators, and others interested in a wide range of ceramics applications, including medicine, aerospace, fiber optics, electronics, automobiles, and the environment. *Programs/services:* Program linking scientists to schools nationwide to serve as mentors, to make in-school presentations, and to invite students to the workplace; through these links, the society fosters scientist-teacher collaborations and partnerships that provide teachers and students access to the society's publications and materials. *Publications/materials: Science on Wheels* (experiment manual); ceramic sample kit; *Ceramics—Into the Future* (video); *Career Opportunities in Ceramics* (brochure).

11.6 American Cetacean Society, P.O. Box 1391, San Pedro, CA 90733
(310) 548-6279
http://www.acsonline.org

Volunteer organization of more than 2,500 scientists, educators, and lay persons interested in education about and devoted to the protection of whales, dolphins, and porpoises. *Programs/services:* Information hotline; volunteer opportunities for teachers; research library. *Publications/materials: Gray Whale Teaching Kit; Whalewatcher* (journal); newsletter; bibliography; information sheets available free of charge to children.

11.7 American Chemical Society, 1155 16th St., N.W., Washington, DC 20036
(202) 872-4600; (800) 227-5558
http://www.acs.org
http://www.chemcenter.org

Principal professional society of chemists, with 150,000 members. *Publications/materials:* Foundations and Challenges to Encourage Technology-based Science (FACETS)—integrated science curriculum for grades 6-8; supplemental activities; *WonderScience*—hands-on physical science magazine for grades 4-6; audiovisual materials; catalog of teaching resources; newsletter; posters.

11.8 American Forest Foundation, 1111 19th St., N.W., Suite 780, Washington, DC 20036
(202) 463-2462
http://www.affoundation.org

Nonprofit environmental education and forest conservation organization. *Programs/services:* Cosponsored with the Council for Environmental Education: **Project Learning Tree (PLT)**—comprehensive environmental education program for students (PreK-12) in 50 states and 6 foreign countries, focused on a broad range of environmental issues and designed to develop critical-thinking skills. Project Learning Tree is also a distribution network for PLT curriculum and other materials; workshops, with accompanying instructional materials, are provided for teaching PLT. *Publications/materials:* PLT curriculum units and teacher's guides; computer-based and other materials distributed mostly through the PLT network; newsletter.

11.9 American Geological Institute, 4220 King St., Alexandria, VA 22302-1507
(703) 379-2480

Federation of more than 25 professional, scientific, and technical associations in the earth sciences; concerned with improving earth science education in schools, colleges, and universities. *Publications/materials:* Text-based instructional materials; leaflet describing careers in the geosciences; dictionary of geological terms; book on planning for field study; *Earth Science Content Guidelines*—report, including activities, to guide the inclusion of earth science content in curriculum for grades K-12, with ideas and activities in the areas of solid earth, water, air, ice, life, and earth in space.

11.10 American Geophysical Union, 2000 Florida Ave., N.W., Washington, DC 20009
(202) 462-6900; (800) 966-AGU1

Professional society with more than 35,000 members, focused on geophysics. *Programs/services:* **Geophysical Information For Teachers (GIFT)** workshops for K-12 teachers at annual meetings; support for science Olympiads. *Publications/materials*: *Earth in Space*—topical geophysical information journal for students and teachers; annotated slide sets; career information.

11.11 American Institute of Aeronautics and Astronautics, 1801 Alexander Bell Dr., 5th Floor, Reston, VA 20191-4344
(703) 264-7500
http://www.aiaa.org

Principal technical society for engineering and science in aviation and space, with 30,000 members. *Programs/services:* Volunteer efforts, usually through local sections of the institute, available to provide teacher workshops, tutor and mentor students, judge science fairs, sponsor essay contests, hold paper airplane contests, and work with teachers and students. *Publications/materials:* Brochures; videos; career information.

11.12 American Institute of Biological Sciences, 1444 I St., N.W., Suite 200, Washington, DC 20005
(202) 628-1500; (800) 992-AIBS
http://www.aibs.org

Umbrella organization of professional life science societies and institutions; concerned with policy issues affecting the biological community, with biological education and research, and with interactions among biology societies and disciplines. *Programs/services:* Sessions on innovative teaching methods at annual meetings; database of scientists who are available to help teachers. *Publications/materials:* *BioScience* (monthly magazine); brochure on careers in biology.

11.13 American Institute of Physics, American Center for Physics, One Physics Ellipse, College Park, MD 20740-3843
(301) 209-3100
http://www.aip.org

Organization of 10 professional societies (totaling 100,000 members) and 19 affiliated societies in physics and related fields; concerned with collecting and disseminating information

about physics, physics education, and the history of physics. *Publications/materials:* *WonderScience*—hands-on science activity magazine for grades 4-6; *Physics Education Newsletter*—electronic newsletter for teachers and administrators.

11.14 American Meteorological Society, 1200 New York Ave., N.W., Suite 410, Washington, DC 20006
(202) 466-5728

Professional scientific society of more than 11,000 members; focused on meteorology, climatology, and oceanography. *Programs/services:* Two national projects—**Project ATMOSPHERE,** on meteorology and climatology, and the **Maury Project,** on oceanography—to train teachers (grades K-12), through 2-week institutes for master teachers, and monitoring of subsequent workshops nationwide in which the master teachers train other teachers. Available through a third major initiative, the **DataStreme Project**—distance-learning course emphasizing the study of current weather, with data delivered via the Internet [http://atm.geo.nsf.gov/devo]. *Publications/materials:* Teacher's guides; DataStreme study guides; materials; hands-on activities solely for use in the projects; audiovisual and computer-based materials; newsletter; career publications.

11.15 American Nature Study Society, c/o Pocono Environmental Education Center, R.R. 2, Box 1010, Dingmans Ferry, PA 18328
(717) 828-2319

Society of about 850 amateur and professional naturalists, conservationists, and teachers; focused on nature and environmental education. *Programs/services:* Workshops at society meetings. *Publications/materials: Nature Study*—journal with in-depth articles, teaching tips, and book reviews; newsletter.

11.16 **American Nuclear Society,** 555 N. Kensington Ave., La Grange Park, IL 60526
(708) 579-8230
http://www.ans.org

International scientific and educational organization composed of physicists, chemists, engineers, educators, and other professionals involved in nuclear science or engineering. *Programs/services:* Multifaceted **Public Education Program (PEP);** PEP Educational Outreach from local sections of the society, providing scientist collaborations, educator workshops, speaker resources, information hotlines; science competitions. *Publications/materials:* Curriculum units with hands-on materials; posters; career publications; newsletter.

11.17 **American Physical Society,** American Center for Physics, One Physics Ellipse, College Park, MD 20740
(301) 209-3200
http://aps.org/educ

Principal professional society for physicists and physics students, with more than 40,000 members; focused primarily on physics and also on physics education. *Programs/services:* **Teacher-Scientist Alliance Institute**—national cooperative effort operated with the American Association of Physics Teachers (*see* 11.3) to mobilize scientists in support of efforts at systemic reform of science education.

11.18 **American Physiological Society,** 9650 Rockville Pike, Bethesda, MD 20814-3991
(301) 530-7132
http://www.faseb.org/aps

Professional society of about 7,000 scientists; fosters scientific research on how the body functions. *Programs/services:* Database of scientists who are available to help teachers; summer research program for middle and high school teachers; online information service on educational materials, programs, and activities. *Publications/materials:* Curriculum units with hands-on, inquiry-based materials; resource sheets (e.g., list of resources, criteria for gender and race equity, and issues in animal research); audiovisual and computer-based materials; career information.

11.19 **American Plastics Council,** 1801 K St., N.W., Suite 701 L, Washington, DC 20006
(202) 371-5339; (800) 2-HELP-90
http://www.plasticsresource.com

National trade association representing the U.S. plastics industry on resource conservation issues. *Programs/services:* Workshops at National Science Teachers Association conventions and other conferences. *Publications/materials: Hands On Plastics: A Scientific Investigation Kit*—includes background information, recycled plastic resin samples, and lesson plans to teach chemical structures, identification codes, and recycling; video on plastics in everyday living.

11.20 **The American Society for Cell Biology,** 9650 Rockville Pike, Bethesda, MD 20814
(301) 530-7153
http://www.ascb.org/ascb

Society of more than 8,000 scientists in cell biology and allied fields. *Pro-*

grams/services: Cell biology symposium for teachers at each annual meeting of the National Association of Biology Teachers; database of scientists who are available to help teachers; letter-answering service for students; speakers.

11.21 **American Society for Microbiology,** 1325 Massachusetts Ave., N.W., Washington, DC 20005-4171
(202) 942-9283
http://www.asmusa.org/edusrc/edu1.htm

Oldest biological science society in the world, with 40,000 members. *Programs/services:* **Scientist-Educator Network**—consisting of scientists who are available to provide assistance as presenters, resource people (for advice and classroom visits), advisers to teachers on curriculum and projects, providers of laboratory tours, judges at science fairs, and, sometimes, mentors to students (to advise on projects and to be shadowed during the workday); database of members of this network is available to science teachers. *Publications/materials:* "How-to" manual for scientists involved in outreach efforts at schools; instructional materials for teachers; career information, including posters and booklet.

11.22 **American Society of Plant Physiologists,** 15501 Monona Dr., Rockville, MD 20855-2768
(301) 251-0560
http://aspp.org

International society of more than 5,000 plant-science researchers, professors, teachers, and students. *Programs/services:* Encourages teacher-scientist partnerships and scientist collaborations with individual teachers; develops partnerships with school systems and science outreach programs; supports the creation and development of teaching tools for plant science. *Publications/materials:* Career information; *Investigating Plants: Hands-on, Low-Cost Laboratory Exercises in Plant Sciences*, primarily for middle schools (available through National Association of Biology Teachers—see 11.69); videotape for scientists on conducting plant science labs for education outreach; brochure/teaching aid on functions and uses of plants; *Plant Physiology* and *The PLANT Cell* (journals).

11.23 American Solar Energy Society, 2400 Central Ave., Suite G-1, Boulder, CO 80301
(303) 443-3130
http://www.ases.org/solar

Academic society of more than 4,000 scientists, researchers, solar professionals, architects, and engineers, with a focus on increasing public awareness of the environmental and economic benefits of solar energy. *Publications/materials: Solar Today*—magazine providing background information on solar energy technologies and real-world applications; *Science Projects in Renewable Energy and Energy Efficiency*—workbook for grades K-12.

11.24 American Water Works Association, 6666 W. Quincy Ave., Denver, CO 80235
(303) 347-6140; (800) 926-7337
http://www.awwa.org

International scientific and educational society for water supply professionals, with more than 54,000 members, including utilities employees, water treatment operators, researchers, manufacturers, educators, and university students; dedicated to providing safe drinking water. *Programs/services:* Public education programs on improving

the quality of drinking water. *Publications/materials: The Story of Drinking Water* (curriculum unit); *How to Create a Successful Science Fair* (teacher's guide); activity books; audiovisual and computer-based materials; bookcovers; catalog of materials.

11.25 American Zoo and Aquarium Association, 7970-D Old Georgetown Rd., Bethesda, MD 20814
(301) 907-7777
http://www.aza.org

Association of more than 180 zoos, zoological parks, and aquariums, supporting membership excellence in conservation, education, science, and recreation. *Programs/services:* **Suitcase for Survival**—national program that provides suitcases filled with confiscated wildlife products and accompanied by educational materials to educate youth about protected wildlife and how illegal trade threatens the extinction of certain species. Program cosponsors: U.S. Fish and Wildlife Service, World Wildlife Fund, National Fish and Wildlife Foundation, and American Zoo and Aquarium Association (AZA); program coordinator: AZA. Teacher-training workshops held at selected zoological parks and aquariums nationwide; complete list of zoos and aquariums that disseminate Suitcase for Survival available from AZA. *Publications/materials:* Brochure on careers at zoos and aquariums.

11.26 The Annenberg/CPB Math and Science Project, 901 E St., N.W., Washington, DC 20004-2037
(202) 879-9654
http://www.learner.org

Project funded by the Annenberg Foundation as a project of the Corporation for Public Broadcasting (CPB), focused on improving math

and science education. *Programs/services:* Support provided for media and communications projects that help educators, administrators, and policymakers understand, appreciate, and implement mathematics and science education reform in the classroom; interactive TV and Web service. *Publications/materials:* Video professional development packages and a free resource database for teachers; *The Guide to Math and Science Reform*—interactive database; *SAMI (Science and Math Initiatives)*—database of Internet teaching resources; catalog of multimedia and print resources.

11.27 Association for Supervision and Curriculum Development (ASCD), 1250 N. Pitt St., Alexandria, VA 22314-1403
(703) 549-9110
http://www.ascd.org

Nonprofit educational association with more than 190,000 members. *Programs/services:* Dissemination of information on educational research and practice, and activities addressing teaching and learning in all fields; sessions at annual conference; **Professional Development Institutes** of 1 to 3 days in major U.S. cities; sponsorship of networks (usually with newsletters) that meet at annual conferences. *Publications/materials: ASCD Curriculum Handbook; Brown's Directories of Instructional Programs* (annual guide to commercial materials); *Only the Best* (annual guide to highest-rated computer-based materials); *Curriculum Materials Directory* (annual guide to noncommercial curriculum materials); *Educational Leadership* (journal); ASCD books; audio-/videotapes; newsletters.

11.28 **Association for the Education of Teachers in Science**, University of West Florida, 11000 University Pkwy., Pensacola, FL 32514-5753
(904) 474-2860
http://science.coe.uwf.edu/aets/aets.html

Educational association with 850 members, focused on the professional development of science teachers. *Programs/services:* Sessions at association meetings; workshops. *Publications/materials:* *Journal of Science Teacher Education;* a section of *Science Education;* yearbooks; newsletter.

11.29 **Association for the Promotion and Advancement of Science Education**, 1111 Homer St., Suite 200, Vancouver, British Columbia, Canada V6B 2Y1
(604) 687-8712
http://www.apase.bc.ca

Nonprofit organization devoted to increasing awareness, understanding, appreciation, and teaching of science and technology. *Programs/services:* Speakers at career days; scientist-mentors for students; teacher-scientist partnerships; database of scientists available for helping teachers; workshops at association meetings. *Publications/materials:* Curriculum units with hands-on materials; audiovisual and computer-based materials; interactive science resources for children, teachers, and parents on Web site; *PRISM*—newsletter to help adults guide and instruct children in learning about science and technology.

11.30 **Association of Science-Technology Centers (ASTC)**, 1025 Vermont Ave., N.W., Suite 500, Washington, DC 20005-3516
(202) 783-7200
http://www.astc.org/astc

Worldwide organization of science centers and museums, planetariums, space theaters, nature centers, aquariums, zoos, natural history museums, children's museums, and other facilities, with more than 400 members in the United States and Canada. *Programs/services:* Created and operates **YouthALIVE!**—a program for underserved adolescents (grades 5-12) delivered by 52 museums that are members of ASTC or the Association of Youth Museums (*see* 11.31). Offered through YouthALIVE! (for students ages 10-17): developmentally appropriate service-learning experiences and hands-on enrichment activities with structured opportunities, such as clubs, camps, classes, workshops, and field trips, to heighten interest and involvement in the physical and life sciences. Individual programs designed by museums, often working with community-based organizations, and seeking minimum involvement of 120 hours per year for 2 or 3 years for each student. Technical assistance and professional development provided by ASTC for museum staff members. *Publications/materials:* Current list of museums disseminating YouthALIVE! program; newsletter, directory of programs, and "how-to" manual for youth programs; *The ASTC/CIMUSET Directory* of member institutions (CIMUSET is the International Committee of Science and Technology Museums, of the International Council of Museums); publications catalog.

11.31 **Association of Youth Museums**, 1775 K St., N.W., Suite 595, Washington, DC 20006
(202) 466-4144

Professional service organization serving more than 360 member museums and professionals worldwide. *Programs/services:* Provides for interaction, information and professional development, and collaboration among youth museums and traditional museums with a special interest in children and family audiences; provides information on children's museums with a focus on interdisciplinary education.

11.32 **Astronomical Society of the Pacific**, 390 Ashton Ave., San Francisco, CA 94112
(415) 337-1100
http://www.aspsky.org

A 108-year-old scientific and educational society with members from 50 states and more than 60 countries, with the goal of sharing the excitement of astronomy with teachers, students, and the public. *Programs/services:* **Project ASTRO**—program linking teachers and students in grades 4-9 with amateur and professional astronomers; summer workshops on teaching astronomy in grades 3-12; astronomy information hotline. *Publications/materials:* Instructional materials; information packets; *The Universe at Your Fingertips* (resource guide for teachers); audiovisual and computer-based materials; posters; catalog of materials; *The Universe in the Classroom* (newsletter on teaching astronomy in grades 3-12).

11.33 **Atlantic Center for the Environment**, 55 S. Main St., Ipswich, MA 01938-2396
(508) 356-0038
http://www.qlf.org

Environmental arm of the Quebec-Labrador Foundation, a nonprofit community service and education organization supporting rural communities and the environment of eastern Canada and New England. *Programs/services:* Teacher-training workshops and sessions; scientist-teacher collaborations; lab visits and research opportunities for students.

11.34 Biological Sciences Curriculum Study (BSCS), 5415 Mark Dabling Blvd., Colorado Springs, CO 80918-3842
(719) 531-5550
http://www.bscs.org

Research and development organization, focused on improvement of science education and professional development of teachers. *Programs/ services:* Workshops and teacher-education opportunities to help teachers use BSCS programs. *Publications/materials: Middle School Science & Technology* (curriculum for grades 6-8).

11.35 Challenger Learning Centers, Challenger Center for Space Science Education, 1029 N. Royal St., Suite 300, Alexandria, VA 22314
(703) 683-9740
http://www.challenger.org

Network of 30 centers in the United States and Canada, at museums and on school and university campuses, focused on space science, and using simulation, teamwork, creative problem solving, and responsible decision making. *Programs/services:* Space flight simulators with hands-on learning experiences and classroom-based projects for students; workshops for teachers using hands-on activities and mission simulation models, with faculty drawn largely from National Aeronautics and Space Administration (NASA) Teacher-in-Space finalists; speakers bureau. *Publications/materials:* Hands-on instructional units and teacher activity guides on space topics; audio-visual and computer-based materials; newsletter.

11.36 Cornell Lab of Ornithology, 159 Sapsucker Woods Rd., Ithaca, NY 14850-1999
(607) 254-2440
http://www.ornith.cornell.edu

International center for the study, appreciation, and conservation of birds and an authoritative source of information about birds. *Programs/ services:* Provides up-to-date ornithological data to scientists and communications media worldwide; developed the following "citizen-science" projects allowing participation in hands-on, inquiry-based activities:

- **Birds in Forested Landscapes Project**—to determine the habitat needs of North American birds.
- **Cornell Nest Box Network**—to study the biology and behavior of cavity-nesting birds.
- **Project/Classroom FeederWatch**—to help scientists track winter bird populations at feeders.
- **Project PigeonWatch**—to help scientists answer questions about pigeon biology and behavior.

Publications/materials: Research kits for all public projects; bird sound recordings on cassettes and CDs; slide collection, with copies at nominal fee; *Living Bird* (magazine); *Birdscape* (newsletter).

11.37 Council for Exceptional Children, 1920 Association Dr., Reston, VA 20191-1589
(703) 620-3660; (703) 264-9446 (TTY)
http://www.cec.sped.org

Professional association for special educators, related service providers, and parents working to improve the educational success of individuals with disabilities and/or who are gifted. *Programs/services:* Annual convention; topical conferences; symposiums; workshops; conferences of state feder-

ations; operation of the ERIC Clearinghouse on Disabilities and Gifted Education and the National Clearinghouse for Professions in Special Education. *Publications/materials:* Extensive literature on special education and gifted education, including curriculum materials, with semiannual catalog; *TEACHING Exceptional Children* and *Exceptional Children* (journals); newsletter; publications of the council's various divisions; career information.

11.38 Council of State Science Supervisors, c/o Council President, Colorado Department of Education, 201 E. Colfax Ave., Denver, CO 80203
(303) 866-6764
http://www.k12.ar.us/csss/index.htm

Organization consisting of a state-level science supervisor/specialist/consultant from each of the 50 states and other jurisdictions (e.g., the District of Columbia, Puerto Rico, Guam). *Programs/services:* Sessions at National Science Teachers Association conventions (regional and national); program of **Presidential Awards for Excellence in Science and Mathematics Teaching;** coordination of individual members' work in creating curriculum guidelines, frameworks, assessments, and standards within their respective areas; information dissemination, primarily to members.

11.39 Ecological Society of America, 2010 Massachusetts Ave., N.W., Suite 400, Washington, DC 20036
(202) 833-8773
http://esa.sdsc.edu

Professional society of more than 7,000 educators, ecologists, and other scientists; focused on the study of plants, animals, and humans in relation to their environment. *Publications/materials: Ecology Education for Children: A Framework of Excellence* (curriculum guidelines); *Careers in Ecology* (brochure); *Ecosystem Services* and *Human Alteration of the Global Nitrogen Cycle* (booklets); fact sheets; *Ecology* (journal).

11.40 **Education Development Center**, 55 Chapel St., Newton, MA 02158-1060
(617) 969-7100
http://www.edc.org

International education research and development organization, with a Center for Science Education and a Center for Learning, Teaching, and Technology among its subdivisions. *Programs/services:* Workshops at meetings of National Science Teachers Association and other organizations; technical assistance to several school districts in implementing systemic reform, with special emphasis on urban schools. *Publications/materials: Insights: An Inquiry-Based Middle School Science Curriculum* (available in Spring 1998)—6 modules for grades 7 and 8 that develop science concepts in the life, earth, and physical sciences; *A World in Motion II: The Design Experience*—interdisciplinary middle school curriculum focusing on engineering, physics, social studies, and mathematical applications; teacher's guides; posters.

11.41 **Eisenhower National Clearinghouse for Mathematics and Science Education (ENC)**, The Ohio State University, 1929 Kenny Rd., Columbus, OH 43210-1079
(614) 292-7784; (800) 621-5785
http://www.enc.org

Clearinghouse for science and mathematics education information (grades K-12), financed by U.S. Department of Education. *Services/materials:* Comprehensive collection of curriculum resources in many formats (print, audio, multimedia, video, kits, games). *ENC Resource Finder,* a detailed catalog of these resources, is available at the ENC Web site ENC Online, which is accessible via World Wide Web [http://www.enc.org], modem [1-800-362-4448 or 1-614-292-9040], and Telnet [enc.org]. Products and services available in print and electronic format, and include newsletters (e.g., *ENC Update*), topical catalogs (e.g., *ENC Focus*), CD-ROMs, and a database of federal programs. Professional development programs conducted nationwide; reference services and technical support provided for ENC users [e-mail: info@enc.org]. Products free to qualified users.

11.42 **Environmental Action Coalition**, 625 Broadway, 9th Floor, New York, NY 10012
(212) 677-1601

Nonprofit organization concerned with education in the areas of household hazardous waste, recycling, waste prevention, and urban forestry. *Publications/materials: Woods and Water*—curriculum on protection of forests and watersheds.

11.43 **EPIE Institute**, 103-3 W. Montauk Hwy., Hampton Bays, NY 11946
(516) 728-9100
http://www.epie.org

Consumer-oriented organization that evaluates educational products. *Programs/services:* LINCT (Learning and Information Network for Community Telecomputing)—program to help communities achieve universal, equitable access to electronic information and learning resources. *Publications/materials: TESS (The Educational Software Selector)*—database with information on more than 3,000 educational software programs ranging over all the sciences and social sciences (including citations to reviews), available on CD-ROM.

11.44 **ERIC Clearinghouse for Science, Mathematics, and Environmental Education**, The Ohio State University, 1929 Kenny Rd., Columbus, OH 43210-1080
(614) 292-6717; (800) 276-0462; 800-LET-ERIC (for new users)
http://www.ericse.org

Clearinghouse and international information network, 1 of 16 in the ERIC (Educational Resources Information Center) system, which is supported by the U.S. Department of Education (*see* 11.119). *Services/programs:* Collects, catalogs, and provides access to educational materials; offers reference and referral services; produces bibliographic information; maintains extensive database of reports, curricular and instructional materials, evaluations, and information on programs, practices, and policies in science, mathematics, and environmental education; accessible and searchable on CD-ROM or over the Internet: e-mail [ericse@osu.edu]; Gopher [gopher.ericse.ohio-state.edu]; World Wide Web [http://www.ericse.org].

11.45 **4-H Series Project**, Human and Community Development, University of California, Davis, CA 95616-8523
(916) 752-8824

Office at the University of California, Davis, that created and operates the **4-H SERIES (Science Experiences and Resources for Informal Education Settings) Program**—national program in which 9- to 12-year-olds are led by trained teens in science activities in out-of-school settings, and then follow up with related community service projects. Program conducted at 4-H SERIES Regional Leadership Centers at the University of California, Davis; University of Missouri, Cooperative Extension of Lawrence County, Mount Vernon, Mo.; Cornell University, Cooperative Extension, Broome County, Binghamton, N.Y.; and Garrad County Extension Service, Lancaster, Ky.

11.46 Geological Society of America, 3300 Penrose Pl., P.O. Box 9140, Boulder, CO 80301-9140
(303) 447-2020; (800) 472-1988
http://www.geosociety.org

Professional scientific society of geologists, with more than 15,000 members. *Programs/services:* **Partners for Education Program (PEP)**—national network with 1,500 partners committed to enhancing science education for children and fostering collaborations and partnerships between teachers and scientists; sessions for teachers at annual meeting; free PEP membership. Available through PEP: national database of scientist and educator partners (for grades K-12); e-mail geoscientist partners and subject-area experts. *Publications/materials:* Geoscience career packets; video; newsletter.

11.47 Geothermal Education Office, 664 Hilary Dr., Tiburon, CA 94920
(415) 435-4574; (800) 866-4436
http://marin.org/npo/geo

Nonprofit educational office focused on K-12 education about geothermal energy. *Programs/services:* Free workshops for teachers; scientist collaborations and information from a scientist database; 24-hour 800 number for free materials; referrals

for more technical information; classroom speakers; class visits to geothermal power plants; scientist mentors for students; poster and essay contests. *Publications/materials:* Curriculum unit (grades 4-8); curriculum guidelines and activity suggestions offered by phone; audiovisual materials; *Steam Press*—fact sheet about geothermal and renewable energy resources as they relate to environmental issues; brochures, booklets, bookmarks, and other free materials for students.

11.48 The GLOBE Program, 744 Jackson Pl., N.W., Washington, DC 20503
(800) 858-9947
http://www.globe.gov

Worldwide network of students (grades K-12) making environmental measurements related to soil, hydrology, atmosphere, and biology, and sharing findings with one another and with the scientific community via the Internet and World Wide Web. The National Oceanic and Atmospheric Administration (NOAA) is lead agency in this program. *Programs/services:* Sessions at GLOBE Program meetings; extensive training workshops; information hotline; scientist collaborations with teachers; database of scientists available for helping teachers. *Publications/materials:* Curriculum units with hands-on materials; audiovisual and computer-based materials; instructional materials for teachers; Web-based magazine for students.

11.49 Great Lakes Planetarium Association (GLPA), c/o D. David Batch, Abrams Planetarium, Michigan State University, East Lansing, MI 48824
(517) 355-4676
http://www.pa.msu.edu/abrams/glpa.html

Regional association of professionals from planetariums (including many

that are school-based) in Illinois, Indiana, Michigan, Minnesota, Ohio, and Wisconsin; association focus is on astronomy and space science, but also includes geology, earth science, and meteorology. *Programs/services:* Workshops for teachers at annual conference; information about the region's planetariums and their programs. *Publications/materials:* Resource banks of slides; planetarium show scripts; booklets on teaching astronomy and on the use of a planetarium for astronomy education; newsletter.

11.50 Harvard-Smithsonian Center for Astrophysics, Science Education Department, 60 Garden St., MS-71, Cambridge, MA 02138
(617) 495-9798
http://cfa-www.harvard.edu/cfa/sed

Small department in a large astrophysical research center; focused on curriculum development, teacher enhancement, and applications of advanced technology. *Services:* **Project SPICA**—program providing teacher workshops in astronomy education (grades K-12), supported by a teacher manual with 37 activities, developed by teachers recruited nationwide; workshops at National Science Teachers Association meetings. *Publications/materials: Project IMAGE: Investigative Materials About Global Environments*—manual of image-based activities for use in earth science and environmental science classes (grades 7-9), with a separate teacher's guide; *Project STAR: The Universe in Your Hands*—astronomy-based science course (grades 8-12), available as a text with hands-on activities; *Harvard-Smithsonian Case Studies in Science Education*—videos, with accompanying guide materials, giving visual models of science education reform, for in-service and preservice teacher education programs; newsletter.

11.51 **Industry Canada**, 155 Queen St., 4th Floor, Ottawa, Ontario, Canada K1A 0H5
(800) 268-6608
http://www.schoolnet.ca/math_sci

Among its activities, Industry Canada offers the following services of interest to middle school science educators. *Programs/services:*

- **Computers for Schools and Libraries Program**—coordinates the repair and distribution of refurbished government and industry surplus computers to Canadian elementary and secondary schools and libraries.
- **SchoolNet**—an extensive on-line educational resource site, with more than 1,500 student and teacher resources.

11.52 **Institute for Chemical Education**, University of Wisconsin, Department of Chemistry, 1101 University Ave., Madison, WI 53706
(608) 262-3033
http://ice.chem.wisc.edu/ice

National organization centered at the University of Wisconsin-Madison, with a network of field centers and affiliates across the country devoted to helping teachers at all grade levels (kindergarten through college) revitalize science in the schools. *Programs/services:* Two-week workshops at various regional sites; 2-to-3-week workshops in Madison; summer fellowships; **Chem Camps** for students (grades 5-8). *Publications/materials:* Supplemental activities; instructional materials for teachers; kits and devices; newsletter.

11.53 **Institute for Earth Education**, Cedar Cove, Greenville, WV 24945
(304) 832-6404
http://slnet.com/cip/iee

International nonprofit organization of educators; focused on environmental education. *Programs/services:* Earth Education interest sessions and workshops conducted by associates around the country; International Earth Education Conferences. *Publications/materials:* Complete educational programs developed and disseminated; *Talking Leaves* (journal); *Earth Education Sourcebook* (annual); other books and program materials.

11.54 **Institute of Food Technologists**, 221 N. LaSalle St., Suite 300, Chicago, IL 60601
(312) 782-8424
http://www.ift.org

Scientific educational society with 28,000 members; focused on food science and technology. *Programs/services:* Collaborations between teachers and professional food scientists; teacher-scientist partnerships through selected food company programs; databases of food scientists available for helping teachers. *Publications/materials:* Series of videotapes and support materials for grades 5-8 on the science of foods, food processing, food safety, and food nutrition; set of classroom experiments in food science; career information.

11.55 **International Society for Technology in Education,** University of Oregon, 1787 Agate St., Eugene, OR 97403-1923
(541) 346-4414; (800) 336-5191 (for materials)
http://www.iste.org

Nonprofit organization with 10,000 members, focused on the improvement of education through the appropriate use of technology; serves as a clearinghouse on the use of technology in education. *Programs/services:* Workshops and seminars at Tel-Ed/Multimedia Conference. *Publications/materials:* Curriculum units; books; educational software packages; curriculum guidelines for accreditation; computer-based materials; *Learning and Leading with Technology* and *Journal of Research on Computing in Education* (journals); *Update* (newsletter).

11.56 **International Wildlife Coalition**, 70 E. Falmouth Hwy., East Falmouth, MA 02536
(508) 548-8328; (800) 548-8704

Nonprofit organization that rescues and protects wildlife and wild habitat, and operates the Whale Adoption Project. *Programs/services:* **Whale Adoption Project**—supports marine mammal research and protection. *Publications/materials: Whales of the World* (teacher kits); newsletter.

11.57 **Izaak Walton League of America**, IWLA Conservation Center, 707 Conservation Lane, Gaithersburg, MD 20878-2983
(301) 548-0150; (800) BUG-IWLA
http://www.iwla.org

National conservation organization with more than 54,000 members, focused on protecting the nation's natural resources. *Programs/services:*

- **Sustainability Education Project**—an educational effort for researching the carrying-capacity issues of human population growth, natural resource consumption, environmental impacts of technologies, and sustainability.
- **Save Our Streams Program**—for stream monitoring and restoration, with workshops, an information hotline, and a database of scientists available for helping teachers.

Publications/materials: Hands On Save Our Streams: Science Project Guide for Students; curriculum materials; books; videotapes; youth guides; *Environments for Life* (newsletter for Sustainability Education Project); *Outdoor America* (magazine); newsletter.

11.58 **JASON Project**, JASON Foundation for Education, 395 Totten Pond Rd., Waltham, MA 02154
(617) 487-9995
http://www.jasonproject.org

Interactive field trip, taking half a million students on remote scientific expedition via satellite and the Internet; emphasis on wide range of earth science and environmental research topics; available at 27 Primary Interactive Network Sites (PINS), including 7 museums and 3 NASA field centers (*see* 11.66)—Ames, Goddard, Johnson. *Programs/services:* Live-broadcast programs from expeditions, with interactive features; simulation of expedition site at each PINS; participation in actual expedition by selected students and teachers; e-mail, and World Wide Web home page with expedition reports, data, and other educational electronic resources. *Publications/materials:* Curriculum units on expeditions available 6 months before each expedition. For further information: e-mail [info@JASON.org]; World Wide Web (at address given above).

11.59 **Keystone Center**, P.O. Box 8606, 1503 Soda Ridge Rd., Keystone, CO 80435-7998
(303) 468-5824; (800) 215-5585
http://www.keystone.org

Nonprofit public policy, scientific, and educational organization, focused on the beneficial and intelli-

gent use of science, technology, and the environment in society. *Programs/services:*

- **Classroom Access to Science Education**—year-round residential programming for teachers and their students.
- **Key Issues Institute**—national, middle-level teacher-training program using environmental issues as a means of understanding and learning science.
- **Keys to Science**—summer training program for high school teachers, with emphasis on cellular and molecular biology.
- **On the Wing: Field Studies in Ornithology**—collaborative field project for young adults in conjunction with the Colorado Bird Observatory.

Publications/materials: Instructional materials for teachers.

11.60 **Los Alamos National Laboratory**, Box 1663, MS P278, Los Alamos, NM 87545
(505) 667-1919
http://www.education.lanl.gov/resources

National laboratory with an active program in science education for New Mexico teachers and students. *Programs/services:* Workshops for teachers; student research internships; summer programs for students; educational technology programs.

11.61 **Microscopy Society of America**, 4 Barlows Landing Rd., No. 8, Pocasset, MA 02559
(707) 964-9460; (800) 538-3672
http://www.msa.microscopy.com

Organization with more than 4,000 members, serving as a center for education and information dissemination for microscopy-related knowledge. *Programs/services:* Project **MICRO** (Microscopy in Curriculum-Research Outreach)—educational

outreach program for putting high-quality microscopy-based science materials and member-volunteers of the society in middle school classrooms nationwide; "Ask-a-Microscopist" service for teachers. *Publications/materials: Microscopic Investigations*—a Lawrence Hall of Science GEMS guide currently under development; career publications; Internet bibliography of children's books on microscopy.

11.62 **Middle Atlantic Planetarium Society (MAPS)**, c/o Laura Deines, MAPS President, Southworth Planetarium, P.O. Box 9300, Portland, ME 04104-9300
(207) 780-4249
http://www.voicenet.com/~mcdonald/MAPS.html

Regional association of professionals from planetariums (including many that are school-based) in Connecticut, Delaware, the District of Columbia, Maine, Maryland, Massachusetts, New Hampshire, New Jersey, New York, Pennsylvania, Rhode Island, Vermont, Virginia, and West Virginia; association focus is on astronomy and space science. *Programs/services:* Workshops for teachers at society meetings; teacher-scientist partnerships; facilitation of loans of Starlab portable planetariums among member planetariums; information about the region's planetariums and their programs. *Publications/materials: Under Roof, Dome, and Sky*—collection of activities developed and used by member planetariums; newsletter.

11.63 **Mineral Information Institute**, 475 17th St., Suite 510, Denver, CO 80202
(303) 297-3226

Private organization supported by professional associations, private companies, and foundations; focused on educating the public about the importance of mineral and energy resources in everyday life. *Publications/materials:* Supplementary activities; audiovisual and computer-based materials; posters.

11.64 **The Museum Institute for Teaching Science,** 79 Milk St., Suite 210, Boston, MA 02109-3903 (617) 695-9771 http://www.mits.org

Nonprofit organization focused on improving the teaching of science, mathematics, and technology. *Programs/services:* Hands-on inquiry-mode summer science workshops for K-8 teachers, taught by the museums of Massachusetts. *Publications/materials: Science Is Elementary* (topical resource magazine for K-6 teachers); newsletter.

11.65 National Aeronautics and Space Administration (NASA), Central Operation of Resources for Educators, Lorain County Joint Vocational School, 15181 Rte. 58 S., Oberlin, OH 44074 (216) 774-1051, Ext. 293 and 249 http://spacelink.msfc.nasa.gov/CORE

Worldwide distribution center for NASA audiovisual educational materials. *Publications/materials:* Free catalog in response to request on school letterhead.

11.66 National Aeronautics and Space Administration (NASA), Education Division, Code FE, NASA Headquarters, 300 E St., S.W., Washington, DC 20546 (202) 358-1110 http://www.hq.nasa.gov/office/codef/education

The following programs and services of the National Aeronautics and Space Administration (NASA) are delivered via 9 NASA field centers

that serve multistate areas. These field centers are located at NASA Marshall Space Flight Center, Ala.; NASA Ames Research Center, Moffett Field, Calif.; Jet Propulsion Laboratory, Pasadena, Calif.; NASA Kennedy Space Center, Kennedy Space Center, Fla.; NASA Goddard Space Flight Center, Greenbelt, Md.; NASA Stennis Space Center, Stennis Space Center, Miss.; NASA Lewis Research Center, Cleveland, Ohio; NASA Johnson Space Center, Houston, Tex.; and NASA Langley Research Center, Hampton, Va. Two other field centers serving only their own states are the NASA Dryden Flight Research Facility, Edwards Air Force Base, Calif.; and Wallops Flight Facility, Wallops Island, Va. *Programs/services:*

- The **Aerospace Education Services Program** consists of traveling aerospace-education units with classroom programs, teacher-enhancement workshops (1 hour to 2 weeks long) on integrating aerospace into the curriculum, and assembly programs (grades K-12).
- The **Community Involvement Program,** an intensive community program emphasizing aerospace, seeks to involve service clubs, government officials, and the private sector, in addition to schools: offers in-service workshops (1 week to 1 month long), assemblies, exhibits, public events.
- **NASA Educational Workshops for Mathematics, Science, and Technology Teachers (NEWMAST)** provides outstanding teachers of mathematics, science, and technology an opportunity to spend 2 weeks at a NASA field center studying NASA's latest technological information.
- The **NASA Space Science Student Involvement Program** includes the **Mission to Planet Earth Project** (grades 6-8), in which teams of students develop an interdiscipli-

nary program that would use space technology to investigate the effects of human activity on the earth's ecosystem.

- The **NASA Teacher Resource Center Network** comprises 9 Teacher Resource Centers, located at the 9 NASA field centers listed above in this entry. The Teacher Resource Centers disseminate NASA educational materials (videotapes, slides, audiotapes, publications, lesson plans, and activities) on science, mathematics, and technology. These materials are also disseminated by 47 Regional Teacher Resource Centers in 36 states, and by NASA's Central Operation of Resources for Educators (*see* 11.65).
- NASA's **Urban Community Enrichment Program** trains lead-teacher teams to conduct interdisciplinary aerospace activities in schools and to train other teachers.

11.67 National Aeronautics and Space Administration, NASA Marshall Space Flight Center, Mail Code CL-01, Huntsville, AL 35812-0001 (205) 961-1225 http://spacelink.nasa.gov

One of 9 NASA field centers serving multistate areas. *Programs/services:* NASA Spacelink—electronic resource providing access to NASA aeronautics and space information, educator guides, and other materials of interest to teachers, faculty, and students.

11.68 National Association for Research in Science Teaching (NARST), c/o Arthur L. White, NARST Executive Secretary, 1929 Kenny Rd., Rm. 200E, The Ohio State University, Columbus, OH 43210 (614) 292-3339 http://science.coe.uwf.edu/narst/narst.html

Professional association of more than 1,400 science teachers, supervisors, and science educators worldwide, organized to improve science teaching through research and teacher education. *Programs/services:* Annual convention, with more than 200 research papers; promotion and coordination of science education research, with interpretation and reporting of the results; NARSTNET listserv [listserve@science.coe. uwf.edu]. *Publications/materials: Journal of Research in Science Teaching; NARST Research Matters— to the Science Teacher;* monographs; newsletter.

11.69 **National Association of Biology Teachers**, 11250 Roger Bacon Dr., No. 19, Reston, VA 20190-5202
(703) 471-1134; (800) 406-0775

Professional society of more than 7,000 biology educators and administrators, representing all grade levels. *Programs/services:* Annual convention; 1- and 2-day regional summer workshops; student achievement and science fair awards. *Publications/materials:* Curriculum materials; curriculum guidelines; monographs and special publications; *The American Biology Teacher* (journal); catalog of materials; career information (video and publications); posters; newsletter.

11.70 **National Association of Geoscience Teachers**, Department of Geology-9080, Western Washington University, Bellingham, WA 98225-9080
(360) 650-3587

Professional education society with 2,000 members, including college and university professors, and geology and earth science teachers. *Programs/services:* Workshops; conferences and field trips for teachers;

annual **Outstanding Earth Science Teacher Award Program;** annual state and regional awards to precollege teachers. *Publications/materials: Journal of Geoscience Education*—with educational articles for secondary and college-level teachers; space poster, with ideas for 18 activities for middle-level students; earth science slide sets.

11.71 **National Audubon Society,** 700 Broadway, New York, NY 10003
(212) 979-3000

Organization with 600,000 members and 40 state and 500 local groups (distinct from Audubon Societies of certain states, which are independent); concerned with ecology, natural resources, wildlife, and habitats. *Programs/services:* Workshops; instructional materials for teachers; information hotline; database of scientists available for helping teachers; Audubon camps. *Publications/materials:* Curriculum units with hands-on materials; audiovisual and computer-based materials; *Audubon* (magazine); posters; newsletter.

11.72 **National Center for Improving Science Education**, 2000 L St., N.W., Suite 603, Washington, DC 20036
(202) 467-0652
http://www.wested.org

Division of WestEd of San Francisco, Calif., an organization dedicated to educational reform. *Programs/services:* Provides guidance for educational policymakers, curriculum developers, and practitioners by synthesizing findings in policy studies, research reports, and exemplary practices and by transforming them into practical resources, with 1 area of emphasis chosen for synthesis work each year; offers workshops by technical assistance teams. *Publica-*

tions/materials: Publications list; curriculum guidelines; guidelines for policymakers; information for parents in resource book and pamphlets; books and monographs, including *Assessment in Science Education: The Middle Years; Building Scientific Literacy: A Blueprint for Science Education in the Middle Years;* and *Science and Technology Education for the Middle Years: Frameworks for Curriculum and Instruction.*

11.73 **National Center for Research on Teacher Learning.** Michigan State University, College of Education, 116 Erickson Hall, East Lansing, MI 48824-1034
(517) 355-9302
http://ncrtl.msu.edu

Center for research on how teachers learn to teach and engage students in active learning. *Programs/services:* Projects specifically focused on science and mathematics. *Publications/materials:* Research reports, issue papers, technical series, videotapes, and special reports on contemporary issues in teaching education.

11.74 **National Earth Science Teachers Association**, 2000 Florida Ave., N.W., Washington, DC 20009
(202) 462-6910; (800) 966-2481

Professional society of 1,000 earth science teachers and others interested in earth science education. *Programs/services:* Workshops and rock swaps at national and regional National Science Teachers Association meetings; summer field trips and field conferences. *Publications/materials: The Earth Scientist* (journal); scripted slide sets.

11.75 **National Energy Foundation**, 5225 Wiley Post Way, Suite 170, Salt Lake City, UT 84116 (801) 539-1406
http://www.nef1.org

Nonprofit educational organization devoted to the development of instructional materials on natural resources and the implementation of innovative teacher-training and student programs. *Programs/services:* Workshops for teachers on mining education; student-team energy patrols; student debate program. *Publications/materials:* Curriculum units with hands-on materials; curriculum guidelines; supplementary materials; posters; newsletter for teachers; catalog of materials.

11.76 **National Gardening Association**, 180 Flynn Ave., Burlington, VT 05401 (802) 863-1308; (800) 538-7476
http://www.garden.org

Organization focused on using plants and gardens as vehicles for learning. *Programs/services:* Teacher development programs and workshops for teachers; Web site focused on garden-based learning; youth garden grant program. *Publications/materials:* *The GrowLab Science Program*—curriculum materials for using indoor classroom gardens; *GrowLab: Activities for Growing Minds* (curriculum); *Growing Ideas: A Journal of Garden-Based Learning*—educator's journal with classroom-tested project ideas.

11.77 **National Geographic Society**, 1145 17th St., N.W., Washington, DC 20036 (202) 857-7000; (800) 368-2728
http://www.nationalgeographic.com

World's largest nonprofit scientific and educational organization. *Publications/materials:* *National Geographic Kids Network*—computer-

and telecommunications-based science curriculum (grades 4-9), developed in cooperation with TERC (*see* 11.114), in which student-scientists investigate real-world scientific issues and exchange information with other students around the world, providing hands-on experience in scientific methods and computer technology; CD-ROMs; interactive videodiscs; films; books; *National Geographic Magazine; National Geographic World*—general interest magazine for ages 8-14.

11.78 **National Information Center for Educational Media (NICEM)**, P.O. Box 8640, Albuquerque, NM 87198-8640 (505) 265-3591; (800) 926-8328
http://www.nicem.com

Center maintaining an international database of educational media and materials, covering all subject areas and age levels. The database of more than 400,000 nonprint materials contains numerous entries for science materials. *Programs/services:* Abstracting and indexing of media materials; contracting to do user-defined searches for special projects requiring media acquisition; providing of custom catalog services based on NICEM's or on a client's media collection. *Publications/materials:* Print indexes; on-line files; CD-ROMs.

11.79 **National Institute for Science Education**, 1025 W. Johnson St., Madison, WI 53706 (608) 263-9250
http://www.wcer.wisc.edu/nise

Center for research on issues related to science, mathematics, engineering, and technology education. *Programs/services:* Conducts and synthesizes research on education in science, mathematics, engineering,

and technology, concentrating on national policy studies, professional development programs, and dissemination programs. *Publications/materials:* *The Why Files*—Web page that examines the science behind the news [http://whyfiles.news.wisc.edu]; newsletter.

11.80 **National Marine Educators Association**, P.O. Box 1470, Ocean Springs, MS 39566-1470 (601) 374-7557
http://www.marine-ed.org

Association of professionals from education (kindergarten through graduate school), science, business, government, museums, aquariums, and marine research, with more than 1,200 members and 16 regional chapters; focused on marine and aquatic studies. *Programs/services:* Teachers' workshops and opportunities for networking with scientists at annual conference and at conferences organized by regional chapters. *Publications/materials:* *Current: The Journal of Marine Education*, with activities; newsletter, with reviews of curricular materials.

11.81 **National Middle Level Science Teachers Association**, c/o Rowena Hubler, Ohio Department of Education, 65 S. Front St., Columbus, OH 43215-4183 (614) 466-2761
http://www.nsta.org/nmlsta/index.htm

Association of middle-level science educators with 1,000 members; affiliate of the National Science Teachers Association. *Programs/services:* With American Plastics Council (*see* 11.19), developed *Hands On Plastics: A Scientific Investigation Kit*; middle-level programs, presented at regional and national conventions of the National Science Teachers Association. *Publications/materials:* *Level Line*—newsletter with ideas for student investigations, demonstrations, inexpensive teaching materials, summer opportunities and professional development for middle-level teachers.

11.82 **National Research Council; Center for Science, Mathematics, and Engineering Education**, 2101 Constitution Ave., N.W., Washington, DC 20418
(202) 334-2353
http://www2.nas.edu/center

The National Research Council (NRC) is the operating arm of three honorary academies: the National Academy of Sciences, the National Academy of Engineering, and the Institute of Medicine. NRC's primary concern is advising the federal government on matters of science and technology policy. Since 1995, the NRC has become increasingly active in efforts to improve science education and has been a leader in the development of standards for precollege science education, completing the development of the *National Science Education Standards* (*see* 7.27) in 1995. The mission of the NRC's Center for Science, Mathematics, and Engineering Education is to promote the improvement of education in science, mathematics, engineering, and technology for all members of society. *Programs/services:*

- [(202) 334-3628] The **National Science Education Standards Project** has a comprehensive outreach strategy to support national, state, and local utilization of the *Standards* through leadership and resource development, partnerships and networks, and targeted symposia and workshops.
- [(202) 334-2110] The Center provides scientists and engineers with information and resources to assist them in contributing effectively to K-12 science education partnerships ranging from classroom interactions to systemic reform programs.

11.83 **National Science Education Leadership Association (NSELA)**, P.O. Box 5556, Arlington, VA 22205
(703) 524-8646

Association with 1,200 members—chairpersons, department heads, science supervisors, coordinators, and other leaders in science education; focused on improving science education through leadership development. *Programs/services:* Miniconferences; leadership institutes; other programs to develop leadership skills. *Publications/materials: Issues in Science Education; NSELA Handbook; The Science Educator* (journal); newsletter.

11.84 **National Science Foundation, Directorate for Education and Human Resources**, 4201 Wilson Blvd., Arlington, VA 22230
(703) 306-1600
http://www.ehr.nsf.gov

The Directorate for Education and Human Resources of the National Science Foundation, an independent federal agency, is a major force for improving science education in the United States; it initiates and sponsors a wide variety of projects to improve education in science, mathematics, and engineering. *Programs/services:* The directorate's work in precollege science education is carried out by several divisions:

- [(703) 306-1690] Division of Educational System Reform (*see* 11.85), concerned with 3 large-scale reform programs: the **Rural Systemic Initiatives Program, Statewide Systemic Initiatives Program**, and **Urban Systemic Initiatives Program.**
- [(703) 306-1620] Division of Elementary, Secondary, and Informal Education (*see* 11.86), concerned with curriculum and teacher enhancement in science, mathematics, and engineering.

- [(703) 306-1640] Division of Human Resource Development (*see* 11.87), concerned with broadening the participation of persons in underrepresented groups in science, mathematics, and engineering.
- [(703) 306-1670] Division of Undergraduate Education, concerned with undergraduate education in science, mathematics, engineering, and technology.

Publications/materials: Guide to Programs (for current fiscal year); *Indicators of Science and Mathematics Education; Indicators of Science and Engineering Education;* other reports; fact sheets.

11.85 **National Science Foundation, Directorate for Education and Human Resources, Division of Educational System Reform**, 4201 Wilson Blvd., Rm. 875, Arlington, VA 22230
(703) 306-1690
http://www.ehr.nsf.gov/ehr/esr

The Division of Educational System Reform, in the National Science Foundation's Directorate of Education and Human Resources (*see* 11.84), operates the following programs that support systemic improvements in science, mathematics, and technology education in grades K-12. *Programs/services:*

- [(703) 306-1684] The **Rural Systemic Initiatives Program**—supports projects to make systemic improvements in science, mathematics, and technology education in rural, economically disadvantaged regions.
- [(703) 306-1682] The **Statewide Systemic Initiatives Program**—supports comprehensive, systemic, statewide efforts to change educational systems and improve science, mathematics, and technology education.

- [(703) 306-1684] The **Urban Systemic Initiatives Program**—supports comprehensive, systemic efforts at fundamental reform of science, mathematics, and technology education in large urban school systems.

11.86 National Science Foundation, Directorate for Education and Human Resources; Division of Elementary, Secondary, and Informal Education, 4201 Wilson Blvd., Rm. 885, Arlington, VA 22230 (703) 306-1620 http://www.ehr.nsf.gov/ehr/esie

The Division of Elementary, Secondary, and Informal Education in the National Science Foundation's Directorate for Education and Human Resources (*see* 11.84) operates the following programs. *Programs/ services:*

- [(703) 306-1615] The **Informal Science Education Program**—supports nonschool projects (e.g., by museums and youth organizations) to increase involvement with science, mathematics, and technology.
- [(703) 306-1614] The **Instructional Materials Development Program**—supports development of innovative, comprehensive, and diverse materials implementing standards-based reform in science, mathematics, and technology.
- [(703) 306-1613] The **Presidential Awards for Excellence in Mathematics and Science Teaching Program**—provides national recognition to outstanding teachers in science and mathematics.
- [(703) 306-1613] The **Teacher Enhancement Program**—supports projects to enhance the content knowledge and pedagogical skills of teachers of science, mathematics, and technology in grades K-12.

- [(703) 306-1616] The **Young Scholars Program**—encourages students in grades 7-12 to investigate careers in science, mathematics, and technology by working with practicing scientists.

11.87 National Science Foundation, Directorate for Education and Human Resources, Division of Human Resource Development, 4201 Wilson Blvd., Rm. 815, Arlington, VA 22230 (703) 306-1640 http://www.ehr.nsf.gov/ehr/hrd

The Division of Human Resource Development, in the National Science Foundation's Directorate for Education and Human Resources (*see* 11.84), operates the following programs. *Programs/services:*

- [(703) 306-1633] The **Comprehensive Partnerships for Mathematics and Science Achievement Program**—supports school systems with significant minority populations in creating partnerships to improve the access of minority students in grades K-12 to science and mathematics education.
- [(703) 306-1636] **Programs for Persons with Disabilities**—supports programs to develop new teaching methods, increase recognition of needs and capabilities of students with disabilities, promote accessibility of appropriate instructional materials and technologies, and increase availability of mentoring resources.
- [(703) 306-1637] **Program for Women and Girls in Science, Engineering and Mathematics**—supports model projects, experimental projects, and information-dissemination activities to improve the science, mathematics, and technology education of women and to increase their numbers in these fields.

11.88 National Science Resources Center, Smithsonian Institution, MRC 403, Arts and Industries Bldg., Rm. 1201, Washington, DC 20560 (202) 357-2555 http://www.si.edu/nsrc

Organization sponsored jointly by the National Academy of Sciences and the Smithsonian Institution to contribute to the improvement of science education in the nation's schools. *Programs/services:* Workshops at National Science Teachers Association and other meetings; **Leadership Institutes** to train teams from school districts across the country on science education reform issues and methods; technical support for school districts involved in science education reform; support of other organizations in reform efforts. *Publications/materials:* Science and Technology for Children—series of 24 core curriculum units (grades 1-6) in the physical, life, and earth sciences; Science and Technology Concepts for Middle School—series of 8 core curriculum units for grades 7-8 (under development); 2 resource guides—*Resources for Teaching Elementary School Science* and *Resources for Teaching Middle School Science; Science for All Children: A Guide to Improving Elementary Science Education in Your School District*—comprehensive guide to systemic science education reform in the nation's elementary schools; newsletter.

11.89 National Science Teachers Association (NSTA), 1840 Wilson Blvd., Arlington, VA 22201-3000 (703) 243-7100 http://www.nsta.org

Organization committed to promoting excellence and innovation in science teaching and learning for all, with membership of more than 53,000, including science teachers, supervisors, administrators, scientists, and business and industry representatives. *Programs/services:* One national and 3 regional conferences per year; certification of science teachers in 8 teaching-level and discipline-area categories; computer bulletin board; educational tours; nearly 25 award programs for teachers and students. *Publications/materials: Science Scope* and *The Science Teacher* (journals); *NSTA Reports!* (newspaper); *NSTA Pathways to the Science Standards* (guidebooks on putting the standards into practice in the classroom); curriculum units; supplementary activities; other instructional materials and publications; posters; complete catalog of titles.

11.90 **National Student Research Center,** Mandeville Middle School, 2525 Soult St., Mandeville, LA 70448
(504) 626-5980
http://yn.la.ca.us/nsrc/nsrc.html

Organization that promotes student research and the use of scientific methods in all areas of the K-12 curriculum. *Programs/services:* Facilitating the establishment of student research centers in schools; electronic network of mentors; electronic libraries of student research, with search and retrieval capabilities. *Publications/materials:* Printed and electronic journals of student research; program development packet for teachers.

11.91 **National Weather Association,** 6704 Wolke Ct., Montgomery, AL 36116-2134
(334) 213-0388
http://www.nwas.org

Professional association supporting and promoting excellence in operational meteorology and related activities. *Programs/services:* Annual awards program; grants to teachers for professional development or purchase of materials and equipment for

the classroom; time donated by members serving as speakers and science fair judges, and in responding to inquiries on science subjects and career planning. *Publications/materials:* Career publications; *National Weather Digest* (journal); newsletter; monographs; audiovisual materials.

11.92 **National Wildlife Federation,** 8925 Leesburg Pike, Vienna, VA 22184-0001
(703) 790-4000
http://www.nwf.org

Federation of 6,500 state and territorial conservation organizations and associate members; focused on conservation of wildlife and other natural resources. *Programs/services:*

• **Animal Tracks**—curriculum materials and teacher-training workshops (grades K-8).
• **Campus Ecology**—student involvement program focused on projects that improve practices on campus and reduce adverse campus impact on the environment; extensive outdoor education programs for all age groups.
• **NatureQuest**—workshops for educators and nature and science counselors.
• **School Yard Habitat**—certification and technical assistance program for developing school grounds into outdoor classrooms.

Publications/materials: National Wildlife Week (annual topical kit of educational activities and posters); *Ranger Rick's NatureScope* (activity manuals for teachers and program leaders); *Conservation Directory* (comprehensive annual listing of state, national, and international environmental organizations and agencies); *Media Guide to Environmental Resources* (annual); *Ranger Rick, National Wildlife,* and *International Wildlife* (magazines); audiovisual materials.

11.93 **Network for Portable Planetariums,** c/o Susan Reynolds, Portable Planetarium Specialist, Onondaga-Cortlandt-Madison BOCES, P.O. Box 4754, Syracuse, NY 13221
(315) 433-2671

International network of users of portable and small stationary planetariums, established to help members deliver planetarium-based educational experiences; focused on astronomy and space science. *Programs/services:* Database of portable-planetarium experts throughout the world who are available for career and technical consultation and workshops; semiannual regional meetings for reviewing materials in the public domain file, demonstrating lessons and techniques, and discussing common problems. *Publications/materials:* Public domain file of curriculum materials and pre-/postvisit materials; booklet of tips for portable planetarium users.

11.94 **North American Association for Environmental Education,** 1255 23rd St., N.W., Suite 400, Washington, DC 20037-1199
(202) 884-8912
http://eelink.umich.edu/naaee.html

Professional organization for persons involved with environmental education; develops and promotes environmental education programs and fosters discussion of important issues. *Programs/services:* Annual conference that includes opportunities and workshops for teachers. *Publications/materials: Directory of Environmental Educators* (updated annually); books, including *Environmental Education in the Schools, Essential Learning in Environmental Education, Environmental Problem Solving,* and many other titles; catalog of materials; newsletter.

11.95 Optical Society of America, 2010 Massachusetts Ave., N.W., Washington, DC 20036 (202) 223-8130; (800) 762-6960

International association of optical scientists and engineers, with 12,000 members; offers a special category of membership for teachers with an interest in optics. *Programs/services:* Educators Day—at the society's annual meeting, science teachers invited by their local society chapter participate in a program of lectures, seminars, and workshops on innovative techniques for using optics in their classrooms; local and student chapter grants, frequently used for local education outreach programs; science fair sponsorship. *Publications/materials:* Optics Discovery Kit (hands-on optics kit); *Careers in Optics and Photonics* (video); monthly magazine columns on optics and science education and on optics experiments for children.

11.96 Pacific Planetarium Association, c/o Jon Elvert, 2300 Leo Harris Pkwy., Eugene, OR 97401 (541) 687-STAR (program information); (541) 461-8227 http://www.efn.org/~esd_plt

Regional association of professionals from 70 planetariums (including many that are school-based) in Alaska, California, Hawaii, Nevada, Oregon, Washington; focused primarily on astronomy and earth and space science for grades K-12. *Programs/services:* State in-service workshops; annual conference; scientist collaborations with individual teachers, and teacher-scientist partnerships supported by individual planetariums; information about the region's planetariums and their programs. *Publications/materials:* Career publications; curriculum units with hands-on materials; curriculum guidelines; audiovisual materials; newsletter.

11.97 Project WET, The Watercourse Program, 201 Culbertson Hall, Montana State University, Bozeman, MT 59717-0057 (406) 994-5392 http://www.montana.edu/wwwwet

Nonprofit supplementary education program for educators and students (grades K-12), focused on water resources and related issues; cosponsored by The Watercourse Program (which was created with funding from the U.S. Department of the Interior's Bureau of Reclamation) and by the Western Regional Environmental Education Council; available through Project WET coordinators in 46 states and the Northern Mariana Islands. *Programs/services:* Workshops and institutes for teachers; teacher-scientist collaborations; information hotline. *Publications/materials:* Project WET Curriculum and Activity Guide, with more than 90 hands-on water activities; *Science Activities* (magazine for teachers); *WETnet Newsletter; WOW! The Wonders of Wetlands Guide; The Water Story* (magazine for students); other publications and modules.

11.98 Project WILD, 5430 Grosvenor Lane, Suite 230, Bethesda, MD 20814 (301) 493-5447 http://eelink.umich.edu/wild

Nonprofit interdisciplinary, supplementary wildlife-based environmental education program for educators (grades K-12), developed jointly by the Council for Environmental Education and the Western Association of Fish and Wildlife Agencies; available in 50 states, the District of Columbia, Puerto Rico, 11 Canadian provinces, and several foreign countries. *Programs/services:* Basic and advanced workshops for educators, available statewide and, in most states, sponsored by the state's wildlife agency and/or department of education. *Publications/materials:* Available only through workshops: *Project WILD K-12 Activity Guide* (emphasizing wildlife and habitat); *Project WILD Aquatic Education Activity Guide* (emphasizing aquatic wildlife and ecosystems).

11.99 Quality Education for Minorities Network, 1818 N St., N.W., Suite 350, Washington, DC 20036 (202) 659-1818

Network devoted to ensuring that minorities in the United States have equal access to educational opportunities. *Programs/services:* Operates the Community Service Centers Project—a pilot effort to establish community service centers on college and university campuses located near low-income public housing, and targeting groups underrepresented in science: Native Americans, African Americans, Mexican Americans, Native Alaskans, and Puerto Ricans. Various educational activities offered at the centers, including some to empower students and parents to become advocates for quality education.

11.100 Raptor Education Foundation, 21901 E. Hampden Ave., Aurora, CO 80013 (303) 680-8500

Organization devoted to promoting environmental literacy, using raptors (birds of prey) as a central focus. *Programs/services:* Introductory program on raptors and owls of America; live-raptor programs with instructional materials; teacher-scientist collaborations; scientist mentors and research opportunities for students; speakers. *Publications/materials:* Curriculum units with hands-on materials; newsletter.

11.101 Rocky Mountain Planetarium Association (RMPA), c/o John Peterson, RMPA President, El Paso Planetarium, 6531 Boeing Dr., El Paso, TX 79925 (915) 779-4316

Regional association of professionals from planetariums (including many that are school-based) in Colorado, Idaho, Montana, New Mexico, Texas, Utah, Wyoming; focused on astronomy and space science. *Programs/ services:* Information about the region's planetariums and their programs, workshops, instructional materials for teachers, research opportunities for students. *Publications/materials:* Some supplemental activities and audiovisual and computer-based materials produced by individual planetariums, available from the association.

11.102 School Science and Mathematics Association, Department of Curriculum and Foundations, Bloomsburg University, 400 E. Second St., Bloomsburg, PA 17815-1301 (717) 389-4915 http://hubble.bloomu.edu/~ssma

Organization with 1,000 members— teacher educators and teachers of K-12 science and mathematics. *Programs/services:* Workshops at annual meetings; small grants. *Publications/materials:* Curriculum units emphasizing science-mathematics integration; *Topics for Teachers* (monograph series); *Classroom Activities* (monograph series); *School Science and Mathematics* (journal); newsletter.

11.103 Science-by-Mail, Museum of Science, Science Park, Boston, MA 02114-1099 (617) 589-0437; (800) 729-3300 http://www.mos.org/mos/sbm/sciencemail.html

National pen pal program that pairs students in grades 4-9 with scientist mentors. *Programs/services:* Participants receive 2 science activity packets, the name and address of a scientist with whom to correspond during the school year, and a certificate upon completion of each packet. *Publications/materials:* Hands-on activity packets, including 6 to 8 activities each, illustrated instruction booklet, and teacher's notes.

11.104 Sigma Xi, The Scientific Research Society, 99 Alexander Dr., P.O. Box 13975, Research Triangle Park, NC 27709 (919) 549-4691; (800) 243-6534 http://www.sigmaxi.org

Interdisciplinary honor society of more than 85,000 research scientists and engineers affiliated with some 500 local Sigma Xi groups throughout North America. *Programs/services:* Available mostly through local Sigma Xi groups: teacher-scientist partnerships; speakers bureaus; classroom demonstrations; curriculum development with teachers; sponsorship of science fairs; lab visits for students; scientist mentors for students. *Publications/materials:* From Sigma Xi headquarters: brochures to promote scientist-teacher partnerships and scientist involvement in reform efforts; names and addresses of the officers of local Sigma Xi groups; *American Scientist* (magazine). From local groups: curriculum guidelines and units; audiovisual and computer-based materials; lab equipment/supplies for loan or as gift.

11.105 Smithsonian Institution, Office of Education, MRC 402, Arts and Industries Bldg., Rm. 1163, Washington, DC 20560 (202) 357-2425 http://educate.si.edu

The Smithsonian Institution's central office for precollege education, drawing on the Smithsonian's complex of museums, exhibitions, collections, and staff expertise to create a range of materials and programs. *Programs/ services:* Summer seminars for teachers; **Smithsonian Institution— National Faculty Program** (regional workshops); museum magnet schools (for students from Washington, D.C., public schools); video programs. *Publications/materials:* Art to Zoo (quarterly free curriculum guide); curriculum booklets; *Resource Guide for Teachers*; *Carousel* (guide to the Smithsonian Institution for teachers and school groups).

11.106 Society for Advancement of Chicanos and Native Americans in Science, Applied Sciences, Trailer #5, University of California at Santa Cruz, Santa Cruz, CA 95064 (408) 459-4272

Society of 600 professionals in science and education seeking to increase the participation of Latinos and Native Americans in science. *Programs/services:* Teacher workshops at annual meeting; scientist collaboration with teachers. *Publications/materials:* Curriculum units with hands-on materials; newsletter, with a section on K-12 programs.

11.107 Society for Developmental Biology, 9650 Rockville Pike, Bethesda, MD 20814-3998 (301) 571-0647 http://sdb.bio.purdue.edu

Professional society of biologists specializing in the development and growth of organisms. *Programs/services:* Science education outreach sessions for K-12 teachers at regional conferences and national annual meeting; Web site on developmental biology and related areas; list of scientists available to help in classrooms and to serve as a resource for teachers and students. *Publications/materials:* Newsletter.

11.108 Society for Sedimentary Geology, 1731 E. 71st St., Tulsa, OK 74136-5108
(918) 493-3361; (800) 865-9765

International organization of geologists who study sediments and sedimentary rocks. *Programs/services:* Workshops for teachers at annual meeting. *Publications/materials: A Sedimentary Geologists' Guide to K-12 Earth Science Education*—providing suggestions about classroom visits and activities and resources; *Hands-on Geology: K-12 Activities and Resources* and *On the Rocks: Earth Science Activities for Grades 1-8*—collections of activities for use in the classroom; *Careers in Sedimentary Geology*—brochure with answers to commonly asked questions.

11.109 Soil and Water Conservation Society, 7515 N.E. Ankeny Rd., Ankeny, IA 50021
(515) 289-2331; (800) THE-SOIL
http://www.swcs.org

Multidisciplinary educational and scientific organization for professionals in natural resource management, with many activities carried out by local chapters. *Programs/services:* Occasional teacher workshops; statewide environmental science fairs sponsored by some chapters. *Publications/materials:* Cartoon booklets on natural resource topics (water cycle, food cycle, plants, wildlife, range management, ecosystem management, wetlands) for students (ages 8-11), and related teacher's guides.

11.110 Southeastern Planetarium Association, c/o Mike Chesman, Bays Mountain Planetarium, 853 Bays Mountain Park Rd., Kingsport, TN 37660
(423) 229-9447

Regional association of professionals from planetariums (including many

that are school-based) in Alabama, Florida, Georgia, Kentucky, Louisiana, Mississippi, North Carolina, South Carolina, Tennessee, Virginia, West Virginia, and Puerto Rico; focused primarily on astronomy and earth science, and also on the physical sciences and biology. *Programs/services:* Sessions at annual meeting; database of scientists who are available to help teachers; promotion of scientist collaboration with individual teachers; information about the region's planetariums and their programs. *Publications/materials:* Newsletter.

11.111 Southwest Association of Planetariums (SWAP), c/o Donna Favour, SWAP President, Richardson Independent School District Planetarium, 9465 Whitehurst Dr., Dallas, TX 75243
(214) 503-2490

Regional association of professionals from planetariums (including many that are school-based) in Arkansas, New Mexico, Oklahoma, and Texas; focused on astronomy and space science. *Programs/services:* Annual conference; information about the region's planetariums and their programs. *Publications/materials:* Newsletter.

11.112 Students Watching Over Our Planet Earth, Rte. 6, Box 211, Fairmont, WV 26554
(304) 363-4309

Environmental education program in more than 1,100 schools in 50 states, the District of Columbia, Puerto Rico, Guam, and several foreign countries; creates and coordinates science research projects on environmental topics for students (grades K-12), and promotes collaborations over the Internet [e-mail: kanawha@aol.com] among schools

nationwide; enrolls only teachers. *Services:* Provides teacher support through electronic newsletters, on-line discussions, and individual support; creates computer protocols and links schools; sets research problems for students; processes and disseminates research results. *Publications/materials:* Background materials; hands-on laboratory activities on water quality.

11.113 Teachers Clearinghouse for Science and Society Education, One W. 88th St., New York, NY 10024
(212) 787-5315

Clearinghouse focused on providing classroom teachers with information on the latest advances in science education, with special emphasis on education in the area of science, technology, and society. *Publications: Teachers Clearinghouse for Science and Society Education Newsletter,* and annual single-topic supplement.

11.114 TERC, 2067 Massachusetts Ave., Cambridge, MA 02140
(617) 547-0430
http://www.terc.edu

Nonprofit education research and development organization focused on science and mathematics learning and teaching. *Programs/services:* LabNet—electronic community of elementary and secondary teachers that fosters science and mathematics teaching [http://labnet.terc.edu/labnet]; **The Hub**—electronic source of materials and information [http://ra.terc.edu]. *Publications/materials: National Geographic Kids Network/Middle Grades* (see 11.77), developed with National Geographic Society; **Global Laboratory**—network of student scientists involved in collaborative environmental investigations; **Tabletop**—software for visualization in data collection and analysis; *Literacy in a*

Science Context—hands-on human physiology curriculum; *Hands On!*—periodical on science, mathematics, and technology education; publications on telecommunications.

11.115 **The Transformations Project,** P.O. Box 1205, Jamaica Plain, MA 02130-1205
(617) 323-4514
http://www.hellgate.k12.mt.us/tp

National, nonprofit partnership program that teams engineers with middle-level educators for an exploration of technology. *Programs/services:* Participants linked through the Internet; outreach training conducted by participants for other teachers and schools in their local community; support provided by a network of engineers to educational programs in these local schools and on an interactive Web site for project activities. *Publications/materials: Transformations: Science, Technology and Society*—set of 8 videotapes with teacher's guides, serving as visual field trips for students and providing real-world applications of technology in society; posters.

11.116 **Triangle Coalition for Science and Technology Education,** 5112 Berwyn Rd., College Park, MD 20740-4129
(301) 220-0870
http://www.triangle-coalition.org

Coalition with representation from more than 160 member organizations, including business, industry, and labor, scientific and engineering societies, education associations, and a national network of local alliances, working to link national efforts at science education reform with local schools and school districts. *Programs/services:* Promotes collaborations and partnerships between

teachers and volunteer scientists through action groups or alliances; **SWEPT**—Scientific Work Experience Programs for Teachers. *Publications/materials:* Available on the World Wide Web: *A Guide for Building an Alliance for Science, Mathematics and Technology Education* and *A Guide for Planning a Volunteer Program for Science, Mathematics and Technology Education*; sent to e-mail addresses 45 times a year: *The Triangle Coalition Electronic Bulletin*.

11.117 **U.S. Department of Agriculture; Cooperative State, Research, Education, and Extension Service (CSREES),** Rm. 3441, South Building, Washington, DC 20250
(202) 720-5853

Agency in U.S. Department of Agriculture that advances science and technology in support of agriculture, forestry, people, and communities in partnership with the State Agricultural Experiment Station System and the State Cooperative Extension System. (For information on specific CSREES programs and services, contact local county Cooperative Extension office.) *Programs/services:*

- [(202) 720-5727] **Ag in the Classroom Program**—provides national coordination for states working to help K-12 students gain a greater awareness of agriculture's role in the economy and society;
- **4-H SERIES Program** (*see* 11.45);
- **National Network for Action in Science and Technology**—supports implementation of science and technology curriculum and processes. [http://www.cyfernet.mes.umn.edu]

11.118 **U.S. Department of Commerce, National Oceanic and Atmospheric Administration (NOAA),** NOAA Public Affairs Correspondence Unit, 1305 East-West Hwy., Stn. 1W204, Silver Spring, MD 20910
(301) 713-1208

Government agency that conducts research and gathers data about the oceans, atmosphere, space, and sun; sponsors a variety of educational outreach initiatives through 5 agencies (National Weather Service; National Marine Fisheries Service; National Environmental Satellite, Data, and Information Service; National Ocean Service; and Office of Oceanic and Atmospheric Research) and through numerous special programs. *Programs/services:* Workshops; hands-on work experiences; lectures; facility tours; donations of weather instruments and computers; mentoring and tutoring programs; professional development opportunities for teachers; speakers bureau. *Publications/materials:* Career publications; curriculum guidelines; computer-based materials; instructional materials.

11.119 **U.S. Department of Education, Office of Educational Research and Improvement,** 555 New Jersey Ave., N.W., Washington, DC 20808-5645
(202) 219-2116
http://www.ed.gov/offices/OERI/oeribro.html

An office of the U.S. Department of Education that supports research and disseminates information. Among its many activities, this office operates or supports the following:

- **Eisenhower National Clearinghouse for Mathematics and Science Education** (*see* 11.41).
- [(202) 219-2116] Ten **Eisenhower Regional Mathematics and Science Education Consortia**—provide information, technical

assistance, and training to states, schools, and teachers to help improve mathematics and science programs and adapt and use exemplary instructional materials, teaching methods, curricula, and assessment tools. Located in Aurora, Colo.; Austin, Tex.; Cambridge, Mass.; Charleston, W.Va.; Honolulu, Hawaii; Oak Brook, Ill.; Philadelphia, Pa.; Portland, Oreg.; San Francisco, Calif.; Tallahassee, Fla. [http://www.enc.org/partners/index.htm]

- [(202) 219-1925] **ERIC (Educational Resources Information Center)**—includes 16 clearinghouses, each specializing in a different subject area of education. (*See* 11.44 for a description of the ERIC Clearinghouse for Science, Mathematics, and Environmental Education.) [http://www.aspensys.com/eric/index.html]

- [(202) 219-2169] **Javits Gifted and Talented Students Education Program**—funds projects to help build a nationwide capability in elementary and secondary schools for meeting the special educational needs of gifted and talented students, including economically disadvantaged individuals, those with disabilities, and those with limited English proficiency. [http://www.ed.gov/prog_info/Javits]

- [(202) 219-1761] **National Assessment of Educational Progress**—measures educational achievement of students in grades 4, 8, and 12, and, for science, uses a hands-on task and portfolio. Teacher and student questionnaires elicit information about instructional practices. [http://www.ed.gov/NCES/naep]

- [(202) 219-2187] Ten **Regional Educational Laboratories**—do applied research and development on educational programs, materials, and professional development and that work with states and localities to implement systemic school improvement. Located in Aurora, Colo.; Austin, Tex.; Charleston, W.Va.; Greensboro,

N.C.; Honolulu, Hawaii; Oak Brook, Ill.; Philadelphia, Pa.; Portland, Oreg.; Providence, R.I.; and San Francisco, Calif. [http://www.nwrel.org]

- [(202) 219-8070] The **Regional Technology in Education Consortia** program—helps states, districts, schools, adult literacy centers, and other institutions use advanced technology to support improved teaching and student achievement. Six consortia focus their activities in 3 major areas—improving teaching and learning, professional development, and infrastructure development—and disseminate information and provide policy support related to those areas. [http://www.rtec/org]

- [(202) 219-2186] **Star Schools Program**—funds partnerships using telecommunications and distance-learning technologies (for example, satellites, fiber optics, computer networks) to improve education. [http://www.ed.gov/prog_info/StarSchools/index.html]

- [(202) 219-1333] **Third International Mathematics and Science Study (TIMSS)**—measured achievement in mathematics and science in 1995 at grades 3, 4, 7, 8, and 12, in up to 41 countries, and also collected information about curriculum, instructional practices, and teachers in each country. [http://www.ed.gov/NCES/timss]

11.120 **U.S. Department of Education, Office of Elementary and Secondary Education (OESE)**, 600 Maryland Ave., S.W., Washington, DC 20202-6100
(202) 401-0113
http://www.ed.gov/offices/OESE

An office of the U.S. Department of Education supporting elementary and secondary education through programs for compensatory education, school improvement, and special student populations. *Programs/ services:* The **Eisenhower Professional Development State Grants**

Program—supports teacher professional development activities through in-service and pre-service training, via state educational agencies to local school systems.

11.121 **U.S. Department of the Interior, Bureau of Reclamation Environmental Education Program**, P.O. Box 25007 (D-5100), Denver, CO 80225-0007
(303) 236-9336, Ext. 223
http://www.usbr.gov

Programs/services: Presents indoor and outdoor programs for students and teachers (grades K-12) on many environmental subjects, especially water, at many locales in all states west of the Mississippi.

11.122 **U.S. Department of the Interior, Earth Science Information Centers**, Reston-ESIC, 507 National Center, Reston, VA 20192
(703) 648-6045; (800) USA-MAPS
http://www.usgs.gov/education

Nationwide information and sales centers for U.S. Geological Survey (USGS) map products and earth science publications. Centers located in Anchorage, Alaska; Denver, Colo.; Menlo Park, Calif.; Reston, Va.; Rolla, Mo.; Salt Lake City, Utah; Sioux Falls, S.Dak.; Spokane, Wash.; Stennis Space Center, Miss. *Programs/services: The Learning Web*, a portion of the USGS Web site dedicated to K-12 education, exploration, and life-long learning. *Publications/materials:* Teacher packets; booklets; posters; fact sheets; CD-ROMs; resource lists.

11.123 **U.S. Department of the Interior, National Park Service**, P.O. Box 37127, Rm. 7312, Washington, DC 20013-7127
(202) 565-1052

The National Park Service assumes principal responsibility for administering the National Park System.

Programs/services: **Parks as Classrooms Program**—arranges workshops for teachers at numerous sites, to encourage building curricula around resources at national parks; many sites have workshops focused at least in part on science.

11.124 U.S. Environmental Protection Agency, 401 M St., S.W. [For Mail Code, see individual program listings, below], Washington, DC 20460

Programs/services of the Environmental Protection Agency (EPA) include the following:

- [(202) 260-8619; Mail Code 1707] **Environmental Education Grants Program**—supports projects of state and local agencies and nonprofit organizations that design, demonstrate, or disseminate new approaches in environmental education, projects with wide potential applicability and addressing high-priority issues. Operated by EPA's Environmental Education Division.
- [(202) 260-0578; Mail Code H-8105] **EPA Research Laboratory-based Education Programs**—offer teaching materials, workshops, lab visits, class presentations, and in-service events (grades K-12) in the localities of 13 EPA research laboratories (4 at Research Triangle Park, N.C.; 2 in Cincinnati, Ohio; and 1 each in Las Vegas, Nev.; Ada, Okla.; Athens, Ga.; Gulf Breeze, Fla.; Duluth, Minn.; Corvallis, Oreg.; and Narragansett, R.I.).
- [(202) 260-7751; Mail Code 3404] Ten **Public Information Centers (PICs)**—offer environmental education materials (such as publications, data, and exhibits) for students and teachers (grades K-12). Located at regional EPA offices in Atlanta, Boston, Chicago, Dallas, Denver, Kansas City, New York, Philadelphia, San Francisco, and Seattle.

11.125 U.S. Space Foundation, 2860 S. Circle Dr., Suite 2301, Colorado Springs, CO 80906-4184 (719) 576-8000; (800) 691-4000 http://www.ussf.org

Nonprofit educational organization that promotes national awareness and support for America's space endeavors. *Programs/services:* **Space Discovery** (5-day graduate course) and **Teaching with Space** (1-to-3-day in-service programs)—providing background information on space, ideas and methods for using space as a theme across the curricula (grades K-12), and ready-to-use activities and lessons for the classroom. *Publications/materials:* Foundation's Education Resource Center, serving as a distributor of free educational printed materials, posters, and videotapes from the National Aeronautics and Space Administration, the Federal Aviation Administration, the Civil Air Patrol, and the National Oceanic and Atmospheric Administration.

11.126 World Wildlife Fund, 1250 24th St., N.W., Washington, DC 20037-1175 (202) 293-4800 http://www.wwf.org

International conservation organization with more than 1 million members in the United States, and sponsoring more than 2,000 projects in 116 countries; dedicated to protecting the world's wildlife and rich biological diversity. *Programs/services:* **Windows on the Wild**—environmental education program on biodiversity. *Publications/materials: Taking Action: An Educator's Guide to Involving Students in Environmental Action Projects; WOW! A Biodiversity Primer and Educator's Guide* (magazine-style primer for middle school students); *Biodiversity! Exploring the Web of Life, Web of Life,* and *Going, Going, Almost Gone! Animals in Danger* (video

education kits); *Environmental Education in the Schools,* (resource book); *Biodiversity—From Sea to Shining Sea* (poster kit).

11.127 Young Astronaut Council, 1308 19th St., N.W., Washington, DC 20036 (202) 682-1984 http://www.yac.org

Corporation formed by the White House in 1984 to administer the **Young Astronaut Program**—national education program promoting the study of science, technology, and mathematics by building on the excitement of space; with more than 27,000 Young Astronaut Chapters formed in every state and in 42 foreign countries. *Programs/services:* Annual student conference; multidisciplinary competitions; broadcast live directly into classrooms, a Young Astronaut television course for grades 4-6. *Publications/materials:* Curriculum materials with hands-on activities; year-long curriculum for school-based Young Astronaut Chapters; newsletter; CD-ROM.

11.128 Young Entomologists' Society, 1915 Peggy Pl., Lansing, MI 48910-2553 (517) 887-0499 http://www.tesser.com/minibeast http://insects.ummz.lsa.umich.edu/yes/yes.html

Educational organization of more than 700 youth and amateur adult entomology enthusiasts. *Programs/services:* Insect science workshops; catalog of materials, offering a wide selection of entomological handbooks, manuals, resource guides, educational materials, and related products. *Publications/materials:* Curriculum and supplementary materials; audiovisual materials; newsletter for teachers and students; extensive bibliography; posters; career information.

INFORMATION ABOUT APPENDIX A

Appendix A provides names, addresses, phone and fax numbers, and e-mail or Web site addresses when available, for publishers and suppliers of books and materials annotated in this guide. The list is arranged alphabetically.

Some companies distribute print publications and curriculum materials or science apparatus as well, and some only one or the other of these categories. Before placing an order, readers should contact the publishers or suppliers directly for current ordering information (including shipping charges).

In compiling the guide, every effort was made to provide accurate, up-to-date bibliographic information. Annually updated information can be found in directories such as *NSTA Science Education Suppliers* (*see* 8.22) or in standard references such as *Books in Print* at local libraries or bookstores.

The annotations in this guide provide International Standard Book Numbers (ISBNs), when those were assigned, to help readers obtain commercially distributed materials. Some publishers use their own catalog numbers, however, so publishers should be consulted before ordering an item.

Readers are urged to seek out local sources for commercial products and recycled materials. They may also want to contact the new suppliers that are continually opening their doors.

AAAS
(*See* American Association for the Advancement of Science)

Active Learning Associates
520 N. Adams St.
Ypsilanti, MI 48197-2482
(800) 993-9499
Fax: (908) 284-0405
e-mail: sevchuk@aol.com
http://www.childrenssoftware.com

Addison-Wesley/Longman
School Services Division
One Jacob Way
Reading, MA 01867
(800) 552-2259
Fax: (800) 333-3328

AIMS Education Foundation
P.O. Box 8120
Fresno, CA 93747-8120
(209) 255-4094
Fax: (209) 255-6396

Air & Space/Smithsonian
P.O. Box 420113
Palm Coast, FL 32142-0113
(800) 766-2149

Air and Waste Management Association (A&WMA)
P.O. Box 915
Hudson, NH 03051
(800) 258-1302
Fax: (603) 880-6520

Alameda County Office of Education
Media Sales
313 W. Winton Ave.
Hayward, CA 94544-1198
(510) 670-4156
Fax: (510) 670-4161

Allyn and Bacon
(*See* Prentice Hall/Allyn and Bacon)

American Association for the Advancement of Science (AAAS)
Directorate for Education and Human Resource Programs
1200 New York Ave., N.W.
Washington, DC 20005
(202) 326-6454
Fax: (202) 371-9849
e-mail: sb&f@aaas.org
http://ehr.aaas.org

American Chemical Society
(To order periodicals)
P.O. Box 2537
Kearneysville, WV 25430
(800) 209-0423
Fax: (800) 525-5562

American Forest Foundation
1111 19th St., N.W.
Washington DC 20036
(202) 463-2462
Fax: (202) 463-2461

American Geological Institute
P.O. Box 205
Annapolis Junction, MD 20701
(301) 953-1744
Fax: (301) 206-9789

American Institute of Mining, Metallurgical and Petroleum Engineers (AIME)
345 E. 47th St., 14th Fl.
New York, NY 10017
(212) 705-7695
Fax: (212) 371-9622

American Library Association
(To order *Booklist*)
434 W. Downer Pl.
Aurora, IL 60506
(800) 545-2433, ext. 5715
e-mail: mwilkins@ala.org
http://www.ala.org/booklist

American Library Association
(To order *Science Books for Young People*)
Order Department
155 N. Wacker Dr.
Chicago, IL 60606
(800) 545-2433, press 7

American Museum of Natural History
Education Department
Central Park West at 79th Street
New York, NY 10024
(212) 769-5304
Fax: (212) 769-5329

American Plastics Council
1801 K St., N.W.
Suite 701-L
Washington, DC 20006-1301
(800) 243-5790
Fax: (202) 296-7119

American Society of Educators
1429 Walnut St.
Philadelphia, PA 19102
(215) 563-6005
Fax: (215) 587-9706
http://www.media-methods.com

American Solar Energy Society
2400 Central Ave., G-1
Boulder, CO 80301
(303) 443-3130
Fax: (303) 443-3212

Appraisal
605 Commonwealth Ave.
Boston, MA 02215

Associated Business Publications International
317 Madison Ave.
New York, NY 10017
Fax: (212) 986-7864

Association for Supervision and Curriculum Development
1250 N. Pitt St.
Alexandria, VA 22314-1453
(703) 549-9110
Fax: (703) 299-4511
e-mail: cbaker@ascd.org
http://www.ascd.org

Association of Science-Technology Centers
1025 Vermont Ave., N.W.
Suite 500
Washington, DC 20005
(202) 783-7200
Fax: (202) 783-7207
e-mail: pubs@astc.org
http://www.astc.org/astc

Astronomical Society of the Pacific
390 Ashton Ave.
San Francisco, CA 94112
(800) 335-2624
(415) 337-1100
Fax: (415) 337-5205
www.aspsky.org

Bakken Library and Museum
3537 Zenith Ave. S.
Minneapolis, MN 55416
(612) 927-6508
Fax: (612) 927-7265

Battle Creek Area Math/Science Center (BCAMSC)
765 Upton Ave.
Battle Creek, MI 49015
(616) 965-9440
Fax: (616) 965-9589

Biological Sciences Curriculum Study
Pikes Peak Research Park
5415 Mark Dabling Blvd.
Colorado Springs, CO 80918-3842
(719) 531-5550
e-mail: cmuonson@cc.colorado.edu
http://www.bscs.org

Blackbirch Press
260 Amity Rd.
Woodbridge, CT 06525
(203) 387-7525
Fax: (203) 389-1596

Bowker
(*See* R. R. Bowker)

California Department of Education
Bureau of Publications Sales Unit
P.O. Box 271
Sacramento, CA 95812-0271
(916) 445-1260
Fax: (916) 323-0823

California Foundation for Agriculture in the Classroom
1601 Exposition Blvd.
Sacramento, CA 95815
(916) 924-4380
Fax: (916) 923-5318

California Instructional Technology Clearinghouse
801 County Center III Court
Modesto, CA 95355-4490
(209) 525-4979
http://www.clearinghouse.k12.ca.us

Captivation
9 Cannongate Dr.
Nashua, NH 03063-1943
(603) 889-1156

Carnegie Corporation of New York
P.O. Box 753
Waldorf, MD 20642

Carolina Biological Supply Co.
2700 York Rd.
Burlington, NC 27215-3398
(800) 334-5551
Fax: (800) 222-7112

Carson-Dellosa Publishing Company
P.O. Box 35665
Greensboro, NC 27425-5665
(800) 321-0943
Fax: (800) 535-2669

Center for Mathematics, Science, and Technology Education
(*See* Illinois State University)

CESI
(*See* Council for Elementary Science International)

Charles Edison Fund
101 S. Harrison St.
East Orange, NJ 07018
(201) 675-9000
Fax: (201) 675-3345

Chemical Industry Education Centre
University of York
Heslington, York YO1 5DD
United Kingdom
(44-1904) 432600
Fax: (44-1904) 432605
e-mail: ciec@york.ac.uk

Children's Book Council
568 Broadway
Suite 404
New York, NY 10012
(212) 966-1990
Fax: (212) 966-2073
e-mail: staff@cbcbooks.org
http://www.cbcbooks.org

Cobblestone Publishing
7 School St.
Peterborough, NH 03458-1454
(800) 821-0115
(603) 924-7209
Fax: (603) 924-7380

College Board Publications
Department W49
P.O. Box 886
New York, NY 10101-0886
(800) 323-7155 (for credit card orders only)
(212) 713-8165

College Entrance Examination Board
(*See* College Board Publications)

Colorado Energy and Resource Educators
8340 W. Massey Dr.
Littleton, CO 80123
(303) 978-0735

The Communication Project
(*See* Scholastic Canada)

Cornell Instructional Materials Service
Kennedy Hall
Cornell University
Ithaca, NY 14853-4203
(607) 255-9252
Fax: (607) 255-7905

Corwin Press
2455 Teller Rd.
Thousand Oaks, CA 91320
(805) 499-0721
Fax: (805) 499-0871
e-mail: order@corwin.sagepub.com

Council for Elementary Science International (CESI)
c/o John Penick
789 Van Allen Hall
University of Iowa
Iowa City, IA 52242
(319) 335-1183
Fax: (319) 335-1188
e-mail: john-penick@uiowa.edu

The Cousteau Society
870 Greenbrier Circle
Suite 402
Chesapeake, VA 23320-9864
(757) 523-9335
Fax: (757) 523-2747

Creative Ventures
P.O. Box 2286
West Lafayette, IN 47906

Critical Thinking Books & Software
P.O. Box 448
Pacific Grove, CA 93950-0448
(800) 458-4849
(408) 393-3288
Fax: (408) 393-3277
e-mail: ct@criticalthinking.com
http://www.criticalthinking.com

CSIRO's Double Helix Science Club
P.O. Box 225
Dickson ACT 2602 Australia
06-276-6641
Fax: 06-276-6643
http://www.csiro.au/communication/doublehe/doublehe.htm

Cuisenaire/Dale Seymour Publications
P.O. Box 5026
White Plains, NY 10602-5026
(800) 237-0338
Fax: (800) 551-7637
http://www.cuisenaire.com

Curriculum Research and Development Group
(*See* University of Hawaii at Manoa)

Dale Seymour Publications
(*See* Cuisenaire/Dale Seymour Publications)

Decision Development Corporation
2680 Bishop Dr.
Suite 122
San Ramon, CA 94583
(800) 835-4332
(510) 830-8896
Fax: (510) 830-0830

Delta Education
P.O. Box 915
Hudson, NH 03051
(800) 258-1302
Fax: (603) 880-6520

Discover
(To order *Discover: The World of Science*)
P.O. Box 420105
Palm Coast, FL 32142-0105
(800) 829-9132

Educational Activities
1937 Grand Ave.
Baldwin, NY 11510
(800) 645-3739
(516) 223-4666
Fax: (516) 623-9282

Educational Products Information Exchange (EPIE) Institute
103 W. Montauk Hwy.
Suite 3
Hampton Bays, NY 11946
(516) 728-9100
Fax: (516) 728-9228
http://www.epie.org

Educators Progress Service
214 Center St.
Randolph, WI 53956
(414) 326-3126
Fax: (414) 326-3127

EDVOTEK
P.O. Box 1232
West Bethesda, MD 20827-1232
(800) 338-6935
(301) 251-5990
e-mail: edvotek@aol.com

Eisenhower National Clearinghouse for Mathematics and Science Education (ENC)
1929 Kenny Rd.
Columbus, OH 43210-1079
(800) 621-5785
(621) 292-7784
Fax: (614) 292-2066
http://www.enc.org

Electronic Learning
P.O. Box 53896
Boulder, CO 80322
(800) 544-2917

Emporia State University
Division of Biological Sciences
P.O. Box 4050
Emporia, KS 66801-5087
(316) 341-5614

Energy and Environmental Alliance
Institute of Science and Public Affairs
C-2200 University Center
Florida State University
Tallahassee, FL 32306-4016
(850) 644-3130

Enslow Publishers
P.O. Box 699
Springfield, NJ 07081-0699
(800) 398-2504
Fax: (201) 379-7940
http://www.enslow.com

ERIC Clearinghouse for Science, Mathematics, and Environmental Education
The Ohio State University
1929 Kenny Rd.
Columbus, OH 43210-1080
(800) 276-0462
Fax: (614) 292-0263

The Exploratorium
3601 Lyon St.
San Francisco, CA 94123
(415) 561-0393
Fax: (415) 561-0307
http://www.exploratorium.edu

Federal Emergency Management Agency
P.O. Box 70274
Washington, DC 20024
(202) 646-3104
Fax: (202) 646-2812

Field Museum of Natural History
Education Department/Books
Roosevelt Road and Lake Shore Drive
Chicago, IL 60605-2496
(312) 922-9410
Fax: (312) 922-6483
http://www.bvis.vic/edu/museum/
harris_loan

Flinn Scientific
P.O. Box 219
Batavia, IL 60510
(630) 879-6900
Fax: (630) 879-6962
e-mail: flinnsci@aol.com

Florida State University and Florida Energy Office
(*See* Energy and Environmental Alliance)

Follett Software Company
1391 Corporate Dr.
McHenry, IL 60050-7041
(800) 323-3397
(815) 344-8700
Fax: (815) 344-8774

Forecast Systems Laboratory
325 Broadway
Mail Code REFS
Boulder, CO 80303
(303) 497-6045
Fax: (303) 497-6064

Franklin Watts
5440 N. Cumberland Ave.
Chicago, IL 60656
(800) 672-6672
Fax: (312) 374-4329

Fulcrum Publishing
350 Indiana St.
Suite 350
Golden, CO 80401-5093
(800) 992-2908
Fax: (800) 726-7112
http://www.fulcrum-books.com

Geothermal Education Office
664 Hilary Dr.
Tiburon, CA 94920
(800) 866-4436
Fax: (415) 435-7737
e-mail: mnemzer@aol.com

Glencoe/McGraw-Hill (Editorial)
936 Eastwind Dr.
Westerville, OH 43081
(614) 890-1111
Fax: (614) 755-5645

Glencoe/McGraw-Hill (Distribution)
P.O. Box 543
Blacklick, OH 43004-9902
(800) 334-7344
Fax: (614) 860-1877

Globe Fearon (Editorial)
1 Lake St.
Upper Saddle River, NJ 07458
(201) 236-7000
FAX: (201) 236-5608

Globe Fearon (Distribution)
4350 Equity Dr.
P.O. Box 2649
Columbus, OH 43216
(800) 848-9500
Fax: (614) 771-7361

Good Year Books
1900 E. Lake Ave.
Glenview, IL 60025
(800) 628-4480, ext. 3038
(847) 729-3000

Greenwood Heinemann
(*See* Heinemann)

Grolier Publishing
Sherman Turnpike
Danbury, CT 06813
(800) 621-1115
Fax: (312) 374-4329

Harcourt Brace and Company
6277 Sea Harbor Dr.
Orlando, FL 32887
(800) 782-4479
Fax: (800) 874-6418

Harcourt Brace and Company, Australia
30-52 Smidmore St.
Locked Bag 16
Marrickville, NSW 2204, Australia
011-61-2-9-517-8999
Fax: 011-61-2-9-517-2249

Heinemann
361 Hanover St.
Portsmouth, NH 03801-3912
(800) 541-2086
(603) 431-7894
Fax: (800) 847-0938
e-mail: custserv@heinemann.com
http://www.heinemann.com

Heldref Publications
1319 18th St., N.W.
Washington, DC 20036-1802
(800) 365-9753
(202) 296-6267
Fax: (202) 296-5149

Holt, Rinehart and Winston
6277 Sea Harbor Dr.
Orlando, FL 32887
(800) 782-4479
Fax: (800) 874-6418

Houghton Mifflin Company
181 Ballardvale St.
Box 7050
Wilmington, MA 01887
(800) 225-3362
Fax: (800) 634-7568

Idea Factory
10710 Dixon Dr.
Riverview, FL 33569
(800) 331-6204
Fax: (813) 677-0373

Illinois-Indiana Sea Grant Program
University of Illinois
65 Mumford Hall
1301 W. Gregory Dr.
Urbana, IL 61801
(217) 333-9448

**Illinois State University
Center for Mathematics, Science, and Technology Education**
Campus Box 5960
Normal, IL 61790-5960
(309) 438-3089
Fax: (309) 438-3592

Incentive Publications
3835 Cleghorn Ave.
Nashville, TN 37215
(800) 421-2830
(615) 385-2967

Information Today
143 Old Marlton Pike
Medford, NJ 08055-8750
(609) 654-6266
Fax: (609) 654-4309
e-mail: custserv@infotoday.com
http://www.infotoday.com

Innovative Learning Publications (Editorial)
10 Bank St.
White Plains, NY 10606

Innovative Learning Publications (Distribution)
Scott Foresman/Addison-Wesley
1 Jacob Way
Reading, MA 01867
(800) 552-2259
Fax: (800) 333-3328

Institute for Chemical Education
Department of Chemistry
University of Wisconsin
1101 University Ave.
Madison, WI 53706-1396
(608) 262-3033
Fax: (608) 262-0381

**International Society for Technology in Education
Administration Office**
1787 Agate St.
Eugene, OR 97403-1923
(541) 346-4414
Fax: (541) 346-5890
e-mail: ISTE@oregon.uoregon.edu
http://isteonline.uoregon.edu

**International Society for Technology in Education
Customer Service Office**
480 Charnelton St.
Eugene, OR 97401-2626
(800) 336-5191
Fax: (541) 302-3778
e-mail: cust_svc@ccmail.uoregon.edu

International Technology Education Association
1914 Association Dr.
Suite 201
Reston, VA 20191-1539
(703) 860-2100
Fax: (703) 860-0353
e-mail: itea@iris.org
http://www.iteawww.org

IRI/Skylight Training and Publishing
2626 S. Clearbrook Dr.
Arlington Heights, IL 60005
(800) 348-4474
(847) 290-6600
Fax: (847) 290-6609
e-mail: info@iriskylight.com
http://www.iriskylight.com

Issues in Science and Technology
Circulation Services
P.O. Box 661
Holmes, PA 19043-9699
(214) 883-6325
e-mail: issuessn@utdallas.edu
http://www.utdallas.edu/research/issues

James A. Kaufman & Associates
192 Worcester Rd.
Natick, MA 01760-2252
(508) 647-0900
Fax: (508) 647-0062
e-mail: jaksafety@aol.com

Jason Foundation for Education
395 Totten Pond Rd.
Waltham, MA 02154
(617) 487-9995
Fax: (617) 487-9999

J. M. Lebel Enterprises
6420 Meadowcreek Dr.
Dallas, TX 75240
(800) 882-0667
Fax: (972) 726-9359

Journal of Chemical Education
Subscription and Book Order
Department
1991 Northampton St.
Easton, PA 18042
(800) 991-5534
(608) 262-7146
Fax: (608) 262-7145
e-mail: jce@aol.com
http://jchemed.chem.wisc.edu

Journal of Geoscience Education
(*See* National Association of
Geoscience Education)

Julian Messner/Simon & Schuster
(*See* Silver Burdette Ginn)

J. Weston Walch
321 Valley St.
P.O. Box 658
Portland, ME 04104-0658
(800) 341-6094
Fax: (207) 772-3105

Kalmbach Publishing Company
21027 Crossroads Circle
P.O. Box 1612
Waukesha, WI 53187
(800) 553-6644
(414) 796-8776
Fax: (414) 796-0126
e-mail: customerservice@kalmbach.com
http://www.kalmbach.com

Karol Media
350 N. Pennsylvania Ave.
P.O. Box 7600
Wilkes-Barre, PA 18773-7600
(800) 526-4773
Fax: (717) 822-8226

Kendall/Hunt Publishing Company
4050 Westmark Dr.
Dubuque, IA 52002
(800) 542-6657
Fax: (800) 772-9165
http://www.kendallhunt.com

Kids Discover
P.O. Box 54205
Boulder, CO 80322
(800) 284-8276

Lab-Aids
17 Colt Ct.
Ronkonkoma, NY 11779
(516) 737-1133
Fax: (516) 737-1286

LaMotte Company
P.O. Box 329
Chestertown, MD 21620
(800) 344-3100
Fax: (410) 778-6394

Lawrence Erlbaum Associates
10 Industrial Ave.
Mahwah, NJ 07430-2262
(800) 9-BOOKS-9 (for orders only)
(201) 236-9500
Fax: (201) 236-0072
e-mail: orders@erlbaum.com
http://www.erlbaum.com

Lawrence Hall of Science
University of California
Berkeley, CA 94720-5200
(510) 642-7771
Fax: (510) 643-0309

Learning Innovations
91 Montvale Ave.
Stoneham, MA 02180
(781) 279-8214
Fax: (781) 279-8220

The Learning Team
84 Business Park Rd.
Armonk, NY 10504
(800) 793-TEAM
Fax: (914) 273-2227

Lebel
(*See* J. M. Lebel Enterprises)

LEGO Dacta
555 Taylor Rd.
P.O. Box 1600
Enfield, CT 06083-1600
(800) 527-8339
Fax: (203) 763-2466

LHS GEMS
Lawrence Hall of Science
University of California
Berkeley, CA 94720-5200
(510) 642-7771
Fax: (510) 643-0309

Libraries Unlimited
Box 6633
Englewood, CO 80155-6633
(800) 237-6124
(303) 770-1220
Fax: (303) 220-8843
e-mail: lu-books@lu.com

Library of Congress
Science and Technology Division
Science Reference Section
10 First St., S.E.
Washington, DC 20540-5580
gopher://marvel.loc.gov.70/11/research/
readingrooms/science/bibs.guides/tracer

Linworth Publishing
480 E. Wilson Bridge Rd.
Suite L
Worthington, OH 43085
(614) 436-7107
Fax: (614) 436-9490
http://linworth.com

Macmillan/McGraw-Hill School
Publishing
(*See* McGraw-Hill Publishing
Company)

Mark Twain Media (Editorial)
100 E. Maine St.
P.O. Box 153
Lewistown, MO 63452
(573) 497-2202
Fax: (573) 497-2507

Mark Twain Media (Distribution)
(*See* Carson-Dellosa Publishing
Company)

McGraw-Hill Order Services
(To order *Endangered Species* and
Wading into Wetlands only)
P.O. Box 545
Blacklick, OH 43005-0545
(800) 262-4729
Fax: (614) 755-5645

McGraw-Hill Publishing Company
(Editorial)
School Division
1221 Avenue of the Americas
New York, NY 10020
(800) 442-9685
(212) 512-2000

McGraw-Hill Publishing Company
(Distribution)
220 East Danieldale Rd.
DeSoto, TX 75115
(800) 442-9685
(214) 224-1111
Fax: (214) 228-1982

Metropolitan Water District of
Southern California
Education Programs
P.O. Box 54153
Los Angeles, CA 90054
(213) 217-6739
Fax: (213) 217-6500

Michigan Department of Education
608 W. Allegan St.
Hannah Bldg.
Lansing, MI 48933
(517) 373-7248

Millbrook Press
P.O. Box 335
Brookfield, CT 06804
(800) 462-4703
Fax: (203) 740-2223

Miller Freeman
P.O. Box 5052
Vandalia, OH 45377
(701) 777-2864
http://www.techlearning.com

Mississippi-Alabama Sea Grant
Consortium
P.O. Box 7000
Ocean Springs, MS 39566-7000
(601) 875-9341
Fax: (601) 875-0528
e-mail: pubs@seahorse.ims.usm.edu

Morrow Junior Books
1350 Avenue of the Americas
New York, NY 10019
(800) 843-9389
Fax: (212) 261-6689

Muse
Box 7468
Red Oak, IA 51591-2468
(800) 827-0227

Museum Institute for Teaching
Science
79 Milk St.
Suite 210
Boston, MA 02109-3903
(617) 695-9771
e-mail: mits@usal.com
http://www.mits.org

NARST
(*See* National Association for
Research in Science Teaching)

NASCO
901 Janesville Ave.
P.O. Box 901
Fort Atkinson, WI 53538-0901
(800) 558-9595
(414) 563-2446
Fax: (414) 563-8296

National Academy Press
2101 Constitution Ave., N.W.
Lockbox 285
Washington, DC 20055
(800) 624-6242
(202) 334-3313
Fax: (202) 334-2451
http://www.nap.edu/bookstore

National Air and Space Museum
Educational Services Department
Smithsonian, MRC-305
Washington, DC 20560
(202) 786-2101
Fax: (202) 633-8928

National Air and Space Museum,
Office of Education
(*See* National Air and Space
Museum, Educational Services
Department)

National Aquarium in Baltimore
Education Department
501 E. Pratt St., Pier 3
Baltimore, MD 21202
(410) 576-3870
Fax: (410) 659-0116

National Association for Research in Science Teaching (NARST)
(For NARST members, to order *Journal of Research in Science Teaching*. For nonmembers: contact John Wiley—(212) 850-6645.)
c/o Dr. Arthur L. White
NARST Executive Secretary
The Ohio State University
1929 Kenny Rd., Rm. 200E
Columbus, OH 43210
(614) 292-3339
e-mail: TS0002@OHSTMVSA.ACS.OHIO-STATE.EDU

National Association of Biology Teachers
11250 Roger Bacon Dr.
Suite 19
Reston, VA 20190-5202
(800) 406-0775
Fax: (703) 435-5582

National Association of Geoscience Education
P.O. Box 5443
Bellingham, WA 98227-5443
(360) 650-3587
(360) 650-3582
Fax: (360) 650-7302
e-mail: xman@henson.cc.wwu.edu

National Audubon Society
Membership Data Center
P.O. Box 52529
Boulder, CO 80322
(800) 274-4201
Fax: (303) 604-7455

National Center for Improving Science Education
2000 L St., N.W.
Suite 616
Washington, DC 20036
(202) 467-0652
Fax: (202) 467-0659
e-mail: info@ncise.org

National Energy Foundation
5225 Wiley Post Way
Suite 170
Salt Lake City, UT 84116
(801) 539-1406
Fax: (801) 539-1451

National Energy Information Center
Forrestal Bldg.—EI-30
1000 Independence Ave., S.W.
Washington, DC 20585
(202) 586-8800
Fax: (202) 586-0727
e-mail: infoctr@eia.doe.gov
http://eia.doe.gov

National 4-H Council
(*See* National 4-H Supply Service)

National 4-H Supply Service
7100 Connecticut Ave.
Chevy Chase, MD 20815
(301) 961-2934
Fax: (301) 961-2937

National Gardening Association
180 Flynn Ave.
Burlington, VT 05401
(800) 538-7476
Fax: (800) 863-5962

National Geographic Society (Editorial)
1145 17th St., N.W.
Washington, DC 20036
(800) 368-2728
(202) 857-7000
http://www.nationalgeographic.org

National Geographic Society
(To order *National Geographic World*)
P.O. Box 63171
Tampa, FL 33663-3171
(800) NGS-LINE
Fax: (202) 429-5712

National Geographic Society (Distribution)
P.O. Box 10768
Des Moines, IA 50340
(800) 368-2728
Fax: (301) 921-1575

National Middle Level Science Teachers Association (NMLSTA)
(Contact National Science Teachers Association [NSTA])

National Middle School Association
2600 Corporate Exchange Dr.
Suite 370
Columbus, OH 43231-1672
(614) 895-4730
Fax: (614) 895-4750

National Science Resources Center
Smithsonian Institution, MRC-403
Arts and Industries Bldg., Rm. 1201
Washington, DC 20560
(202) 357-2555
Fax: (202) 786-2028
http://www.si.edu/nsrc

National Science Teachers Association (NSTA)
(Formerly located in Washington, DC)
1840 Wilson Blvd.
Arlington, VA 22201-3000
(800) 722-NSTA
(703) 243-7100
Fax: (703) 522-6091
e-mail: membership@nsta.org

National Technical Information Service (NTIS)
Springfield, VA 22161
(800) 553-6847
Fax: (703) 321-8547
e-mail: orders@ntis.fedworld.gov
(for orders)
http://www.ntis.gov

National Wildlife Federation (Editorial)
8925 Leesburg Pike
Vienna, VA 22184
(703) 790-4000
http://www.nwf.org/nwf

National Wildlife Federation
(To order *Discovering Deserts* and *Conservation Directory* only)
P.O. Box 9004
Winchester, VA 22604
(800) 477-5560
Fax: (540) 722-5399
e-mail: gordon@nwf.org

National Wildlife Federation
(To order periodicals)
P.O. Box 777
Mount Morris, IL 61054-8276
(800) 588-1650

Natural History
(*See* American Museum of Natural History)

New Mexico Museum of Natural History
P.O. Box 7010
Albuquerque, NM 87194
(505) 841-2871
(505) 841-2811

New York Energy Education Project (NYEEP)
89 Washington Ave., Rm. 678 EBA
Albany, NY 12234
(518) 473-1965
Fax: (518) 473-0858

New York Hall of Science
47-01 111th St.
Flushing Meadows
Corona Park, NY 11368
(718) 699-0005
Fax: (718) 699-1341

New York Science, Technology and Society Education Project (NYSTEP)
89 Washington Ave., Rm. 678 EBA
Albany, NY 12234
(518) 473-1965
Fax: (518) 473-0858

NOAA/ERL/FSL
(National Oceanic and Atmospheric Administration, Environmental Research Laboratories, Forecast Systems Laboratory)
325 Broadway
Mail Code REFS
Boulder, CO 80303
(303) 497-6045
Fax: (303) 497-6064

Northeastern University Center for Electromagnetics Research
Northeastern University
235 Forsyth Bldg.
360 Huntington Ave., 235FR
Boston, MA 02115
(617) 373-2034
Fax: (617) 373-8627

NSTA
(*See* National Science Teachers Association)

NYEEP
(*See* New York Energy Education Project)

NYSTEP
(*See* New York Science, Technology and Society Education Project)

Ohio State University Research Foundation
(*See* Ohio State University at Mansfield)

Ohio State University at Mansfield
1660 University Dr.
Mansfield, OH 44906
(419) 755-4342
Fax: (419) 755-4327
e-mail: tarino.1@osu.edu

Oryx Press
4041 N. Central Ave.
Suite 700
Phoenix, AZ 85012-3397
(800) 279-6799
(602) 265-2651
Fax: (800) 279-4663
e-mail: info@oryx press.com
http://www.oryxpress.com

Oxford University Press (Editorial)
198 Madison Ave.
New York, NY 10016
(212) 726-6000

Oxford University Press (Distribution)
2001 Evans Rd.
Cary, NC 27513
(800) 451-7556
Fax: (919) 677-1303
http://www.oup-usa.org

Helen M. Parke
Rte. 21, Box 38
Greenville, NC 27834
(919) 328-6736
Fax: (919) 328-6218

Pennsylvania Biotechnology Association
1524 W. College Ave.
Suite 206
State College, PA 16801
(800) 796-5806
Fax: (814) 238-4081
e-mail: 73150.1623@compuserve.com

PLANETS Educational Technology Systems
P.O. Box 22477
San Diego, CA 92192-2477
(619) 587-2138

Polystyrene Packaging Council
1801 K St., N.W.
Suite 600K
Washington, DC 20036
(202) 974-5341
Fax: (202) 296-7354
e-mail: awalton@socplas.org
http://www.polystyrene.org

Popular Science
Box 5100
Harlan, IA 51537
(212) 779-5000

Prentice Hall (Editorial)
1 Lake St.
Upper Saddle River, NJ 07458
(201) 236-7000
Fax: (201) 236-5608

Prentice Hall (Distribution)
4350 Equity Dr.
Columbus, OH 43216
(800) 848-9500
Fax: (614) 771-7361

Prentice Hall/Allyn and Bacon
200 Old Tappan Rd.
Old Tappan, NJ 07675
(800) 223-1360

Project WILD
707 Conservation Lane, Suite 305
Gaithersburg, MD 20878
(301) 527-8900
Fax: (301) 527-8912
http://eelink.umich.edu/wild

Roberts Rinehart
5455 Spine Rd.
Boulder, CO 80301
(800) 352-1985
(303) 530-4400
Fax: (303) 530-4488

RonJon Publishing
3730 E. McKinney St.
Suite 101
Denton, TX 76208-4637
(817) 383-3060
Fax: (817) 387-0505

R. R. Bowker
P.O. Box 31
New Providence, NJ 07974
(800) 521-8110
Fax: (908) 665-6688
e-mail: info@reedref.com

SAE International
400 Commonwealth Ave.
Warrendale, PA 15096
(800) 457-2946
(724) 772-8519
Fax: (724) 776-0890
http://www.sae.org

Sargent-Welch/VWR Scientific
911 Commerce Ct.
P.O. Box 5229
Buffalo Grove, IL 60089-5229
(800) 727-4368
Fax: (800) 676-2540
e-mail: sarwel@sargentwelch.com
http://www.sargentwelch.com

Schlitz Audubon Center
1111 E. Brown Deer Rd.
Milwaukee, WI 53217
(414) 352-2880
Fax: (414) 352-6091

Scholastic Canada and The Communication Project
164 Tomlinson Circle
Markham, Ontario L34 9K2
Canada
(905) 940-2973

Scholastic (Editorial)
Instructional Publishing Group
555 Broadway
New York, NY 10012
(212) 343-6100

Scholastic
(To order *ScienceWorld* and
SuperScience Blue)
P.O. Box 3710
2931 E. McCarty St.
Jefferson City, MO 65102-3710
(800) 631-1586

Scholastic (Distribution)
P.O. Box 7502
2931 E. McCarty St.
Jefferson City, MO 65102
(800) 724-6527
Fax: (573) 635-5881

School Library Journal
P.O. Box 57559
Boulder, CO 80322-7559
(800) 456-9409
Fax: (800) 824-4746

School Science and Mathematics Association
400 E. Second St.
Bloomsburg, PA 17815-1301
(717) 389-4915
Fax: (717) 389-3615
e-mail: ssm@ucs.orst.edu
http://www.orst.edu/Dept/
sci_mth_education/SSM

Science Books & Films
Department SBF
P.O. Box 3000
Denville, NJ 07834
(202) 326-6454
Fax: (202) 371-9849

Science Curriculum
24 Stone Rd.
Belmont, MA 02178
Phone/fax: (617) 489-2282

Science Service
Subscription Department
P.O. Box 1925
Marion, OH 43305
(800) 247-2160
Fax: (614) 382-5866
e-mail: scinews@scisvc.org
http://sciencenews.org

Scientific American
P.O. Box 3186
Harlan, IA 51593-2377
(212) 355-0408
e-mail: info@sciam.com
http://www.sciam.com

Scientific American Frontiers School Program
105 Terry Dr.
Suite 120
Newtown, PA 18940-3425
(800) 315-5010
Fax: (215) 579-8589
e-mail: saf@pbs.org
http://www.pbs.org/saf

Scott Foresman/Addison-Wesley (Editorial)
1900 E. Lake Ave.
Glenview, IL 60025
(847) 729-3000

Scott Foresman/Addison-Wesley (Distribution)
1 Jacob Way
Reading, MA 01867
(800) 552-2259
Fax: (800) 333-3328
http://www.sf.aw.com

PUBLISHERS AND SUPPLIERS

Sea World
(*See* Sea World of Florida)

Sea World of Florida
Education Department
7007 Sea World Dr.
Orlando, FL 32821
(407) 351-3600
Fax: (407) 363-2399

SEPM
(*See* Society for Sedimentary
Geology)

Silver Burdett Ginn (Editorial)
299 Jefferson Rd.
Parsippany, NJ 07054-0480
(973) 739-8000

Silver Burdett Ginn (Distribution)
Education School Group
P.O. Box 2649
Columbus, OH 43216
(800) 848-9500
Fax: (614) 771-7361

Singing Rock Press
P.O. Box 1274
Minnetonka, MN 55345
Phone/fax: (612) 935-4910

Sky and Telescope
P.O. Box 9111
Belmont, MA 02178-9917
(800) 253-0245
Fax: (617) 864-6117
e-mail: orders@skypub.com
http://www.skypub.com

Smithsonian Institution
(To order *Smithsonian* magazine)
Membership Data Center
P.O. Box 420309
Palm Coast, FL 32142-9143
(800) 766-2149

Smithsonian Office of Education
Arts & Industries Bldg.
Room 1163, MRC-402
Washington, DC 20560
(202) 357-2425
Fax: (202) 357-2116
e-mail: education@soe.si.edu
http://educate.si.edu/intro.html

**Society for Sedimentary Geology
(SEPM)**
1731 E. 71st St.
Tulsa, OK 74136-5108
(800) 865-9765
Fax: (918) 493-2093
http://www.ngdc.noaa.gov/mgg/sepm/
sepm.html

Sopris West
1140 Boston Ave.
Longmont, CO 80501
(303) 651-2829
Fax: (303) 776-5934

Southern Illinois University
Box 2222
Edwardsville, IL 62026-2222
(618) 692-3788
Fax: (618) 692-3359

**Southwest Educational
Development Laboratory**
211 E. 7th St.
Austin, TX 78701-3281
(512) 476-6861
Fax: (512) 476-2286
http://www.sedl.org

Springer-Verlag New York
P.O. Box 2485
Secaucus, NJ 07096-2485
(800) 777-4643
(201) 348-4033 (in New York)
Fax: (201) 348-4505

StarDate
2609 University Ave., Rm. 3-118
The University of Texas at Austin
Austin, TX 78712
(800) STA-RDATE
(512) 471-5285
Fax: (512) 471-5060
http://pio.as.utexas.edu

Stipes
P.O. Box 526
Champaign, IL 61824-0526
(217) 356-8391
Fax: (217) 356-5753

**Superintendent of Documents
U.S. Government Printing Office**
P.O. Box 371954
Pittsburgh, PA 15240-7954
(202) 512-1800
Fax: (202) 512-2250

Teacher Created Materials
P.O. Box 1040
Huntington Beach, CA 92647
(714) 891-7895
(800) 662-4321
Fax: (800) 525-1254
http://www.teachercreated.com

Teacher Ideas Press
P.O. Box 6633
Englewood, CO 80155-6633
(800) 237-6124
Fax: (303) 220-8843
e-mail: lu-books@lu.com
http://www.lu.com

Teachers College Press
Teachers College
Columbia University
1234 Amsterdam Ave.
New York, NY 10027
(212) 678-3929
Fax: (212) 678-4149
http://www.tc.columbia.edu/~tcpress

Teacher's Laboratory
P.O. Box 6480
Brattleboro, VT 05302-6480
(800) 769-6199
Fax: (802) 254-5233
e-mail: connect@sover.net

Team Labs
6390B Gunpark Dr.
Boulder, CO 80301
(800) 775-4357
Fax: (303) 530-4071
http://www.teamlabs.com

Texas Learning Technology Group (TLTG)
7703 N. Lamar Blvd.
Austin, TX 78752
(800) 580-8584
(512) 467-0222, ext. 6101
Fax: (512) 467-3554

3-2-1 Contact Magazine
P.O. Box 51177
Boulder, CO 80322-1177
(800) 678-0613

Tom Snyder Productions
80 Coolidge Hill Rd.
Watertown, MA 02172-2817
(800) 342-0236
Fax: (617) 926-6222

TOPS Learning Systems
10970 S. Mulino Rd.
Canby, OR 97013
(503) 266-8550
Fax: (503) 266-5200

Twenty-First Century Books
115 W. 18th St.
New York, NY 10011
(800) 628-9658, ext. 9387
(212) 886-9387
e-mail: 21cb@hholt.com

UCAR LEARN Center
P.O. Box 3000
Boulder, CO 80307-3000
(303) 497-8107
Fax: (303) 497-8610

UCS Publications
Two Brattle Square
Cambridge, MA 02238-9105
(617) 547-5552
Fax: (617) 864-9405
e-mail: ucs@ucsusa.org

Union of Concerned Scientists (UCS)
(*See* UCS Publications)

University Corporation for Atmospheric Dynamics
(*See* UCAR LEARN Center)

University of Hawaii at Manoa Curriculum Research and Development Group
Castle Memorial Hall 120
1776 University Ave.
Honolulu, HI 96822-2463
(800) 799-8111
(808) 956-7863
Fax: (808) 956-9486
e-mail: young@uhunix.uhcc.hawaii.edu

University of Texas M. D. Anderson Cancer Center
1515 Holcomb Blvd.
P.O. Box 240
Houston, TX 77030
(713) 745-1205
Fax: (713) 792-0800

University of Wisconsin
Center for Biological Education
Department of Plant Pathology
1630 Linden Dr.
495 Russell Labs
Madison, WI 53706
(608) 262-6496
Fax: (608) 263-2626

U.S. Department of Energy, National Energy Information Center
(*See* National Energy Information Center)

U.S. Environmental Protection Agency
Office of Research and Development
401 M St., S.W.
Washington, DC 20460
(202) 260-8619
Fax: (202) 260-4095

U.S. Forest Service, Intermountain Region
Public Affairs Office
324 25th St.
Ogden, UT 85501
(801) 625-5827
Fax: (801) 625-5240
http://www.fs.fed.us/outdoors/mrce/iye/contents.htm

U.S. Government Printing Office
(*See* Superintendent of Documents)

Von Holtzbrinck Publishing Services (VHPS)
175 Fifth Ave.
New York, NY 10010
(800) 488-5233
Fax: (212) 633-0748

Walch
(*See* J. Weston Walch)

Wards Natural Science Establishment
P.O. Box 92912
Rochester, NY 14692-9012
(800) 962-2660
Fax: (800) 635-8439

WGBN Boston
Attn: Print and Outreach
125 Western Ave.
Boston, MA 02134
(617) 492-2777, ext. 3848
Fax: (617) 787-1639

Wheelock College
200 The Riverway
Boston, MA 02215
(617) 734-5200, ext. 256
Fax: (508) 468-0073

WHOI Publication Services
P.O. Box 50145
New Bedford, MA 02745
(508) 457-2000
Fax: (508) 457-2180
e-mail: oeanusmag@whoi.edu
http://www.whoi.edu/oceanus

John Wiley (Corporate/Editorial Office)
605 Third Ave., Fl. 5
New York, NY 10158
(212) 850-6000
(212) 850-6088

John Wiley
(To order *Science Education* only)
P.O. Box 7247-8491
Philadelphia, PA 19170-8491
(212) 850-6645
Fax: (212) 850-6071
e-mail: info@jwiley.com

John Wiley (Distribution Office)
1 Wiley Dr.
Somerset, NJ 08873
(908) 469-4400
Fax: (908) 302-2300

Bob Williams
P.O. Box 2222
Southern Illinois University
Edwardsville, IL 62026
(618) 692-3788
Fax: (618) 692-3359

J. Michael Williamson
Wheelock College
200 The Riverway
Boston, MA 02215
(617) 734-5200, ext. 256
Fax: (508) 468-0073

Young Naturalist Company
1900 N. Main
Newton, KS 67114
(316) 283-4103
Fax: (316) 283-4103

ZED Consulting
P.O. Box 1678
Port Angeles, WA 98362-0083
(604) 246-0084

Introduction to Appendix B

Consistent with the National Science Resources Center's (NSRC's) philosophy of science teaching and with the *National Science Education Standards* of the National Research Council, the materials included in *Resources for Teaching Middle School Science* are hands-on and inquiry-centered. Briefly described, such materials provide opportunities for students to learn through direct observation and experimentation; they engage students in experiences not simply to confirm the "right" answer but to investigate the nature of things and to arrive at explanations that are scientifically correct and satisfying to young adolescents; and they offer students opportunities to experiment productively, to ask questions and find their own answers, and to develop patience, persistence, and confidence in their ability to tackle and solve real problems.

To produce evaluation criteria for identifying the most effective instructional materials available, the NSRC drew upon three primary sources:

- the National Science Education Standards (see appendix C in this guide);
- the experience gained by the NSRC in its ongoing review of science curriculum materials under the auspices of the National Academy of Sciences and the Smithsonian Institution; and
- the experience of teachers, superintendents, principals, and science curriculum coordinators across the United States.

The NSRC's "Evaluation Criteria for Middle School Science Curriculum Materials" were used by panels of teachers and scientists in the structured review of curriculum materials for this guide. The criteria are organized in the following sections:

- **Pedagogical Appropriateness** These criteria elaborate on the following key questions: Do the materials promote effective middle school science teaching and learning? Are inquiry and activity the basis of the learning experiences? Are the topics addressed in the unit and the modes of instruction developmentally appropriate?
- **Science Content and Presentation** These criteria address whether the science content is accurate, up to date, and effectively presented. Specific issues addressed include these: Do the suggested investigations lead to an understanding of basic science concepts and principles? Is the writing style interesting and engaging, while respecting scientific language? Which of the subject matter standards from the *National Science Education Standards* does the material focus on?
- **Organization and Format; Materials, Equipment, and Supplies; and Equity Issues** The criteria on organization and format include questions about the presentation of information—for example, whether the suggestions for instructional delivery are adequate and whether the print materials for students are well written, age-appropriate, and compelling in content. The criteria concerning hands-on science materials focus on questions such as the clarity and adequacy of instructions on manipulating laboratory equipment and the inclusion of appropriate safety precautions. Criteria addressing equity issues include the question of whether the material is free of cultural, racial, gender, and age bias.

At the end of each section, reviewers are asked to summarize the strengths and weaknesses of the material being reviewed. Final recommendations are based on a synthesis of the comments in the three sections.

Because instructional materials are designed to be used in different ways, the NSRC has identified three categories for classifying different types of science curriculum materials:

- **Core instructional materials,** which are substantial enough to form the foundation of a comprehensive middle school science curriculum.
- **Supplementary units,** which often consist of a series of activity-centered lessons. These units can provide enrichment for inquiry-based science teaching but may not have the depth or focus of core curriculum units.
- **Science activity books,** which offer a selection of ideas and activities to facilitate science learning. These materials are generally too broad in scope or specific in focus to serve as the foundation of a comprehensive science program.

The evaluation criteria not only apply to materials at these different levels, but they can help identify the most effective use of a particular instructional resource by focusing reviewers' attention on its strengths and weaknesses.

The following considerations should be kept in mind when one is using the criteria. The expectations for core materials are more comprehensive than for supplementary materials. For example, core materials need to provide assessment strategies, whereas this is not an expectation for science activity books. Likewise, core materials need to allow students to study a concept in depth, while supplementary units may provide only a general introduction to a topic.

The NSRC's "Evaluation Criteria for Middle School Science Curriculum Materials" are reprinted in full in this appendix. Teachers, curriculum specialists, curriculum developers, principals, superintendents, and those involved in various aspects of science education reform may find the criteria not only instructive, but useful as an instrument for reviewing instructional materials for local adoption.

NATIONAL SCIENCE RESOURCES CENTER
SMITHSONIAN INSTITUTION • NATIONAL ACADEMY OF SCIENCES
Resources for Teaching Middle School Science

EVALUATION CRITERIA FOR MIDDLE SCHOOL SCIENCE CURRICULUM MATERIALS

TITLE: *or name of resource*

SERIES TITLE: *if applicable*

AUTHOR(S): *if applicable*

CITY/STATE: *where published*

PUBLISHER/SOURCE:

COPYRIGHT DATE: ISBN NO: ADVERTISED GRADE LEVEL(S): *grades(s)*

SUPPLIES: *availablity of materials and kits for core curriculum materials*

COST: *suggested list price*

RESOURCE TYPE: *student activity book, teacher's guide, books on teaching science, etc.*

SUBJECT: *selected from major content categories*

Please supply the following information:

REVIEWER: _____   DATE: _____
                     (reviewer's name)   *(date of review)*

RECOMMENDED USER:

(check each that applies)   _____ stu   _____ tchr   _____ adm   _____ other (_____)

GRADE LEVEL(S) RECOMMENDED BY REVIEWER IF DIFFERENT FROM THE ADVERTISED LEVEL(S) STATED ABOVE:

(Please circle the specific grade level(s) for which you believe these materials are most appropriate.)

K   1   2   3   4   5   6   7   8   9   10   11   12

Reviewer: _____

1

NATIONAL SCIENCE RESOURCES CENTER
Smithsonian Institution • National Academy of Sciences

PEDAGOGY

Instructions: The following questions are designed to help you identify the important elements of each criterion. Please respond by selecting "Yes" if the material meets this goal and "No" if it does not. If "No" is selected, please explain the reason in the space provided below the question. In some instances, the question may not be applicable; then mark "NA."

CRITERIA	RATING		
I. DOES THE MATERIAL ADDRESS THE IMPORTANT GOALS OF MIDDLE SCHOOL SCIENCE TEACHING AND LEARNING?			
Does the material focus on engaging students in concrete experiences with science phenomena? Reason:	Yes	No	NA
Does the material enable students to investigate an important science concept(s) in depth over an extended period of time? (Especially necessary for core materials.) Reason:	Yes	No	NA
Does the material contribute to the development of scientific reasoning and problem-solving skills? Reason:	Yes	No	NA
Does the material stimulate student interest and relate to their daily lives? Reason:	Yes	No	NA
Does the material allow for or encourage the development of scientific attitudes and habits of mind, such as curiosity, respect for evidence, flexibility, and sensitivity to living things? Reason:	Yes	No	NA
Are assessment strategies aligned with the goals for instruction? Reason:	Yes	No	NA
Will the suggested assessment strategies provide an effective means of assessing student learning? Reason:	Yes	No	NA

Reviewer: _____

NATIONAL SCIENCE RESOURCES CENTER
Smithsonian Institution • National Academy of Sciences

NSRC EVALUATION CRITERIA FOR CURRICULUM MATERIALS

CRITERIA	RATING		
II. DOES THE MATERIAL FOCUS ON INQUIRY AND ACTIVITY AS THE BASIS OF LEARNING EXPERIENCES?			
Does the material engage students in the processes of science? Reason:	Yes	No	NA
Does the material engage students in planning and conducting scientific investigations? Reason:	Yes	No	NA
Does the material provide opportunities for students to develop questioning skills related to scientific investigations? Reason:	Yes	No	NA
Does the material provide opportunities for students to make and record their own observations? Reason:	Yes	No	NA
Does the material provide opportunities for students to gather data and defend their own evidence? Reason:	Yes	No	NA
Does the material provide opportunities, where appropriate, for students to use mathematics in the collection and treatment of data? Reason:	Yes	No	NA
Does the material provide opportunities for students to express their results in a variety of ways? Reason:	Yes	No	NA
Does the material encourage students to construct and analyze alternative explanations for science phenomena? Reason:	Yes	No	NA
Does the material provide opportunities for students to work collaboratively with others? Reason:	Yes	No	NA

Reviewer: _____

NATIONAL SCIENCE RESOURCES CENTER
Smithsonian Institution • National Academy of Sciences

NSRC EVALUATION CRITERIA FOR CURRICULUM MATERIALS

CRITERIA	RATING		
III. ARE THE MODES OF INSTRUCTION DEVELOPMENTALLY APPROPRIATE?			
Does the material present a logical sequence of related activities that will help students build conceptual understanding over several lessons? Reason:	Yes	No	NA
Does the suggested instructional sequence take into account students' prior knowledge and experiences? Reason:	Yes	No	NA
Do the suggested student activities develop critical thinking and problem-solving skills? Reason:	Yes	No	NA
Are the tools and techniques recommended for gathering, analyzing, and interpreting data appropriate for middle school students? Reason:	Yes	No	NA
Does the material incorporate examples of technological applications of science and the interactions among science, technology, and society? Reason:	Yes	No	NA
Does the material include historical examples to help students understand the nature of scientific inquiry and the interactions between science and society? Reason:	Yes	No	NA
Does the material include suggestions for integrating science with other important areas in the middle school curriculum, such as mathematics, language arts, and social studies? Reason:	Yes	No	NA

Reviewer: _____

NATIONAL SCIENCE RESOURCES CENTER
Smithsonian Institution • National Academy of Sciences

ASSESSMENT AND RECOMMENDATION—
PEDAGOGICAL APPROPRIATENESS OF MATERIALS

Instructions: Provide brief responses to the three requests below. It is not necessary to use complete sentences; words and phrases are sufficient. Then complete the recommendation statement.

Please provide a *brief* overview of the concepts taught and the activities suggested in this material.

With the above criteria in mind, please comment on any particular strengths in this material.

With the above criteria in mind, please comment on any particular weaknesses in this material.

After reviewing this material with only the above criteria for pedagogical appropriateness in mind,

_____ I **recommend** this material.

_____ I **do not recommend** this material.

Reviewer: _____

5

SCIENCE CONTENT AND PRESENTATION

Instructions: The following questions are designed to help you identify the important elements of each criterion. Please respond by selecting "Yes" if the material meets this goal and "No" if it does not. If "No" is selected, please explain the reason in the space provided below the question. In some instances, the question may not be applicable; then mark "NA."

CRITERIA	RATING		
I. SCIENCE CONTENT			
Is the science content in the materials accurately represented? Reason:	Yes	No	NA
Is the science content consistent with current scientific knowledge? Reason:	Yes	No	NA
Are important ideas included? Reason:	Yes	No	NA
Are generalizations adequately supported by facts? Reason:	Yes	No	NA
Are facts clearly distinguished from theories? Reason:	Yes	No	NA
Do the suggested investigations lead to an understanding of basic concepts and principles of science? Reason:	Yes	No	NA
Do experiments and activities promote student understanding of how scientists come to know what they know and how scientists test and revise their thinking? Reason:	Yes	No	NA

Reviewer: _____

6

NSRC EVALUATION CRITERIA FOR CURRICULUM MATERIALS

CRITERIA	RATING		
II. SCIENCE PRESENTATION			
Is science shown to be open to inquiry and free of dogmatism? Reason:	Yes	No	NA
Are different scientific viewpoints presented when appropriate? Reason:	Yes	No	NA
Are personal biases avoided? Reason:	Yes	No	NA
Is the writing style interesting and engaging, while respecting scientific language? Reason:	Yes	No	NA
Is vocabulary used to facilitate understanding rather than as an end in itself? Reason:	Yes	No	NA
Is science represented as an enterprise connected to society? Reason:	Yes	No	NA

Reviewer: _____

NATIONAL SCIENCE RESOURCES CENTER
Smithsonian Institution • National Academy of Sciences

CRITERIA
III.   TOPICS ADDRESSED FROM NATIONAL SCIENCE EDUCATION STANDARDS

Instructions: Following is a concise listing of the subject matter standards for physical science, life science, and earth and space science, as well as the science and technology standards, identified for grades 5 to 8 in the *National Science Education Standards.* (The list is from Tables 6.2 through 6.5, pp. 106–107, in the *Standards.*) For each standard addressed in the material, place a check mark in the column on the right.

STANDARD	ADDRESSED
PHYSICAL SCIENCE	
• Properties and changes of properties in matter	
• Motions and forces	
• Transfer of energy	

STANDARD	ADDRESSED
LIFE SCIENCE	
• Structure and function in living systems	
• Reproduction and heredity	
• Regulation and behavior	
• Populations and ecosystems	
• Diversity and adaptations of organisms	

STANDARD	ADDRESSED
EARTH AND SPACE SCIENCE	
• Structure of the earth system	
• Earth's history	
• Earth in the solar system	

STANDARD	ADDRESSED
SCIENCE AND TECHNOLOGY	
• Abilities of technological design	
• Understandings about science and technology	

Reviewer: _____

8

ASSESSMENT AND RECOMMENDATION—
SCIENCE CONTENT AND PRESENTATION

Instructions: Provide a brief written response to the first two requests below. It is not necessary to use complete sentences; words and phrases are sufficient. Then respond to the multiple choice question on level of quality.

With the above criteria in mind, please comment on any particular strengths in this material.

With the above criteria in mind, please comment on any particular weaknesses in this material.

What is the overall quality of the science presented in this instructional material?

_____ Low   _____ Medium   _____ High

After reviewing this material with only the above criteria for science content and presentation in mind,

_____ I **recommend** this material.

_____ I **do not recommend** this material.

Reviewer: _____

9

ORGANIZATION AND FORMAT, MATERIALS, AND EQUITY

Instructions: The following questions are designed to help you identify the important elements of each criterion. Please respond by selecting "Yes" if the material meets this goal and "No" if it does not. If "No" is selected, please explain the reason in the space provided below the question. In some instances, the question may not be applicable; then mark "NA."

CRITERIA	RATING		
I. ORGANIZATION AND FORMAT			
Teacher materials (whether module or textbook):			
Does the background material provide sufficient information for the teacher on the scientific content? Reason:	Yes	No	NA
Does the background material provide sufficient information on common student misconceptions? Reason:	Yes	No	NA
Is the format easy to follow? Reason:	Yes	No	NA
Are the directions for conducting laboratory activities and investigations clear? Reason:	Yes	No	NA
Are the suggestions for instructional delivery adequate? Reason:	Yes	No	NA
Are the suggested times for instructional activities reasonable? Reason:	Yes	No	NA
Does the material include appropriate suggestions for incorporating instructional technology? Reason:	Yes	No	NA

Reviewer: _____

NATIONAL SCIENCE RESOURCES CENTER
Smithsonian Institution • National Academy of Sciences

CRITERIA	RATING		
I. ORGANIZATION AND FORMAT, *CONTINUED*			
Student materials (whether module or textbook):			
Are the print materials for students well-written, age-appropriate, and compelling in content? Reason:	Yes	No	NA
Do the illustrations and photographs reinforce the concepts presented? Reason:	Yes	No	NA
Is the overall readability of the materials appropriate for middle school students? Reason:	Yes	No	NA
Textbooks:			
Are major concepts, principles, and ideas adequately developed? Reason:	Yes	No	NA
Are major concepts, principles, and ideas presented in logical sequence throughout the textbook? Reason:	Yes	No	NA
Is each chapter well-organized? Reason:	Yes	No	NA

Reviewer: _____

11

NATIONAL SCIENCE RESOURCES CENTER
Smithsonian Institution • National Academy of Sciences

CRITERIA	RATING		
II. HANDS-ON MATERIALS, EQUIPMENT, AND SUPPLIES			
Are the equipment, materials, and supplies recommended for use appropriate for middle school students? Reason:	Yes	No	NA
Are instructions on manipulating laboratory equipment and materials clear and adequate? Reason:	Yes	No	NA
Is a master source list of materials provided? Reason:	Yes	No	NA
Is a list of materials included for each activity? Reason:	Yes	No	NA
Is a complete set of materials readily available at a reasonable cost? Reason:	Yes	No	NA
Are consumable materials easily obtained and affordable? Reason:	Yes	No	NA
Are appropriate safety precautions included? Reason:	Yes	No	NA
III. EQUITY ISSUES			
Is the material free of cultural, racial, ethnic, gender, and age bias? Reason:	Yes	No	NA
Are appropriate strategies included to address the diversity of middle school students' needs, experiences, and backgrounds? Reason:	Yes	No	NA

Reviewer: _____

NATIONAL SCIENCE RESOURCES CENTER
Smithsonian Institution • National Academy of Sciences

NSRC EVALUATION CRITERIA FOR CURRICULUM MATERIALS

ASSESSMENT AND RECOMMENDATION—
ORGANIZATION AND FORMAT, MATERIALS, AND EQUITY

Instructions: Provide a brief response to the request below. It is not necessary to use complete sentences; words and phrases are sufficient. Then complete the recommendation statement.

With the above criteria in mind, please comment on particular strengths or weaknesses in this material.

After reviewing this material with only the above criteria for organization and format, materials, and equity issues in mind,

_____ I **recommend** this material.

_____ I **do not recommend** this material.

Reviewer: _____

13

NSRC EVALUATION CRITERIA FOR CURRICULUM MATERIALS

RECOMMENDATION BASED ON ALL CRITERIA

Instructions: Complete the section below. If you "recommend with reservations" or "do not recommend" a material for inclusion, briefly state your primary reason in the space provided.

Based upon all aspects of my review of this material,

_____ I **highly recommend** this material.

_____ I **recommend** this material.

_____ I **recommend** this material **with reservations.**

Primary reason for reservations:_____

_____

_____

_____ I **do not recommend** this material.

Primary reason for rejection: _____

_____

_____

Reviewer: _____

NATIONAL SCIENCE RESOURCES CENTER
Smithsonian Institution • National Academy of Sciences

ABOUT APPENDIX C

The content standards in this appendix are reprinted, with permission, from *National Science Education Standards* (NSES), developed by the National Research Council (Washington, D.C.: National Academy Press, 1996). © 1996 National Academy of Sciences. Included in this appendix are "Content Standard: K-12, Unifying Concepts and Processes" (NSES, pp. 115-19); "Content Standards: 5-8" (NSES, pp. 143-45, 148-49, 154-61, 165-71).

Ordering Information
National Science Education Standards (ISBN 0-309-05326-9) is available from the National Academy Press, 2101 Constitution Ave., N.W., Lockbox 285, Washington, D.C. 20055; phone: (800) 624-6242; (202) 334-3313 (Washington, D.C., metropolitan area); fax: (202) 334-2451. Price per copy: $19.95; quantity discounts available. NSES can also be ordered via the Internet, at http://www.nap.edu

NSES On-Line
The complete text of the *Standards* is available on-line, at the following Web site address: http://www.nap.edu/readingroom/books/nses

- The "Assessment Standards" identify characteristics of exemplary assessment practices and provide criteria that should be used in evaluations of students, teachers, programs, and policies.
- The "Science Content Standards" describe what students should know, understand, and be able to do in the natural sciences from kindergarten through high school.
- The "Science Education Program Standards" focus on issues at the school and district levels and describe conditions needed for quality school science programs.
- The "Science Education System Standards" provide criteria for judging the performance of all parts of the science education system—including school districts, state school systems, and the national education system.

The National Science Resources Center (NSRC) drew upon all of the above categories in developing its criteria for evaluating middle school curriculum materials. The category entitled "Science Content Standards" is particularly relevant with respect to the middle school criteria. (The NSRC's "Evaluation Criteria for Middle School Science Curriculum Materials" are contained in appendix B.)

Not only were the NSES content standards a basic component in the development of the evaluation criteria, but they are an important consideration for those adopting and using science curriculum in the classroom. For the convenience of readers, the "Science Content Standards" for grades 5 through 8 are reprinted here.

The "Science Content Standards" include the traditional subject areas of physical, life, and earth and space sciences. They also include standards on unifying concepts and

Introduction to Appendix C
Many readers of *Resources for Teaching Middle School Science* will already be familiar with the *National Science Education Standards* (NSES). The following information is provided for those who have not yet had the opportunity to study this document.

The National Research Council developed the *National Science Education Standards,* published in 1996, with the assistance of thousands of science teachers, scientists, science educators, and many other experts throughout the United States. The purpose of the standards, as described in the NSES (p. 11), is "to guide our nation toward a scientifically literate society."

The six categories of standards included in the NSES document together form a coordinated, interconnected whole. All of the following six categories need to be addressed for the vision of science education described in the National Science Education Standards to be attained:

- The "Science Teaching Standards" describe what teachers at all grade levels should know and be able to do to teach science effectively.
- The "Professional Development Standards" indicate the experiences teachers need for developing their knowledge and skill as professionals before they start teaching and throughout their careers.

processes (for grades K through 12), the nature of scientific inquiry, technological design and the connections between science and technology, science in personal and social perspectives, and the history and nature of science.

In chapters 1 through 5 of this guide, each annotation of core and supplementary curriculum material includes a list labeled "Key to Content Standards: 5-8." This key indicates the content standards addressed in depth in the material.

Readers can turn to this appendix to review the full text of all content standards listed in each key. (No key is given for student activity books, since they are not usually intended to focus on science concepts in depth.)

Each NSES content standard in this appendix has fundamental concepts and principles (which appear under the subheading "Guide to the Content Standard"). However, it is important to recognize that the listing of a standard in an annotation does not necessarily imply that the instructional material addresses all of the fundamental concepts and principles included under that NSES standard.

The NSES document also includes content standards for grades K-4 and 9-12. Although many of the curriculum materials annotated here may address concepts described in the standards for levels K-4 and 9-12, it was beyond the scope of this guide to provide correlations with the K-4 and 9-12 standards.

Content Standard: K–12

Unifying Concepts and Processes

STANDARD: As a result of activities in grades K-12, all students should develop understanding and abilities aligned with the following concepts and processes:
- **Systems, order, and organization**
- **Evidence, models, and explanation**
- **Constancy, change, and measurement**
- **Evolution and equilibrium**
- **Form and function**

DEVELOPING STUDENT UNDERSTANDING

This standard presents broad unifying concepts and processes that complement the analytic, more discipline-based perspectives presented in the other content standards. The conceptual and procedural schemes in this standard provide students with productive and insightful ways of thinking about and integrating a range of basic ideas that explain the natural and designed world.

The unifying concepts and processes in this standard are a subset of the many unifying ideas in science and technology. Some of the criteria used in the selection and organization of this standard are

- The concepts and processes provide connections between and among traditional scientific disciplines.
- The concepts and processes are fundamental and comprehensive.
- The concepts and processes are understandable and usable by people who will implement science programs.
- The concepts and processes can be expressed and experienced in a developmentally appropriate manner during K-12 science education.

Each of the concepts and processes of this standard has a continuum of complexity that lends itself to the K-4, 5-8, and 9-12 grade-level clusters used in the other content standards. In this standard, however, the boundaries of disciplines and grade-level divisions are not distinct—teachers should develop students' understandings continuously across grades K-12.

Systems and subsystems, the nature of models, and conservation are fundamental concepts and processes included in this standard. Young students tend to interpret phenomena separately rather than in terms of a system. Force, for example, is perceived as a property of an object rather than the result of interacting bodies. Students do not recognize the differences between parts and whole systems, but view them as similar. Therefore, teachers of science need to help students recognize the properties of objects, as emphasized in grade-level content standards, while helping them to understand systems.

As another example, students in middle school and high school view models as physical copies of reality and not as conceptual representations. Teachers should help students understand that models are developed and tested by comparing the model with observations of reality.

Teachers in elementary grades should recognize that students' reports of changes in such things as volume, mass, and space can represent errors common to well-recognized developmental stages of children.

GUIDE TO THE CONTENT STANDARD
Some of the fundamental concepts that underlie this standard are

SYSTEMS, ORDER, AND ORGANIZATION The natural and designed world is complex; it is too large and complicated to investigate and comprehend all at once. Scientists and students learn to define small portions for the convenience of investigation. The units of investigation can be referred to as "systems." A system is an organized group of related objects or components that form a whole. Systems can consist, for example, of organisms, machines, fundamental particles, galaxies, ideas, numbers, transportation, and education. Systems have boundaries, components, resources flow (input and output), and feedback.

The goal of this standard is to think and analyze in terms of systems. Thinking and analyzing in terms of systems will help students keep track of mass, energy, objects, organisms, and events referred to in the other content standards. The idea of simple systems encompasses subsystems as well as identifying the structure and function of systems, feedback and equilibrium, and the distinction between open and closed systems.

Science assumes that the behavior of the universe is not capricious, that nature is the same everywhere, and that it is understandable and predictable. Students can develop an understanding of regularities in systems, and by extension, the universe; they then can develop understanding of basic laws, theories, and models that explain the world.

Newton's laws of force and motion, Kepler's laws of planetary motion, conservation laws, Darwin's laws of natural selection, and chaos theory all exemplify the idea of order and regularity. An assumption of order establishes the basis for cause-effect relationships and predictability.

Prediction is the use of knowledge to identify and explain observations, or changes, in advance. The use of mathematics, especially probability, allows for greater or lesser certainty of predictions.

Order—the behavior of units of matter, objects, organisms, or events in the universe—can be described statistically. Probability is the relative certainty (or uncertainty) that individuals can assign to selected events happening (or not happening) in a specified space or time. In science, reduction of uncertainty occurs through such processes as the development of knowledge about factors influencing objects, organisms, systems, or events; better and more observations; and better explanatory models.

Types and levels of organization provide useful ways of thinking about the world. Types of organization include the periodic table of elements and the classification of organisms. Physical systems can be described at different levels of organization—such as fundamental particles, atoms, and molecules. Living systems also have different levels of organization—for example, cells, tissues, organs, organisms, populations, and communities. The complexity and number of fundamental units change in extended hierarchies of organization. Within these systems, interactions between components occur. Further, systems at different levels of organization can manifest different properties and functions.

EVIDENCE, MODELS, AND EXPLANATION Evidence consists of observations and data on which to base scientific explanations. Using evidence to understand interactions allows individuals to predict changes in natural and designed systems.

Models are tentative schemes or structures that correspond to real objects, events, or classes of events, and that have explanatory power. Models help scientists and engineers understand how things work. Models take many forms, including physical objects, plans, mental constructs, mathematical equations, and computer simulations.

Scientific explanations incorporate existing scientific knowledge and new evidence from observations, experiments, or models into internally consistent, logical statements. Different terms, such as "hypothesis," "model," "law," "principle," "theory," and "paradigm" are used to describe various types of scientific explanations. As students develop and as they understand more science concepts and processes, their explanations should become more sophisticated. That is, their scientific explanations should more frequently include a rich scientific knowledge base, evidence of logic, higher levels of analysis, greater tolerance of criticism and uncertainty, and a clearer demonstration of the relationship between logic, evidence, and current knowledge.

CONSTANCY, CHANGE, AND MEASUREMENT Although most things are in the process of becoming different—changing—some properties of objects and processes are characterized by constancy, including the speed of light, the charge of an electron, and the total mass plus energy in the universe. Changes might occur, for example, in properties of materials, position of objects, motion, and form and function of systems. Interactions within and among systems result in change. Changes vary in rate, scale, and pattern, including trends and cycles.

Energy can be transferred and matter can be changed. Nevertheless, when measured, the sum of energy and matter in systems, and by extension in the universe, remains the same.

Changes in systems can be quantified. Evidence for interactions and subsequent change and the formulation of scientific explanations are often clarified through quantitative distinctions—measurement. Mathematics is essential for accurately measuring change.

Different systems of measurement are used for different purposes. Scientists usually use the metric system. An important part of measurement is knowing when to use which system. For example, a meteorologist might use degrees Fahrenheit when reporting the weather to the public, but in writing scientific reports, the meteorologist would use degrees Celsius.

Scale includes understanding that different characteristics, properties, or relationships within a system might change as its dimensions are increased or decreased.

Rate involves comparing one measured quantity with another measured quantity, for example, 60 meters per second. Rate is also a measure of change for a part relative to the whole, for example, change in birth rate as part of population growth.

EVOLUTION AND EQUILIBRIUM Evolution is a series of changes, some gradual and some sporadic, that accounts for the present form and function of objects, organisms, and natural and designed systems. The general idea of evolution is that the present arises from materials and forms of the past. Although evolution is most commonly associated with the biological theory explaining the process of descent with modification of organisms from common ancestors, evolution also describes changes in the universe.

Equilibrium is a physical state in which forces and changes occur in opposite and off-setting directions: for example, opposite forces are of the same magnitude, or off-setting changes occur at equal rates. Steady state, balance, and homeostasis also describe equilibrium states. Interacting units of matter tend toward equilibrium states in which the energy is distributed as randomly and uniformly as possible.

FORM AND FUNCTION Form and function are complementary aspects of objects, organisms, and systems in the natural and designed world. The form or shape of an object or system is frequently related to use, operation, or function. Function frequently relies on form. Understanding of form and function applies to different levels of organization. Students should be able to explain function by referring to form and explain form by referring to function.

Content Standards: 5-8

Science as Inquiry

CONTENT STANDARD A: As a result of activities in grades 5-8, all students should develop
- **Abilities necessary to do scientific inquiry**
- **Understandings about scientific inquiry**

DEVELOPING STUDENT ABILITIES AND UNDERSTANDING

Students in grades 5-8 should be provided opportunities to engage in full and in partial inquiries. In a full inquiry students begin with a question, design an investigation, gather evidence, formulate an answer to the original question, and communicate the investigative process and results. In partial inquiries, they develop abilities and understanding of selected aspects of the inquiry process. Students might, for instance, describe how they would design an investigation, develop explanations based on scientific information and evidence provided through a classroom activity, or recognize and analyze several alternative explanations for a natural phenomenon presented in a teacher-led demonstration.

Students in grades 5-8 can begin to recognize the relationship between explanation and evidence. They can understand that background knowledge and theories guide the design of investigations, the types of observations made, and the interpretations of data. In turn, the experiments and investigations students conduct become experiences that shape and modify their background knowledge.

With an appropriate curriculum and adequate instruction, middle-school students can develop the skills of investigation and the understanding that scientific inquiry is guided by knowledge, observations, ideas, and questions. Middle-school students might have trouble identifying variables and controlling more than one variable in an experiment. Students also might have difficulties understanding the influence of different variables in an experiment—for example, variables that have no effect, marginal effect, or opposite effects on an outcome.

Teachers of science for middle-school students should note that students tend to center on evidence that confirms their current beliefs and concepts (i.e., personal explanations), and ignore or fail to perceive evidence that does not agree with their current concepts. It is important for teachers of science to challenge current beliefs and concepts and provide scientific explanations as alternatives.

Several factors of this standard should be highlighted. The instructional activities of a scientific inquiry should engage students in identifying and shaping an understanding of the question under inquiry. Students should know what the question is asking, what background knowledge is being used to frame the question, and what they will have to do to answer the question. The students' questions should be relevant and meaningful for them. To help focus investigations, students should frame questions, such as "What do we want to find out about . . .?", "How can we make the most accurate observations?", "Is this the best way to answer our questions?" and "If we do this, then what do we expect will happen?"

The instructional activities of a scientific inquiry should involve students in establishing and refining the methods, materials, and data they will collect. As students conduct investigations and make observations, they should consider questions such as "What data will answer the question?" and "What are the best observations or measurements to make?" Students should be encouraged to repeat data-collection procedures and to share data among groups.

In middle schools, students produce oral or written reports that present the results of their inquiries. Such reports and discussions should be a frequent occurrence in science programs. Students' discussions should center on questions, such as "How should we organize the data to present the clearest answer to our question?" or "How should we organize the evidence to present the strongest explanation?" Out of the discussions about the range of ideas, the background knowledge claims, and the data, the opportunity arises for learners to shape their experiences about the practice of science and the rules of scientific thinking and knowing.

The language and practices evident in the classroom are an important element of doing inquiries. Students need opportunities to present their abilities and understanding and to use the knowledge and language of science to communicate scientific explanations and ideas. Writing, labeling drawings, completing concept maps, developing spreadsheets, and designing computer graphics should be a part of the science education. These should be presented in a way that allows students to receive constructive feedback on the quality of thought and expression and the accuracy of scientific explanations.

This standard should not be interpreted as advocating a "scientific method." The conceptual and procedural abilities suggest a logical progression, but they do not imply a rigid approach to scientific inquiry. On the contrary, they imply codevelopment of the skills of students in acquiring science knowledge, in using high-level reasoning, in applying their existing understanding of scientific ideas, and in communicating scientific information. This standard cannot be met by having the students memorize the abilities and understandings. It can be met only when students frequently engage in active inquiries.

GUIDE TO THE CONTENT STANDARD
Fundamental abilities and concepts that underlie this standard include

ABILITIES NECESSARY TO DO SCIENTIFIC INQUIRY

IDENTIFY QUESTIONS THAT CAN BE ANSWERED THROUGH SCIENTIFIC INVESTIGATIONS. Students should develop the ability to refine and refocus broad and ill-defined questions. An important aspect of this ability consists of students' ability to clarify questions and inquiries and direct them toward objects and phenomena that can be described, explained, or predicted by scientific investigations. Students should develop the ability to identify their questions with scientific ideas, concepts, and quantitative relationships that guide investigation.

DESIGN AND CONDUCT A SCIENTIFIC INVESTIGATION. Students should develop general abilities, such as systematic observation, making accurate measurements, and identifying and controlling variables. They should also develop the ability to clarify their ideas that are influencing and guiding the inquiry, and to understand how those ideas compare with current scientific knowledge. Students can learn to formulate questions, design investigations, execute investigations, interpret data, use evidence to generate explanations, propose alternative explanations, and critique explanations and procedures.

USE APPROPRIATE TOOLS AND TECHNIQUES TO GATHER, ANALYZE, AND INTERPRET DATA. The use of tools and techniques, including mathematics, will be guided by the question asked and the investigations students design. The use of computers for the collection, summary, and display of evidence is part of this standard. Students should be able to access, gather, store, retrieve, and organize data, using hardware and software designed for these purposes.

DEVELOP DESCRIPTIONS, EXPLANATIONS, PREDICTIONS, AND MODELS USING EVIDENCE. Students should base their explanation on what they observed, and as they develop cognitive skills, they should be able to differentiate explanation from description—providing causes for effects and establishing relationships based on evidence and logical argument. This standard requires a subject matter knowledge base so the students can effectively conduct investigations, because developing explanations establishes connections between the content of science and the contexts within which students develop new knowledge.

THINK CRITICALLY AND LOGICALLY TO MAKE THE RELATIONSHIPS BETWEEN EVIDENCE AND EXPLANATIONS. Thinking critically about evidence includes deciding what evidence should be used and accounting for anomalous data. Specifically, students should be able to review data from a simple experiment, summarize the data, and form a logical argument about the cause-and-effect relationships in the experiment. Students should begin to state some explanations in terms of the relationship between two or more variables.

RECOGNIZE AND ANALYZE ALTERNATIVE EXPLANATIONS AND PREDICTIONS. Students should develop the ability to listen to and respect the explanations proposed by other students. They should remain open to and acknowledge different ideas and explanations, be able to accept the skepticism of others, and consider alternative explanations.

COMMUNICATE SCIENTIFIC PROCEDURES AND EXPLANATIONS. With practice, students should become competent at communicating experimental methods, following instructions, describing observations, summarizing the results of other groups, and telling other students about investigations and explanations.

USE MATHEMATICS IN ALL ASPECTS OF SCIENTIFIC INQUIRY. Mathematics is essential to asking and answering questions about the natural world. Mathematics can be used to ask questions; to gather, organize, and present data; and to structure convincing explanations.

UNDERSTANDINGS ABOUT SCIENTIFIC INQUIRY

- Different kinds of questions suggest different kinds of scientific investigations. Some investigations involve observing and describing objects, organisms, or events; some involve collecting specimens; some involve experiments; some involve seeking more information; some involve discovery of new objects and phenomena; and some involve making models.
- Current scientific knowledge and understanding guide scientific investigations. Different scientific domains employ different methods, core theories, and standards to advance scientific knowledge and understanding.
- Mathematics is important in all aspects of scientific inquiry.

- Technology used to gather data enhances accuracy and allows scientists to analyze and quantify results of investigations.
- Scientific explanations emphasize evidence, have logically consistent arguments, and use scientific principles, models, and theories. The scientific community accepts and uses such explanations until displaced by better scientific ones. When such displacement occurs, science advances.
- Science advances through legitimate skepticism. Asking questions and querying other scientists' explanations is part of scientific inquiry. Scientists evaluate the explanations proposed by other scientists by examining evidence, comparing evidence, identifying faulty reasoning, pointing out statements that go beyond the evidence, and suggesting alternative explanations for the same observations.
- Scientific investigations sometimes result in new ideas and phenomena for study, generate new methods or procedures for an investigation, or develop new technologies to improve the collection of data. All of these results can lead to new investigations.

Physical Science

CONTENT STANDARD B: As a result of their activities in grades 5-8, all students should develop an understanding of
- **Properties and changes of properties in matter**
- **Motions and forces**
- **Transfer of energy**

DEVELOPING STUDENT UNDERSTANDING

In grades 5-8, the focus on student understanding shifts from properties of objects and materials to the characteristic properties of the substances from which the materials are made. In the K-4 years, students learned that objects and materials can be sorted and ordered in terms of their properties. During that process, they learned that some properties, such as size, weight, and shape, can be assigned only to the object while other properties, such as color, texture, and hardness, describe the materials from which objects are made. In grades 5-8, students observe and measure characteristic properties, such as boiling points, melting points, solubility, and simple chemical changes of pure substances and use those properties to distinguish and separate one substance from another.

Students usually bring some vocabulary and primitive notions of atomicity to the science class but often lack understanding of the evidence and the logical arguments that support the particulate model of matter. Their early ideas are that the particles have the same properties as the parent material; that is, they are a tiny piece of the substance. It can be tempting to introduce atoms and molecules or improve students' understanding of them so that particles can be used as an explanation for the properties of elements and compounds. However, use of such terminology is premature for these students and can distract from the understanding that can be gained from focusing on the observation and description of macroscopic features of substances and of physical and chemical reactions. At this level, elements and compounds can be defined operationally from their chemical characteristics, but few students can comprehend the idea of atomic and molecular particles.

The study of motions and the forces causing motion provide concrete experiences on which a more comprehensive understanding of force can be based in grades 9-12. By using simple objects, such as rolling balls and mechanical toys, students can move from qualitative to quantitative descriptions of moving objects and begin to describe the forces acting on the objects. Students' everyday experience is that friction causes all moving objects to slow down and stop. Through experiences in which friction is reduced, students can begin to see that a moving object with no friction would continue to move indefinitely, but most students believe that the force is still acting if the object is moving or that it is "used up" if the motion stops. Students also think that friction, not inertia, is the principle reason objects remain at rest or require a force to move. Students in grades 5-8 associate force with motion and have difficulty understanding balanced forces in equilibrium, especially if the force is associated with static, inanimate objects, such as a book resting on the desk.

The understanding of energy in grades 5-8 will build on the K-4 experiences with light, heat, sound, electricity, magnetism, and the motion of objects. In 5-8, students begin to see the connections among those phenomena and to become familiar with the idea that energy is an important property of substances and that most change involves energy transfer. Students might have some of the same views of energy as they do of force—that it is associated with animate objects and is linked to motion. In addition, students view energy as a fuel or something that is stored, ready to use, and gets used up. The intent at this level is for students to improve their understanding of energy by experiencing many kinds of energy transfer.

GUIDE TO THE CONTENT STANDARD
Fundamental concepts and principles that underlie this standard include

PROPERTIES AND CHANGES OF PROPERTIES IN MATTER

- A substance has characteristic properties, such as density, a boiling point, and solubility, all of which are independent of the amount of the sample. A mixture of substances often can be separated into the original substances using one or more of the characteristic properties.
- Substances react chemically in characteristic ways with other substances to form new substances (compounds) with different characteristic properties. In chemical reactions, the total mass is conserved. Substances often are placed in categories or groups if they react in similar ways; metals is an example of such a group.
- Chemical elements do not break down during normal laboratory reactions involving such treatments as heating, exposure to electric current, or reaction with acids. There are more than 100 known elements that combine in a multitude of ways to produce compounds, which account for the living and nonliving substances that we encounter.

MOTIONS AND FORCES

- The motion of an object can be described by its position, direction of motion, and speed. That motion can be measured and represented on a graph.
- An object that is not being subjected to a force will continue to move at a constant speed and in a straight line.
- If more than one force acts on an object along a straight line, then the forces will reinforce or cancel one another, depending on their direction and magnitude. Unbalanced forces will cause changes in the speed or direction of an object's motion.

TRANSFER OF ENERGY

- Energy is a property of many substances and is associated with heat, light, electricity, mechanical motion, sound, nuclei, and the nature of a chemical. Energy is transferred in many ways.
- Heat moves in predictable ways, flowing from warmer objects to cooler ones, until both reach the same temperature.
- Light interacts with matter by transmission (including refraction), absorption, or scattering (including reflection). To see an object, light from that object—emitted by or scattered from it—must enter the eye.

- Electrical circuits provide a means of transferring electrical energy when heat, light, sound, and chemical changes are produced.
- In most chemical and nuclear reactions, energy is transferred into or out of a system. Heat, light, mechanical motion, or electricity might all be involved in such transfers.
- The sun is a major source of energy for changes on the earth's surface. The sun loses energy by emitting light. A tiny fraction of that light reaches the earth, transferring energy from the sun to the earth. The sun's energy arrives as light with a range of wavelengths, consisting of visible light, infrared, and ultraviolet radiation.

Life Science

CONTENT STANDARD C: As a result of their activities in grades 5-8, all students should develop understanding of
- **Structure and function in living systems**
- **Reproduction and heredity**
- **Regulation and behavior**
- **Populations and ecosystems**
- **Diversity and adaptations of organisms**

DEVELOPING STUDENT UNDERSTANDING

In the middle-school years, students should progress from studying life science from the point of view of individual organisms to recognizing patterns in ecosystems and developing understandings about the cellular dimensions of living systems. For example, students should broaden their understanding from the way one species lives in its environment to populations and communities of species and the ways they interact with each other and with their environment. Students also should expand their investigations of living systems to include the study of cells. Observations and investigations should become increasingly quantitative, incorporating the use of computers and conceptual and mathematical models. Students in grades 5-8 also have the fine-motor skills to work with a light microscope and can interpret accurately what they see, enhancing their introduction to cells and microorganisms and establishing a foundation for developing understanding of molecular biology at the high school level.

Some aspects of middle-school student understanding should be noted. This period of development in youth lends itself to human biology. Middle-school students can develop the understanding that the body has organs that function together to maintain life. Teachers should introduce the general idea of structure-function in the context of human organ systems working together. Other, more specific and concrete examples, such as the hand, can be used to develop a specific understanding of structure-function in living systems. By middle-school, most students know about the basic process of sexual reproduction in humans. However, the student might have misconceptions about the role of sperm and eggs and about the sexual reproduction of flowering plants. Concerning heredity, younger middle-school students tend to focus on observable traits, and older students have some understanding that genetic material carries information.

Students understand ecosystems and the interactions between organisms and environments well enough by this stage to introduce ideas about nutrition and energy flow, although some students might be confused by charts and flow diagrams. If asked about common ecological concepts, such as community and competition between organisms, teachers are likely to hear responses based on everyday experiences rather than scientific explanations. Teachers should use the students' understanding as a basis to develop the scientific understanding.

Understanding adaptation can be particularly troublesome at this level. Many students think adaptation means that individuals change in major ways in response to environmental changes (that is, if the environment changes, individual organisms deliberately adapt).

GUIDE TO THE CONTENT STANDARD
Fundamental concepts and principles that underlie this standard include

STRUCTURE AND FUNCTION IN LIVING SYSTEMS
- Living systems at all levels of organization demonstrate the complementary nature of structure and function. Important levels of organization for structure and function include cells, organs, tissues, organ systems, whole organisms, and ecosystems.
- All organisms are composed of cells—the fundamental unit of life. Most organisms are single cells; other organisms, including humans, are multicellular.
- Cells carry on the many functions needed to sustain life. They grow and divide, thereby producing more cells. This requires that they take in nutrients, which they use to provide energy for the work that cells do and to make the materials that a cell or an organism needs.
- Specialized cells perform specialized functions in multicellular organisms. Groups of specialized cells cooperate to form a tissue, such as a muscle. Different tissues are in turn grouped together to form larger functional units, called organs. Each type of cell, tissue, and organ has a distinct structure and set of functions that serve the organism as a whole.

- The human organism has systems for digestion, respiration, reproduction, circulation, excretion, movement, control, and coordination, and for protection from disease. These systems interact with one another.
- Disease is a breakdown in structures or functions of an organism. Some diseases are the result of intrinsic failures of the system. Others are the result of damage by infection by other organisms.

REPRODUCTION AND HEREDITY
- Reproduction is a characteristic of all living systems; because no individual organism lives forever, reproduction is essential to the continuation of every species. Some organisms reproduce asexually. Other organisms reproduce sexually.
- In many species, including humans, females produce eggs and males produce sperm. Plants also reproduce sexually—the egg and sperm are produced in the flowers of flowering plants. An egg and sperm unite to begin development of a new individual. That new individual receives genetic information from its mother (via the egg) and its father (via the sperm). Sexually produced offspring never are identical to either of their parents.
- Every organism requires a set of instructions for specifying its traits. Heredity is the passage of these instructions from one generation to another.
- Hereditary information is contained in genes, located in the chromosomes of each cell. Each gene carries a single unit of information. An inherited trait of an individual can be determined by one or by many genes, and a single gene can influence more than one trait. A human cell contains many thousands of different genes.
- The characteristics of an organism can be described in terms of a combination of traits. Some traits are inherited and others result from interactions with the environment.

REGULATION AND BEHAVIOR
- All organisms must be able to obtain and use resources, grow, reproduce, and maintain stable internal conditions while living in a constantly changing external environment.
- Regulation of an organism's internal environment involves sensing the internal environment and changing physiological activities to keep conditions within the range required to survive.
- Behavior is one kind of response an organism can make to an internal or environmental stimulus. A behavioral response requires coordination and communication at many levels, including cells, organ systems, and whole organisms. Behavioral response is a set of actions determined in part by heredity and in part from experience.

- An organism's behavior evolves through adaptation to its environment. How a species moves, obtains food, reproduces, and responds to danger are based in the species' evolutionary history.

POPULATIONS AND ECOSYSTEMS

- A population consists of all individuals of a species that occur together at a given place and time. All populations living together and the physical factors with which they interact compose an ecosystem.
- Populations of organisms can be categorized by the function they serve in an ecosystem. Plants and some micro-organisms are producers—they make their own food. All animals, including humans, are consumers, which obtain food by eating other organisms. Decomposers, primarily bacteria and fungi, are consumers that use waste materials and dead organisms for food. Food webs identify the relationships among producers, consumers, and decomposers in an ecosystem.
- For ecosystems, the major source of energy is sunlight. Energy entering ecosystems as sunlight is transferred by producers into chemical energy through photosynthesis. That energy then passes from organism to organism in food webs.
- The number of organisms an ecosystem can support depends on the resources available and abiotic factors, such as quantity of light and water, range of temperatures, and soil composition. Given adequate biotic and abiotic resources and no disease or predators, populations (including humans) increase at rapid rates. Lack of resources and other factors, such as predation and climate, limit the growth of populations in specific niches in the ecosystem.

DIVERSITY AND ADAPTATIONS OF ORGANISMS

- Millions of species of animals, plants, and microorganisms are alive today. Although different species might look dissimilar, the unity among organisms becomes apparent from an analysis of internal structures, the similarity of their chemical processes, and the evidence of common ancestry.
- Biological evolution accounts for the diversity of species developed through gradual processes over many generations. Species acquire many of their unique characteristics through biological adaptation, which involves the selection of naturally occurring variations in populations. Biological adaptations include changes in structures, behaviors, or physiology that enhance survival and reproductive success in a particular environment.
- Extinction of a species occurs when the environment changes and the adaptive characteristics of a species are insufficient to allow its survival. Fossils indicate that many organisms that lived long ago are extinct. Extinction of species is common; most of the species that have lived on the earth no longer exist.

Earth and Space Science

CONTENT STANDARD D: As a result of their activities in grades 5-8, all students should develop an understanding of
- **Structure of the earth system**
- **Earth's history**
- **Earth in the solar system**

DEVELOPING STUDENT UNDERSTANDING

A major goal of science in the middle grades is for students to develop an understanding of earth and the solar system as a set of closely coupled systems. The idea of systems provides a framework in which students can investigate the four major interacting components of the earth system—geosphere (crust, mantle, and core), hydro-sphere (water), atmosphere (air), and the biosphere (the realm of all living things). In this holistic approach to studying the planet, physical, chemical, and biological processes act within and among the four components on a wide range of time scales to change continuously earth's crust, oceans, atmosphere, and living organisms. Students can investigate the water and rock cycles as introductory examples of geophysical and geochemical cycles. Their study of earth's history provides some evidence about co-evolution of the planet's main features—the distribution of land and sea, features of the crust, the composition of the atmosphere, global climate, and populations of living organisms in the biosphere.

By plotting the locations of volcanoes and earthquakes, students can see a pattern of geological activity. Earth has an outermost rigid shell called the lithosphere. It is made up of the crust and part of the upper mantle. It is broken into about a dozen rigid plates that move without deforming, except at boundaries where they collide. Those plates range in thickness from a few to more than 100 kilometers. Ocean floors are the tops of thin oceanic plates that spread outward from mid-ocean rift zones; land surfaces are the tops of thicker, less-dense continental plates.

Because students do not have direct contact with most of these phenomena and the long-term nature of the processes, some explanations of moving plates and the evolution of life must be reserved for late in grades 5-8. As students mature, the concept of evaporation can be reasonably well understood as the conservation of matter combined with a primitive idea of particles and the idea that air is real. Condensation is less well understood and requires extensive observation and instruction to complete an understanding of the water cycle.

The understanding that students gain from their observations in grades K-4 provides the motivation and the basis from which they can begin to construct a model that explains the visual and physical relationships among earth, sun, moon, and the solar system. Direct observation and satellite data allow students to conclude that earth is a moving, spherical planet, having unique features that distinguish it from other planets in the solar system. From activities with trajectories and orbits and using the earth-sun-moon system as an example, students can develop the understanding that gravity is a ubiquitous force that holds all parts of the solar system together. Energy from the sun transferred by light and other radiation is the primary energy source for processes on earth's surface and in its hydrosphere, atmosphere, and biosphere.

By grades 5-8, students have a clear notion about gravity, the shape of the earth, and the relative positions of the earth, sun, and moon. Nevertheless, more than half of the students will not be able to use these models to explain the phases of the moon, and correct explanations for the seasons will be even more difficult to achieve.

GUIDE TO THE CONTENT STANDARD
Fundamental concepts and principles that underlie this standard include

STRUCTURE OF THE EARTH SYSTEM
- The solid earth is layered with a lithosphere; hot, convecting mantle; and dense, metallic core.
- Lithospheric plates on the scales of continents and oceans constantly move at rates of centimeters per year in response to movements in the mantle. Major geological events, such as earthquakes, volcanic eruptions, and mountain building, result from these plate motions.
- Land forms are the result of a combination of constructive and destructive forces. Constructive forces include crustal deformation, volcanic eruption, and deposition of sediment, while destructive forces include weathering and erosion.
- Some changes in the solid earth can be described as the "rock cycle." Old rocks at the earth's surface weather, forming sediments that are buried, then compacted, heated, and often recrystallized into new rock. Eventually, those new rocks may be brought to the surface by the forces that drive plate motions, and the rock cycle continues.
- Soil consists of weathered rocks and decomposed organic material from dead plants, animals, and bacteria. Soils are often found in layers, with each having a different chemical composition and texture.
- Water, which covers the majority of the earth's surface, circulates through the crust, oceans, and atmosphere in what is known as the "water cycle." Water evaporates from the earth's surface, rises and cools as it moves to higher elevations, condenses as rain or snow, and falls to the surface where it collects in lakes, oceans, soil, and in rocks underground.
- Water is a solvent. As it passes through the water cycle it dissolves minerals and gases and carries them to the oceans.
- The atmosphere is a mixture of nitrogen, oxygen, and trace gases that include water vapor. The atmosphere has different properties at different elevations.
- Clouds, formed by the condensation of water vapor, affect weather and climate.
- Global patterns of atmospheric movement influence local weather. Oceans have a major effect on climate, because water in the oceans holds a large amount of heat.
- Living organisms have played many roles in the earth system, including affecting the composition of the atmosphere, producing some types of rocks, and contributing to the weathering of rocks.

EARTH'S HISTORY
- The earth processes we see today, including erosion, movement of lithospheric plates, and changes in atmospheric composition, are similar to those that occurred in the past. Earth history is also influenced by occasional catastrophes, such as the impact of an asteroid or comet.
- Fossils provide important evidence of how life and environmental conditions have changed.

EARTH IN THE SOLAR SYSTEM
- The earth is the third planet from the sun in a system that includes the moon, the sun, eight other planets and their moons, and smaller objects, such as asteroids and comets. The sun, an average star, is the central and largest body in the solar system.
- Most objects in the solar system are in regular and predictable motion. Those motions explain such phenomena as the day, the year, phases of the moon, and eclipses.
- Gravity is the force that keeps planets in orbit around the sun and governs the rest of the motion in the solar system. Gravity alone holds us to the earth's surface and explains the phenomena of the tides.
- The sun is the major source of energy for phenomena on the earth's surface, such as growth of plants, winds, ocean currents, and the water cycle. Seasons result from variations in the amount of the sun's energy hitting the surface, due to the tilt of the earth's rotation on its axis and the length of the day.

Science and Technology

CONTENT STANDARD E: As a result of activities in grades 5-8, all students should develop
- **Abilities of technological design**
- **Understandings about science and technology**

DEVELOPING STUDENT ABILITIES AND UNDERSTANDING

Students in grades 5-8 can begin to differentiate between science and technology, although the distinction is not easy to make early in this level. One basis for understanding the similarities, differences, and relationships between science and technology should be experiences with design and problem solving in which students can further develop some of the abilities introduced in grades K-4. The understanding of technology can be developed by tasks in which students have to design something and also by studying technological products and systems.

In the middle-school years, students' work with scientific investigations can be complemented by activities in which the purpose is to meet a human need, solve a human problem, or develop a product rather than to explore ideas about the natural world. The tasks chosen should involve the use of science concepts already familiar to students or should motivate them to learn new concepts needed to use or understand the technology. Students should also, through the experience of trying to meet a need in the best possible way, begin to appreciate that technological design and problem solving involve many other factors besides the scientific issues.

Suitable design tasks for students at these grades should be well-defined, so that the purposes of the tasks are not confusing. Tasks should be based on contexts that are immediately familiar in the homes, school, and immediate community of the students. The activities should be straightforward with only a few well-defined ways to solve the problems involved. The criteria for success and the constraints for design should be limited. Only one or two science ideas should be involved in any particular task. Any construction involved should be readily accomplished by the students and should not involve lengthy learning of new physical skills or time-consuming preparation and assembly operations.

During the middle-school years, the design tasks should cover a range of needs, materials, and aspects of science. Suitable experiences could include making electrical circuits for a warning device, designing a meal to meet nutritional criteria, choosing a material to combine strength with insulation, selecting plants for an area of a school, or designing a system to move dishes in a restaurant or in a production line.

Such work should be complemented by the study of technology in the students' everyday world. This could be achieved by investigating simple, familiar objects through which students can develop powers of observation and analysis—for example, by comparing the various characteristics of competing consumer products, including cost, convenience, durability, and suitability for different modes of use. Regardless of the product used, students need to understand the science behind it. There should be a balance over the years, with the products studied coming from the areas of clothing, food, structures, and simple mechanical and electrical devices. The inclusion of some nonproduct-oriented problems is important to help students understand that technological solutions include the design of systems and can involve communication, ideas, and rules.

The principles of design for grades 5-8 do not change from grades K-4. But the complexity of the problems addressed and the extended ways the principles are applied do change.

GUIDE TO THE CONTENT STANDARD
Fundamental abilities and concepts that underlie this standard include

ABILITIES OF TECHNOLOGICAL DESIGN

IDENTIFY APPROPRIATE PROBLEMS FOR TECHNOLOGICAL DESIGN. Students should develop their abilities by identifying a specified need, considering its various aspects, and talking to different potential users or beneficiaries. They should appreciate that for some needs, the cultural backgrounds and beliefs of different groups can affect the criteria for a suitable product.

DESIGN A SOLUTION OR PRODUCT. Students should make and compare different proposals in the light of the criteria they have selected. They must consider constraints—such as cost, time, trade-offs, and materials needed—and communicate ideas with drawings and simple models.

IMPLEMENT A PROPOSED DESIGN. Students should organize materials and other resources, plan their work, make good use of group collaboration where appropriate, choose suitable tools and techniques, and work with appropriate measurement methods to ensure adequate accuracy.

EVALUATE COMPLETED TECHNOLOGICAL DESIGNS OR PRODUCTS. Students should use criteria relevant to the original purpose or need, consider a variety of factors that might affect acceptability and suitability for intended users or beneficiaries, and develop measures of quality with respect to such criteria and factors; they should also suggest improvements and, for their own products, try proposed modifications.

COMMUNICATE THE PROCESS OF TECHNOLOGICAL DESIGN. Students should review and describe any completed piece of work and identify the stages of problem identification, solution design, implementation, and evaluation.

UNDERSTANDINGS ABOUT SCIENCE AND TECHNOLOGY

* Scientific inquiry and technological design have similarities and differences. Scientists propose explanations for questions about the natural world, and engineers propose solutions relating to human problems, needs, and aspirations. Technological solutions are temporary; technologies exist within nature and so they cannot contravene physical or biological principles; technological solutions have side effects; and technologies cost, carry risks, and provide benefits.
* Many different people in different cultures have made and continue to make contributions to science and technology.
* Science and technology are reciprocal. Science helps drive technology, as it addresses questions that demand more sophisticated instruments and provides principles for better instrumentation and technique. Technology is essential to science, because it provides instruments and techniques that enable observations of objects and phenomena that are otherwise unobservable due to factors such as quantity, distance, location, size, and speed. Technology also provides tools for investigations, inquiry, and analysis.
* Perfectly designed solutions do not exist. All technological solutions have trade-offs, such as safety, cost, efficiency, and appearance. Engineers often build in back-up systems to provide safety. Risk is part of living in a highly technological world. Reducing risk often results in new technology.
* Technological designs have constraints. Some constraints are unavoidable, for example, properties of materials, or effects of weather and friction; other constraints limit choices in the design, for example, environmental protection, human safety, and aesthetics.
* Technological solutions have intended benefits and unintended consequences. Some consequences can be predicted, others cannot.

Science in Personal and Social Perspectives

CONTENT STANDARD F: As a result of activities in grades 5-8, all students should develop understanding of
* **Personal health**
* **Populations, resources, and environments**
* **Natural hazards**
* **Risks and benefits**
* **Science and technology in society**

DEVELOPING STUDENT UNDERSTANDING

Due to their developmental levels and expanded understanding, students in grades 5-8 can undertake sophisticated study of personal and societal challenges. Building on the foundation established in grades K-4, students can expand their study of health and establish linkages among populations, resources, and environments; they can develop an understanding of natural hazards, the role of technology in relation to personal and societal issues, and learn about risks and personal decisions. Challenges emerge from the knowledge that the products, processes, technologies and inventions of a society can result in pollution and environmental degradation and can involve some level of risk to human health or to the survival of other species.

The study of science-related personal and societal challenges is an important endeavor for science education at the middle level. By middle school, students begin to realize that illness can be caused by various factors, such as microorganisms, genetic predispositions, malfunctioning of organs and organ-systems, health habits, and environmental conditions. Students in grades 5-8 tend to focus on physical more than mental health. They associate health with food and fitness more than with other factors such as safety and substance use. One very important issue for teachers in grades 5-8 is overcoming students' perceptions that most factors related to health are beyond their control.

Students often have the vocabulary for many aspects of health, but they often do not understand the science related to the terminology. Developing a scientific understanding of health is a focus of this standard. Healthy behaviors and other aspects of health education are introduced in other parts of school programs.

By grades 5-8, students begin to develop a more conceptual understanding of ecological crises. For example, they begin to realize the cumulative ecological effects of pollution. By this age, students can study environmental issues of a large and abstract nature, for example, acid rain or global ozone depletion. However, teachers should challenge several important misconceptions, such as anything natural is not a pollutant, oceans are limitless resources, and humans are indestructible as a species.

Little research is available on students' perceptions of risk and benefit in the context of science and technology. Students sometimes view social harm from technological failure as unacceptable. On the other hand, some believe if the risk is personal and voluntary, then it is part of life and should not be the concern of others (or society). Helping students develop an understanding of risks and benefits in the areas of health, natural hazards—and science and technology in general—presents a challenge to middle-school teachers.

Middle-school students are generally aware of science-technology-society issues from the media, but their awareness is fraught with misunderstandings. Teachers should begin developing student understanding with concrete and personal examples that avoid an exclusive focus on problems.

GUIDE TO THE CONTENT STANDARD
Fundamental concepts and principles that underlie this standard include

PERSONAL HEALTH
- Regular exercise is important to the maintenance and improvement of health. The benefits of physical fitness include maintaining healthy weight, having energy and strength for routine activities, good muscle tone, bone strength, strong heart/lung systems, and improved mental health. Personal exercise, especially developing cardiovascular endurance, is the foundation of physical fitness.
- The potential for accidents and the existence of hazards imposes the need for injury prevention. Safe living involves the development and use of safety precautions and the recognition of risk in personal decisions. Injury prevention has personal and social dimensions.
- The use of tobacco increases the risk of illness. Students should understand the influence of short-term social and psychological factors that lead to tobacco use, and the possible long-term detrimental effects of smoking and chewing tobacco.
- Alcohol and other drugs are often abused substances. Such drugs change how the body functions and can lead to addiction.
- Food provides energy and nutrients for growth and development. Nutrition requirements vary with body weight, age, sex, activity, and body functioning.
- Sex drive is a natural human function that requires understanding. Sex is also a prominent means of transmitting diseases. The diseases can be prevented through a variety of precautions.

- Natural environments may contain substances (for example, radon and lead) that are harmful to human beings. Maintaining environmental health involves establishing or monitoring quality standards related to use of soil, water, and air.

POPULATIONS, RESOURCES, AND ENVIRONMENTS
- When an area becomes overpopulated, the environment will become degraded due to the increased use of resources.
- Causes of environmental degradation and resource depletion vary from region to region and from country to country.

NATURAL HAZARDS
- Internal and external processes of the earth system cause natural hazards, events that change or destroy human and wildlife habitats, damage property, and harm or kill humans. Natural hazards include earthquakes, landslides, wildfires, volcanic eruptions, floods, storms, and even possible impacts of asteroids.
- Human activities also can induce hazards through resource acquisition, urban growth, land-use decisions, and waste disposal. Such activities can accelerate many natural changes.
- Natural hazards can present personal and societal challenges because misidentifying the change or incorrectly estimating the rate and scale of change may result in either too little attention and significant human costs or too much cost for unneeded preventive measures.

RISKS AND BENEFITS
- Risk analysis considers the type of hazard and estimates the number of people that might be exposed and the number likely to suffer consequences. The results are used to determine the options for reducing or eliminating risks.
- Students should understand the risks associated with natural hazards (fires, floods, tornadoes, hurricanes, earthquakes, and volcanic eruptions), with chemical hazards (pollutants in air, water, soil, and food), with biological hazards (pollen, viruses, bacterial, and parasites), social hazards (occupational safety and transportation), and with personal hazards (smoking, dieting, and drinking).
- Individuals can use a systematic approach to thinking critically about risks and benefits. Examples include applying probability estimates to risks and comparing them to estimated personal and social benefits.
- Important personal and social decisions are made based on perceptions of benefits and risks.

SCIENCE AND TECHNOLOGY IN SOCIETY
- Science influences society through its knowledge and world view. Scientific knowledge and the procedures

used by scientists influence the way many individuals in society think about themselves, others, and the environment. The effect of science on society is neither entirely beneficial nor entirely detrimental.

- Societal challenges often inspire questions for scientific research, and social priorities often influence research priorities through the availability of funding for research.
- Technology influences society through its products and processes. Technology influences the quality of life and the ways people act and interact. Technological changes are often accompanied by social, political, and economic changes that can be beneficial or detrimental to individuals and to society. Social needs, attitudes, and values influence the direction of technological development.
- Science and technology have advanced through contributions of many different people, in different cultures, at different times in history. Science and technology have contributed enormously to economic growth and productivity among societies and groups within societies.
- Scientists and engineers work in many different settings, including colleges and universities, businesses and industries, specific research institutes, and government agencies.
- Scientists and engineers have ethical codes requiring that human subjects involved with research be fully informed about risks and benefits associated with the research before the individuals choose to participate. This ethic extends to potential risks to communities and property. In short, prior knowledge and consent are required for research involving human subjects or potential damage to property.
- Science cannot answer all questions and technology cannot solve all human problems or meet all human needs. Students should understand the difference between scientific and other questions. They should appreciate what science and technology can reasonably contribute to society and what they cannot do. For example, new technologies often will decrease some risks and increase others.

History and Nature of Science

CONTENT STANDARD G: As a result of activities in grades 5-8, all students should develop understanding of
- **Science as a human endeavor**
- **Nature of science**
- **History of science**

DEVELOPING STUDENT UNDERSTANDING

Experiences in which students actually engage in scientific investigations provide the background for developing an understanding of the nature of scientific inquiry, and will also provide a foundation for appreciating the history of science described in this standard.

The introduction of historical examples will help students see the scientific enterprise as more philosophical, social, and human. Middle-school students can thereby develop a better understanding of scientific inquiry and the interactions between science and society. In general, teachers of science should not assume that students have an accurate conception of the nature of science in either contemporary or historical contexts.

To develop understanding of the history and nature of science, teachers of science can use the actual experiences of student investigations, case studies, and historical vignettes. The intention of this standard is not to develop an overview of the complete history of science. Rather, historical examples are used to help students understand scientific inquiry, the nature of scientific knowledge, and the interactions between science and society.

GUIDE TO THE CONTENT STANDARD
Fundamental concepts and principles that underlie this standard include

SCIENCE AS A HUMAN ENDEAVOR
- Women and men of various social and ethnic backgrounds—and with diverse interests, talents, qualities, and motivations—engage in the activities of science, engineering, and related fields such as the health professions. Some scientists work in teams, and some work alone, but all communicate extensively with others.
- Science requires different abilities, depending on such factors as the field of study and type of inquiry. Science is very much a human endeavor, and the work of science relies on basic human qualities, such as reasoning, insight, energy, skill, and creativity—as well as on scientific habits of mind, such as intellectual honesty, tolerance of ambiguity, skepticism, and openness to new ideas.

NATURE OF SCIENCE
- Scientists formulate and test their explanations of nature using observation, experiments, and theoretical and mathematical models. Although all scientific ideas are tentative and subject to change and improvement in principle, for most major ideas in science, there is much experimental and observational confirmation. Those ideas are not likely to

change greatly in the future. Scientists do and have changed their ideas about nature when they encounter new experimental evidence that does not match their existing explanations.

- In areas where active research is being pursued and in which there is not a great deal of experimental or observational evidence and understanding, it is normal for scientists to differ with one another about the interpretation of the evidence or theory being considered. Different scientists might publish conflicting experimental results or might draw different conclusions from the same data. Ideally, scientists acknowledge such conflict and work towards finding evidence that will resolve their disagreement.
- It is part of scientific inquiry to evaluate the results of scientific investigations, experiments, observations, theoretical models, and the explanations proposed by other scientists. Evaluation includes reviewing the experimental procedures, examining the evidence, identifying faulty reasoning, pointing out statements that go beyond the evidence, and suggesting alternative explanations for the same observations. Although scientists may disagree about explanations of phenomena, about interpretations of data, or about the value of rival theories, they do agree that questioning, response to criticism, and open communication are integral to the process of science. As scientific knowledge evolves, major disagreements are eventually resolved through such interactions between scientists.

HISTORY OF SCIENCE

- Many individuals have contributed to the traditions of science. Studying some of these individuals provides further understanding of scientific inquiry, science as a human endeavor, the nature of science, and the relationships between science and society.
- In historical perspective, science has been practiced by different individuals in different cultures. In looking at the history of many peoples, one finds that scientists and engineers of high achievement are considered to be among the most valued contributors to their culture.
- Tracing the history of science can show how difficult it was for scientific innovators to break through the accepted ideas of their time to reach the conclusions that we currently take for granted.

APPENDIX D:
Overviews of Core and Supplementary Programs
with Titles Annotated in This Guide

INFORMATION ABOUT APPENDIX D

Appendix D contains three sections:

- Annotated Titles in Core Programs (D.1-D.20)
- Annotated Titles in Supplementary Series (D.21-D.43)
- Individual Supplementary Units (D.44)

The information is arranged as follows:

- The first two sections contain alphabetical listings of core programs and supplementary series, respectively. For each of these programs and series, a descriptive overview is provided, together with a list of the titles from that program or series which are annotated in the guide.
- The third section contains an alphabetical listing of supplementary units that are not in series.
- For ease of reference, the entry number is shown with each title.

This appendix is not meant to be a catalog-style listing of all titles published in each program or series, but to provide quick reference to the materials annotated in the curriculum chapters of this volume. Readers seeking a comprehensive, current list of all of the titles in any program or series should contact the publisher of the curriculum materials directly. (Appendix A provides contact information.)

Appendix D does not include science activity books. Readers are referred to the "Science Activity Books" sections of the curriculum chapters and to the indexes in this volume for locating information on activity books.

ANNOTATED TITLES IN CORE PROGRAMS

D.1 **Concepts and Challenges in Life, Earth, and Physical Science series** The series entitled Concepts and Challenges in Life, Earth, and Physical Science consists of 3 textbooks—1 in life science, 1 in earth science, and 1 in physical science.

Each year-long course contains about 20 units. Teaching materials, ancillary student materials, and some optional components are available for each course.

- *Concepts and Challenges in Earth Science,* 4.1

D.2 **Foundational Approaches in Science Teaching (FAST)** The Foundational Approaches in Science Teaching (FAST) series is an interdisciplinary science program consisting of 3 courses for middle, junior, and senior high school students. Each 1-year course is organized in 3 strands—physical science (chemistry and physics), ecology (biological and earth sciences), and relational study. The ecology and physical science strands, which provide the formal science content, are intended to be presented concurrently by alternating short sequences of investigations from each strand. The relational study strand integrates the sciences, technology, and society. Components of the program include the student book, teacher's guide, several reference booklets for each course, and other optional teacher support materials.

- *The Local Environment,* 5.7
- *Matter and Energy in the Biosphere,* 5.8

D.3 **Full Option Science System (FOSS) series** The Full Option Science System (FOSS) program is a K-6 science curriculum consisting of 27 stand-alone modules. The 8 modules for grades 5-6 are organized under topics in the life, physical, and earth sciences and in scientific reasoning and technology. They can be used in any order. The FOSS program is designed to engage students in scientific concepts through multisensory, hands-on laboratory activities. All modules of the program incorporate 5 unifying themes—pattern, structure, interaction, change, and system. The components of a FOSS module are a teacher's guide and a kit of materials.

- *Environments,* 3.1
- *Food and Nutrition,* 2.7
- *Landforms,* 4.6
- *Levers and Pulleys,* 1.10
- *Mixtures and Solutions,* 1.13
- *Models and Designs,* 5.12
- *Solar Energy,* 4.9
- *Variables,* 5.28

D.4 **Glencoe Life, Earth, and Physical Science series** The Glencoe Life, Earth, and Physical Science series includes 3 full-year courses— 1 in life, 1 in earth, and 1 in physical science—for students in grades 8 and above. Four major themes are developed: energy, systems and interactions, scale and structure, and stability and change. An extensive set of materials and resources, including many optional components, is available for students and teachers.

- *Glencoe Earth Science,* 4.5
- *Glencoe Life Science,* 2.8
- *Glencoe Physical Science,* 1.6

D.5 **Insights series** The Insights program, for grades K-6, consists of 17 modules, several of which are appropriate for middle school. Topics in the program reflect a balance of life, physical, and earth sciences. Insights modules integrate science with the rest of the curriculum, particularly with language arts and mathematics. The activities support cultural, racial, and linguistic diversity. Each module requires about 25 class sessions to complete. The components of an Insights module are a teacher's guide and a kit of materials.

- *Human Body Systems,* 2.11
- *Structures,* 1.16
- *There Is No Away,* 3.3

D.6 **Integrated Science series** The Integrated Science series includes 3 full-year courses that integrate chemistry, physics, and the life, earth, and space sciences with environmental issues and emphasize the development of critical-thinking skills. Four major themes are incorporated in the program: energy, changes over time, systems and structures, and environmental interactions. Designed for students of different ability levels, the lessons are graded as "starting off," "going further," or "for the enthusiast." In addition to the student edition and teacher's manual, the program offers a variety of support materials.

- *Integrated Science: Book One,* 5.2
- *Integrated Science: Book Two,* 5.3

D.7 **Introductory Physical Science** *Introductory Physical Science* is a full-year course focused on the study of matter leading to the development of the atomic model. The course addresses 3 broad areas: the empirical framework for developing an atomic model, an introduction to the atomic model, and the electric dimension of the atomic model. This division provides natural breaking points for spreading the course over more than a year, if preferred.

- *Introductory Physical Science,* 1.9

D.8 **Middle Grades Science series** The Middle Grades Science series is an integrated science program for middle school students (grades 6, 7, and 8). The program uses a "spiral" approach to teaching science content and is designed around an evolving story line. Each year-long course is based on investigations of a series of questions that focus on scientific concepts and their relationship to the real world. Concepts are drawn from biology, chemistry, earth and space science, and physics. Components of the program

include teacher's guides—1 for each grade level, a program handbook, and a technology supplement.

- *Middle Grades Science: A Problem-Solving Approach, Sixth Grade,* 5.9
- *Middle Grades Science: A Problem-Solving Approach, Seventh Grade,* 5.10
- *Middle Grades Science: A Problem-Solving Approach, Eighth Grade,* 5.11

D.9 **Middle School Life Science** *Middle School Life Science* is a full-year course organized around a series of learning cycles during which students work independently, with partners, and in small groups. They engage in hands-on laboratory activities to explore an idea or concept, develop the concept during class discussion and/or through readings or additional experiments, apply the concepts learned to other situations, and form connections between their new knowledge and other areas of inquiry.

- *Middle School Life Science,* 2.13

D.10 **Middle School Science and Technology series** The Middle School Science and Technology series is a 3-year thematic program that integrates the life, earth, and physical sciences and emphasizes technology as a process for solving problems. The curriculum includes investigations, simulations, debates, plays, outdoor activities, research projects, and creative-writing projects. The titles of the 3 year-long courses—*Investigating Patterns of Change, Investigating Diversity and Limits,* and *Investigating Systems and Change*—reflect the program's unifying themes. Each course incorporates cooperative learning strategies. Components of the program include the student book, teacher's edition, teacher's resource package, implementation guide, and kit of materials.

- *Investigating Diversity and Limits,* 5.4
- *Investigating Patterns of Change,* 5.5
- *Investigating Systems and Change,* 5.6

D.11 **Prentice Hall Exploring Life, Earth, and Physical Science series** The Prentice Hall Exploring Life, Earth, and Physical Science series is a program for middle school students. Designed to cover all relevant areas of science, this integrated program consists of 3 textbooks (1 for each major discipline) and incorporates 7 science themes—energy, evolution, patterns of change, scale and structure, systems and interactions, unity and diversity, and stability. Each of the 3 year-long courses contains about 6 units. The units are also available, possibly with some modifications, as individual textbooks in the Prentice Hall Science Integrated Learning System series (*see* D.12). For each course, teaching materials, ancillary student materials, and some optional components are available.

- *Exploring Earth Science,* 4.2
- *Exploring Life Science,* 2.6
- *Exploring Physical Science,* 1.3

D.12 **Prentice Hall Science Integrated Learning System series** The Prentice Hall Science Integrated Learning System series is a program for middle school or junior high school students. Designed to cover all relevant areas of science, this program consists of 19 books, each in a particular topic area, such as sound and light, the planet earth, and cells—building blocks of life. Seven science themes are incorpo-

rated into the program; the themes are energy, evolution, patterns of change, scale and structure, systems and interactions, unity and diversity, and stability. For each unit, teaching materials, ancillary student materials, and some optional components are available.

- *Cells: Building Blocks of Life,* 2.1
- *Chemistry of Matter,* 1.1
- *Ecology: Earth's Living Resources,* 2.2
- *Electricity and Magnetism,* 1.2
- *Exploring Earth's Weather,* 4.3
- *Exploring Planet Earth,* 4.4
- *Evolution: Change over Time,* 5.1
- *Heat Energy,* 1.8
- *Heredity: The Code of Life,* 2.9
- *Human Biology and Health,* 2.10
- *Matter: Building Block of the Universe,* 1.12
- *Motion, Forces, and Energy,* 1.14
- *The Nature of Science,* 5.13
- *Parade of Life: Animals,* 2.14
- *Parade of Life: Monerans, Protists, Fungi, and Plants,* 2.15
- *Sound and Light,* 1.15

D.13 **Prime Science series** The Prime Science series is an interdisciplinary science program for middle and high school students. It consists of 5 textbooks (Levels A, B, and C for grades 6, 7, and 8, respectively, and Levels 1 and 2 for grades 9 and 10). The program uses a "spiral" approach to teaching science content and skills. Concepts from biology, chemistry, earth and space science, and physics, as well as the applications of science, are incorporated throughout the program. Science topics are introduced in personal and social contexts—for example, ideas about speed and motion are presented in the context of travel and road safety. Each course consists of a student textbook, a teacher's guide, and a test bank on a diskette.

- *Prime Science: Level A,* 5.14
- *Prime Science: Level B,* 5.15
- *Prime Science: Level C,* 5.16

D.14 **Project STAR** Project STAR is a full-year course that uses astronomy as a vehicle for teaching students about real-world applications of mathematics and physics. The activities were written for high school students but can be adapted for middle school. The course stresses the importance of measurements, observations, and building models. The program includes a student textbook, a teacher's guide, an activity book, and several kits.

- *Project STAR: The Universe in Your Hands,* 4.8

D.15 **Science and Technology for Children (STC) series** The Science and Technology for Children (STC) series consists of 24 inquiry-centered curriculum units for grades 1-6, with 4 units at each grade level. Students learn about topics in the life, earth, and physical sciences. The technological applications of science and the interactions among science, technology, and society are addressed throughout the program. The STC units, each of which takes about 16 class sessions to complete, encourage participatory learning and the integration of science with mathematics, language arts, social studies, and art. The components of an STC unit are a teacher's guide, a student activity book with simple instructions and illustrations, and a kit of materials.

- *Ecosystems,* 2.4
- *Experiments with Plants,* 2.5
- *Floating and Sinking,* 1.4
- *Food Chemistry,* 1.5
- *Magnets and Motors,* 1.11
- *Measuring Time,* 4.7
- *Microworlds,* 2.12
- *The Technology of Paper,* 5.27

D.16 Science Education for Public Understanding Program (SEPUP) series The Science Education for Public Understanding Program (SEPUP) series consists of 2 year-long courses—1 for middle and early secondary school (*Issues, Evidence, and You*) and 1 for high school (*Science for Citizenship in the 21st Century*). The program focuses on science and technology and on interactions of science and technology with people and the environment. The series promotes the use of scientific principles, processes, and evidence in public decision making. Materials include a teacher's guide, student books, and a kit of materials. (SEPUP is the second phase of a project that began as CEPUP—Chemical Education for Public Understanding Program.)

• *Issues, Evidence and You*, 3.2

D.17 Science Interactions series
The Science Interactions series is a complete program for middle or junior high school students, consisting of 3 textbooks—*Course 1, Course 2*, and *Course 3*. This integrated program is based on the premise that many areas of science depend on the fundamentals of physics and chemistry. During the 3-year program, each course first introduces basic concepts of physics and chemistry, followed by related topics in life and earth sciences and further topics in physics and chemistry. Each course also incorporates 4 science themes—energy, systems and interactions, scale and structure, and stability and change. In addition, connections are made among the sciences and with other subjects such as art and literature. Extensive sets of materials and resources, including some optional components, are available.

• *Science Interactions: Course 1*, 5.17
• *Science Interactions: Course 2*, 5.18
• *Science Interactions: Course 3*, 5.19

D.18 SciencePlus Technology and Society series The SciencePlus Technology and Society series consists of 3 year-long courses for middle school students. Each of the 3 textbooks—designated Level Green, Level Red, and Level Blue—integrates the life, earth, and physical sciences and incorporates the program's 5 science themes: energy, systems, structures, changes over time, and cycles. Cross-disciplinary connections are emphasized, and the impacts of scientific, technological, and science-related social issues are explored. For each course, an extensive set of materials and resources, including some optional components, is available for students and teachers.

• *SciencePlus Technology and Society: Level Green*, 5.20
• *SciencePlus Technology and Society: Level Red*, 5.21
• *SciencePlus Technology and Society: Level Blue*, 5.22

D.19 Science 2000 series The Science 2000 series is an integrated, multimedia science curriculum designed to introduce middle school students (grades 5 through 8) to 6 important themes of science: energy, evolution, patterns of change, scale and structure, stability, and systems and interactions. A separate, year-long course containing 4 units is offered for each grade. Each unit in a course takes from 7 to 9 weeks to complete. Students use videodisc imagery, software simulations, databases, hands-on investigations, and worksheets to explore real-world scientific questions. For each course,

an extensive set of materials is available for students and teachers.

• *Science 2000: Grade 6*, 5.23
• *Science 2000: Science 1 (Grade 7)*, 5.24
• *Science 2000: Science 2 (Grade 8)*, 5.25

D.20 SCIS [Science Curriculum Improvement Study] 3 The SCIS series focuses on the concepts and processes of science for grades K-6. The current version of the series—SCIS 3—consists of 13 units: a kindergarten unit and 2 sequences of 6 units each in physical-earth science and life-environmental science for grades 1 through 6. Two units are designed for grade 6. The components of a SCIS 3 unit are a teacher's guide and a kit of materials.

• *Ecosystems*, 2.3
• *Scientific Theories*, 5.26

ANNOTATED TITLES IN SUPPLEMENTARY SERIES

D.21 Biotechnology series The Biotechnology series consists of 3 units—1 each for grades 5-6, 7-8, and 9-12. These volumes—Books 1, 2, and 3 of *An Introduction to Biotechnology*—are designed to introduce teachers and students to the science of biotechnology through hands-on activities and analysis.

• *An Introduction to Biotechnology: Book 2*, 2.31

D.22 Changes in the Environment Series The Changes in the Environment Series was produced as part of the GLOBE-NET Project, a partnership of science teachers and research scientists working on aspects of global change. The scientists make presentations and lead visits to laboratories and field sites and the teachers use this information to develop activities and instructional materials for grades 4-12.

- *Lyme Disease: A Sourcebook for Teaching about a Major Environmental Health Problem,* 2.35

D.23 Chemical Education for Public Understanding Program (CEPUP) series The Chemical Education for Public Understanding Program (CEPUP) series consists of 12 modules for grades 7-9. The modules focus on chemicals and the interaction of chemicals with people and the environment. The series promotes the use of scientific principles, processes, and evidence in public decision making. The components of a CEPUP module are a teacher's guide and a kit of materials. (SEPUP—the Science Education for Public Understanding Program—is the second phase of the project that began as CEPUP.)

- *Chemicals in Foods: Additives,* 5.29
- *Chemical Survey and Solutions and Pollution,* 3.10
- *Determining Threshold Limits,* 5.32
- *Investigating Chemical Processes: Your Island Factory,* 5.43
- *Investigating Groundwater: The Fruitvale Story,* 3.19
- *Investigating Hazardous Materials,* 3.20
- *Plastics in Our Lives,* 3.25
- *Risk Comparison,* 2.43
- *Toxic Waste: A Teaching Simulation,* 3.30
- *The Waste Hierarchy: Where Is "Away"?* 3.32

D.24 Delta Science Module (DSM) series The Delta Science Module (DSM) series has 51 life, physical, and earth science units for grades K-8 that emphasize science concepts, science content, and process skills. The series includes 12 modules for grades 5-6 and 8 modules for grades 6-8. Each requires about 3 to 4 weeks to complete and includes a teacher's guide and materials for a class of 32 students.

- *Chemical Interactions,* 1.20
- *Color and Light,* 1.23
- *DNA—From Genes to Proteins,* 2.19
- *Earth, Moon, and Sun,* 4.14
- *Earth Processes,* 4.15
- *Electrical Connections,* 1.25
- *Electromagnetism,* 1.26
- *Erosion,* 4.19
- *Fungi—Small Wonders,* 2.25
- *If Shipwrecks Could Talk,* 5.41
- *Lenses and Mirrors,* 1.32
- *Newton's Toy Box,* 1.34
- *Plants in Our World,* 2.39
- *Pollution,* 3.26
- *Pond Life,* 2.40
- *Rocks and Minerals,* 4.29
- *Simple Machines,* 1.37
- *Solar Energy,* 4.31
- *Weather Forecasting,* 4.37
- *You and Your Body,* 2.44

D.25 Eco-Inquiry: A Guide to Ecological Learning Experiences for the Upper Elementary/Middle Grades The modules in *Eco-Inquiry: A Guide to Ecological Learning Experiences for the Upper Elementary/Middle Grades* contain real-world projects and investigations in ecology. The modules build students' understanding of ecological processes in their local environment.

- *Eco-Inquiry: A Guide to Ecological Learning Experiences for the Upper Elementary/Middle Grades,* 3.13

D.26 Environmental Action series The Environmental Action series consists of 6 stand-alone modules for middle and secondary school students. The series focuses on environmental issues and on the impact of these issues on human health and environmental quality. Each module includes a student edition and a teacher's resource guide.

- *Chemicals: Choosing Wisely,* 3.9
- *Energy Conservation,* 3.15
- *Waste Reduction,* 3.34

D.27 Event-Based Science series The Event-Based Science series is a program for middle school students in grades 6-9. Each module tells the story of a real event—such as the 1995 outbreak of the Ebola virus in Zaire—through reprinted newspaper articles and personal interviews; sections of background information explain relevant scientific concepts. A central task related to the module's story line leads to a final product that allows students to apply the science they have learned. For each module, a student book, teacher's guide, and videotape and/or videodisc are available.

- *Asteroid!* 4.10
- *Earthquake!* 4.16
- *Flood!* 4.21
- *Hurricane!* 4.23
- *Oil Spill!* 3.24
- *Outbreak!* 2.38
- *Volcano!* 4.35

D.28 Foundations and Challenges to Encourage Technology-based Science (FACETS) series The Foundations and Challenges to Encourage Technology-based Science (FACETS) program consists of 3 series of 8 modules each for grades 6-8. Each module focuses on a topic in the life, earth, or physical sciences. The time needed to complete FACETS modules varies from 2 to 4 weeks. Each module consists of a student book and a teacher's guide.

- *Acid Rain,* 3.5
- *Cleaning Water,* 3.11
- *Climate and Farming,* 5.31
- *Communicable Diseases,* 2.18
- *Earthquakes,* 4.17
- *Food from Our Land,* 2.23
- *Growing Older,* 2.26
- *Handling Information,* 5.36
- *Keeping Fit,* 2.32
- *Managing Crop Pests,* 3.22
- *Packaging,* 5.48
- *Shrinking Farmlands,* 4.30
- *A Sunken Ship,* 5.51
- *Threads,* 5.52
- *Weather and Health,* 4.36
- *What's in Our Food?* 1.40

D.29 Great Explorations in Math and Science (GEMS) series The Great Explorations in Math and Science (GEMS) series includes more than 50 teacher's guides and handbooks for preschool through grade 10. About 35 of these are appropriate for middle school. The series also includes several assembly presenter's guides and exhibit guides. New guides and handbooks continue to be developed, and current titles are revised frequently. The series is designed to teach key science and mathematics concepts through activity-based learning. The time needed to complete GEMS units varies from about 2 to 10 class sessions.

- *Acid Rain,* 3.4
- *Animals in Action,* 2.16
- *Bubble Festival,* 1.17
- *Bubble-ology,* 1.18
- *Chemical Reactions,* 1.21
- *Color Analyzers,* 1.22
- *Convection: A Current Event,* 4.11
- *Discovering Density,* 1.24
- *Earth, Moon, and Stars,* 4.13

- *Earthworms,* 2.20
- *Experimenting with Model Rockets,* 1.28
- *Global Warming and the Greenhouse Effect,* 3.16
- *Height-o-Meters,* 5.37
- *Hot Water and Warm Homes from Sunlight,* 5.38
- *Mapping Animal Movements,* 2.36
- *Mapping Fish Habitats,* 2.37
- *More Than Magnifiers,* 1.33
- *Moons of Jupiter,* 4.24
- *Of Cabbages and Chemistry,* 1.35
- *Oobleck: What Do Scientists Do?* 1.36
- *Paper Towel Testing,* 5.49
- *River Cutters,* 4.28
- *Stories in Stone,* 4.32
- *Vitamin C Testing,* 1.39

D.30 Integrated Mathematics, Science, and Technology (IMaST) series The Integrated Mathematics, Science, and Technology (IMaST) series for middle school includes 6 modules. The materials in each are designed to be used by a team of mathematics, science, and technology teachers concurrently over a 9-week period. Each module includes a teacher's guide and a student book.

- *Energy Transformations: Fourth Module in Bio-Related Technologies Unit,* 5.33
- *Food Production: Second Module in Bio-Related Technologies Unit,* 5.34
- *Forecasting: Discovering, Simplifying, and Applying Patterns,* 5.35
- *Manufacturing,* 5.47
- *Waste Management: Third Module in Bio-Related Technologies Unit,* 3.33
- *Wellness: First Module in Bio-Related Technologies Unit,* 5.53

D.31 JASON Project Series Each year, the JASON Project—administered by the JASON Foundation for Education—embarks on a 2-week scientific expedition to a remote location. The project develops a science and technology curriculum module to prepare students to participate in the expedition using interactive telecommunication. The JASON Project series currently consists of 9 such modules.

- *JASON IV Curriculum: BAJA California Sur,* 5.44
- *JASON VI: Island Earth, Hawai'i Expedition Curriculum,* 5.45

D.32 Life in the Universe series The Life in the Universe Series consists of 6 units, including the 3 volumes in the SETI Academy Planet Project. Each book in the SETI Academy Planet Project is designed to be a complete unit in itself as well as a subunit of a 3-unit course. During the activities in the 3 units, each student plays the role of a "cadet" at the SETI [Search for Extraterrestrial Intelligence] Academy, a fictitious institution. (The SETI Institute is an actual scientific organization.)

- *The Evolution of a Planetary System,* 4.20
- *How Might Life Evolve on Other Worlds?* 5.39
- *Life: Here? There? Elsewhere? The Search for Life on Venus and Mars,* 5.46

D.33 Living Lightly series The Living Lightly series is a program for grades K-12. Each volume focuses on the environment and on decision making related to environmental issues. The series includes 4 volumes, 1 of which is designed for grades 7-9.

- *Living Lightly on the Planet: A Global Environmental Education Guidebook,* 3.21

D.34 Macmillan/McGraw-Hill Science series The Macmillan/McGraw-Hill Science series is a comprehensive, activity-based, K-8 science curriculum made up of 42 stand-alone units, 18 of which are designed for grades 6-8. The series is constructed around 7 major themes: systems and interactions, scale and structure, stability, energy, evolution, patterns of change, and models. The subject of each unit—for example, changes in matter—is presented from the perspective of one or more of these themes. One theme is designated as the "major theme" for a unit, and any others are treated as "related themes." For each unit, a wide range of materials, including some optional components, is available for students and teachers.

• *Changes in Ecosystems*, 3.8
• *Changes in Matter*, 1.19
• *Earth and Beyond*, 4.12
• *Earth's Ecosystems*, 3.12
• *Earth's Solid Crust*, 4.18
• *Forces and Machines*, 1.30
• *Life Changes through Time*, 2.33
• *Using Energy*, 1.38

D.35 National Geographic Kids Network series The National Geographic Kids Network series is a telecommunications-based program for grades 3-9 that emphasizes collaborative student research on real-world issues. The series includes 7 units for grades 3-6 and 9 units for grades 6-9. Each unit includes a kit and an 8-week telecommunications package.

• *Acid Rain*, 3.6
• *Too Much Trash?* 3.29
• *What's in Our Water?* 3.36

D.36 New Directions Teaching Units The New Directions Teaching Units focus on developing scientific literacy and conceptual understanding. They were designed to reflect the ideas about teaching, learning, and curriculum in the Michigan Essential Goals and Objectives for K-12 Science Education, which were developed by the Michigan Science Education Resources Project. Several New Directions Teaching Units can be used with middle school students.

• *Food, Energy, and Growth*, 2.22
• *Hard As Ice*, 1.7
• *The Lives of Plants*, 2.34
• *Steamed Up!* 5.50

D.37 Problem-Solving Activities for Middle-Level Science series The Problem-Solving Activities for Middle-Level Science series consists of 8 stand-alone modules. Each module contains 2 to 6 units focused on technological and/or ethical aspects of issues involving science, technology, and society. The series was designed so that teachers might select modules and units that address local needs and draw on local community resources. A module requires 3 to 8 weeks to complete, depending on the units selected. Supplies and equipment may be required that are not typically part of a school's science inventory.

• *Energy and Communications: How Can We Send and Receive Information?* 1.27
• *Epidemics: Can We Escape Them?* 2.21
• *The Human Body: How Can I Maintain and Care for Myself?* 2.28
• *Solid Waste: Is There a Solution?* 3.28
• *Using Earth's Resources: What Are the Tradeoffs?* 4.34
• *Water: Can We Keep It Fit for Life?* 3.35
• *Wildlife and Humanity: Can We Share the Earth?* 3.37

D.38 Project Earth Science series The Project Earth Science series consists of 4 volumes for students in middle and junior high school. Each volume focuses on a single area in earth science—astronomy, geology, meteorology, or physical oceanography—and contains a collection of hands-on activities and a series of readings related to the topic area. The central theme of the series is the uniqueness of the earth among the planets in the solar system.

• *Project Earth Science: Astronomy*, 4.25
• *Project Earth Science: Geology*, 4.26
• *Project Earth Science: Meteorology*, 4.27

D.39 Real-World Mathematics through Science series The Real-World Mathematics through Science series consists of 10 units for grades 6-8. Each unit combines pre-algebra topics with science explorations to motivate students in both areas of study. Students work in cooperative groups to solve open-ended problems and make connections between real-world mathematics and science.

• *Classifying Fingerprints*, 5.30

D.40 Scholastic Science Place series The Scholastic Science Place series is a K-6 program with 42 units, 6 for each grade level. The 6 units for grade 6 are organized under topics in the life, earth, and physical sciences. Three key themes—scale and structure, systems and interactions, and patterns of change—are incorporated into the program. For each unit, teaching materials, student materials, and some optional components are available.

• *Biodiversity: Understanding the Variety of Life*, 2.17
• *How Telecommunications Works: How People Use Energy to Communicate*, 5.40
• *The Universe: Exploring Stars, Constellations, and Galaxies*, 4.33

D.41 Science Technology and Reading (STAR) series Designed for the upper elementary grades, the Science Technology and Reading (STAR) series consists of 8 thematic "labs" in the natural and physical sciences. Each lab focuses both on science activities and on a genre of children's literature, developing correlations between the science process and the process of reading. In addition to a teacher's guide for each of the 8 labs, the STAR program includes a mentor's guide for scientists, engineers, and others assisting in the classroom.

- *Ecology Lab,* 3.14
- *Flight Lab,* 1.29
- *Geology Lab,* 4.22
- *Inventor's Lab,* 1.31

D.42 TLTG [Texas Learning Technology Group] Environmental Science Series The TLTG Environmental Science Series is a multimedia program for grades 7-12. Designed for the single-computer classroom, the 4 units in this series focus on environmental pollution and health-related issues from a variety of perspectives. For each unit, all video, graphics, and text-based materials—including the teacher's and students' guides—are contained on a CD-ROM.

- *Health Risk: Shadow over Crystal Valley,* 3.17

D.43 A World in Motion II: The Design Experience series A World in Motion II: the Design Experience series consists of 3 units on using science, mathematics, and technology to explore the process of design. Each unit engages students in a problem-solving context for which they must create a design or solution to address a particular need or problem. The active participation of volunteers in the classroom is a distinguishing feature of this series.

- *A World in Motion II: The Design Experience, Challenge 2,* 5.54

INDIVIDUAL SUPPLEMENTARY UNITS

D.44 The following units, which are not part of formal series, are annotated in the Supplementary Units sections of chapters 1 through 5.

- *Biology Is Outdoors! A Comprehensive Resource for Studying School Environments,* 3.7
- *From Genes to Jeans: An Activity-Based Unit on Genetic Engineering and Agriculture,* 2.24
- *How Much Is Too Much? How Little Is Too Little? Factors That Affect Plant Growth,* 2.27
- *Hydroponic Instructional Package,* 2.29
- *The Interrelationships of Soil, Water, and Fertilizers and How They Affect Plant Growth,* 2.30
- *Investigating and Evaluating Environmental Issues and Actions: Skill Development Program,* 3.18
- *Investigating and Evaluating STS Issues and Solutions: A Worktext for STS Education,* 5.42
- *The Monitor's Handbook,* 3.23
- *The Pondwater Tour,* 3.27
- *Power Plants: A Plant-Based Energy Curriculum for Grades 5 through 8,* 2.41
- *Rainforest Researchers,* 2.42
- *Understanding Basic Ecological Concepts,* 3.31
- *Zebra Mussel Mania,* 2.45

THE INDEXES

The eight indexes that follow are designed to allow easy access to the information, materials, and organizations annotated in this guide. The titles of the indexes and their general focus and coverage are as follows:

- The Title Index locates curriculum and other book and periodical titles annotated or referred to in the guide.
- The Index of Authors, Series, and Curriculum Projects focuses on chapters 1 through 9 and on appendix D ("Overviews of Core and Supplementary Programs with Titles Annotated in This Guide").

- The General Subject Index contains information on the structure and development of the guide as described in the front matter, introductions, overviews, and appendixes. This index also covers the subjects addressed by reference materials annotated in chapters 6 through 9.
- The Index of Topics in Curriculum Materials covers chapters 1 through 5.
- The Index of Content Standards Addressed in Core and Supple-

mentary Curriculum Materials applies to chapters 1 through 5.
- The Index of Grade Levels of Curriculum Materials by Scientific Area covers chapters 1 through 5.
- The Index of Scientific Areas of Curriculum Materials by Grade Level covers chapters 1 through 5.
- The Index of Ancillary Resources (Places to Visit/Organizations) covers chapters 10 and 11.

Throughout the indexes, the locator numbers in italic refer to page numbers. All other references are to entry numbers.

Title Index

Index of Authors, Series, and Curriculum Projects

Index of Authors, Series, and Curriculum Projects

General Subject Index

GENERAL SUBJECT INDEX

The General Subject Index refers readers to information on the structure and development of the volume contained in the front matter, introductions, overviews, and appendixes. It also covers the subjects addressed by reference materials annotated in chapters 6 through 9. (For references to the science content of the curriculum materials annotated in chapters 1 through 5, see the Index of Topics in Curriculum Materials.)

The locator numbers in italic refer to page numbers. All other references are to entry numbers.

Index of Topics in Curriculum Materials

INDEX OF TOPICS IN CURRICULUM MATERIALS

The Index of Topics in Curriculum Materials covers chapters 1 through 5. (See the General Subject Index to locate information on reference materials in chapters 6 through 9, and in the front matter, introductions, overviews, and appendixes.)

The locator numbers in italic refer to page numbers. All other references are to entry numbers.

INDEX OF TOPICS IN CURRICULUM MATERIALS

INDEX OF TOPICS IN CURRICULUM MATERIALS

Index of Content Standards Addressed in Core and Supplementary Curriculum Materials

INDEX OF CONTENT STANDARDS ADDRESSED IN CORE AND SUPPLEMENTARY CURRICULUM MATERIALS

The Index of Content Standards Addressed in Core and Supplementary Curriculum Materials applies to chapters 1 through 5. The locator numbers used are entry numbers of the annotations.

Index of Grade Levels of Curriculum Materials by Scientific Area

GRADE 6

Earth and Space Science
  Core Materials, 4.3, 4.6, 4.7, 4.9
  Supplementary Units, 4.11, 4.13, 4.14, 4.15, 4.17, 4.19, 4.20, 4.22, 4.24, 4.26, 4.27, 4.28, 4.29, 4.30, 4.31, 4.32, 4.33, 4.36, 4.37
  Science Activity Books, 4.38, 4.39, 4.40, 4.41, 4.42, 4.43, 4.44, 4.45, 4.47, 4.48, 4.49, 4.50, 4.51, 4.53, 4.54, 4.55, 4.56, 4.59, 4.60, 4.61, 4.62, 4.63, 4.65, 4.66, 4.68, 4.69

Environmental Science
  Core Materials, 3.1, 3.3
  Supplementary Units, 3.4, 3.6, 3.13, 3.14, 3.26, 3.29, 3.36, 3.37
  Science Activity Books, 3.38, 3.39, 3.40, 3.41, 3.42, 3.43, 3.45, 3.46, 3.47, 3.50, 3.52, 3.53, 3.55, 3.56, 3.57, 3.58, 3.59, 3.60, 3.62, 3.63

Life Science
  Core Materials, 2.3, 2.4, 2.5, 2.7, 2.11, 2.12
  Supplementary Units, 2.16, 2.17, 2.20, 2.25, 2.27, 2.32, 2.34, 2.36, 2.37, 2.39, 2.40, 2.41, 2.42, 2.44, 2.45
  Science Activity Books, 2.46, 2.48, 2.49, 2.51, 2.52, 2.53, 2.55, 2.56, 2.57, 2.58, 2.59, 2.60, 2.62, 2.64, 2.66, 2.67, 2.69, 2.70, 2.72

Multidisciplinary and Applied Science
  Core Materials, 5.5, 5.9, 5.12, 5.14, 5.17, 5.20, 5.23, 5.26, 5.27, 5.28
  Supplementary Units, 5.30, 5.37, 5.38, 5.40, 5.41, 5.42, 5.44, 5.45, 5.48, 5.49, 5.50
  Science Activity Books, 5.55, 5.56, 5.57, 5.58, 5.59, 5.60, 5.61, 5.62, 5.64, 5.65, 5.66, 5.67, 5.68, 5.72, 5.73, 5.75, 5.76, 5.77, 5.78, 5.79, 5.80, 5.81, 5.83, 5.85

Physical Science
  Core Materials, 1.4, 1.5, 1.7, 1.10, 1.11, 1.13, 1.16
  Supplementary Units, 1.17, 1.18, 1.22, 1.23, 1.24, 1.25, 1.26, 1.28, 1.29, 1.31, 1.32, 1.33, 1.34, 1.35, 1.36, 1.37, 1.39, 1.40
  Science Activity Books, 1.42, 1.43, 1.44, 1.45, 1.47, 1.48, 1.49, 1.50, 1.51, 1.52, 1.53, 1.54, 1.55, 1.56, 1.57, 1.58, 1.59, 1.60, 1.62, 1.64, 1.65, 1.66, 1.69, 1.70, 1.76, 1.78, 1.79, 1.85, 1.88, 1.90, 1.91, 1.92, 1.93, 1.94, 1.95, 1.96, 1.99, 1.100, 1.101, 1.104, 1.105, 1.108, 1.110, 1.111, 1.112, 1.113, 1.115

GRADE 7

Earth and Space Science
  Core Materials, 4.1, 4.2, 4.3, 4.4, 4.5
  Supplementary Units, 4.10, 4.11, 4.12, 4.13, 4.14, 4.15, 4.16, 4.17, 4.18, 4.19, 4.21, 4.23, 4.24, 4.25, 4.26, 4.27, 4.28, 4.31, 4.32, 4.33, 4.34, 4.35
  Science Activity Books, 4.38, 4.39, 4.40, 4.41, 4.42, 4.43, 4.44, 4.46, 4.47, 4.48, 4.50, 4.51, 4.53, 4.54, 4.55, 4.59, 4.60, 4.61, 4.62, 4.63, 4.64, 4.65, 4.66, 4.67, 4.68, 4.69

Environmental Science
  Core Materials, 3.2
  Supplementary Units, 3.4, 3.5, 3.7, 3.8, 3.9, 3.10, 3.11, 3.12, 3.13, 3.15, 3.16, 3.17, 3.18, 3.19, 3.20, 3.21, 3.23, 3.24, 3.25, 3.27, 3.28, 3.32, 3.33, 3.34, 3.35, 3.37
  Science Activity Books, 3.38, 3.39, 3.40, 3.41, 3.43, 3.44, 3.45, 3.46, 3.47, 3.48, 3.49, 3.50, 3.51, 3.52, 3.53, 3.54, 3.55, 3.56, 3.57, 3.58, 3.59, 3.60, 3.61, 3.62, 3.63

Life Science
  Core Materials, 2.1, 2.2, 2.6, 2.9, 2.10, 2.13, 2.14, 2.15
  Supplementary Units, 2.16, 2.17, 2.18, 2.19, 2.20, 2.21, 2.23, 2.24, 2.25, 2.26, 2.27, 2.28, 2.29, 2.34, 2.35, 2.36, 2.37, 2.38, 2.39, 2.41, 2.42, 2.43, 2.45
  Science Activity Books, 2.46, 2.47, 2.48, 2.49, 2.50, 2.51, 2.52, 2.53, 2.54, 2.55, 2.58, 2.59, 2.60, 2.62, 2.63, 2.64, 2.65, 2.66, 2.67, 2.68, 2.69, 2.70, 2.72

Multidisciplinary and Applied Science
  Core Materials, 5.1, 5.2, 5.3, 5.4, 5.5, 5.7, 5.10, 5.13, 5.15, 5.17, 5.18, 5.20, 5.21, 5.24
  Supplementary Units, 5.29, 5.30, 5.32, 5.33, 5.34, 5.37, 5.38, 5.39, 5.40, 5.41, 5.42, 5.43, 5.44, 5.45, 5.46, 5.47, 5.49, 5.50, 5.51, 5.53, 5.54
  Science Activity Books, 5.55, 5.56, 5.57, 5.58, 5.59, 5.60, 5.61, 5.62, 5.64, 5.65, 5.66, 5.67, 5.68, 5.69, 5.70, 5.72, 5.74, 5.75, 5.76, 5.77, 5.78, 5.79, 5.80, 5.81, 5.82, 5.83, 5.84, 5.85

> INDEX OF GRADE LEVELS OF CURRICULUM MATERIALS BY SCIENTIFIC AREA
>
> Identical information is presented in the two grade-levels indexes. The information is simply arranged differently:
>
> - In this index, the disciplines (Earth and Space Science, Environmental Science, Life Science, Multidisciplinary and Applied Science, and Physical Science) are arranged under the grades (6, 7, and 8).
> - In the Index of Scientific Areas of Curriculum Materials by Grade Level, the grades are arranged under the disciplines.
>
> As in chapters 1 through 5, to which these two indexes refer, the curriculum materials for each discipline are divided in the categories core materials, supplementary units, and science activity books.

Physical Science
  Core Materials, 1.3, 1.15
  Supplementary Units, 1.17, 1.18, 1.19, 1.20, 1.21, 1.22, 1.24, 1.25, 1.26, 1.27, 1.28, 1.29, 1.30, 1.32, 1.33, 1.34, 1.35, 1.36, 1.37, 1.38, 1.39, 1.40
  Science Activity Books, 1.41, 1.42, 1.43, 1.44, 1.45, 1.46, 1.47, 1.48, 1.49, 1.50, 1.51, 1.52, 1.53, 1.54, 1.55, 1.56, 1.57, 1.59, 1.60, 1.61, 1.62, 1.63, 1.66, 1.67, 1.68, 1.69, 1.70, 1.71, 1.72, 1.73, 1.74, 1.75, 1.76, 1.77, 1.78, 1.79, 1.80, 1.81, 1.82, 1.83, 1.84, 1.85, 1.86, 1.87, 1.88, 1.89, 1.91, 1.92, 1.93, 1.94, 1.95, 1.96, 1.97, 1.98, 1.99, 1.100, 1.101, 1.102, 1.103, 1.104, 1.105, 1.108, 1.109, 1.110, 1.111, 1.112, 1.113, 1.115

GRADE 8

Earth and Space Science
  Core Materials, 4.1, 4.2, 4.3, 4.4, 4.5, 4.8
  Supplementary Units, 4.10, 4.11, 4.12, 4.13, 4.14, 4.15, 4.16, 4.19, 4.21, 4.23, 4.24, 4.25, 4.26, 4.27, 4.28, 4.32, 4.34, 4.35
  Science Activity Books, 4.38, 4.39, 4.40, 4.41, 4.42, 4.43, 4.44, 4.46, 4.47, 4.48, 4.50, 4.51, 4.52, 4.53, 4.54, 4.55, 4.57, 4.58, 4.59, 4.60, 4.61, 4.62, 4.63, 4.64, 4.65, 4.66, 4.67, 4.68

Environmental Science
  Core Materials, 3.2
  Supplementary Units, 3.4, 3.7, 3.8, 3.9, 3.10, 3.13, 3.15, 3.16, 3.17, 3.18, 3.19, 3.20, 3.21, 3.22, 3.23, 3.24, 3.25, 3.27, 3.28, 3.30, 3.31, 3.32, 3.34, 3.35, 3.37
  Science Activity Books, 3.38, 3.41, 3.44, 3.45, 3.46, 3.47, 3.48, 3.49, 3.50, 3.51, 3.52, 3.53, 3.54, 3.55, 3.56, 3.57, 3.58, 3.59, 3.60, 3.61, 3.63

INDEX OF GRADE LEVELS OF CURRICULUM MATERIALS BY SCIENTIFIC AREA

Index of Scientific Areas of Curriculum Materials by Grade Level

INDEX OF SCIENTIFIC AREAS OF CURRICULUM MATERIALS BY GRADE LEVEL

Identical information is presented in the two grade-levels indexes. The information is simply arranged differently:

- In this index, the grades (6, 7, and 8) are arranged under the disciplines (Earth and Space Science, Environmental Science, Life Science, Multidisciplinary and Applied Science, and Physical Science).
- In the Index of Grade Levels of Curriculum Materials by Scientific Area, the disciplines are arranged under the grades.

As in chapters 1 through 5 to which these two indexes refer, the curriculum materials for each discipline are divided in the categories core materials, supplementary units, and science activity books.

INDEX OF SCIENTIFIC AREAS OF CURRICULUM MATERIALS BY GRADE LEVEL

Index of Ancillary Resources (Places to Visit/Organizations)

INDEX OF ANCILLARY RESOURCES (PLACES TO VISIT/ORGANIZATIONS)

CREDITS

Front cover: Design and photo illustration by Francesca Moghari; original photo, © 1997, Comstock, Inc.; line illustrations by Max-Karl Winkler.

Pages xvi-1: Dane Penland, Smithsonian Institution/courtesy of National Science Resources Center, Washington, D.C.

Pages 6-7, 15, 116, 256, 262-63, 269, 283, 292: Matt Smith/courtesy of National Science Resources Center, Washington, D.C.

Page 70: Robert Allen Strawn/courtesy of National Science Resources Center, Washington, D.C.

Page 154: Rick Vargas, Smithsonian Institution/courtesy of National Science Resources Center, Washington, D.C.

Page 198: Hugh Talman, Smithsonian Institution/courtesy of National Science Resources Center, Washington, D.C.

Pages 304-305: Courtesy of Smithsonian Institution, Washington, D.C.

Page 311: Courtesy of National Air and Space Museum, Smithsonian Institution, Washington, D.C.

Page 373: Eric Long, Smithsonian Institution/courtesy of National Science Resources Center, Washington, D.C.

ORDER CARD
(Customers in North America Only)

Resources for Teaching
Middle School Science

Use this card to order additional copies of **Resources for Teaching Middle School Science** and the books described on the reverse. All orders must be prepaid. Please add $4.00 for shipping and handling for the first copy ordered and $0.50 for each additional copy. If you live in CA, DC, FL, MA, MD, MO, TX, or Canada, add applicable sales tax or GST. Prices apply only in the United States, Canada, and Mexico and are subject to change without notice.

___ I am enclosing a U.S. check or money order.

___ Please charge my VISA/MasterCard/American Express account.

Number: _____

Expiration date: _____

Signature: _____

PLEASE SEND ME:

Qty.	Code	Title	Price
___	MIDDLT	Middle School Science, single copy	$24.95
___	MIDDLB	2-9 copies	$20.50ea*
___	MIDDLB	10+ copies	$17.95ea*
___	ELESCT	Elementary School Science, single copy	$17.95
___	ELESCB	2-9 copies	$13.50ea*
___	ELESCB	10+ copies	$11.95ea*
___	SCISTT	National Science Educ. Standards, single copy	$19.95
___	SCISTB	2-9 copies	$16.50ea*
___	SCISTB	10+ copies	$13.95ea*

*No other discounts apply.

Please print.

Name _____

Address _____

City _____ State _____ Zip Code _____

MIDC

FOUR EASY WAYS TO ORDER
By phone: Call toll-free 1-800-624-6242 or (202) 334-3313 or call your favorite bookstore.
By fax: Copy the order card and fax to (202) 334-2451.
By electronic mail: Order via Internet at http://www.nap.edu/bookstore.
By mail: Return this card with your payment to NATIONAL ACADEMY PRESS, 2101 Constitution Avenue, NW, Lockbox 285, Washington, DC 20055.
Quantity Discounts: 5-24 copies, 15%--25-499 copies, 25%. To be eligible for a discount, all copies must be shipped and billed to one address.
All international customers please contact National Academy Press for export prices and ordering information.

ORDER CARD
(Customers in North America Only)

Resources for Teaching
Middle School Science

Use this card to order additional copies of **Resources for Teaching Middle School Science** and the books described on the reverse. All orders must be prepaid. Please add $4.00 for shipping and handling for the first copy ordered and $0.50 for each additional copy. If you live in CA, DC, FL, MA, MD, MO, TX, or Canada, add applicable sales tax or GST. Prices apply only in the United States, Canada, and Mexico and are subject to change without notice.

___ I am enclosing a U.S. check or money order.

___ Please charge my VISA/MasterCard/American Express account.

Number: _____

Expiration date: _____

Signature: _____

PLEASE SEND ME:

Qty.	Code	Title	Price
___	MIDDLT	Middle School Science, single copy	$24.95
___	MIDDLB	2-9 copies	$20.50ea*
___	MIDDLB	10+ copies	$17.95ea*
___	ELESCT	Elementary School Science, single copy	$17.95
___	ELESCB	2-9 copies	$13.50ea*
___	ELESCB	10+ copies	$11.95ea*
___	SCISTT	National Science Educ. Standards, single copy	$19.95
___	SCISTB	2-9 copies	$16.50ea*
___	SCISTB	10+ copies	$13.95ea*

*No other discounts apply.

Please print.

Name _____

Address _____

City _____ State _____ Zip Code _____

MIDC

FOUR EASY WAYS TO ORDER
By phone: Call toll-free 1-800-624-6242 or (202) 334-3313 or call your favorite bookstore.
By fax: Copy the order card and fax to (202) 334-2451.
By electronic mail: Order via Internet at http://www.nap.edu/bookstore.
By mail: Return this card with your payment to NATIONAL ACADEMY PRESS, 2101 Constitution Avenue, NW, Lockbox 285, Washington, DC 20055.
Quantity Discounts: 5-24 copies, 15%--25-499 copies, 25%. To be eligible for a discount, all copies must be shipped and billed to one address.
All international customers please contact National Academy Press for export prices and ordering information.

Resources for Teaching Elementary School Science

This book is an annotated guide to hands-on, inquiry-centered curriculum materials and sources of help for teaching science from kindergarten through sixth grade. The guide annotates about 350 curriculum packages, describing the activities involved and what students learn. Each annotation also lists recommended grade levels, accompanying materials and kits or suggested equipment, and ordering information. This guide also features sections with references for teachers and information about facilities such as museums and other organizations from which teachers can obtain resources and assistance.

ISBN 0-309-05293-9; 1996, 312 pages, 8.5 x 11, indexes, paperbound, single copy, $17.95; 2-9 copies, $13.50 each; 10 or more copies, $11.95 each (no other discounts apply)

National Science Education Standards

This book offers a coherent vision of what it means to be scientifically literate, describing what all students regardless of background or circumstance should understand and be able to do at different grade levels in various science categories. The book describes the exemplary teaching practices that provide students with experiences that enable them to achieve scientific literacy, criteria for assessing and analyzing students' attainments in science, and the learning opportunities that school science programs afford. In addition, it describes the nature and design of the school and district science program, and the support and resources needed for students to learn science.

ISBN 0-309-05326-9; 1996, 272 pages, 8 x 10.5, index, paperbound, single copy, $19.95; 2-9 copies, $16.50 each; 10 or more copies, $13.95 each (no other discounts apply)

Use the form on the reverse of this card to order your copies today.

Resources for Teaching Elementary School Science

This book is an annotated guide to hands-on, inquiry-centered curriculum materials and sources of help for teaching science from kindergarten through sixth grade. The guide annotates about 350 curriculum packages, describing the activities involved and what students learn. Each annotation also lists recommended grade levels, accompanying materials and kits or suggested equipment, and ordering information. This guide also features sections with references for teachers and information about facilities such as museums and other organizations from which teachers can obtain resources and assistance.

ISBN 0-309-05293-9; 1996, 312 pages, 8.5 x 11, indexes, paperbound, single copy, $17.95; 2-9 copies, $13.50 each; 10 or more copies, $11.95 each (no other discounts apply)

National Science Education Standards

This book offers a coherent vision of what it means to be scientifically literate, describing what all students regardless of background or circumstance should understand and be able to do at different grade levels in various science categories. The book describes the exemplary teaching practices that provide students with experiences that enable them to achieve scientific literacy, criteria for assessing and analyzing students' attainments in science, and the learning opportunities that school science programs afford. In addition, it describes the nature and design of the school and district science program, and the support and resources needed for students to learn science.

ISBN 0-309-05326-9; 1996, 272 pages, 8 x 10.5, index, paperbound, single copy, $19.95; 2-9 copies, $16.50 each; 10 or more copies, $13.95 each (no other discounts apply)

Use the form on the reverse of this card to order your copies today.